# BRAHMS STUDIES

*Analytical and Historical Perspectives*

# BRAHMS STUDIES
## *Analytical and Historical Perspectives*

Papers delivered at the
International Brahms Conference
Washington, DC
5–8 May 1983

Edited by
GEORGE S. BOZARTH

CLARENDON PRESS · OXFORD
1990

Oxford University Press, Walton Street, Oxford OX2 6DP
Oxford New York Toronto
Delhi Bombay Calcutta Madras Karachi
Petaling Jaya Singapore Hong Kong Tokyo
Nairobi Dar es Salaam Cape Town
Melbourne Auckland
and associated companies in
Berlin Ibadan

Oxford is a trade mark of Oxford University Press

Published in the United States
by Oxford University Press, New York

© Oxford University Press 1990

British Library Cataloguing in Publication Data
International Brahms Conference (1983: Washington, D.C.)
Brahms studies : analytical and historical perspectives:
papers delivered at the International Brahms Conference,
Washington, DC 5–8 May 1983.
1. German music. Brahms, Johannes, 1833–1897
I. Title II. Bozarth, George S.
780.92
ISBN 0–19–311922–6

Library of Congress Cataloging in Publication Data
International Brahms Conference (1983: Washington, D.C.)
Brahms studies : analytical and historical perspectives : papers
delivered at the International Brahms Conference, Washington, DC,
5–8 May 1983 / edited by George S. Bozarth.
Includes bibliographical references.
1. Brahms, Johannes, 1833–1897—Congresses. I. Bozarth, George S.    II   Title.
ML410.B815   1983    780'.92—dc20    89–71027
ISBN 0–19–311922–6

Typeset by Pentacor PLC.
Printed in Great Britain by
Butler & Tanner Ltd., Frome, Somerset

# PREFACE

SYSTEMATIC and critical study of the nineteenth century by music historians is a fairly recent endeavour. For the first generations of scholars, nineteenth-century music was contemporary music, and, with a few notable exceptions, most of those involved in critical research devoted their energy and limited resources to charting the course of music in centuries prior to their own, to broadening and deepening their knowledge of earlier, more remote eras. The study of early music remained the preoccupation of historical musicology well into our own century. In the last two decades the situation has changed dramatically. At sufficient temporal distance, and equipped with sharpened style-analytical and source-critical methods, scholars have begun to delve into 'musicology's lost century'. Dissertations on nineteenth-century topics have proliferated; new collected editions for Beethoven, Schubert, Berlioz, Wagner, and Verdi, among others, have been launched; research conferences on various nineteenth-century composers and topics have been convened, their proceedings published; and for the last dozen years, scholars of nineteenth-century music have had a pre-eminent journal of their own.

Research on Johannes Brahms has followed much the same path, though somewhat more belatedly than other areas of nineteenth-century studies. Ironically, this delay may have been caused, at least in part, by the publications which the first generation of Brahms scholars produced as testimony of their devotion to their late friend and colleague—Max Kalbeck's monumental biography (1904–22), the sixteen-volume set of correspondence issued by the Deutsche Brahms-Gesellschaft (1906–22) and Berthold Litzmann's collection of the extant letters between Clara Schumann and Brahms (1927), and the *Johannes Brahms sämtliche Werke* edited by Eusebius Mandyczewski and Hans Gál and released under the auspices of the Gesellschaft der Musikfreunde in Vienna (1926–8). During the same period Florence May produced a two-volume reminiscence/biography (1905), and Walter Niemann (1920) and Richard Specht (1928) released important biographical studies viewing Brahms, respectively, as a North German and within his adoptive Viennese environment. Furthermore, numerous friends and colleagues published accounts of their encounters with Brahms; Max Friedlaender (1922) and Paul Mies (1923) wrote monographs on Brahms's Lieder (Friedlaender's research was done in conjunction with the preparation of a critical edition of the songs for C. F. Peters); and in the 1920s articles by Mies and Alfred Orel afforded the first glimpses of Brahms's compositional process. In these publications so much information was brought forth, so much seemed to be based firmly on primary sources and first-hand experience, that many assumed all the important work of Brahms research had been done, that Brahms's position in the musical pantheon was set, secure, and clearly defined.

The decade between the completion of the *Brahms Werke* and the onset of the Second World War was not without significant contributions. In 1935 the correspondence between Brahms and the Viennese surgeon Theodor Billroth, an important confidant of Brahms on artistic matters, was published, with extensive annotation, by Otto Gottlieb-Billroth, and in the same year Karl and Irene Geiringer released a biography of Brahms written in the fresh light of hundreds of letters recently become accessible in the Brahms estate. Rudolf Gerber (1932) and Friedrich Brand (1937) contributed monographs on Brahms's songs and chamber music, respectively, and articles by Gerber, Geiringer, Mies, Orel, and others continued to elucidate facets of Brahms's character and work. It was also at this time that Heinrich Schenker released his study of Brahms's collection of 'octaves and fifths' (1933), Arnold Schoenberg produced the first version of his seminal essay on 'Brahms the Progressive' (1933), Edwin Evans completed his panoramic account of the works of Brahms (1912–38), and Donald Francis Tovey wrote his survey of Brahms's chamber music (1929) and began a series of analytical essays on Brahms's music (1935–44). Still, Brahms scholarship tended to rest on the triple pillars of Kalbeck, the collected correspondence, and the *Brahms Werke*.

After the war, scholarly study of Brahms resumed in much the same vein. A number of significant dissertations focused on specific aspects of Brahms's music, including his use of dynamics (Imogen Fellinger, 1956), his works for solo voice (Konrad Giebeler, 1959) and for choir (Siegfried Kross, 1958), his use of sonata form (Arno Mitschka, 1959), his chamber music (Werner Czesla, 1968; Klaus Stahmer, 1968), and the influence of folk-song (Werner Morik, 1965; Siegmund Helms, 1967); in 1961 Hans Gál contributed a volume of insightful essays (*Brahms: Werk und Persönlichkeit*). It is not to belittle the work of these scholars to note that documentary and source-critical questions were not their primary concern and that for the most part Kalbeck and the *Brahms Werke* remained trusted research tools. Yet new documentary materials continued to be brought to light, allowing Brahms to be viewed more fully and from slightly different angles. Foremost among these materials were the correspondence with the engraver/photographer Julius Allgeyer (Alfred Orel, 1964), the poet Klaus Groth (Volquart Pauls, 1956), the Hamburg composer and conductor Julius Spengel (Annemarie Spengel, 1959), and the Brahms family (Kurt Stephenson, 1973); the letters from Fritz Simrock to Brahms (Stephenson, 1961); and the letters and memoirs of Richard Barth, Richard Heuberger, and the Petersen family (Kurt Hofmann, 1976 and 1979).

During this same period, a large number of primary musical and documentary sources for Brahms began making their way into public collections. In Hamburg, the Staats- und Universitätsbibliothek purchased the engraver's models for more than two dozen opera, ·creating a repository of Brahms manuscripts that rivals the collection of the Gesellschaft der Musikfreunde in Vienna as a centre for Brahms research. On this side of the Atlantic, the New York Public Library acquired the Brahms collection of the pianist Paul Wittgenstein, the Pierpont Morgan Library became heir to the Brahms manuscripts in the Mary Flagler Cary Collection and repository for Robert Owen Lehman's Brahms holdings, and the Library of Congress purchased the famed Jerome and Margaret Stonborough collection—over five dozen music manuscripts and the complete Brahms–Hermann Levi correspondence. All three libraries have subsequently enriched their

Brahms collections, and additional items have found their way into other European and American libraries. By the mid-1970s American scholars found themselves in the enviable position of being able to study the original sources for such masterpieces as the First Piano Concerto and the first three symphonies, for numerous chamber and keyboard pieces, and for dozens of choral works and songs. Through the cataloguing efforts of the late Donald M. McCorkle and Margit L. McCorkle, information on the location and nature of these and hundreds of other autographs and manuscript copies has become public knowledge. At last Brahms scholars have at hand the means with which to begin a full re-examination of the traditional wisdoms of their field.

The unprecedented accessibility of primary sources is only now beginning to be appreciated, its effect seen in a handful of studies in compositional process, chronology, and textual criticism (dissertations by George Bozarth, 1978, and Camilla Cai, 1985; articles, critical editions, and prefaces to facsimile editions by Bozarth, Walter Frisch, Ernst Herttrich, Margit McCorkle, Robert Pascall, and James Webster). As the standards of modern scholarship are applied, the shortcomings in the methods of Kalbeck and the editors of the *Brahms Werke* are starting to be revealed. The most important result has been the launching of a pilot project for a new collected edition under the supervision of Friedhelm Krummacher at the University of Kiel.

Throughout the 1970s and early 1980s, though, the primary emphasis in Brahms studies has remained on analysis of style and the placement of Brahms's music within its historical context. Scholars in Germany, now joined by colleagues in England and America, have produced monographs, dissertations, and extended studies on Brahms's songs (Max Harrison, 1972; Eric Sams, 1972; Christiane Jacobsen, 1975; Ira Braus, 1986); on motivic-thematic interactions (Christian Martin Schmidt, 1970) and the use of hemiola (Franz Hermann Wolfgang Plyn, 1984) in the instrumental music, and on motivic and rhythmic contrapuntal structure in the chamber music (Peter Breslauer, 1984); on sonata form (Robert Pascall, 1973; James Webster, 1978–9), structural ambiguity (David Epstein, 1979; Jonathan Dunsby, 1981), Brahms's codas (Matthias Rohn, 1986), and the principle of developing variation in Brahms's music (Walter Frisch, 1984); on Brahms's interest in Renaissance and Baroque music (Virginia Hancock, 1983); on his editing of Schubert Ländler (David Brodbeck, 1984); on the aesthetic bases for the music of Brahms and Bruckner (Constantin Floros, 1980); on Brahms's response to issues in composition in the late nineteenth century (Carl Dahlhaus, 1980); on the reception of Brahms's music in the contemporary press (Angelika Horstmann, 1986); and on the relationship of Schoenberg and Brahms (Klaus Velten, 1976; Michael Musgrave, 1980). Filling out the picture were scores of articles—in seven volumes of *Brahms Studien* issued by the Johannes Brahms-Gesellschaft Internationale Vereinigung e.V., Hamburg (1974–87), and in two volumes of Brahms studies published by the Cambridge University Press (edited by Robert Pascall, 1983, and Michael Musgrave, 1988)—treating a wide variety of topics.

In 1980 the International Brahms Congress organized by Ellwood Derr in Detroit provided the first major forum for the presentation of recent research on Brahms, and during the sesquicentennial year of 1983 other conferences took place in Assisi, Florence, Hamburg, Kiel, Leipzig, Linz, London, Marburg, Vienna, and Washington, DC. (To date, proceedings from the Hamburg, Kiel, London, and Vienna conferences have been published.) Re-evaluations resulting from recent Brahms studies range from fresh analytical and historical insights into single works to a new picture, now being sketched and fleshed out, of Brahms as a pivotal composer in the late nineteenth century, an artist demonstrably the musical heir to Schubert and Beethoven and the progenitor of Schoenberg and his Viennese contemporaries. There can be little doubt that musicological and analytical investigation into the life, music, and historical position of Brahms is in the midst of a strong and sustained resurgence.

The papers published in the present volume were delivered at the International Brahms Conference held at the Library of Congress in Washington, DC, 5–8 May 1983, as part of a five-day Brahms Festival. The participants in this symposium were chosen either because they were currently involved in Brahms research or because their expertise in other areas—Renaissance and Baroque studies, the music of Haydn, Mozart, Schubert, Schumann, and Wagner—is relevant to Brahms scholarship. The scholars assembled came from the United States, Canada, Great Britain, and Germany, and represented a wide range of theoretical and musicological approaches and interests.

The conference was organized into seven sessions, devoted to papers on 'Brahms and Viennese Classicism', 'Brahms the Progressive', 'Brahms Theory' (theoretical thinking inspired by Brahms's music), 'Brahms's Symphonic Music', 'Brahms and Early Music', 'Brahms as Editor', and 'Brahms as Song Composer'. These divisions have in general been retained here, though two of the sessions have been combined under the rubric 'Brahms and Musical Tradition' and the papers of another, 'Brahms Theory', have been distributed into other categories, including a new one, 'Performance Practice'. Some of the papers appear here as originally presented, but most have been expanded, several into extended investigations.

Karl Geiringer's keynote address 'Brahms the Ambivalent' views Brahms as a product of the more conservative decades of the mid-nineteenth century, not always able to reconcile the contradictory elements of his personality, but fully able in his music to draw inspiration from the masterworks of the past while remaining experimental, progressive. The first two groups of papers then examine, from various perspectives, the traditional and the progressive elements in Brahms's music. The investigation of 'Brahms and Musical Tradition' begins with Christoph Wolff's essay placing the antiquarian interests of Brahms and Wagner within the context of nineteenth-century historicism. Theorist David Lewin then explores the nature of the dialectic synthesis of historical modes of musical thought in Brahms's music, focusing on conflicting Mozartean and Beethovenian rhetorical models in the String Quartet in C minor, Op. 51 No. 1, on cantus firmus technique and *Grundgestalt* formation in the String Sextet in G major, Op. 36, on cantus firmus technique, serial formation, and structural voice-leading in the Rhapsody in G minor, Op. 79 No. 2, and on Franconian rhythm, dissonance treatment, and form in the Intermezzo in E minor, Op. 116 No. 5.

Drawing upon evidence gleaned from her study of Brahms's extensive library of early music, Virginia Hancock examines works from three periods in Brahms's compositional career—the *Begräbnisgesang*, Op. 13; three *Chorlieder* from Op. 62; and the motet 'Ich aber bin elend', Op. 110 No. 1—in light of his contemporaneous study and performance of music by Johann Sebastian Bach, Heinrich Isaac, Antonio Scandello, Johannes Eccard, and Heinrich Schütz. Using statistical methods, James Webster investigates the internal proportions of Brahms's later sonata movements (from the Op. 51 String Quartets to the Op. 115 Clarinet Quintet) and their relationship to Viennese Classical tradition; then, with a closer focus, he examines the ways in which Brahms tailored the most variable of the large sections, the retransition into the recapitulation. Elaine Sisman demonstrates how Brahms reinterpreted Classical sectional structures in his slow movements, achieving new syntheses which retain Haydn's and Beethoven's patterns of repetition, recurrence, contrast, and development, but revise the relationships and limits among these principles. And, rounding out this section and pointing towards the next, Charles Rosen discusses Brahms's subversion of Classical forms—his methods of weakening tonal relations, his use of varied sequences, his blurring of traditional articulations of form with 'weak' cadences, his dislocation of sense between bass and melody, and his individualistic treatment of dissonance.

Borrowing its title from Schoenberg's famous essay 'Brahms the Progressive', the second section of the book begins with Michael Musgrave's observations on Schoenberg's penetrating, but highly selective view of Brahms. Schoenberg's remarks on Brahms also provide a starting-point for Walter Frisch's survey of the manner in which Brahms used displacement of metre both to create metrical ambiguity on the local level and to articulate the larger structures of his instrumental movements; the closing section in his study considers metrical displacement in the third of the *Vier ernste Gesänge*, a song in which the shifting bar lines become intimately bound up with both the medium and the message. In the final paper in this section, Edward Cone explores the ways in which Brahms deploys the same material both horizontally and vertically, an aspect of Brahms's progressivism which Schoenberg the serialist must surely have recognized, but on which he remained silent.

A single study focuses on 'Performance Practice'. Working from the premises that motion is the most important quality of music and that Brahms built into each of his compositions the manner and quality that its motion must have in performance, David Epstein investigates how Brahms used rhythm and metre to extend and maintain motion until the point of closure. Epstein further proposes that Brahms's use of tempo as a control of movement relied upon the concept of the *tactus* prevalent in Renaissance music.

The four papers in 'Brahms as Editor' view the composer's editorial activities on behalf of Schubert and Schumann and the steps to publication for his own works. David Brodbeck gives an account of the manuscript sources from which Brahms selected the twenty Schubert Ländler that he edited in 1869 (D. 366 and 814) and considers the compositional criteria that led Brahms to order these dances as he did. Based in part on passages in the Brahms–Clara Schumann correspondence omitted from the published letters, Linda Roesner reveals Brahms's involvement behind the scenes in the preparation of posthumous editions of Schumann's *Scherzo* and *Presto passionato* (1869), the five additional *Études symphoniques* (1873), and the 1841 version of the D minor Symphony (in the Schumann *Gesamtausgabe*). In the final two papers of this section, Robert Pascall reconstructs the history of the problem-fraught publication of the Third Symphony and Margit McCorkle documents Brahms's trial performances and other preparations for the publication of his orchestral and large-scale choral compositions.

Two papers in 'Brahms as Song Composer' treat the issue of word-tone relationships in compositions by the young Brahms. In his study of the early songs, Ludwig Finscher assesses the alterations that Brahms made in the lyrics of the minor poets of his youth and the special manner in which he treated the poetry of Eichendorff. Shifting the focus to the early instrumental works, George Bozarth demonstrates how all of the Andantes in the three piano sonatas develop in a manner which mirrors the broad emotional progress as well as many details of the poems associated with them, and how, in the case of the Sonata in F minor, Op. 5, the melodic and tonal procedures characteristic of its two Andantes thoroughly condition the nature of the remaining movements, creating an entire sonata which can be understood in 'poetic' as well as 'absolute' terms. In the third paper of this section, Imogen Fellinger lays the historical groundwork for the investigation of cyclic tendencies in Brahms's collections of songs.

The final section of the book demonstrates various approaches to the study of Brahms's orchestral works. The *Tragic Overture*, a work which has received close scrutiny by Donald Francis Tovey and again recently by James Webster, is the subject of Claudio Spies's essay, an adjuration to those who view music as conforming (or not conforming) to 'formal norms', rather than perceiving the continuities and inferring the coherences in music in terms of materials and techniques whose interaction in the unfolding of a piece might better be encompassed within the concept of 'processes'. John Rahn contemplates the nature of the perceptual interaction which occurs from the comparison of two works by Brahms in the key of D, the Second Symphony and the Violin Concerto. Robert Bailey assesses the relationship of musical language and structure in the Third Symphony, viewing this masterpiece within the context of the tonal language of Wagner and the formal practices of Schumann, the two composers whose music is evoked through citation in the Third Symphony. And Siegfried Kross examines Brahms's exploration of the potential for shaping musical forms from ongoing thematic processes; in addition to the symphonies, Kross considers the three piano sonatas, the First Piano Concerto, the Piano Quartets in G minor and A major, the String Quartet in C minor, and a number of vocal works.

With its premier collection of Brahms manuscripts and letters, the Library of Congress was the natural site for a convocation of American Brahms scholars and their colleagues. The idea for the festival/conference was first advanced by the late Donald Leavitt, then Chief of the Music Division, and it was his planning that made it possible for the conferees and for Washington's music-lovers to enjoy a series of concerts by some of the world's finest performers. The cordiality and industry of the staff of the Music Division at the Library of Congress, most notably Elizabeth Auman, who co-ordinated local arrangements, created an atmosphere congenial to intellectual deliberation and musical performance. In conjunction with the conference and festival, the Library mounted an exhibition of Brahms autographs, including several manuscripts acquired in anticipation of these events, and issued a catalogue of its Brahms holdings and a facsimile edition of its autographs for Brahms's Schack Lieder. On the day before the conference, a round-table discussion was held on the future of Brahms research, and on 7 May, the sesquicentenary of Brahms's birth, the American Brahms Society was officially founded.

The International Brahms Conference was sponsored by the University of Washington (Seattle), with assistance from the School of Music and the Graduate School of Research Fund at the University of Washington and with major funding from the National Endowment for the Humanities and the Mercedes-Benz Corporation. The publication of these papers has been aided by subventions from the Graduate School Research Fund and the College of Arts and Sciences at the University of Washington; the American Brahms Society; the Oscar G. T. Sonneck Fund, Music Division, Library of Congress; Princeton University; and the Massachusetts Institute of Technology. All musical examples from compositions by Brahms are based on the *Johannes Brahms sämtliche Werke* and those photographically reproduced are published with permission of Breitkopf & Härtel, Wiesbaden; attributions of other examples reproduced from published texts are given with the example. For permission to publish fascimiles of manuscripts, we are indebted to the Library of Congress and the Deutsche Staatsbibliothek, Berlin. Special thanks are due to Denise Von Glahn Cooney, who prepared the index for this volume; Rose Mauro, who prepared some of the musical examples; Maria Easton, Tamara Friedman, and Robert Kingston, who assisted with the proof-reading; and the editorial staff of the Oxford University Press.

GEORGE S. BOZARTH
*Seattle*

# Contents

# PERFORMANCE PRACTICE

# BRAHMS AS EDITOR

# BRAHMS AS SONG COMPOSER

# BRAHMS'S SYMPHONIC MUSIC

# Notes on the Contributors

ROBERT BAILEY has taught at Princeton, Yale, the University of California at Berkeley, and the Eastman School of Music, and is currently a member of the faculty of New York University. His writings focus on problems of Wagner's compositional method and of the tonal system in late nineteenth-century Germany.

GEORGE S. BOZARTH was director of the 1983 International Brahms Conference at the Library of Congress. He is on the faculty of the University of Washington. His articles on Brahms include studies on compositional process, problems in chronology, documents, and editorial issues. He has prepared a critical edition of the organ works of Brahms and is currently editing the correspondence between Brahms and Robert Keller.

DAVID BRODBECK has taught at the University of Southern California and is currently on the faculty of the University of Pittsburgh. His work on Brahms has focused on Brahms's editions of Schubert Ländler and on the *Liebeslieder Walzer*. He has also published studies on Beethoven and Schubert and undertaken research on Mendelssohn's sacred music and Schumann's sonata style.

EDWARD T. CONE is a Professor Emeritus at Princeton University. A composer and pianist as well as a theorist, he has written works for piano, voice, chamber combinations, and orchestra. He has served as an editor of the journal *Perspectives of New Music* and is the author of *Musical Form and Musical Performance* and *The Composer's Voice*, which won an ASCAP-Deems Taylor Award.

DAVID EPSTEIN, who is on the faculty of the Massachusetts Institute of Technology, is a composer, conductor, and theorist. He has appeared as guest conductor with major orchestras in the United States and abroad, among them the Royal Philharmonic, the Orchestre de la Suisse Romande, and the Cleveland Orchestra, and is the author of *Beyond Orpheus: Studies in Musical Structure*.

IMOGEN FELLINGER is Wissenschaftlicher Oberrat at the Staatliches Institut für Musikforschung Preußischer Kulturbesitz in Berlin. She is the author of *Über die Dynamik in der Musik von Johannes Brahms*, *Verzeichnis der Musikzeitschriften des 19. Jahrhunderts*, and *Periodica musicalia: 1789–1830*, as well as numerous articles on Brahms and other composers and topics from the eighteenth to twentieth centuries.

LUDWIG FINSCHER earned his doctorate with a dissertation on Loyset Compère and completed his *Habilitation* with a study of the emergence and early history of the string quartet. He has taught at the University of Frankfurt am Main, and is currently on the faculty at the University of Heidelberg. His main research interests are the Josquin period and Viennese Classicism.

WALTER FRISCH, who is on the faculty of Columbia University, is an editor of *19th-Century Music* and the author of *Brahms and the Principle of Developing Variation*. He has also published a study of Schubring's critical writings on Brahms and written the introduction for a facsimile edition of the Alto Rhapsody. His current work is on the early tonal compositions of Schoenberg.

KARL GEIRINGER (1899–1989) served as curator of the collections of the Gesellschaft der Musikfreunde in Vienna (1930–8) and taught at Boston University and the University of California, Santa Barbara. In collaboration with his wife, Dr Irene Geiringer, he wrote *Brahms: His Life and Work*, which has become the standard Brahms biography in English. He was also author of books on Haydn, Bach, the Bach family, and instruments in the history of Western music.

VIRGINIA HANCOCK, after earning degrees in chemistry and being involved in teaching and research in science, began a second career in music, as a musicologist, choral conductor, and singer specializing in the performance of early music. She currently teaches at Indiana State University and is the author of *Brahms's Choral Compositions and His Library of Early Music*, as well as numerous articles on Brahms and early music.

SIEGFRIED KROSS is Dean of the Faculty of Philosophy at the University of Bonn. He is the author of *Die Chorwerke von Johannes Brahms* and *Brahms-Bibliographie*, as well as numerous articles on the Schumann–Brahms circle. He has also written on Beethoven and Telemann, and is the editor of *Dokumentation zur Geschichte des Deutschen Liedes*.

DAVID LEWIN is a composer and theorist who has taught at Yale University and is currently on the faculty of Harvard University. As a scholar, he is primarily known for his writings on Schoenberg, atonality, and serialism. He has also published articles on Mozart, Schubert, and Brahms, as well as studies involving the theories of Rameau, Hauptmann, and Riemann.

MARGIT L. MCCORKLE began her musical career as a recitalist and teacher of piano and harpsichord. She is the author of the monumental *Johannes Brahms Thematisch-bibliographisches Werkverzeichnis*, the first comprehensive catalogue of the sources for Brahms's music, prepared in collaboration with the late Donald M. McCorkle. She has also published critical editions of Brahms's Schumann Variations, Op. 9, and Variations, Op. 21, Nos. 1 and 2.

MICHAEL MUSGRAVE is on the faculty of Goldsmiths' College, University of London. He is the author of *The Music of Brahms* and the editor of *Brahms 2: Biographical, Documentary and Analytical Studies*, a collection of essays stemming from the 1983 London Brahms Conference, of which he was the director. His studies have focused on Schoenberg's interest in the music of Brahms.

ROBERT PASCALL is Professor of Music at the University of Nottingham. A contributor to *MGG* and *Grove 6*, he has also published numerous articles on Brahms and his contemporaries, and has prepared editions of their music. He served as the editor of

*Brahms: Biographical, Documentary and Analytical Studies*, a collection of articles issued during the Brahms sesquicentenary.

JOHN RAHN is a member of the composition and theory faculty at the University of Washington. The author of the textbook *Basic Atonal Theory*, he has served as editor of *Perspectives of New Music* since 1983. He has written articles in a wide variety of areas, including tonal and serial theory, thirteenth-century music and musical grammars, computational models of music theory, computer software systems for music synthesis, and ethnomusicology.

LINDA CORRELL ROESNER's articles and reviews dealing with manuscript and printed sources for works by Schumann and Brahms have appeared in various journals and collections. She is editor of new critical editions of the Schumann symphonies (Edition Eulenburg) and co-editor of the symphonies for the forthcoming complete edition of Schumann's works.

CHARLES ROSEN is internationally renowned as a concert pianist, with an extensive discography of works by composers from the eighteenth through twentieth centuries to his credit. He is the author of *The Classical Style: Haydn, Mozart, Beethoven*, which won a National Book Award, and *Sonata Forms*, and is a member of the faculty at the State University of New York at Stony Brook.

ELAINE SISMAN has taught at the University of Michigan and is currently on the faculty of Columbia University. She has published studies on the instrumental music of Haydn and on eighteenth-century theoretical treatises. At present she is completing a book on variation forms in the eighteenth and early nineteenth centuries.

CLAUDIO SPIES is a composer and conductor who has taught at Harvard, Vassar, Swarthmore, and the Salzburg Seminar in American Studies, and is currently on the faculty of Princeton University. His compositions have earned him several distinctions, including an award from the National Institute of Arts and Letters and a Fellowship Grant from the National Endowment for the Arts.

JAMES WEBSTER is Professor of Music at Cornell University and has also taught at Princeton, Columbia, and Brandeis universities. The author of numerous articles about Haydn, Mozart, Beethoven, Schubert, and Brahms, Viennese Classical chamber music, sonata form, and editorial practice, he has also prepared editions for the *Neue Bach-Ausgabe* and the *Joseph Haydn Werke*.

CHRISTOPH WOLFF is on the faculty of Harvard University. He previously taught at Erlangen, Toronto, Columbia, and Princeton universities, and is the author of *Der Stile Antico in der Musik J. S. Bachs*. He has contributed several volumes to the *Neue Bach-Ausgabe* and the *Neue Mozart-Ausgabe*, and has published widely on the history of music from the fifteenth to the nineteenth centuries.

# KEYNOTE ADDRESS

# BRAHMS THE AMBIVALENT

—

## KARL GEIRINGER

WEBSTER's *Dictionary of the English Language* defines the word *ambivalence* as 'simultaneous attraction toward and repulsion from an object . . . or action'. Very few persons in the history of music experienced such a state of mind more frequently than did Johannes Brahms. In his actions and thoughts, and even in his creative activities, he was full of contradictions. Zerlina's immortal 'vorrei, e non vorrei' ['I would like to and I would not like to'] could be used as a kind of motto for his attitude.

To some extent Brahms may have inherited this disposition from his father. Johann Jakob Brahms was born into a respectable, narrow bourgeois family. But he did not want to follow in the footsteps of his forebears; he yearned for the imagined freedom of a musical career. Before long he played various string instruments, as well as flute and horn, tolerably well, and went with high expectations to the city of Hamburg. After a prolonged struggle he achieved a modest position as a double-bass and horn player, settled down, got married, and raised a family. However, his restlessness made itself felt again. Jakob tried various kinds of financial experiments—started raising rabbits, pigeons, and chickens, opened a small store which soon was sold again at a loss, and even considered emigrating to America. Eventually he refused to live with his wife and moved out of the apartment they had shared for many years. When Brahms's mother, who was seventeen years older than her husband, died, the man of fifty-nine married again, this time a woman eighteen years his junior.

In Johann Jakob, who, after all, had only modest talents, opposing forces were still to some extent compatible. In the genius Johannes, however, they created substantial difficulties: an urge for bourgeois respectability and bourgeois comfort warred with a desire for independence and an unwillingness to suffer any restraint.

In his daily life Brahms displayed very simple tastes. His clothing was plain and inexpensive; he ate in cheap restaurants and spent little on his food. He never owned a house, but lived in a rented apartment and used furniture belonging to his landlady. He did not even spend much for his beloved collection of musical autographs by great composers.

Brahms kept pedantic order among his books and music. He prided himself on being able to find immediately—even in the dark—any of the books of which he was particularly fond, such as, for instance, the Bible in Martin Luther's translation. He was an avid reader and liked to underline sentences which particularly appealed to him, while correcting every mistake he noticed in a book or piece of music. If he found something remarkable, he would write a big 'NB' in the margin. Brahms even made a special collection of parallel fifths and octaves he found in compositions of the past.

In financial matters too Brahms showed a typically bourgeois mentality. He displayed a certain shrewdness in affairs of business and liked to be well paid for his compositions.

Most of all he longed for a fixed position which would enable him to settle down and give up his life of perpetual concert tours. Specifically, he was anxious to be appointed as the conductor of the Hamburg Philharmonic orchestra and of the chorus connected with it, because he wanted to live as a respected citizen in the city in which he was born and had spent his youth. His greatest wish was to find a congenial partner with whom to share his life, get married, and raise children, of whom he was particularly fond.

All these traits in Brahms's character were opposed, however, by others diametrically different. While as a rule he made it a point to eat very plain and inexpensive fare, and was always satisfied with the simplest meals, he loved to be invited by some of his wealthy friends and admirers to quite sumptuous feasts. Frau von Miller, the wife of a rich music-lover, kept a diary of the food she served to Brahms on each of his frequent visits, so as to avoid embarrassing repetitions. We find there, for instance, that she offered him on 20 February 1892 brain consommé, lobster salad, *fillet de bœuf* garnished with vegetables, ham cooked in Madeira wine, hazel grouse, ice cream, pastry, champagne, and coffee. Other meals always included soup, fish, and three kinds of meat. Brahms's ample girth in later years thus finds an easy explanation.

Brahms's insistence on neatness and order in the arrangement of his books and music was not, however, carried over to his personal appearance and the state of the rest of his property. His suits were always hopelessly creased, his trousers pulled up too far. Instead of an overcoat he liked to wear a plaid over his shoulders, held in place by a huge safety-pin. His hat was always in his hand, never on his head. Brahms's cupboard for his clothing and linen was, as a rule, in the most terrible disarray, although his landlady did her best to keep everything neat and in good order.

Brahms, who was pleased when he had an opportunity to earn money, displayed no interest in it once he owned it. He kept bundles of banknotes uncounted in his closet and gave money away easily. Family members and friends were given generous financial gifts. He never checked his bank account, and left the management of his considerable fortune to his publisher Fritz Simrock. Once when Simrock speculated with Brahms's money and lost the substantial sum of 20,000 Marks, the composer consoled him with the following letter: 'Dear Friend, do not make an unnecessary fuss . . . of course, I have not worried for a moment about the matter . . . because I think of money only while I am talking about it.'

Brahms's ardent desire to occupy a permanent position in his home town was certainly based on self-delusion. In 1863 he was appointed as leader of the distinguished Wiener Singakademie, and later he served as the highly respected artistic director of the Gesellschaft der Musikfreunde in Vienna, but in both cases he resigned after a while because he was unable to put up with a settled activity which interfered with his creative work. He likewise refused tempting offers from Berlin and Cologne, and even when the coveted invitation from Hamburg finally arrived, the man of sixty-one did not accept it, claiming that it was now too late for him. He never admitted, even to himself, that he was tempermentally and mentally unsuited to become a steady member of a well-organized bourgeois society.

The ambivalence of Brahms's feeling manifested itself with particular clarity in his attitude towards marriage. It is characteristic that his first and greatest love belonged to a woman who was fourteen years his senior (an echo of his father's attitude) and the mother of seven children. It was obvious that the almost penniless young composer could not possibly have married Clara Schumann, who was a widow at the age of thirty-seven. Later, after the first great passion for Clara had turned into a life-long friendship, he was captivated several times by the charms of other members of the fair sex, particularly when the young lady was endowed with a fine voice. As he was very handsome, famous, and wealthy, he could easily have succeeded in finding a partner for life. However, he found it impossible to take the last decisive step and form a permanent connection. He was basically unwilling and unable to exchange his unfettered freedom for the bliss of a shared existence. To a friend he once uttered: 'Here in my room, I am quite alone and undisturbed. Oh, this is wonderful.'

It appears particularly fortunate that a genius with such ambivalent feelings lived in an artistic period which, to some extent, seemed to produce a certain number of contradictory elements. In a way Brahms was just the right person for his time. In order to explain this statement, it is necessary to consider the year of his birth—1833—in a larger context.

Between 1810 and 1813 no less than five of the greatest composers in the field of Romantic music were born: in 1810, Robert Schumann and Frederic Chopin; in 1811, Franz Liszt; and in 1813 Richard Wagner and Giuseppe Verdi. Half a century later, between 1860 and 1864, four other outstanding composers were born who gave Romantic music a new direction and imbued it with a different meaning: in 1860, Gustav Mahler and Hugo Wolf; in 1862, Claude Achille Debussy; and in 1864, Richard Strauss. In between these two peaks of revolutionary artistic activity we find a valley of comparatively quiet, unhurried, conservative thinking, an instinctive return to the values of the past. In this period of moderate retrenchment occurred the compositional activity of Johannes Brahms, whose date of birth lies approximately midway between 1810 and 1860. He was, as we all know, a Romantic composer, writing music with numerous progressive features; at the same time he felt strongly attracted by the ideas of earlier musical thinking. Thus the ambivalence of his nature found expression in his art. Brahms was, as Wagner rather derisively stated, a classical romanticist.

In 1933, Arnold Schoenberg offered his famous lecture 'Brahms der Fortschrittliche' ['Brahms the Progressive'], which he later transformed into an extensive essay. In the same centennial year, not knowing of Schoenberg's lecture, I published an article 'Brahms als Musikhistoriker'. Since that time, numerous studies which emphasize either the modernistic or the retrospective nature of Brahms's art have been published. The richness of his harmonies, the frequent inclusion of non-harmonic notes in his chords, and his predilection for unconventional modulations are pointed out; in addition, his use of asymmetric phrases, irregularities of metre, and complicated rhythmic structures—peculiarities of his style which point into the future—surpass in certain respects even the innovations of the revolutionary Wagner. On the other hand, as we are well aware, Brahms gained inspiration from works of the past. The great masters of earlier times, from Palestrina and Schütz to Schubert and Schumann, served as godfathers to some of his works. Hardly any great composer of the nineteenth century felt so completely at home in the strict forms of the past, such as the fugue, canon, chorale prelude, and motet; and no other great composer was so easily induced to change his role and do purely editorial work in order to save valuable music of the past from oblivion.

We have learned that Brahms was in some respects unable to reconcile the contradictory elements in his character. In his art, however, he succeeded magnificently in fusing opposing forces into a glorious new unity. In Brahms's music there is no conflict between old and new, between experimental and traditional; instead, a peaceful dialogue leads to a harmonious solution. In his compositions, diametrically opposed artistic elements are completely reconciled. Goethe's famous saying, 'Und das Gesetz nur kann uns Freiheit geben' ['Observance of the law alone leads to freedom'], might well have been coined for Brahms's work. We may begin to comprehend the true nature of the composer's art if we keep in mind that in Brahms's music strictness and freedom have reached an indivisible, unique union.

# BRAHMS
## AND
# MUSICAL TRADITION

—

A real tradition is not the relic of a past that is irretrievably gone; it is a living force that animates and informs the present. . . . a tradition is carried forward in order to produce something new.

IGOR STRAVINSKY
from *Poetics of Music in the Form
of Six Lessons* (1947)

# BRAHMS, WAGNER, AND
# THE PROBLEM OF HISTORICISM
# IN NINETEENTH-CENTURY MUSIC:
# AN ESSAY

—

## CHRISTOPH WOLFF

THE dialectic interrelationship of 'old' and 'new' represents one of the more decisive factors in the history of music. In this respect, however, music does not differ from other socio-cultural phenomena. Connotations and implications of newness change and keep changing, and since every new idea or object is bound to become an old one, it is most difficult to determine newness adequately in retrospect. And, of course, individual perspectives vary broadly as well. Hence it follows that disagreement can hardly be avoided, particularly when value-judgements are involved.

The term 'historicism' includes a polemical facet, as do most other '-isms', because the issue of relative versus absolute values invariably invites conflict. The application and definition of the term 'historicism' also invites problems because philosophers and historians have understood the idea of historicism in many different ways, ranging from the early nineteenth-century discussions of the general principle of historical variability, relativity, and perfectability to theories in the social sciences of historical trends and laws, which Karl Popper criticizes in *The Poverty of Historicism*. Carl Dahlhaus, who devotes a whole chapter to the topic of historicism in his recent survey of issues in nineteenth-century music,[1] emphasizes its many paradoxical aspects that extend from the nineteenth century into the twentieth, but primarily discusses issues of a historiographical nature.

Among the premises of historicism, the historical consciousness that spread early in the nineteenth century figures most prominently. Musical life and thought no longer restricted 'music of the past' to that of the immediately preceding generation. The works of Bach, for instance, like those of Shakespeare or Michelangelo, became the corner-stone of an ever-expanding and deepening background, against which the accomplishments of the recent past and present—in terms of simultaneous cultivation of contemporary and historical repertories—could be recognized as a matter of course.

[1] *Die Musik des 19. Jahrhunderts*, 269–76.

Consciousness of past and present, quite naturally, had to raise the question of the future. It is therefore not surprising that the philosopher Ludwig Feuerbach, who played a major role in giving the term 'historicism' a decidedly negative ring, wrote in 1843 his *Grundsätze der Philosophie der Zukunft*. Only a few years later, in 1849, Richard Wagner published 'Das Kunstwerk der Zukunft', an essay clearly indebted to Feuerbach's work.[2] Indeed, on the basis of a newly established historical consciousness, future developments moved into focus. It is this context which prompted Robert Schumann, in 1853, to write the prophetic article 'Neue Bahnen', in which he introduced the young genius Johannes Brahms to a wider public.[3] What then did the musical future hold in store for an observer in the early 1850s? Wagnerian music drama and Brahms. And indeed in 1853 Brahms, like other aspiring young composers before and after him, made the pilgrimage to Weimar to visit Liszt; moreover, Brahms's piano sonatas of the early 1850s share certain musical procedures with contemporaneous works by Liszt, as Walter Frisch has recently demonstrated.[4] But less than ten years later, Brahms and Wagner, twenty years his senior, were seen as opposite poles: the list of signatures on the 1860 Manifesto against the threatening predominance of Liszt's and Wagner's 'Neudeutsche Schule' was headed by Brahms and his colleague Joseph Joachim.[5] The irreconcilable aesthetic schism between Brahms and Wagner was at this point established beyond any doubt. And since progressiveness sided conveniently with 'the artwork of the future', Brahms, from the Wagnerians' vantage-point, could only be portrayed as unprogressive, if not downright reactionary.

We have long left behind the polemics of the nineteenth century, and our perspectives have become much more differentiated. By associating Brahms with historicism, we have replaced the negative labels 'unprogressive' and 'conservative', yet because of the latent pejorative meanings of historicism, and by generally dissociating Wagner from it, some facets of the original labelling have been retained. It seems important, however, to see both Brahms and Wagner in their relationship to nineteenth-century historicism in order to understand better what they have in common and what separates them with regard to their practical as well as conceptual dealing with historical materials. As for Brahms in particular, we are in danger of taking so-called historicist attitudes for granted without thoroughly analysing impact and context. There is, unfortunately, a tendency to look for individual works or isolated passages of an expressly retrospective nature rather than at the picture as a whole, or to emphasize obvious resemblances rather than the essential differences. A case in point: discussions of Brahms's Piano Sonata in C major, Op. 1, seem all too frequently limited to its—undeniable—indebtedness to Beethoven, leaving aside what sets it apart—unquestionably too—from the Beethoven tradition.

---

[2] *Sämtliche Schriften und Dichtungen*, 3: 42–177.

[3] *Neue Zeitschrift für Musik* 20 (28 Oct. 1853).

[4] *Brahms and the Principle of Developing Variation*, 46 ff.

[5] The manifesto (first published in the newspaper *Berliner Echo*) is reprinted in Kalbeck, *Brahms*, 1: 404–5.

Music historians have always been keenly aware of Brahms's familiarity with, and genuine interest in, the music of the past, extending from the Mendelssohn–Schumann generation back into the Renaissance, even the Middle Ages.[6] That, of course, has helped to make Brahms a perennial favourite of musicologists, not necessarily with respect to scholarly scrutiny of his music, but due to a truly congenial, if not emotional, affinity. Naturally this has something to do with the fact that the early modern history of our discipline reaches right into Brahms's backyard, so to speak, with men such as Nottebohm, Pohl, Chrysander, and Spitta belonging to his circle of friends. There were no similarly intimate connections between such leading scholars and the seemingly 'anti-musicological' Wagner. This is not to suggest that these facts matter a great deal from a late twentieth-century perspective. They have, however, unquestionably influenced the musicological reception of both Wagner and Brahms in the earlier decades of this century and during the formative stages of the discipline of musicology. Thus, we have long been thoroughly aware of the book and music shelves surrounding Brahms's composing desk and more recent studies, particularly by Imogen Fellinger,[7] Siegmund Helms,[8] Siegfried Kross,[9] and Virginia Hancock,[10] have substantially increased our knowledge.

Brahms's followers, however, rarely recognize Richard Wagner as a man of learning. His library was even bigger than that of Brahms, although it clearly lacked the musicological breadth and depth of Brahms's collection and, instead, contained much historical, mythological, philosophical, and generally humanistic literature.[11] Still, among the musical items, we find quite a few histories of music, theoretical works (even including a new edition of Boethius), hymnological books (for example, Philipp Wackernagel's edition of Luther's chorales), biographical literature (both Carl Heinrich Bitter's and Philipp Spitta's Bach books, Otto Jahn's Mozart biography, etc.), and a very large collection of editions, including Carl Proske's *Musica divina* series, Palestrina, Hassler, and other—mostly Italian—Renaissance music, Bach (B minor Mass, St Matthew Passion, and several cantata volumes from the Bach Gesellschaft edition, plus many single editions), Handel, Gluck, Haydn, Mozart, Beethoven, and so on.

In both Wagner's and Brahms's libraries, German music and books about German music predominated, which is not surprising since this material was much more readily available. Yet it must not be overlooked that nineteenth-century historicism was closely connected with nationalistic movements, which rose at about the same time all over Europe. In Germany this link between historicism and nationalism was

---

[6] Documented in his library (cf. Kurt Hofmann, *Die Bibliothek von Johannes Brahms*) and editorial activities (Couperin, W. F. and C. P. E. Bach, Mozart, Beethoven, Schubert, Chopin, and Schumann).

[7] 'Brahms und die Musik vergangener Epochen'.

[8] 'Johannes Brahms und Johann Sebastian Bach'.

[9] *Die Chorwerke von Johannes Brahms*.

[10] *Brahms's Choral Compositions and His Library of Early Music*, as well as various articles, including her contribution to the present volume.

[11] *Katalog der Bibliothek von Richard Wagner in Wahnfried*.

particularly strong. German nationalism reached its peak in 1870–1 during the Franco-Prussian War, and it is quite interesting to see how both Wagner and Brahms sided with the Prussians and enthusiastically welcomed the founding of the Second Reich.[12] Indeed, Brahms's *Triumphlied*, Op. 55, originated in this connection and was enthusiastically dedicated by its composer (from the foreign and faraway Vienna) to the new German Emperor Wilhelm I. While the events of 1870–1 were related to widespread militant nationalism, one can also observe in Germany many nationalist trends of a peaceful nature. Especially in evidence—and related to the struggle for unification of the politically fragmented German nation—was an almost religiously serious search for national identity and Germanic origins. Both Brahms and Wagner took a genuine interest in the German heritage—Wagner mainly in Germanic mythology, Brahms primarily in German folk-song—and both pursued these matters systematically and broadly since they proved highly relevant for their artistic plans and concerns.

Musical works of the past were objects of study for both composers as well, but again their experiences appear to be rather different. Wagner, by no means an introverted person, dealt with the historical repertory mainly by reading, listening, and occasionally playing (Bach's *Well-Tempered Clavier* was among his perennial favourites). Brahms, on the other hand, was not only privately, but also publicly involved with the music of the past through his concert activities as well as his editorial work. These differences are closely related to the striking dissimilarity in the way the two composers applied their knowledge and experience to their creative work.

For Wagner, retrospective elements often serve for special effects as, for instance, in *Die Meistersinger*, a music drama with obvious historicist tendencies. Here, not only does the first scene open with an imitation church chorale, but the orchestral prelude also prominently displays polyphonic features which Wagner himself referred to as 'applied Bach'; he also called the *Meistersinger* assembly a 'continuation of Bach'.[13] But neither Bach's polyphony nor Beethoven's developmental techniques nor any other historical features are ever fully explored and elaborated in his music. Wagner preferred more of a suggestive, cursory approach, and allusions ordinarily suffice. He once wrote, in 1878: 'Much of what Bach wrote is subconscious, dreamlike; there the "unendliche Melodie" is predestinated.'[14] This comment appears to be quite characteristic of Wagner's vague ideas and his more intuitive than accurate historical premises.

To Brahms, the study of music by other composers, contemporary or historical, meant first and foremost a learning process which formed an integral part of his working habits. Unlike Wagner, who hardly ever turned to someone else for compositional advice,

---

[12] Cosima Wagner, *Die Tagebücher*, 1 (1871–2), *passim*.

[13] 'Angewandter Bach' and 'Fortsetzung von Bach', cf. ibid., 2: 260 (15 Dec. 1878).

[14] 'Alles ist im Keim da, was dann in einen üppigen Boden wie Beethoven's Phantasie weiter wucherte; unbewußt wie im Traum ist vieles von Bach niedergeschrieben; die unendliche Melodie ist da prädestiniert'; ibid., 2: 229 (13 Nov. 1878); cf. also Carl Dahlhaus, 'Wagner und Bach'.

Brahms very much depended on the constructive criticism of his friends and colleagues, and had no problems subjecting his work to their critical review.[15] Study of the works of other composers served to deepen this process by providing him with materials to challenge his own compositional critique.

Applying the term 'historicism' in nineteenth-century music creates manifold problems.[16] For example, to use it as a convenient label to define the context of Brahms's music, *vis-à-vis* that of Wagner's, leads to a juxtaposition based on false premises. The age of historicism has left, without a doubt, a deeper mark in Brahms's than in Wagner's music, although Brahms never went as far as, for instance, Liszt did in his *Missa Choralis*, which represents an exemplary emulation of Caecilianist style. It seems inappropriate to apply to Brahms the definition of 'historicism' given by the art historian Nikolaus Pevsner: 'Historicism is the belief in the power of history to such a degree as to choke original action and replace it by action which is inspired by period precedent'.[17]

For Brahms, musical forms such as the sonata, symphony, song, *Clavierstück*, and motet were primarily processes and principles rather than architectonic structures, and he used his historical experience not to conserve traditions but to reinterpret and change established practices—at times radically. His historical knowledge provided him with a frame of reference and with concrete material with which to bring about change. And this change takes place on many compositional levels, both large- and small-scale. Perhaps most noticeable and typical is Brahms's emphasis on local events (which in Wagner play a very secondary role): especially dense and highly differentiated texture, complex modal harmony (by which I mean a kind of harmonic design that is not chromatic in the Liszt–Wagnerian sense, but fundamentally diatonic and emphatically coloured by chromaticism as well as church modality), and clearly articulated rhythmic-melodic features of suggestive forcefulness (with an overt preference for hemiola), to mention only a few aspects. (Incidentally, the prevailingly 'melancholic' character in Brahms's music seems related to his predilection for similarly expressive qualities in Mozart's Piano Concerto in D minor, K. 466, several Bach cantata movements, for example, BWV 150/7), Schütz's sacred concerto 'Saul, Saul, was verfolgst du mich', Eccard's motet 'Übers Gebirg Maria geht', and certain tunes, mainly of modal quality, from folk-song collections like the *Deutsche Volkslieder* of Kretzschmer and Zuccalmaglio.

Brahms's strength as a composer consists to a large degree in his ideas of reinterpretation, in his scholarly synthetic power, and in his constructivist penetration of the musical material. Although he never claimed to write music of the future, he nevertheless did so, in his own way. He indeed pursued 'new paths' as predicted by Schumann and, from the vantage-point of today rather than the biased perspective of the late nineteenth century, Brahms need not stand in second place as regards newness of musical language.

---

[15] Cf. Paul Mies, 'Der kritische Rat der Freunde und die Veröffentlichung der Werke bei Brahms'.
[16] Cf. Erich Doflein, 'Historismus in der Musik'.
[17] *Studies in Art, Architecture, and Design*, 2:243.

# BRAHMS, HIS PAST, AND MODES OF MUSIC THEORY

―

## DAVID LEWIN

### I

As we listen to the compositions of Brahms, his musical past has a special kind of immanence for us. It is not so much that we are aware of specific models, quotations, or traditional procedures. We notice these to some extent in virtually all music. Rather, it is the way in which Brahms uses his models that is so striking: much more than just patches of material or aspects of his technique, they manifest historical modes of musical thought, and as such contribute to an ongoing process of dialectic synthesis that lies at the centre of his compositional discourse.

To explore this point, let us consider the opening of the String Quartet in C minor, Op. 51 No. 1 (1873). Example 1 sketches aspects of this passage. In bars 1 to 8 we recognize the gist of a rhetorical form which Schoenberg called a sentence: a motivic model is stated, progressively developed, and 'liquidated', leading to a cadence. The rhetoric is characteristic of Beethoven, especially at the opening of a sonata movement. Beethoven uses it, for example, in the main themes of the Piano Sonata in F minor, Op. 2 No. 1, the *Waldstein*, the *Appassionata*, and the Fifth Symphony. In each of these cases the motivic rhetoric leads to a climactic half-cadence on the dominant, followed by a pregnant pause.

The Brahms theme follows its rhetorical models in this respect, as in others, up to bar 9; but then a curious phenomenon becomes manifest. According to the Beethovenian paradigm, the climactic dominant of bars 7–8 should be followed by an immediate return to the opening motivic model, forcefully plunging on into a bridge section, and indeed Brahms's piece contains just such a return, but here it is delayed until bar 23. During the

EXAMPLE 1. Brahms, String Quartet in C minor, Op. 51 No. 1, I, bars 1–11.

EXAMPLE 2. Brahms, String Quartet in C minor, Op. 51 No. 1, I. Voice-leading sketch of bars 7–24.

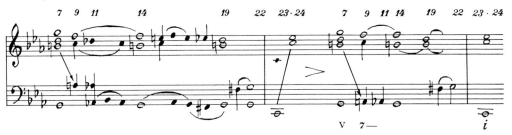

intervening bars, Brahms temporarily relaxes the tension of the climactic dominant (bars 9–10), and then launches a lyrical section (bars 11–22) that explores the dominant in a complex and lengthy trope. Example 2 shows the large-scale elaboration of dominant harmony during this passage. The bass line on the right side of Example 2 is governed by a structural linear gesture that encircles G chromatically: A (bar 9), A♭ (bar 11), G (bar 14), F♯ (bar 20), and G (bar 22). It is highly appropriate that this structural gesture, governing a tension-releasing span of the music, should retrograde a characteristic linear gesture embedded in the opening bars of the melody, where tension was building. The earlier gesture can be read off Example 1; it consists of G (bar 1), F♯ (bar 2), G (bar 2), A♭ (bar 3), and A♮ (bars 3–4).

The relaxation of dominant tension, during bars 9–10 and the lyric trope of bars 11–22, is utterly foreign to the sentence rhetoric. Indeed, Brahms uses very balanced periodic motive structure in bars 11–22. We observe here an abrupt shift of rhetorical mode, temporarily negating the peremptory demands of the Beethovenian sentence by indulging the lyric luxuriance of Mozartean dominant prolongation. It is not hard to locate specific models for this music in Mozart, even instances in C and for string ensemble: the harmonic idea of Brahms's seventh to tenth bars is essentially that governing the first eight bars of Mozart's 'Dissonance' Quartet, K. 465, without the characteristic cross-relations; and the striking entrance of the Neapolitan six-four harmony, over the first two beats in bar 11 of Brahms's quartet, recalls the same harmonic turn in the opening theme of Mozart's String Quintet in C major, K. 515.[1] Like both of these passages from Mozart, the comparable portion of Brahms's quartet involves leisurely prolongation of a large-scale dominant.

The purpose of making these observations is not, however, to locate the sources of Brahms's material or technique in this or that specific model; rather it is to appreciate how two radically different historical modes of musical rhetoric can interact as an essential feature of his compositional discourse. That discourse, in synthesizing the relation of these modes, attributes a special kind of function to various musical events.

---

[1] Compare Brahms's bars 13–14 to Mozart's bars 43–4; indeed, compare Brahms's bars 11–13 to Mozart's bars 48–50 in general. Note specifically the first violin part in Brahms's eleventh bar and the same part in Mozart's bars 48–9.

For instance, the dominant harmonies at bar 7 and at bar 22, as they articulate the raising and lowering of musical tensions, each carry a sort of dialectic historical baggage peculiar to Brahms's style.

## II

Brahms's penchant for historical synthesis extends beyond matters of rhetorical *Gestus*, to involve aspects of organizational technique. David Epstein has commented aptly on the interrelationship between large-scale voice-leading and motivic *Grundgestalt* formations in Brahms's music.[2] Brahms's cantus firmus techniques contribute to this special interrelationship in a characteristic way: they interact with both motivic formations and middle-ground voice-leading, thereby involving both of these nineteenth-century means of organization with modes of sixteenth-century discourse as Brahms understood them.

Example 3 shows the opening melody from the second movement of the String Sextet in G major, Op. 36. The opening G of the passage is also included, for reasons that will become clear. This melody is developed and leads to a cadence on the minor dominant (in D minor) at bar 17, where a second theme appears, unaccompanied harmonically. That second theme, transposed to its dominant and put in the bass, acquires a syncopated countersubject in bars 21–4. Then at bar 25 the second theme is put back in its original key and register; the countersubject, now unsyncopated, is transposed accordingly and moved into the bass, while a (syncopated) third line appears above the whole texture. Example 4 demonstrates the counterpoint of bars 25–8, without octave doublings.

EXAMPLE 3. Brahms, String Sextet in G major, Op. 36, II, bars 1–4.

The ornaments in the cello line, together with the incipit D in the low register, help us to hear that the unsyncopated 'countersubject' is actually the opening theme in melodic inversion. Example 4 can be regarded as an exercise (with some liberties) in mixed species, using the inverted form of the main theme as its cantus firmus and the second theme as one of its counterpoints. Again we note an abrupt shift in modes of musical discourse and the characteristic historical component of the dialectic. The original theme becomes a *Gegensatz*, specifically as (syncopated) countersubject to the second theme, and then asserts itself (unsyncopated) as a cantus firmus over which the second theme itself is a *Gegensatz*. Here the historical discourse is specially complicated by the

---

[2] *Beyond Orpheus*, passim.

EXAMPLE 4.  Brahms, String Sextet in G major, Op. 36, II, bars 25–8.

third line

second theme

countersubject

archaism of the species exercise itself, which reflects aspects of sixteenth-century practice only as they are filtered through eighteenth-century pedagogical sensibility.

But the species exercise does more than make a historical gesture here. By investing the formation of the opening theme with a special structural function as cantus firmus, it fixes that formation as locally stable and referential. This is important because the formation is part of a *Grundgestalt* complex that has been unusually mobile over the first movement of the piece.

To touch on this briefly, we can note that the opening theme of the first movement begins with a rising figure G–D–E♭ and then brings the E♭, after prolonging it as a harmonic root, back down to D again; compare this to the opening of Example 3. And compare to the end of Example 3 the cadence of the initial phrase in the first movement—a descending figure A–G–D–D, where the first D anticipates the second. The cadential leap in this figure is extended by a chain of echoes in the music; the same happens after the corresponding upward-leaping figure that closes the cantus firmus of Example 4. The latent Dorian incipit G–D–E♭–D of the first-movement theme, an incipit which also underlies the beginning of Example 3, is made manifest by the first ending to the exposition in the opening movement: that passage, which arrives at D minor just before a big repeat (like Example 4), makes a first-species stretto on the motive D–A–B♭–A. This gesture also prepares a sixteenth-century contrapuntal mode of discourse for the events which occur later in the piece, around the passage given in Example 4. In the third movement, *Grundgestalt* motivic formations develop yet more radically. Amidst all of this plasticity, the cantus of Examples 3 and 4 stands firm.

Let us turn now to the Rhapsody in G minor, Op. 79 No. 2, and examine the use of cantus firmus technique in connection with middle-ground voice-leading. Example 5 is a combined serial, cantus firmus (tenor), and voice-leading sketch, asserting a main structural line for the piece through its exposition. The motive D–E♭–E–F, which I have marked *S*, plays a role of cantus firmus or structural tenor here, as well as that of a serial *Grundgestalt* formation and a voice-leading gesture. The synthesis of these categories is of course characteristically Brahmsian. Schenker, around 1921, might have termed *S* an *Urreihe*.[3]

As the example shows, *S* is followed by its retrograde *R*, its transposition *T₄* up four semitones, and the retrograde *RT₄* of that transposition. The E♭ of the retrograde form is displaced down an octave to the original *S* register, where the entire *R* form is doubled in an inner voice. We shall see later to what uses Brahms puts this displacement.

When we listen to the line of Example 5 by itself, without the concomitant harmonization of the piece, it clearly sounds as an elaboration of D harmony. Below the notes of Example 5 I have written their degree functions with respect to that D root, a root which later expands to a key, taking the cadential weight of the exposition. Specifically, the cantus firmus forms *S*, *R*, *T₄*, and *RT₄*, when heard unaccompanied within Example 5, imply the respective *Züge* $\hat{1}$–$\hat{2}$–$\hat{3}$, $\hat{3}$–$\hat{2}$–$\hat{1}$, $\hat{3}$–$\hat{4}$–$\hat{5}$, and $\hat{5}$–$\hat{4}$–$\hat{3}$ over an underlying D root.

The $\hat{2}$-to-$\hat{1}$ gesture of bars 9–10 develops that idea, as it grows out of *R*. We do not hear a structural closure here in the piece itself, for $\hat{2}$ is tonicized at the E minor harmony of bar 9. Within the $\hat{2}$–$\hat{1}$ gesture at this point, the chromatic E♭ is missing. This event was prepared by the octave displacement of the high E♭ within *R* itself at bar 3. Bars 11 and 12 restore the high E♭ in a variant of the $\hat{2}$-to-$\hat{1}$ gesture; this passage also puts a $\hat{4}$-to-$\sharp\hat{3}$ gesture in descant above that ♭$\hat{2}$-to-$\hat{1}$. The descant $\hat{4}$–$\sharp\hat{3}$ bears the same relation to *RT₄* as ♭$\hat{2}$-to-$\hat{1}$ bears to *R*. The high E♭ and G of bar 11 are exactly the pitches displaced

EXAMPLE 5. Brahms, Rhapsody in G minor, Op. 79 No. 2. Serial, cantus firmus, and voice-leading sketch, bars 1–21.

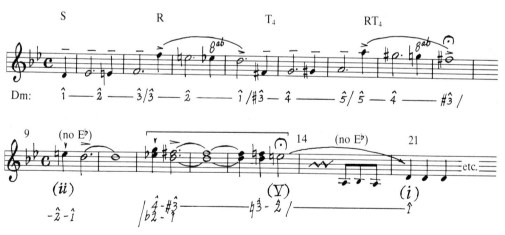

[3] Heinrich Schenker, *Beethoven, Die letzten Sonaten, Sonate A dur Op. 101.* On p. 53 Schenker designates his motivic cantus firmus for the Adagio an *Urreihe*. His linear analysis of the Finale, which proceeds on the basis of rising and falling four-note conjunct (diatonic) gestures, bears a kinship to the analysis of Brahms's Rhapsody which follows here: my analysis too surveys rising and falling forms of a four-note conjunct (chromatic) gesture, the gesture *S*.

downward an octave within $R$ and $RT_4$, respectively; they are marked '8$^{ab}$' in the example.

The $\hat{4}$-to-$\sharp\hat{3}$ gesture continues into bar 13, expanding to become a complete motive form G–F♯–F–E. (The form is bracketed in the example.) The E that was tonicized at bar 9 now recurs as the unique goal of a motive form that is not a $\hat{1}$, $\hat{3}$ ($\sharp\hat{3}$), or $\hat{5}$ in D. And E is now supported by a powerful dominant harmony (in D), as a good Schenkerian second degree (of D) should be. The E and the dominant harmony are prolonged in the music of bars 14–20; they move at bar 21 to the cadential melodic D of Example 5 and a strong supporting D minor tonic harmony, with a characteristic new theme that ends the exposition. The high E♭ is again absent between the structural E of bar 14 and the structural D of bar 21. On the one hand, this absence of high E♭ characterizes retrograde motive forms as they descend; on the other hand, it is also an integral element of the strong tonal melodic closure, $\hat{2}$–$\hat{1}$ in D.

The cantus firmus technique, as well as the serial procedure, interacts with structural voice-leading on yet a larger scale. Bars 1–8 of Example 5 are concerned with third-degree events, specifically with motive forms that either begin or end on the minor or major $\hat{3}$ of D. In contrast, bars 9–13 of the example focus on second-degree events: E is tonicized at bar 9 and the G–F♯–F–E gesture, aiming at E, is the only motive form in the example that does not end on some note of some D triad. Finally, after the second degree of D is prolonged over bars 14–20, the last section of the exposition emphatically reiterates the first degree of D, as does its theme. There emerges clearly an overall sense of a structural $\hat{3}$–$\hat{2}$–$\hat{1}$, co-ordinated with these three sections.

Example 6 takes our analysis further into the piece, up to the return of the second theme in B minor at bar 54. The sequence of serial forms in this example refers strongly to the model of Example 5. Instead of $S$, $R$, $T_4$, and $RT_4$, we now have $S$, $R$ (aborted), $T_8$, and $RT_8$. $T_8$ is the 'dual' of $T_4$. The $R$ form at bar 37 is aborted precisely because the high E refuses to descend to a high E♭. The E finally does descend, at bar 48, but here the pitch is spelled D♯ rather than E♭. This descent occurs within a serial form that aims for the second degree of B minor, over dominant support, in a manner analogous to the G–F♯–F–E form of bars 11–13 (though the concomitant foreground events of bars 47–9 are quite different from those of bars 11–13). The descent of E to D♯ at bar 48 also suggestively recalls the earlier tonicization of E at bar 9, where E was approached from a preceding D♯ (not E♭) in bar 8.[4]

# III

We have seen how modes of Classical rhetoric and Renaissance technique enter into dialectic relations, both among themselves and in connections with nineteenth-century—

---

[4] The D♯ of bar 8 does not appear on Example 5: there I hear it as structurally subordinate to F♯, which fits into the basic linear scheme I have just analysed. I disagree here, and in other aspects of my analysis, with some of the priorities Jonas assigns in his interesting reading of the passage (Heinrich Schenker, *Harmony*, ed. and annotated by Oswald Jonas, 345).

EXAMPLE 6. Brahms, Rhapsody in G minor, Op. 79 No. 2. Serial, cantus firmus and voice-leading sketch, bars 33–54.

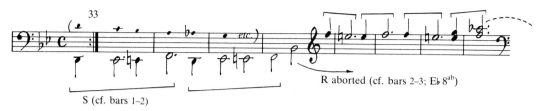

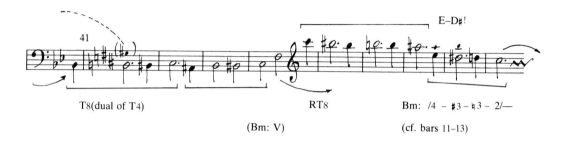

even twentieth-century—modes of discourse, when we listen to Brahms's music. I should now like to carry my point to an extreme and suggest that the discourse of Franconian mensuration is appropriate to our perception of the Intermezzo in E minor, Op. 116 No. 5, a creation which is in many ways the most modern of Brahms's compositions.

One might well ask if Brahms knew anything about Franconian theory. In a sense this does not matter, for I am interested in discussing our responses to Brahms's music today, not his conscious procedures in 1891, and there is no reason why one should not find Franconian terminology as pertinent as serial technique in discussing the structure of our perceptions. Still, it is quite possible that Brahms had some knowledge of mensural theory. As I will show in the appendix to this paper, Brahms was very likely to have been aware of several works on this subject by various scholars of his day, not only writings by August Wilhelm Ambros, but also, and in particular, essays and books by Heinrich Bellermann and Gustav Jacobsthal, where one finds ideas about the perfection and the relationship of *modus* to *metrum* that are strikingly relevant to controversies in scholarship today. But for now, let us examine the music.

EXAMPLE 7. Brahms, Intermezzo in E minor, Op. 116 No. 5, bars 1–12.

Example 7 reproduces the opening section of the piece, a passage which has many modern features, not the least of which is the dissonance treatment. We are used to the 'inside out' metrical notation of the opening; we have encountered such notation in earlier works by Brahms. But what are we to make of the dissonance treatment around bars 7 and 8? How can we even begin to describe what is happening, let alone analyse it? Some sort of suspension technique is clearly at work. Yet it is difficult to say where the suspensions are prepared and where they resolve, since the suspensions themselves are syncopated in some way which is not immediately clear. In this connection, the metrical notation of bars 1–6 confuses matters still more.

What *is* clear about the metrical situation, at least in modern terms, is that bars 1–6 are notated 'inside out', while the cadential bars 11–12 in the first ending come out 'right' notationally. The notation continues 'right side out' after the second ending until the reprise of the theme. The strange treatment of the suspensions in bars 7–8 is therefore involved with a large-scale rhythmic modulation of some sort that connects bars 1–6, in one mode of rhythmic behaviour, to bars 11 ff. in another.

With the introduction of such terminology, the discourse of mensural rhythm irresistibly suggests itself. Instead of worrying about nineteenth-century conventions of metre and metrical notation, might we not more exactly describe the situation by saying that the piece begins in the second mode and modulates into the first mode at bar 11, where the written bar line, taking the tonal weight of the harmonic arrival, also coincides with the beginning of the new perfection?

Franco himself tells us how to modulate from second to first mode, or vice versa: one inserts a rest of appropriate length into the durational series and then picks up again in the other mode.[5] That, in fact, is essentially what Brahms does in the bar preceding the repeat, in order to return to second mode. The modulation into the first mode at bar 11, which starts from the last chord of bar 6 and involves the thorny bars 7–10, is not so simple. Without becoming deeply immersed in those bars yet, we can still hear where Brahms's durational editing takes place: it involves the extra eighth-notes of bars 8 and 10 which bridge over the rests that until this point have articulated the perfections. These extra eighth-notes elaborate cadential dominant seventh harmonies, and one might fancifully entertain the idea that the approach to the tonal cadence at bar 11, with its nineteenth-century species of metric weight, plays a compositional role equivalent to that of the Franconian rest, so far as mensural discourse is concerned. That is, the discourse of tonality, obtruding itself into the rhythmic chain of perfections as we approach bar 11, temporarily breaks that chain, which is then free to resume later in another rhythmic mode.

Exactly the same use of a tonal articulation—to break a mensural chain and change Franconian mode—can be observed at the reprise of the theme, shown in Example 8. The bass pedal on B, which began with the second ending at bar 11, has essentially persisted up to bar 25, where the B recurs in the bass with cadential weight as a dominant in E minor. The first-mode rhythm that set in with the second ending for bar 11 has also persisted, continuing until the last eighth-note of bar 28, where the tonal arrival severs the Franconian chain once again, allowing the reprise to commence in second mode. Example 9 attempts to reconstruct a hypothetical series of transformations, analysing a path from the banal paradigm of Example 9a, through the plagal deception of 9b, to the event in the music itself (Example 9c). (Actually, I hear Example 9b and the music not so much as a plagal deception, but more as a sort of 'Phrygian half-cadence'. We will do well, though, to avoid bringing the topic of sixteenth-century melodic modes into the present context.)

EXAMPLE 8. Brahms, Intermezzo in E minor, Op. 116 No. 5, bars 25–9.

---

[5] *Ars Cantus Mensurabilis*, 150. The discussion of this passage by Leo Treitler is much to the point in the present connection ('Meter and Rhythm in the *Ars Antiqua*', especially 554–6).

EXAMPLE 9. Brahms, Intermezzo in E minor, Op. 116 No. 5. Hypothetical transformations for bars 28–9.

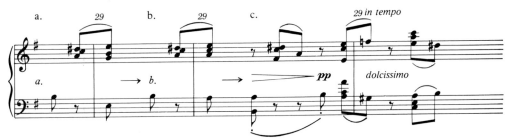

The point of the transformation from the first-mode version of Example 9*b* to the actual event is that the melodic tonic E in the soprano must arrive here not only at the beginning of a perfection, which happens in Example 9*b*, but also on a *brevis*. That is an essential aspect of the way in which the note E behaves as a tonic at the very opening of the piece, an aspect audibly clarified by the repeat. After eighteen bars of dominant build-up in the first mode, it would be virtually impossible to hear Example 9*b arriving* in any other mode than the first, no matter what rhythms might follow. The actual music clarifies and emphasizes the thematic-rhythmic character of the arrival in E, just before bar 29, exactly because the rhythmic expectations of Example 9*a–b* are so powerfully prepared, by the tonal harmony *inter alia*, before being thwarted.

It is fascinating to analyse the changing roles of the characteristic half-step relations E–D♯, D♯–E, B–C, and C–B, as they interact with *brevis/longa* structure, the beginnings of perfections in the two rhythmic modes, and the notated bar lines. Compare, for example, the opening of the piece in these respects with Examples 8 and 9. The mensural role of D♯–E is of course crucial to the reprise.

The F♮ which appears after the notated bar line of bar 29 becomes increasingly prominent over the last part of the piece, giving rise to a strong plagal or Phrygian aura. The F♮ must be referred not only to the F♮ at the beginning of bar 6, but also to the E♯ at the end of that bar. We shall soon discuss the E♯ within a rhythmic context; the rest of this investigation must be left to the interested reader.

Let us return to the puzzle of bars 7–8, where our exploration began. Since the first rhythmic mode is associated with the dominant region of this piece and the second mode with the tonic, it is logical that the disruption of the second mode should begin precisely at the last chord of bar 6, where the bass of the rising motive attains the tonicized fifth degree of the key. We have heard diminished harmonies before this, both as diatonic (at the end of bar 2, etc.) and as secondary dominants (within bars 5 and 6). But we respond to the chord at the end of bar 6 as peculiarly dissonant, for we are expecting the diatonic B minor chord which has been prepared.

The rhythmic complications of bars 7–8 are launched by this dissonant E♯. We expect F♯ (within the B triad), not E♯. And E♯, once heard, does not resolve to F♯ where we anticipate that it will, at the onset of bar 7. Indeed, by the time F♯ finally arrives, the harmony has changed and the F♯, which ought to resolve matters, behaves at once like a dissonant suspension, as if it had already been there before!

Soon we shall investigate this more closely. In the meantime, let us return to the diminished harmony at the end of bar 6, considering the mensural implications of the psychological dissonance it projects. Unlike the diatonic harmony at the close of bar 2, this harmony is essentially and problematically dissonant. And thus it cannot support the beginning of a traditional perfection in the second mode, which the earlier consonant harmonies could, including the 'consonant' diminished triad at the end of bar 2. Of course the sheer acoustical similarity of the two diminished triads delays our recognition of this fact. So too does the F♯ at the beginning of bar 6, which fleetingly suggests that the E♯ might be an F♮, and the B–D–E♯ sonority a diatonic diminished triad, B–D–F, in A minor. These are subtleties which smooth an otherwise jarring impact here. Still, we hear the second mode already beginning to disintegrate at the end of bar 6, despite the continuing rhythmic and textural pattern.

Example 10a sketches the harmonic progression underlying bars 7–8. It is not hard to hear the progression itself; the question is, how does the dissonance treatment elaborate it? In Examples 10b and 10c, I have sketched what seems to me to be the two strongest transformational models which the music suggests. Example 10b is faithful to the rhythms of attacks and rests, and to the location of the bass line in the score. This reading, however, relies crucially upon hearing the E♯ move to F♯ at the beginning of bar 7,

EXAMPLE 10. Brahms, Intermezzo in E minor, Op. 116 No. 5. Underlying harmonic progression (*a*) and two transformational models (*b*, *c*) for bars 7–8.

and that, as we have just noted, is something which emphatically does not happen. In contrast, Example 10*c* faithfully transcribes the events surrounding the bar line of bars 7–8. It is also faithful to the temporal placement of the 'suspending' voice itself at this point. But Example 10*c* must analyse the rest of the music as rhythmically displaced from the score, to accommodate an imaginary B minor harmony on the fourth eighth of the example, a harmony that supports an imaginary consonant F♯ in the melody; the consonant F♯ then prepares 'correctly' the subsequent F♯ 'suspension' on the fifth eighth of the example. The rhythmic displacements and imaginary events of Example 10*c* thus distort the actual music as much as the alternate displacements and imaginary events of Example 10*b*.

As a purely tonal gesture, Example 10*b* is notated metrically inside out; Example 10*c* in contrast is right side out. Example 10*b*, with its inside out metre, harks back to the opening of the piece; Example 10*c* anticipates the 'correct' metre of bar 11 etc. Consistently enough, Example 10*b* is a 'second-mode' reading of the passage at issue, while Example 10*c* is a 'first-mode' reading of the same passage. The brackets on Example 10 indicate the quasi-perfections in these two readings.

I say 'quasi-perfections' because we have no business invoking harmonic rhythm, as I have done here, to group a modal rhythmic passage into perfections. Having noted that, one becomes aware of an even more startling dialectic here, involving tonal and mensural discourse: the quasi-perfections are defined not only by the harmonic rhythm, but also by the accents of the appoggiaturas or suspensions which appear at the beginnings of the groupings and resolve into their endings. In Example 10*b*, namely, the accent/release pattern of the appoggiatura/resolution relation is coextensive with the second mode perfections *BL*, while in Example 10*c* accent/release and suspension/resolution are coextensive with the first mode perfections *LB*. The use of dissonance to mark the *beginning* of a rhythmic group in this way is a characteristic feature of tonality (and other post-Renaissance practices); it runs expressly counter to the injunction of Franco, who instructs us to mark the beginnings of perfections with *consonances*.[6] As we noted earlier, it is precisely the psychological dissonance of the final chord in bar 6 that begins to shatter the purity of Franconian discourse in this piece. But now, by invoking the discourse of tonality and suspension technique over bars 7–8, Brahms shows us that it is precisely the attacks of dissonances that determine the locations of the quasi-perfections, and thus decide the mensural issue at stake—the rhythmic mode of the passage. A more far-reaching dialectic synthesis of musical contradictions, extending over a broader historical period, would be hard to imagine.

---

[6] This injunction is discussed in the Appendix, along with Bellermann's response to it.

## APPENDIX

I CAN present no conclusive evidence that Brahms ever read the discussion on mensural theory in August Wilhelm Ambros's *Geschichte der Musik*, of which a new edition appeared in 1891, the year that Brahms composed the E minor Intermezzo.[7] But it seems reasonable to suppose that at some point he did, if only while examining Ambros's historical treatment of folk-song, which lies close by in the book.[8] That would surely have interested him, and he definitely knew other writings by Ambros, which he took seriously, though with some disparagement.[9]

One of the few scholars whose work Brahms actually did praise was Heinrich Bellermann. Around New Year's Day, 1883, Brahms advised Richard Heuberger to study two, and only two, theoretical works: Bellermann's *Contrapunkt* (1862) and Nottebohm's *Beethoven's Unterricht bei J. Haydn, Albrechtsberger und Salieri* (1873).[10]

This collocation of Bellermann with Nottebohm is significant. Brahms's warm relations with Nottebohm are well known. The two musicians actually resided together in 1870, and Brahms helped to further Nottebohm's scholarly work, according to Douglas Johnson.[11] Brahms clipped and collected many of Nottebohm's *Beethoveniana* articles that started appearing in the *Allgemeine musikalische Zeitung* in 1869.[12]

In 1868 Bellermann had joined the editorial board of the *AmZ*, and during subsequent years, while Nottebohm's articles on Beethoven were being published in that journal, Bellermann was extraordinarily active in mensural scholarship, writing extensively and conspicuously on this subject, among others, in the pages of the *AmZ*. It is difficult to suppose that Brahms would have ignored Bellermann's work. He certainly had the opportunity to peruse it. Consider, for instance, volume 58 of the *AmZ*, for 1870, the year cited by Johnson. In this volume is an essay by Bellerman entitled 'Über die Eintheilung der Intervalle in Consonanzen und Dissonanzen bei den ältesten Mensuralisten' which was split into three instalments, each a lead article, in issues Nos. 11, 12, and 13 (16 March, 23 March, and 30 March). The first instalment, devoted primarily to John of Garland, Aristotle, and Anonymous I, appears on pp. 81–2; on p. 83, a verso, begins one of Nottebohm's *Beethoveniana* pieces. Thus, if Brahms did clip this Nottebohm article, he would literally have held Bellermann's work in his hand. The second instalment of Bellermann's essay (pp. 89–91) is primarily devoted to Franco and contains a translation of the *Compendium Discantus*. Again, this instalment is followed directly by a Nottebohm article.

Bellermann had earlier translated Chapter 11 of Franco's *Ars Cantus Mensurabilis*, for the 1868 volume of the *AmZ*. The 1870 volume contains essays by Bellermann on other subjects which would certainly have attracted Brahms's attention, for instance 'Zur Quintenfrage' and

---

[7] *Geschichte der Musik*, 2: 395–436.

[8] Ibid., 300–27.

[9] See Paul Mast, 'Brahms's Study, Octaven u. Quinten u. A.', 42–3, 104–5, and 177–9.

[10] Richard Heuberger, *Erinnerungen an Johannes Brahms*, 18–19. Brahms also belittled Hugo Riemann's *Lehrbuch des Kontrapunktes* to Heuberger in 1889 (p. 41); one doubts he would have been much interested in the mensural study that appears in Riemann's *Geschichte der Musiktheorie*, even if he had somehow come across this work by 1891 (it was first published in 1898).

[11] 'Nottebohm', *The New Grove Dictionary of Music and Musicians*, 13: 429.

[12] Alfred Orel, 'Johannes Brahms' Musikbibliothek', 40 (p. 159 in Hofmann reprint).

'Einige Bemerkungen über die consonierende Quarte bei den Componisten des 16. Jahrhunderts'. The 1873 volume contains a review by Bellermann of Nottebohm's *Beethoveniana* in book form, and also of that author's *Beethoven's Unterricht bei J. Haydn, Albrechtsberger und Salieri*, a work which Brahms was to recommend ten years later to Heuberger.

In 1870 the *AmZ* published the inaugural dissertation of Gustav Jacobsthal, who identified himself in a lead footnote as 'ein Schüler von Prof. Heinr. Bellerman'. This monograph, the earliest modern work on mensural theory cited by *The New Grove* and *MGG*, is entitled 'Die Mensuralnotenschrift des XII. und XIII. Jahrhunderts'. It was released in five instalments, which appeared in issues Nos. 32–6 (10 August–7 September). The instalment for issue No. 34 (21 August) finishes on p. 271, the recto of the last sheet of that issue; on the back of that page follows a list of Brahms compositions available from J. Rieter-Biedermann (up to the *German Requiem*, Op. 45). The Jacobsthal instalments in issues Nos. 35 and 36 both discuss Franco's ideas about the transmutation of first and second modes through the use of rests.

This evidence by itself is of course only circumstantial. But Brahms's interest in early music is well documented, and one would expect such matters as Bellermann and Jacobsthal were discussing in their mensural studies to have been of at least passing interest to Brahms. The work of these two scholars is especially interesting to us now because the theoretical positions they took anticipate and support some of the views only recently advanced (again) by Leo Treitler (see n. 5). Bellermann, in his translation of Chapter 11 from the *Ars Cantus Mensurabilis*, tropes Franco's prose in an interesting manner: where Franco tells us 'that in all modes consonances are always to be used at the beginning of the perfection', Bellermann translates 'that in all modes one must put a consonance at the beginning of the perfection, i.e., on the strong beat'.[13] He realizes full well what he is about here, for in another work he introduces the reader to the Franconian dot as 'a little mark . . . that they call the *Divisio modi*, which stands for the modern bar line'. Shortly thereafter he has the following to say: 'If the *Divisio* stands directly following a triple *Longa*, Franco calls it a *Sign of Perfection*; for without the *Divisio*, the *Longa* would be duple or imperfect. But this name, "Sign of Perfection", is quite beside the point, since here too the dot stands for a bar line.'[14]

So much for the relation of the perfection to the modern bar. Bellermann's position on the subject, whatever its merit, is clear. As for the relation of metric modes to poetic metres, Jacobsthal, discussing Odington in issue No. 35 of the 1870 *AmZ*, is more diplomatic, but not much less firm: 'In the Iamb, the stress falls on the long syllable, so that the short serves as an upbeat, and the complete bar begins with the long syllable. Whether or not the same is true for the corresponding mode, though, that is, whether the perfection, the complete bar, begins with

---

[13] Franco writes 'quod in omnibus modis utendum est semper concordantiis in principio perfectionis', which Bellermann translates 'daß man in allen Modi zu Anfang der *Perfectio* d. h. auf den guten Takttheil, eine Concondanz setzen muß'. The *AmZ* translation of 1868 does not include the Latin text. Bellerman later published his translation as a bilingual edition along with historical, bibliographical, and editorial commentary (*Franconis de Colonia Artis Cantus Mensurabilis . . .* ). The passage at issue appears on p. 22.

[14] The first passage reads: 'ein kleines Zeichen . . . welches man die *Divisio modi* nennt und welches die Stelle des modernen Taktstriches vertritt'. The second passage asserts: 'Steht die *Divisio* unmittelbar hinter einer dreizeitigen *Longa*, so nennt sie Franco ein *Signum perfectionis*; dann ohne die *Divisio* würde hier die *Longa* . . . zweizeitig oder imperfekt sein. Doch ist dieser Name "*Signum perfectionis*" höchst unwesentlich, da auch an dieser Stelle der Punkt an Stelle des Taktstriches steht.' Both passages appear on p. 119 of *Die Mensuralnoten und Taktzeichen des XV. und XVI. Jahrhunderts*, where they contribute to an appendix on the history of notation. The first edition of this book was published in 1858; it seems to have been written in preparation for the well-known treatise on counterpoint, which appeared in 1862.

the *longa imperfecta* (which is then stressed, so that the note thereby unstressed, the *brevis recta*, serves as upbeat), or on the other hand, whether the perfection begins with the shorter note, thereby stressed, the *brevis recta* (so that the longer note, the *longa imperfecta*, remains unstressed)—on all this the treatises have nothing to say. Still, rhythmic configurations corresponding to the latter model, in which the shorter syllable is stressed, are not uncommon in [the poetry of] the Middle Ages, while they were not sanctioned by the Greeks.'[15]

Can we suppose that Brahms, as he conceived and elaborated his Intermezzo in E minor, was entertaining memories of writings like these, however consciously or vividly? We shall never know, but the thought of his doing so is intriguing.

---

[15] 'Bei dem Jambus liegt die Betonung auf der lange Silbe, so daß die kurze als Auftakt gilt, und der volle Takt mit der langen Silbe beginnt. Ob bei dem entsprechenden modus aber dasselbe gilt, d. h. ob die Perfection, der volle Takt mit der *longa imperfecta*, die dann betont wird, beginnt, so daß die den unbetonte kurze Note, die *brevis recta* den Auftakt bildet, oder aber, ob die Perfection mit der dann zu betonenden kürzeren Note, der *brevis recta*, beginnt, so daß die längerer Note, die *longa imperfecta*, unbetont bleibt, darüber sagen die Tractate nichts; doch kommen solche dem letzten Fall entsprechende rhythmische Gliederungen, in denen die kürzere Silbe betont wird, im Mittelalter nicht selten vor, während sie von den Griechen nicht gebilligt werden' (p. 279).

# BRAHMS AND EARLY MUSIC: EVIDENCE FROM HIS LIBRARY AND HIS CHORAL COMPOSITIONS

——

## VIRGINIA HANCOCK

THE evidence to which the title of this paper refers is of two principal types: that which can be gathered from study of materials in Brahms's library and that which results from analysis of his choral compositions. The interpretation of each type is subject to difficulties, but still more problems arise when one attempts to interrelate the two kinds of evidence in order to describe the influence of early music on Brahms's original compositions. These problems are compounded by Brahms's extreme reticence in matters he considered private (which included nearly everything having to do with the sources of his inspiration and his methods of composition), so that those seeking insight into why and how he wrote his music have traditionally had to rely on intuition and more or less informed guesswork. Recently, however, research has been directed towards ascertaining exactly what materials are still available for study and beginning to explore these sources for the new and more reliable evidence they might contain. Discussion and interpretation of these materials may now begin.[1]

For the study of Brahms's interest in early music, one major resource has been preserved essentially intact and is available for examination: Brahms's personal library of books, music, and manuscripts, housed in the Archive of the Gesellschaft der Musikfreunde in Vienna. The contents of this library were first catalogued and described, at least in part, by Brahms's friend Eusebius Mandyczewski, head of the Archive at the time of the composer's death.[2] Max Kalbeck used the materials when preparing his biography of Brahms;[3] they were later examined by Karl Geiringer and described in several articles and in his book on the composer;[4] and in the 1950s Imogen Fellinger consulted some of the performance materials for her study of Brahms's dynamics.[5] In

---

[1] For a recent discussion of Brahms's use of models from Mozart and Beethoven, see Charles Rosen, 'Influence: Plagiarism and Inspiration'; also cf. the papers by David Lewin, Elaine Sisman, and James Webster in the present volume. On general problems facing the research scholar wishing to study Brahms, see Donald M. McCorkle, in collaboration with Margit L. McCorkle, 'Five Fundamental Obstacles in Brahms Research'.

[2] 'Die Bibliothek Brahms'.

[3] *Johannes Brahms*, passim.

[4] 'Brahms als Musikhistoriker', 'Brahms as a Reader and Collector', and 'Brahms as a Musicologist'; in collaboration with Irene Geiringer, 'The Brahms Library in the "Gesellschaft der Musikfreunde", Wien' and *Brahms: His Life and Work*, passim.

[5] *Über die Dynamik in der Musik von Johannes Brahms*.

1934 Alfred Orel published a transcription of Brahms's 'fair copy' catalogue of the musical contents of his library, and that list was reprinted by Kurt Hofmann as an appendix to his own catalogue of all the non-musical items.[6]

This writer's efforts have been directed toward examining all the Renaissance and Baroque vocal music still found in Brahms's collection, cataloguing and describing it, and attempting to assess Brahms's study of these materials in relation to his career as a choral composer, in order to provide, whenever possible, documentary evidence of relationships between the music of Brahms and that of his predecessors.[7] In the present paper these methods will be used to examine selected works by Brahms; as far as possible, interpretations will be based on materials in the library itself. The variety of the sources suggests several different ways to approach Brahms's compositions. Often his own annotations provide direct evidence of his awareness of specific details and techniques in early music, and thereby provide the most convincing evidence available that he was conscious of the origins of such practices when he employed them in his own works. When such annotations are lacking, Brahms's use of techniques reminiscent of those appearing in early music can be observed and discussed as purely musical evidence.

The compositions to be treated span Brahms's compositional career and styles: the *Begräbnisgesang*, Op. 13 (1858), three of the *Sieben Lieder*, Op. 62 (1874), and the motet for double choir 'Ich aber bin elend', Op. 110 No. 1 (1889). For the first and last compositions, relationships to works by J. S. Bach and Heinrich Schütz, respectively, will be stressed; the three Lieder will be assessed in terms of compositional practices of the Renaissance.

# I

Brahms composed the *Begräbnisgesang* in the autumn of 1858, during his second season at the court of Detmold.[8] By that time, his library already contained a substantial quantity of early music. He had begun his collection even before meeting Joseph Joachim and the Schumanns in 1853: the earliest datable book which demonstrates his developing interests is a 1743 print of David Kellner's *Treulicher Unterricht im General-Baß*, acquired in 1848; the earliest datable manuscript copy, which contains short choral pieces by Palestrina, Corsi, Durante, and Lotti, closes with two Hungarian melodies added after the choral works and dated 17 January 1853. During the years of Robert Schumann's hospitalization, when Brahms lived in Düsseldorf to be near the Schumann

---

[6] Alfred Orel, 'Johannes Brahms' Musikbibliothek'; Kurt Hofmann, *Die Bibliothek von Johannes Brahms: Bücher- und Musikalienverzeichnis*. On Brahms's catalogues, see Virginia Hancock, *Brahms's Choral Compositions and his Library of Early Music*, 9–10, and George S. Bozarth, 'Brahms's Lieder Inventory of 1859–60 and Other Documents of his Life and Work', 105–7.

[7] *Brahms's Choral Compositions*, as well as 'Sources of Brahms's Manuscript Copies of Early Music in the Archiv of the Gesellschaft der Musikfreunde in Wien' and 'The Growth of Brahms's Interest in Early Choral Music, and its Effect on His Own Choral Compositions'.

[8] Siegfried Kross, *Die Chorwerke von Johannes Brahms*, 77. Kross's valuable study cites most of the available information about the compositional history of this and all other choral works by Brahms.

family, he worked in Schumann's library, organizing and studying its contents, and making handwritten copies of what interested him. The copies still in Brahms's collection contain chorale tunes and settings (often showing his interest in the histories of the melodies and in their variant versions), folk-songs, and a number of sacred works by Italian composers, the largest of which is Palestrina's *Missa Papae Marcelli*.[9]

Another important addition to Brahms's collection of early music was made during his residence in Düsseldorf: the first volume of the Bach complete works, which Clara Schumann gave him on Christmas Eve in 1855, with the inscription 'to my beloved friend Johannes Brahms, as a beginning' ['meinem geliebten Freunde Johannes Brahms als Anfang']. Soon afterwards Brahms registered his own subscription; his name first appears in the list of subscribers in 1856, in the volume containing the B minor Mass. Unaware of his subscription, the Princess Frederike of Detmold gave him a second set for Christmas 1858.[10]

During the autumn of 1858, the Princess had had ample opportunity to become acquainted with Brahms's enthusiasm for Bach. Among the works he conducted with the court choir were Cantata 4, 'Christ lag in Todesbanden', and Cantata 21, 'Ich hatte viel Bekümmernis', both of which he had found in the *Gesamtausgabe*.[11] Brahms's annotations in the two volumes containing these works show how carefully he studied them as they arrived. He corrected printing errors and noted parallel octaves and fifths, and his interest in the architecture of movements led him to enter repeat signs to indicate large-scale repetitions and *vi-de* signs to point out smaller repetitions or parallel constructions, such as sequences. Frequently he marked imitation, indicating entrances either with brackets or, when he wanted to make more careful distinctions, with numbers: in Cantata 21, for example, numbers from 1 to 5 label choral and oboe entries in the section 'daß er meines Angesichtes Hülfe und mein Gott ist'. In the first choral fugue of the same cantata, Brahms labelled and numbered the exposition and stretto entries, identified the principal key areas, and showed the relationships between entering voices by drawing lines between the pairs (ST and AB in bars 2 and 5, respectively, for example, and then TS and AB in bars 8 and 10, with the note 'umgekehrt' ['reversed'] ).

The performance annotations Brahms entered into others of his scores of Renaissance and Baroque vocal music also reveal features he thought important. Most of the surviving

---

[9] A full list and description of the copies of early music which Brahms prepared appears in Hancock, *Brahms's Choral Compositions*, 11–59 and Appendix 2, and a list of manuscript copies of early music made by other copyists and found in his library is included on pp. 59–69.

[10] Brahms wrote to Clara Schumann asking that she suggest a deserving person to whom the duplicate copies could be given. See Berthold Litzmann, ed., *Clara Schumann–Johannes Brahms Briefe*, 1: 240.

[11] In early October 1858, Brahms wrote to Joachim about rehearsing Cantata 4, complaining about the inadequacy of his performing forces and asking for suggestions about how to perform the work without an organ and how to reinforce those voices that needed support. Joachim had conducted the cantata himself and responded with a detailed list of suggestions. In late November, Brahms again wrote to Joachim, this time to report that he was very pleased with the way his performance had gone, and that he now wanted to work on Cantata 21. Joachim responded that he would try to help again, but that in this case he did not know the cantata already and might not have time to learn it. See *Brahms Briefwechsel*, 5: 215–16, 221, 224, 230. According to Florence May, in *The Life of Johannes Brahms*, 1: 273, Brahms conducted four performances of Cantata 21 during his third season at Detmold.

information of this nature comes from performances that took place some years later than those in Detmold.[12] Study of these materials shows that when Brahms conducted a piece more than once, or when he altered his original decisions about performance, he tended to simplify or eliminate written dynamics (the same is true in his own music); such alterations usually represent a simplification of detail rather than a change in essence or emphasis.

The materials from Brahms's performance of Cantata 4 at the Gesellschaft der Musikfreunde in 1872 are preserved in the Archive of that institution. For the second strophe— the soprano-alto duet—the dynamics Brahms added demonstrate his attention to the structure of the movement as a whole, to the meaning of the text, and to the movement's many suspensions; his tendency is to emphasize the shape of each single phrase, with the peak in volume occurring at the point of highest vocal range and greatest harmonic tension. Many of his other performance copies, especially those for slow movements of Baroque works, show this same kind of attention to the harmonic features that accompany affective texts.

The annotations Brahms made for the 1872 performance of Cantata 4 appear not in his own copy of the first volume of the *Gesamtausgabe*, but rather in the one owned by the Archive at the time of the performance. Some confusion has arisen in the Brahms literature because of Brahms's habit of entering performance markings into his personal copies *only* when another copy was not available—that is, if the group he was conducting did not already own a full score. Thus, his season as conductor of the Vienna Singakademie in 1863–4 is quite fully documented in scores in his own library, but evidence about his performances of works by Bach and Handel in 1872–5 as director of the Gesellschaft der Musikfreunde must be sought in the scores owned by that organization. Here, however, we encounter a problem, because after Brahms gave up the directorship, these scores were used by other conductors who sometimes altered Brahms's markings, sometimes added their own. Furthermore, after Brahms's death and the transfer of his library to the Archive, his own volumes of Bach and Handel were occasionally used and annotated by other conductors. Thus, many of Brahms's performance scores were not his personal copies, and not all of the markings now present in the scores are in his hand. In the case of Cantata 4, after entering his performance decisions into the Gesellschaft's score, Brahms transferred them, adding more detail, into a second copy of the score, which was subsequently used as a model by the copyist who prepared the parts. A later conductor partially obliterated Brahms's markings in this second score, and added his own. Thus, for example, Brahms cannot be held responsible for the decision to double the alto cantus firmus in Versus 4 with four trumpets.[13]

Brahms's *Begräbnisgesang* is a setting of seven strophes of a Renaissance funeral hymn

---

[12] See Virginia Hancock, 'Brahms's Performances of Early Choral Music', 128.

[13] Siegmund Helms, in 'Johannes Brahms und Johann Sebastian Bach', apparently did not know that Brahms made use of the Gesellschaft's volumes of the Bach complete works; he does discuss the second copy of Cantata 4 and refers to the noisy four-trumpet doubling as 'recht originelle' (p. 72). Dynamic markings added to 'Jesu, meine Freude' in a separate copy of the Bach motets have also been mistaken by Helms and others as being by Brahms.

by Michael Weisse. Brahms probably found this sacred text in Philipp Wackernagel's *Das deutsche Kirchenlied* of 1841 (a collection of texts only), where it is entitled 'Zum Begrebnis'.[14] Whether he was familiar with the tune traditionally associated with this text is unknown, but if he was, he chose not to use it; indeed, in the autumn of 1858 he explicitly wrote to Julius Otto Grimm that he had employed no pre-existing melody.[15] Thus, any resemblances to chorale tunes set by Bach are coincidental, perhaps arising from the predictable pattern and narrow compass of the phrases. A more meaningful comparison may be made between the melody of this piece and some of those in other Brahms works associated with the idea of death; note, for example, the similar beginnings of the *Begräbnisgesang*, the second movement of *Ein deutsches Requiem*, Op. 45, 'Magdalena' from the *Marienlieder*, Op. 22, and the first of the *Vier ernste Gesänge*, Op. 121. These parallels have been generally recognized by writers on Brahms's music, as have several others which specifically link the *Begräbnisgesang* with the *German Requiem*.

The rhythm of Brahms's melody fits the first strophe of the text well—much better, in fact, than the metric version of the traditional tune does. When the same music is used for strophes 3 and 7, however, the relationship between the text and the rhythmic accentuation of the melody deteriorates markedly because of continual shifts in metric arrangement within lines of the poem. Siegfried Kross is undoubtedly correct in his observation that Brahms's toleration of this situation—indeed, his emphasis of it—is a signal that he was writing in a consciously 'historical' manner. His setting of the second strophe is melodically monotonous, cast in a style resembling psalmody, until the sopranos enter for the first time at the reference to 'Gottes Posaun', and a crescendo leads to a fortissimo reappearance of the original tune at the start of the third strophe.

'Historical' influences do not appear to have had any effect on the C major melody which Brahms composed for the fourth and sixth stanzas: the text underlay is altered to fit the second appearance of this new melody. Only at the beginning of stanza four does a serious clash again occur between text accentuation and metre.

The fifth stanza begins with an obvious resemblance between Brahms's vocal parts and the opening of the soprano–alto duet in Bach's Cantata 4 (Example 1) which Grimm

[14] No. 373. If Brahms did use this collection as the source for his text, he must have had access to a copy other than the one now in his library, which he signed and dated 'Weihnacht 1862' on the inside of the front cover. (His copy of Wackernagel's *Kleines Gesangbuch geistlicher Lieder*, published in 1860, he inscribed 'Johs. Brahms / 1864.') Brahms modernized the spelling of the title of the poem; other changes in the title are discussed in Kross, *Die Chorwerke*, 77–8. The most likely explanation of the confusion over the title is that it was caused by Brahms himself, who in his correspondence with the publisher Rieter-Biedermann (*Brahms Briefwechsel*, 14: 44–50) refers to the work casually as the 'Grabgesang' and formally as the 'Begräbnisgesang', and who on his autograph manuscript entitled it 'Gesang zum Begräbnis'. Brahms cited Carl von Winterfeld's *Der evangelische Kirchengesang* to support his preference for the last of these titles, but it seems likely he really meant Wackernagel's collection, since Winterfeld's reference to this hymn (1: 277), used in passing in his text and not as a title, is 'des Begräbnißgesanges von Michael Weisse'.

[15] *Brahms Briefwechsel*, 4: 79. In spite of Brahms's statement to the contrary, a number of writers have said that he used either the traditional tune or some other chorale melody. Robert Haven Schauffler, in *The Unknown Brahms*, 393, identified it as 'Erhalt uns, Herr, bei deinem Wort', which Bach used in Cantata 6. The notes of the first phrase are indeed the same, though the bar line is displaced by one beat; but after this phrase the close resemblance ends.

EXAMPLE I. (*a*) J. S. Bach, Cantata 'Christ lag in Todesbanden', BWV 4, II, bars 1–7.
(*b*) Brahms, *Begräbnisgesang*, Op. 13, bars 61–5.

observed and mentioned in a letter to Brahms.[16] It seems clear that Brahms intended the resemblance, and just as clear that he turned away from it in the upward leap of a sixth (followed by the alto in exact imitation) and in his cadence on F major—this tonal move unexpected because in each cadence in Bach's movement a similar approach leads not to the relative major, but downward to what would, in Brahms's key, be D minor (in Example 1*a*, B minor).

As the stanza continues with the entrance of the tenor–bass pair, any harmonic resemblance to Bach's cantata movement disappears, although suspensions continue to be emphasized by dynamics in the same manner Brahms employed in his later performance of Cantata 4, as described above. Moreover, unlike Bach's parts, Brahms's are canonic for the first several bars of each of the three sets of entrances in the stanza; the third, for alto, tenor, and bass, illustrates the word 'Freude' with another upward leap of a sixth. Indeed, the way in which the contours of the vocal lines in this stanza closely reflect the meaning of the text suggests a reason why its setting is unique: the living soul ascends in the women's voices, the body sleeps in the downward motion of the men's

---

[16] *Brahms Briefwechsel*, 4: 83.

voices, and then eternal joy is assured as the canon in the alto, tenor, and bass rises once more.

The text of the fifth strophe also refers to the last judgement and, although the subject is not specifically illustrated by the vocal parts, Brahms's doubling of the voices with trombones may refer to the traditional associations of this instrument. He may also have recalled the manner in which Bach doubled the vocal lines in Cantata 4; when he wrote to Joachim about his plans to rehearse the cantata, he had been concerned that the voices might be drowned out.[17] Another resemblance to Cantata 4 is the trio-sonata texture of these canonic duets, where the true bass appears first in the bassoon, then in the low brasses. Throughout this section, and indeed in most of the rest of the piece, the true bass is performed not by the vocal bass, but rather by an independent instrumental part. Thus, in the alto–tenor–bass canon for strophe 5, the bass line is played by the third trombone and tuba; although it is not part of the canon, it is necessary none the less if the passage is to make sense harmonically, for it provides a foundation upon which the dissonances in the voices are constructed. The clarinet and bassoon parts decorate this outline and, in the second phrase, anticipate the sequential developments in the harmony in a way which makes logical what would otherwise be startling turns in the vocal lines.

In the second stanza, the instrumental group supports the chanting of the choir with a two-bar descending ostinato, imitated in different parts, over a tonic pedal in the timpani. Similar bass lines and pedals, of course, occur repeatedly in the music of Bach; in just the volumes of Bach cantatas which Brahms knew by late 1858 there are too many examples to list. By contrast, characteristically Brahmsian instrumental practices employed in the *Begräbnisgesang* and apparently having no connection with early music include the pounding triplets of the third stanza and at the conclusion (compare again the *German Requiem*), the liquid clarinet triplets which accompany the fourth and sixth stanzas, and the parallel sixths which fill the inner parts of the instrumental interludes between the first and second and the third and fourth stanzas. There is enough of Brahms the Romantic in this work, despite its often conscious archaism, that one must question the musical sophistication of the student who figures in an anecdote told to Florence May by Carl von Meysenbug, a friend of Brahms from Detmold who had sung in Grimm's choir at Göttingen:

As Grimm was distributing the parts of the 'Ave Maria' and the 'Begräbnisgesang' at one of the practices . . . my neighbour, a glib University student with the experience of several terms behind him, said to me in a surprised tone: 'Brahms! who is that?' 'Oh, some old ecclesiastic of Palestrina's time', I replied—a piece of information which he accepted and passed on.[18]

# II

To explore the relationship between Brahms's secular a cappella choral writing and German music of the Renaissance, I have selected three Chorlieder which Brahms

[17] Ibid., 5: 215–16.
[18] *The Life of Johannes Brahms*, 264.

completed in 1874, at about the middle of his career—'Waldesnacht', 'Dein Herzlein mild', and 'All meine Herzgedanken', Op. 62 Nos. 3–5. These pieces have been chosen not because they contain the most obvious uses of Renaissance models by Brahms, but because they are generally representative of his methods of adapting practices from earlier music to the expression of secular texts which are fully at home in the Romantic era (all three are settings of poems from Paul Heyse's *Der Jungbrunnen*). Earlier or later works could equally well have been selected.[19]

The earliest evidence of Brahms's acquaintance with music of the German Renaissance appears in the manuscript copies he made in 1854 in connection with his study of folk-song melodies and chorale settings (see Section I above); these include works by Isaac, Hassler, Gesius, and Praetorius (Vienna, Gesellschaft der Musikfreunde, A 128, ff. 1–4; A 134, ff. 39–40).[20] During the mid- to late 1850s and early 1860s—the period during which Brahms studied counterpoint intensively and directed choirs in Detmold, Hamburg, and at the Vienna Singakademie—he extended his exploration of German compositions based on chorales and folk-song to include Tenorlieder and other late Renaissance settings.[21] Much of his examination of this repertoire was devoted to comparison of different versions of texts and melodies, as numerous cross-references and other markings in his copies show. But more general musical questions engaged his interest as well.

Certain nineteenth-century 'scientific' collectors of folk-songs dismissed the early settings as primitive, but Brahms disagreed with them on this issue, as well as on many others. Next to the following statement by Franz Böhme in the introduction to his 1877 collection Brahms entered a large and obviously indignant exclamation mark:

The medieval musical settings of the fifteenth and sixteenth centuries, even those of the so-called classic period of counterpoint in Palestrina's and Lasso's time, are basically *foreign* to us modern people of the nineteenth century; and for the public as well as the modern artist, who is not accustomed to historic things, they have become *tedious*.[22]

Judging from the extent of his study of this repertoire, Brahms found these settings anything but tedious. One of the richest sources in his library for evidence of his observations on this music is a manuscript copy of all five volumes of Georg Forster's collection *Ein außbund schöner Teutscher Liedlein . . .* (1553–60).[23] The transcription from partbooks into score had been made by a music teacher in Karlsruhe, and another

[19]  For a fuller discussion of the influence of Renaissance models on Brahms's choral music composed up to the mid-1860s, see Virginia Hancock, 'Brahms's Links with German Renaissance Music'.

[20]  See Hancock, *Brahms's Choral Compositions*, 14–15, 49–50.

[21]  Ibid., 20–3, 62–3, 122. Also see George S. Bozarth, 'Johannes Brahms und die Liedersammlungen von David Gregor Corner, Karl Severin Meister und Friedrich Wilhelm Arnold'.

[22]  *Altdeutsches Liederbuch*, p. lxxii. 'Jene mittelalterlichen Tonsätze des 15. und 16. Jahrhunderts, selbst die der sogenannten klassischen Periode des Contrapunktes zu Palestrina's, O. Lasso's Zeit sind uns modernen Menschen des 19. Jahrhunderts grundlich *fremdartig* und für die Menge wie für den modernen Künstler, der sich nicht gerade in das Historische hineingelebt hat, *ungenießbar* geworden.'

[23]  RISM 1560²⁵, 1553³⁰, 1552²⁸, 1556²⁸, and 1556²⁹.

copy was commissioned by the management of the Karlsruhe orchestra for presentation to Brahms to commemorate a performance of the *German Requiem* in 1869. In these volumes, Brahms, as usual, entered cross-references to different settings of certain melodies and to settings in other collections, and corrected or questioned possible errors. He also added accidentals (mainly to create cadential leading-tones), marked imitative entries, added missing portions of text, and filled in canonic parts (in one piece he entered an entire second chorus which sings in canon with the first chorus). He was especially intrigued by the group of quodlibets in the second volume and bracketed the different tunes as they appear; in one of these quodlibets he also used brackets to point out a cadential hemiola and marked a short section where the soprano has triplets against duple metre in the lower parts.

In other works of the German Renaissance in his library, Brahms noted passages where the true metre is not the same as that shown by editorial bar lines. For example, in the copy of Isaac's 'Innsbruck, ich muß dich lassen' which he had made from Winterfeld's *Der evangelische Kirchengesang*, he entered alternative bar lines in red pencil. This piece was barred in $\frac{4}{2}$, but Brahms noted that the soprano is really in $\frac{3}{1}$ during the first part of the piece (Example 2; note values reduced by one-half). He did not, however, pursue this idea into the copies prepared for his performance of the work at the Gesellschaft der Musikfreunde in 1872; perhaps he realized that the cross-rhythms of the other three voices indeed defy *any* kind of rational barring.

Another piece Brahms copied (source unknown) which exhibits formidable complexity in rhythm because of the independence of its vocal lines is a setting of 'Schein uns, du liebe Sonne' by Antonio Scandello (1517–80), an Italian who served as Kapellmeister in Dresden and composed in the German tradition. This piece is remarkable not only for its rhythm, but also for the concentration and sweetness of its dissonances, all of which are diatonic and arise because of the independence and integrity of the parts. The first few bars of this Lied are shown in Example 3. Similar dissonance treatment is found in much of the music of Johannes Eccard, whose 'Übers Gebirg Maria geht' was one of Brahms's

EXAMPLE 2. Heinrich Isaac, 'Innsbruck, ich muß dich lassen', bars 1–7.

EXAMPLE 3. Antonio Scandello, 'Schein uns, du liebe Sonne', bars 1–8.

favourites (the copy which Clara Schumann made for him is preserved in his library; see Example 4 for the closing bars), and also, of course, in many of the most poignant moments of Brahms's own music.

'Waldesnacht', Op. 62 No. 3, is one of Brahms's best-known choral works, probably the most often performed of his secular a cappella Chorlieder. The setting is strophic, and although the discreet text-painting was presumably written to correspond to the first strophe, it does not distort the meaning of the other two strophes. The texture is primarily homophonic, but individual voices are employed in quasi-Vorimitation to bridge some of the gaps between phrases (Brahms used true Vorimitation extensively in other works). The middle section (bars 12–16) consists of a double canon at the lower

EXAMPLE 4. Johannes Eccard, 'Übers Gebirg Maria geht', bars 32–6.

fifth, led by the soprano and alto moving together in thirds, and answered by the tenor and bass a beat later. The resultant dissonance and metric disorientation vividly create a 'träumerisch' mood and demonstrate how a typically atmospheric Romantic moment can be achieved by means of the strictest of counterpoint and other techniques that extend back through the history of German music into the Renaissance.

On the surface Brahms's setting of 'Dein Herzlein mild' seems like a simple rendition of a charming poem that compares the opening of a heart to love with the flowering of a bud.[24] The triple metre which Brahms chose, however, gave him the opportunity to create a complex pattern of overlapping hemiolas. As in 'Waldesnacht', the second part of each strophe begins with the soprano and alto in thirds, imitated after a single beat by the tenor and bass in thirds, this time at the octave. The hemiola which occurs in the middle two bars of the phrase in the upper voices is therefore followed at the distance of one beat by a similar pattern in the lower voices, before all parts come together at the conclusion of the stanza. The third stanza is a variation of the first two, formed by the addition of three bars (bars 21*b*–24*a*). These bars contain a second hemiola in the soprano, with the other parts following one beat later with a pattern of eight beats divided into groups of two; the end of the extension is coloured by an unexpected Neapolitan sixth chord. This expansion and increased activity, of course, express in musical terms the text '[das Knösplein] ist erschlossen' ['the bud has opened']. The playfulness of this work is unusual for Brahms, but entirely in the spirit of his German Renaissance predecessors.

The three stanzas of 'All meine Herzgedanken' are set strophically. For this piece Brahms employed six parts, with the altos and basses doubled—a configuration of voices which he used in six-part vocal writing as a matter of course, but which does not appear

[24] This setting of 'Dein Herzlein mild' is actually Brahms's second. The first setting (WoO 19), discovered by Henry Drinker in the partbooks of Brahms's Hamburg *Frauenchor* and published by him in 1938, probably dates from the late 1850s; it is also preserved in a recently discovered autograph located under a paste-over in the autograph manuscript of the *12 Lieder und Romanzen*, Op. 44 (Library of Congress).

in any of the works in his collection of early music (although he did own copies of a number of works for six voices by Palestrina and Gabrieli). Again the texture is partly chordal, partly imitative, but in this piece no rhythmic dislocation occurs; imitation among the six voices (bars 11 ff.) is used to achieve a straightforward intensification of the choral sound. The surprising feature is the harmonic adventurousness of the setting, and the logic which confines these excursions to a very few bars. (Brahms's Op. 104 Chorlieder exhibit similar harmonic compression.) The imitation begins in the unexpected key of A major, the major mediant, but before long this tonal centre is unsettled by the intrusion of a G♮ which appears first in the tenor in cross-relation with the G♯ persisting in the other voices (bars 13–14) and is then echoed in canon by the soprano (bar 15); finally the G♮ is perceived to have been part of a dominant seventh, introduced well in advance but leading to a cadence on D major, which itself sets up a rapid return to the tonic. The long closing phrase is filled with some of Brahms's tenderest diatonic dissonance, but is also spiced by chromaticism reminiscent of the middle section.

In spite of the skill used in its construction, 'All meine Herzgedanken' leaves the listener with the impression that a Romantic sentiment has been expressed quite naturally—without sophistication or artifice. Brahms, in his own way, shares this achievement with the great composers of the past.

# III

My last example, the motet 'Ich aber bin elend', a work for double choir like its companion pieces in Opp. 109 and 110, was written at the end of Brahms's career as a choral composer. It allows us to demonstrate certain connections between his late choral writing and compositions by Heinrich Schütz which he had recently been studying. These parallels are much more specific than the comparisons made in Sections I and II of this paper.

The music of Schütz was first called to the attention of nineteenth-century musicians by Carl von Winterfeld in 1834 in his three-volume study *Johannes Gabrieli und sein Zeitalter*. Winterfeld devoted an entire chapter to Schütz and published three complete Schütz pieces and eleven fragments in his volume of musical examples. In 1863 Brahms conducted one of these examples, 'Saul, Saul, was verfolgst du mich?' with the Vienna Singakademie; his performance markings, as preserved in his own copy of Winterfeld and in surviving parts, show detailed attention to the expressive possibilities of the text. After that performance, however, Brahms apparently encountered few other compositions by Schütz until the first volume of the Schütz *Gesamtausgabe*, edited by Philipp Spitta, appeared in 1885.[25]

As with the music of Bach, Brahms studied the Schütz volumes with great thoroughness. Pencil strokes in the margins and page corners turned down call attention

---

[25] See Hancock, *Brahms's Choral Compositions*, 24, 33, 66, 127–8.

to entire pieces; textual errors and musical parallels are marked, as they often are in other scores in his library; and some passages are designated for special attention, without explanation. Only one verbal comment occurs, in the *Johannes-Passion*: 'schöne Nachahmung' ['nice imitation'], a special tribute from a composer who customarily noticed and marked examples of musical imitation in early music and who was himself a master contrapuntist.

A number of the passages Brahms marked in the Passions, the *Psalmen Davids*, and the Italian Madrigals he also copied out into a collection of fragments which he kept (Vienna, Gesellschaft der Musikfreunde, A 130, ff. 21–4). For some of these passages the nature of his interest can be surmised. Many appear to illustrate the long-range parallel octave and fifth motions and methods of avoiding consecutive parallels which Brahms compiled in his collection of 'Octaven und Quinten'.[26] For example, the one Schütz fragment found in both collections (Example 5), taken from *Psalm 2*, presumably attracted Brahms's attention because its parallel fifths, separated by intervening notes that form parallel octaves, are clearly audible. At the same time, he cannot have failed to notice the other striking features of this passage—the cross-relations and vivid illustration of the text's mocking laughter ('aber der im Himmel wohnet, lachet ihr' ['but he who dwells in heaven laughs at them'] ).

By the 1880s Brahms was familiar with the style of Palestrina and some of his successors, like Lotti and Durante, where dissonance, however compounded, is carefully controlled; he was also, of course, well acquainted with late Baroque practice, in which even the most dissonant or chromatic effects are nearly always obtained by strictly logical means. He had had relatively little acquaintance, however, with late Renaissance madrigals or with early Baroque music of any kind, and many of Schütz's contrapuntal practices and methods of text illustration were quite new to him. He marked or copied out a number of passages where striking chromaticism, sharp or unprepared dissonance, or unusual leaps in the vocal lines occur.

All the Schütz fragments to be cited in connection with the discussion of Brahms's motet 'Ich aber bin elend' come from the *Psalmen Davids* (1619), which were published

EXAMPLE 5. Heinrich Schütz, *Psalm 2*, SWV 23, bars 31–8.

[26] Johannes Brahms, *Oktaven und Quinten u. a.*, which reproduces this collection in facsimile, with commentary by Heinrich Schenker; and Paul Mast, 'Brahms's Study, Octaven u. Quinten u. A., with Schenker's Commentary Translated', which reproduces the collection in facsimile and in annotated transcription.

in the second and third volumes of the *Gesamtausgabe* in 1886 and 1887, respectively. The polychoral writing in these works may well have prompted Brahms to compose the double-choir settings in his late motets, as a number of scholars have suggested.

Example 6 reproduces a passage from Schütz's setting of Psalm 115 which Brahms marked but did not copy out. The chromaticism and long notes used to illustrate the reference to 'the dead' are striking, as are also the descending passages that literally 'go down into silence'.

In annotations made years earlier in Winterfeld's *Gabrieli*, Brahms had expressed his disapproval of two specific features of early Baroque chromaticism: he drew large Xs next to passages in which cross-relations occur and where the diminished fourth (or its complement, the augmented fifth) is employed melodically or harmonically. The Schütz passages which he copied at this later time, however, contain both, and on these occurrences Brahms made no comment. One of these passages, from *Psalm 8* (Example 7), illustrates how highly chromatic counterpoint can grow from a seemingly innocuous subject when imitation is pursued to its logical conclusion and normal cadential patterns employing suspensions are added. A passage where similar features are more closely linked to the meaning of the text is shown in Example 8: a harmonic diminished fourth on the word 'Tiefe' is followed by upward leaps to the imitative entries on the word 'ruf'. Here Brahms pointed out the tenor, bass, and alto entrances with brackets, as he often did when marking strict imitation.

More imitation, this time in a tightly confined chromatic subject, appears in a passage Brahms copied from Schütz's *Psalm 84*, 'Wie lieblich sind deine Wohnunge'—a setting he would surely have examined with special interest since he had already used this text in his *German Requiem*. The phrase shown in Example 9 again demonstrates Schütz's manner of reflecting the meaning of an affective text with chromaticism.

Schütz's setting of Psalm 84 also contains verses in falsobordone (passages of unmeasured homophonic psalmody sung by all the voices)—a rhythmic-textual practice which Brahms could not help but have noticed. Falsobordone also appears in Schütz's setting of Psalm 110, in another place where Brahms must have observed it because it follows a passage which he copied. The rhythm of this latter phrase corresponds exactly with the textual accents and produces a temporary triple metre which runs counter to the bar lines (Example 10; Spitta's edition and Brahms's copy are barred in $\frac{4}{2}$).

In a fragment which Brahms copied from Schütz's *Psalm 6* (Example 11), the bass begins each of the two choral entries of the line 'denn ich bin schwach'. The upper three parts follow homophonically, at the distance of half a beat, with a rhythm that exactly matches the text, melodic lines that drop a third on the word 'schwach', and harmony coloured by cross-relations. When the four parts are heard together, the offset rhythmic effect, coupled with the dissonance resulting when the bass moves before the other parts, produces a striking illustration of 'weakness' followed by 'healing', as the four voices move together into an authentic cadence.

Brahms's motet 'Ich aber bin elend', on a text taken from Psalm 69 and Exodus 34, is in

EXAMPLE 6. Schütz, *Psalm 115*, SWV 43, bars 139–53.

EXAMPLE 7.  Schütz, *Psalm 8*, SWV 27, bars 107–16.

EXAMPLE 8.  Schütz, *Psalm 8*, SWV 27, bars 1–8.

EXAMPLE 9. Schütz, *Psalm 84*, SWV 29, bars 100–10.

EXAMPLE 10. Schütz, *Psalm 110*, SWV 22, bars 36–43.

EXAMPLE 11. Schütz, *Psalm 6*, SWV 24, bars 25–30.

three sections which correspond to the major divisions in its text.[27] Many features of the setting are strongly reminiscent of passages in Schütz's *Psalmen Davids*. In the first section, the eight available parts are deployed in two different five-part configurations— the sopranos in unison accompanied by four-part men's chorus, then the basses in unison, repeating the soprano melody an octave and a fourth lower, accompanied by

[27] Kross, *Die Chorwerke*, 458–60, has an extensive discussion of the motet.

four-part women's chorus. The melody of the sopranos and basses contains leaps of an octave up to the word 'elend' and a diminished fourth downwards on the first 'wehe' (compare bars 1–4 and 9–13 with Example 8), with continued stepwise motion downwards for the repetition of 'wehe' (compare bars 5–6 and 14–15 with Example 6). The accompanying voices weave a free contrapuntal fabric based on imitation of a chromatic head motive (compare bars 7–10 with Examples 7 and 9) and include imitation of the melody's diminished fourth. The result is a Schützian combination of sharp dissonances, cross-relations, and harmonic as well as melodic diminished fourths.

The second section of the motet is a litany: the first choir recites the text in short phrases, while the second choir responds 'Herr, Herr Gott'—always differently, but always including a rising fourth in one of the voices. The reciting choir has a mainly homophonic texture which resembles not only the falsobordone passages in the Schütz *Psalms*, but also those sections where the metre of the text is independent of the bar lines; see, for example, the phrase 'und von großer Gnade und Treue' (Example 12*a*; compare Example 10). For the phrase 'und vergibst Missetat, Übertretung und Sünde' ('and forgive iniquity, transgression, and sin'; Example 12*b*) the bass moves just ahead of the other voices. The result is an effect of confusion and dissonance remarkably similar to the passage from Schütz's *Psalm 6* described above (compare Example 11).

The last response 'Herr, Herr Gott' also serves as the transition to and first phrase of

EXAMPLE 12. (*a*) Brahms, 'Ich aber bin elend', Op. 110 No. 1, bars 22–3. (*b*) Bars 28–9.

the third section of the motet. Here true eight-part writing and diatonic confidence in God's protection bring the work to a ringing conclusion.

# IV

The three groups of works discussed in this paper illustrate different uses of the types of evidence mentioned at the outset. In every case the contents of Brahms's library may be observed, and so likewise, of course, may the musical content of the early works and of his own compositions. However, once the documentary evidence is gathered, its interpretation is the responsibility of the scholar, since Brahms himself left virtually no information on his opinions or methods. It would be a fruitless exercise to search for instances where Brahms actually 'lifted' material from early music for his own compositions; the nature of influence is much subtler. It is equally unnecessary to state the obvious once again—that Brahms knew a great deal about early music. One has only to listen to his choral music to hear the results. My intention has been to pursue a course between these two extremes: to provide actual evidence of Brahms's knowledge of Renaissance and Baroque music, and to suggest specific examples where such knowledge may have had an effect—direct or indirect—on his own music.

To provide a variety of examples for this 'case study', I have deliberately chosen Brahms works that by their nature suggest a range of relationships with the tradition of early music. One would certainly expect closer connections in the case of an a cappella motet than with a secular choral song, for instance. Likewise, it should surprise no one that Brahms's later works show a more thoroughgoing assimilation of elements from early music than does the earlier and less unified *Begräbnisgesang*. My aim has been to demonstrate that, although Brahms's interest in and love for music of earlier periods was a factor in his life and work throughout his career, its effects were neither constant nor predictable, and his choral compositions should not be viewed as mere imitations or extensions of tradition. These works ultimately have their own value, which overrides all questions and arguments about 'influence'.

# THE GENERAL AND THE PARTICULAR IN BRAHMS'S LATER SONATA FORMS

———

## JAMES WEBSTER

CHARLES Rosen writes provocatively:

The concept 'style' is not historical; it is critical, and it always arises after the fact. Haydn was not creating 'Classical style'; he never heard of it. Insofar as Classical style exists (and of course it does not exist at all), it was invented by people like [Heinrich Christoph] Koch in the 1790s. . . . It is a unity, but it's *post facto*. Classical style was a style for Brahms; he knew what he was imitating or recreating.[1]

With but one or two reservations, one can only agree. The term 'classic' was never applied to Haydn, Mozart, or Beethoven until the nineteenth century, at first by literati and later by musicologists. Rosen's formulation thus propounds the paradox that Brahms's style was an imitation or re-creation of something that never really existed. One might object that Brahms and his contemporaries probably did believe in a Classical style, and that his music is doubtless based in part on developments and refinements of that style. But Rosen has already anticipated this criticism by moving the discussion towards the concept of influence, very broadly defined. Ridiculing the tired habit of spying thematic borrowings and similarities, he focuses instead on general relationships between compositional ideas, which may be formal, gestural, textural, instrumental, and so on, as well as thematic, and which can operate indirectly and unconsciously as well as on the surface.[2] In this context, I would merely go one step further and, for influence, substitute the idea of compositional *tradition*, which seems better suited to describe and explain the kinds of complex transmissions and renewals of artistic heritages in which Brahms was engaged.[3]

As far as Brahms's large-scale instrumental music is concerned, tradition is of course represented primarily by his cultivation of long-established genres of orchestral and chamber music; and by his apparently firm stance against programmatic interpretation, the 'music of the future', and the rest of it. His originality is represented by his chromatic

---

[1] *Haydn Studies*, ed. Jens Peter Larsen *et al.*, 345–6.
[2] 'Influence: Plagiarism and Inspiration' (including numerous examples drawn from Brahms).
[3] See also James Webster, 'Traditional Elements in Beethoven's Middle-Period String Quartets'.

language, constant motivic development and thematic transformation, metric and rhythmic complexity, and an increasing tendency towards 'total organization', allied, however, with a pervasive functional and formal ambiguity. Likewise, he cultivated traditional gestural and formal models, notably sonata form and variation form, but he imbued them with new tonal and structural content appropriate to his novel thematic, harmonic, and rhythmic style. According to Gustav Jenner, Brahms insisted on the need to avoid schematic approaches to large-scale composition, and to let the form grow organically out of the musical ideas.[4] These sentiments are remarkably similar to Tovey's frequent accounts of the organic nature of Brahms's forms,[5] and to today's conventional proscriptions against textbook models in formal analysis. The Schoenbergian and Schenkerian traditions in recent Brahms studies also take his mastery of organic growth for granted.

Given all this, it seems surprising that certain aspects of Brahms's later sonata forms are regular, even 'predictable'. I have in mind not only his almost invariable tendency to recapitulate the second group literally and in full, but also a certain apparent arbitrariness, a certain lack of Beethovenian 'necessity' in his developments and codas; but also an apparent uniformity of proportions, of internal dynamics, of large-scale rhythmic structure. This apparent predictability might seem to reopen Rosen's implied question whether Brahms was not after all a classicizing composer in some respects.[6] But a paradox at once emerges: the closer one looks at any given movement or passage, the more this apparent predictability fades into the background, and the more compelling Brahms's formal mastery and rhetorical skill appear. This paradox suggested the organization of the present study.

First, the internal proportions of the later sonata-form first movements are investigated with respect to their extent of variability (Section II), and some preliminary comparisons drawn with other groups of movements (Section IV). (I assume that these movements, from the String Quartets, Op. 51, onwards, constitute a single coherent repertory, defined by Brahms's resumption of activity in this domain following the long hiatus beginning in 1865, and by the absence of clear chronological divisions within them. Some possible distinctions of period and genre within this repertory are explored in Sections III and IV.) The methodology used here is experimental, but it seems to offer wide potential for further application in comparative studies of form. Second, the most variable and individual of the large sections—the retransitions to the recapitulation—are analysed as unique and individual solutions appropriate to the context of each individual movement (Section V). This contrast should increase our understanding of the relationship between the general case and the particular artistic solution in Brahms's later sonata forms.

---

[4] *Johannes Brahms als Mensch, Lehrer und Künstler*, 6, 60. Cf. Walter M. Frisch, 'Brahms, Developing Variation, and the Schoenberg Critical Tradition', 232.

[5] Donald Francis Tovey, 'Brahms's Chamber Music', 254, condensing a longer discussion from his analysis of the Piano Quartet in C minor, in *Essays in Musical Analysis: Chamber Music*, 205–8.

[6] Rosen does not give voice to such implications in 'Influence: Plagiarism and Inspiration'; his attitude in the passage from *Haydn Studies* (n. 1) is perhaps less clear.

# II

There are twenty-one sonata-form first movements in Brahms's later instrumental cycles. The internal proportions of their main sections are listed in Table 1, according to the four main genres (symphonies; string chamber music including the Clarinet Quintet; trios and quartet with piano; duo sonatas with piano). The twelve columns in the main section of Table 1 give, in order, the percentage of the movement occupied by the exposition, first group, second group, (ratio of first group to second group), development, 'main' section of the development, retransition, (ratio of development to exposition), entire recapitulation, recapitulation of the first group, recapitulation of the second group, and coda. (Columns 2 and 3 are subdivisions of column 1, to which they total; similarly columns 6 and 7 total to 5, and 10 and 11 to 9.) In no case was any difficulty encountered in locating the boundary between the first group and second group, or between the exposition and development. Occasionally such problems arise with respect to the development and recapitulation, the main section of the development and retransition, and the recapitulation and coda. (Such ambiguities are even more common in slow movements and finales.)[7]

It will be most useful to begin with the repertory as a whole, summarized in the row labelled 'MEAN' just below the main section of Table 1. In Brahms's later sonata-form movements, the exposition occupies on average almost precisely one-third of the whole, the development almost precisely one-quarter, and the coda just over one-seventh. The recapitulation is considerably shortened compared with the exposition; in fact, it is closer in length to the development. The cuts (usually involving substantial recomposition) occur almost entirely in the first group, which is reduced by almost exactly one-third of its original length, while Brahms almost always repeats the second group literally (as is well known). Indeed the slight shortening of the second group (less than 4 per cent of its length) is attributable primarily not to cuts as such, but to Brahms's habit of breaking off just short of the point corresponding to the end of the exposition, so as to lead seamlessly into the coda. The only movement with a substantial cut within the second group is from the Third Symphony, in which the second statement of the second theme (for oboe and violas) is omitted. (Throughout this paper, except where explicitly stated to the contrary, any mention of a specific work refers to its first movement.) All these recapitulatory features originated in Brahms's earliest works and were maintained more or less consistently throughout his life.[8]

In two cases, it seemed of interest to calculate the *ratio* between sections. Column 4 gives the ratio between the length of the first group and transition, and the second and closing groups. Depending on the method of calculating the average, the mean ratio is

---

[7] Ambiguities regarding the demarcation of the parts of Brahms's sonata forms are discussed in Frisch, *Brahms and the Principle of Developing Variation*; Jonathan Dunsby, *Structural Ambiguity in Brahms*; and Rosen, *Sonata Forms*. It cannot be denied that different decisions regarding, say, the location of the beginning of the retransition would lead to different results in Tables 1 and 2. The retransitions from these movements are discussed in detail in Section V.

[8] See Webster, 'Schubert's Sonata Form and Brahms's First Maturity', Part 2, 58–9 *et passim.*

TABLE 1. Internal proportions in Brahms's later sonata-form first moveme[...]

| | % EXP[m] | % 1Gr+Tr | % 2Gr+Cl | $\left(\dfrac{1Gr}{2Gr}\right)$ | % DEV | % Main | % Re[...] |
|---|---|---|---|---|---|---|---|
| [a]Sym 1 | 31[s] | 17 | *14−* | 1.22 | *32+* | 17 | *14* |
| Sym 2 | 35 | 15.5 | 19 | 0.80 | 23 | *12−* | *11* |
| [b]Sym 3 | 32 | 15 | 18[b] | 0.82 | 23 | *12−* | *11* |
| Sym 4 | 33 | *12−* | *21+* | *0.565−* | 23 | 19 | *4* |
| [c]4et c | 33.5 | 13 | 20.5 | 0.63 | 21 | 19 | *1* |
| [d]4et a | *39+* | 13 | *26[d]+* | *0.52−* | *16−* | *11−* | *5* |
| 4et B♭ | *30−* | *9−* | *21+* | *0.435−* | *30+* | *24+* | *6* |
| [e]5et F | 33 | *19[s]* | *14−* | *1.40+* | 25 | 14 | *11* |
| 5et G | *31−* | 14 | 17 | 0.81 | 27 | 20.5 | *7* |
| [f]Cl–5et | *31−* | 16 | *15−* | 1.06 | *33+* | *26[f,s]+* | *7* |
| Pf 4et c | *37+* | *21+* | 16 | *1.325+* | 23 | 17 | *7* |
| [g]Pf Tr C | 36 | 16 | 20 | 0.78 | 22 | 17 | *6* |
| Pf Tr c | 34 | 16 | 18 | 0.86 | 23 | 19 | *4* |
| [h]Pf Tr B | *39+* | *26[h]+* | *13−* | *1.97[t]+* | 25 | *24+* | *4* |
| [i]Cl Tr a | 36 | *19[s]* | 17 | 1.10 | *19−* | 16 | *3* |
| V Son G | 33 | 14 | 19 | 0.76 | *30.5+* | 21 | *6* |
| Vc Son F | *31−* | 16 | *15[s]* | 1.03 | *29+* | *13−* | *10* |
| V Son A | 34 | 18 | 16 | 1.09 | 22 | *22[s]* | *0* |
| V Son d | 31.5 | 15 | 16.5 | 0.91 | *17−* | *13.5−* | *4* |
| [j]Cl Son f | 36 | 15 | *21+* | 0.71 | *19−* | 19 | *6* |
| [k]Cl Son E♭ | *31−* | *12−* | 19 | 0.62 | 26 | 18.5 | *8* |
| MEAN | 33.7 | 15.7 | 17.9 | $(0.925)^{n}$ $(0.88)^{n}$ | 24.3 | 17.8 | *6* |
| **VARIABILITY** | | | | | | | |
| Std. Dev. | *2.75[r]−* | 3.6 | 3.0 | $(0.35)^{n}$ | *4.7[r]+* | *4.2[s]+* | |
| Rank[q] | 1 | 5–6 | 2 | — | 10 | 8 | |
| % of MEAN | *8.2[r]−* | 23.1 | 17.0 | (38.2) | 19.4 | 23.5 | *6* |
| Rank[q] | 1 | 6 | 3 | — | 5 | 7 | *1* |
| Size | 1 | 7 | 4–5 | — | 3 | 4–5 | *1* |

[a] Bars 495–511 calculated at 1.5 per notated bar; basis of percentages = 483 bars (introduc[...] omitted).

[b] Second-theme bars in $\frac{9}{4}$ calculated at 1.5 per notated bar; bars 112–19 calculated at 1.5 notated bar; basis of percentages = 239 bars.

[c] Bars 224–60 (*alla breve*) calculated at ⅔ per notated bar; basis of percentages = 247 ⅔ ba[...]

[d] Bars 98–103, 266–71 calculated at 1.5 per notated bar; 305–35 calculated at 25 instead o[...] bars; basis of percentages remains at 335 bars.

[e] Bars 205–21 calculated at 27 instead of 17 bars; basis of percentages = 234 bars.

[f] Bars 98–126 calculated at 40 instead of 29 bars; basis of percentages = 229 bars.

[g] Bars 309–36 calculated at 0.75 per notated bar; basis of percentages = 360 bars.

[h] Four bars in $\frac{3}{2}$ late in first group calculated at 1.5 per notated bar; bars 225–74 in [...] calculated at 1.25 per notated bar; basis of percentages = 296 bars.

[i] Bars 212–24 (*Meno allegro*) calculated at 1.25 per notated bar; basis of percentages = [...] bars.

[j] Bars 214–36 calculated at 35 instead of 23 bars; basis of percentages = 248 bars.

[k] Bars 162–73 calculated at 1.5 per notated bar; basis of percentages = 179 bars.

[m] Repetitions of the exposition are ignored.

[n] The upper of the two figures in the row MEAN represents the mean of the values fo[...] individual movements; the lower figure represents the ratio of the MEAN values. (These

| | % RECAP | % 1Gr+Tr | % 2Gr+Cl | % CODA | Signif. Variant Sections | Relative Variability[p] |
|---|---|---|---|---|---|---|
| + | 25 | 11 | 14 | 12[a] | 4/0 | 0.86 |
| | 28 | 9 | 18.5 | 15 | 2/0 | *0.44−* |
| | 27 | 10.5 | 16[b] | 18[s] | 2/0 | *0.49−* |
| | 29 | 11 | 17 | 15.5 | 3/0 | *0.43−* |
| 5 | **36+** | *16+* | 20 | *10[c]−* | 3/1 | 1.02 |
| − | *32.5+* | 9 | 23[d]+ | 12[d] | +6/2+ | **1.31+** |
| + | 31[s] | 10 | 21+ | 9− | +9/0 | 1.06+ |
| | 29 | *15+* | *14−* | 13[e] | 5/0 | 0.84 |
| | *23−* | 8 | 15 | *19+* | 3/0 | 0.67 |
| 5+ | 23− | 10 | *13−* | 13.5 | +7/0 | 0.92 |
| | 30 | 12 | 18 | 9.5− | 4/0 | 0.69 |
| | 28 | 7[s] | 21+ | 14[g] | −1/0 | *0.45−* |
| 5 | 25 | 6− | 18 | 18[s] | −1/0 | *0.49−* |
| | 23− | 9 | *13.5−* | 13.5[h] | 5/3+ | 1.22+ |
| − | 26 | 11 | 15.5 | 19[i]+ | 3/0 | 0.65 |
| + | 28 | 7[s] | 20 | 9− | 3/0 | 0.715 |
| 5+ | *24−* | 8 | 16 | 16 | 5/1 | 0.89 |
| | *22−* | 10 | *11.5−* | **22+** | 2/2+ | 0.97 |
| 5− | *33+* | **18+** | 15 | 18[s] | 4/1 | 1.035 |
| − | 27 | 6− | 21+ | 17[j] | +6/0 | 0.80 |
| | 28.5 | 9.5 | 19 | 14.5[k] | 2/0 | *0.455−* |
| )[n] | 27.4 | 10.2 | 17.2 | 14.6 | 3.8/0.5 | 0.78 |
| )[n] | | | | | | |
| )[n] | 3.8 | 3.1 | 3.2 | 3.6 | 2.0/0.9 | 0.27 |
| | 7 | 3 | 4 | 5–6 | — | — |
| ) | 13.7 | 30.3 | 18.8 | 24.7 | — | — |
| | 2 | 9 | 4 | 8 | — | — |
| | 2 | 9 | 6 | 8 | — | — |

will be identical only in special cases.) The standard deviation, limits of significance, ...ngly deviant individual values in these two columns are necessarily based on the former ...(the upper value given for the MEAN).

figure is the mean, for each work, of the *ratios* between the absolute values of its actual ...s from the MEAN figures and the corresponding standard deviations. (Only the ten ...having real length are included.) For example, the exposition of the First Symphony is ...cent of the movement, a deviation of 2.4 per cent from the mean, which is 0.87 of the ...deviation of 2.75; the deviation for the first group, 1.5, is 0.41 of the standard deviation ...nd so forth. The result, 0.86, is the mean of the ten ratios so calculated. This method of ...g variance is independent of the sizes both of the sections and of the standard ...s.

rank '1' is most stable (lowest standard deviation; lowest % of MEAN); '10' is least

mean of the values of the standard deviations of the individual sections is 3.6, with ...d deviation of 0.6. The mean of the values for '% of MEAN' is 24.6 per cent, with a ...deviation of 16.3 per cent.

...e figures only appear to equal the minimum deviations for 'significance' (given at the ...f Table 1), owing to rounding off; in fact they are closer to the means.

figure exceeds the mean by *three* standard deviations; cf. Table 2, note *d*.

0.88 or 0.92 (see Table 1, note *n*); that is, the first group and transition occupy nearly half the entire exposition, while the second and closing groups occupy barely more than half. Column 8 shows the ratio between development and exposition; the means 0.72 and 0.73 indicate that on average Brahms's development is just under three-quarters as long as the exposition.

The sections differ substantially in their relative stability (that is, the extent to which they vary from their respective mean proportions); see the bottom portion of Table 1, labelled 'VARIABILITY'. Here are given, first, the standard deviation of the values in each column, and a ranking of these figures; then, the *ratio* of each standard deviation to the mean proportion (expressed as a percentage), along with rankings of those figures and, for comparison, of the average sizes themselves. In general, the larger the section, the less will be its percentage of variability (see the last two of the five rows just cited). That is, the exposition is the longest of the ten sections and by this measure the most stable, and the recapitulation is the next longest and likewise the next most stable; whereas the most variable sections, in order, are the retransition to the recapitulation, recapitulation of the first group, and coda, and this agrees precisely with their degrees of brevity. This seems reasonable, in that the addition or deletion of a four-bar phrase, for example, would hardly affect the proportions of an entire exposition of perhaps a hundred bars, but would represent a change of more than 20 per cent in the typical retransition of only nineteen bars.

In both absolute terms (magnitude of standard deviation) and relative terms (% of MEAN), the exposition is the most stable section. It not only ranks highest by both measures, but in both cases it is the only section that is significantly more stable than average. (Such sections are indicated by italic type and by + or – signs; see the Appendix, third paragraph, and Table 1, note *r*.) In absolute terms, the second group of the exposition is the next most stable, while in relative terms, as mentioned, it is the recapitulation. The development, on the other hand, is clearly the most variable area of the movement in absolute terms; all three highest rankings of variability appear here, two of them significantly higher than average. In relative terms, the development section as a whole and the main part of the development section occupy a middle ground, but the retransition emerges as exceedingly volatile, more than twice as variable as any other section, and by statistical measures highly significantly deviant (indicated here by bold-face type).

The stability of the exposition and volatility of the development are futher indicated by those rankings of relative variability and size of section which fail to correspond (last two rows of Table 1). The second group, in both exposition and recapitulation, is significantly *more* stable (more than one rank higher) than would be predicted from its size alone. The first group in the exposition is also more stable in this sense, but by only one rank, a degree of difference which may not be significant. The development as a whole and its main section, by contrast, are *less* stable than their size would indicate. (The consistency with which *all* the exposition sections are stable and development sections variable would seem to preclude the possibility that this correlation is valid only at the large and small extremes of the range, but varies randomly for sections of average size. The second group and the main part of the development are for practical purposes the same size, but the relative variability of the latter section is 38 per cent higher. A similar comparison can be drawn between the entire development and recapitulation, which are close in size.) All these results suggest that in his maturity Brahms had a more or less clear sense of normal proportions for the exposition, and in particular for the second group (the latter remains stable in the recapitulation as well), but that these stable expositions served as the basis for much more widely differing types of construction later in the movement.

A somewhat different picture emerges from the two columns so far left out of account, which measure *ratios* between sections: first group to second group and development to exposition.[9] The relative proportional stability of the exposition and the second group, when considered as independent sections, is compatible with many different methods of constructing the exposition as a whole. The second group can be more than twice as long, as in the Bb major String Quartet; or nearly so, as in the Fourth Symphony and the A minor String Quartet. On the other hand, the *first* group can be twice as long, as in the extreme case of the Piano Trio in B major; in fact, no fewer than eight movements devote more than half of the exposition to the first group and transition, and in the F major Quintet and the C minor Piano Quartet this imbalance is significantly large. Statistically, less variability is found between development and exposition. Still, in the First Symphony, the Bb major Quartet, and the Clarinet Quintet the development actually equals or exceeds the exposition in length; whereas in the A minor String Quartet it is astonishingly only two-fifths as long, and it barely exceeds half the length in the Clarinet Trio, the D minor Violin Sonata, and the F minor Clarinet Sonata.

Several movements greatly shorten the first-group recapitulation: the Piano Trio in B major, whose gigantic first group could in any case not bear full recapitulation; the Piano Trio in C minor, whose first theme is not recapitulated at all until the coda; and the Clarinet Sonata in F minor, whose first theme is displaced back to the end of the development in the minor Neapolitan, in what amounts to a disguised retransition (see Section V). Other movements, however, actually lengthen this section. In the C minor String Quartet, the beginning of the main theme (bar 135) is tentatively augmented (as in the Fourth Symphony), and its later extension is substantially expanded (bars 143–50 vs. 7–10). The Violin Sonata in D minor includes an extensive 'secondary development', as Rosen would call it (bars 153–67 vs. 24–9),[10] creating proportionally the longest recapitulated first group in any later Brahms first movement.

Let us now focus on individual movements taken as wholes. Eighty individual entries in the main section of Table 1 (from a total of 252) are significantly shorter or longer than the mean for the column in question and are indicated by italic type; an additional ten entries are highly significantly deviant and appear in bold-face type. (See the third

---

[9] See Pascall, 'Formal Principles in the Music of Brahms', 100–1 *et passim*.
[10] *Sonata Forms*, 104–10, 276–80, *et passim*.

paragraph of the Appendix.) The total numbers of both types of deviation in each movement are given at the far right of Table 1, in the column labelled 'Signif. Variant Sections'; the number to the left of the virgule indicates italic entries, the number to the right, bold-face entries. The second column at the far right gives a measure of the general level of variability for each movement (see Table 1, n. *p*). Both of these columns also indicate significantly and highly significantly deviant averages.

Depending on which measure is preferred, Brahms's most extreme or atypical later sonata-form first movements, measured against the norms for all the movements, are those of the String Quartets in A minor and B♭ major and the Piano Trio in B major. The Quartet in B♭ major has nine significantly deviant proportions (out of a possible twelve); but the A minor Quartet and B major Trio include, respectively, two and three highly significantly deviant proportions among their total of eight, and they substantially exceed the Quartet in B♭ major in average variability. The variability in the A minor Quartet is not only higher than for any other work, but achieves the rare highly significant level of deviance. Its deviant profile results primarily from its very long second group (a full quarter of the entire movement), which includes a sixteen-bar second theme (bar 46) given twice in contrasting scorings; a long extension of the counter-statement (bar 78), leading to a big climax in the minor; a *subito piano* (bar 94) with much cadential extension; the formal closing theme (bar 104), itself stated twice and with the second cadence extended in turn; and a substantial retransition on the head motive (bar 120). As a result, the exposition as a whole is also very long (and the ratio of the first group to the second group very small); both long values recur in the recapitulation. By contrast, the development is almost necessarily the shortest in the repertory (and, except for the beautiful and subtle retransition, it seems a little distracted and aimless), and its ratio to the exposition is likewise the lowest of any movement.

The unusual proportions of the B major Trio result from Brahms's well-known *tour de force* of recycling the entire gigantic first group from the 1854 version of this work. This first group alone occupies a full quarter of the movement, and carries very significantly high values for the exposition and first group/second group ratio along with it. The second group is very short, but Brahms nevertheless contrives to compress all the essentials into it: second theme (bar 76), a full antecedent-consequent period; a modulating crescendo extension (bar 84); forte return of the second theme (bar 96), leading to a grand melodic climax (bar 100); and clear closing theme (bar 110). Given this huge exposition, it is perhaps surprising that the development and coda are of normal length (the main section of the development is actually longer than average, but the retransition is tiny). The compensating short value appears in the recapitulation, with its drastically shortened (i.e. normal) first group and short second group. In the B♭ major String Quartet, the first group is by far the shortest in the repertory, and the second group is longer than usual, producing not only the lowest ratio of first to second group of any movement, but the shortest exposition; the coda is also unusually short, while the balance is restored by a relatively long development. Despite the high number of significantly deviant sections in this movement, its average level of deviance is lower than those in the A minor Quarter and B major Trio (in fact, it exceeds the threshold for significance by only 0.01); that is, the individual deviations are considerably smaller than those in the other two works.

Other movements with relatively many deviant sections (but only ordinary levels of average deviance) include the Clarinet Quintet (its ratio of development to exposition is the highest in the repertory), the Clarinet Sonata in F minor, and the Violin Sonata in A major (two highly deviant sections: a 'missing' retransition and the longest coda in the repertory). Other movements with relatively high average variability (but only ordinary numbers of deviant sections) include the String Quartet in C minor and the Violin Sonata in D minor. Both, as noted, take the unusual step of lengthening the first group in the recapitulation, and hence the complete recapitulation is longer as well (in the Quartet it is the longest in the repertory). In the Sonata, this long first group appears to compensate for the unusually short development, which is cast entirely over a dominant pedal, thus motivating the secondary development in the recapitulation, which both extends the process of development and explores new tonal regions (F# minor, hinted at in the development). The Violoncello Sonata in F major, finally, includes the only remaining highly significant deviation, an astonishing retransition section that not only exceeds the main part of the development in length but is largely in the tonic (see Section V below).

Since the main section must total 100 per cent, one or more very short (or long) sections are usually balanced by unusually long (or short) sections elsewhere. But this need not be so: the First Symphony, the Piano Trios in C major and C minor, and the Clarinet Sonata in E♭ major exhibit significant deviations in only one direction. In these cases, the 'compensating' deviations are distributed amongst several sections, and so none of them is 'significant'. For example, in the First Symphony, the long development is balanced by a somewhat shorter exposition, recapitulation, and coda, but of these only the exposition is even close to being significantly short.

It may also be of interest to look at 'unusually typical' movements (in terms of the averages for all of them). According to the incidence of significantly variant sections, Brahms's most 'normal' later sonata-form first movements are the Piano Trios in C major and C minor, which have but one apiece; the Second and Third Symphonies (with the identical pattern of a long retransition in a normal development) and the Clarinet Sonata in E♭ major have but two. According to general variability, however, the Fourth Symphony best fits the norms, followed very closely by the Second Symphony, the Trio in C major, and the Clarinet Sonata; the Third Symphony and the Trio in C minor are also significantly typical. The six works just named also stand out collectively in that they are grouped together within 0.05 of a standard deviation (0.44 to 0.49), while the next lowest figure (0.65) is already more than twice as close to the mean (0.78).

It is not easy to interpret such findings. The concept of statistical normality in an artistic context is inherently problematic, particularly when applied to a composer as 'organic' as Brahms. Could the 'typicality' of the Trio in C major be related to the fact of its being the only work in C major, perhaps even for Brahms the most intelligible key? Is the first movement of the Fourth Symphony properly understood as 'normal', in the face of its unusual and sophisticated motivic and tonal exploitation of descending thirds and the resultant B–C neighbour relations, and its leading position in a work which as a whole is unique in form? Should the low variability in the Piano Trio in C minor (a statistical average) weigh heavily against its conspicuous failure to recapitulate the first theme in the tonic until the coda? (The latter feature is to be sure reflected in the significant variants; the first-group recapitulation is shorter than average.) I do not presume to offer answers to these questions here; but the problematic aspects of the concepts normality and typicality in this context must never be ignored.

### III

One is naturally interested to know how the proportions in Brahms's later sonata-form movements vary according to genre, date, key, and so forth. Some information on these points is provided in Table 2. The mean values and standard deviations (from Table 1) appear at the top. The next five rows give the mean values for each of the main genres (the string chamber music, for reasons that will become clear, is subdivided into the quartets and the quintets, the latter still including the Clarinet Quintet); the next four rows do the same for four different coherent subsets of the repertory which might reasonably be supposed to be similar in external form: the five relatively early works (up to the First Symphony), the last three symphonies, the three works for piano and strings completed in 1886,[11] and the late works with clarinet.

In terms of the criteria used in Table 1, the most 'atypical' of the five genres is the string quartet. (These works can reasonably be said to constitute a subgenre, by virtue of their double distinction of early date and scoring.) Whereas on average no other genre has more than two clearly significantly deviant entries in Table 2, the quartets have six. The internal construction of the exposition is weighted decisively in favour of the second group; the recapitulation of the first group does not undergo the customary cut, and this, combined with the long second group, makes the recapitulation as a whole longer than usual; the coda, by contrast, is short. These deviations are consistent in all three quartets. The development sections of the individual works also exhibit significant deviations (cf. Table 1), but the latter are of opposite tendency (+ or –) and hence 'cancel out', yielding a normal reading in Table 2. Their influence is seen, however, in the very high figures for the number of variant sections and for variability (first two columns in the right-hand part of Table 2). But the string quartets are more consistent as a genre than these results might suggest; see the last column of Table 2, which gives a measure of variability within each genre or group of works in terms of that genre's own averages (rather than in terms of the repertory as a whole, as in the preceding column). The quartets' internal variability, though higher than average, is not significantly high. It is the duo sonatas which exhibit significantly high internal variability, despite merely average incidences with respect to the overall norms (the former cancelling out with respect to the latter in

---

[11] See, for example, Tovey, 'Brahms's Chamber Music', 259–63.

TABLE 2. Internal proportions in selected groups of movements

| | % EXP | % 1Gr+Tr | % 2Gr+Cl | $\left(\frac{1Gr}{2Gr}\right)$ [a] | % DEV | % Main | % Retr | $\left(\frac{Dev}{Exp}\right)$ [a] | % RECAP | % 1Gr+Tr | % 2Gr+Cl | % CODA | Mean Signif. Variants | Relative Variability (Table 1) [b] | Internal Variability (Table 2) [c] |
|---|---|---|---|---|---|---|---|---|---|---|---|---|---|---|---|
| MEAN | 33.7 | 15.7 | 17.9 | 0.925 | 24.3 | 17.8 | 6.5 | 0.73 | 27.4 | 10.2 | 17.2 | 14.6 | 3.8/0.5 | 0.78 | 3.13 |
| Std. Dev. | 2.75 | 3.6 | 3.0 | 0.35 | 4.7 | 4.2 | 4.4 | 0.19 | 3.8 | 3.1 | 3.2 | 3.6 | 2.0/0.9 | 0.27 | 0.53 |
| Sym. | 33 | 15 | 18 | 0.85 | 25 | 15 | 10 | 0.78 | 27 | 10 | 16.5 | 15 | 2.75/0 | 0.555 | 2.54− |
| Str. 4et | 34 | 12− | 22+ | 0.53− | 22 | 18 | 4 | 0.68 | 33+ | 12 | 21.5+ | 10− | +6.0/1.0 | 1.13+ | 3.53 |
| Str. 5et | 31.5 | 16 | 15(−) | 1.09 | 28.5(+) | 20 | 8 | 0.91(+) | 25 | 11 | 14− | 15 | 5.0/0 | 0.81 | 2.97 |
| Pf. Ch | 36.5+ | 19.5+ | 17 | 1.21 | 22.5 | 18.5 | 4 | 0.62 | 26 | 9 | 17 | 15 | 2.8/0.6 | 0.70 | 2.78 |
| Pf. Duo | 33 | 15 | 18 | 0.85 | 24 | 18 | 6 | 0.74 | 27 | 10 | 17 | 16 | 3.7/0.7 | 0.81 | 3.81+ |
| Relatively Early (Op. 51, 60, 67, 68) | 34 | 15 | 19.5 | 0.825 | 24 | 17.5 | 7 | 0.735 | 31+ | 11.5 | 19 | 11− | 5.2/0.6 | 0.99 | 4.06+ |
| Sym. 2–4 | 33 | 14 | 19 | 0.73 | 23 | 14 | 9 | 0.695 | 28 | 10 | 17 | 16 | 2.3/0 | 0.45− | 1.75− |
| 1886 (Op. 99–101) | 33 | 16 | 17 | 0.99 | 25 | 18 | 7 | 0.755 | 23− | 8 | 15 | 19+ | 2.7/1.0 | 0.78 | 3.19 |
| Late clar. (Op. 114, 115, 120) | 33 | 15 | 18 | 0.87 | 24.5 | 20 | 5 | 0.75 | 26 | 9 | 17 | 16 | 4.5/0 | 0.71 | 3.37 |
| Slow Mvts. (Op. 60, 73, 90, 99, 114) | 42[d]+ | 26+ | 15.5 | 2.03[d] | 20(−) | —[e] | —[e] | 0.56(−) | 28 | 18.5+ | 9− | 10− | — | — | 6.03[d,e]+ |
| [omit Op. 99] | 45[d]+ | 27[d]+ | 18 | 1.59+ | 17− | —[e] | —[e] | 0.38− | 28 | 17.5+ | 11− | 10− | — | — | 4.53[d]+ |
| Finales (Op. 60, 73, 88, 90, 101, 111) | 31− | 16 | 15(−) | 1.09 | 24.5 | 20 | 4 | 0.805 | 26 | 11 | 15 | 18+ | — | — | 4.20+ |
| 'First Maturity' (Op. 18, 25, 26, 34, 36, 38) (1st mvts.) | 35 | 14.5 | 20.5 | 0.77 | 22 | 18 | 4 | 0.64 | 32+ | 14+ | 18 | 11− | — | — | 3.10 |

[a] Cf. Table 1, note *n*. The figures in these columns in Table 2 all are means of the ratios obtained for the individual works, not ratios of the mean values for the sections in question.

[b] Cf. Table 1, right-hand column. The figures given here are simply the means of the means of the values in Table 1 for the works in each category.

[c] This figure represents the mean of the standard deviations obtained for the ten 'real' sections (omitting the two ratios) for each category of works listed in Table 2 *taken as a repertory in its own right* (rather than with respect to Table 1). The mean value in this column, 3.13 with standard deviation 0.53, is derived from the figures for the five subgenres following (that is, for the entire repertory as thus broken down into subgenres, not from any results in Table 1. (The + and − indications for significant deviance are drawn from this figure, not from any results in Table 1. (The analogous mean of the standard deviations for the ten sections in Table 1 is 3.64, standard deviation 0.64.)

[d] These figures differ from the mean by at least *three* standard deviations (not merely two, as otherwise with bold-face entries); in a normal population, such a value would be encountered less than 1 per cent of the time.

[e] Retransition and 'main' development section cannot reliably be distinguished in these movements. The average value for the standard deviation in the right-hand column is therefore based on eight rather than ten values.

the manner just described), and despite their total absence of significantly deviant individual sections.

The quintets, piano chamber music, and duo sonatas exhibit average levels of variability with respect to the repertory as a whole. The quintets have short second groups, and the combination of modestly short expositions and modestly long developments produces a high ratio of development to exposition. The piano-chamber works have long first groups, and therefore long expositions, and the ratio between first and second group is unusually high and that between development and exposition unusually low, although neither approaches statistical significance. The high figure for first groups of course reflects the special case of the Piano Trio in B major, but in fact the tendency appears consistently (cf. Table 1); the same is true for the ratio of development to exposition (this feature is strikingly consistent among all five works). It is tempting to posit a correlation between these long first groups and the need or desire to bring alternating presentations of the main theme, once for the strings and once for the piano, but this does not seem to be decisive. By this reasoning, duo sonatas ought also to have longer first groups, but they do not; and the complex methods by which Brahms extends his first groups seem to operate independently of any simplistic correlation with genre or scoring.[12]

The symphonies, by contrast, are both unusually typical and unusually consistent. They have no significantly deviant sections; the low relative variability (0.555) is very close to the threshold for significance (0.51); and their internal variability is significantly low. This is even clearer in the case of the Symphonies Nos. 2–4, that is, if the apparently much earlier, and in any case quite different, first movement of No. 1 is left out of account (see the next section of Table 2). The relative variability of these three works is significantly low, and internally they are highly consistent, the only group of works from the repertory to attain this distinction in either direction. Perhaps Brahms strove, consciously or unconsciously, for a more 'predictable', unexceptionable approach to sonata form in this largest and most public among his mature instrumental genres—a consistency of procedure he felt unnecessary to maintain in the freer, more intimate world of chamber music. (Of course, this conjecture must not be interpreted as critical of Brahms. As noted above, consistency of proportions is entirely compatible with freedom and inspiration in other domains; and the later movements in all four symphonies amply demonstrate formal originality, both in individual movements and in the construction of the cycle as a whole.)

Among the other subgenres in the second main section of Table 2, the only significant deviations are that the 'relatively early' works (the three string quartets, the Piano Quartet in C minor, and the First Symphony) have long recapitulations and short codas, while the 1886 piano-chamber works have short recapitulations and long codas. It is remarkable that a group of works so clearly distinguishable by both date and scoring as the late clarinet works exhibits no significant variations from Brahms's norms in formal proportions. On the other hand, they vary from the overall norms as much as any

---

[12] See Arno Mitschka, *Der Sonatensatz in den Werken von Johannes Brahms*, Ch. 1 (a richly detailed and useful account).

average groups of works, and their internal variability is also average; in this they differ decisively from the 'normal' and 'consistent' later symphonies.

In general, the main sections of Table 2 present a picture of striking uniformity, especially apparent when reading down the columns. Except for the few deviations just cited, every group of expositions averages 33 or 34 per cent of the whole, every remaining group of developments between 22 and 25 per cent; even the volatile ratios between first group and second group, and development and exposition, stay cautiously near the overall means. Statistically, only 15 of 108 entries, or 14 per cent, are significantly deviant, whereas one might expect 30 to 35 per cent (this of course reflects in part the effect of individual values cancelling out within the various genres). The most variable individual sections, those located within the development, show not a single significantly high or low reading.

Attempts to find meaningful correlations with other variables usually failed. Among those investigated were length of movement (admittedly a problematical quantity), other chronological subgroups, works with a minor tonic, and works in the same key. (In all these cases, an 'average' deviation seems meaningful only where it reflects a consistent pattern in the individual works in question, as opposed to a single very large deviation. All such individual cases can be seen in Table 1.) Several interesting patterns appear in the relatively early works; these will be discussed below in another context. The only other significant chronological pattern affects—once again—the retransitions. From the Second Symphony up to the F major Violoncello Sonata, they are much longer than average (four of seven are significantly long, and the other three are average; the mean value, 9.8, is close to significant); whereas from the A major Violin Sonata onwards they are short (three of nine are significantly short, while the other six are average; the mean value, 3.8, is close to significant). The only significant key-related results are that in all three F major works (which date from the brief period 1882–6) the main sections of the development are short and the retransitions extremely long (as is also the case in the first three symphonies); in the two G major works, both the developments and likewise their ratio to the expositions are significantly long; and in the two A minor works, the exposition is rather long, while all the values affecting the development are significantly low. This is hardly a rewarding harvest. No significant variants of proportion, by contrast, are correlated with such potentially interesting variables as movements with a minor tonic, or movements in which the exposition is not repeated.

# IV

It is tempting to compare these proportions to the ones obtained from those of Brahms's works which I have elsewhere interpreted as constituting his 'first maturity' as an instrumental composer (see the last row of Table 2).[13] Compared to the later works, these have a significantly long recapitulation of the first group, owing to the lack of what was later to become the customary cut in this section. Hence the recapitulation as a whole is

[13] 'Schubert's Sonata Form', Part 2; the Horn Trio, Op. 40, is omitted here because of the lack of a first movement in sonata form.

longer, while the coda is significantly shorter. (The full recapitulation of the first group is especially interesting, inasmuch as Brahms's three early piano sonatas resemble the later works in shortening this section compared to the exposition.) In addition, the second group in the exposition is modestly longer compared to the first group, and the development modestly shorter compared to the expositon. Still more unusual would be the apparent cut in the recapitulation of the *second* group, were it not that this merely reflects a single special case, the Piano Quartet in G minor.

But these proportions are similar to those found in the three string quartets. Every deviant feature just cited recurs there, usually in exaggerated form. On the other hand, the other two C minor works completed in the early 1870s, the First Symphony and the Piano Quartet, differ from the string quartets, and resemble many later works, in their avoidance of short retransitions and in including cuts in the first-group recapitulation; and they differ from both the earlier works and most later ones in their emphasis on the first group in the exposition at the expense of the second group. In short, although the hypothetical 'relatively early' group is apparently less deviant than the quartets alone (because these opposing tendencies cancel out), it is actually wildly variable, as indicated by its very high figure for internal variability. This reflects the differences between the string quartets on the one hand and the symphony and piano quartet on the other. It also presumably reflects the unknowable extent to which drafts of several of these movements, from widely differing periods in the 1850s and 1860s, were retained unchanged in the final versions. By comparison, the internal variability in Brahms's first-maturity movements is virtually identical to the average for the later works, thereby confirming their coherent origins and their consistent musical procedures.

These observations suggest a hypothesis regarding Brahms's development as a sonata-form composer. In his first maturity, along with a convincing synthesis of Beethovenian, Schubertian, and more recent styles, he worked out a relatively consistent set of norms for the formal proportions. After the prolonged hiatus of c.1865–71, he returned decisively to large-scale instrumental composition in the early and middle 1870s, completing and publishing long-gestating works in the central genres string quartet and symphony (as well as the Piano Quartet in C minor, Op. 60), and he produced instrumental sonata forms continuously thereafter. The similarities of construction between the first maturity and the three string quartets suggest continuity of development, but the proportions of the two other C minor works are quite different. Since these five diverse movements are both similar and dissimilar to both the (more consistent) first-maturity and the (more consistent) later movements, and since they originated during a long period which overlapped with the earlier one, it is difficult to resist interpreting them as being in these respects 'transitional'. By this interpretation, the real period of consolidation begins later, approximately with the Second Symphony and the G major Violin Sonata (1877–8).[14] (The clear distinction between the extraordinarily

---

[14] The only account I have seen that makes a division at about this point is Mitschka, *Der Sonatensatz*, 304–5, but his criteria are much too vague and general for my taste. He sees the period of 'consolidation' extending up to the Second Symphony, the one of consummate mastery beginning with the Violin Concerto.

consistent Symphonies Nos. 2–4 and the First Symphony may reinforce this interpretation, as may Brahms's later abandonment of the piano quartet and string quartet in favour of duos and trios with piano and the string quintet.)

Another obvious basis of comparison for our repertory is with Brahms's later slow movements and finales. However, only a minority of such movements are clearly in sonata form—a number of difficulties in the analysis of these movements are only now being recognized—and so only a few can unambiguously serve as a basis for comparison.[15] The results are nevertheless suggestive (see Table 2). The five slow movements studied, from the C minor Piano Quartet, the Second and Third Symphonies, the F major Violoncello Sonata, and the Clarinet Trio, show far greater differences from the first-movement norms than any subgroup within that repertory. The exposition is vastly enlarged, to over 40 per cent of the whole, owing entirely to a similarly vast expansion of the first group (the second group is actually a little smaller), and this expansion occurs at the expense of every other major part of the form. The development is marginally smaller absolutely, but of course very much so in comparison to the exposition. In the recapitulation not only is the first group shortened, but the second group as well (even compared to its relative brevity in the exposition), and the coda is only two-thirds the size. If the slow movement of the F major Violoncello Sonata is omitted (its analysis as an example of sonata form is somewhat problematic), the diminished importance of the development is even more pronounced.

The reason for these differences is obvious: in slow movements, Brahms writes long, beautiful themes, often in small 'closed' forms with leisurely extensions and codettas or double statements based on contrasting scoring. The curtailment of the second group, development, and coda are thus not merely 'reciprocals' of the long first group, but logical consequences of the different aesthetic presuppositions. In many respects, the second group and the development function more like episodes than primary constituents of the form. The second group need not (should not) be a weighty or extended counterpoise to the first group; the development need not (should not) storm the heights or plumb the depths; the coda's rounding-off should be more suggestive than explicit, and a final climax is ordinarily not in place. (The biggest climax in Brahms's slow movements, for example in the Second Symphony, often comes in a secondary development in the recapitulation of the first group.) A particular feature is that often no clear distinction exists between the 'main' part of the development and the retransition, whether because the boundary is impossible to locate, as in the Second Symphony, or because the entire (short) development functions simultaneously as the retransition, as in the C minor Piano Quartet. Another feature of these slow movements, however, is their huge internal variability, dwarfing any other group of movements; this well confirms their flexible and in part ambiguous formal construction. Even here, however, distinctions can be made. If the Violoncello Sonata in F major is omitted, the variance

[15] See Pascall, 'Some Special Uses of Sonata Form by Brahms', 58–63, and the paper by Elaine Sisman on Brahms's slow movements in the present volume.

declines by 25 per cent (although it still remains very high). More strikingly, the symphonies remain extraordinarily consistent, in that the slow movements in both Nos. 2 and 3 conform uncannily closely to the average for all four slow movements—their figures for relative variability (0.32 and 0.29, respectively) are far lower than those for *any* first movement.

Brahms's sonata-form finales (the Second and Third Symphonies, both string quintets, and the Piano Quartet and Piano Trio in C minor) resemble his first movements far more closely. The only tangible differences are that the expositions are relatively brief, owing to a shorter second group, and that the codas are longer. (The second and third of these tendencies also distinguish sonata-form finales of the Classical period.) Their variability is very high, however, almost as high as in the slow movements (omitting Op. 99). All this suggests that, particularly with respect to slow movements, the position and function of a movement within the cycle was a more important determinant of Brahms's formal proportions than any other variable, and that he followed conscious or unconscious norms of construction more closely in first movements than elsewhere. It also suggests that the highly unusual constructions in the *Tragic Overture* and the *Academic Festival Overture* (the exposition of the latter comprises 56 per cent of the whole!) are not freakish at all, but rather reflect the quite different context of the independent concert overture.[16]

## V

It is clear from Table 1 that the retransition is by far the most volatile and variable section in Brahms's sonata form. This section therefore seems ideally suited to provide a test case for the analysis of his individual artistic solutions within a given formal context. Obviously, a sonata-form retransition will ordinarily be distinguishable from the 'main' development section or sections; and it will ordinarily arouse expectations of the reprise, usually by harmonic preparation of the tonic, adumbration of the opening theme, or both. Just as obviously, a composer as wedded to formal and tonal ambiguity as Brahms will scarcely have avoided opportunities for subtlety and misdirection in preparing his reprises, and so we must expect to find doubtful and difficult cases, particularly regarding the beginning of the retransition and the reprise.[17] (The term 'reprise' here specifically designates the return to the main theme in the tonic or, by extension, the first gesture of the recapitulation.) Rather than attempt to establish firm criteria for making such decisions, however, it will suffice to discuss characteristic examples, pointing out ambiguities as they arise.

Table 3 lists the retransitions in our twenty-one movements according to several

[16] I know of no serious recent discussion of the *Academic Festival Overture*; on its tragic companion, see my 'Brahms's *Tragic Overture*: The Form of Tragedy', and the paper by Claudio Spies in the present volume.

[17] On retransitions in general, see Beth Shamgar, 'On Locating the Retransition in Classic Sonata Form'; Shelley Davis, 'H. C. Koch, the Classic Concerto, and the Sonata-form Retransition'; Rosen, *Sonata Forms*. For Brahms in particular, Frisch (n. 7) offers numerous stimulating analyses. The interesting essay by Reinhold Brinkmann, 'Anhand von Reprisen', came to my attention too late for use in the present paper.

characteristics: percentage of the whole development section; keys used; principal musical material; phrase structure; and principal aesthetic effect. The column headed 'Blurred Beginning?' indicates (as appropriate) a veiled or ambiguous beginning of the retransition. The next column indicates comparable blurrings at the reprise itself, while the last column cites significant recompositions of or substitutions for the opening theme.

These retransitions run the gamut from nullity—in the A major Violin Sonata—to fully half the development section. (The mean length is 26 per cent of the development, with a standard deviation of 15.5 per cent; significantly short and long retransitions appear in italics and bold-face, as in Table 1.) The A major Sonata moves from the final cadences of the new, contemplative versions of the original closing theme (bar 146; cf. 79), now in C♯ minor and major, directly to the reprise; the remote tonality (III♯) links seamlessly, by common-tone, to the opening $\hat{3}$ of the main theme. (Perhaps this C♯ theme could count, retrospectively, as a covert retransition, although it apparently prepares nothing, and the development is still shorter than average at this point.)

Very short retransitions occur in the String Quartet in C minor, Piano Trio in B major, and Clarinet Sonata in F minor. In all three, the development slides from the foreign key into the reprise by beginning the first theme on the foreign sonority, but modulating into the tonic within its course, so that we discover to our surprise that the reprise has already begun without our realizing it. In the C minor Quartet, a tonally obscure progression involving C♯ minor and A major is suddenly transformed into C minor when the dominant of the Neapolitan in first inversion turns into the plain submediant built on the tonic ($V^6/\flat II = VI^6$, bar 133). An augmentation of the initial motive follows immediately, similar to the familiar augmentation at the reprise of the Fourth Symphony, and leads directly into the reprise. The harmonic progression in the Clarinet Sonata is identical, but it assumes a more elemental and inevitable form that is closely integrated with the material and its tonal implications (see below). In the B major Trio, the theme begins in the plain relative minor, before moving to the dominant (bar 190 = 22; bars 188–9, clearly the arrival at the reprise, correspond to no particular bars of the exposition!); this apparently prosaic key however plays an equally central role in the overall tonal plan of the work, as does F♯ minor in the Violoncello Sonata.

A converse procedure occurs when an apparently orthodox dominant preparation leads to a reprise 'off' the tonic, as in the submediant main-theme recapitulation in the C minor Piano Quartet. Other movements in which Brahms slides into the reprise include the String Quartet in A minor and the Quintet in G major;[18] in these cases, however, the retransition is of normal length and has unmistakably prepared the reprise in advance. Another movement in which the tonic enjoys no dominant preparation is the Third Symphony (see below).

At the other extreme we have the first three symphonies and two additional F major works—the Quintet and the Violoncello Sonata—all of whose retransitions occupy

---

[18] The latter retransition is analysed by Rosen in *Sonata Forms*, 322–4.

TABLE 3. Retransitions in Brahms's later sonata-form move

RETRANSITION

| | Bars | % of Dev. | Tonality | Material[a] | Constru |
|---|---|---|---|---|---|
| Sym. 1 | 273–342 | 45 | Long V pedal [Surprise vii] | Basic motives | 3 paragr |
| Sym. 2 | 246–301 | 47 | IV–♭VI–♭III–iii–V–♭III–iii–I–ii$^7$ | Basic motives | 3(4) par |
| Sym. 3 | 101–23 | 48 | ♭VII–V/iv–♭VI–I | Motto as horn melody; 1P | 2 paragr + motto |
| Sym. 4 | 227–46 | 19 | V/♯iii–V$^7$ | 1Pb (bar 9) | 1 paragr |
| 4et c | 133–4 | 8 | V$^6$/♭II = VI$^6$ | 1Pa$^1$ (augm.) | 2 mm. |
| 4et a | 165–82 | 33.5 | v–(i–iv)–i | 1P/var's + K | 2 paragr |
| 4et B♭ | 184–204 | 21 | vi–V$^9$ | Special dev. theme (= 106) | 1 paragr |
| 5et F | 111–36 | 44 | Long V pedal [Surprise ♭VI] | 1Pa' + Tr; 1Pa'' | 2 paragr |
| 5et G | 94–105 | 24 | IV–vi–♭VI–I$^6_4$ | Dev. motives + 1Pab | 2 paragr |
| Cl. 5et | 121–35 | 22 | V pedal (of I; then of i) | 3Pb + 2P; 1Pa | 2 paragr |
| Pf. 4et c | 176–97 | 29 | Long V pedal | 1S, Var. 2 (!) | 1 paragr |
| Pf. Tr. C | 189–208 | 25 | V/vi–♭VI; VI–(V)–I | 3P; 1Pa' | 2 paragr |
| Pf. Tr. c | 126–34 | 16 | V pedal | 2P; K'? | 1(2?) pa |
| Pf. Tr. B | 185–7 | 4 | vi–V | 1Pa | 1 phrase |
| Cl. Tr. a | 119–25 | 16 | V$^6_5$–V | 2P'' (cf. 34); 16ths = dev. | 1 phrase |
| V. Son. G | 134–55 | 30 | i [*sic*]; to V | 4S' + 1P; 2P (1Pa cad's) | 3 paragr (2 + 1) |
| Vc. Son. F | 94–127 | 55 | V$^7$; I [*sic*]; ii–V | 'Themeless' + tremolo (cf. 1P); Tr | 3 paragr |
| V. Son. A | — | 0 | — | — | — |
| V. Son. d | 120–9 | 22 | V$^7$ | ? | 1 paragr |
| Cl. Son. f | 136–7 | 4 | V$^6$/♭II = VI$^6$ | [Cadence] | 2 bars |
| Cl. Son. E♭ | 89–102 | 30 | V/V; ♭VI/V; V$^7$ | Primarily 1Pa (97,99 = 1Sa'?) | 3 short paragr |

[a] The symbols used here resemble those developed by Jan LaRue for labelling th material (see his *Guidelines for Style Analysis* [New York, 1970], 154 ff.). 1P, 2P, etc., d the first and second themes in the first group ('P'), respectively; 1S, 2S, etc., the same

| | REPRISE | | |
|---|---|---|---|
| ‌ect | Blurred Beginning? | Blurred?[a] | Altered?[a] |
| ‍cresc. to *pp*; esc.—climax | 294? (*pp*/cresc.) 263? (V) | 339? Motto 343? Theme | |
| ‍rcling round max; then *p* | 262? (V) 282? (*ff*) 290? (1Pa in I) | | 1P + 2P simult. |
| ‍omantic'; ‍lection | 112? (1P/cresc.) | 120? Motto 124? Theme | |
| ‍cresc./rit. | 219? (1P') | | Augmented (1Pa$^1$ only) |
| ‍rupt *p*; ‍ntative | | 'Slides in' | Augmented (1Pa$^1$ only) |
| ‍. + reflect | | 'Slides in' | |
| ‍cresc. to *pp* | | | |
| ‍resc.—climax | (V already 103) | | Th. compl. |
| ‍gitated cresc. climax | 100? (1P) | 'Slides in' | |
| ‍eet tune; cresc. to sad | | | 1P + 2P simult. |
| ‍resc.—climax; ‍nse counterpoint | | 198? A-flat 199? 1P | |
| ‍resc.—climax; ‍nse counterpoint | | 206? | Th. compl. |
| ‍resc./*p*/cresc. | 113? (2P) | Repr. is to 1Pb (134b = 4b) | |
| ‍ld cresc. | | 189 (= 21) (Repr. = m.1) | |
| ‍resc.—climax | 105?? (16ths; related prog's) | Repr. is to 2P (126 = 14) | Th. compl. of 2P! |
| ‍cal swells ‍hile relaxing | | Tonic minor before repr. | |
| ‍ee text] | [See text] | 112 ff. = I + outline of 1P structure | |
| ‍ommon-tone I♯—I; no ‍tr. (157–8) | — | | |
| ‍Vhispering' ‍ntinues; e$^3$ | [Entire dev. on V] | | |
| ‍ee text] | [See text] | Repr. is to 2P (138 = 5) | |
| ‍cresc. | 86? (V arrives) | | |

‌d group ('S'); K is the closing theme; phrases or other subparts are designated by a, b,
‌suffixed to P, 2S, etc.

effectively half the development. These very long passages immediately raise the question of whether the beginning of the retransition has been properly located; this amounts to the question of definition outlined above. Whenever two or more possibilities seem to exist, the alternatives are cited in the column 'Blurred Beginning?' in Table 3. In the First Symphony, the dominant arrives as a half cadence as early as bar 263, preceding the long decrescendo to the pianissimo (bar 294) from which, in turn, the ensuing gigantic crescendo arises. By bar 274 the return of the rising chromatic motto and the coalescence of the ominous timpani motive on to an ostinato dominant pedal (clearly reminiscent of the transition to the finale of Beethoven's Fifth Symphony) seem unambiguously retransitional, despite the fact that the crescendo begins only twenty bars later. The dominant retransition in the C minor Piano Quartet is similar in character and intensity, although more overtly contrapuntal and constructed as a single paragraph rather than three or four. In the later Quintet in F major, however, the retransition is remarkably similar in construction to that in the First Symphony. Not only is it divided into several paragraphs on the dominant, preceded by still earlier preparatory dominants (bars 103–10), and based on a gigantic crescendo, but its surprise deviation to the remote tonality of Db, a semitone away (bar 134), is precisely analogous to the surprise B minor in the symphony (bar 335).

The long retransitions in the Second and Third Symphonies are not based on dominant pedals. The Second Symphony is particularly subtle; the various musical features that seem to imply retransitional function appear gradually, one after the other: (1) the fortissimo outburst in bar 246 reintroduces the head motive of the main theme (bar 2) and then the second theme from the first group (bar 44); furthermore, they stand in the subdominant—but they do not yet seem to point clearly towards the dominant; (2) the dominant arrives, as a pedal, in bar 262, but it is not articulated as a crucial arrival, and the harmonizations of the pedal do not behave like those in a normal preparation for the tonic; (3) the fortissimo head motive returns in bar 282, now clearly more impatient; (4) finally, a clearly recognizable preparation arrives with the augmented motto-motive (bar 1) in the tonic at bar 290. A final subtlety is that, following all this, the actual progression into the reprise (bars 300–2) is not a V–I progression at all, but $\mathrm{II}^7_{5\flat}$–$\mathrm{I}^6_4$ that is, the tonic reprise enters tentatively as an unstable sonority over the dominant in the bass, recalling its disposition on its initial appearance in bar 2.[19]

The delayed entry of the reprise in the First Symphony illustrates yet another kind of blurring, which can arise when the movement begins with a motto preceding the 'main theme' proper. In these cases the motto and the theme can articulate different aspects of the function 'reprise', or the motto can serve as retransition, the reprise coinciding with

---

[19] Two splendid recent analyses of this movement, by David Epstein in his *Beyond Orpheus*, 67, 162–75, and by Carl Schachter, 'The First Movement of Brahms's Second Symphony: The Opening Theme and its Consequences', both point out many features (primarily in the exposition) relevant to this retransition and blurred reprise, without focusing on it as a distinct topic. (The clear rhythmic function of bar 302 as a downbeat on the four-bar level seems to support Schachter's interpretation of bar 2, as against Epstein's.)

the theme. The effect is startling in the Third Symphony, where we pause late in the development for a romantic horn solo in the remote key of Eb major and minor (bar 101), leading to ominous unisons on the main-theme head motive (bar 112). Abruptly, the motto awakens us from these reveries (bar 120) and, amazingly, reinterprets the F in the bass (which we had thought was V/V in Eb minor) as the home tonic. Here the motto clearly functions as part of the retransition, swinging back to the tonic via Db, and the reprise proper enters with the main theme (bar 124). To call the horn melody in bar 101 the beginning of the retransition is clearly debatable—the tune does not sound like a preparation—and yet the motto motive, bar 111, is the head motive of the theme, and both phrases are united by the Eb tonality which persists until the eruption of the motto in its original form.

In these cases no real ambiguity arises regarding the proportions of the large sections of the form. But when (as is common) the first group is based on two or more distinct ideas, each having its own thematic identity and rhythmic construction, the potential for large-scale formal ambiguity is difficult for Brahms to resist. An obvious case in point is the Clarinet Sonata in F minor (see Example 1). Its first theme (bar 1) is restated in F♯ minor, the minor Neapolitan (bar 130), itself an outgrowth of the mysterious unexplained Gb at the end of bar 4. (But this F♯ minor simultaneously sounds like a subdominant of the C♯ which has ruled since bar 116, until the D–C♯ progressions of bars 132–6 clinch C♯ as dominant—note the difference from bar 4.) Even apart from being in a remote key, this thematic return does not sound like a reprise. Indeed, its differences from bar 1 in scoring, tonal orientation, and complexity of texture are precisely what one might expect of a first theme when it turns up in the middle of a development. Only after the bare, mysterious transformation of this dominant C♯ into Db, VI of the home tonic (bars 136–7), can we realize that the *second* theme is now truly being recapitulated (bar 138 = 5 and 25), and hence that the preceding F♯ in some sense constitutes a reprise. One could therefore call bar 130 the beginning of the recapitulation (although where then would be *its* preparation?—and the whole development would occupy only 16 per cent of the movement); or one could call the entire phrase bars 130–7 the retransition (which would then be of normal length). But I prefer to emphasize not only the lack of any audible retransition preceding bar 130, or of any reprise-like effect there, but even more the importance of bars 136–7 as a pivot. It is not merely a harmonic pivot which reinterprets C♯ as Db and therefore restores the tonic, and not merely a parallel to bar 4 (see the bass in bars 134–5), but, like the shifting perspectives in an ambiguous drawing, a profound reinterpretation of the musical ideas themselves. The sense of inevitability in this reprise, of eternal rhythms manifested in those swings from C♯ = Db to B♮ to C, depends, paradoxically, on its having been thoroughly prepared (C♯ as dominant in bars 126–9) without our being aware of it—as if a god were performing a transformation of matter from one state to another, whose effects we can see but whose causes we cannot presume to understand. A prosaic recognition of bar 130 as a 'Neapolitan reprise of the

EXAMPLE 1. Brahms, Clarinet Sonata in F minor, Op. 120 No. 1, I. (*a*) Bars 1–12. (*b*) Bars 125–43.

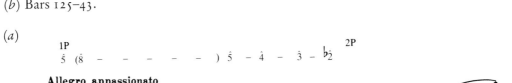

(*a*)

(*b*)

main theme' would shatter this illusion, which depends on our delayed realization that it is taking place only after the process is already long under way.[20]

Still further removed from textbook sonata form are those movements in which Brahms omits the first theme entirely at the reprise. This happens in the C minor Piano Trio and the Clarinet Trio, as well as in a number of finales. The effect is more striking in the former work, because the first idea that returns in the tonic was the second idea in the exposition (bar 135 = 5) and originally stood on the dominant. It therefore sounds like part of the retransition here, but it leads surprisingly to the transition theme from the *end* of the first group, also on the home dominant (bar 140 = 26), and so directly to the recapitulation of the second group. On the other hand, the retransition actually begins a little earlier, with the march-like third theme from the first group (bar 126 = 11)—albeit in remote keys; this idea is thus accounted for as well. Only the opening theme is omitted, to return decisively in the coda.

Other special effects at the reprise include the contrapuntal combination of two or more first-group themes hitherto heard separately, as in the familiar example of the Second Symphony; this also occurs in the Clarinet Quintet. These telescoped reprises not only intensify the expression, but simultaneously effect the necessary foreshortening of the first-group recapitulation without the need to omit any important ideas. This type of intensification is Brahms's mellow analogue to Beethoven's technique of reserving the climactic version of the opening idea for the reprise (or the coda), a procedure which Joseph Kerman has often described and which may be called 'thematic completion'.[21] But Brahms himself indulged in this type of climactic reprise in the F major Quintet, the C major Trio, and the Clarinet Trio, all prepared by highly organized crescendo passages. In the last of these movements, however, it is astonishingly the *second* idea from the first group that returns as the climax; the first theme, which had already been analogously transformed in the first group and development, is not recapitulated in its original form at all.

One last method by which Brahms blurs the boundary between retransition and reprise is to return to the tonic in the retransition itself. In the Violin Sonata in G major this tonic is minor, and it is articulated primarily by a theme from late in the second group—compare the Sonata in A major—and so the effect is not as unusual as the abstract concept 'tonic in the development section' might suggest. But the tonic retransition in the Violoncello Sonata in F major is extraordinary. The development centres around a long contemplative passage in F♯ minor (the minor Neapolitan again); when this begins to modulate, it eventually impinges on B, the leading-tone of the home dominant (bar 92; see Example 2). This event is emphasized by a drastic change in

---

[20] See my analysis of similarly complex recapitulations of two-theme first groups in 'Schubert's Sonata Form', Part 1, 31–3 (with further references), Part 2, 60, 64. The profound recomposition of the recapitulation in the first movement of the Piano Quintet in F minor depends on the same return from F♯ minor, articulated in a similar way (ibid., 68); it gives a comparable impression of a gigantic 'hinge', as inevitable as it is silent. (A precedent for the attribution of divine inevitability to Brahms's descending-third progressions can be found in Tovey, 'Brahms', 266, on the finale of the Clarinet Trio.)

[21] 'Beethoven', 381; 'Notes on Beethoven's Codas', 149–50.

EXAMPLE 2. Brahms, Violoncello Sonata in F major, Op. 99, I. (*a*) Bars 1–6, 17–18. (*b*) Bars 92–128.

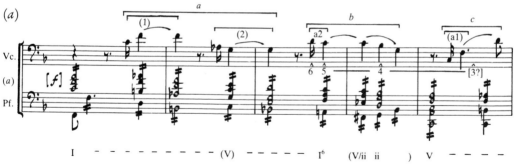

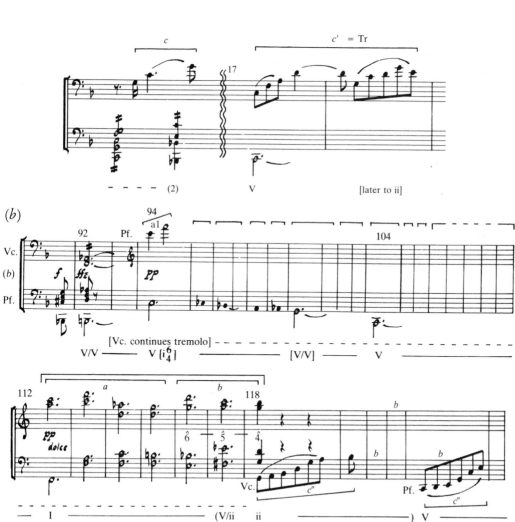

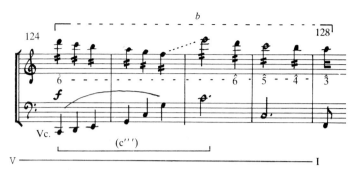

texture: the piano right-hand drops out momentarily, and the cello initiates a long tremolo passage which recalls the beginning of the movement, while the piano resumes on the dominant with a long succession of statements of the head motive from the main theme itself. This conjunction of home dominant, opening motive, and analogue to opening texture unambiguously establishes bar 94 as the beginning of the retransition. But the entire long passage that follows is not only without overt thematic content, it is mysteriously distant from the hustle and bustle that otherwise characterize this movement; it is almost themeless and almost timeless. The dominant eventually returns and leads to the tonic itself at bar 112, but this tonic arrival is also drastically under-articulated; the low cello tremolo and the pianissimo whole-bar chords in the piano continue unabated. However, the contour and harmony of bars 112–18 constitute an almost literal, if heavily disguised, repetition of the main theme itself (see again Example 2). We recall the theme as if in a vision, or like a vague memory of something we cannot quite place. The G minor chord in bar 118—compare bar 4; in both cases a melodic progression $\hat{6}$–$\hat{5}$–$\hat{4}$ over a supertonic harmony breaks off without achieving the descent to $\hat{3}$—gives the excuse for reverting, unexpectedly, to the second half of the transition theme (which had also touched on G minor in the exposition). This resembles nothing so much as an awakening into the light of common day, although we cannot know what it is from which we are awakening, nor where we are. This passage leads yet again to the dominant and the tremolos (bar 124); but these tremolos are in the piano, where they belong; and so this dominant can at last lead to the true reprise (bar 128), simultaneously reinterpreting the $\hat{6}$–$\hat{5}$–$\hat{4}$ progression as part of the dominant and leading it in the most forceful way imaginable to the long-awaited $\hat{3}$. (The end of the coda, in turn, reverts to this $\hat{4}$–$\hat{3}$ and repeatedly leads it down to the tonic.)

What is perhaps most remarkable is that following all this Brahms nevertheless fully recapitulates the essential material of the first group. That is, the dreamlike retransition does not merely 'stand for' the reality of the recapitulation, but takes its place as an autonomous constituent of the world of this movement. Why? Doubtless because of the whispering, chromatic, reflective main section of the development, so great a contrast and in so remote a key. How was Brahms to integrate this section into the movement as a whole? Not by simply awakening from it, for that would make *it* merely a dream. Rather, he moves from it *into* a dream of the real world (the main theme), but one that will not fade. Hence, even though the development stands in a peculiarly complex and mysterious relationship to the rest of the movement, it retains its power, by the mediation of a 'real' dream of reality. That power then reveals itself again in the tonality of the slow movement.

# VI

From examples like these it is clear that norms of formal procedure, whether the bad old textbook models or the numerical averages developed earlier in this paper, can never satisfactorily account for the reality of individual compositions. In fact, when Brahms's technique seems most paradoxical—as in the timeless, themeless, tonic retransition we have just analysed—the artistic result is often the most poetic. By the same token, it would be absurd to argue that, merely because his expositions vary much less in length than his developments, they are less interesting or less fully achieved. The measures of variability themselves can also be misleading. The complete omission of any retransition in the Violin Sonata in A major, for example, is perhaps as significant a deviation in artistic terms as the very long retransition in the Violoncello Sonata; yet the ratio of 'relative deviation' for the retransition is considerably lower in the former work than in the latter. If not precisely a falsification, this relationship represents at the least a partial distortion of their artistic meaning. (See, too, the remarks on 'typical' works at the end of Section II above.)

Still, it must be useful to be able to demonstrate, more or less precisely, the extent to which Brahms's irregularities of proportion are concentrated in certain genres, or certain parts of the movement, or certain subperiods in his long final maturity, at the expense of others; to know not merely that the first group in the B major Trio is proportionally longer than that in any other work, but how much longer; to know that the String Quartet in A minor has proportionally the shortest development section and the Clarinet Quintet the longest, that the Violin Sonata in D minor has the longest 'secondary development', that the Sonata in A major has the longest coda and the Sonata in G major the shortest (and how long in each case); and so forth indefinitely. Many potentially fascinating studies are suggested by the various groups and pairs of works which in this or that respect are quite similar (or quite dissimilar); a number of such groups have been cited above. It is equally apparent that similar studies could be carried out on more detailed aspects of the form, for example the relationship between first and second group, the role of the transition section and the closing group, and so forth. A positive feature of the method would seem to be that, unlike many recent numerical and statistical analyses of common-practice repertories, the results relate directly and meaningfully to the actual musical constituents of the works so analysed.[22]

---

[22] A responsible and useful application of statistical method to formal analysis of sonata movements is Roger Kamien, 'The Opening Sonata-Allegro Movements in a Randomly Selected Sample of Solo Keyboard Sonatas Published in the Years 1742–1774 (Inclusive)'; cf. the extracts from it published as 'Style Change in the Mid-18th-Century Keyboard Sonata'. With appropriate alterations to account for the fact that my repertory is the entirety of a finite class of works, while his was a random sample of a very large population, I have implicitly followed many of Kamien's principles regarding statistical significance.

The real potential of this type of investigation appears to be *comparative*. Although its limitations are manifold and severe, and (it must be stressed) it is open to abuse, it appears to offer the possibility of a more or less objective description of the proportions and formal construction in any repertory of sonata-form movements, in a manner which permits convenient and meaningful comparison with any other repertory. Surely different composers, styles, and periods must exhibit greater variations than can be found within the limited, coherent, mature output of a single master such as Brahms. In short, one could imagine a comprehensive and highly differentiated morphological history of the sonata form (or any other form). Although we do not yet possess the groundwork for such research, the present study may perhaps be a first step in that direction.

It is already clear, for example, that Brahms's mature sonata forms differ substantially from those of the Classical period. The typical proportions in his first-movement expositions are quite different from Haydn's and Beethoven's (their average second group is half again as long as the first group, rather than Brahms's mere 9 to 14 per cent longer), and also from Mozart's (his average first group seems to be fully as long). Perhaps the short first group, long second group, and short coda in Brahms's B♭ major String Quartet constitute what he thought of as 'Classical' proportions, in conjunction with its strong and self-conscious reflections of Classical style in many other ways. It has already been estimated that Mozart, Haydn, and Beethoven typically wrote developments of quite different proportions;[23] of these only Haydn's average seems close to Brahms's (about three-quarters the length of the exposition). A related question would be the extent to which other composers join Brahms in writing 'stable' expositions as opposed to variable developments.

From another angle, the extent of variability, particularly regarding extreme cases, seems to be far greater in Beethoven than in Brahms. No Brahms first movement extends the second group to anything like two and two-thirds or four and a half times the length of the first group, as Beethoven appears to do in the Piano Sonatas, Op. 10, Nos. 2 and 3; no Brahms development is even 10 per cent longer than the exposition, whereas that in the *Eroica* is more than half again as long; no Brahms coda even approaches being the longest of all four main sections of the form, as in Beethoven's *Les Adieux* (not to mention many of his finales). Perhaps Beethoven was in this sense the more 'radical' composer. Be all this as it may, the question of what Brahms accepted as 'norms' or principles in writing sonata-form movements seems to me to have been taken too much for granted. Whatever their limitations, the 'numbers' presented here may offer a sound basis for further research into Brahms's sonata form.

[23] Webster, 'Sonata Form', 502.

# APPENDIX

THE percentages of the whole movement occupied by each section, as given in Tables 1 and 2, were calculated on the basis of notated bars. Sections involving changes of metre (e.g., the second theme in the Third Symphony) or explicit changes of tempo such as 'sostenuto', 'animato', and the like (e.g., the coda in the First Symphony) were calculated using estimates of the ratio by which such changes affect the proportions based on notated bars. The particulars of these recalculations are given in the notes to Table 1.

The percentages were calculated to three significant figures, but (except in the row MEAN) are rounded off to two, because the lengths of the sections (an exposition, a 'main' development section, a coda, etc.) fall generally into the range of 30 to 100 bars; that is, a range in which only two digits (whole percentages) can be significant. An exception was made for remainders between 0.45 and 0.55 per cent inclusive, which are given as 0.5 per cent. The decimal values in the columns $\frac{1Gr}{2Gr}$ and $\frac{Dev}{Exp}$ are likewise given only to the nearest 0.01; but they were calculated on the basis of the three-figure values in the raw data, and hence occasionally differ from those that would be obtained from the figures in the tables. For example, in Table 1, the Third Symphony, the figure 0.82 for the ratio of first group to second group results from dividing 14.6 by 17.8, whereas the rounded-off values 15 and 18 might suggest 0.83. (See also Table 1, note *n*, and Table 2, note *a*.) For the same reason, 'identical' figures may yield different results, as in the first group and second group for the Clarinet Quintet and the Violoncello Sonata in F major; both appear as 16 and 15, respectively, but the resultant ratio appears as 1.06 in the former case ($15.7 \div 14.8$), 1.03 in the latter ($15.6 \div 15.2$); see also Table 1, note *s*. Similarly, the occasional apparent failure of 'subsidiary' columns to sum correctly to 'main' columns results from rounding off; for example, again in Table 1, the Third Symphony, the raw values for the first group (14.6) and second group (17.8) sum to 32.4 (exposition), but these appear as 15, 18, and 32, respectively.

The italic and bold-face entries in the tables indicate those proportions in each column which, respectively, deviate 'significantly' and 'highly significantly' from the MEAN value for that column. (The values in the *rows* 'Std. Dev.' and '% of MEAN' are analysed in the same way; cf. Table 1, note *r*.) The minimum limits 'qualifying' for these classes were determined by adding (or subtracting), for italic entries, one standard deviation (given in the first row under VARIA-BILITY) from the MEAN; and two standard deviations for bold-face entries. In a random sample of a population with a 'normal' distribution (the type graphically representable by a 'bell-shaped curve'), the proportion of the sample further than one standard deviation from the mean will approximate 32 per cent, while the proportion further than two standard deviations will approximate 5 per cent. In the main section of Table 1, with 252 entries, the corresponding figures are 80 italic entries and 10 bold-face, or 36 and 4 per cent, respectively. It thus seems reasonable to interpret the 80 italic sections as 'exceptional' in length, and the 10 bold-face ones as 'highly exceptional', within Brahms's mature sonata-form first movements.

The significance of these results might be disputed, on the grounds that any array of figures of this type (any measures of proportional length in a group of sonata-form movements) will have means and standard deviations, and hence will by definition contain 'exceptional' and 'highly exceptional' sections in approximately the same proportions. But the method employed here distinguishes between relatively stable sections (e.g., the exposition) and relatively variable ones (e.g., the development); between relatively 'typical' movements (those labelled – in the last column of Table 1) and relatively 'unusual' ones (those labelled +); between relatively 'stable' genres and relatively variable ones (last column in Table 2); and so forth. It also singles out exceptional individual movements (and the particular sections responsible); and it offers possibilities for comparative studies of a sort as yet unknown, as discussed in Sections II and VI of the main text.

# BRAHMS'S SLOW MOVEMENTS: REINVENTING THE 'CLOSED' FORMS

—

## ELAINE R. SISMAN

WHEN Gustav Jenner showed Brahms a slow movement of which he was especially proud, Brahms's response completely deflated the young man. 'Because I had focused too much attention on the inessential at the expense of the essential', Jenner recalled, ' . . . the magnificence of my beloved Adagio collapsed before my eyes into an empty void. But for my pain, with which Brahms actually could sympathize, he had only this dubious consolation: "Such a long Adagio is the most difficult".'[1]

Indeed, Brahms was no stranger to the agonies of Adagio composition. Many years earlier, he had sent Joseph Joachim the slow movement of his Piano Concerto in D minor, Op. 15, with a request for decisive criticism; 'if only I could finally rejoice over a well-made Adagio!' was his wistful, ambiguous comment.[2] Perhaps he was still remembering his problems with the Adagio of his Piano Trio in B major, Op. 8, whose revision he desired even as he sent it off for publication in 1854 (it was recast in 1889).[3] His tone when asking for Clara Schumann's verdict on the Adagio of the Serenade in A major, Op. 16, was anxious.[4] And even in the 1870s he confessed to Joachim that he was 'stumbling' over the Adagio and Scherzo of his Violin Concerto.[5]

Composing slow movements may well have given Brahms difficulty, as these remarks and certain revised autographs suggest.[6] Yet on the face of it, these movements seem to explore no greater range of formal options than those long since sanctified by the

---

[1] 'Brahms zeigte mir, wie mein Blick mit wahrhaft rührender Zärtlichkeit an unwesentlichen Dingen gehangen hatte, während das Wesentliche, worauf es ankam, unbeachtet geblieben war. Naturgemäß traten diese Mängel im langsamen Satz besonders stark hervor; doch ist es leichtverständlich, wenn ich bekennen muß, daß gerade dieser Satz voll jugendlicher Schwärmerei mein Stolz war: und so fiel denn die ganze Pracht dieses geliebten Adagios als eine bittere Enttäuschung vor meinen sehenden Augen in ein leeres Nichts zusammen. Für meinen Schmerz aber, den Brahms wohl mitempfinden mochte, hatte er nur den zweifelhaften Trost: "Ein so langes Adagio ist das Schwerste".' Gustav Jenner, *Brahms als Mensch, Lehrer, und Künstler*, 7. Jenner later says that Brahms had him start out with variations because with them one could best distinguish between essential and inessential (p. 48).

[2] 'Könnte ich mich doch endlich über ein gelungenes Adagio freuen!' Letter of Jan. 1857. *Brahms Briefwechsel*, 5: 168.

[3] 'Das Trio hätte ich auch gern noch behalten, da ich jedenfalls später darin geändert hätte.' Letter to Joachim, 19 June 1854. *Brahms Briefwechsel*, 5: 47.

[4] Letter of 10 Sept. 1859. Berthold Litzmann, ed., *Clara Schumann–Johannes Brahms Briefe*, 1: 277. Clara responded enthusiastically on 18 Sept. 1859 (p. 278).

[5] Letter of 23 Oct. 1878. *Brahms Briefwechsel*, 6: 146.

[6] Extensive revisions to the slow movements of the Piano Quartet in G minor, Op. 25, and the String Quartet in B♭ major, Op. 67, will be discussed below. Cf. also Karl Geiringer, *Brahms: His Life and Work*, 228, 229, 234–5, 241.

Viennese Classical composers— the 'closed forms' of variation, rondo, and ternary form (ABA), with their small sections and recurring cadences, and the more dynamic sonata forms.[7] Haydn, Mozart, Beethoven, and Schubert had themselves already created a whole subset of hybrid structures through various syntheses of these formal principles. How, then, did Brahms deal with his inheritance? I would suggest that Brahms's own reinterpretations of this tradition allowed him to develop a new stance appropriate to a slow movement, especially when employing ternary form, the most straightforward of the 'closed forms'.[8] In addition to assimilating the long-established formal designs for repetition, recurrence, contrast, and development within the circumscribed dimensions of slow movements, Brahms was able to create new ambiguities, and hence to impart new aesthetic meaning to the traditional gestures of these forms. In turn, these reinterpreted 'closed form' gestures were used to enrich his more dynamic sonata forms.

I believe that Brahms in his slow movements was able to overcome his notoriously self-conscious relationship with his Classical predecessors. Walter Frisch writes: 'One senses that, outside the bright spotlight of the first-movement position, Brahms felt freer to give rein to his compositional imagination'.[9] It may be that in slow movements, which make no single form obligatory, the Classical masters had not staked out as compelling a claim in Brahms's imagination, so that his wrestling with the past, or what Harold Bloom calls 'the anxiety of influence', abated somewhat. In Bloom's words, 'weaker talents idealize; figures of capable imagination appropriate for themselves. But . . . self-appropriation involves the immense anxieties of indebtedness.'[10] W. Jackson Bate's argument also seems tailor-made for Brahms: 'We could, in fact, argue that the remorseless deepening of self-consciousness, before the rich and intimidating legacy of the past, has become the greatest single problem that modern art (art, that is to say, since the later seventeenth century) has had to face . . .'[11] I take my cue from a passage later in Bloom's book: 'But poetic influence need not make poets less original . . . . The profundities of poetic influence cannot be reduced to source-study, to the history of ideas, to the patterning of images'.[12] I will not attempt here to seek out all the features of Brahms's slow movements which reveal him appropriating or transforming his Viennese Classical models, though I do not fault such investigations, for, as Charles Rosen recently pointed out, 'when the study of sources is at its most interesting, it becomes indistinguishable from pure musical analysis'.[13] Rather, I will keep the Classical

---

[7] These four types still appear as the full range of possibilities in Arrey von Dommer's 1865 revision of Koch's *Musikalisches Lexicon* (1802), an edition admired by Brahms, who wrote of it approvingly in letters to Fritz Simrock (25 Nov. 1888 and 23 Jan. 1894; *Brahms Briefwechsel*, 11: 205 and 12: 116, respectively).

[8] The notion of a 'stance appropriate to a slow movement' I take from Joseph Kerman, *The Beethoven Quartets*, 180. For an interesting recent discussion of Brahms's formal innovations, see Robert Pascall, 'Ruminations on Brahms's Chamber Music'.

[9] *Brahms and the Principle of Developing Variation*, 123. I am grateful to Professor Frisch for showing me part of this book before publication and for many generous communications about Brahms.

[10] *The Anxiety of Influence*, 5.

[11] *The Burden of the Past and the English Poet*, 4.

[12] *The Anxiety of Influence*, 7.

[13] 'Influence: Plagiarism and Inspiration', 100. Among the more recent studies to examine the role of other

background more or less at bay, and focus on Brahms's original and profound rethinkings of slow-movement forms that constitute, as Bloom might say, a 'creative correction' of his warily embraced inheritance.

# II

A survey of Brahms's slow movements will set the stage for closer examination of his most original creations. Six of the slow movements are sets of variations (see Table 1).[14] Surface melodic elaboration and colourful harmonic substitution, the essence of the variations in the two piano sonatas (Opp. 1 and 2), were later repudiated in the two string sextets (Opp. 18 and 36), in which Brahms consciously 'purified' the form according to his often-quoted dictum—'in a theme for [a set of] variations, it is almost only the bass that *actually* means anything to me'.[15] Not coincidentally, the latter movements suggest that Beethoven and Schubert were among Brahms's models.[16] Also Beethovenian is the Andante con moto of the Piano Trio in C major, Op. 87, whose theme is split into two melodies presented simultaneously in strings and piano, then varied in turn.[17] Finally, the slow movement of the String Quintet in G major, Op. 111, makes mysterious, even fantasy-like, its otherwise transparent variations—even Tovey failed to recognize the forces at work here[18]—by means of two bold strokes: the theme is an 'open' period, ending away from the tonic, and is linked to an affectively rich transition, the role of which is greatly expanded each time it returns between the 'open' variations. Indeed, Brahms locates the progressive increase of tension within these transitional passages, and thus outside the traditional theme-and-variation sequence, in order to enhance the

composers' works on Brahms are Imogen Fellinger's 'Brahms's View of Mozart', Constantin Floros's 'Studien zu Brahms Klaviermusik' and *Brahms und Bruckner: Studien zur musikalischen Exegetik*, Virginia Hancock's 'The Growth of Brahms's Interest in Early Choral Music, and its Effect on his own Choral Compositions' and *Brahms's Choral Compositions and His Library of Early Music*, Oliver Neighbour's 'Brahms and Schumann: Two Opus Nines and Beyond', Robert Pascall's 'Musikalische Einflüße auf Brahms', James Webster's 'Schubert's Sonata Form and Brahms's First Maturity', Helmut Wirth's 'Nachwirkungen der Musik Joseph Haydns auf Johannes Brahms', and the papers by Virginia Hancock and David Lewin in the present volume.

[14] The Andante variations which serve as finales in the Clarinet Quintet, Op. 115, and the second Clarinet Sonata in Op. 120 appear in the Appendix to Table 1 as 'outside slow-movement position'; the latter work, though, is problematic, because it contains no other slow movement. Of the three variation finales (including the Allegretto of the String Quartet in B♭ major, Op. 67), only one—Op. 115—is in minor, whereas six of the eight slow movements in minor are variations (all but the Serenade in A major, Op. 16, and the Horn Trio, Op. 40). It should also be noted that nearly every slow movement uses variation technique extensively in thematic repetitions and returns.

[15] Letter to Adolf Schubring of Feb. 1869. *Brahms Briefwechsel*, 8: 217. See Elaine R. Sisman, 'Brahms and the Variation Canon'; cf. also the paper by George Bozarth in the present volume.

[16] For example, the variations in the Sextet, Op. 18, resemble the slow movements of Beethoven's Seventh Symphony and Schubert's String Quartet in D minor ('Death and the Maiden'); cf. Webster, 'Schubert and Brahms (II)', 62; and the old Folia chord progression. The Sextet, Op. 36, apparently takes over certain techniques from the slow movement of Beethoven's String Quartet in A major, Op. 18 No. 5.

[17] Geiringer (*Brahms*, 237) points this out, noting how this imparts to the movement a rondo-like character, but he does not mention the similarity to Beethoven's procedure in the finale of the 'Eroica' Symphony. See Elaine R. Sisman, 'Tradition and Transformation in the Alternating Variations of Haydn and Beethoven'.

[18] Donald Francis Tovey, 'Brahms's Chamber Music', 265.

TABLE 1. Brahms's Slow Movements.

| Opus | Work, key | Tempo, key (movement other than II) | Form |
|------|-----------|-------------------------------------|------|
| 1 | Piano Sonata, C | Andante, c | Variations |
| 2 | Piano Sonata, f♯ | Andante con espr., b | Variations |
| 5 | Piano Sonata, f | Andante espr., A♭ (D♭) | ABA B/coda |
| 8 | Piano Trio, B | Adagio non troppo, B (III) | ABA Allegro |
| 11 | Serenade, D | Adagio non troppo, B♭ (III) | Sonata |
| 15 | Piano Concerto, d | Adagio, D | ABA coda |
| 16 | Serenade, A | Adagio non troppo, a (III) | Sonata/ABA |
| 18 | String Sextet, B♭ | Andante ma moderato, d | Variations |
| 25 | Piano Quartet, g | Andante con moto, E♭ (III) | ABA coda |
| 26 | Piano Quartet, A | Poco Adagio, E | Rondo (ABCABA) |
| 34 | Piano Quintet, f | Andante, un poco Adagio, A♭ | ABA |
| 36 | String Sextet, G | Adagio, e (III) | Variations |
| 40 | Horn Trio, E♭ | Adagio mesto, e♭ (III) | ABA |
| 51/1 | String Quartet, c | Romanze. Poco Adagio, A♭ | ABA B/coda |
| 51/2 | String Quartet, a | Andante moderato, A | ABA B/coda |
| 60 | Piano Quartet, c | Andante, E (III) | Sonata/ABA |
| 67 | String Quartet, B♭ | Andante, F | ABA |
| 68 | Symphony, c | Andante sostenuto, E | ABA coda |
| 73 | Symphony, D | Adagio non troppo, B | Sonata/ABA |
| 77 | Violin Concerto, D | Adagio, F | ABA |
| 78 | Violin Sonata, G | Adagio, E♭ | ABA B/coda |
| 83 | Piano Concerto, B♭ | Andante, B♭ (III) | ABA |
| 87 | Piano Trio, C | Andante con moto, a | Variations |
| 88 | String Quintet, F | Grave/Allegretto vivace/Presto, c♯ | ABABA |
| 90 | Symphony, F | Andante, C | Sonata/(ABA) |
| 98 | Symphony, e | Andante moderato, E | Sonata |
| 99 | Cello Sonata, F | Adagio affettuoso, F♯ | ABA/Sonata |
| 100 | Violin Sonata, A | Andante tranquillo/Vivace, F | ABABA B/coda |
| 101 | Piano Trio, c | Andante grazioso, C | ABA |
| 102 | Double Concerto, a | Andante, D | ABA B/coda |
| 108 | Violin Sonata, d | Adagio, D | 'Cavatina' |
| 8 | Piano Trio (rev.), B | Adagio, B (III) | ABA |
| 111 | String Quintet, G | Adagio, d | Variation/Fantasy |
| 114 | Clarinet Trio, a | Adagio, D | Sonata/Rondo |
| 115 | Clarinet Quintet, b | Poco Adagio, B | ABA |
| 120/1 | Clarinet Sonata, f | Andante un poco Adagio, A♭ | ABA |

APPENDIX. Slow movements outside 'slow-movement position'

| | | | |
|------|-----------|-------------------------------------|------|
| 40 | Horn Trio, E♭ | Andante, E♭ (I) | ABABA coda |
| 115 | Clarinet Quintet, b | Andante con moto, b (IV) | Variations |
| 120/2 | Clarinet Sonata, E♭ | Andante, E♭ (III) | Variations |

intensity of the movement's climax within the D major/minor variation, which is the dynamic, developmental culmination of the movement. Earlier composers might have distributed the weight of their variations towards arrival in the final segment—Brahms himself did this through modal change in the piano sonatas and the Op. 36 Sextet—or, more often, in a coda, but the potential force of transitions, especially developmental ones, had never before been explored as fully. Brahms's slow-movement variations, then, draw upon classical models, yet create new expressive contexts for this most repetitive of forms.

Brahms wrote four slow rondo movements, three of which feature an alternating pattern with varied returns (ABA′B′A″).[19] This format, invented by C. P. E. Bach (*Sonatas with Varied Reprises*, W. 50/6, H. 140), was standardized by Haydn in numerous works and subsequently transformed by Beethoven to include changes in key and tempo in the B sections (slow movements of the Ninth Symphony and the String Quartet in A minor, Op. 132).[20] Schubert also continued the tradition in his later piano sonatas (D major, D. 850; G major, D. 894; C minor, D. 958). Brahms's practices follow no specific precedents, however. In the first movement of the Horn Trio, Op. 40, anomalous anyway by not being in sonata form (and not fully pertinent here because of the presence of a 'true' slow movement in the work), the faster B sections are unstable, and each centres around a different key. While this may recall Beethoven's Ninth, the second B section here is not used as the chance to resolve the first; instead, it provides a pretext for bringing back the opening A theme in a remote key (bar 200). This false tonal return, in a key closer to the B than to the A sections, is a technique straight out of Brahms's ternary forms, as we shall see.

The slow-movement rondos in both the String Quintet in F major, Op. 88, and the Violin Sonata in A major, Op. 100, actually appear to conflate slow movement and scherzo: their episodes are scherzandos and no separate scherzo movement follows.[21] While the extreme tempo change suggests Beethoven, the scherzando character of the B sections does not. Brahms also tends to let the B sections have the last word, but without creating the double-strophe balancing act of, say, Haydn's Symphony No. 103 ('Drumroll'). Brahms's ternary movements also often end with reminiscences of the B section in the coda, and both the String Quintet and the Violin Sonata join the Horn Trio in adopting the false tonal returns of those ternary movements: affected are the final A section in the Quintet (and the very end as well) and both returns of the A section in

[19] The Adagio of the First Symphony was originally also a type of rondo movement; the two episodes were later fused into the central B section. Cf. Robert Pascall, 'Brahms's First Symphony slow movement: The initial performing version', and Frithjof Haas, 'Die Erstfassung des langsamen Satzes der ersten Sinfonie von Johannes Brahms', which includes a reconstruction of the original movement.

[20] See Elaine R. Sisman, 'Haydn's Hybrid Variations' and 'Tradition and Transformation'.

[21] Cf. Hans Gál, *Johannes Brahms: His Work and Personality*, 165–8. On the Sarabande and Gavotte on which the slow movement of Op. 88 is based, see Robert Pascall, 'Unknown Gavottes by Brahms'. That the second episode or 'scherzo' is a faster variation of the first in both Op. 88 and Op. 100 certainly resembles the third movement of the Second Symphony; on this point, see Karl Michael Komma, 'Das "Scherzo" der 2. Symphonie von Johannes Brahms'.

the Sonata. Brahms's one other slow rondo, in the Piano Quartet in A major, Op. 26, is a unique structure, with which I will deal presently.

The only full-scale sonata form movement, that is, 'first-movement form', among Brahms's slow movements is in his first orchestral piece, the Serenade in D major, Op. 11, and the only 'slow-movement sonata form' (without development proper, but, in this case, with secondary development) appears in the Fourth Symphony, Op. 98.[22] (The slow movement of the Violin Sonata in D minor, Op. 108, may also fall in this latter category. Praised by Elisabeth von Herzogenberg, who 'rejoiced to find the Adagio undisturbed by any middle section',[23] this piece is, as Tovey has it, a cavatina: his comparisons of it with Haydn's String Quartet in D minor, Op. 42, and Beethoven's Quartet in B♭ major, Op. 130, are apt.[24]) Every other sonata-type movement is a hybrid of sorts, requiring qualification in terms of ABA form, when the second theme and its return raise problematic issues, or of rondo form. In the Clarinet Trio, Op. 114, Brahms's only combination of rondo and sonata (although not corresponding to Rosen's 'rondo-slow-movement form'[25]), the main theme returns in the tonic after the exposition, diverges into a development section, is recapitulated in the subdominant, and returns in the tonic during the coda:

$$
\begin{array}{ccccccc}
A & B & A & \text{dev} & A & B & \text{coda}/A \\
I & V & I & & IV & I & I
\end{array}
$$

While a subdominant recapitulation has many precedents, a comparison between this 'wrong-key' return and those in Brahms's ABA slow movements does seem suggestive.

As for the sonata movements with ABA features themselves, the second theme does not return in the Serenade in A major nor in the Second and Third Symphonies; in the last of these pieces, the theme does reappear, but in the finale.[26] In the Piano Quartet in C minor, Op. 60, the second theme returns at the close of the movement, acting as an abbreviated coda, and in retrospect, its extensive earlier statement takes on the characteristics of a B section. A curious case is the Violoncello Sonata in F major, Op. 99: four unprepared bars in the dominant (bars 16–19) close the A section after a tonic coda has resolved all the earlier subdominant activity. These same bars reappear at the appropriate spot in the reprise (bars 60–3), in the tonic and now elided with a final coda (the earlier 'tonic coda' had returned in the 'wrong' key, the flat submediant). Yet their function is never clear in terms of sonata form, and their brevity and harmonic purpose, even their opening upbeat, create more of a linkage with the B section than a foil to the tonic themes. (The particular mixture of forms in the Second Symphony will be discussed below.)

---

[22] These categories are taken from Charles Rosen, *Sonata Forms*, 96–110. Cf. also the paper by James Webster in the present volume.

[23] Letter of 30 Oct. 1888. *Brahms Briefwechsel*, i: 212; in English translation, 362. Her dislike of contrast in slow movements is a recurring idea in the letters.

[24] Tovey, 'Brahms's Chamber Music', 264.

[25] Rosen, *Sonata Forms*, 110.

[26] See the sensitive discussion of this piece in Frisch, *Brahms and the Principle of Developing Variation*, 129–42. Cf. also the paper by Robert Bailey in the present volume.

Ternary (ABA) movements themselves comprise fully half of Brahms's slow movements, and their influence on the form of other movements has been apparent in the preceding summary. On the surface, no form holds fewer surprises: the succession of lyrical, closed periods in the first part, the inevitable contrast, often with its own closed format and without a preparatory transition, the equally inevitable return—all create a set of firm expectations in the listener. And Brahms often satisfies these expectations directly, as in the Piano Trio in C minor, Op. 101. Even in the intensely lyrical movements of the String Quartet in C minor, Op. 51 No. 1, and the Violin Concerto, Op. 77, the nature of the contrast, a different set of recognizable gestures, is 'familiar' in advance. Movements with transitions between A and B may provide a measure of ambiguity, as in the Piano Concerto in D minor, Op 15, but this is easily resolved.[27] Ambitious codas may be similarly problematic; examples include the Piano Sonata in F minor, Op. 5, and the first version of the Piano Trio in B major, Op. 8. Yet Brahms found his most intimate voice in this form, which he transformed with a profound change in the relationships among the expected three sections. As the following discussion will show, Brahms developed a powerful set of 'ABA signals' that redesigned not only his ternary movements, but also his slow sonata movements as well.

# III

Significant departures from the norms of Brahms's ABA forms occur in the slow movements of the first two piano quartets (Opp. 25 and 26), the centre-pieces of his 'first maturity', that period of crucial stylistic syntheses in his sonata forms.[28] Both movements have in common the exceptional length of their main themes and high degree of contrast within these themes, and both are also the first to have B sections in unusual keys—the ternary movements in the Piano Sonata, Op. 5, and the Piano Trio, Op. 8, had modulated to the subdominant (never to be used again), while the First Piano Concerto had moved to the relative minor. Their most significant breaks with past works, though, are the shearing off of the huge codas that had concluded both sonata and trio, and the apparent abandonment of programmatic (or at least allusive) elements.[29]

The Andante con moto of the Piano Quartet in G minor, Op. 25, is Brahms's longest ternary movement, a full 235 bars. In degree of contrast, length of transitions, and harmonic alteration of reprise, it became the model for many of his later, albeit more compact, ternary movements. The forty-bar theme (bars 1–8 quoted in Example 1) itself expands the traditional binary design by generating its own contrasting section (bars 17–26, partially quoted in Example 2), which is based on the rhythm of bars 5 and 6, and

---

[27] Perhaps because of these transitions, Arno Mitschka considers many ABA movements as somehow sonata-form hybrids; see his book *Der Sonatensatz in den Werken von Johannes Brahms*, 221–39.

[28] Cf. Webster's discussion of this period in 'Schubert and Brahms (II)', 53–5.

[29] On the latter point, see Constantin Floros, *Brahms und Bruckner*, 144–7, on the slow movement of Op. 15; Eric Sams, 'Brahms and his Clara themes', 432–4, on the slow movement of Op. 8; and on the slow movement of Op. 5, Detlef Kraus, 'Das Andante aus der Sonate Op. 5 von Brahms: Versuch einer Interpretation', Walter Frisch, 'Brahms and Schubring: Musical Criticism and Politics at Mid-Century', 277, and the paper by George Bozarth in the present volume.

combines pulsating triplets, pedal-point, and chromatically ascending melody with appoggiaturas to execute a tension-filled move to the mediant minor by bar 21. As if to underscore the unusual quality of this passage, Brahms avoids even a brief modulation back to the tonic, choosing instead to complicate the return of the opening phrase with a joltingly unprepared tonic chord in a weak bar (bar 26). At the close of the theme, two transitional passages await (bars 40–58 and 59–74). The first, a large, two-part sequence (Example 3), juxtaposes the opening phrase and the tenser contrasting phrase, creating a new countermelody to the former by linking it rhythmically to the latter. At bar 59, we reach G major, the third step of the tonal sequence, and a dominant pedal which we assume will soon yield the standard relative minor (the overall proportions of the piece would seem to demand a quick resolution to a new theme or stable section). Instead, another transition (Example 4) introduces a martial dotted rhythm which accompanies a new, restlessly imitated melodic figure.

A stirring B section in C major finally arrives, but despite its apparent contrast to the A section, it has already been prepared: its structure parallels that of the A section, though with its first part ending at bar 107 in the new tonic of C major (after touching on E♭ major, the key of the movement, and previewing A♭ major, the key of the second section); its second part (bars 107–18) includes a big textural contrast, complete with triplets and a restless melodic figure which, like the one in the transition from A to B, is treated imitatively; and even the contour of the first eight bars of the B section corresponds to that of the first four bars of A, in a kind of eye-rhyme, since the melodies are in different keys (see Example 5).[30] Brahms exploits this resemblance by deploying the fully prepared reappearance of the main theme in C major, the key of the B section, rather than E♭ major (bar 152). The preparation for this key consists of an obviously false return in C minor (bars 148 ff.) which serves as a magnet drawing our attention towards the imminent arrival of the A theme in C major. The dominant pedal which underlies the opening bars of the ensuing statement of that theme might suggest that true arrival is avoided here. But when the theme finally does return in E♭, again it is over a dominant pedal, and with a syncopated delay of the melody (bars 168 ff.). Only in the first coda (bars 207 ff., Example 6) are some of the rhythmic similarities of the movement's motives reconnected: coming together are the rhythm and melodic contour of both contrasting phrases, as well as the triplet pulsation, now with the joyous martial character of the B section.

The autograph manuscript of this quartet, extant in the archive of the Gesellschaft der Musikfreunde in Vienna, reveals compositional changes that are nearly all concerned with the transitional phrases and the return of the A section. For example, the texture of the piano in the transitional phrases at bars 44–7 and 52–5 was originally thicker, similar to that at bars 21–5. Most striking is Brahms's original conception of the return (Examples 7 and 8): he initially thought to bring back the brilliant figuration of the 'first

---

[30]  Actually, Brahms himself disavowed less than explicit melodic relationships, in the letter to Schubring cited in note 15: cf. Frisch *Brahms and the Principle of Developing Variation*, 31–2.

EXAMPLE 1. Brahms, Piano Quartet in G minor, Op. 25, III, bars 1–8: A theme.

EXAMPLE 2. Brahms, Piano Quartet in G minor, Op. 25, III, bars 17–20: contrasting phrase in A section.

EXAMPLE 3. Brahms, Piano Quartet in G minor, Op. 25, III, bars 40–4: transition 1 after A section (alternates with contrasting phrase).

piano left hand (arpeggios in right hand)

EXAMPLE 4. Brahms, Piano Quartet in G minor, Op. 25, III, bars 59–62: transition 2 after A section.

EXAMPLE 5. Brahms, Piano Quartet in G minor, Op. 25, III: 'eye-rhyme' between A and B sections.

EXAMPLE 6. Brahms, Piano Quartet in G minor, Op. 25, III, bars 207–11: final version of coda.

EXAMPLE 7. Brahms, Piano Quartet in G minor, Op. 25, III: autograph, first version of ultimately rejected coda. First two bars have arpeggios in strings, all crossed out. (NB: Most of piano right hand is approximate in this transcription, because it is scratched out and over-written with the arpeggios of Example 8.)

EXAMPLE 8. Brahms, Piano Quartet in G minor, Op. 25, III: autograph, second version of ultimately rejected coda; bars 1B and 2B replace 1A and 2A; the remaining bars are written over the bars in Example 7.

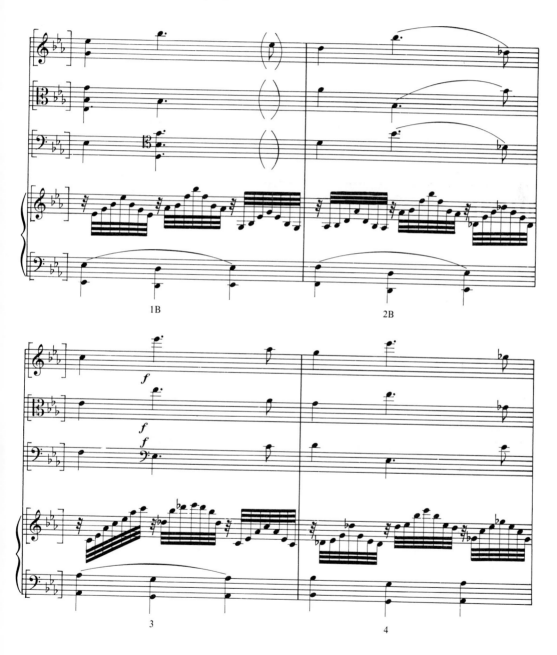

*Elaine Sisman*

transition' (bars 40 ff.) between sections A and B (after bar 206), now recast as a coda with the typical move to the subdominant. This idea he revised, before ultimately cutting it out entirely: first he laid out the whole passage placing the arpeggios in the strings, the A section melody in the left hand, and the dotted countermelody in the right hand

(Example 7); then he scratched out the right-hand melody, giving it to the strings, and, as in the first A section, restored the arpeggios to the right hand (Example 8). It cannot be discerned from the autograph at what point Brahms decided to shorten the return. The present coda, however, rehearses the harmonic motion of the rejected original, and with the same triplets. The cut section Brahms correctly deemed structurally unnecessary.[31]

Thus, the G minor Piano Quartet reveals a startlingly expanded set of sections, with considerable time spent preparing each departure; events are unified both musically and dramatically. The false return becomes a characteristic gesture for Brahms after this work, and he continually refines its use. Its power always derives from its preparation, which in most cases causes us to recognize another moment as the 'real' false return—as in the C minor return here—so that we are lulled into thinking that the next return is indeed the real one. For instance, in the A major slow movement of the String Quartet in A minor, Op. 51 No. 2, the B section has two strongly contrasting ideas (the dramatic canon plus tremolo, bars 43 ff. and 52 ff., and the lyrical phrase reminiscent of Wagner, bars 48 ff. and 60 ff). An obviously transitional 'return' in D major allows us to think that the second return, in F major, is the true one. Only gradually does the tonic re-emerge. Similarly striking, but without the first false return, is the F major slow movement of the String Quartet in B♭ major, Op. 67, again with two quite different ideas in the B section (this time appropriating gestures from the French overture at bars 29 ff. and from the ethereal progression in the first movement of Beethoven's String Quartet in F major, Op. 59 No. 1, and the 'Heiliger Dankgesang'). Brahms originally intended a short transition to a varied return in F major, as his autograph shows.[32] But, in a paste-over, he expanded this passage into a disorienting, chromatically modulatory transition that launches a varied return in D major. The key of F major appears only after an entire D major statement. The typical three-phrase construction of a Brahmsian slow-movement theme (aba or aba') here aids in its own harmonic reinterpretation.[33]

The slow movement of the Piano Quartet in A major, Op. 26, has long been recognized as the only rondo of its type among Brahms's slow movements. I would propose to read the movement in a new way, one that places it in the context of Brahms's experiments with ABA form.[34] The gently oscillating, squarely irregular, five-plus-five-bar theme

[31] My thanks to Dr Otto Biba, Peter Riethus, and the staff of the Gesellschaft der Musikfreunde for their helpfulness with this and other materials during a research trip to Vienna.

[32] Geiringer, *Brahms*, 234–5, shows the original version.

[33] A similar, though less complex example of this appears in Brahms's earlier Ballade in D major, Op. 10 No. 2, where the A section returns in the 'wrong' key. The phrase structure of the A section is abcb, in which c is in B minor; the form of the return, on the other hand, is acb, where a is in B major and c and b then follow in the 'right' keys, B minor and D major, respectively. There is no real 'false' return here. Brahms's later piano pieces, of course, offer many rich examples of reinterpreted ternary structures; they are, however, outside the scope of this paper.

[34] Christoph Wolff presented a similar ABA formulation for this movement in a paper given later in the Brahms year, adducing Brahms's sketch in its support. See his 'Von der Quellenkritik zur musikalischen Analyse: Beobachtungen am Klavierquartett A–Dur op. 26 von Johannes Brahms', 156–8. The sketch, found in the autograph of the Handel Variations, Op. 24, has been discussed by Jane A. Bernstein and used to support her own contention that the movement is in sonatina form; see 'An Autograph of the Brahms "Handel Variations" ', 275–8.

(Example 9) is extended at its close to a cadential, neighbour-note figure (bar 13) that then generates the entire transitional part of the A section (Example 10). (This transition is presumably the *Gegensatz* that Joachim found awkward but grew to appreciate.[35]) Dark appeggios move us from a preparation of G minor to one of F minor, but the beautifully varied A section re-emerges, dreamlike, without a resolution (bars 24 ff.). I regard this entire three-part structure as an A section, based on the model of Op. 25, rather than as a theme, episode, and refrain (ABA'), and I think subsequent events bear this out. The first real episode, then, is the piano's entrance with an impassioned new theme in B minor (Example 11), partially derived from the fourth and fifth bars of A, and with the strings continuing the regular eighth-note accompaniment of A as well. (A resemblance to Chopin's Fantasy in F minor, Op. 49, bars 93 ff. is not far-fetched.) The peaceful 'interlude' theme, or C section, which follows (Example 12) has a pivotal role: as the one passage in the movement where the eighth-note pattern does not appear—it features only ethereal strings in linear part-writing—it is the antithesis of the B minor theme; yet, because it is in B major, it complements the B minor statement, thus completing the identification of a middle section in the dominant. Furthermore, its climax in bars 77 ff. is patently based on the melody of B, with its descending eighth-notes, and it sets up a return to A that is much more of a 'real' return than that heard earlier (after the arpeggios, at bar 24), because the strings now sing out the unvaried melody, *senza sordini* (bars 86 ff.).[36]

We expect a full return of the A section, arpeggios and all, and we get it—up to a point. But Brahms's greatest surprise is to defeat our structural expectations while at the same time satisfying our tonal ones: after section A and the arpeggios, the B theme suddenly bursts out in F minor—the key now twice prepared by the arpeggios—with the melody

---

[35] Letter of 15 Oct. 1861: 'The Adagio is glorious! At first I thought that the contrasting section to the E major would be infelicitous; but when I (in my hesitant way) played it through on the piano, I became quite warmly disposed towards it; and when the golden thread of the theme shone through the uncertain passion to calm it, that was just so lovely.' ['Herrlich ist das Adagio! Erste meinte ich, der Gegensatz zum E dur wäre nicht glücklich; aber als ich's (selbst auf meine stockende Weise) auf dem Klavier durchspielte, wurde ich doch ganz warm dabei; und wenn dann der goldene Faden des Themas in die unbestimmte Leidenschaft beruhigen hineinschimmert, so ist das gerade ganz wunderschön.'] *Brahms Briefwechsel*, 5:313.

[36] The reviewer of this movement for the *Allgemeine musikalische Zeitung* (No. 37, 9 Sept. 1863, 626–7) may have heard it the same way. After poetically describing the opening E major section and arpeggios, he wrote: 'Thereupon follows a middle section for the piano in B minor, broadly laid out melodically [and] somewhat harsh, then a solo spot for strings in B major, which is thereupon varied by the piano and accompanied by [the strings] in rhythmic alternation. Finally the movement turn back to E major and repeats the whole main section, with variation of the tone colour and with different enrichments, together with the sinister arpeggios and the middle section (this time in F minor) etc. The piece ends quietly in E major, but not without yet another reminiscence of the ghostly spectre.— Invention and design appear to us here just as significant and original as the realization [is] consequential and rich.' ['Darauf folgt in H-moll ein melodisch breit ausgelegter, etwas herbe klingender Mittelsatz des Claviers, dann in H-dur eine Solostelle der Streichinstrumente, welche darauf vom Clavier variirt und von jenen in rhythmischem Wechsel begleitet wird. Endlich lenkt der Satz nach E-dur zurück und es wiederholt sich mit Veränderungen der Klangfarben und mit verschiedenen Bereicherungen der ganze Hauptsatz zusammt der unheimlichen Arpeggiostelle und dem Mittelsatz (diesmal in F-moll) u.s.w. Das Stück endet ruhig in E-dur, jedoch nicht ohne nochmalige Erinnerung an den geisterhaften Spuk.—Erfindung und Anlage scheinen uns hier ebenso bedeutend und originell als die Ausführung consequent und reich.']

EXAMPLE 9. Brahms, Piano Quartet in A major, Op. 26, II, bars 1–5: A them...

EXAMPLE 10. Brahms, Piano Quartet in A major, Op. 26, II, bar 15: contrasting transition (*Gegensatz*) within A theme.

EXAMPLE 11. Brahms, Piano Quartet in A major, Op. 26, II, bars 42–4: B theme (B minor).

EXAMPLE 12. Brahms, Piano Quartet in A major, Op. 26, II, bars 58–61: C theme (B major).

in the strings and accompanied by both eighth-note motive and arpeggios in the piano (bars 109 ff.). Consider the effect of this passage: it finally resolves the dangling dominant of F minor; it reinterprets the transition by giving it structural weight, as the piano continues its patterns in an episode; and it maintains the segregation of material between strings and piano, rather than having them trade off the melody, as they had done in every previous section. Ultimately, it forces us to reimagine the form. The outline of a rondo is indeed present (ABCABA), but as a result of what we might term an 'interrupted' ternary structure, now gigantically conceived:

A  B  A
aba  B C abBa

And after the transition, the final A, long anticipated, emerges just as tentatively as we expected it would (bars 127 ff.). The final B theme, now inserted irresistibly into the middle of the last segment of the arch form, is thus simultaneously the delayed harmonic resolution and the structural analogue of the transition. As in Op. 25, transitional passages have crucial formal consequences.

Indeed, to Brahms the very idea of 'transition' seems a challenge, one which he takes up later in the Horn Trio, Op. 40, and the Second Piano Concerto, Op. 83. In the Trio, composed at the end of his 'first maturity', the transition begins a fugato whose main motive then delves into mysterious keys in a developmental sequence of descending thirds. Only after the main theme returns do we realize that the transition has been the B section. (The situation here is further complicated by the half-cadence that concludes the A section; the 'open' A and following fugato seem to promise sonata form.)

In the Piano Concerto, Brahms adapted the lessons of his earlier ABA movements to the concerto genre for the first time.[37] In both the First Piano Concerto and the Violin Concerto, the eloquent ritornello theme is picked up by the soloist in a varied display. In Op. 83, on the other hand, the piano enters first on a cadential figure (Charles Rosen has shown its indebtedness to Beethoven's *Emperor* Concerto[38]), which then becomes the accompaniment to the solo variation of the tutti theme. Yet this theme diverges almost immediately, giving way to a lengthy, figural transition bounded by several ritornello-like reappearances of the tutti theme (bars 35 and 42 on V/V, bars 55 and 57 on i). The ritornello thus acts as both harmonic and thematic ground to the frequently changing solo figuration. The sheer size of this section and the establishment of the tonic minor, together with the possible implications of the ritornello as projecting a false return, make it not implausible that we identify this as the B section; the return of the piano's dreamy ascending cadential figure would seem to confirm this. But the arrival of a new section, in F♯ major, on an almost motionless chord progression, now fully elaborates the piano's initial arpeggios. In fact, this 'true' B section acts as the solo's counterpoise to the tutti theme. The piano has little to say after this, and a false return of the tutti theme in F♯ major, typical by now, ushers in only an abbreviated A section: the piano's arpeggios lead simply to the cadenza. In this piece, then, the unexpected differentiation between solo and tutti material, together with the unusually extensive transition, create a striking and somewhat ambiguous ABA design. If its tightened structural logic reflects the economy of the later Brahms, its formal procedures recall his 'first maturity'.

# IV

Brahms thus fully reinvented the ABA form by demonstrating that one can no longer take for granted its most basic premises: what is A and what is B, where the return is, and what transitions mean. These mixed signals also turn up in his slow sonata-type movements, often resulting in a kind of synthesis of sonata and ABA. The foregoing discussion has pointed out some problematic sonata-form procedures in several slow movements, such as the Violoncello Sonata in F major and the Horn Trio. The coda-like return of the second theme in the Piano Quartet in C minor, Op. 60, recalls another feature of Brahms's ABA practice—the re-emergence of the B theme in the coda (cf. the C minor String Quartet, the F minor Piano Sonata, the G major Violin Sonata, and so

---

[37] Carl Dahlhaus speaks of the 'dialectical' complications of the ABA form in Op. 15, in his monograph *Johannes Brahms—Klavierkonzert Nr. I d-moll, op. 15*, 17: 'The simplicity of the form appears as the support and at the same time the adversary of a differentiated structure.' ['Die Simplizität der Form erscheint als Stütze und zugleich als Widerpart einer differenzierten Struktur.']

[38] Rosen, 'Influence', 65–6.

on). Even movements with a transition between the A and B sections may raise the expectation of sonata form (cf. the Piano Concerto in D minor, the Piano Quintet, and the Horn Trio). My final examples will show Brahms, as a symphonist, overcoming the burden of the past and using his ternary innovations to influence his slow-movement sonata forms. The discussion will focus on the Second Symphony.

For his First Symphony, Brahms wrote a ternary form that was by no means uncomplicated. Recent research has uncovered the original quasi-five-part structure,[39] and the arrangement of materials in the final version represents an increase in complexity rather than the reverse. I refer not merely to the quotation from the introduction of the first movement (bars 5–6), but also to the coda/transition between sections A and B, the references to A in the B section, and the return of material from A in a different key (bars 9–16 come back at bars 76–84, now with a six-bar extension, but in a key further away from the tonic; in fact, tonal logic would suggest that the key relations be reversed). And the coda is proportionally one of the longest in any slow movement. Still, this remains the most 'straightforward' ABA form in the symphonies.

Brahms provided his own precedent for symphonic *Mischformen* in his Serenade in A major, Op. 16, where, as James Webster has pointed out, sonata and ABA form are combined: the second theme, a huge lyric contrast, is never recapitulated.[40] This is hardly new—the slow movements of Mozart's Piano Concerto in A major, K. 488, and Beethoven's Piano Concerto in C minor, Op. 37, also fail to resolve their second themes. But in each of these earlier cases, the expressive effect of that second theme was similar to the first.[41] Here, the second theme is an enormous episode bearing no relation to the first. It is perhaps significant that Brahms later plundered this movement for symphonic material: the oscillating figure that forms the fugato in the Second Symphony's slow movement as well as the second theme of that movement comes from this piece. If the Serenade shows Brahms reworking classical models,[42] the Second Symphony reveals him reinterpreting himself.

The principal formal issue at stake in the slow movement of the Second Symphony is the nature of the recapitulation; that there is a real sonata-style exposition and development is beyond question. The slow tempo and leisurely unfolding of the first theme, complete with metrical ambiguities and developing variation, enforce the perception of a 'progressive' sonata exposition, each of whose particles generates the next functional area.[43] Yet the 'character' of the theme and whether or not it cadences in the

[39] See n. 19.

[40] Webster, 'Schubert's Sonata Form (II)', 60.

[41] Of K. 488, Charles Rosen writes: 'There is a direct expository movement from first to second theme, but no recapitulation of the second theme: however, the themes are closely related, and a recapitulation of the first ritornello is used as a substitute'. *The Classical Style: Haydn, Mozart, Beethoven*, 245, n. 1.

[42] Webster, 'Schubert's Sonata Form (II)', 60, also points out the undeniable relevance of the slow movement of Beethoven's String Quartet in C major, Op. 59 No. 3, to this movement. Clara Schumann, for her part, called the opening 'Bachisch' and the character of the whole 'somewhat churchlike; it could be an Eleison' ['etwas Kirchlicher, es könnte ein Eleison sein']; the middle section she referred to as the 'neue Gesang'; letter of 18 Sept. 1859, Litzmann, *Schumann–Brahms Briefe*, 1: 278–9.

[43] Frisch offers a compelling analysis of this movement in *Brahms and the Principle of Developing Variation*, 123–9.

tonic cannot be used as a determinant of form: a closed first group may be either ABA or sonata. The First, Third, and Fourth Symphonies all have main themes with tonic cadences, each of which is immediately elided with a closing-type passage that becomes a modulating transition; but, while the closing/transitional passage of the First Symphony leads to a contrasting B section in the relative minor, the analogous passages in the Third and Fourth Symphonies lead to bridge material and the dominant. The situation is complicated in the Third Symphony by the ambiguous character of the remaining themes in the exposition. In this context, then, the firm cadence in the tonic at bar 17 of the Second Symphony forecasts neither ternary nor sonata form, nor does the ostensible reiteration of the cadence by the horn, which instead turns the figure into a fugato (bars 17 ff.). (We have seen in the Horn Trio how a fugato-transition may 'become' a B section.) And yet, how are we to hear the return of the climactic subdominant-tonic of bar 3—the one we thought the horn was going to play—when it comes back in bar 28 and creates a real point of arrival? It is only a single step above the tonic (in V/V) and sounds like the cadence that has been delayed. The theme that next appears—a lilting, triadic melody in the winds with light pizzicato accompaniment (bars 33 ff.)—might well be either second theme or B section; only the obvious coda (bars 45 ff.) makes us interpret this section as the end of the exposition. The development that follows (bars 49 ff.) confirms this identification.

Yet at the end of the development, after the apparently inevitable neighbour-note transition figure, Brahms swerves back into his ternary mode. The appearance of the main theme in G major (bars 57 ff.) is a double surprise, first, because it comes in over a dominant pedal—it takes a second to remember that the theme itself was first over a dominant pedal—and then because it is in the wrong key. This statement of the theme breaks off, interrupted by the end of the development and the neighbour-note bar. Of the next return of the theme, one is a little warier. But instead of an interruption, a chromatic descent brings on a false recapitulation in the correct key (bars 65 ff.). When the real, varied recapitulation finally arrives (bar 68), it is less a surprise than a retrospective revelation perceived during the culminating third bar of the theme (bar 70). The fugato episode of the exposition, shorter and prepared differently, now generates the real climax of the movement—the transformation of the third-bar motive into a huge brass fanfare that ushers in a secondary development. Replaced by development, the lyrical second theme has no place here, and even the coda theme now acts as a deceptive subdominant interpolation (bars 92 ff.). Locating in the A theme itself the primary material of the movement, this secondary development completes the identification, paradoxically enough, with ternary form: with hindsight, the B theme functions as a gestural contrast, much like that in the Serenade, Op. 16 (the contrapuntal developments in the two movements are even similar). The movement might also be considered analogous to the Op. 26 Adagio, in which the return of the theme was interrupted so that an earlier impassioned outbreak might be satisfactorily resolved. A reading such as

A B  C+dev  A+dev  C A
    on C      on A

(with C as coda theme) is quite similar to the ABCABA proposed for the earlier movement. That the A material here is an opposite extreme from Op. 26 goes without saying, but the differences show Brahms reformulating his movement to fit his theme—one of his most important concerns, as Gustav Jenner reported.[44]

## V

In Brahms's slow movements, one must always mediate between the received musical messages and their unexpected resolutions—a step-by-step process—and the larger sections and their assigned weights and relationships—a retrospective process. Brahms the classicist delighted in reinterpretations of conventions, as did Haydn before him,[45] and in progressively unfolding structures in which the sense of process is as important as the actual material, as did Beethoven. Hybrid forms and many-faceted connections between repeating, recurring, contrasting, or developing sections were nothing new. But Brahms found a way to deal with the burden of his inheritance. From the very beginning, he conceived his slow movements on a grand scale; those in the Piano Sonata, Op. 5, and the Piano Trio, Op. 8, are among the largest he wrote, and both contain codas that nearly overwhelm the ABA design itself. The slow sonata form of the Serenade, Op. 11, is likewise highly differentiated and extensive. Shortly thereafter, however, in the Serenade, Op. 16, and the Sextet, Op. 18, Brahms turned to formal exploration and trimming of excess. The Serenade reveals a compact structure whose ambiguity rests on Brahms changing the rules of the game twice before the movement is through, while staying faithful to a contrast principle. The Sextet variations, charting a course from the austere and minor to the heavenly and major, and back again, show the influence of ABA on this form. This method of organization, exploited by many earlier composers, is examined here by Brahms for the first and only time.

Having pared down and reorganized—having regrouped his forces around the ABA, in a sense—Brahms proceeded in the two piano quartets radically to redefine the limits of the slow movement, not coincidentally, for his Viennese début. Gigantic in scope, his ambitious reappraisals of convention created apparent contrast with hidden connecting threads in Op. 25, and formal expansiveness tightly reined in by motivic unity and long-range harmonic goals in Op. 26. In both, his most important innovation was to transform the moment of return into an entity far more elusive than in earlier music. While any return after contrast carries with it a set of expectations—and its inevitability is one such expectation—Brahms traded on them to a quite unprecedented degree, using transitions (often based on neighbour-note motives); changes of character, tempo, and metre; key relationships more remote than even those of Schubert (though often without Schubert's exuberant daring); and rhythmic and tonal ambiguity. His ubiquitous use of variation technique in the returning A sections, while already a common feature in the slow movements of Haydn, Beethoven, and Schubert, sets a new level of expressiveness, but

---

[44] Jenner, *Brahms als Mensch*, 61.
[45] See, for example, Edward T. Cone, 'The Uses of Convention: Stravinsky and his Models'.

also reflects a deeper structural purpose. After all, variation in a section whose beginning is somehow blurred (the Second Symphony, Op. 73) or which is in the wrong key (the String Quartet, Op. 67) may either point up or else further obscure the structural significance of that idea, and has a very different effect from variation that creates a new radiance around something that was merely lovely. Yet, both of these effects can be found in Op. 26, where the variation technique helps us to differentiate between returns within the A section and returns of the entire section.

After the piano quartets, nearly every slow movement is shadowed by ABA forms in which Brahms synthesizes a shifting relationship among the components by redefining the nature of contrast and the limits of return or recurrence. The contrasts, while often apparently antithetical to the opening material, may also be based on a deep relationship with it; this may be put to good use during the return. And false tonal returns, not a feature of Brahms's big first-movement sonata forms, become a crucial feature to his slow-movement aesthetic, and play an important role not only in the ternary structures for which they were developed, but also in ABA concerto and ABA sonata hybrids, like the Second Piano Concerto and the Second Symphony, respectively. Elisabeth von Herzogenberg may have found too much contrast in Brahms's slow movements, but we would find it hard to object to an aesthetic that, in reinventing the most commonplace of compositional givens, makes the Andantes expansive and the Adagios profound.

# BRAHMS THE SUBVERSIVE

—

## CHARLES ROSEN

WRITING about Brahms's Rhapsody in G minor, Op. 79 No. 2, Carl Dahlhaus makes an interesting mistake. I hasten to add that to me Dahlhaus is one of the most provocative and intelligent writers on music in this century; it is therefore all the more curious that Brahms could have misled someone so distinguished and so perceptive. The error occurs in Dahlhaus's discussion of 'expanded' and 'wandering' tonality (the fourth section of his essay 'Issues in Composition').[1] Dahlhaus ascribes 'wandering' or 'floating' tonality to Wagner and Liszt, and he wishes to demonstrate that such procedures can also be found in Brahms. This he tries to prove with the opening of the Rhapsody in G minor, Op. 79 No. 2 (see Example 1), though he realizes that he has not much of a case, for this passage really does sound a lot in G minor. Dahlhaus himself, in fact, finds very good reasons, from a linear point of view, for explaining why these bars are in G minor. Still, when he comes to the second theme, he claims that G minor has been so little established and the new tonality that now unfolds is so ambiguous that we accept it as D minor only because the dominant is the traditional key for a second group.

What is interesting is that in almost no piece in G minor is D minor the key for the 'second group'; that we know that the second theme is in the key of D cannot be due to some kind of tradition.[2] There are a few movements in the major mode where Brahms used the minor dominant for a second group, but that is in fact not a tradition, but rather the breaking of one. The traditional key for the second group would, of course, be B♭ major.

The opening of this piece is so curious that it is reasonable for Dahlhaus and anyone else to be puzzled. For one thing, it begins with what appears to be a full sequence; yet, although the two opening bars sound like a sequence, one of its members is not parallel to the other, for details have been changed: the opening fourth in the bass becomes a sixth, the opening fifth in the right hand becomes a diminished fifth. Both bars are essentially V–I progressions, both with surprise resolutions. Varied sequences existed long before Brahms, of course, but it is instructive to compare Brahms's practice with that of, say, Vivaldi and Bach. Whereas in Vivaldi the sequences tend to come with unvaried rigidity, Bach usually attempts to vary his, generally by means of voice-leading,

---

[1] *Between Romanticism and Modernism: Four Studies in the Music of the Later Nineteenth Century*, 69–71.

[2] After 1825, composers occasionally used the dominant minor as a secondary tonality, but examples are very rare (e.g. Mendelssohn's String Quartet in A minor, Op. 13, and the *Scottish* Symphony, Op. 56); the dominant *major* may be found in Schubert's Piano Sonata in A minor, D. 784, and in Mendelssohn's Piano Trio in D minor, Op. 49, but this relationship is equally infrequent.

EXAMPLE 1. Brahms, Rhapsody in G minor, Op. 79 No. 2, bars 1–13.

though without strong variation of harmony. In Brahms, the typical variation is more radically of a harmonic nature, as in the example here.

Another peculiar thing about the opening of the Rhapsody in G minor is that almost all the cadences are what might be called 'weak cadences' ('weak' in a descriptive, not a pejorative sense). The strongest form of cadence is, of course, the V–I cadence. The normal plagal cadence is already a weakened form, and there are even weaker forms of the plagal cadence. Almost all the progressions of this opening page appear to be plagal, but are in fact ambiguous. Take the one in bars 3 and 4:

EXAMPLE 2.

The G major chord at the opening of bar 4 is heard clearly as a tonic (as our ears have accepted the opening two beats of the Rhapsody as a V–I progression with a surprise resolution to VI); at the same time, it is weakened by the diminished seventh and sounds as the dominant of IV. The cadence is not plagal, but IV to V of IV. It is a half-cadence on a dominant, in this case a tonic chord used momentarily as a dominant to IV. This sense of going from I to V is enforced by what precedes:

EXAMPLE 3.

This sets the pattern for the harmonic structure of the whole page:

EXAMPLE 4.

These four half-cadences define G minor and the move to D minor completed by bar 21: the establishment of G minor is achieved not only by line, but also harmonically.

This ambiguity (plagal cadence with a touch of minor or half-close on a local dominant) may help us understand the nature of Brahms's relation to the Classical tradition. If we reverse each of these four cadences, we have 'strong' cadences:

EXAMPLE 5.

Cadences 1, 3, and 4 are, already in the correct order, the three cadences that open Beethoven's First Symphony: they define G as Beethoven's defined C. (Beethoven's cadences are only slightly more powerful; his three dominants are dominant sevenths.) In short, Brahms's method of establishing his tonic is a simple although radical subversion of a traditional classical way of establishing a key. I do not mean to imply that Brahms intentionally added VI to Beethoven's IV–I–V, and then played each of the cadences backwards, but that the ambiguity that induced Dahlhaus's error does not come from a 'floating' or 'wandering' view of tonality, but from a thoroughly systematic and original treatment of basic Classical procedures. Reversing a Classical means of establishing a tonality allows Brahms here to define G at the same time that he establishes the move to D. This is significant, as we shall find that what is characteristic of Brahms's style is an overlapping of functions normally kept separate in Classical procedure.

These weakened cadences are typical of Brahms: when he uses tonic-dominant relationships, he tends to weaken them, and not only on a small scale, as in this piece, but on a very large scale as well. Two of the best examples occur in the first movements of the Second Piano Concerto and the Violin Concerto; both are pieces in major in which the dominant minor is used as the second key. Perhaps there is a precedent for this, for there is a precedent for almost everything in Brahms—he was an extraordinarily learned composer, and I have become convinced that if in any instance I do not know the precedent, it is because I have not looked hard enough. Nevertheless, the use of the minor dominant as the secondary key in an exposition, and the extent to which Brahms uses it, does seem to me very innovative. And I do not think this can be related to the brief allusion to the dominant minor in the second group of sonata expositions which is frequent in mid-eighteenth-century composers such as Monn and Wagenseil and which continues as a sort of tradition (see Mozart's Piano Sonata in F major, K. 332, for an example). In a way, Brahms's use of the minor dominant is better considered as an extension of Beethoven's use of the minor in pieces such as the *Appassionata*, compositions in minor which proceed to the relative major but mix a great deal of minor into the relative major.

Another innovation of Brahms is his use of what might be called a dislocation of sense between bass and melody. Melody in eighteenth- and nineteenth-century music traditionally implied its own harmony; in other words, the harmony has two values, horizontal and vertical; in general these two are in phase. Of course a composer can also harmonize a melody in a way that is not implied by the melody itself, creating a surprise. What is interesting about Brahms is the extent to which the horizontal and vertical are out of phase, with the harmony moving on to the next step before the melody has got there. A typical example occurs at the beginning of the Third Symphony (see Example 6). Even though a suggestion of F minor is in evidence in the diminished seventh chord which follows the opening tonic F major, still the minor of the second bar of the melody (bar 4) comes as something of a shock, even today when one knows the piece. I think this is very different from the way it was done by eighteenth-century composers. One does find harmonic anticipation in Haydn, Mozart, and Beethoven, so it is not absolutely new with Brahms, but the shock he derives from it is fairly new. In Mozart a change of harmony of this sort always has a very peculiar expressive value related to the intervals of the theme itself, as in the slow movement of the Piano Trio in E major, K. 542 (see Example 7, the initial, and a subsequent, harmonization of the opening theme). This is as

EXAMPLE 6. Brahms, Symphony No. 3 in F major, Op. 90, bars 1–6.

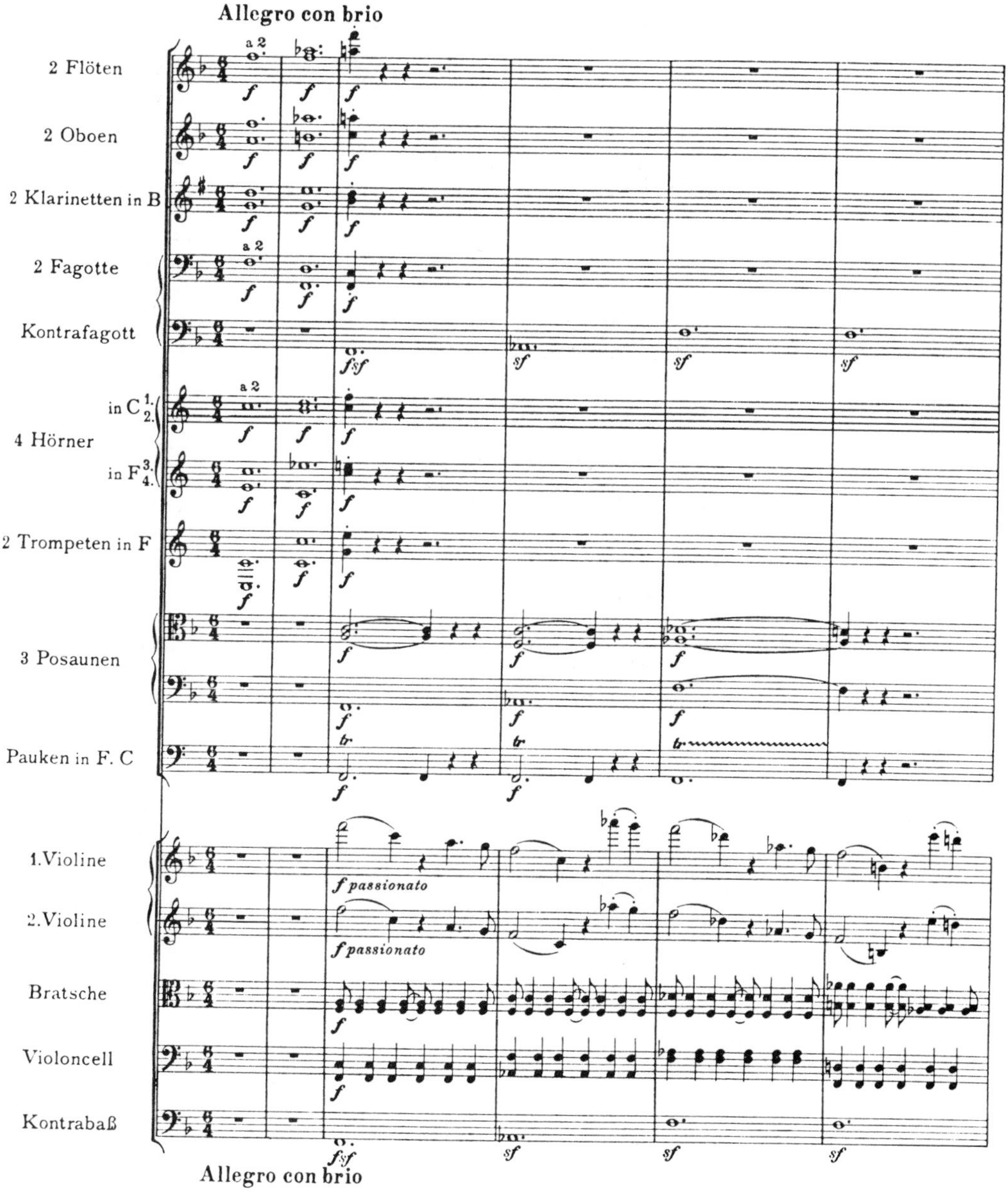

EXAMPLE 7. (*a*) Mozart, Piano Trio in E major, K. 542, bars 1–4. (*b*) Bars 12–16.

astonishing as anything in Brahms, but the reharmonization is inspired by the minor seventh E down to F♯ outlined by the theme. The new harmonies only realize in advance this dissonance and its resolution to a D, but in Brahms the minor that initiates the fourth bar of the Third Symphony appears almost gratuitously independent of the melody, even though, as in Mozart, it implies what is to come in the melody. One finds the same thing, for example, in the middle section of the Ballade in G minor, Op. 118 No. 3 (Example 8). The melody by itself in bars 41 and 42 implies G♯ minor, while the bass defines B major. In bar 43 the melody implies B major, at which point the bass begins to shift to G♯ minor. When the melody reaches a G♯ in bar 44, the bass moves toward F♯ major. This interplay is exceptionally fluid, and explains why Brahms's style rarely shows the hard-edged quality of the Viennese Classical tradition, where the vertical and horizontal components of harmony are much more in phase.

EXAMPLE 8. Brahms, Ballade in G minor, Op. 118 No. 3, bars 41–4.

Once again this is a technique Brahms derived from compositions of the generation following Beethoven. Largely he takes this, I think, from Schubert, who was a master at such things. As a precedent for the beginning of the Third Symphony, we could cite Schubert's Quintet in C major, which has exactly the same kind of shock value as the Brahms (Example 9). Schubert also has a piece of B major in which he harmonizes what ought to be a B major chord with a G♯ minor chord, the final Variation of the Andantino varié in B minor for piano four hands (the slow movement of the *Divertissement sur des motifs origineaux français*, D. 823; Example 10). It is interesting that when Schubert does this, he sounds most like Brahms. I cannot comment on what direct connection this piece may have to the slow movement of Brahm's Second Symphony.

This kind of dislocation between melody and bass is something at which Brahms became very expert, and I think he went further than any other composer before him.

EXAMPLE 9. Schubert, Quintet in C major, Op. 163, D. 956, I, bars 1–4.

EXAMPLE 10. Schubert, Andantino varié from *Divertissement sur des motifs originaux français*, D. 823, bars 65–8.

One example, from the finale of the Horn Trio, Op. 40, is particularly striking (Example 11). How disconcerting it must be to the violinist concentrating on his own melody, with the harmony it implies, to find the third bar completely reinterpreted by the bass of the piano part in a way impossible to predict from the melody. Such procedures occur in a great deal of Brahms's music, and what they do is to loosen the fairly strict ties in Viennese Classical style between harmony and melody.

The idea of having harmony and melody out of phase with each other is not new. Of course, it occurs in Schumann all the time. The difference between Brahms and Schumann is that in Schumann the dislocation of harmony and melody is generally systematic. In 'Paganini' from *Carnaval*, for instance, the left hand begins off the beat, a sixteenth-note before the bar line and fortissimo, while the right hand begins on the bar line and piano, so that one is sure that it is the left hand which is on the bar line, the right hand which is off (Example 12). But then both hands play softly, and it is clear that the right hand is on the bar line, which seems to have shifted. Here the harmony changes systematically out of phase with the melody. In Brahms, such changes are not systematic, but fluctuate, as the example from the Horn Trio demonstrates, and bar line displacement is only momentary.

Dislocation of sense is of course a rhythmic device, and it can be used very strictly by

EXAMPLE 11. Brahms, Trio in E♭ major for Violin, Horn, and Piano, Op. 40, Finale, bars 1–12.

Brahms to displace the accent. But again it is not, as in Schumann, an ongoing systematic displacement. Consider the sixth piece of the *Davidsbündlertänze*, Op. 6 (Example 13). A tarantella normally has accents on the first and fourth beats, and the one on beat 4 should be quite strong (which performers sometimes forget). Yet Schumann consistently accents beats 3 and 6 in the right hand, beat 2 and 5 in the left hand. This sort of systematic displacement Brahms, on the whole, avoids. Displacement is certainly present, and, I think, probably derived from his study of Schumann, but it is very much more fluid than in the music of his predecessor.

Returning to the opening of the finale in the Horn Trio (Example 11), we see here what I would call a dislocation of sense between the horizontal harmonic meaning and the vertical harmonic meaning, for, while the harmony in the upper voices goes off to vi in bars 3 and 4, the bass continues to play I–V–I–V–I. As the passage continues, the changes

EXAMPLE 12. Schumann, 'Paganini' from *Carnaval*, Op. 9, bars 1–10.

EXAMPLE 13. Schumann, *Davidsbündlertänze*, Op. 6 No. 6, bars 1–4.

of harmony occur basically on the sixth beat, but not consistently so. Note also how Brahms puts the harmonic change into relief by the position of the chord: root position occurs, very clearly defined, at a point where you would not be expecting it, and the weak beats are accented by this very strongly, though not, as I have said, with the regularity one finds in Schumann. Indeed, Schumann would probably have carried this on until finally you were convinced that the sixth beat was the first beat of the bar (compare, for example, the penultimate page of the Toccata, Op. 7).

The Intermezzo in C major, Op. 119 No. 3, shows how these various factors can influence large-scale structure, although in a short piece. First of all, the overall tonal structure is that of a fairly weak progression to relative minor and back: it begins in C major, moves to A minor by the end of the twelfth bar, and then repeats this exposition (Example 14). In the third bar, the way in which the E minor chord is spaced on the sixth beat causes it to receive a slight and unexpected accent. Later in the piece, at bars 29, 30, 31, and 32 (Example 15), this aspect is developed: new harmonies in root-position chords appear on the sixth beat of the bar; changes of harmony and melody occur out of phase with the basic rhythm of the piece. In these bars the changes of harmony are also foreshadowed by the left hand on the weak third beat in the middle of each bar: the one bass note that is held becomes the root of the harmony of the next bar.

Brahms's treatment of sequence is at its most subtle in bars 3 to 7. Bars 3 to 4 imply a rising sequential movement (see Example 16a), immediately abandoned for a descending one. The new sequence implies a simple pattern (Example 16b), but this too is inflected by Brahms. A sequence has a forward-moving energy, and Brahms's alterations act as brakes to this motion. That is why one of his works always seems to move more slowly than those of the Classical tradition from which his style derives.

Brahms's treatment of dissonance subverts practices handed down from the late eighteenth- and early nineteenth-century styles, and again he seems to be following Schumann. Whereas Schumann, though, often leaves dissonance hanging over unresolved into subsequent beats in a fairly systematic manner, Brahms tends to add the dissonance just at the moment when resolution is expected, but without, however, denying the resolution. In the sixth bar of the Intermezzo, for example, the dissonant E♭s appear just as resolution is expected. I mean this as no criticism, but in Brahms the relationship of consonance and dissonance is constantly eaten from within as if by termites. His music is full of holes, of frustrated expectations; this gives it its very unusual quality, and explains why nobody mistakes a piece by Brahms for one by the composer that he seems to be ostentatiously imitating, why Brahms never really sounds like Haydn, Beethoven, Schubert, or Mendelssohn, except, perhaps, in a few early pieces.

Brahms modulates to A minor in this Intermezzo, but the key is not fully confirmed. This confirmation is only implied—Brahms reaches A minor, then changes to the major (bar 10), as if to confirm A, but always sounds A as a six-four chord, not in a proper root position. Indeed, he never allows a clear V–I progression (until bars 24–5, when the resolution remains unharmonized). Every attempt is undercut by a dissonance that not only hangs over, but is resolved, if at all, too late to count, with the A minor and A major

EXAMPLE 14.  Brahms, Intermezzo in C major, Op. 119 No. 3, bars 1–13.

EXAMPLE 15.  Brahms, Intermezzo in C major, Op. 119 No. 3, bars 29–32.

EXAMPLE 16*a*.                              EXAMPLE 16*b*.

chords being tossed on to the end of bars 9 and 10 and coloured by dissonance in bars 11 and 12.

One of the ways in which Brahms does establish A minor as a secondary key (and it is quite clearly established) is through expressive alterations of rhythm: he writes 'sostenuto' over all of bar 10 and at the end of bar 12. (My readings come from the Breitkopf & Härtel collected edition, which is based on the first edition; in the autograph which Brahms gave to Clara Schumann in 1893, now owned by Dr Friedrich G. Zeileis, Gallspach, Austria, neither 'sostenuto' is present; the copyist's manuscript used as the engraver's model, now in private possession in West Germany, was not available for consultation.) The first of these establishes the key, the second occurs as Brahms quits the key. It is extraordinary how Brahms depends on the weakest possible harmonic progressions and how masterful he is at convincing us by rubato and texture that they work, as they do indeed here. (It is also interesting to see how the overlapping phrases in this opening passage subvert the usual twelve-bar structure of three four-bar phrases.)

The retransition in this piece provides another example of a false sequence, this one radically so (Example 17). After a typical sequence of descending thirds (bars 35–6), Brahms begins preparation for the return, which is ultimately effected through a minor plagal cadence. In the intervening bars Brahms first moves to a root-position D♭ major chord, and then, in the second half of the false sequence, to F minor in first inversion. In this case, the dynamics serve to enforce the falsity of the parallelism: the peak of the crescendo emphasized a D♭ major chord in root position in bars 37–8, and it sounds as if Brahms is moving to an A♭ major chord at the peak of the crescendo in bar 39. It is left to the bass to bring out the real harmonic progression, which is confirmed only at the last possible moment with the F on the last beat of bar 40.

The return itself is interesting. Brahms creates here on a small scale what he does in very large works, like the Fourth Symphony: an augmented return, and a particularly ingenious one. It is impossible to determine exactly where the return takes place; if we judge by the reappearance of the original rhythm, the return does not begin until bar 45. But once you have heard bar 45, and by the time you reach bar 47, you realize that this is an answer and that an elliptical return has already taken place at bars 41 to 45.

Adding to the ambiguity is the minor plagal cadence that leads to the return at bar 41; it is not until four bars later (at bar 44) that a dominant occurs, and even here there is a dislocation, for the bass of the dominant first appears as the third of an E minor chord (bar 44, beat 1), sounding quite clearly as if it is part of that chord, although its textural displacement immediately indicates that this pitch has a different meaning, that this G does not belong to the E minor chord, but is the bass for the G dominant seventh that follows. This is one of the subtlest examples of Brahms's use of this kind of displacement, and one of the wittiest: it presents us with the paradox of a dominant preparation for a return occurring four bars after the return has already begun. One might say that Brahms provides us with the dominant-tonic relationship after it is no longer necessary. That would be an exaggeration. The V⁷ 'preparation' is still necessary as a confirmation of the return. A basic classical device is given once again by Brahms in reverse order, and its

EXAMPLE 17. Brahms, Intermezzo in C major, Op. 119 No. 3, bars 35–48.

function becomes ambiguous. The continuity of the music is considerably enriched: the symmetry of the two four-bar phrases (41–4 and 45–8) makes us hear the V⁷ chord of bar 44 as part of an already ongoing process, instead of in its traditional role as the end point of a retransition. Nevertheless, it actually fulfills its traditional function even in its displacement: we do hear bar 45 as the beginning of the reprise, and only retrospectively recognize that it had already started with bar 41.

Displacement again occurs at the end of the piece (Example 18). Now, though, instead of using the dominant seventh to confirm the return to the tonic *after* the fact, Brahms sets up the dominant well ahead of time, as a pedal (bars 56 ff.). But a very peculiar process then takes place: after four bars of dominant-tonic progressions (but with resolutions on the weakest beats), he suddenly calls for two bars 'un poco ritardando' (this is in the autograph version), which delays the final V–I cadence to the point where one hardly feels a need to attach much importance to it when it finally arrives, 'a tempo'. The return to the tonic has actually taken place during the ritardando on the six-four

EXAMPLE 18. Brahms, Intermezzo in C major, Op. 119 No. 3, bars 55–70.

chord at the end of the dominant pedal (bar 62). It almost looks as if Brahms had been reading one of those Schenkerian models, in which he noticed that the important final V–I takes very little time, and so he decided he was going to get it over with as fast as possible. This gives the V–I cadence its relaxed grace. Interpretation of this passage also depends on an understanding of the traditional Viennese waltz.

One last detail: Just before the six-four chord, the pitch A starts to assert itself in both treble and bass (bars 60–1) and is important until the end of the piece. Indeed, this pitch, and in this same context, played an important role at the very beginning of the piece. Its final appearance, and a prominent one, is in the 'throw-away' passage which closes the piece (bars 66 ff.), where it actually gives the final cadence a kind of plagal colour. The way Brahms has removed the emphasis from the firm traditional V–I cadence is the source of this page's heavy-handed but engaging charm.

What I have hoped to show with these various observations—and the only justification I can offer for this paper appearing with others devoted to Brahms and Viennese Classicism—is that, although Brahms is still dealing with almost all the traditional elements of late eighteenth- and early nineteenth-century music, he tends to play with them, to manipulate them, dislocating their traditional relationships with each other and setting them off one against the other for purposes that no composer before him had ever envisaged. Brahms is both subverting the Classical tradition and at the same time exploiting it with a learning greater than any of his contemporaries.

# BRAHMS THE PROGRESSIVE

# SCHOENBERG'S BRAHMS

—

# MICHAEL MUSGRAVE

## I

THE time is still within easy recall when the coupling of the names Brahms and Schoenberg caused surprise, indeed shock in circles Schoenbergian as well as Brahmsian, for it seemed to threaten the pattern of relationships on which a whole view of history rested secure. What could they conceivably have in common? Was not Brahms the great Conservative, the sovereign custodian of the Classical inheritance of abstract instrumental music, steadfast in the face of the rising tide of Wagnerism and the lure of the programme? A noble figure, certainly, but hardly one relevant to the present or future. And Schoenberg? Was he not the very opposite, the very incarnation of modernism? Not only an experimenter, but sufficiently visionary to create a new system, a new language of his own, and one so strictly organized that it seemed to represent a new aesthetic, a complete rejection of the intuitive world of Brahms? Of course, each had shown other tendencies in his youth. The young Brahms was a fiery Romantic who had impressed the New Germans; but he had soon settled down to his real life's work as a composer of chamber music and symphonies, inclining to the conservative values of Clara Schumann and Joachim, of Billroth and Hanslick. And true, Schoenberg had started off as the composer of such Romantic works as *Verklärte Nacht*; but he had soon tired of this style and had quickly moved into an entirely new world, allying himself with such progressives as Mahler, Strauss, Loos, Kraus, Kandinsky, and Kokoschka.

That such a polarized view could have remained binding for so long offers a fascinating illustration of the way we receive musical experiences and arrange our view of the past to suit our need for mental order—thus the power of the image, so familiar to the modern world of advertising. But this view is spectacularly at odds with reality. Brahms was never in any sense, other than a most superficial one, a conservative composer. His language was advanced and vital and continues to challenge and attract. And Schoenberg? His modernism was certainly not achieved at the expense of the past. On the contrary, his progressive style was founded in intimate relationship with the styles of his predecessors. Indeed, with the passage of time, a broader audience is now privy to what a close circle knew all along: that the worlds of Schoenberg and Brahms represent a continuity. But it was only with the publication of certain major writings—by circumstance more in English than in German—that this was revealed.

The spirit of the relationship between Schoenberg and his past is preserved for us with great immediacy in a recorded interview with him. In response to Halsey Stevens's questions concerning the technical aspects of his serial works, Schoenberg replied:

I think there is a possibility to learn something of my technical achievements. But I think it is even better to go back to those men from whom *I* learnt them; I mean to Mozart, Beethoven, Brahms, and Bach. I owe very much to Mozart, and if one studies, for instance, the way in which I write for string quartet, then one cannot deny that I have learned this directly from Mozart—and I am proud of it.[1]

Perhaps it was the lack of any formal academic training—his proud position as an essentially self-taught composer—which caused Schoenberg to feel such a bond with the past, the capacity to relate to past techniques without any barrier of didactic conditioning. The strong emphasis he placed on Mozart as his greatest teacher reflects a tendency during his later years to see his own work against an increasingly broad historical background, to take stock, as it were, after the perfection of the 'twelve-note' method. He himself admitted that he came to view the past with even more insight as he progressed further into his new world of ideas. He even spoke of incorporating the new perceptions drawn from the 'twelve-note' method into his analyses of the classics.[2] And in the article 'National Music' he gave a vivid illustration of the strength of his ties to the past: disarmingly he reeled off the influences on his music—'my teachers were primarily Bach and Mozart, and secondarily Beethoven, Brahms, and Wagner. From *Bach* I learned . . .'(then follow three topics), 'from *Mozart* . . .' (five more topics), and so on. 'I also learned much from Schubert and Mahler, Strauss and Reger too,' he continued, 'I shut myself off from no one . . .'[3]

Although the nineteenth-century composers fall into subsidiary categories here, I do not believe this was the case during Schoenberg's youth. The world in which he grew up and created his early masterworks was dominated more by Brahms, Wagner, and Beethoven than by Mozart and Bach. And indeed the Brahmsian world was the most immediate, for the Brahmsian aesthetic was dominant in Vienna, and Schoenberg absorbed it and the relationship to the past which it implied. Of course, such a background did not ordain that Brahms remain the most influential model for Schoenberg. But the intense involvement with his music which we may deduce from the article 'Brahms the Progressive' and many other writings and from the instrumentation of the Piano Quartet in G minor is significantly confirmed by the views of an early and perceptive pupil, Egon Wellesz. In his lecture *The Origins of Schoenberg's Twelve-Note System*, after pointing to other early models, Wellesz declares, 'but the composer who influenced him decisively throughout his life, and whom he rated highest among modern composers, was Brahms. It was Brahms whose way of constructing and developing a theme, of making an unnoticeable transition from the first theme to the second,

[1] Brentwood, California; July 1949. Arnold Schoenberg, *The Music of Arnold Schoenberg*, vol. 3 (sound recording).
[2] See Josef Rufer, *Composition with Twelve Notes*, vii.
[3] pp. 173–4.

influenced him in his *Sextet* and in his string quartets . . . '[4] And one can see Wellesz's point: the influence of Wagner could hardly have extended into the post-tonal works with the same directness. But the whole world of Brahmsian thematicism—of motivic structure, of transition processes, of strict contrapuntal working in 'free' contexts—all this remained to function afresh, not least in the serial context.

That Brahms was very important to Schoenberg is not in question. But how can one approach this subject? It is tempting to seize upon the article 'Brahms the Progressive', the most familiar source for the association of the two names, and examine it critically. But that would perhaps obscure the broader picture. That particular article was written with a clear purpose—to rectify the traditional view of Brahms, on the occasion of the centenary of his birth—and it is extreme in many ways. Furthermore, it takes much for granted, perhaps raising more questions than it answers. Indeed, it needs to be seen against a broader background, that of Schoenberg's theoretical writings. Of course, these too pose a large problem, for they are many, various, not always complete, and not the work of a consistent theorist. Schoenberg's writings cannot, for example, be compared with those of Heinrich Schenker. Schoenberg was an active composer, much more intuitive than is often granted, yet one with a remarkable capacity for learning from the past and for expressing his discoveries conceptually. One may have to look long and hard to get the measure of his conceptual view of individual composers, but it is worth the effort.

The main theoretical writings relevant to our investigation are the following: *Harmonielehre* (1911, revised by Schoenberg, 1922), translated as *Theory of Harmony* (1978); *Style and Idea* (1950; expanded by Leonard Stein, 1975); *Structural Functions of Harmony* (1954; revised by Leonard Stein, 1969); *Preliminary Exercises in Counterpoint* (1963); and *Fundamentals of Musical Composition* (1967). These cover four principal areas: harmony, theme, counterpoint, and form. In varying degrees they cross-relate, reflecting underlying and constant preoccupations. With his many published articles, especially those of *Style and Idea*, to add clarification, Schoenberg's writings offer a rich field from which to draw, and I will touch on several of them in the remaining two sections of this paper, which offer thoughts on how Schoenberg's view of Brahms relates to his theoretical outlook and what was the significance of this relationship.

## II

In the interest of brevity and, I believe, with no violence to the essential drift of Schoenberg's thought, his ideas on Brahms and their relationship to harmony, theme, counterpoint, and form may be broadly surveyed under two headings: that is, factors relating to the short-term consideration of themes—their motivic structures, their harmonic contexts—and those relating to the longer term—to structural integration on a broad span, to the process of transition from one area to another. First, the question of local harmony and theme. Schoenberg's views in this area turn on two crucial conceptual

[4] p. 4.

distinctions. One concerns theme, the other, harmony, and both are ultimately complementary. In the 'advanced' music of the later nineteenth century Schoenberg observed two kinds of harmony, both of which he termed 'expanded' or 'extended harmony' or 'tonality'. The one kind is a harmony unclear in its consequence, a harmony which is either suspended in meaning or which fluctuates between possible goals, is adventurous because ambiguous. The second kind is also adventurous, but is not ambiguous: it simply moves very quickly at times when one would expect stability. The first type he entitled 'suspended' or 'fluctuating harmony'; the second he gave no comparable term, but it can be described as a special form of 'roving harmony'. I should, at this juncture, pause to mention the difficulties inherent in Schoenberg's terminology with regard to harmony. The terms 'suspended' and 'fluctuating harmony' translate, respectively, the German terms 'aufgehobene' and 'schwebende Tonalität' employed in the *Harmonielehre* of 1911. But by the time of *Structural Functions of Harmony*, a book derived from materials developed while teaching at UCLA, 1936–43, 'schwebende' had come to mean what 'aufgehobene' had formerly meant, that is, suspended, avoiding reference to a tonic, while 'aufgehobene' had disappeared entirely, to be supplanted by the term 'roving harmony', a designation of very wide application whose freedom of use reflects the vagueness of the concept of monotonality, of which it is a part, a freedom which also affects the clear use of the term modulation.

As with harmony, so there are two views of theme: as that which proceeds by direct repetition on another degree, and as that which develops from within itself. The first he characterized with the traditional expression 'model and sequence'—statement, repetition through sequence—while the second he termed 'developing variation'—a variation which is not local or decorative, but organic, which creates a continuous 'prose-like' growth, the consequence of which is likely to be extreme irregularity of phrasing due to the inner life of the motive. Schoenberg describes these views in *Structural Functions* and in *Fundamentals*, respectively.

Both sets of distinctions—harmonic and thematic—reflect a desire, central to 'Brahms the Progressive', to see Wagner and Brahms as complementary as well as independent figures. Although for Schoenberg 'suspended' and 'fluctuating harmonies' belong essentially to the province of Wagner, 'developing variations' to that of Brahms, I hope I do not oversimplify if I suggest that there is an intimate relationship between the two sets of distinctions. For composers employ the practice of 'model and sequence' in passages of 'suspended' or 'fluctuating harmony' as a means of making them clear, of ensuring, in Schoenberg's recurrent term, 'comprehensibility'. The one needs the other, and likewise with theme, for a harmony which moves purposefully through numerous 'regions', which roves adventurously, is going to be the complement of an evolving theme, and a theme is unlikely to evolve continuously within a tonal context without implying such fluidity.

In his writings Schoenberg repeatedly illustrated these distinctions through the same musical examples. The Prelude to *Tristan und Isolde* served as Schoenberg's classic example of the treatment of a harmony which implies goals that are never confirmed and which finally denies these goals altogether by means of a larger movement into another tonal area (Example 1).[5] Thus the opening phrase seems to repose on the dominant of A minor, but this is denied through a sequential repetition which leads to an implied dominant in C major, and thence to the dominant of E minor, from which it seems to return to the true dominant of A minor, only to veer dramatically to F major. Whether we call this 'suspended harmony', because it avoids a tonic statement, or 'roving harmony', because it implies several goals, the tonal character is complemented by an equally distinctive thematic process, that of 'model and sequence'.

In quite a different mood, Schoenberg's favoured illustration of Brahms's speed of deviation into 'regions' in themes is the first subject of the String Quintet in G major, Op. 111 (Example 2a).[6] He does not cite this as an example of 'developing variation' as such, but merely points to its harmony. His classic demonstration of 'developing variation' seems to be the second subject of the Violoncello Sonata in E minor, Op. 38, where 'all the motive-forms and phrases of this melody develop gradually out of the first three notes, or perhaps even out of the first two notes' (Example 2b), though the theme is

EXAMPLE 1. Wagner, Prelude to *Tristan und Isolde*, bars 1–17. Adapted from Example 85a in Schoenberg's *Structural Functions of Harmony* (W. W. Norton & Co. Inc.), p. 77.

---

[5] *Structural Functions of Harmony*, 77.
[6] Ibid., 82–4.

actually very short.[7] But the method of composition is the same in the Quintet theme: a continuously evolving theme in which the latter part of the first idea is repeated to initiate a seamless process of growth. Here thematic evolution and the exploration of a wide harmonic territory are indivisible.

Brahms's music was crucially important to Schoenberg because it demonstrated how to move adventurously where one would expect stability, and how to do this without any extra-musical stimulus. Brahms was a rare phenomenon: a virtuoso in the handling of abstract music. Even Mozart's subtleties Schoenberg interprets against the implied background of dramatic music.[8]

# III

Schoenberg recognized Brahms as a composer of organic music, and this must have prompted him to consider the application of 'developing variation' over longer spans of time in Brahms's music—the evolution of ideas from one section to the next and, furthermore, over more than one movement. Unfortunately, we know very little about the details of this interest. Schoenberg made tantalizing references to the principle of total organization in tonal works, to the activity of the Grundgestalt, or 'basic shape' or 'form', but he never honed his definition or provided tangible examples. This task was taken up by his pupil Josef Rufer, who gave a 'basic shape' analysis of Beethoven's Piano Sonata in C minor, Op. 10 No. 1, in the appendix to his book *Composition with Twelve Notes*.[9] Schoenberg seems to have wanted to leave the possibilities open. He saw that

EXAMPLE 2*a*. Brahms, String Quintet in G major, Op. 111, I, bars 1–16, as reduced and annotated in Schoenberg's *Structural Functions of Harmony* (W. W. Norton & Co. Inc.), pp. 82–4.

---

[7] *Fundamentals of Musical Composition*, 62 (cf. Example 61*b* on p. 80).
[8] On the potential relationship Schoenberg perceived between Brahms's methods of composition and the demands of opera, see 'Brahms the Progressive', 440–1.     [9] pp. I–II.

EXAMPLE 2b. Brahms, Violoncello Sonata in E minor, Op. 38, I, bars 58–65, as reproduced and annotated in Schoenberg's *Fundamentals of Musical Composition* (Faber & Faber Ltd), p. 80.

great music is deeply unified and, by the same token, contains rich contrasts, and he must have recognized in the music of Brahms prime illustrations of this, for in few works of the tonal era is both all-pervasive unity and tonal contrast manifest so greatly, or in so many endlessly subtle ways, as in the compositions of Brahms. There are hints, though, of Schoenberg's awareness of this. In 'Brahms the Progressive' he pointed to the permeating influence of the interval of the third in the Fourth Symphony, and noted the relationship between the first movement and the variation finale, where 'Brahms, towards the end of the last movement . . . carries out some of the variations by a succession of thirds, [and thereby] unveils the relationship of the theme of the Passacaglia to the first movement', and where 'the theme of the passacaglia in its first half admits the contrapuntal combination with the descending thirds' (Example 3).[10]

More tangibly, Schoenberg observed the subtlety of Brahms's transitions, his way of moving from one type of texture to another, as Wellesz pointed out. Schoenberg described how the characteristic features of a theme are gradually eliminated—a process

---

[10] pp. 405–6.

he termed 'liquidation'—until all that remains are uncharacteristic features which no longer demand continuation. If the music is continuous, rather than cadencing, this process represents the thematic aspect of transition, and is thereby the natural corollary of 'developing variation'. Schoenberg drew no extensive example from Brahms, but an obvious one exists in the String Quartet in C minor, Op. 51 No. 1—the passage in the first movement extending from the second subject to the closing group, bars 54–66 (Example 4). Here the mobile dotted figure is gradually confined intervallically and repeated so as to admit easily the contrast of the singing upper line (bars 62 ff.), which at its final cadence sets up the conditions for the return of the first subject, introduced by its inversion (bars 73–5).

Yet it seems a very long way from a passage such as this to the one which Wellesz quotes from Schoenberg's First String Quartet, Op. 7—the first major transition (bars 85–96) of the vast and complex work which lasts for forty-five minutes and yields nothing whatsoever to the comfort of the listener.[11] If the processes employed here were influenced by Brahms, the result is radically different. And if we set aside the theoretical writings, which make clear intellectually what is indeed far from apparent aurally, we are left with the antithesis with which we began. To be sure, Schoenberg's Brahms was not everyone's Brahms. What resemblance does his Brahms bear to the Brahms we all know and love, the Brahms who fills the concert-halls, the great melodist, the lover of the dance, of irresistible waltzes, passionate gypsy songs, touching German folk-songs? Perhaps it is wrong, though, to criticize Schoenberg for not giving a rounded picture of the man and his music—indeed, he never claimed to have sought to do so. Surely he would have acknowledged these points, for no one was more appreciative of Viennese popular music than Schoenberg. But this was not what was most important to him. We can see this clearly from the way in which he discusses the popular form of the waltz, in order to show how far Brahms's music was from it. Strauss's 'Blue Danube Waltz' was Schoenberg's symbolic illustration of simplicity in music: literal repetition, rudimentary harmonies, symmetrical phrasing, nothing to strain the mind, music for children.[12] But, as Schoenberg noted on more than one occasion, adults need not be told things twice; what they require is varied repetition. Each statement must add something, and what it adds must point to what follows as well as to what precedes. Thus Schoenberg's interest in Brahms, who represented the end of a tradition which he intimately understood, creating some of its most sophisticated works—sophisticated in harmonic richness, thematic ingenuity, structural integration—who therefore was for Schoenberg the epitome of the mature, and thus progressive composer, one who explored fully the consequences of his ideas, who conceived an entire work 'in a single spontaneous vision', who showed a deep 'responsibility to his materials'. Add to this Brahms's ruthless self-criticism and his demanding work ethic, and we achieve the perfect Schoenbergian model—Schoenberg's Brahms, Brahms in Schoenberg's own image. He conveniently

[11] 'The Origins of Schoenberg's Twelve-Note System', 5.
[12] Cited in numerous writings, for example in 'Brahms the Progressive', 399.

EXAMPLE 3. Brahms, Fourth Symphony in E minor, Op. 98, I, bars 1–8, as compared to IV, bars 1–4 in Schoenberg's 'Brahms the Progressive', p. 406.

EXAMPLE 4.  Brahms, String Quartet in C minor, Op. 51 No. 1, I, bars 54–66.

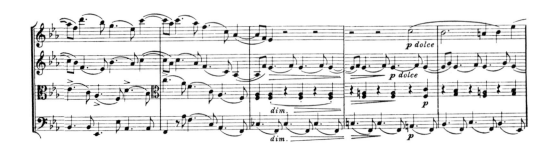

ignores what he observed elsewhere—that Brahms quite sincerely regarded the 'Blue Danube Waltz' as 'unfortunately not by Johannes Brahms'.[13]

Thus Schoenberg's Brahms is not the 'complete' Brahms, but rather a composite of all those aspects of Brahms's approach to art that he felt ought to be present in the best music and which he championed to the inevitable exclusion of others. And indeed Schoenberg's choice of examples for technical discussion exhibits this same extreme partiality and selectivity: the theme from the String Quintet, Op. 111, is unique for a sonata-form first subject; the song 'Meine Liebe ist grün', Op. 63 No. 5, cited by Schoenberg for its quick modulation and tonal instability, is unlike any other; the Rhapsody in G minor, Op. 79 No. 2, is more adventurous, in its avoidance of tonic confirmation in the first subject, than the other Rhapsodies, with their predictable harmonic schemes; and there *are* sequences and literal repetitions in Brahms's music. Although Schoenberg says a great deal about phrasing, he comments little on rhythm, on the pattern of relationships against a pulse. Of course he knew this was important— 'When Brahms demanded that one hand of the pianist play twos or fours while the other played threes, people disliked this and said it made them seasick. But this was probably the start of the polyrhythmic structure of many contemporary scores'[14]—yet it interested him less, so he said less about it. Likewise, although he did speak about the relationship of harmony and theme in principle, he rarely demonstrated this in his examples from the music of his predecessors. For instance, the motivic significances which he finds in the slow movement of the String Quartet in A minor, Op. 51 No. 2, prove much less striking when considered against their harmonic background. The first subject of the Violoncello Sonata in F major, Op. 99 (Example 5) provides a less familiar but equally striking example (Schoenberg discussed this melody in the introduction of a radio talk on his Orchestral Variations, Op. 31, as a means of 'softening up' his audience): 'Younger listeners will probably be unaware that at the time of Brahms's death this sonata was still very unpopular and was considered indigestible . . . at that time

[13] Brahms inscribed this remark—'Leider nicht von Johannes Brahms'—together with the opening bars of the 'Blue Danube Waltz', on the autograph fan of Strauss's stepdaughter. See Geiringer, *Brahms*, facing p. 225, for a photograph of this fan; cf. also the facsimile of Schoenberg's copy of this inscription and his variation on it—'Leider von Johannes Brahms [opening bars of the Piano Quartet in G minor, Op. 25] only orchestrated by Arnold Schoenberg'—in Frisch, *Brahms and the Principle of Developing Variation*, 76.

[14] 'Criteria for the Evaluation of Music', 131.

EXAMPLE 5. Brahms, Violoncello Sonata in F major, Op. 99, I, bars 1–8.

the unusual rhythm within . . . $\frac{3}{4}$ time, the syncopations which give the impression that the third phrase is in $\frac{4}{4}$ . . . and the unusual intervals, the ninths contained in this phrase, made it difficult to grasp. I felt all this myself, so I know how seriously it must be taken!'[15] All of this is true about the theme itself, which is all Schoenberg quoted, but with its harmony—broad simple progressions in the piano—the point he tries to make seems artificial.

What interested Schoenberg was not rounded analysis, but historical tendency, and, to be more precise, tendency towards his own music. I believe that this point can be illustrated most strikingly through reference to two small, but tell-tale examples from his writings. The first of these concerns the Fourth Symphony. At the beginning of *Fundamentals of Musical Composition*, Schoenberg gives examples of the ways in which

[15] 'The Orchestral Variations Op. 31: A Radio Talk, 1931', 29.

motives may be transformed, and he makes a distinction between 'exact repetitions' and 'modified repetitions': 'Exact repetitions preserve all features and relationships. Transpositions to a different degree, inversions, retrogrades, diminutions, and augmentations are exact repetitions if they preserve strictly the features and note relations.'[16] These stand in contrast to 'modified repetitions', which are 'local' and have no effect other than decorative, or 'developmental'. His aim is to distinguish between that which is, at least in his terms, essentially the same, and that which is essentially different, and in the process he proposes Brahms as a proto-serialist (Example 6). But he has improved upon his model because not all of these features are present in the Fourth Symphony. There are only tendencies. Aspects of these forms appear in the work, but never in the precise forms Schoenberg gives. The most aurally apparent is probably the augmentation, his item *c*. This comes at the recapitulation, where Brahms effects yet another subtle retransition, through variation. But it only points towards a proto-serial mode of thought. Schoenberg does the rest.

The second example is from the Third Symphony. The harmonic interest of the opening could never be mere colour for Schoenberg. An A♭ at the beginning of a piece in F major by Brahms must have consequence. Thus he writes in the *Theory of Harmony*, 'when Brahms introduces the second theme of his Third Symphony (F major [first movement]) in the key of A major, it is not because one "can introduce" the second theme just as well in the key of the mediant. It is rather the consequence of a principal motive, of the bass melody (harmonic connection!) F–A♭ (third and fourth measures),

EXAMPLE 6. Brahms, Fourth Symphony in E minor, Op. 98, I, bars 1–8, as annotated in Schoenberg's *Fundamentals of Musical Composition* (Faber & Faber Ltd), p. 11.

[16] p. 9.

whose many repetitions, derivations, and variations finally make it necessary, as a temporary high point, for the progression F–A♭ to expand to the progression F–A (F, the initial key, A, the key of the second theme).' Such is Schoenberg's belief in the organic logic of Brahms's music that he simply has to find an explanation for the A♭, even if it means making a statement which seems forced, or even unclear, as in his conclusion: 'Thus, the basic motive is given by the initial key and the key of the second theme'.[17] The movement's basic motive is F–A♭–F, and the relation to A major is purely a matter of interpretation. The point could have been better made with reference to the contemporaneous String Quintet in F major, Op. 88, whose parallel tonal scheme can well be seen as 'the consequence' of the striking cadence on A, as dominant of D, at bar 8, suddenly revealing the sharp side of the tonality whilst it is being established.

Yet we should not be alarmed by these examples. If every analyst sought to give a perfectly balanced view of the past, there would be no future. Progress happens because people see what they want to see, what they need to see. The idea of an objective view becomes the more elusive the more one thinks about it. And as much was to happen to Schoenberg's music itself. He might have wished his work to be seen in the great tradition of Bach, Mozart, and Brahms, but what interested the younger generation was what made it different—the strictnesses, the symmetries, the control, the system. Hence the image referred to at the outset of this paper. Yes, Schoenberg's was only one view— and he certainly was not along in regarding Brahms as progressive: Donald Francis Tovey and Charles F. Abdy-Williams also demonstrated in their writings a sensitivity to the advanced nature of Brahms's musical language.[18] In a period when it is no longer necessary to play advocate for Brahms, Schoenberg's view may well seem partial and extreme. Yet there can be few responses to the musical past that have gone so deeply into crucial processes; for all that comes under the heading of thematicism and integration in Schoenberg's discussions is indeed essential to Brahms's manner of compositional thinking, a vital aspect of his language, and a means toward the expression of a deeply reflective mind. And it *is* the crucial link to Schoenberg, as he himself tells us in connection with *Verklärte Nacht*: the second subject of the first exposition uses both 'developing variation' and 'model and sequence', Brahms as well as Wagner, creating five bars from four by an internal extension involving variation, and giving us a key to Schoenberg's early thematicism (Example 7). And in turn, once we have learned to see Brahms's themes through Schoenbergian eyes—even when these themes are not of the extreme type on which he focused in 'Brahms the Progressive'—they never seem the same again. 'Style' becomes a transient feature, 'Idea', the true historical continuity. Much of the audience who heard Schoenberg's first broadcast of 'Brahms the Progressive' in 1933 were probably bewildered by his remarks. By now his message is

---

[17] p. 164.

[18] Tovey's views are apparent throughout his writings on Brahms's music in the various volumes of his *Essays in Musical Analysis*; Abdy-Williams lays great stress on Brahms in *The Rhythm of Modern Music*, most notably the Second Symphony (pp. 210–36).

EXAMPLE 7. Schoenberg, *Verklärte Nacht*, bars 50–4.

much more familiar, yet it still represents a challenge: to recognize and esteem only the highest values in musical art, values supremely expressed for Schoenberg in the music of Brahms.

# THE SHIFTING BAR LINE: METRICAL DISPLACEMENT IN BRAHMS

## WALTER FRISCH

## I

Of all the musical analyses presented by Schoenberg in his essay 'Brahms the Progressive', the most suggestive treat issues of metre and rhythm. Schoenberg does not concern himself with hemiola, with patterns of three against two, or some of the other devices frequently cited by commentators. Rather, he demonstrates that in Brahms continuous motivic development—what he often called 'developing variation'—can temporarily obscure the notated bar lines, generating a highly flexible, fluid metrical universe.

Schoenberg's principal example is the theme from the Andante of the String Quartet in A minor, Op. 51 No. 2 (Example 1a). He divides the theme into six 'phrases' and shows how each one is built by intensive reinterpretation and reduplication of the interval of a second.[1] He then points out that during this development, or really because of it, the theme overrides its notated metre of $\frac{4}{4}$. The first three phrases and the last each occupy one and a half bars, or six beats (inclusive of the upbeat eighth-note of the subsequent phrase), and the fourth and fifth each a single bar, or four beats (p. 435). Schoenberg rebars Brahms's theme to reflect this pattern, giving each phrase its own bar. The result, seen in Example 1b, is that the first three phrases fall into $\frac{6}{4}$ or $\frac{3}{2}$, the fourth and fifth into $\frac{4}{4}$. But Schoenberg also indicates with an asterisk above bar 6 that the last phrase would not be adequately represented by this plan, since it places unwanted stress on the high C♯ in the middle of the last phrase.

In fact, Schoenberg's proposed rebarring does little to illuminate the structure of the theme. As Carl Dahlhaus has suggested, there is little justification for equating one phrase with one bar. Brahms's notation of the theme is more appropriate than Schoenberg's, he notes, for, although it seems at first to give unusual emphasis to the concluding D of phrase 1, it represents phrase 2 properly by placing on a downbeat the E, which is strong because of its dotted-quarter value and its harmonization by the tonic triad.[2] Moreover, the theme in its original form falls into a relatively symmetrical, antecedent-consequent structure of eight bars, dividing after phrase 3. Schoenberg

---

[1] 'Brahms the Progressive', 430–1. All further references to this essay will be given in the text.
[2] 'Musikalische Prosa', in Dahlhaus, *Schönberg und Andere*, 137.

EXAMPLE 1. (*a*) Brahms, String Quartet in A minor, Op. 51 No. 2, II, bars 1–8. (*b*) Schoenberg's rebarring.

himself admits the rightness of Brahms's own notation in accommodating what he calls the theme's 'subcutaneous beauties'—the elegant way in which Brahms builds the theme from the elaboration of the basic interval. He adds, 'if eight measures constitute an aesthetic principle, it is preserved here in spite of the great freedom of construction' (p. 436).

Schoenberg was the first major critic to point to the ambiguity between notated and perceived metre in Brahms and to suggest that it comprises a fundamental and innovative aspect of Brahms's art.[3] Yet his writings on the subject are neither systematic nor exhaustive. As suggested above, Schoenberg tends to ignore the vertical dimension, the metrical implications of the harmony and accompanying parts. Moreover, the analyses never advance beyond the level of the individual theme, making no attempt to show how the shifting bar lines might affect the larger framework or dimension of a piece. Nor does Schoenberg consider how Brahms adapts or refines such procedures during his career. These tantalizing subjects have also been ignored by most subsequent commentators, even those that fall within what I have elsewhere referred to as the Schoenberg critical tradition. Rudolf Réti, Karl Wörner, Carl Dahlhaus, Jonathan Dunsby, and David Osmond-Smith, for example, concentrate almost exclusively on thematic and formal issues in isolated works of Brahms.[4] Only David Epstein appears openly to have

---

[3] An earlier adumbration of the topic is in Hugo Riemann, 'Die Taktfreiheiten in Brahms' Liedern'.

[4] See Rudolf Réti, *The Thematic Process in Music*, esp. 70–2, 81, and 139–51; Karl Wörner, *Das Zeitalter der*

acknowledged 'the apparent metrical and rhythmic confusion that is so often encountered in [Brahms's] scores, where attacks that seem qualitatively strong . . . are placed on metrically weak beats'.[5] This paper will attempt to address that 'apparent confusion'—to characterize Brahms's techniques of metrical displacement, and to explain where and why he employs them.

## II

In his early instrumental works Brahms often seems readier to tamper with phrase lengths than with the metrical framework. For example, in the first movement of the ambitious Piano Sonata in F minor, Op. 5 (1853), the one-bar head motive is continually reshaped and transformed, but is never subjected to displacement (except for the hemiola in bars 49–50). Instead, Brahms divides his exposition into a series of articulated phrases comprising, respectively, 6, 5, 5, 6, 8, 8, 9, 7, and 7 bars. (The last bar of the first seven-bar phrase (bar 62) overlaps with the start of the second phrase.) Phrases of irregular or variable length are, to be sure, a significant aspect of Brahms's language—and were recognized as such by Schoenberg in 'Brahms the Progressive' (see pp. 416–22). But they differ fundamentally from actual metrical displacement.

A striking example of displacement occurs, however, in the G major episode (bars 42–86) of the Rondo finale of the Piano Sonata in C major, Op. 1 (1853), where the notated $\frac{9}{8}$ metre is overridden by groupings of six eighth-notes. The opening of this episode (Example 2) consists of two phrases functioning as antecedent and consequent, each moving harmonically from G to D. As indicated in the example, the antecedent (bars 42–5) might be heard on a higher level as three bars of $\frac{12}{8}$, but the consequent (bars 46–50) fails to conform to that pattern, for it contains an 'extra' six beats: the cadence to D is delayed until the downbeat of bar 50 (and the harmony is sustained for five more beats). With this downbeat the notated metre is restored (only to be disrupted again ten bars later).

The conflict between $\frac{6}{8}$ and $\frac{9}{8}$ (or between duple and triple articulation of the bar) is in fact central to the movement as a whole. The groupings of six, latent in the G major episode just discussed, become explicit in the subsequent A minor episode (bar 107 ff.), which is actually notated in $\frac{6}{8}$. The time signature reappears again in the Presto coda to conclude the movement. Although far from subtle, Brahms's manipulation of metre is thus an integral part of the design of the Op. 1 finale. The metrical 'compression' of the coda is made to seem logical, to grow out of what has preceded.

Still more prophetic of the later Brahms is a passage in variation 6 of the *Variations on*

---

*thematischen Prozesse in der Geschichte der Musik*, esp. 113; Carl Dahlhaus, 'Issues in Composition', in his *Between Romanticism and Modernism*; Jonathan Dunsby, *Structural Ambiguity in Brahms*; and David Osmond-Smith, 'The Retreat from Dynamism: A Study of Brahms's Fourth Symphony'. For a more extended discussion of this critical tradition, see Frisch, *Brahms and the Principle of Developing Variation*, Ch. 1.

[5] *Beyond Orpheus*, 169.

*a Theme of Robert Schumann*, Op. 9 (1854) (Example 3). In bar 20 the framework of a strongly accented $\frac{6}{8}$ metre—compound metres seem to invite this kind of manipulation—is suddenly disrupted by what at first seems to be a hemiola, or groups of two eighth-notes (see brackets in the example). But the third group (marked 'sostenuto') is extended into the next bar by the addition of a third eighth-note. The original triple grouping of the $\frac{6}{8}$ metre is thus restored, but no longer adheres to the notated bar line. For three bars the music continues in this pattern, with the notated beats 5 and 2 coming to sound like 1 and 3. The harmony, the bass note, and the phrasing fully reinforce the displacement by changing every third beat. On the last two beats of bar 23 the original metrical grid begins to re-emerge much as it had first vanished, with groupings of two eighth-notes (see brackets). A crescendo leads to the accented downbeat of bar 25 (the penultimate in this variation), with which the notated $\frac{6}{8}$ is at last fully re-established.[6]

Passages like those from Opp. 1 and 9 remain relatively rare in the early instrumental works. It is not really until the early 1860s, the period Donald F. Tovey called Brahms's 'first maturity',[7] that the composer begins to explore such 'progressive' techniques in a

EXAMPLE 2. Brahms, Piano Sonata in C major, Op. 1, IV, bars 42–50.

<hr/>

[6] This passage is mentioned in Marcia Citron, 'Metric Conflict in Brahms'.

[7] 'Brahms's Chamber Music', 243. It should be noted that I am not considering here the kind of metrical irregularity frequently encountered in Brahms's 'Hungarian' music, for example, the *Variations on a Hungarian Song*, Op. 21 No. 2, where the theme alternates between $\frac{3}{4}$ and $\frac{4}{4}$. Such techniques owe more to 'local colour' than to any significant compositional procedure.

EXAMPLE 3. Brahms, *Variations on a Theme by Robert Schumann*, Op. 9, variation 6, bars 19–26.

more systematic and thoroughgoing fashion. Perhaps the first piece to attain the fluency that Schoenberg was to admire in Op. 51 is the first movement of the Piano Quartet in A major, Op. 26 (1861).

The closing theme of the exposition (preceded by a portion of the transition) is given as Example 4. The transition concludes with a hemiola (bars 104–5), which, rather than merely ruffling the metrical surface (as in Op. 5), triggers a more complex process. Although the first beat of bar 106 provides a clear downbeat and a cadence to E major, the new thematic idea begins only on the second and third beats. Our ears reorient themselves metrically to hear B–E, the motive with a dotted rhythm, as an upbeat to the G♯. Because it is tied over the bar line, this G♯ suppresses the notated first beat of bar 107 and takes on the character of a downbeat. For two bars the theme seems to move in a displaced triple metre, as suggested by the dotted bar lines and time signatures above the theme in Example 4. But the material proves too volatile even for this framework, for in bars 108–10 a duple pattern emerges, suggesting a grouping of $\frac{2}{4}$. On a higher level the six beats extending from the tied B may suggest a $\frac{3}{2}$ grouping (for which the hemiola in the transition has provided a precedent). On the last beat of the notated bar 110, Brahms reintroduces the dotted rhythm. It seems at first to be an 'extra' beat in the prevailing duple pattern—but proves in fact to be an upbeat, now aligning properly with the bar line and guiding us back at last into the notated triple metre. In my hypothetical rebarring of the theme in Example 4, I adopt the same principles that Schoenberg used in his analysis of the theme of the String Quartet in A minor: analogous notes or figures are placed in the same part of a bar. The dotted rhythm appears as an upbeat; rhythmic or melodic accents appear as downbeats or strong beats.

As with Schoenberg's example, however, this rebarring is not really adequate, for it fits only the melody. The accompaniment in the cello (indicated in Example 4) adheres strictly to the written metre, arpeggiating on every downbeat and thus remaining in conflict with the theme.

# III

The metrical procedures of Opp. 1, 9, and 26 are taken up on a much more ambitious scale in the Piano Quintet in F minor, Op. 34, composed in 1862, the year after the Piano Quartet. First drafted as a string quintet (no longer extant), then arranged during the winter of 1862–3 as a sonata for two pianos, the work attained its final instrumentation only in 1864. But, as the sources reveal, throughout the process of rescoring from sonata to piano quintet it retained the same musical structure—with one fairly significant exception, to be discussed below.

As in Op. 26, the metrical displacement occurs at the close of the exposition in the first movement. But instead of a constantly shifting bar line, we encounter here a more persistent dislocation, whereby the bar line seems to move to the right, first an eighth-

EXAMPLE 4. Brahms, Piano Quartet in A major, Op. 26, I, bars 103–14.

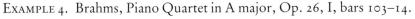

note, then a full beat. The closing theme (Example 5) begins conventionally enough, with two parallel four-bar phrases, an antecedent (bars 74–7) and a consequent (bars 78–81). But now the symmetry begins to break down rapidly. Brahms first reduces the theme to one of its component motives, a descending stepwise third with a dotted rhythm (bars 81–2). (This process, called 'liquidation' by Schoenberg, is a basic one in Classical and Romantic music.) The motive continues to evolve, assuming the rhythm of three equal eighth-notes. Here the first note loses its upbeat character and sounds stressed or accented. The original rhythmic groupings and the notated metre are thereby disrupted, as the piano virtually creates its own independent $\frac{9}{8}$ metre beginning on the second eighth-note of bars 83 and 84 (the pattern is supported by Brahms's own slurs). This represents the first stage of metrical displacement: the perceived bar line has shifted half a beat.

As the three-note groups continue to pour forth, overlapping in the piano and strings,

EXAMPLE 5. Brahms, Piano Quintet in F minor, Op. 34, I, bars 73–97.

even the most astute listener will become utterly disoriented. For Brahms not only obscures the metrical framework of the basic motive, but in bars 85–6 continues to modify its pitch content. The original descending third expands to become a leap of a third followed by a step, then a fourth followed by a semitone—thus Db–Ab–G♮. These bars display Brahms's art of developing variation at its most intense.[8]

As if to assert its status as the goal of the motivic-rhythmic process, the Db–Ab–G figure is now broadened out to even quarter-notes. The metre seems also to be stabilized: a pattern of three quarter-notes followed by a quarter rest is established in all parts. Brahms thus restores a $\frac{4}{4}$ metrical framework—but one which does not coincide with the notated bar line! Because the notated third beat is empty in bars 90–5 and the first beat is empty in bars 87–95 (in both first and second endings), they tend to sound like weak second and fourth beats respectively. That is, notated beats 2 and 4 are perceived as 1 and 3. The bar line has thus drifted still further to the right, now a full beat, as suggested by the dotted bar lines above Example 5.

The most striking difference between this passage and the one in the A major Piano Quartet is that now there is no accompaniment adhering to the written metre; with no metrical background, the notated second and fourth beats cannot be heard as syncopated. In short, there is no element that aurally contradicts the displaced $\frac{4}{4}$ metre.

This phenomenon has another psychological or perceptual dimension. After the confusion of bars 83–5, the listener without a score (or without previous knowledge of the music) may not realize that the forte chord of bar 86 falls on the notated second beat. He will become aware of the displacement only at the repeat of the exposition (first ending), and again at the violin entrance at the beginning of the development section (second ending, bar 96); in both instances (shown in Example 5) bar 95 will suddenly seem one beat too short.

The only substantive change Brahms made when transcribing the two-piano sonata as a piano quintet involves the closing theme, which in the sonata (Example 6) contains an additional bar. The exposition of the sonata is ninety-six bars long, that of the quintet ninety-five. The 'extra' bar is 83, in which the dotted rhythms are first transformed into three equal eighth-notes. The autograph of the Piano Quintet, in the Whittall Collection at the Library of Congress, reveals that this truncation was an afterthought.[9] Brahms first wrote out the manuscript with the 'extra' bar, as shown in the facsimile given as Illustration 1, comprising bars 80–93. At some later point, before sending the work off to his publisher in July 1865, he pasted five bars over the last three bars of the top system, then crossed out the first three bars of the bottom system (see Illustration 2). This yielded a net loss of one: six bars were replaced by five. Brahms also rescored the passage. Throughout the closing group of the quintet, the piano had originally taken over the second piano part of the sonata. But in the paste-over Brahms redistributes the material

---

[8] For further discussion of the pitch-related aspects of developing variation in this movement, see Frisch, *Brahms and the Principle of Developing Variation*, 83–6.

[9] The quintet autograph has been published in facsimile in *Johannes Brahms Autographs*, 75–156.

EXAMPLE 6. Brahms, Sonata for Two Pianos in F minor, Op. 34 *bis*, I, bars 81–9.

differently: at bar 85 the piano takes over what had been played by the strings (or, in the sonata, by the first piano).[10]

It was, I think, the 'progressive' in Brahms that encouraged him to make the change. In the sonata, bars 81–6 fall into a regular pattern of 2 + 2 + 2 bars, as shown by my brackets in Example 6. In each two-bar unit, the motive is traded between the two pianos. The two-bar pattern continues even after the displacement is established, in bars 87–90. By removing bar 83, Brahms disrupts this somewhat predictable symmetry,

[10] Although Op. 34 *bis* was not published until 1872, seven years after the release of Op. 34, Brahms apparently made no attempt to reconcile the two-piano version to the revised quintet version. For a fuller account of the sources for Op. 34 and Op. 34 *bis*, and of the differences between the versions, see Elizabeth Jean Lamberton, 'Brahms's Piano Quintet, Op. 34, and Duo-Piano Sonata, Op. 34 *bis*: A Critical Study'. Since this dissertation was written, an additional source for Op. 34 *bis* has appeared, a partly autograph manuscript in the possession of the descendants of Princess Anna von Hesse, the work's dedicatee. See the brief account by Margit McCorkle, 'Filling the Gaps in Brahms Research', 285.

accelerating the development of the motive and, concomitantly, the disintegration of the metrical framework. It is the kind of compositional change that would have been understood by Schoenberg, who on numerous occasions expressed approval of the way in which Brahms's themes avoid repetition and symmetry, proceeding immediately to develop the basic material.

# IV

Two more questions might be asked at this point about Brahms's characteristic metrical procedures, one historical, the other critical. Where might Brahms have encountered such devices in earlier or contemporary music? And, just what aesthetic or compositional function do they serve in his music?

The first question seems appropriate because, as is well known, Brahms was one of the most historically conscious—self-conscious, we might say—of all nineteenth-century composers. He was a serious collector, student, and (for a time) conductor of Renaissance and Baroque vocal music. In his personal collection, preserved at the Gesellschaft der Musikfreunde in Vienna, are not only many printed editions—he was among the early subscribers to the *Gesamtausgaben* of Bach, Handel, and Schütz—but also many works he copied out by hand. Virginia Hancock has revealed that Brahms frequently marked interesting rhythmic and metrical phenomena, such as hemiola figures in Bach. More significantly, he would also correct or modify editorial bar lines with which he disagreed. In his own handwritten copy of Isaac's 'Innsbruck, ich muß dich lassen', made from Carl von Winterfeld's edition probably in 1857–60, Brahms bracketed in red pencil an implied triple metre that had been obscured by the editor's duple notation.[11] Similarly, when encountering unbarred early melodies, he carefully pondered what metre or metres the text demanded; for example, in sketches for his choral arrangements of 'Wach auf, mein Kind' (*Deutsche Volkslieder* of 1864 [WoO 34], No. 12), a melody taken from David Gregor Corner's *Groß Catolisch Gesangbuch* of 1631, we find him experimenting with barrings that yield various solutions in regular and mixed metres.[12] There is no doubt that the metrical elasticity Brahms admired in early music found its way into his own choral music, as Hancock suggests. That the instrumental music was also thereby enriched represents perhaps an even greater achievement; it shows Brahms adapting these techniques to a completely different medium and syle.

There are, of course, more immediate precedents within the common-practice period

[11] See Virginia Hancock, *Brahms's Choral Compositions and his Library of Early Music*, 161–2. See also Hancock's article, 'The Growth of Brahms's Interest in Early Choral Music, and its Effect on His Own Choral Compositions'. For a full bibliographic description of Brahms's *Abschriften*, see Margit McCorkle, *Johannes Brahms: Thematisch-Bibliographisches Werkverzeichnis*, 733–7.

[12] See George S. Bozarth, 'Johannes Brahms und die Liedersammlungen von David Gregor Corner, Karl Severin Meister und Friedrich Wilhelm Arnold', 194–5 and 198.

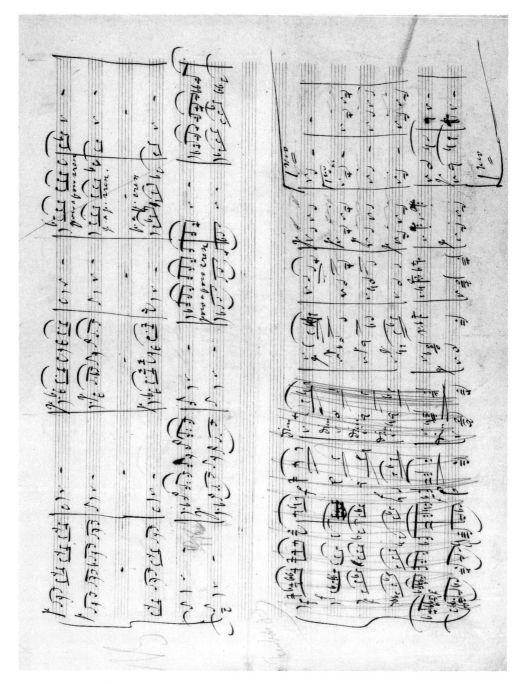

ILLUSTRATION 1. Brahms, Piano Quintet in F minor, Op. 34. Facsimile of eighth page of autograph manuscript (I, bars 80–93) before revision. Reproduced by permission of the Library of Congress, Washington, DC.

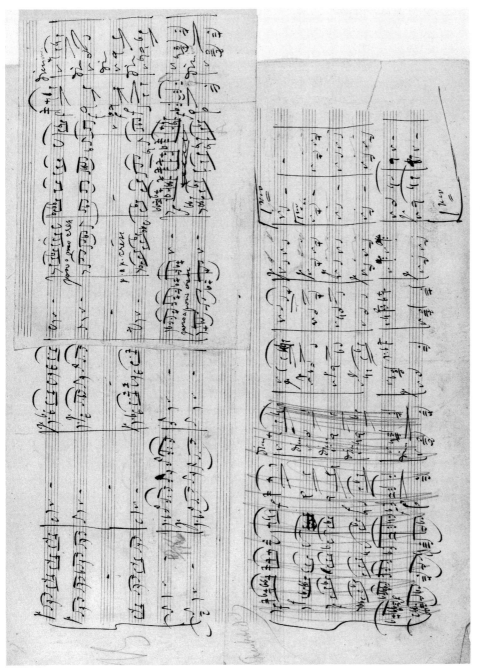

ILLUSTRATION 2. Brahms, Piano Quintet in F minor, Op. 34. Facsimile of eighth page of autograph manuscript (I, bars 80–92) after revision. Reproduced by permission of the Library of Congress, Washington, DC.

for Brahms's procedures. Haydn's music is filled with metrical ambiguities, as in the Trio from the *Oxford* Symphony. One striking example of a mobile bar line in Mozart is even cited by Schoenberg in 'Brahms the Progressive', involving the closing theme of the exposition in the first movement of the Piano Quartet in G minor, K. 478.[13] But it is in Beethoven and Schumann that one finds the most pervasive exploration of the kind of metrical processes I have described. In the first movement of the *Eroica* Symphony such passages as the familiar one given in Example 7 disrupt the prevailing triple metre with strong *sforzandos* on every other beat. From bar 27 on this pattern asserts itself so forcefully that a duple metre may be said momentarily to displace the triple, as indicated by the dotted lines in the example.[14] Many theorists would characterize these *sforzando* accents as strong syncopations. But, as implied in the discussion of the Brahms quintet, we can hear syncopations only if the written metre is reinforced in some way. Or, in the words of the nineteenth-century theorist Moritz Hauptmann, if 'a series [of notes] is to appear syncopated, then the unsyncopated series must at the same time be present with it; for without the normal series, of which the syncopated forms the metrical contradiction, the syncopated would itself be shown normally accented'.[15]

However an individual listener chooses to organize the succession of accents in this and other similar passages in middle-period Beethoven, it is clear that the composer is exploiting the tension, and exploring the threshold, between strong syncopation and actual metrical displacement.[16] In Schumann this kind of tension becomes a more basic element of style. Many passages in his scores wreak havoc with the notated metre by means of either groupings that change constantly or by a more consistent and uniform displacement. The sixteenth piece of the *Davidsbündlertänze* provides a good example of the former type (Example 8). Although notated as an upbeat, the opening chord, a strong root-position tonic, tends to be heard as downbeat. It initiates a rhythmic-melodic pattern of three beats (marked by brackets in the example). After two statements the pattern is extended to four beats, then contracted to two at the cadence of bar 4. The forte chords here constitute a wittily over-emphatic reinforcement of a cadence that is already sufficient: Schumann seems to be having his little laugh ('mit gutem Humor') at the disruption of the three-beat pattern. The second phrase (bars 4–8) repeats the same design: two statements of three, followed by one each of four and two.

Although the aural effect is bewildering, the overall plan is quite regular. In essence Schumann is dividing six beats in two different ways, first as 3 + 3, then as 4 + 2.

---

[13] See Schoenberg, 'Brahms the Progressive', 436–7.

[14] The metrical displacement becomes more persistent in the development section of the first movement. See Philip Downs, 'Beethoven's "New Way" and the *Eroica*'.

[15] Moritz Hauptmann, *The Nature of Harmony and Metre*, 342. Hauptmann appears to be the only theorist in the nineteenth century to have acknowledged the possibility of such displacement.

[16] The late works of Beethoven contain numerous such passages, often introduced with greater subtlety and less ostentation than in the *Eroica*. Marcia Citron ('Metric Conflict') mentions the second movement of the *Archduke* Trio, Op. 97, bars 34–40, and the first movement of the *Hammerklavier* Sonata, Op. 106, bars 91–5. To these examples may be added several passages in the Diabelli Variations, Op. 120, including variation 17, bars 12–5, and variation 19, bars 24–8.

EXAMPLE 7. Beethoven, Symphony No. 3, Op. 55, I, bars 23–37.

EXAMPLE 8. Schumann, *Davidsbündlertänze*, Op. 6 No. 16, bars 1–8.

Moreover, the metrical legerdemain conceals a conventional antecedent-consequent design (like the Brahms theme analysed by Schoenberg), which falls into a tidy eight bars divided symmetrically as 4 + 4.

Schumann's other principal metrical procedure avoids such mercurial shifting in favour of a more sustained displacement, whereby perceived and notated metres remain out of phase for long stretches of time. One well-known passage occurs in the last movement of the Piano Concerto, where for forty bars the second theme floats blithely in $\frac{3}{2}$, disregarding the notated $\frac{3}{4}$ (bars 461 ff.). The solo piano music also abounds in these devices.

I would propose for Brahms's metrical procedures a dual pedigree, in both Beethoven and Schumann, although in fact his music rarely sounds like that of either composer. It has neither the elemental, visceral energy of the *Eroica*, nor the wit and capriciousness of Schumann. Brahms's procedures are, on the whole, very sober and, as might be expected, eminently logical and rational. This brings us to consider the second question asked earlier: what structural role do such devices play in Brahms's music? There are, I believe, two principal, related functions—formal articulation and motivic development. Always carefully prepared, metrical displacements tend to occur at certain spots in Brahms's scores—in sonata forms, normally at the end of the exposition and/or in the retransition. In this respect Brahms is more systematic than Beethoven or Schumann.

The example discussed above in the first movement of the Piano Quartet in A major, Op. 26 (Example 4), appears shortly before the double bar line, in the most 'developmental' part of the sonata-form exposition. The same is true of the Piano Quintet (Example 5), which bears closer examination here.

During the second group Brahms paves the way for the metrical dislocation by placing a progressively greater stress on the second beat of the bar. The principle motive of the initial theme of the second group (bar 33) cuts off abruptly and conspicuously on the second beat, as well as on the fourth beat. A few bars later (37–8), the stress on beat 2 becomes strong enough to obscure momentarily the notated metre. At the analogous spot in the counter-statement of this theme (bars 51–2) Brahms's additional crescendos and decrescendos draw still more attention to beats 2 and 4. Genuine sycopation in bars 69–73 carries the process a step further and leads directly to the fortepiano on the second beat of bar 74 (see Example 5). Upon reaching the closing theme, a listener is thus sensitized to the equivocal status of beat 2, which receives sharp, consummatory fortepiano accents in bars 74 and 78.

Although the displacement comes about step by step, the restoration of the original metrical framework is astonishingly sudden. In the last bars of the exposition (bars 91–4) the piano meditates quietly upon a fragment of the opening theme of the movement, F–G–A♭. The motive climbs slowly in a sequence based on the notes of the tonic triad, beginning on F, then A♭, then C. But at this third leg of the sequence, the double bar intervenes to thrust us back to the beginning of the exposition (shown in Example 5). As the opening theme gets under way with the same three-note motive, beginning a beat 'early', we become aware that the metrical framework has been abruptly straightened. The downbeat of bar 1 serves as what David Lewin has called a 'transformational beat', one that brings the heard and notated metres into agreement.[17] The repeat of the exposition is essential, of course, for it juxtaposes the two versions of the opening motive—or more precisely, its two metrical universes. The displacement has thus served Brahms as a means of modifying or developing thematic material. The repeated exposition takes on a new dimension as we, metrically wiser, listen for the process that concludes with the displacement of the F–G–A♭ head motive.

After the second ending, at the start of the development section, Brahms proceeds to superimpose the two metrical grids. At bar 96 the main theme returns in the first violin on the notated downbeat, while the displaced pattern continues underneath in the piano part. Although we can appreciate intellectually this superimposition, we cannot, I think,

---

[17] See Lewin's very stimulating article 'Vocal Meter in Schoenberg's Atonal Music, with a Note on a Serial Hauptstimme', esp. 25.

experience real metrical conflict—at least not for long. For when the violin enters in the notated framework, the displaced pattern becomes perceived as syncopated. In other words, it is unlikely that we can hear *two* successive beats as downbeats. An analogous situation in the visual arts has been discussed by E. H. Gombrich, who suggests that the eye cannot in fact perceive ambiguity. When confronted by an optical tease like a drawing by Escher, or the figure that can be seen as either a duck or a rabbit (or any similar figure-ground image), we must, says Gombrich, choose one image. We see the stairway coming towards us, or we see the rabbit; the other possible readings disappear, for we 'cannot experience alternative readings at the same time'.[18] Similarly, when the first violin enters in bar 96 of Brahms's development, we will not experience two metres at once; rather, our ears select the most comfortable metrical 'reading', that provided by the notated bar line.

## V

The kinds of metrical procedures we have examined in the Piano Quintet become a fundamental part of Brahms's musical language after the mid-1860s, informing almost every large-scale instrumental or vocal work. In each case, as in Op. 34, the mobile bar lines can be shown to be intimately, and ever more elegantly, linked to both motivic development and formal articulation. In the turbulent first movement of the String Quartet in C minor, Op. 51 No. 1 (1873), as in the quintet, the metre is dislocated towards the end of the exposition (bars 62–74) as a culmination of earlier developmental activity; the notated metre is restored with the double bar line. A similar process takes place in the briefer, more lyrical Allegretto movement of the quartet (bars 15–24). On a much larger scale—but occurring in the analogous place—is the massive canonic and metrically disorienting episode in the first movement of the Second Symphony (1877) (bars 136–56).[19]

Perhaps the most impressive—indeed, encyclopaedic—work in this respect is the Third Symphony (1883). The first movement is governed by two different processes: on the one hand, a tendency of the sixth beat to assert itself as a downbeat, and on the other, a conflict between the notated metre of $\frac{6}{4}$ and the frequently implied $\frac{3}{2}$. The former procedure, which works similarly to that in Op. 34, need not be traced in detail here. Like the second and fourth beats in the quintet, the sixth and third here gradually gain in prominence over the course of the exposition, especially from bar 49 on; the eventual result is a full displacement of the $\frac{6}{4}$ metrical framework on to those beats by bar 61 (or perhaps 66), just before the double bar line. As in the quintet, all accompanying parts reinforce the displacement, so that it is virtually impossible (unless one has one's eyes on a conductor) to hear syncopation alone.

[18] *Art and Illusion: A Study in the Psychology of Pictorial Representation*, 5. Chapters 7 and 8 contain a more extended discussion of this topic. See also p. 43.

[19] This passage is discussed by David Epstein in *Beyond Orpheus*, 166–7, as part of a broader treatment of metre and rhythm in the first movement of the Second Symphony.

More distinctive and sophisticated in the first movement of the symphony is the other process, which involves less the shifting of the bar line than the reordering of the internal division of the bar. The conflict between duple and triple is projected at the very opening. Each of the first two chords of the initial F–A♭–F 'motto' lasts a full bar; the absence of internal articulation makes it impossible to perceive any definite metre. The main theme, entering in the violins in the third bar, begins to project a metrical profile, but one that fits more clearly into $\frac{3}{2}$ than $\frac{6}{4}$. Only in bar 7 is the duple division of the bar firmly supported in all parts: the theme, the 'motto', and the harmonic voices move every half bar. The second group of the exposition raises the duple-triple issue in a different fashion. The new A major theme (bar 36) is notated in $\frac{9}{4}$, which is heard as an expansion or broadening of the original metre into triple time (and not an inner reordering of the bar, as at the opening).

These matters are brought to a stunning climax at the close of the development section (Example 9), which, as was mentioned above, constitutes a primary location for metrical displacement. At bar 112 the main theme appears in E♭ minor, now following in all parts its natural tendency to unfold in $\frac{3}{2}$ (although it is still notated in $\frac{6}{4}$). The last two bars of the retransition (118–19) are marked 'ritardando'; then at bar 120 the recapitulation begins abruptly in the *Tempo primo*. Unlike in the exposition, the duple $\frac{6}{4}$ is now clearly articulated from the outset: the 'motto' chords are subdivided by the strings into two per bar. The proper metrical framework for the main theme is thus restored. The aural effect is that the recapitulation is generated by a kind of metrical contraction or compression from a broad $\frac{3}{2}$ to a fast $\frac{6}{4}$. Brahms has thus linked the metrical processes closely to articulation of the formal design, specifically to the juncture of the end of the development and beginning of the recapitulation.

Brahms reinforces this metrical and formal juxtaposition with an equally sudden harmonic compression, in which the traditional dominant, C major, is bypassed entirely. In bars 117–19 the prevailing key, E♭ minor, moves towards its own dominant, B♭; an F pedal-point, heard as V/V in E♭ minor, is present throughout. This F originates as a *thematic* note, as the end point of the descending scale figures in dotted rhythms. But at bar 118 it begins to function as the *harmonic* bass note of an F⁷ chord. On the last beat of bar 119 this harmony is intensified by an Italian augmented sixth chord, G♭–B♭–E♮, which resolves on the downbeat of bar 120 to an F major triad. We still assume this chord to be functioning as V of B♭, but in fact the F has suddenly asserted itself as the tonic and as the first note of the main theme. This abrupt change in function—from F as V/V in E♭ minor to F as tonic—is a corollary to the metrical shift from the 'developmental' $\frac{3}{2}$ to the 'tonic' $\frac{6}{4}$.

The Andante movement of the Third Symphony is a more understated, but no less remarkable, example of a similar conjunction of thematic, metrical, formal, and harmonic procedures. The opening theme (Example 10*a*) can be said to pose a metrical 'problem' involving the status of the fourth or last beat of the bar, about which melody and accompaniment disagree. The melody, phrased or slurred within the bar, interprets the fourth beat as a weak, concluding element; but in the accompanying parts, the fourth

EXAMPLE 9. Brahms, Symphony No. 3, Op. 90, I, bars 110–23.

EXAMPLE 10. (*a*) Brahms, Symphony No. 3, Op. 90, II, bars 1–4. (*b*) Bars 80–7. Reproduced from Walter Frisch, *Brahms and the Principle of Developing Variation* (*University of California Press*).

(*a*)

beat *begins* a slurred group and thus pushes forward into the next bar. There is a harmonic corollary to the rhythmic conflict: the root-position tonic triad appears not only on the first beat of bar 1 (where it is expected) but again on the last beat and on the second beat of bar 2, where it alternates with a subdominant triad. We are thereby made aware of the potential ambiguity of the tonic harmony: it can be strong, as I, or weak, as the dominant of IV.

Throughout the exposition (especially after bar 29) the fourth beat threatens to displace the metrical framework, just like the second beat in the Piano Quintet and the sixth in the first movement of the symphony. The mysterious second theme (bar 40) is an extraordinary study in the rhythmic fluidity of beats 4 and 2. As in the first movement, Brahms reserves the greatest tension and ambiguity for the retransition (Example 10*b*). In bar 80, the development reaches a climax with a fortissimo statement, in diminution, of the head motive of the main theme, C–D–B–C. The last note is sustained, and harmonized by a diminished seventh chord built on C. Above this the clarinet quietly takes up the motive again. Its metrical background is now blurred (although not, I think, displaced): the motive begins on the notated fourth beat, and its first note is tied over the bar line. Flute, oboe, and bassoon successively take up this figure over harmonies that shift restlessly, but remain rooted on C.

In the fourth statement of the theme fragment (bar 84), the eighth-note figure D–B is augmented to become two quarter-notes; this augmentation delays the arrival of the C until the fourth beat. Simultaneously with that C, the flute and oboe begin another statement of the fragment, which is now further modified: Brahms retains the augmentation of the D–B but removes the tie across the bar line; the D thus arrives on the downbeat of bar 85. When the second motive of the main theme follows (G–A–G–A), we suddenly realize that the augmented fragment has in fact stood in for the opening motive—in other words, that the recapitulation has begun. The phrasing, however, is still locked into the grid of the preceding retransition, for melody and accompaniment are both slurred across the bar line. Not until the next bar (87) are the proper downbeat and the original phrasing restored.

As with the first movement, let us retreat momentarily to examine the harmonic component of this passage. The entire retransition unfolds over a well-entrenched pedal on C, although (as with the F pedal in the first movement retransition) we cannot yet recognize this pitch as the tonic. At bar 84, the harmony settles on to a D major chord ($D^7$ in third inversion, if one takes account of the pedal-point). Then, as the motivic fragment completes its evolution into the main theme, the D shifts suddenly to C major on the second beat of bar 85. Brahms thus bypasses altogether the dominant of C: much as in the first movement, the pedal note simply asserts itself as tonic underneath the thematic return. We are disoriented not only by the harmonic ellipsis, but also by the lack of synchronization between melody and harmony. In bar 85 the melody has adjusted itself to the notated downbeat, while the harmony continues to move in the pattern of the retransition, changing on the second beat. The tonic chord thus clashes exquisitely with the melodic B♮.

Although the technical means are strikingly similar to the first movement, the effect is very different. In the first movement the return is achieved through a kind of violent paroxysm; in the Andante the whole process by which the recapitulation emerges is so gradual that one cannot point to a single moment where it 'begins'. It evolves literally element by element, as theme, metre, and harmony coalesce into what we finally recognize as the recapitulation.

The retransition passages from both the first and second movements of the Third Symphony show how impressively Brahms has refined his technique in the two decades since the Piano Quintet. As in Op. 34, two different metrical spheres abut at an important juncture in the sonata form—here between development and recapitulation. (In the first movement, the two spheres are $\frac{3}{2}$ and $\frac{6}{4}$; in the second, the two out-of-phase $\frac{4}{4}$ frameworks.) Brahms again uses the head motive of the main theme as the transitional element, or (to switch metaphors) as the common denominator. In the two symphony movements, however, less attention is drawn to the bar line itself, because it is only one element of a tension involving thematic, harmonic, and formal processes. Brahms has fully integrated the nuances of metrical displacement into his musical vocabulary.

# VI

We have up to now considered metrical displacement principally in large-scale instrumental works. What of the smaller vocal forms at the opposite end of the compositional spectrum? Brahms did not employ such techniques as systematically or consistently in his Lieder, probably because he felt that a regular poetic text demanded closer adherence to the bar line and because the medium does not invite extensive thematic development or formal articulation. For his very last vocal works, however, the

*Vier ernste Gesänge*, Op. 121 (1896), Brahms selected prose passages from the Bible with no rhyme or metre, texts that seem to have freed his most sophisticated compositional tendencies. Especially in the third song, 'O Tod', he deploys his characteristic metrical devices with unprecedented fluidity; and now these 'absolute' techniques are put directly in the service of textual expression.

The words of this song comprise two verses from chapter 41 of Ecclesiasticus, from the Apocrypha:

> 1. O Tod, wie bitter bist du, wenn an dich gedenket ein Mensch, der gute Tage und genug hat und ohne Sorge lebet, und dem es wohl geht in allen Dingen und noch wohl essen mag!
>
> 2. O Tod, wie wohl tust du dem Dürftigen, der da schwach und alt ist, der in allen Sorgen steckt, und nichts Bessers zu hoffen, noch zu erwarten hat!
>
> [1. Oh death, how bitter is the thought of you to a man who has a good life and sufficient possessions and who lives without sorrow; and who is fortunate in all things and may still eat well.
>
> 2. Oh death, how well you serve the needy man, who is feeble and old, who is beset by all sorrows and has nothing better to hope for or to expect.]

We are given two contrasting viewpoints on death; it is dreaded by the healthy and happy man, and welcomed by the broken and needy one. Brahms articulates the distinction most obviously by a change of mode from minor to major; and, as has often been pointed out, the two aspects of death are conveyed as musical transformations of a single theme: the harsh descending thirds of the first 'O Tod' become blissful ascending sixths at the conclusion.

Metre also plays a significant role in this process. Examples 11*a* and 11*b* present, respectively, the first six phrases of the song in their original notation and rebarred to take account of the implied shift in metre. No sooner is the $\frac{3}{2}$ metre established by the double statement of 'O Tod' than it is disrupted by the implied $\frac{4}{2}$ metre of the twofold 'wie bitter'. Brahms extends the first syllable of 'bit-ter' so that it occupies two beats; phrase 2 therefore concludes on the third beat of the real bar 3, usurping the upbeat that would be occupied by the next 'wie', if the second phrase of the song were parallel to the first. We thus hear 'wie bitter' as a metrical expansion from $\frac{3}{2}$ to $\frac{4}{2}$. With the addition of 'bist du', the second 'wie bitter' (phrase 3) moves more firmly and quickly towards a perceived downbeat, thus restoring the original triple metre—but one which no longer corresponds to the notated bar line.

In phrase 3 the metrical framework continues to contract, from the restored $\frac{3}{2}$ to $\frac{2}{2}$, and even to a single-beat bar, $\frac{1}{2}$. In my rebarring I have placed important musical and verbal stresses on downbeats. But this metrical plan is complicated or obscured by the canonic imitation between voice and piano beginning at bar 5. Here the two quarter-note Bs of the piano sound like upbeats, but so do the first two Es of the imitative response by the voice. Phrases 5 and 6 function much like phrases 3 and 4; the $\frac{3}{2}$ metre is re-established, then once again contracted successively to $\frac{2}{2}$ and $\frac{1}{2}$.

EXAMPLE 11. (*a*) Brahms, 'O Tod', Op. 121 No. 3, bars 1–9. (*b*) Rebarring of bars 1–9. (*c*) Bars 31–40. Reproduced from Walter Frisch, *Brahms and the Principle of Developing Variation* (University of California Press).

(c)

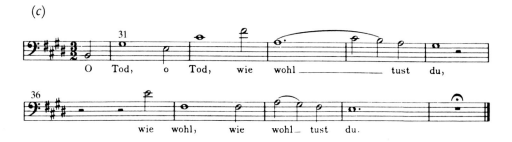

No notation can accurately capture the listener's experience of such a fluent passage. But there can be little disagreement about the effect of explosion at the first 'bitter', both melodically and metrically. It is as if the metre is responding as an aftershock to the opening of a huge gap, an augmented octave, in the voice.

This then is how Brahms captures the anguish, the despair of death. But when the text and the mode change, the metrical profile of the music also changes. In the middle section of the song (bars 18–30; the song has an A B A' form), the notated $\frac{3}{2}$ and implied $\frac{2}{2}$ and $\frac{1}{2}$ metres of the beginning, in which upbeats and downbeats fall (so to speak) uncomfortably close together, are broadened out to a more tranquil $\frac{4}{2}$, notated by Brahms in cut time. The feminine rhythms at 'wohl' and 'du' (bars 21 and 22) now soften the impact of the downbeats.

Despite the tranquility of much of the middle section, resolution of metrical tensions set up at the opening happens only with the return to triple metre for the final ten bars of the song (Example 11c). Here the $\frac{3}{2}$, which had been disrupted at the opening and abandoned in the middle section, is fully restored; all downbeats align comfortably with the bar line. The 'wohl' is now extended, by analogy to the first 'bitter'. The extension creates a five-bar phrase (31–5) but does not—as it did at the beginning—obscure or undermine the metre. The 'wie wohl tust du' is given a parallel response (bars 36–9), which confirms or stabilizes the notated metre.

The repose of death is thus conveyed not only by the change from minor to major and by the inversion of the thirds to sixths, but by metrical resolution. Although the scale is vastly different, the technique is essentially the same as in the two movements of the Third Symphony: the opening presents a metrical 'problem' or tension, which is further explored in the 'development' section, here the central portion of the song in ₵; and at the moment of 'recapitulation' (A') the original notated metre is restored and stabilized. As in the symphony, there is even a harmonic component to this process: the bars preceding the return at 31 (not shown in Example 11) seem to be moving towards the key of C♯ minor, but with the A minor six-four chord of bar 29 turn suddenly towards the tonic E. What we expect is the tonic *minor*, as at the opening of the song; but the return enters instead in the *major*. In this composition, then, Brahms has fused thematic, formal, harmonic, and metrical processes in a way no less compelling than in the larger Third Symphony.

Besides the Andante from the A minor String Quartet, 'O Tod' is the only Brahms work to which Schoenberg devotes extended analysis in 'Brahms the Progressive'. As with the quartet, Schoenberg pays most attention to intervallic economy, demonstrating how virtually every thematic shape in the song is derived from permutations, extensions, inversions, etc., of the interval of a third (pp. 431–5). He gives rather short shrift to what he called 'the beauties of its phrasing' (p. 440), alluding only briefly to the fluid metrical processes we have just examined. But his words on the song as a whole form an appropriate conclusion to this study. He writes, 'the sense of logic and economy and the power of inventiveness which build melodies of so much natural fluency deserve the admiration of every music lover who expects more than sweetness and beauty from music (p. 435). . . . I am pressed to say that this third of the *Vier ernste Gesänge*, "O Tod, O Tod, wie bitter bist du", seems to me the most touching of the whole cycle—in spite of its perfection, if not *because* of it' (p. 439).

What impressed Schoenberg above all—and what is perhaps still too little appreciated in Brahms—is the close relationship in 'O Tod' between technique and expression, between purely compositional procedures and the aesthetic or emotional impact. Or, to use a metaphor from the title of one of Schoenberg's other essays, no valid distinction between 'heart' and 'brain' can be made in music such as this. The same can be said for the Piano Quintet, the Third Symphony, and many other great compositions, where the shifting bar lines become wonderfully expressive elements of Brahms's musical language.

# HARMONIC CONGRUENCE IN BRAHMS

## EDWARD T. CONE

### I

'THE two-or-more dimensional space in which musical ideas are presented is a unit'.[1] Thus Schoenberg (in startling capitals, which I have not reproduced) expressed the basic concept underlying musical composition in general, serialism in particular, and the twelve-tone method especially. He continued:

A musical idea, accordingly, though consisting of melody, rhythm, and harmony, is neither the one nor the other alone, but all three together. The elements of a musical idea are partly incorporated in the horizontal plane as successive sounds, and partly in the vertical plane as simultaneous sounds. The mutual relation of tones regulates the succession of intervals as well as their association into harmonies; the rhythm regulates the succession of tones as well as the succession of harmonies and organizes phrasing. And this explains why, as will be shown later, a basic set of twelve tones can be used in either dimension, as a whole or in parts.

Of course it explains nothing of the kind: unity does not necessarily imply uniformity. The fact that music is composed of tones combined successively as melodies and simultaneously as harmonies does not entail that the same type of organization governs both dimensions. And both Renaissance polyphony and functional tonality demonstrate that it is possible to produce highly organized music in which the two are largely determined by different classes of intervals—the melodic second as opposed to the harmonic third and fifth.

What Schoenberg was trying to justify is one of the potentials of serial music: the availability of the same material for both horizontal and vertical deployment. One type of texture (though not the only one) that may result is that in which melodic lines on the one hand and successive chords on the other exhibit the same notes (pitch-classes) or the same intervals. This melodic-harmonic identity I call harmonic congruence, in contrast to harmonic functionality, which relates all simultaneities to a limited vocabulary of hierarchically related chords.

Congruence and functionality are by no means mutually exclusive, for a single passage can exhibit both at the same time. Indeed, since serialism, as Schoenberg was eager to

---

[1] Arnold Schoenberg, 'Composition with Twelve Tones (1)', 220.

point out, was a natural if not inevitable development, we should suspect nineteenth-century composers of occasionally indulging in congruent harmony—without, to be sure, renouncing functionality. And if Schoenberg was right in labeling Brahms a progressive, it should not surprise us to find among his works examples of precisely that sort.

We must be careful, however. It is easy to infer intention where there is in fact only coincidence. I recall a conversation between Milton Babbitt and Roger Sessions about the opening chord of the *Eroica* Symphony. Babbitt pointed out that from the bass up it spells out, in serial fashion, the arpeggiated motif of the first theme. 'True', replied Sessions, 'but I have always felt that Beethoven's object was the special sound of the low third'.

Just so; and correspondingly unrelated considerations may often have prompted traditionally tonal composers to employ what may sound, to our ears, as harmonic congruence. Thus I cannot accept it as anything but a delightful coincidence that in the opening phrase of Mozart's Piano Sonata in F major, K. 332, whereas the accompaniment of the first bar anticipates the melody of bars 1–2, the retention of the tonic pedal allows the harmony of the fourth bar to reflect the melody of bars 3–4 (Example 1). On the other hand, Wagner's well-known horizontal deployment of the *Tristan* chord[2] occurs too often and too openly throughout the work to be accidental; and there are points of melodic-harmonic congruence in the other music dramas as well.

It is not to Wagner, however, that we should look for a source of Brahms's usage, at least during his earlier works, but to more congenial composers. A move towards a simple form of harmonic congruence can be discerned in the tendency among certain Romantic composers to derive harmonic accompaniments motivically from the very melodies that they support functionally. One can find clear instances in the works of Schumann and Chopin, to name two composers with whose music Brahms was thoroughly familiar. Charles Rosen, who calls the device 'heterophonic accompaniment', points to its use in Schumann's Fantasy and in Chopin's Prelude in G major and Scherzo in C♯ minor.[3] Chopin develops the technique still further in the finale of the Sonata in B♭ minor, where the sequential steps of the opening theme repeat, in augmentation, the arpeggio that is at the same time a melody and its own accompaniment (Example 2). And if we accept the controversially dissonant reading of the famous chord in bar 7 of the First Ballade, we can find in that single sonority an extraordinarily wide forecast of the principle harmonic areas of the piece: G, B♭, D, and E♭, or i, III, V, VI in G minor—harmonic congruence on the largest scale.

## II

Brahms, in the same spirit, liked to enrich his textures by fashioning accompaniment figures from diminutions of thematic motives, especially in his early instrumental works.

---

[2] See, for example, Ernst Kurth, *Romantische Harmonik und ihre Krise in Wagners 'Tristan'*, 84. For a less obvious case, see Milton Babbitt, 'Responses: A First Proximation', 21.

[3] *Sonata Forms*, 315–17.

EXAMPLE 1. Mozart, Piano Sonata in F major, K. 332, I, bars 1–4.

EXAMPLE 2. Chopin, Piano Sonata in B♭ minor, Op. 35, IV, bars 1–3.

There, however, the diminutions are used not so much to harmonize the parent themes themselves as to support transitions or other subsequent ideas. (The openings of the Piano Quintet and the First Piano Concerto are thus manipulated, to name two familiar examples.) But we can look to the later songs for examples of self-accompaniment: to 'Mein wundes Herz', Op. 59 No. 7, which exemplifies a favourite procedure whereby successive motives of the melody in diminution yield an accompaniment figure (Example 3); or to the subtler method of 'Es liebt sich so lieblich im Lenze', Op. 71 No. 1, in which the melody arises as an augmented retrograde of the accompaniment (Example 4).

EXAMPLE 3. Brahms, 'Mein wundes Herz', Op. 59 No. 7, bars 5–6.

EXAMPLE 4. Brahms, 'Es liebt sich so lieblich im Lenze', Op. 71 No. 1, bars 1–3.

Still denser texture, resulting in a closer approach to true congruence, is exhibited by passages of very close canon, at a rhythmic interval of a beat or a fraction thereof. Examples are the opening of the finale of the Clarinet Trio, Op. 114, and the famous canonic variation in the finale of the Fourth Symphony (bars 241–52), passages to which I shall return later.

Those canons illustrate, and to a certain extent depend on, another well-known characteristic of the composer: his love for arpeggiated melodies. Obviously a tune that proceeds by chordal skips is more adaptable to verticalization in a tonal context than one that moves by step. Quintessentially Brahmsian in this respect is 'Feldeinsamkeit', Op. 86, No. 2. Does the melody arise as an arpeggiation of the chords, or are the chords simultaneous projections of the melody? Each of the four extended vocal phrases, except where cadentially directed, can be heard predominantly as a series of broken chords, occasionally filled in by passing-tones. The accompaniment elaborates the same chords harmonically, sometimes over a tonic pedal, sometimes independently.

Even the non-harmonic tones are pressed into service to maintain the identity of horizontal and vertical (see bars 5–6, Example 5). This type of polyphony, in which passing-tones or neighbours are sounded against their preparations or resolutions (or both), produces another typically Brahmsian texture that encourages the tendency toward harmonic congruence. The technique is often extended to embrace contrapuntally passing triads; these can be seen at work in 'Von ewiger Liebe', Op. 43 No. 1,

EXAMPLE 5. Brahms, 'Feldeinsamkeit', Op. 86 No. 2, bars 5–6.

bars 14–17 (Example 6). Similarly, passing-tones and appoggiaturas contribute to the identity of a melody and its gradually unfolding harmony in the opening of 'Die Schale der Vergessenheit', Op. 46 No. 3: by bar 5, when the chord is at last complete, all elements of the one have been accounted for in the other (Example 7).

The use of pedal-points, noted incidentally in 'Feldeinsamkeit', can likewise contribute to congruence; for the sustained pedal, in addition to playing a harmonic role, often doubles an important melodic tone, which is thus independently maintained against all the other tones of the same melody. Suspensions, too, have a similar though more local

EXAMPLE 6. Brahms, 'Von ewiger Liebe', Op. 43 No. 1, bars 14–17.

EXAMPLE 7. Brahms, 'Die Schale der Vergessenheit', Op. 46 No. 3, bars 1–5.

effect, since they result in the simultaneous sounding of elements from two contiguous chords. Both devices are used together to produce an effect of congruence in the opening of 'Sommerabend', Op. 85 No. 1 (Example 8). The suspended D in bar 4, aided by the passing F, creates a harmonic complex that incorporates all the elements of the vocal phrase-member of bars 3–4. The suspended C of bar 6, again aided by a passing-tone, E♭, functions analogously for bars 5–6. At the same time, a pedal on the tonic, B♭, exerts its sway over both members, suggesting that the whole melody can be heard as a single

EXAMPLE 8. Brahms, 'Sommerabend', Op. 85 No. 1, bars 1–9.

complicated tonic chord arpeggiated through four bars. The pedal in fact lasts for three more bars, with suspensions and passing-tones again contributing to an overall harmonic unity that is maintained until the entrance of the chromatic tone Ab, which proclaims the transformation of Bb into an applied dominant. (It is interesting to compare 'Mondenschein', the second song in the opus, in which the same melody is now supported by a dominant pedal.)

Brahms's love for syncopated accompaniment figures often gives him an occasion for very brief suspensions. Fleeting though they are, a careful performance will produce a series of overlapping sonorities that will blend horizontal and vertical. Brahms was precise about this. Throughout the 'Sapphische Ode', Op. 94 No. 4, for example, the piano distinguishes carefully between those bars that exploit the overlapping of the two hands and those that avoid it by the use of rests.

Related to Brahms's predilection for arpeggiated melodies is his method of constructing basses by moving downward in thirds. Such basses effect not only a gradual shift in function but often a constant harmonic enrichment as well, for each successive bass-note may be retained as an element of the chords that follow. The resulting ninths, elevenths, or even thirteenths, embrace many—sometimes all—the tones they are called on to harmonize. Thus in the Intermezzo in B minor, Op. 119 No. 1, each of the chords implied by the arpeggiations of the first three bars summarizes the melody so far (Example 9a). It is not surprising to find the Intermezzo concluding with a cadence employing a tonic thirteenth, which (with the exception of the obligatory raised seventh) embraces the entire scalar melody of the preceding phrase (Example 9b).

EXAMPLE 9. Brahms, Intermezzo in B minor, Op. 119 No 1.
(*a*) Diagram of bars 1 ff.　　　　　　(*b*) Diagram of bars 58–66.

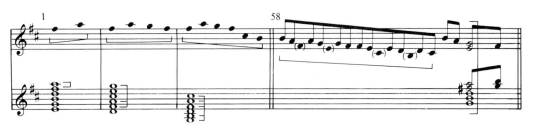

# III

So far I have enumerated several pervasive characteristics or mannerisms that help to define Brahms's style. All of them are explicable within the framework of tonality and functional harmony; yet at the same time all of them occasion moments of harmonic congruence. There are a number of passages that further suggest that such congruence is more than merely coincidental; their cumulative evidence may even demonstrate that harmony of this kind in itself constitutes an important aspect of the composer's style. As Alan Walker puts it, 'The attitude of mind which led Schönberg to invent his twelve-note system had already made itself manifest *on a conscious level* in Brahms'.[4]

One indication of such a predilection is the frequent use of a peculiar keyboard texture in which arpeggio and chord are inextricably blended. In the principal theme of the Capriccio in G minor, Op. 116 No. 3, are the arpeggiations to be heard melodically, harmonically, or as the elements of four polyphonic lines? The first page of this Fantasy (Example 10) suggests that no single answer is correct, that the basic motivic sonority—

EXAMPLE 10. Brahms, Capriccio in G minor, Op. 116 No. 3, bars 1–2, 5–6, 9–14.

4 'Brahms and Serialism', 17. Emphasis in the original.

the chordal seventh in all its varieties— is to be heard vertically, horizontally, even diagonally! Another Capriccio in this opus, No. 7 in D minor, exhibits similar texture.

Especially striking are the numerous cases in which an arpeggiated melody is associated with a vertical form of a similar chord, chromatically altered. The opening phrases of the Violin Sonata in A major, Op. 100, exploit this effect (Example 11). So do a number of the songs: notably 'Die Mainacht', Op. 43 No. 2, whose climactic 'Träne' (bars 29–30) is given added poignance by such alteration (Example 12); and 'Der Tod, das ist die kühle Nacht', Op. 96 No. 1, where the opening arpeggio of the voice, a half diminished seventh, is changed during its course into a fully diminished seventh by the piano (Example 13).

EXAMPLE 11. Brahms, Violin Sonata in A major, Op. 100, bars 3–4, 8–9.

EXAMPLE 12. Brahms, 'Die Mainacht', Op. 43 No. 2, bars 29–30.

EXAMPLE 13. Brahms, 'Der Tod, das ist die kühle Nacht', Op. 96 No. 1, bars 1–3.

Movement in the reverse direction, in which a chord gives way to a melody arpeggiating another form, occurs at a crucial point in the Rhapsody in G minor, Op. 79 No. 2. The development section ends uniquely, with a fermata on a tonic minor chord with an added major sixth (E♮). It is succeeded by the return of the principal theme, which is based on an arpeggiation of the same chord, but with E♮ replaced by E♭ (Example 14). That configuration—a minor triad plus a minor sixth, or an inverted major seventh chord—is an important motivic germ. It assumes numerous forms—horizontal, vertical, and mixed—that not only produce the melody of the main theme but also contribute prominently to the rest of the piece.

The pervasion of an entire movement in this way by one or two sonorities, usually seventh chords, is of course a procedure that reminds one of the role of Schoenberg's *Grundgestalt*.[5] It can be seen at work also in the half and fully diminished sevenths of the Capriccio in D minor, Op. 116 No. 1, in the sevenths and augmented triads of the song 'Meerfahrt', Op. 96 No. 4, in the motivic germ (third plus second) of 'An die Nachtigall', Op. 46 No. 4, and in a number of other short compositions. But it can function in longer movements as well. In the opening Allegro non troppo of the String Quartet in A minor, Op. 51 No. 2, those sections relating to the first theme are dependent on various forms of the opening four-note motive and the chord or chords it implies. And in the finale of the Piano Trio in C major, Op. 87, the first bar presents two chords, one horizontally and one vertically (again the half and fully diminished sevenths, respectively), that will determine the course of the first theme and its developments.

Sometimes the chordal nature of a linear motive is obscure, its explanation being held in reserve, as in the Intermezzo in E♭ minor, Op. 118 No. 6. The opening melody could hardly be less conducive of arpeggiation. Even its harmonization, which treats the sustained F as an accented passing-tone over a diminished seventh, hides the truth. That, although frequently intimated, is revealed only at the climax in bar 53: the opening melody, together with its accompanying arpeggio, horizontalizes a chord of the minor ninth (Example 15).

EXAMPLE 14. Brahms, Rhapsody in G minor, Op. 79 No. 2, bars 85–6.

5 For a discussion of what Schoenberg meant by this term, see David Epstein, *Beyond Orpheus*, 17–33.

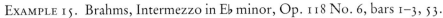

EXAMPLE 15. Brahms, Intermezzo in E♭ minor, Op. 118 No. 6, bars 1–3, 53.

Still closer to twelve-tone technique are those passages in which a line yields a progression of two or more chords. The examples in this category may seem short and unpredictable. Yet they are not desultory; they occur far too prominently for that. Often they give the effect of a free variation of the original material, as in the passage that immediately succeeds the greatly extended opening phrase of the Piano Trio in C major (bars 13–18). While the strings develop in sequence a rhythmic variant of the first triadic motive, the piano transforms the opening unison line into a series of chords and arpeggios (Example 16). The process is repeated in the recapitulation (bars 213–18), but the congruence is not so exact.

The variation effect is even clearer in 'Nachklang', Op. 59 No. 4, a song that is in itself a condensation of its predecessor in the opus, 'Regenlied'. In that model, the second stanza began strophically, repeating the music of the first. In the second stanza of 'Nachklang' the voice is given a new melody, but the accompaniment slowly unfolds a partly verticalized form of the original tune—a process already set in motion by the preceding interlude (Example 17).

In both trio and song, the verticalized versions are more relaxed and extended than their originals. That need not be the case, for the technique affords obvious opportunities for harmonic compression. Thus at the outset of the Violoncello Sonata in F major, Op. 99, the piano accompaniment in bars 7–8 summarizes in chordal form the entire melody of bars 1–4 (Example 18).

By compression of this kind Brahms occasionally creates an entirely new theme. In the first movement of the Trio in B major, Op. 8 (revised version), the second subject, so treated, is startlingly transformed into a contrasting closing figure (cf. bars 75–8 and 110–11, Example 19).

Cadences are favourite places for harmonic summaries that compress previous melodic action. The late songs afford a number of examples. One of the most elaborate is the coda of 'Auf dem Kirchhofe', Op. 105 No. 4. First reducing the vocal cadence on 'Genesen' to one chord, it continues by harmonically summarizing the melody of the entire preceding phrase (Example 20). A beautiful instrumental example is afforded by the Violin Sonata in G major, Op. 78: just before the closing theme of the first movement, the cadential chords sum up the descent of a melody that has already partially harmonized itself (Example 21).

EXAMPLE 16. Brahms, Piano Trio in C major, Op. 87, I, bars 1–4 vs. 13–18.

EXAMPLE 17. Brahms, 'Nachklang', Op. 59 No. 4, bars 1–4, 16–25.

EXAMPLE 18. Brahms, Violoncello Sonata in F major, Op. 99, I, bars 1–4, 7–8.

EXAMPLE 19. Brahms, Piano Trio in B major, Op. 8 (revised version), I, bars 76–9, 110–11.

EXAMPLE 20. Brahms, 'Auf dem Kirchhofe', Op. 105 No. 4, bars 27–36.

Wie stur.mes.tot die Sär . ge schlum.mer.ten, auf al.len Grä.bern tau .te

still: Ge . ne . . . sen.

EXAMPLE 21. Brahms, Violin Sonata in G major, Op. 78, I, bars 56–60.

More numerous, and more obvious in their adaptation of congruent harmony, are those melodies that are indeed self-harmonized, the supporting chords being composed of the tones and intervals of the melody itself. In contrast to those cases where the melody is predominantly the arpeggiation of a single underlying chord, the harmony in the present instances, based on a series of chords, declares a certain independence. Since horizontal and vertical projections of a chord will normally move at different rates of speed, the harmony is often out of synchronization, as it were. Some examples, nevertheless, are regular and predictable, for example, the last page of the Piano Trio in C major (bars 214–18; Example 22). For four bars there is an almost exact identity between melody (violin) and bass (cello): bar by bar they contain the same notes, though in different order. (As the piano doubling shows, the two parts actually cross in the third bar.) The piano chords are composed of the same material in the same order, but gathered together in overlapping clusters, until bar 217 prepares for the climax by a substitution—D♯ for E. But the E has only been postponed; it is saved for a piano sonority that comprises not only the melodic lines of the preceding bar but also the G that resolves them in bar 218—a cumulative sonority for a climactic point.

The *Vier ernste Gesänge*, Op. 121, are full of both clear and concealed examples. In addition to the obvious arpeggiations that initiate Nos. 2 and 3, there are details like the little motive that introduces the second period of No. 2, at bars 15–16 (Example 23). Its three occurrences—the first in the piano, the remaining two in the voice—are given successively richer harmonizations, gradually approaching the complete harmonic congruence of the last. In the same song, the approach to the final cadence contains noteworthy suspensions and syncopations. And I cannot forbear mentioning a little phrase in No. 3, bars 26–7, that is harmonized by a progression based on its own retrograde. That the device was intentional is indicated by its continuation—now purely melodic—in bars 27–8 (Example 24).

EXAMPLE 22. Brahms, Piano Trio in C major, Op. 87, IV, bars 214–18.

EXAMPLE 23. Brahms, *Vier ernste Gesänge*, Op. 121 No. 2, bars 15–16, 19–20, 31–2.

EXAMPLE 24. Brahms, *Vier ernste Gesänge*, Op. 121 No. 3, bars 26–8.

# IV

Brahms sometimes broadens the principle of congruence in his treatment of non-chordal tones in otherwise arpeggiated melodies. Such a tone, because of its dissonant nature, may at first be unavailable as part of the underlying harmony; in that case it is often given special status as the root or bass (or both) of a new chord. In the opening of the G major Violin Sonata, that is what happens to the passing C, the only non-chordal element in the initial motive: it becomes the root of the neighbouring subdominant that inflects the prevailing tonic of the phrase. At the same time, a short chain of suspensions permits the linear connections D–C and D–E to be heard vertically. Finally, the piano chords conceal complex augmentations of the complete motive, both directly and in retrograde (Example 25).

EXAMPLE 25. Brahms, Violin Sonata in G major, Op. 78, I, bars 1–4.

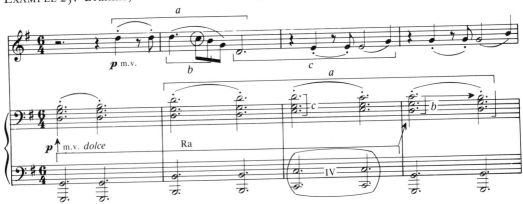

A similar technique is used in the initial phrase of 'Wie Melodien zieht es mir', Op. 105 No. 1: note the vocal appoggiatura, D, of bar 2 reflected in the harmonic bass of bar 3. In 'Auf dem See', Op. 106 No. 2, the opening melody contains two unprepared but unaccented neighbours, C♯ and F♯ (bar 5), which serve as chordal roots in bars 6–7.

As the above examples show, the enhancement of a non-chordal tone may throw the bass into unusual relief. That situation has interesting consequences in the opening Allegro amabile of the A major Violin Sonata. In the first statement of the second theme (bars 50–66), the opening melody arpeggiates the new tonic chord of E (Example 26). Its two passing-tones, A and F♯, are immediately restated as chordal elements—bass and root respectively of the supertonic (bar 53). The new passing-tone at that point, D♯, is differently treated: the entire melodic complex of that bar is to return (bar 59), transposed and compressed into a single dissonant chord—a half diminished seventh— to initiate a new continuation of the theme. But that continuation has an even closer progenitor in the bass. Altering its own enhanced passing-tone A (bar 53) to A♯ (bar 56), the bass produces a line that forecasts not only the dissonance of bar 59 (with no transposition necessary) but its resolution in bar 61 as well.

The first subject of the same movement demonstrates how the convertibility of horizontal and vertical can operate on the most detailed level (Example 27). Four versions of the opening three-note figure (bars 11–12, 13–14, 31–2, 33–4) exhibit the motive respectively (a) stated melodically, (b) compressed by the simultaneous statement of its first two elements, (c) frankly divided between the two voices thus implied, which nevertheless preserve the original attack-pattern, and (d) simultaneously divided and compressed. The closing theme as well (bar 79) can be heard as a variant, although the two preceding bars suggest yet another, more complex source.

EXAMPLE 26. Brahms, Violin Sonata in A major, Op. 100, I, bars 51–61.

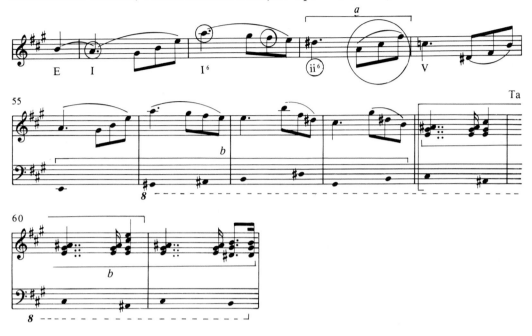

EXAMPLE 27. Brahms, Violin Sonata in A major, Op. 100, I, bars 11–12, 13–14, 31–2, 33–4, 77–9.

# V

Even if the foregoing excerpts are convincing as instances of congruent harmony, it must be admitted that most of them are indeed just that: excerpts. One may therefore well ask whether Brahms ever used the technique consistently over a lengthy movement. The answer must be: consistently, no; persistently, yes. Consistency would be virtually impossible for one working wholly within the tonal framework; yet a number of compositions—late ones especially—owe their unique sound to a texture permeated by congruent sonorities and progressions. The Clarinet Trio in A minor, Op. 114, is a case in point, of which I can mention only a few highlights here. In the first movement, each of the three principle themes of the exposition develops its own version of congruence. The opening motive is stated as an unharmonized cello solo (Example 28*a*). The preparation for its tutti statement begins in bar 18, at the return of the initial tonic arpeggio, now harmonized by VI–i$_3^6$. Four bars later, the definitive return of the theme is expanded to contain both chords. So does the new bass; but at the same time it includes the descending tetrachord that originally served as a continuation of the arpeggiated melody. And when that tetrachord reappears in its normal soprano position one bar later, its harmonization devolves on a tonic seventh that, with its resolution (through iv $_4^6$ to i), sums up the entire motive. (The practice of breaking a line in two and presenting both halves simultaneously is oddly anticipatory of a familiar serial device. For another example, involving a theme already congruently harmonized on its first appearance, look at bar 12 of the finale of the Violin Sonata in A major.)

The second subject, presented melodically by the cello, is imitated in a partly horizontal, partly vertical diminution by the piano (Example 28*b*). The closing theme, not to be outdone, is stated in three simultaneous versions: in the right hand of the piano part as a melody, in the left hand as accompanying arpeggios, and in the clarinet and cello as a duet (Example 28*c*).

EXAMPLE 28. Brahms, Clarinet Trio in A minor, Op. 114, I.
(*a*) Bars 1–2, 18, 22–4.

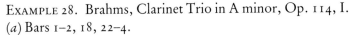

(*b*) Bars 44–8.

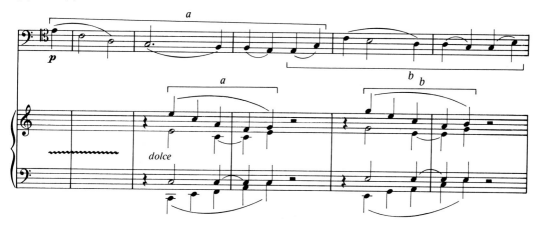

(*c*) Bars 67–70.

The clarinet melody of the Adagio is accompanied by anticipatory imitations in the piano (Example 29). These, together with the sustained cello bass, suggest but do not explicitly state a series of dissonant chords congruent to the successive slurs of the clarinet. The goal is almost perfectly achieved, however, in the coda, in the combination of the piano's countermelody and the accompanying arpeggios.

The finale begins with a return to harmonies familiar from the opening of the first movement, deployed in a unique confluence of horizontal and vertical (Example 30*a*). The typically Brahmsian close canon presents its intervals both successively and simultaneously. But while the leaping sixths of the melody (E–C, A–F) suggest tonic and submediant (E–C–A, C–A–F), they are actually harmonized by tonic and subdominant. Not until the following bars, when the sixths are inverted into descending thirds, are they supported by $i_3^6$ and $VI_3^6$. It is not long before these are combined into the chord, characteristic for this movement, of VI⁷ (bar 8). The same chord, horizontalized and inverted, introduces the second theme (bars 38–9). The connection is made even more obvious when this new motive is combined with its own inversion—which is of course a transposition of the original form (bars 46–8). When that passage returns in the recapitulation, now untransposed (bars 144–6), the identification is complete.

Descending thirds again underlie the development initiated in bar 79, in which they are harmonically combined to produce cycles of descending fifths (ascending fourths; Example 30*b*). The passage closes with such a progression strikingly superimposed on a tonic pedal. And the same thirds, compressed still further, yield the final cadence of the movement, which preserves consistent congruence by substituting an augmented mediant for the expected dominant.

EXAMPLE 29. Brahms, Clarinet Trio in A minor, Op. 114, II, bars 1, 49–50.

EXAMPLE 30. Brahms, Clarinet Trio in A minor, Op. 114, IV.
(*a*) Bars 1–4, 8, 46–8, 144–6.

(*b*) Bars 84–5, 101–5, 189–91.

## VI

The descending-third formula was a favourite of Brahms, appearing in many guises. Its prevalence in the Fourth Symphony has often been noted, and no discussion of Brahms's congruent harmony can avoid at least a cursory glance at that work. Here if anywhere the evidence of the text points strongly to an intentional use of the technique, not only within movements but also as a device for binding them together. The canon in the finale, cited above, is one of the last stages of a process set in motion by the first subject of the first movement—a source-theme for the entire symphony.[6] The first eight bars of the melody, consisting of a chain of descending thirds (or rising sixths) followed by one of rising thirds, are ready made for verticalization—or rather for various verticalizations, depending on how many successive elements are taken in each chord (Example 31*a*). At the very outset, five notes (B–G–E–C–A) spell out overlapping triads of E minor, C major, and A minor—a condensed reference to the key of the first movement, the Phrygian introduction of the second, the key of the third, and the opening of the finale. (The Phrygian nature of the C major is supported by the F♮ in the ensuing four-bar group.) But the actual harmonization of the theme is based on i–iv–V[7] over a tonic pedal, and soon the first authentic cadence (bars 17–19) suggests yet another verticalization: i–V[9].

A new version of the source-theme, based on a major triad, underlies the figure that announces and then accompanies the second subject (bars 53 ff.). Other variations are found in the development; I shall call attention only to the inception of the striking

---

[6] Alan Walker discusses the melodic aspects of the process in 'Brahms and Serialism', 19.

canon (bars 168–70) that conceals still another verticalized form (Example 31*b*). Anyone who has followed these steps will have no difficulty in recognizing the derivation of the final cadences of the movement (bars 434–8).

EXAMPLE 31. Brahms, Fourth Symphony in E minor, Op. 98, I.
(*a*) Pitches of theme; bars 17–19.

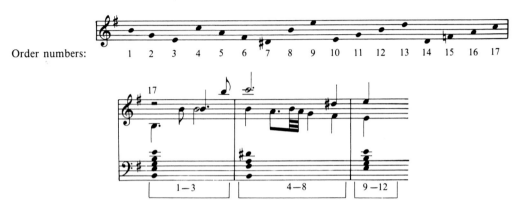

(*b*) Bars 159, 434–40.

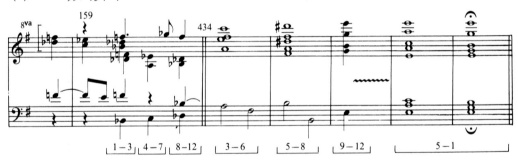

Distant as the Andante moderato may sound from what has preceded it, its Phrygian introduction, as we have seen, betrays a connection. So, too, does the cantilena that follows, for buried in its harmonization is a major version of the source-theme (Example 32). The Allegro giocoso departs further from that material; yet even here, the opening statement seems to be composed of verticalized fragments of the basic idea in retrograde (Example 33). I put forward this suggestion tentatively, but it is supported by the opening statement of the finale, which combines fragmentary retrograde with modal transposition (Example 34*a*). Some of the variations sound much closer to the source: the one beginning at bar 33, for example, or the major version at bar 113. And the subject of the canonic variation, itself based on a transposition of the basic idea, is first presented as the bass of an untransposed form (Example 34*b*).

EXAMPLE 32. Brahms, Fourth Symphony in E minor, Op. 98, II, bar 5.

EXAMPLE 33. Brahms, Fourth Symphony in E minor, Op. 98, III, bars 1–4.

EXAMPLE 34. Brahms, Fourth Symphony in E minor, Op. 98, IV.
(*a*) Bars 1–4.　　　　　　　　　　　　　(*b*) Bars 233–5.

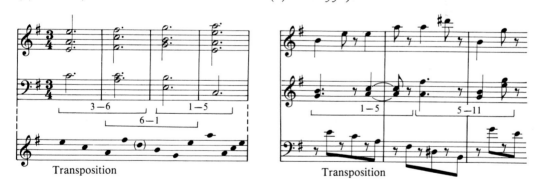

# VII

Schoenberg naturally refers to that canon in his well-known essay 'Brahms the Progressive', but only to call attention to its relation to the first movement.[7] No mention is made of its harmonic interest. Schoenberg does come closer to a recognition of Brahms's progressivism in that respect when he discusses the third of the *Vier ernste Gesänge*. But even here, although the musical examples clearly reveal the congruent

[7] pp. 405–6.

aspects of the harmony, the text is concerned with the motivic treatment of ascending and descending thirds, and later with the phrase-rhythm.[8] As Walker says,

The essay 'Brahms the Progressive' reveals a comparatively unknown aspect of this composer but rather tantalisingly ignores the logical conclusion of the argument it presents. For example, Schönberg knew Brahms's E-minor Symphony well enough to point out the vital connection between the outer movements, and it is inconceivable to me that having got this far he failed to recognise the embryo serialism that occurs throughout the work.[9]

One can only guess at the reasons for such an omission. Could Schoenberg have failed to hear the harmonic results of the motivic manipulation he so painstakingly describes, or could he have failed to appreciate the significance of what he heard? Could he, subconsciously or even consciously, have suppressed his recognition of a technique that came too close to what he considered an important innovation of his own? Very soon after his first experiments in his new method he was proclaiming, as the 'weightiest assumption behind twelve-tone composition', a basic law—a law which, he insisted, 'I was the first to utter and accord its true significance'. By now it should have a familiar ring:

Whatever sounds together (harmonies, chords, the result of part-writing) plays its part in expression and in presentation of the musical idea in just the same way as does all that sounds successively (motive, shape, phrase, sentence, melody, etc.), and it is equally subject to the law of comprehensibility.[10]

Schoenberg may well have been 'the first to utter' the principle, but surely Brahms had caught a glimpse of 'its true significance'.

---

[8] Ibid., 431–5, 440.
[9] 'Brahms and Serialism', 17.
[10] 'Twelve-Tone Composition', 207.

# PERFORMANCE PRACTICE

# BRAHMS AND THE MECHANISMS OF MOTION: THE COMPOSITION OF PERFORMANCE

———

## DAVID EPSTEIN

THE paradoxes of Zeno of Elea may seem a curious starting-point for a study of Brahms. Yet the problems Zeno discussed have points in common with practices that permeate Brahms's music, particularly as they concern motion. This shrewd Greek philosopher reappears continually in the history of thought. His paradoxes, and the dilemmas of logic and of observation that he posed, have confronted us through the centuries, for they rest not upon any vogue, or modishness of thought, but upon basic physical principles. Indeed they strike even now at the roots of contemporary physics, and though Zeno was no musician, what he poses bears directly upon our art.

Recall Zeno's case of Achilles seeking to catch up with the tortoise, or his question whether the arrow in flight is at rest or in motion. A common thread runs through these paradoxes. Each points out our inadequate means for dealing with motion. Indeed our confrontation with motion is itself paradoxical, for as Zeno shows, we lack the concepts to deal with motion in dynamic terms—in terms, that is, consistent with the intrinsic quality of movement that in fact constitutes motion. Instead we use static concepts, dividing the space through which something moves into segments which we can study separately and which, perhaps, we can ultimately integrate. There seems an inescapable dilemma we must grapple with when dealing with motion. We can describe it 'objectively', and thereby precisely, or subjectively—and imprecisely—by poetic means. It seems impossible to capture both qualities simultaneously.

This is an issue of no mean importance for music, for motion is a vital quality, perhaps the quintessential quality, of music. Motion pervades music. Without motion a performance is dead, if not deadly. Without its unique and proper sense of motion a work is frustrating to hear. Motion is intimately related to affect, musical character, emotion (the etymological connection is significant). Motion, as an overall umbrella concept, would seem to subsume gesture and character as they relate to themes, phrases, sections. Articulation, accent, stress, all serve to effect and to assist motion. Musicians at work talk of how the piece 'moves'—how it goes. The great repertoire is filled with indications to clarify these matters of motion: *doppio movimento*, *accelerando*, *hold back*, *nicht schleppen*, *drängen*, *tenuto*; not to mention tempo markings and subsidiary indications of character—*grazioso*, *scherzando*, and the like.

Yet for all this, the paradoxical percepts of Zeno persist. We deal with motion inadequately in music, forced to precise if sometimes misleading indications (metronome markings, for example), or to poetic, gestural language. Or perhaps we deal with motion not at all, simply assuming what we know we know, but cannot indicate. Certainly our technical equipment for discussing this all-important aspect of music is weaker than that for any other area of musical discourse. And while musicians at work may sing, grunt, gesture to convey their sense of things mobile, this communication is less adequate when written music must be the mode to communicate with us across oceans or across centuries. We need a richer vocabulary of motion.

This study is an effort in that direction. Its starting-point and its inspiration is the music of Brahms, who reveals in his scores a profound awareness of these problems, and who developed special means for dealing with them. Many of these means involve those seeming paradoxes and ambiguities of rhythm and metre that themselves are hallmarks of Brahms's style. This richness of ambiguity, in the perspective of this study, suggests that Brahms built into his scores as part of their structure, and accordingly built into his compositional craft, unusual techniques for the control and the continuity of musical motion.

No musician can deal with the music of Brahms without encountering these ambiguities. In their most common form they involve a disparity between how the music is heard and the way it is embodied in score. Rhythmically strong points of phrases, for example, felt as downbeat articulations, are often notated on weak portions of bars. The disparity leads not only to questions of perception but to those of performance as well. Which bar, for instance, can we consider the downbeat of the opening phrase in the Second Symphony, first movement (Example 1)? Different criteria will suggest either bar 1 or 2. If bowings in the cellos and double-basses are to be consistent with the phrasing, the question must be resolved, yet no clear answer is evident.[1]

A more disconcerting case, perhaps, is found early in the Allegro, first movement, of the First Symphony (Example 2). The arrival at a *ff* as the result of a crescendo begun five bars before; the two-note phrase groupings, with their second notes shortened in the tradition of classical practice; the weighted texture created by the addition of winds in bar 53—all these features and more make the initial beat of the two-beat groupings sound strong. Yet they are written as weak second beats in each bar.

Yet more paradoxical, and a moment of extra attentiveness if not anxiety for all orchestral players (especially the horns!), is the passage in the Second Symphony, first movement (Example 3) where the music floats in a sea of rhythmic and metric uncertainty. The melodic motives, derived from the rhythm of the opening bars of the movement (see Example 1), fit within the $\frac{3}{4}$ metric pattern and tend to sound as if their first notes lie on the downbeats of the bars. They are not written that way however, and the eternal syncopations of the horns further remove any sense of a clear beat or, for that matter, any idea of where in fact the music may be in relation to a downbeat.

[1]  I discuss this passage in greater detail in my book *Beyond Orpheus*, 165–9.

EXAMPLE 1. Brahms, Symphony No. 2 in D major, Op. 73, I, bars 1–6.

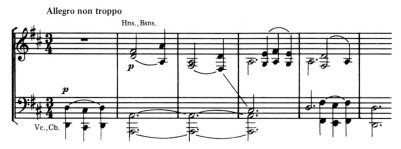

EXAMPLE 2. Brahms, Symphony No. 1 in C minor, Op. 68, I, bars 51–7.

EXAMPLE 3. Brahms, Symphony No. 2 in D major, Op. 73, I, bars 136–41.

Inevitably these phrases conclude, but their conclusion does not always mean ambiguity resolved. For cadences themselves often seem misplaced within a bar, their articulation or their metric weight seemingly on the wrong beat. Equally often the cadence will be incomplete—foreshortened through an elision, or thrown into a weaker and perhaps surprising light by a false or partial resolution. The ambiguities persist in these scores, woven into the warp and woof of the musical fabric. They even appear at times when we think them absent.

The opening of the Third Symphony is such a case (Example 4). Everything that we hear in these opening bars convinces us that the music begins with a strong structural downbeat. Everything, that is, until the third bar. The opening chord, firmly emblazoned in sonorities of brass and winds, is a solid, root-position tonic. The diminished chord that follows resolves to the tonic in bar 3. F major, stability, normalcy thus reign supreme in a conventional two-bar group.

Bar 3 changes all this. The high melody in the violins is clearly more interesting than the opening motive; the character and musical weight of this richer idea suggest that the 'real' piece starts here, and that the first two bars, despite their stability, were some sort of upbeat introductory phrase. The recurrence of the introductory motive in the bass at bar 3 reinforces this impression, as it now seems not the main motive but a countermotive over which the main melody is built. Yet how does a stable tonic passage like the opening serve as an upbeat? The enigma, as ever in Brahms, lies deep within the music, to be utilized for various purposes later in the piece.

We can delight in the aesthetic pleasure of these rich and complex matrices of ambiguity, but their analysis has given trouble to generations of musicians. It is difficult to delineate boundaries of musical ideas and phrases in these passages, or even to determine the criteria by which these delineations might be made. It is equally difficult for the performer to know how to shape these phrases in the absence of a clear sense of their structure.

Brahms's ambiguity arises not from a muddled view on his part of his own music. Quite the contrary; it is obviously deliberate. His mastery over his music suggests that there must be a key to this lack of clarity—some level or some perspective which, when revealed, makes sense of these conflicting concepts and points to a higher purpose that they all serve. This may well be the case, and rhythm and movement may well be this purpose. To illustrate the point, however, requires as a prelude a sorting out of the structural elements and priorities of rhythm and metre themselves.

EXAMPLE 4. Brahms, Symphony No. 3 in F major, Op. 90, I, bars 1–5.

In *Beyond Orpheus* I propose such a sorting out through the rhythmic/metric *schema* reprinted here in Table 1. (Interested readers should refer to Chapter 4 of the book for the finer details of that discussion.)

TABLE 1.

Musical Time

| Metre | Rhythm |
| --- | --- |
| Beat | Pulse |
| Measure | Motive |
| Hypermeasure | Phrase |
| Larger periods | Larger periods |

The *schema*, utilizing in part the work of Cone[2] and of Cooper and Meyer[3], rests upon premises that are pertinent to general properties of time, of which musical time is seen as a special case. These premises are:
(1) Hierarchy
(2) Duality
(3) The need for demarcation
(4) Means of demarcation (i.e., emphasis).

Musical motion is the product of this rhythmic/metric structure. The structure in fact is the necessary undergirding to ensure not only the event of motion, but its continuity and ultimate cessation at a predetermined and desired point of closure. Indeed this closure—the resolution of forces at a designated moment—is perhaps the ultimate disposition of compositional craft, for only by this means can a work proceed to conclusion. Motion may be a shared event between the work, which embeds this quality in its construction, and the performer, who propels the music in part by his own energies. Closure and conclusion, however, must be a *compositional* function. If we rarely think about this point, the reason may lie largely in the fact that our repertoire is formed of works by masters—music in which these matters are artfully designed and controlled. Anyone who has performed lesser music may well be aware of the matter, however, for he may have encountered pieces where musical energy bogs down *en route* due to structural lapse, thus forcing the performer to 'push' the work to its concluding bars, much as we must push a car to the mechanic's shop after a breakdown, with no help from the car's own source of power.

Of the premises listed above, hierarchy is virtually a self-evident aspect of temporal structure. Relatively little has been done in music theory, however, with larger levels of hierarchy, so that no terminology exists to define these broader levels and their periods with precision, as the *schema* suggests.[4]

---

[2] Edward T. Cone, *Musical Form and Musical Performance.*
[3] Grosvenor Cooper and Leonard Meyer, *The Rhythmic Structure of Music.*
[4] The level of beat and pulse—the smallest practical time units—will not concern us in this discussion. They are useful concepts, however, when discussing performance matters like rubato, for they distinguish between two different kinds of time units which in this case either synchronize or work against each other.

Equally well known is the fact of duality—that time can be experienced in two basic modes: the steady passage of 'clock time', and the unique time of events. Metre is akin to clock time, dividing music into (presumed) evenly spaced units. Rhythm, on the other hand, is unique and integral to each piece and to each musical event.

The remaining premisses are part of a larger concern. Time undemarcated is an unusable (though perhaps a poetic) concept. Demarcation is thus a necessity, and every mode of time-keeping must establish its means of demarcation.[5] What, then, are the means by which music demarcates time? More often than not we use the term 'accent' in referring to these markers, though Cooper and Meyer make a valuable distinction between 'accent', which is structural, and 'stress', which is non-structural. Hence the term 'emphasis', used here as a generic category to cover both modes of demarcation.

Accents, as structure, are built into the inner workings of music. To destroy them is to destroy the music in some fundamental way. Stresses, being non-structural, are surface elements, lending interest and life to a passage but not critical to its very existence or recognizability. Stresses could thus be extracted from a musical fabric without destroying the fabric itself.

A sudden loud noise, therefore, does not necessarily establish an accent, though the force of a resolution to tonic harmony from prior dissonance may well be a downbeat and an accent, however loud or soft it is. By contrast, those off-beat *sforzandi* in the midst of many Beethoven passages, powerful and exciting as they are, are not structural but rather stresses. Were we to remove them, we could still easily recognize the music.

This distinction is often clouded by the fact that our small repertoire of words and markings for articulations (·, >, ∧, *sf*, *rf*, marcato, tenuto, etc.) does double duty, often serving to designate stresses as well as accents. It seems, in fact, that these marks, which we have habitually associated with accents, denote stresses more often than they do true structural articulations. For structural articulations make their point 'naturally', so to speak, and thus need little, if any, reinforcement.

The means for articulating accents are various and different for each mode of the *schema* in Table 1, and for each of its levels. At and before the time of Brahms, the bar received a metric accent on its initial beat, the product of a long-established tradition. Motives, as a norm—and this does not in the main account for Brahms—took their accent pattern from the bar, within which they usually fit. Upbeats in a motive—an anacrusis, for example—were weak, the accent falling on the metric downbeat that followed.

---

[5] In discussing the demarcation of temporal periods, it is important to recognize a major paradox about time—namely, that time cannot define itself by an intrinsic terminology. We cannot, in other words, define time by time, as we can define space by space. For no self-contained chronometry exists for the domain of time comparable to the closed spatial system of geometry, whose descriptive terms (high, low, long, short . . .) are themselves spatial.

Furthermore, unlike space, time is unavailable to the senses; we cannot hear, see, taste, feel, or smell it. Consequently we 'tell time' and define time with metaphors and markers drawn from the world of space; markers which, moreover, are themselves sensual (the beat's aural click; the clock's visual face). Not to distinguish these points causes confusion about what time is, and what we may be doing—and using—when we designate, or think we designate, time.

Matters are not as clear on longer time levels. The four-bar hypermeasure, for instance, is a staple of Classical music and generally has a metric pattern of accent in which the initial bar is stronger than subsequent ones.[6] Four-bar phrases generally fit within this hypermeasure frame, to some extent sharing this same accent pattern. Phrases often extend beyond four bars, however, or shorten to smaller lengths. What happens to hypermeasures at these points is an open question, though the conflict between metre and phrase is obvious. Phrase predominates at these places, for musical interest here lies not in a standardized metric unit but in the qualities and directions of a musical idea— properties that are integral to the phrase.

Phrases moreover have additional patterns of accents, accents that inhere in contours, beginnings, cadences, etc. Always in the background, on this and larger levels, is the powerful force of harmony, which is often the ultimate force of articulation. The resolution of a harmonic progression, from instability to the stability of the tonic, exerts a powerful downbeat accent, while the tension and dissonance inherent in unresolved progressions are upbeat in nature. They add direction and impetus to musical motion. The structural downbeat plays an important role in this system, as Cone has shown, for it co-ordinates all musical elements to create a downbeat force so strong as to turn all that precedes it into its own upbeat.

Musical structure emerges from this discussion as a multi-levelled, bi-modal matrix. As with many hierarchic structures, different levels within this matrix interact, possibly synchronized or even nested within one another, or working in opposition, with the heightened tensions that result. Moreover, metric or rhythmic time segments—at every level—have their own manner of accent, and particular means for articulating such accents. These accents, rhythmic and metric, at all levels, are qualitatively unique and qualitatively different. We experience these various accents with differing degrees of intensity, character, inflection, articulation, meaning. For the most part, we are intuitively clear about their meaning, as they are part of a code we have learned to understand. Were this not the case, Classic-Romantic music (the focus of this discussion) could not be as widely performed as it is with such degrees of control and basic agreement.[7]

The rhythmic and metric aspects of Brahms's technique, particularly the anomalous aspects on which we focused earlier, can be understood more clearly in the light of this discussion. Brahms obviously works against the norms of this system in examples such as

---

[6] Hypermeasures might be two- as well as four-bar units, but duple in nature.

[7] It is the fine points of this music for which we seek greater understanding. They lie within a larger framework of which there is basic comprehension. This argument presumes major theoretical positions developed in recent linguistics and aesthetics. It runs parallel, for example, to Noam Chomsky's hypothesis that human beings universally possess an innate capacity to comprehend grammar in language. We presume a similar capacity here— very likely also universal—with respect to the grammatical properties of music. We further agree with the important point made by Nelson Goodman that a work of art communicates by means of a code, and that successful communication requires that both the sender and the receiver of the work be familiar with this code. This code, obviously, must be learned, and its comprehension exists in varying degrees within any population. Geography, historical era, culture, style, and many other factors all condition such a code.

we have shown, placing motives and phrases out of phase with the measures and hypermeasures that would be their normal metric frame. He offsets cadential accents by similar metric displacements, and dilutes harmonic resolution with false or partial cadences, or with phrase elisions. These are but the main and the obvious parts of his technique. A close scrutiny of his scores reveals an almost endless variety of yet subtler means for achieving similar effects, the skill and imagination by which these are devised indicating, as well as any index might, the creative artistry of the composer.

This incongruence and dissynchrony between rhythm and metre on so many levels results in continual imbalance and counterbalancing of forces, maintaining levels and modes of tension at virtually all times. Tension resolved in one way (a cadence, perhaps) will be deflected by other means (a false resolution, a metric displacement). Always tension remains, ever graduated in its intensities and varied in the manner by which it is effected, but always felt and ever functioning. It is notable that structural downbeats—those big moments of full release—are rare in Brahms. When they do occur they are often elided with the following phrase to mitigate their force.

Tension means energy unresolved, and unresolved energy ultimately means forward motion. Indeed, this is the purpose of it all. Motion is the key to the anomalies and the ambiguities we have discussed, and it is the perspective within which these incongruities resolve. What Brahms achieved is a unique kind of musical structure, whose anomalous opposition and counterbalancing of elements build into the music not only the means of forward motion but the means as well for its control, pacing, and ultimate resolution.

This is a remarkable achievement and at the same time a most practical one, for by these means the music in a fundamental sense is performance proof. It can be spoiled in performance in numerous ways (ours, alas, is not a safe profession) but not in one most basic way: its forward motion cannot be destroyed. Let the performer play the notes and the rhythms as they are written and the music must move, since motion in Brahms's scores is not a function of the energy that a player may lend a work; motion is built into the notes themselves, the inevitable product of their structure.

This is not the case in all music, even the finest of music. Works of composers before Brahms have moments when musical motion may flag, the result not of flawed craft, to be sure, but rather because the means for achieving motion are of a different kind, more vulnerable in the hands of unperceptive performers. A passage may rest in temporary harmonic stasis, for example, the focus of interest lying for the moment in other aspects—a by-play of line and colour, perhaps, or an interplay of motives. Given the wrong perspective, these passages risk losing tension in performance, the player failing to understand in which dimension activity prevails, thereby responding to the stasis of harmony and 'dropping the line' as a result. This cannot happen with Brahms. His music is structured with a canny sense for making what must happen inevitably happen, and what must move, move.

The puzzling passages cited earlier in this study make better musical sense in the light of this perspective. In discussing them I quote myself to some extent, with the thought that interested readers can pursue fuller studies of these examples in other of my writings, as there are limitations of time (and space) here.

The ambiguous opening bars of the Second Symphony, first movement, seen in Example 1 cannot be resolved locally, for the ambiguity serves a higher function of large-scale movement. The resolution, as shown in *Beyond Orpheus* (p. 67 ff.), comes at bar 44, where the first structural downbeat arrives and where the music, on a broader level, truly begins to move forward. The first forty-four bars are in fact an extended upbeat resting on dominant harmony—in a sense, a broad introductory phrase. The fuller discussion of this movement in the same book (pp. 162–75) shows numerous ways through which Brahms maintains the balance of tensions by means described earlier. It also points out the remarkable symmetry by which the movement is framed, for the only two unclouded structural downbeats on the tonic are found in the opening, at bar 44, and part-way through the coda, at bar 477, forty-seven bars from the end. With the (supposed) wisdom of hindsight I would further point out, more than a decade after writing *Beyond Orpheus*, that neither of these two downbeats are fully unimpeded. Each is an elision, so that even here the forward impetus of the music is enforced.

Brahms uses a somewhat similar strategy of ambiguity with regard to the epigrammatic phrase that opens the Third Symphony (see Example 5). The uncertain role of this opening figure—whether it is primary or introductory, a true structural downbeat or somehow preliminary—are all played upon at the recapitulation (bars 120 ff.) and at the close of the coda (bars 216 ff.). The initial two-bar figure, with its subsequent elision, is expanded at these places to four bars, also elided, and with these elisions the sense of a structural downbeat is likewise obscured. There is in fact no pure structural downbeat in the movement. Even the final bar is an elision, as are the parallel moments at bars 15 and 136 where large opening phrases of exposition and recapitulation temporarily cadence in F, the tonic.

*Beyond Orpheus* briefly discussed the Intermezzo in A major, Op. 118 No. 2, pointing out that whenever tonic harmony appears in the A sections of this ABA form it is either on a weak beat of the bar, or on the downbeat but in an unstable harmonic inversion or a delayed harmonic resolution. (The illustration is reproduced here as Example 6.) All this, again, embodies the same rhythmic-metric-harmonic approach. Only the sectional cadence places the tonic unambiguously on the downbeat.

Even this cadence is less clear than it may seem; though it is on the downbeat of the bar, the bar itself is the second of a two-bar hypermeasure. The cadence is thus of a weaker nature, and as such it adds a closing touch to the musical affect of the entire piece. There is about this intermezzo a quality of melancholy, or resignation, with which the cadence is thoroughly consistent, its weak or 'resigned' closure making a final statement of a feeling that runs through the work.

The slow movement of the Second Symphony is one of the most stunning examples of this technique of continuous, controlled motion and minimal use of structural downbeats (Example 7). In this case there is but one such downbeat—the final bar of the movement. (It, too, has aspects of an elision.) Cone's insight into the function of a structural downbeat is particularly exciting to contemplate in this instance, for by this perspective the movement in its entirety is seen to be an upbeat to this last bar. One need not know this to play the movement properly; the structure exerts its own control. It is a gripping

EXAMPLE 5. Brahms, Symphony No. 3 in F major, Op. 90, I, bars 1–3, 120–4, 216–24, 14–17.

EXAMPLE 6. Brahms, Intermezzo in A major, Op. 118 No. 2, bars 1–4, 16–20, 27–30, 36–8, 46–8.

EXAMPLE 7. Brahms, Symphony No. 2 in D major, Op. 73, II, bars 1–7, 9–12, 16–18, 31, 33–4, 39, 45, 48–9, 59–60, 72–4, 100–4.

experience, however, to perform the movement with this in mind, for the eloquence of the music is enhanced all the more by the sense of one single long breath.

To be sure, there are moments of respite here. The second thematic group at bar 33 (the movement is in sonata form) is essentially stable, the melodic anticipations creating more a slight lilt than anything else. Counterbalancing this local stability, however, is the large-scale force of tonality, for the passage lies in the dominant, the harmony thus exerting an underlying tension.

Elsewhere virtually every passage reveals the techniques we have discussed. The opening melody sounds as if it begins on a strong pulse, but is displaced to the weakest part of a $\frac{4}{4}$ bar. The long phrase slurs, of course, make all this inaudible. Though there is no question that we are in B major at bar 3, the full resolution of the harmony is delayed until the last and weakest beat of the bar. The cadence on the downbeat at bar 6 is left ambiguous, harmonically, and when harmony is clarified on the following beat it is found not to be the tonic but a 'false' chord instead. Even when the tonic chord does fall on a downbeat, at the beginning of bar 17, it lacks downbeat force, since the metric scheme of the preceding passage is intrinsically unclear. Either the second or the third beats of bar 16 could be heard as strong, with the result that the resolution at bar 17 feels weak or, at best, uncertain in its metric weight. The music continues in like manner, the closing theme in bar 45 both starting a beat 'late' (it feels downbeat-like) and lying on a six-four chord; the new phrase at bar 49 opening on an elision; and so on.

Musicians sometimes ask whether in situations like the opening phrase of this movement metre actually matters at all, since hearing the music without knowledge of the score would give no idea that the phrase is out of phase with the written bar. If we cannot hear the metre, the argument goes, then does it exist in any real sense, since what we perceive through the ear is the ultimate test?

Indeed the metre does exist, and in fact plays an important role at these moments, but only a different perspective can show this. If motion is a quintessential aspect of music, then inflection and articulation are its principal means of effect. For it is by articulation that we convey those ever subtle and varied accents that inflect the features of a structure and in turn allow us to feel the structure in motion. The end result of all this is communication—not necessarily to a trained musician sitting in the audience with a mental picture of the score, but to general listeners who, if attuned to the musical flow, receive its message.

For this communication an audience need know nothing about how music looks in score. The player, however, not only knows how the score reads but is introduced to the music and must contend with it—conceptualize it and struggle with its attributes—in the shape that it is presented in score. Herein lies the point of this important argument: The player cannot help but feel conflicted, if not internally contorted, by the contradictory accents caused by the notation of a phrase and by its metrical displacement. This conflict must inevitably speak through one's instrument, thereby articulating the music with the inflections Brahms meant it to have. Played with these inflections, the music must move—move, in fact, to Brahms's calculated schedule of tensions and intensities.

The flow of movement is thus controlled by Brahms through the unique manner in which he casts the rhythmic and metric structure of his music, often working deliberately against the structural system of his day specifically for this purpose. His control of movement is yet more extensive, however, for Brahms controls as well the *pace* by which this movement proceeds. This control is achieved by a system of structured tempos, a system which acts in complementary fashion to the rhythmic-metric controls by which flow and forward motion are achieved.

The means for this control of tempo is at once simple and yet profound, and it has its roots in the practice of earlier music in European history. Simply put, a steady basic pulse runs continuously throughout a work of Brahms, underlying all segments, sections, and movements of the work and serving as the referential basis—indeed, the temporal module—for explicit changes of tempo. New tempos relate to this basic pulse in such a way that the two tempos can be characterized by simple ratios, ratios made of low-order whole numbers—for the most part 1 : 1, 1 : 2, 2 : 3, 3 : 4, and their inverse.[8]

---

[8] Ratios, rather than 'beat-relation formulas' (e.g. ♩ = ♪ ), are the simplest ways to indicate these proportions. For one thing, the formulas read differently in different eras. ( ♩ = ♪ in Romantic music means ♩ = ♪ ; in our time

This is in fact the principle of the *tactus* found in Renaissance music—that even flow of beats that regulated this music so fully that changes of movement within all parts of a piece were *tactus*-bound through a system of mathematical proportions. Brahms, with his interest and knowledge of Renaissance music, may well have been impressed by the coherence and unity this system provided, for unity and coherence were corner-stones of his own musical ethos. For that matter there is evidence that the tactus concept underlay European music beyond the Renaissance. It may well have prevailed until Brahms's day, though the degree to which this is true remains an open question. To some extent it may have been a musical undercurrent, tacitly assumed by Classical and early Romantic composers. It is discussed explicitly in the writings of some composers and theorists of these years. Certainly this kind of tempo correlation can be demonstrated in the music of this period, as I have done in *Beyond Orpheus*, and as have other writers. There is also growing evidence that time-keeping of this sort is a basic and possibly universal practice, very likely resting upon neurophysiological mechanisms. A forthcoming book of mine deals with historical, structural, and physiological bases of this question in some detail.[9]

The continuous pulse principle is demonstrable in Brahms; there is explicit evidence of it in his scores, as well as implicit indications. As with everything else in this music there are also ambiguities in these scores, as they concern tempo. More than anything else these ambiguities stem from Brahms's use of tempo descriptions, rather than from any innate propensities of the music itself. It is not always clear what Brahms means by certain tempo terms, which in his hands suggest different (often slower) tempos than in the music of his predecessors. More puzzling are the connotations of the adjectives by which he modifies terms for tempo. As often as not these seem to pertain to musical character and gesture more that to speed.

Ambiguous also is Brahms's indication of new tempos, in sections of his works where the underlying pulse in fact remains unchanged. In this, however, lies one of the most subtle and sophisticated aspects of his art. For Brahms often creates the sense of a new tempo by changing the amount of rhythmic activity that takes place within a beat which itself remains constant. He changes as well the character of the music within a new section—altering its articulations, inflection, its total *Gestalt*, without in fact altering the pulse itself. This same technique is used to effect a sense of acceleration or ritard in many passages where, again, the underlying pulse remains unchanged. These moments embody changes of activity within the beat, or even across several beats, the changes frequently characterized by a simple arithmetic progression in the inner rhythmic life of the beat. Thus within a prevalent quarter-note pulse the inner articulations may reduce from

it signifies the reverse and is often written ⟵♩ = ♩⟶. There is a historical 'no-man's land' when the symbols are used both ways.) Ratios also convey more information simply. If we read 'beat' for each number, the ratio indicates how many sub-pulses are prevalent across a change of tempo and how they fit, or nest, within the new beat. Thus 1 : 2 is an obvious doubling of beat length (that is, slowing down to half-speed). A faster tempo of 3 : 2, on the other hand, indicates a sub-pulse that remains constant, regrouped by differing amounts of such sub-pulses to form the new beat.

---

[9] An article that speaks to this subject and which suggests that a continual pulse may be a human universal has already appeared. Cf. 'Tempo Relations: A Cross-Cultural Study', *Music Theory Spectrum* 7 (1985), 34–71.

sixteenths to eighth-triplets to eighth-notes to quarter-notes, the 4 : 3 : 2 : 1 series giving the effect of slowing down.

There are two ways to decelerate or accelerate in time. One is progressively to change the actual duration of successive beats that mark the passage of time. This is the common notion of accelerando or ritardando. To do it well takes artistry of the highest kind, for the continual shrinking or swelling of the beat must convey some miniscule modulus whose step-by-step accretion or deletion gives the series a controlled and graduated character. This rule is probably observed more in the breach that in its obeyance; it also risks the further danger of overshooting its goal, and thereby missing a new tempo that is in 'right' proportion. (Good Romantic rubato playing makes similar demands, and has about as dismal a record of performance success.)

The other approach to acceleration/ritard is the earlier technique described above, which in a way is safer since it provides a stable underlying beat that serves as a control. Especially if the underlying pulse is silent, the effect can be much the same as acceleration/ritard proper, for only the surface of the music is audible, and this surface reflects a graduated change of speed, though its gradations are fewer and less subtle.

There are true fluctuations of pulse in Brahms, to be sure, and there is room for flexibility in his phrasing as well. These occur more in the sense of rubati within a local purview, however; they do not change the underlying structural pulse that gives shape and unity to temporal motion. By retaining this fundamental pulse, and by changing the activity within it, Brahms often achieves the shrinking and swelling of flow and feeling that are characteristic of his music. The tempo plan of the *Academic Festival Overture* in Example 8 is typical of this, the trumpet passage at bar 63 feeling almost static, the section of bar 345 seeming placid and flowing, the phrases at bars 156 and 379 respectively animated and majestic, as Brahms indicates. (The metronome marking, incidentally, is my suggested tempo. Tempo proportions read in the modern style, aligned with the progression of the music. In this work the proportions are all implicit except for the final one, which is Brahms's indication.)

Examples 9–13 list a number of other works where Brahms makes explicit the proportions achieved through a continuous pulse.[10] Note that the pulse of the second tempo in the Romance, Op. 118 No. 5 (*Allegretto grazioso*) is the same as the opening *Andante*. But the second section indeed sounds faster, for it begins with beats filled by eighth-note activity, whereas the quarter-note pulse of the chorale-like opening has no inner motion. The 1 : 1 pulse relationship is indicated by Brahms not at this second section, but just before the return to Tempo 1. In the light of hindsight, we see that the ritard which closes the first section is really a rubato; it leads nowhere, that is, but returns to the ground pulse at the start of the *Allegretto*, albeit to music of different character and motion.

Where Brahms changes tempos through a true alteration of beat duration, he invariably sets up some rhythmic figure prior to the change which serves as the reference

---

[10] The close of the Second Piano Concerto is discussed in *Beyond Orpheus*, 94–5.

EXAMPLE 8. Brahms, *Academic Festival Overture*, Op. 80, bars 1–2, 63–7, 88–9, 156–9, 241–4, 290–1, 345–7, 379–80.

EXAMPLE 9. Brahms, *Tragic Overture*, Op. 81, bars 1–4, 208–9, 264–5.

EXAMPLE 10. Brahms, Symphony No. 2 in D major, Op. 73, III, bars 1–2, 63–4, 101–6, 107–8, 124–5, 126–7, 188–94.

EXAMPLE 11. Brahms, Piano Concerto No. 2 in B♭ major, Op. 83, IV, bars 1–3, 365–6, 377–9.

EXAMPLE 12. Brahms, Intermezzo in A minor, Op. 116 No. 2, bars 1–2, 19–20, 51.

EXAMPLE 13. Brahms, Romance in F major, Op. 118 No. 5, bars 1–2, 17, 45–9.

* Brahms's marking    ** Implicit

for the changed pulse itself. The change is thus composed into the music, so to speak; the durations and proportions are heard and felt, so that in a sense there is no other way for the music to go, so forcefully are the signals felt that shepherd this change. A most vivid example of this is the transition in the *Haydn Variations* from Variation 5 to Variation 6, shown in Example 14. The tempo proportion is 3 : 4, the music obviously riding upon the fast sub-pulse in each motive—the sub-pulse itself remaining at the same speed for both variations.[11]

This passage is an ideal example of implicit tempo relations in Brahms. The tempo in these two sections of the *Haydn Variations* are rarely, if ever, heard other than in this way. Yet this transition, in its characteristic Brahms fashion, is not without its enigmas. For even the most accurate tempo change here can leave one wondering about its accuracy. The doubt stems from the remarkable variety of character between the two variations. The bright sounds and clear, sharp articulations of the winds which speak in the fifth variation are so different from the horns, as they open Variation 6, that the latter music seems cut of other cloth indeed. This perception speaks to the very essence of variation, and may be as good an index as any of Brahms's mastery of composition as musical transformation.

Examples 15–19 show further cases of implicit tempo relations in other works. As with

[11] Tempo relations in the Brahms Haydn Variations have been dealt with in depth by Allen Forte, 'The Structural Origin of Exact *Tempi* in the Brahms–Haydn Variations', and by me, *Beyond Orpheus*, 83–6. Both studies share a number of significant premises, foremost among them, perhaps, that the tempos are proportional and are integrated as part of the basic structural plan of the work. Both studies further agree that the precise specifications of tempos reside in rhythmic/structural aspects of the music, rather than in verbal indications of tempo, which are mainly suggestive. The proportions arise largely from motivic properties of the music. The studies differ in their views of these rhythmic motives, leading to some differences in tempos for particular variations, though much of the tempo plan is seen in common.

EXAMPLE 14. Brahms, *Variations on a Theme by Haydn*, Op. 56, bars 206–7, 264.

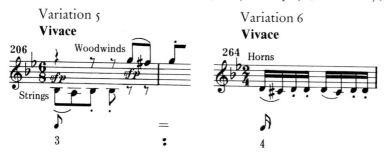

EXAMPLE 15. Brahms, Violin Concerto in D major, Op. 77, III, bars 1–2, 271–2.

the Haydn Variations, each of these instances provides rhythmic clues—or, more properly, signals—which, heard and felt, make almost inevitable the change within the designed proportions. The 1 : 1 correspondence of the motive at the close of the Violin Concerto (Example 15) makes it seemingly impossible to hear this moment otherwise. Both this work and the First Symphony (Example 16) are discussed in *Beyond Orpheus* and reprinted here, as they are such rich examples of this practice. The First Symphony in particular may reward extended study, as it shows Brahms casting and maintaining a time structure of some forty minutes' duration, all based upon the primacy of a basic pulse which modulates by the most careful yet subtle means, so that changes occur through measured, controlled gradations of acceleration or ritard, all of them built into the music. The signals are not always obvious in this case, however. Ones like the brief duplet figure in the cellos prior to the coda of the first movement must be noted through study, or they can easily be missed and the proportions lost. The built-in 'rallentando-without-rallentando' that precedes the *Più Andante* (fourth movement) is another case where the music will play itself if given a chance. But this requires that one understand the function of this movement, which seems to have eluded many performers. More of this later.

The two tempos of the Capriccio in G minor, Op. 116 No. 3 (Example 17) are virtually the same—at most, slight flexible variants of the basic pulse, if even that, which Brahms's two tempo terms themselves suggest. Yet again the second section sounds considerably slower, the result of its totally different character which, not unlike a sober processional, treads a slower pace based on the half-note pulse. The passionate opening, by contrast, virtually throbs with inner activity. This change is carefully prepared through the six or seven bars that precede it. The two half-bar rests not only add force to the (partial)

EXAMPLE 16. Brahms, Symphony No. 1 in C minor, Op. 68.

resolution of the preceding *Steigerung*; they further cut down in one dramatic stroke the inner pulsation that drives the music earlier, in this way introducing still another species of rallentando-without-rallentando: the reduction of inner-beat activity, as suggested in the example, from 4 to 3 sub-pulses to a single, half-bar pulse and, ultimately, to a closing chord that is two pulses long.

The *Più Adagio* of Op. 117 No 1 (Example 18) is really a character indication (that is, 'more broadly') rather than one of tempo, for the two sections of this Intermezzo share the same pulse. Brahms transforms the motion, however, so that the middle section seems to move by quarter-notes (a semi $\frac{3}{4}$). This, together with the sombre character of the music, indeed creates a sense of much slower movement. Wilhelm Kempff, in an eloquent performance thoroughly within the Brahms tradition (DGG record No. LPM 18903) plays the *Andante moderato* at ♩. = 2.00 sec. and the *Più Adagio* at ♩. = 2.20 sec., an increment of 10 per cent. By the criteria of current psycho-acoustical and psycho-physiological research it is doubtful, or at best marginal, whether this degree of change can be perceived.[12] It is, at most, a flexible stretching of the pulse which, within the context of the music, does not disturb the prevalent time structure.[13]

[12] This is confirmed by tests of the Weber fraction, a common standard of psychophysics, by Ernst Mach, 'Untersuchungen über den Zeitsinn des Ohres', and by D. J. Getty, 'Discrimination of Short Temporal Intervals: a Comparison of Two Models'. See also C. D. Creelman, 'Human Discrimination of Auditory Duration'.

[13] In preparing this study I checked by stop-watch Kempff's opening tempos for each of the three intermezzi that constitute Op. 117. They are given below:

| Transition<br>poco a poco | Coda<br>piu tranquillo | IV. Introduction - - - - - - - ⌐<br>Adagio  Più andante ┊ Allegro non troppo | Coda<br>Più allegro |
|---|---|---|---|

♩. = 48–52    ♩ = 64–69    ♩ = 96–104    ♩ = 96–104

|  |  | 2 | : 1½ | : 1 | : | 1 |
|---|---|---|---|---|---|---|
|  |  | 4 | : 3 | : 2 | : | 2] |

2 : 3    : 4 : 3 : 2 : 2

Strings. Winds    Strings    Tutti    Horn    Violin I    Strings. Bassoon

2 = 3    = 4 = 3 = 2 = 2

4 : 5 : 6

** Measure 28

**Adagio**        [4 : 3 Tempo increment]

       **Più andante**

Orchestra

Timpani

Timpani roll equals    unmeasured : 16 : 12    : [8 X 3/4 = 6]

The final Intermezzo of Op. 117 (Example 19) employs tempo constructs similar to those seen in earlier examples. A common pulse underlies all sections of the piece, but by changes of musical character now familiar to this discussion three distinct tempo 'families' are arrived at. A pulse of M.M. *c.* 80 works well in this piece, but different rhythmic units embody this pulse. The somewhat brooding opening *Andante con moto*

| Op. 117, No.: | 1 | 2 | 3 |
|---|---|---|---|
| Tempo: | Andante moderato | Andante non troppo<br>con molto espressione | Andante con moto |
| Metre: | 6/8 | 3/8 | 2/4 |
| Pulse: | ♩. = 2.00 sec. | ♩. = 2.23 sec. | ♩ = 2.26 sec. |
| Pulse in metronome equivalent: | 30 | 27 | 27 |

The tempos suggest an extension of this time concept: they reveal the entire opus as perhaps a unified work springing from a common pulse. Very likely there are other facets of unity of a *Grundgestalt* nature as well; one can almost predict this from our existing knowledge of Brahms and his compositional thinking. The correlated tempos would certainly play a large role in this unification, the more so as they serve as ground pulses, within which the individual works impose many different rhythmic constructs. Compare also George Bozarth's observations, in his paper in the present volume, about the common poetic inspiration of the first two intermezzi.

EXAMPLE 17. Brahms, Capriccio in G minor, Op. 116 No. 3, bars 1–2, 28–36.

EXAMPLE 18. Brahms, Intermezzo in E♭ major, Op. 117 No. 1, bars 1–2, 21–2, 37–8.

EXAMPLE 19. Brahms, Intermezzo in C# minor, Op. 117 No. 3, bars 1–2, 39–47.

moves via the eighth-note, while the flowing *Più mosso ed espressivo* of the middle section moves by the quarter-note. The intermediary in this transition is the *Poco più lento* that ends the first section (and the entire piece as well). This is another of those passages in which Brahms works his tempo modulation by creating music that indeed seems slower, as he indicates, though its ground structure is not truly slower. The ritard that precedes the *Poco più lento* helps this effect, for it does not actually ritard but acts more like a rubato, leading to the *Poco più lento* whose slowness lies in its slower inner rhythmic life. Sixteenth-note inner motion in the beginning section now gives way to true eighth-note movement, so that the *Poco più lento* indeed sounds much slower, though it basically moves at ♪ = *c.* 80. The transition to the faster *Più mosso* is likewise smoothed out by the long fermata that precedes it, which effectively takes any sense of beat out of the picture, thus making less clear what pulse does in fact prevail when the music gets under way once more in the new tempo.

The recapitulation of the slow movement of the Third Symphony (Example 20) is another place where Brahms, this time on a large time-scale, creates a sense of broadening, if not an outright rallentando, when in fact there is no actual change of speed. The broadening effect here is powerful, perhaps due to the massed sounds of a symphony orchestra and the wide spectrum of sonorities it can create. So powerful is this effect that the closing segment of the section in fact suggests a different tempo, though this is not the case.

What begins the movement as a simple folk-like melody, flowing in quarter-note motion, becomes enlivened by sixteenth-note motion in its repetition at bar 24. Brahms initiates the disguised recapitulation with this faster motion, gradually reducing the inner life of successive themes to triplets, eighth-note, quarter- and half-note motion by the start of the closing theme at bar 115. A pause in bar 115, just before this closing theme, is used to the same effect as we have seen elsewhere: it gently interrupts the motion, and confuses slightly the sense of what inner pulse the music may actually be riding upon at this moment.[14]

The process to this point is the familiar one of inner sub-pulse reduction by the series 4 : 3 : 2 : 1 [:½] that we have seen elsewhere. Its effect is to create a sense of time at the closing section (bar 115 ff.) that feels slower than it actually is. By contrast to the passages that precede this point, one may sense here almost no motion for a brief moment. This is a place where some conductors actually *do* slow down the tempo, with the disastrous result of truly destroying the pulse that underlies and structures the entire movement. Not only is this unnecessary (Brahms has already provided for the effect); it hurts the performance. A perspective of the entire movement, rather than a local purview of this moment alone, makes such a distortion virtually unviable.

There are places in Brahms's works where the tempo actually does change—where the

---

[14] The reduction of speed in sub-pulses is somewhat mixed in the segment beginning at a bar 108. The inner voices retain a prior triplet figure; however, the melody (violins) and countermelody (cellos and basses) contain primarily eighth-note and quarter-note rhythms. All of this leads to the theme at bar 115, where the pulse embodies the feel of the quarter- and/or half-note.

EXAMPLE 20. Brahms, Symphony No. 3 in F major, Op. 90, II, bars 1, 24, 84–5, 100–1, 106–9, 115–17.

duration of the beat, that is, is altered to become longer or shorter. This of course is the complementary process to that which we have been discussing, which has shown an *apparent* change in the passage of time created *within* an unchanging pulse. In places where the beat truly changes, the seamless sense of sectional linkage and of time flow is maintained by a true rallentando or accelerando; or, it may be effected by the psychological sense of such a gradual change, created within the confines of a steady beat by the technique we have just studied. The difference at these new places is one of purpose: the techniques serve to link real alterations of beat. The care that Brahms lavished upon these passages, to ensure that in performance they would flow as he wished, is further evidence of the depth to which his craft served nuances of expression.

Two instances of this time usage are shown here. One is the First Piano Concerto; the other is the First Symphony, seen in Example 16. The symphony is one of the most impressive temporal constructs in the Brahms repertoire, maintaining an underlying pulse for well over forty minutes' playing time, and modifying this pulse through subtle means that make its changes appear either to change not at all or, at most, to seem a mere expressive flexibility—when, that is, the music is played as indicated.

This aspect of the symphony is discussed in *Beyond Orpheus* (pp. 91–4) with detail not possible in these pages. We can however look at several tempo changes here. One is the transition, via the coda of the first movement, to the second movement. The slower movement is twice as slow as the first (that is, 1 : 2—or 2 : 4). Brahms uses the coda to modify the sense of this forthcoming change. It is a subtle use of transition, and even its arrival is created by subtle means. Shortly before the coda an unobtrusive cello figure moving in the prevalent $\frac{6}{8}$ pattern (it is, in fact, the extension of a motive heard just previously) reduces to duplets within the beat, and then to one note per beat, all this accompanied by a diminuendo. The effect is of broadening, without true broadening actually happening. The duplets serve a further function as well: they occur just before the new, slower tempo and serve as the basis for the new eighth-note pulse at the *Meno allegro*, heard in horns and timpani. (This new pulse, too, is motivic, recalling the opening of the symphony. Motive and tempo are inextricably bound in Brahms's scores.) The tempo thus slows by ratio of 2 : 3, and the slower pulse, if extended to 4 sub-pulses, provides the tempo of the second movement (2 : 3 : 4)—its tempo thus twice as long as in the first movement.[15]

The rest of the symphony follows a somewhat similar plan. The third movement is twice as fast as the second, thus reverting to the original tempo. Its coda (*Più tranquillo*), as with the first movement, serves as a transition, in this case to the *Adagio* that introduces the final movement, whose tempo is twice as slow as the third movement. The coda of the third movement thus mediates the 1 : 2 (or 2 : 4) relationship between these last two movements, its interpolation extending the ratio 2 : 3 : 4. This is shown in Example 16, the means for this series inhering in the rhythmic figures of the music. Even

[15] Herbert von Karajan, whose conception of the symphony follows Brahms's tempo scheme described here, varies in one interesting and rich respect: his tempo for the second movement is the same as that of the coda in the first movement. The closing pulse of the coda thus carries across to the second movement, resulting in an appropriate and somewhat flexible tempo for the later movement. Triplets played pizzicato in the lower strings at the close of the second movement provide the rhythmic cipher for the transition to the third movement, for two of these three triplet notes provide the new tempo of the third movement (thus a return to Tempo I via 3 : 2).

There is a lovely unity to this conception, particularly at this transition between the second and third movements, for the pizzicato triplets not only effect the tempo change but carry across these two movements a similar musical effect, since the third movement begins with similar pizzicato motion in the same lower strings.

the transition to the coda itself follows a similar series (that is, 2 : 3, or 4 : 5 : 6). This short transition, indicated *poco a poco* over the space of two bars, allows the conductor to increase the sixteenth-note sub-pulses bar by bar from 4 to 5 to 6, at which point the coda has arrived. (This incremental inner count may seem complex, but in reality happens quite naturally.)

Most impressive is the final reduction of tempo within the introduction of the final movement, arriving at the *Allegro non troppo* via a 4 : 3 : 2 series (see again Example 16). The rhythmic cipher for the transition to *Più andante* at bars 28–30 is the syncopated figure shown in the example, which sounds for only three-quarters of the beat. It thus embodies the beat duration for the following section (that is, a transition via 4 : 3). Again, to ease the moment of transition, Brahms has the timpani effect a psychological transition across this break (bars 28–30), reducing the number of timpani strokes progressively from an unmeasured fast trill to sixteen to twelve strokes. Clearly what is happening here is another of the 4 : 3 : 2 reductions we have seen before. Following this formula to its conclusion, the timpanist should go from twelve to eight strokes in the new tempo. However, since the new beat is three-quarters as long as the former beat, the strokes must likewise be reduced in number: $\frac{3}{4} \times 8 = 6$, which explains why timpani and violins in the new tempo play sextuplets.

The First Piano Concerto, in its first movement exposition, makes a tempo transition from first to second group by similar means (Example 21). Six bars before the change the music begins one of Brahms's broadenings-without-change-of-beat. The orchestra moves from music which up till now has had prominent sub-pulses by threes, to a bar of an implied $\frac{3}{2}$ half-note beat (the hemiola, bar 153) to a calmer dotted half-note pulse, and finally to a pulseless sustained chord (the final two bars of the old tempo). The solo piano during the last three bars of this transition creates its own sense of rallentando by similar means, moving from nine notes to the dotted half-note (the prevalent pulse) to six eighth-notes in the final bar. These six notes themselves can be heard two ways, as the example shows, the first group of six being 2 x 3, thus following the prevalent inner pulse, and the second group being 3 x 2. 3 x 2 produces a dotted-quarter inner pulse; the beat feels divided in two, and this new dotted-quarter pulse becomes the natural new tempo for the second group (*Poco più moderato*). The ratio of the two related tempos (Tempo I and *Poco più moderato*), established by the change of inner sub-pulses at the transition, can be seen in several ways. In terms of the length of the dotted half-note in each section, the ratio is 2:3 (i.e., the new section is slower, its dotted half-note longer). The *Poco più moderato*, however, moves by the quarter-note, whereas Tempo I moves by the dotted half-note. The quarter-note in the new tempo is actually faster than the dotted half-note by a ratio of 2:1—that is, half the old pulse of dotted half-note equals the new quarter-note.

The return to Tempo I at bar 226 is most easily felt by reversing the 2:1 ratio defined above. In effect, the returning pulse of Tempo I (dotted half-note) is twice as slow as the quarter-note by which Tempo II moved. Simply doubling the beat provides the returning pulse of Tempo I.

EXAMPLE 21.  Brahms, Piano Concerto No. 1 in D minor, Op. 15, I, 151–7.

*Solo in 4 octaves

Brahms beclouds this fact, however, by making unclear what the true pulse is at the return of Tempo I. As shown in the example, the new rhythmic figure in the piano at bar 226 can be heard either in terms of the quarter-note, the half-note (thus a $\frac{3}{2}$ meter), or the dotted half-note ($\frac{6}{4}$). The passage emanates from the almost pulseless cadence (b. 224–5), and Brahms retains the metrical ambiguity in the arpeggios of the solo piano, which are grouped in $\frac{3}{2}$ patterns for several bars before reverting to a clear $\frac{6}{4}$. Ambiguity here helps to create a seamless joint to a clear $\frac{6}{4}$. The 'real' development section begins at bar 231 with the return of the opening theme. The intervening five bars are a transition, but not a simple one. Added to the mix is Brahms's extension here to two bars of the one-bar D pedal that opens the concerto. This tonic pedal, at the outset of the concerto, leaves unclear where the 'real' downbeat is—is it on the tonic D, or at the entrance of the 'real' theme a bar later (the Third Symphony paradigm)? The extension of this D pedal to two bars here plays to a further degree with this thematic-ambiguity-within-phrase-ambiguity-within-temporal-ambiguity.

A discussion of the Intermezzo in E minor, Op. 119 No. 2, will close this paper. The work, as viewed in the autograph copy[16] and the published version, presents insights into Brahms's working procedures and his creative perceptions (Example 22). In this case there seems to have been a somewhat puzzled perception, which only heightens the interest of this evidence.

Brahms seems to have had some difficulty either understanding an aspect of tempo in this work or deciding how best to convey it. The autograph shows an original tempo of *Allegretto un poco agitato*, with the word *Allegretto* crossed out and *Andantino* put in its place. For the middle section Brahms originally wrote in the autograph: ( ♪ = ♪ ) *il doppio Movimento*. In the published score, however, he abandoned the *doppio Movimento* marking *in toto*, together with the relationship formula, in favour of the indication *Andantino grazioso*.

---

[16] See the facsimile of this manuscript, now owned by Dr Friedrich G. Zeileis, Gallsbach, Austria, in *Johannes Brahms, Intermezzi Opus 119 Nr. 2 und 3*.

The difference between *Allegretto* and *Andantino* in the opening tempo would seem more a matter of nuance and character than of clock speed. This may well have been a question, then, of how best to convey a sense of movement already clear in Brahms's own mind. But what do we make of the *doppio Movimento* formula? Convention in Brahms's day dictated that this indication, with the pulse relationship written as it was, meant that the second section should go twice as fast as the first. This is offensive aesthetically and, in the second strain of section II, almost impossible technically. Could Brahms in a momentary lapse have meant it the other way around—section I twice as fast as section II? Very unlikely, in view of a slower tempo marking of *Andantino* substituted for *Allegretto*, and equally unlikely as this tempo, too, is offensive aesthetically and technically. What then of the removal of the *doppio Movimento* tempo direction? Is this mere secrecy—a retention of this new tempo, together with the thought that it is better left implicit? Unlikely, in view of the objections already noted. A final possibility: should section II be twice as *slow* as section I? Also unlikely, as this yields an impossibly slow tempo.

The decisions we are discussing here are post-compositional ones—editorial decisions, not decisions of creation. Nothing basic to the structure of the music is changed between the autograph and the printed score, with the exception of these tempo markings. These markings thus had to be ones to communicate, via the score, music already given life and shape. For compositional ideas conceived on Brahms's level would not allow of pushing and pulling by tempo factors as great as doubling. The compositional *Gestalt* was too complete, too many-faceted. A gross alteration in tempo would have required other major surgery to work out musical ideas successfully, and this would have yielded a piece different in substantial ways from the Op. 119 No. 2 that we know.

Brahms's perception *was* right in a basic and important sense, and what these markings indicate is a search, as part of the later stages of composition, to pin-point the perception of his own creation so that it might be accurately conveyed. The term *doppio* that Brahms originally penned concerned this perception. For something *is* doubled in this second section, though it is not tempo (Brahms rightly withdrew this tempo indication): it is the time frame of the theme in the second section. This theme is an augmentation, by a factor of two, of the theme heard in the opening phrases.

Thematic transformation was a hallmark of Brahms's technique, used true to form in this work.[17] The second section changes character, harmonic mode (minor to major), and inner sense of motion (prevalent sixteenth-note sub-pulses give way to eighth-notes). These latter augmentations only work, however, if the basic pulse of the music remains constant. $\musQuarter = \musQuarter$ is thus the true formula for the tempos; the pulse relates as 1 : 1. In keeping with his own practice, Brahms leads up to this augmentation in the second section by virtually augmenting the three bars preceding the section. The first two of these bars are as much a large $\frac{3}{2}$ bar as they are hemiola, and the last bar before the change virtually stops

---

[17] For a discussion of thematic transformation in Brahms's music, see Walter Frisch, *Brahms and the Principle of Developing Variation*, particularly Ch. 2.

EXAMPLE 22. Brahms, Intermezzo in E minor, Op. 119 No. 2, bars 1–2, 33–7.

\* In autograph, *Allegretto* (un poco agitato) was
crossed out and *Andantino* (un poco agitato)
was substituted.

\*\* Brahms's original marking (autograph),
subsequently abandoned

Phrase comparison

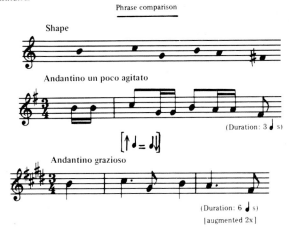

the tempo flow, thus cementing the seamless transition one degree more. Example 22 shows these details.

Seen in this light all becomes clear concerning the final version. The tempo indications—*Andantino un poco agitato* and *Andantino grazioso*—accurately convey a sense of character variance worked upon the same fundamental beat. Withdrawing the equivalence formula (even had it been changed to a correct one) was the right decision by Brahms's standards, for there was no need for it. The music spoke its own right tempo. This perception is further vindicated by the return at the coda of the seemingly slower E major melody from the middle section. No change of tempo is indicated, yet the melody at the coda plays at the same tempo that it had earlier—a function of the unchanging pulse that underlies the entire Intermezzo.

There is a turned-inward quality about Brahms, in his music and in what we know of his personality and his life, that must be evident to any sensitive, perceptive listener. At times it seems almost a secretive husbanding of privacy that shows up even in some actions Brahms took with regard to his music.

To be sure this is not the only side of the rich and complex personality that was Brahms. Yet aspects of Brahms's life and music substantiate this perception: the somewhat melancholy feeling of many works; the composer's unsuccessful yearning for a love relationship which his shyness in part seems to have placed beyond his grasp; his enigmatic and occasionally self-deprecating modesty, particularly about his music ('the long terror' was his description of the Second Piano Concerto, played on two pianos shortly after its completion to 'the victims Billroth and Hanslick';[18] 'this quite worthless rubbish' was his characterization of the Op. 76 Intermezzi and the Op. 74 motets).[19]

The composer's actions with regard to his music further add to this impression of quasi-secrecy, or at times curious lack of certainty. Brahms destroyed many manuscripts of his music late in his life, especially sketches and first drafts. Nor were some performance instructions always firm. The metronome marking of $\downarrow$. = 58 appears at the start of the First Piano Concerto in Brahms's autograph score, but was not carried over into the first edition.[20] Many of his piano works, some of them studied here, lack specific indications of tempo or tempo relationships. Even the Intermezzo, Op. 119 No. 2, which gave him troubles in this respect, as we have just seen, omitted a guide to tempo proportions once the enigma was solved; that very guide was in fact struck from the score.

One can make many things of the incidents in Brahms's life as they indicate his personality. It would be a mistake, however, to view the biographical, as it relates to Brahms's music, purely as suggesting secretiveness in the sense of a possessive or

---

[18] Quoted in Karl Geiringer, *Brahms, His Life and Work*, 147.

[19] Ibid., 134.

[20] Related by Paul Badura-Skoda in his *Revisionsbericht* for the 1963 Eulenberg edition of the score, p. iii. This manuscript is owned by the Deutsche Staatsbibliothek, Berlin; for a facsimile of the initial page of this score, see Carl Dahlhaus, *Johannes Brahms—Klavierkonzert Nr. 1 d-moll, Op. 15*, after p. 16.

unsociable desire for privacy. Another key to these actions suggests itself, one with richer implications for compositional craft and the relationship of composer to score to performer and performance.

Brahms may well have realized the need to structure his music, and to communicate it via score, in such a way that a performance must follow somewhat inevitably along the lines that he wished. Obviously no score can do this for all aspects of music; all composers must depend upon tradition, a common musical code, and numerous other circumstances to guarantee the ideal performance, if such a thing even exists. But in the domain of motion—that all-important envelope in which so much of musical structure, detail, nuance are wrapped—Brahms seems to have found a unique way to achieve his wishes. Part of this way, as we have seen here, was to turn the rhythmic and metric system of his era to his own ends, enigmatic though they appear, so that the music must flow to predestined conclusions if the notes are played as indicated. Likewise he seems to have relied upon the power of his music to suggest its character, and hence its proper tempo and changes of tempo. The fewer the mechanical indications like metronome markings the better, this approach would seem to say, for such exact marks have about them a false precision and a sense of eternal authority that may only divert a musician's attention from an intuitive perception of the music—a perception that strikes deeper at central concerns and carries him further into the special world of a work. By the same token the less said about the origins of musical ideas the better—they can only divert attention from the music in its final form as it enters the world at large. Thus, perhaps, the reason for destroying sketches, manuscripts, and drafts, for these are private matters of the composer's workshop. Doubtless, too, Brahms's experience as pianist and conductor contributed to a sense of the performer's psychology and needs, though in depriving us of the unique insights of manuscripts and sketches it remains an open question whether Brahms's goals were, ultimately, most richly served.

There is no 'hard proof' of this attitude, obviously. Brahms left us no written tract on the matter. Nor would he have, if this attitude was in fact his, for to do so would have contradicted the stance itself. (But this now has us reasoning in a circle.) Yet the approach seems implicit in all that we have seen in his scores, not leastwise in the building in of controls for the forward movement of the music and the modulation of its tempos. A measure of Brahms's success with this approach, as one musician at least observes the musical world about him, is the relative consistency in tempos and in musical motion that one hears in performances of Brahms's music—by comparison, at least, with much else in the great repertoire of the Classic-Romantic era.

We have dealt with enigmas and ambiguities in this paper, each of them yielding answers on higher levels of resolution. It would seem that even this question of general compositional approach can only be resolved on the yet higher level of Brahms's personality, and on the unstated premises by which Brahms worked out his compositional reasoning. These premises themselves must remain partly enigmatic, in the absence of a doctrine, a manifesto, a definitive statement. Thus the enigmas of Brahms continue, on ever higher levels, with ever richer perspectives. It would have been enough if Brahms, like many major composers, had left us no more that the magnificent body of music that was his life's work. He did far more that this, however, as the enigmatic aspects of his music suggest. Brahms saw deeply into the structural possibilities inherent in the system of tonality—the system that was the basis for his music and that of the European tradition. His extensions, revisions, and reworkings of that system, and the effects these had upon musical motion and affect, left us with a new and richer view of the possibilities inherent within this system—and within music itself.

# BRAHMS AS EDITOR

# BRAHMS'S EDITION OF TWENTY SCHUBERT LÄNDLER: AN ESSAY IN CRITICISM

## DAVID BRODBECK

THE 1860s were kind to Schubert. A new generation of Schubertians came of age in Vienna, unearthing works and offering the public a variety of performances and publications. During this decade Heinrich Kreissle released his pioneering biography of Schubert, Gustav Nottebohm began work on his thematic catalogue of the composer's works, and Johann Herbeck programmed many lost and forgotten works, most notably the 'Unfinished' Symphony. Johannes Brahms, who visited Vienna for the first time between September 1862 and May 1863, was no mere bystander to these events. His early experience of the city was scarcely separable from his long-held interest in the music of her native son. As he put it to Adolf Schubring in March 1863, Vienna was filled with 'the sacred memory of the great musicians whose lives and work are brought daily to our minds. In the case of Schubert especially one has the impression of his being still alive. Again and again one meets people who talk of him as a good friend; again and again one comes across new works, the existence of which was unknown'.[1]

Brahms was enraptured by these new works. In a letter to his publisher Rieter-Biedermann he wrote that they provided him with his 'most beautiful hours' in Vienna. Yet, he continued,

as enjoyable and pleasurable as it is to examine them, almost everything else about them is as sad. Thus, for example, I have many things here in manuscript that belong to [the publisher C. A.] Spina or [to Schubert's nephew Eduard] Schneider and of which there is nothing other than the manuscripts—no single copies!—and at Spina's the things are no more kept in a fireproof case than [they are] here . . . How many other things are scattered here and there in the hands of private individuals, who either guard their treasures like dragons, or carelessly let them disappear.[2]

[1] '. . . das heilige Gedächtnis der großen Musiker, an deren Leben und Schaffen hier man täglich erinnert wird. Da ist nun besonders Schubert, bei dem man die Empfindung hat, als lebte er noch! Immer neue Menschen lernt man kennen, die von ihm als einem guten Bekannten sprechen, und immer neue Werke sieht man, von deren Existenz man nichts wußte, und die so unberührt sind, daß man den Sand abscheuern könnte.' Brahms-Briefwechsel, 8: 196–7; translated in Karl Geiringer, Brahms: His Life and Works, 353.

[2] Überhaupt verdanke ich die schönsten Stunden hier ungedruckten Werken von Schubert, deren ich eine ganze Anzahl im Manuskript zuhause habe. So genußvoll und erfreuend aber ihre Betrachtung ist, so traurig ist fast alles, was sonst daran hängt. So z. B. habe ich viele Sachen hier im Manuskript, die Spina oder Schneider gehören, und von denen es nichts weiter als das Manuskript gibt, keine einzige Kopie! und die Sachen werden bei Spina so wenig als bei mir in einem feuerfesten Schrank aufbewahrt . . . Wie viel Sachen sind zerstreut, da und dort bei Privatleuten, die entweder ihren Schatz wie Drachen hüten oder sorglos verschwinden lassen.' Ibid., 14: 77.

Brahms's devotion to Schubert is revealed in more poetic terms in a second letter to Schubring, written in June 1863:

My love for Schubert is a serious one, precisely because it it not a passing fancy.

Where is [there] a genius like his, which soars so boldly and certainly to the heavens, where we see only the greatest few enthroned? He seems to me [to be] like a young god who plays with Jupiter's thunder and handles it a bit oddly now and then. But he plays in such a region, at such a height, to which others do not soar for long. . . .

Now, I hope, we will soon have a chat here about this loved one of the gods.[3]

Private sentiments were soon translated into public action, beginning in 1864 with the publication by Spina of Schubert's *12 Ländler*, Op. 171 (D. 790). Its anonymous editor was none other than the young Brahms, who based his edition upon an autograph of the dances drawn from the rich trove of Schubertiana that he had been adding to his private library since his arrival in Vienna.[4] The Ländler were well received, and in June 1865 Brahms revealed plans for a second collection. To Schubring he reported that he might soon publish some of the other dances at his disposal, since his friends found them to be 'great fun'.[5] But these friends would have to be patient. Even in January 1869, when after nearly four years the dances came up again in Brahms's correspondence, now with the Leipzig publisher Bartholf Senff, the would-be editor was not prepared to deliver them to the press: 'I still have unpublished "dances" [by Schubert], but the manuscripts [are] not ready'.[6] In the ensuing months, however, Brahms did prepare a collection, and finally in May 1869 his friend J. P. Gotthard, a former employee of Spina who had recently set up his own publishing enterprise in Vienna, released the set under the title *20 Ländler für Pianoforte . . . von Franz Schubert (Nachgelassenes Werk)*. The edition noted,

---

[3] 'Meine Schubertliebe ist eine sehr ernsthafte, wohl grade, weil sie nicht flüchtige Hitze ist. Wo ist ein Genie wie seines, das sich so kühn und sicher zu dem Himmel aufschwingt, wo wir dann die wenigen Ersten thronen sehen. Er kommt mir vor wie ein Götterjüngling, der mit dem Donner des Jupiters spielt, also auch gelegentlich ihn absonderlich handhabt. Aber so spielt er in einer Region, in einer Höhe, zu der sich die andern lange nicht aufschwingen . . . Nun, ich hoffe, wir plaudern hier nächstens über diesen Liebling der Götter.' Ibid., 8: 199–200.

[4] Brahms's activity as an editor of Schubert's dances is discussed in my Ph.D. dissertation, 'Brahms as Editor and Composer: His Two Editions of Ländler by Schubert and His First Two Cycles of Waltzes, Opera 39 and 52'; parts of the present essay have been adapted from that study. On Brahms's edition of the *12 Ländler*, see also my article 'Dance Music as High Art: Schubert's Twelve Ländler, Op. 171 (D. 790)'.

In addition to the *12 Ländler* just cited and the *20 Ländler* to be discussed presently, Brahms anonymously prepared the first editions of four other Schubert works: a piano score of the Mass in E♭ major, D. 950 (J. Rieter-Biedermann, 1865), the *Drei Clavierstücke*, D. 946 (J. Rieter-Biedermann, 1868), the 'Quartett-Satz' in C minor, D. 703 (B. Senff, 1870), and the song 'Der Strom', D. 565 (E. W. Fritzsch, 1877). Later he figured prominently in the preparation of the first Schubert *Gesamtausgabe*, for which he edited the two volumes of symphonies in the mid-1880s. On Brahms's relationship with the music of Schubert, also see Robert Pascall, 'Brahms and Schubert', and James Webster, 'Schubert's Sonata Form and Brahms's First Maturity'.

[5] 'Ich habe übrigens mehr der Art von ihm und—auch selbst eine Portion, von denen ich vermutlich, da sie den Freunden gar so gut Spaß machen, den Sommer herausgeben werde.' *Brahms Briefwechsel*, 8: 207.

[6] ' "Tänze" [von Schubert] habe ich noch ungedruckte, doch die Manuskripte nicht zur Hand.' *Brahms Briefwechsel*, 14: 171.

confusingly, as we shall see, that 'Die Original-Handschrift besitzt Hr. Johannes Brahms', but, as before, Brahms's *editorial* work was done anonymously.[7]

Gotthard published the dances simultaneously in arrangements for piano solo and duet. The two-hand edition contains the annotation 'N.º 17 bis 20 nach den Schubert'schen vierhändigen Originalien für zwei Hände eingerichtet'; the four-hand edition contains the correlate: 'N.º 1 bis 16 nach [den] Schubert'schen zweihändigen Originalien für vier Hände eingerichtet.'[8] But these notes give only a hint of the diverse provenances of the dances, which Schubert had written over a period of several years.[9] In this regard, a fundamental difference between Brahms's two editions is evident. By contrast to the *12 Ländler*, whose dances Brahms sent to the press in 1864 exactly as Schubert had left them in a single manuscript, the edition of 1869 comprises twenty Ländler culled from many dances in different sources. In other words, the integrity of the second print stems not from the composer, Schubert, but from the editor, Brahms. This story has several parts. We may begin by linking Brahms to the various sources upon which the edition was based.

---

[7] For complete bibliographical information, see Kurt Hofmann, *Die Erstdrucke der Werke von Johannes Brahms*, 328–31 and Margit L. McCorkle, *Johannes Brahms Thematisch-Bibliographisches Werkverzeichnis*, 624–7. The first edition is reproduced in Brodbeck, 'Brahms as Editor and composer', 275–83. Brahms's editorial involvement is noted, with little additional comment, in Max Kalbeck, *Johannes Brahms*, 1: 278; Otto Erich Deutsch, 'The First Editions of Brahms', 272; and Maurice J. E. Brown, 'The Dance-Music Manuscripts', 231–2.

[8] Knowing that four of the twenty dances were originally duets may explain the erroneous announcement of the edition on 26 May 1869: '24 (bisher ungedruckte) Ländler für Pianoforte zu zwei und vier Händen' (*Allgemeine musikalische Zeitung* 4 [1869]: 168). It seems likely that the number of duets was inadvertently added to the total number of dances to give a sum of twenty-four. According to Gustav Nottebohm (*Thematisches Verzeichniss der im Druck erschienenen Werke von Franz Schubert*, 214), it was Gotthard who made the arrangements. But since Nottebohm respected Brahms's anonymity concerning all other editorial matters, there is reason to believe that in this instance, too, he was merely being tactful. In any case, in 1934 Georg Kinsky published an edition of four-hand dances by Schubert including '11 von J. Br. für vier Hände gesetzten Ländlern', which he took from a copy by Brahms's friend Hermann Levi (Schott Edition, No. 2338; the present location of the Levi manuscript is unknown). These dances are Nos. 1–6, 8–10, 12 and 13 from Brahms's edition (that is, eleven of the sixteen original two-hand pieces). Deutsch, who was not cognizant of the duo edition of 1869, thus assumed that the 1934 print was the first edition of Brahms's four-hand arrangements ('First Editions of Brahms', 271). Brown, who likewise did not know the four-hand edition of 1869, thought that the four original duets (Nos. 17–20) were first published in a supplementary volume of Schubert's four-hand music released by Peters in 1870 ('Dance-Music Manuscripts', 240).

[9] In his thematic catalogue Deutsch assigned the number 366 to the dances in genuine two-hand versions, and the number 814 to the works composed for piano duet, indicating respective years of composition of 1816 and 1824. Schubert arranged the first of the duets as a solo piece for inclusion in a *Sammeldruck* published in December 1824; this dance thus appears twice in Deutsch's catalogue—as D. 366/17 and D. 814/1. Although the appearance of the four duets in a manuscript dated July 1824 (B. 51) justifies their being designated D. 814, the specification of the solo works is rather less felicitous. Several of the dances in D. 366 stem from the years 1819–24, and none can be assigned with confidence to the year 1816. The incipit of D. 366/16 appears with those of several other dances on the back of the autograph of the arietta 'La pastorella al prato', D.528, which is dated January 1817 (B.20); but the dances and the vocal piece constitute separate layers and thus need not have been written in temporal proximity. Indeed, one of the other incipits is of the famous 'Trauerwalzer', D. 365/2, which occurs in complete form in two manuscripts dated March 1818 (B. 25 and B. 26). As Brown observed ('Dance-Music Manuscripts', 219), these incipits probably represent an early effort to gather dances into a publishable collection; it is doubtful that Schubert had such a goal as early as 1816.

TABLE I. *20 Ländler*

| | Key | Source[a] B. 34 | B. 52 | B. 51 | B. 28 | B. 30 | B major copy | Date |
|---|---|---|---|---|---|---|---|---|
| 1 | A | 20 | | | | | | 1819–20 |
| 2 | A | | | 11 | | | | July 1824 |
| 3 | a | | | 13 | | | | July 1824 |
| 4 | a | | | 1 | | | | July 1824 |
| 5 | a | | | 14 | | | | July 1824 |
| 6 | C | | 4 | | | | | 1823–4 |
| 7 | G | | | | 1 | | | 1821–3 |
| 8 | D | | | 12 | | | | July 1824 |
| 9 | B | 13 | | | | | | 1819–20 |
| 10 | b | 15 | | | | | | 1819–20 |
| 11 | B | | | | | | 2 | ᵇ |
| 12 | eb | | | 4 | | | | July 1824 |
| 13 | bb | | 3 | | | | | 1823–4 |
| 14 | Db | | | | 4 | | | 1821–3 |
| 15 | Db | | | | 5 | | | 1821–3 |
| 16 | Ab | | | | | 6 | | ᵇ |
| 17 | Eb | | | 5 | | | | July 1824 |
| 18 | Ab | | | 6 | | | | July 1824 |
| 19 | c | | | 7 | | | | July 1824 |
| 20 | C | | | 8 | | | | July 1824 |
| TOTAL | | 3 | 2 | 10 | 3 | 1 | 1 | |

*Note:* Brahms's editorial work was done anonymously; the title page reads simply: *20 Ländler / für / Pianoforte . . . / von / Franz Schubert / (Nachgelassenes Werk) / Wien, 1869, bei J. P. Gotthard.*

ᵃ The columnar numbers indicate the position of the dances within the various sources.

ᵇ This copy contains works published in Op. 9, whose date of publication (Nov. 1821) provides a probable *terminus ad quem*.

# I

Table 1 summarizes information concerning the sources Brahms used, suggests dates for them, and gives the keys of the twenty dances. (Hereafter several manuscripts will be identified by their registration in Maurice J. E. Brown's inventory of Schubert's dance autographs.[10]) The first manuscript (B. 34) is undated, but on the basis of its paper type can be assigned to the months of October 1819 to January 1820. From among the nine unpublished dances of this large collection, Brahms chose three for his edition. The second manuscript, an undated leaf containing four dances (B. 52), provided the editor

---

10 'Dance-Music Manuscripts', 217–43.

with two other numbers; datable concordant sources suggest that Schubert wrote this manuscript in 1823 or 1824.[11]

Both of these autographs were among the many treasures that Brahms bequeathed to the Gesellschaft der Musikfreunde.[12] The editor's connection with the third manuscript (B. 51), written at the Esterházy estate in Zeléz in July 1824, is less obvious. This source eventually passed into the hands of Helene Hauptmann of Leipzig, daughter of the theorist Moritz Hauptmann. Finally, in August 1928 it was offered for sale by the Berlin firm of Karl Ernst Henrici. The present whereabouts of the manuscript are unknown.

Fortunately Fräulein Hauptmann made a copy of the incipits of the dances (Staatsbibliothek Preußischer Kulturbesitz Berlin, N. Mus. Nachl. 10, 43a), from which the contents of the autograph can be determined. B. 51 evidently transmits fourteen dances—four solo pieces, followed by six duets and four additional solos. Five of the dances were printed in Schubert's lifetime; Nos. 2 and 3, and variants of Nos. 9 and 10, appeared in the popular collection of *Deutsche Tänze*, Op. 33, while a solo version of No. 5 was published in a rare 1824 *Sammeldruck* entitled *Musikalisches Angebindes zum neuen Jahr*. The other nine dances remained unpublished until 1869, when, together with the previously published fifth dance, they were included in Brahms's edition.

The first inkling that Brahms had access to B. 51 is provided by Heinrich Kreissle's pioneering biography of Schubert, published in 1864, wherein we find mention of a catalogue of Schubert dances in Brahms's possession which listed 'no fewer than 79 Ländler, waltzes, and German dances, and 28 Écossaises' (that is, a total of 107 dances).[13] Although the number of Écossaises in Brahms's estate matches the number cited by Kreissle, the number of dances in triple metre (65) is fourteen less than that given in the catalogue (Table 2). But B. 51 contains precisely the number of compositions in triple metre necessary to make a total of seventy-nine. The biographer's remarks, then, raise the possibility that Brahms might once have owned the missing autograph.

Yet another manuscript—an undated copy of fifteen dances in Brahms's own hand— settles the matter. This source, which eventually came into the keeping of Marie Laycock-Gotthard, the publisher's daughter, will hereafter be cited as the Gotthard

---

[11] On the dating of B. 34, see Robert Winter, 'Cataloguing Schubert', 161; Winter's methodology is laid out in detail in his 'Paper Studies and the Future of Schubert Research'. On the dating of B. 52, see Brown, 'Dance-Music Manuscripts', 241.

[12] The musical portion of Brahms's bequest has not been properly catalogued, but his former ownership of its many autographs is acknowledged in Eusebius Mandyczewski, *Zusatz-Band zur Geschichte der k. k. Gesellschaft der Musikfreunde in Wien: Sammlungen und Statuten*. See also Alfred Orel, 'Johannes Brahms' Musikbibliothek'. Orel's catalogue is simply a transcription of Brahms's own handwritten inventory (Stadts- und Landesbibliothek, Vienna, Ia 67.338), whose summary account of the Schubert dance holdings reads: 'T̲änze. Walzer u. Ecossaisen. (im Ganzen $\frac{113}{109}$ Nuṁern)/("Deutsches Tempo" 12 Walzer. Atzenbrucker etc.)'. As we shall see, neither of Brahms's tallies reflects the present holdings of the Gesellschaft der Musikfreunde or, for that matter, conforms to the report of his collection by the early Schubert scholar Heinrich Kreissle.

[13] Heinrich Kreissle von Hellborn, *Franz Schubert*, 212–13, n. 1; notwithstanding its imprint of 1865, Kreissle's study apparently was published in November 1864, at which time it was announced in the *Allgemeine musikalische Zeitung*, n.s. 2 (1864): 815.

TABLE 2. Dance autographs in Brahms's estate

|   | No. of dances | Identification GdM shelf no. | B. listing (no.)[a] | D² listing (no.)[b] |
|---|---|---|---|---|
|   | *Triple Metre* | | | |
| 1 | 6 | A 259 | 42 | 145/W1–3; 365/29–31 |
| 2 | 4 | A 260 | 43 | 145/W2,5; 365/32, 33 |
| 3 | 12 | A 262 | 47 | 790 |
| 4 | 20 | A 263 | 34 | 145/L1–3,5,10, 11,13–17; 366/1, 9,10; 970 |
| 5 | 4 | A 265 | 52 | 146/2; 366/6,13; 783/D16 |
| 6 | 6 | A 266 | 56 | 145/15; 366/4; 783/D2,6,9; 975 |
| 7 | 5 | A 267 | 28 | 366/7,14,15; 974 |
| 8 | 8 | A 268 | 38 | 145/L4,6,9,12; 980C |
| SUBTOTAL | 65 | | | |
|   | *Duple Metre* | | | |
| 9 | 6 | A 258 | 35 | 697 |
| 10 | 12 | A 261 | 44 | 781 |
| 11 | 10 | A 264 | 37 | 145/E2,3; 977 |
| SUBTOTAL | 28 | | | |
| TOTAL | 93 | | | |

[a] These numbers correspond with those assigned by Maurice J. E. Brown in his inventory of Schubert's dance autographs ('The Dance-Music Manuscripts', 217–43).
[b] W= Walzer; L = Ländler; D = Deutscher; E = Écossaise.

copy.[14] Brahms evidently copied five of the dances from B. 34 and B. 52, the other ten from B. 51 (Table 3); the order of dances in his copy in every instance reflects the relative order of dances in the three Schubert autographs.

Because the Gotthard copy is now accessible only in photocopy, it is difficult to date on physical evidence. The manuscript could stem from Brahms's earliest days in Vienna,

[14] This source is entered as No. 10 in Anhang Va in McCorkle, *Johannes Brahms Thematisch-Bibliographisches Verzeichnis*, 739. Although Marie may have inherited the manuscript from her father, she might just as well have received it directly from Brahms, who was close to the publisher's family; see Alexander Weinmann, *J. P. Gotthard als später Originalverleger Franz Schuberts*, *passim*. The daughter, in turn, made a present of the manuscript early in this century, as is apparent from an inscription found on the last page: 'dies Brahms m[sk]r. Herrn T. Konrath freundlich / zugedacht / von M. Laycock-Gotthard / Vätlan 27. Juni 1913'. Dr Martin Bente, director of G. Henle Verlag (Munich), graciously helped me acquire a photocopy of the manuscript, which is in private possession in the Federal Republic of Germany. The eleven two-hand dances in this source are essentially identical to the eleven duets in Brahms's arrangement that Kinsky published in 1934 (see above, n. 5).

TABLE 3. Gotthard copy

|  | Source (B. no.) | 20 *Ländler* (no.) |
|---|---|---|
| 1 | 51/1 | 4 |
| 2 | 51/4 | 12 |
| 3[a] | 51/5 | 17 |
| 4[a] | 51/6 | 18 |
| 5[a] | 51/7 | 19 |
| 6[a] | 51/8 | 20 |
| 7 | 34/13 | 9 |
| 8 | 34/15 | 10 |
| 9 | 34/20 | 1 |
| 10 | 52/3 | 13 |
| 11 | 52/4 | 6 |
| 12 | 51/11 | 2 |
| 13 | 51/12 | 8 |
| 14 | 51/13 | 3 |
| 15 | 51/14 | 5 |

*Note*: This undated manuscript in Brahms's hand is in private possession in the Federal Republic of Germany. At the end of the last dance Brahms wrote: '(No. 1–4 [Nos. 12–15 of this manuscript]/Zelèz 1824 Juli)/dito die Walzer/Seiten 1, 2, u. 3 [Nos. 1–6 of this manuscript].'

[a] Piano duet.

months when he copied numerous works by Schubert.[15] But more likely he set to work on the manuscript only as the plan to publish the dances began to form in his mind. With the exception of B. 51/5 (a version of the dance by Schubert included in the *Angebindes zum neuen Jahr* of 1824, which Brahms almost certainly did not know), no previously published dance appears in the copy. And perhaps more telling, the edition contains none of the unpublished dances from the autographs that were passed over in the copy (B. 34/2–4, 7, 8, and 12). In any event, there is little doubt that Brahms's manuscript was used in the edition, since in those cases where the readings of the copy and the autograph differ, those of the former appear in the print.[16]

Of the five dances in the edition not found in the Gotthard copy, four appear in manuscripts which through documentary evidence can be placed in Brahms's hands by 1869. Since Kreissle's biography establishes 1864 as the *terminus ad quem* of Brahms's acquisition of all his dance autographs, we can presume that the only authentic source in the Brahms estate containing any of the other dances in the print (B. 28) served the editor

[15] See Brodbeck, 'Brahms as Editor and Composer', 16–20.
[16] No. 13 is a case in point. Its published reading transmits the two slight errors that Brahms made when he copied the dance from B. 52. In both the copy and first edition, an accent mark was left out on the third beat of the third bar, and the non-structural eighth-note c″ was omitted from the inner voice of the melody on the second beat of bar 9.

as the source for those three pieces; from its paper type this manuscript can be dated 1821–3.[17]

The other relevant manuscript is inscribed 'Frz. Schubert' but is, in fact, a copy, not an autograph (B. 30). The present whereabouts of this source are unknown. Maurice J. E. Brown once examined it, however, and identified Brahms's hand in the marginal note '?ungedruckt' written next to the last dance in the collection (and the only one not published in the *Original Tänze*, Op. 9, of 1821). This confirms Brahms's examination of the manuscript before the date when the *20 Ländler* were released, of course, for he included the dance as the sixteenth number in his edition.[18]

## II

To summarize our findings so far: five manuscripts known to have come into Brahms's keeping during the 1860s (the autographs B. 51, B. 34, B. 52, and B. 28, and the copy B. 30) are the likely sources of nineteen of the twenty dances. Only the eleventh dance has not been accounted for. The one extant source containing this number is, like B. 30, a manuscript copy found in Brahms's estate (henceforth, the B major copy). But unlike the other manuscripts considered to this point, documentary evidence linking it to Brahms before the 1869 publication date of the *20 Ländler* is lacking. We must, then, rely on stylistic evidence, the evaluation of which, paradoxically, requires us first to examine the three other dances in the source that share the key of B major, which were published in Op. 9 in a slightly different order (Table 4).

The set from the earlier print begins with an extraordinary composition (Example 1). Although rhythmically conventional, the accompaniment in part 1 is characterized by a remarkable modal interchange. The melody is also impressive, sounding the lower neighbour-note E♯ against the B minor harmony in the left hand. The prolongation of G♯ minor throughout part 2 and the attendant lack of tonic closure at the end of the piece are equally noteworthy. The second and third dances, by contrast, are far more conventional, and, on the face of it, not in the least worthy of special note.

Example 2 reproduces Nos. 9–11 of the *20 Ländler*. Like others in the edition, these dances were not ordered by Schubert. The first two pieces appear in B. 34, but there they are separated by another dance, which was published in 1823 as one of the Ländler in Op. 18. Why did Brahms elect to draw these dances together and to follow them with the

---

[17] I wish to thank Professor Robert Winter (private communication) for the dating of this manuscript; for Winter's methodology, see above n. 11. Although another one of Brahms's autographs (B. 56) contains a version of one of the dances in the print (No. 4), Brahms held faithfully to the reading of this dance in B. 51 when preparing the Gotthard copy.

[18] Brown, 'Dance-Music Manuscripts', 231–2, mistakenly identifies this source as an autograph. A number of features of the script point to its being a copy, and, indeed, it is listed among *Abschriften* in the revised Deutsch catalogue. Although its present location is not known, a photocopy of the manuscript is preserved in the Österreichische Nationalbibliothek (Ph A 1100); unfortunately, Brahms's annotation—written in blue pencil—is not visible in this copy. I wish to thank Dr Walpurga Litschauer, editor of the dances in the *Neue Schubert-Ausgabe*, for sending me her findings on this source.

TABLE 4.  B major copy

|   | Key | Identification 1st edn. | $D^2$ (no.) |
|---|-----|------------------------|-------------|
| 1 | Db  |                        | 972/1       |
| 2 | B   | *20 Ländler*/11        | 366/11      |
| 3 | B   | Op. 9/24               | 365/24      |
| 4 | B   | Op. 9/22               | 365/22      |
| 5 | B   | Op. 9/23               | 365/23      |
| 6 | Ab  |                        | 972/2       |
| 7 | A   |                        | 972/3       |

*Note:* This copy is located in the Gesell-schaft der Musikfreunde in Vienna (Q 16 190). The manuscript is undated and untitled.

previously unpublished dance in B whose only known source is the B major copy? One influence on these decisions seems to have been a desire to imitate the arrangement in Op. 9 of the other three B major dances in the copy.

The correspondences between the two groups are numerous and striking. The strongest likeness involves the terminal dances (both found in the B major copy), which, quite extraordinarily, share left-hand parts. The middle dances can also be paired; were they not set in opposite modes, their melodies would begin identically. By the same token, the first dances are analogous. Like Op. 9 No. 22, the ninth Ländler in Brahms's collection begins with a striking use of the tonic minor preceding strong closure in the tonic major at the end of part 1. Taken together, these echoes of Op. 9 in the *20 Ländler* suggest that by 1869 Brahms knew the B major copy—the only surviving source for the eleventh dance in his edition, and one that eventually came into his possession.

The matter would seem to be closed. Since the four autographs and two copies described so far can all be linked to Brahms and together transmit all twenty dances, they would seem to constitute the sources for his edition. Yet according to the annotation found on p. 3 cited earlier—'Die Original-Handschrift besitzt Hr. Johannes Brahms'—the edition was based not on a disparate group of manuscripts, but on a single autograph in the possession of the editor. Was it, then, Schubert who compiled the dances after all?

Although the Ländler are not found gathered together in any extant source, it is not impossible that such a manuscript once existed. In 1870 the *Allgemeine musikalische Zeitung* in fact reported that the readings of the Ländler were taken from a single autograph, in Brahms's keeping, in which Schubert had written the first sixteen dances for piano solo, the last four for piano duet.[19] These comments, however, were probably nothing more that a restatement of the annotation in the print, not a summation of

---

[19] 'Die zu Grunde liegende Originalhandschrift besitzt Hr. Johannes Brahms; dieselbe enthält die ersten sechszehn Nummern in zweihändiger, die letzten vier aber in vierhändiger Bearbeitung.' *Allgemeine musikalische Zeitung* 5 (1870): 305.

EXAMPLE 1. Schubert, *Original Tänze*, Op. 9 Nos. 22–4.

EXAMPLE 2. Schubert, *20 Ländler*, Nos. 9–11.

evidence taken first hand. Indeed, Brahms used the plural when he wrote to Senff about the dances in January 1869, saying that the *manuscripts* were not ready. And subsequent nineteenth-century testimony likewise provides little corroboration for the report in the AmZ. Gustav Nottebohm's somewhat less precise account of the sources of the *20 Ländler* in 1874, for example, claims merely that 'Johannes Brahms owns all the dances in autograph form'.[20] Obviously Nottebohm believed that all the versions were authentic, but his non-committal language implies that he knew that more than one manuscript came into play in the edition.[21] Similarly, in a slightly later inventory of Schubert's works, George Grove made no mention of a single autograph. The ten dances in B. 51 he entered under the year 1824, but the remaining Ländler were grouped under the heading 'pieces without date of month or year'.[22] The weight of the evidence, therefore, supports the view that the dances in Brahms's edition never existed in a single manuscript. To reiterate the most important consequence of this conclusion: the groupings of pieces in the *20 Ländler* can only be traced to the efforts of their editor, not their composer. Interpreting Brahms's conduct of this editorial responsibility must be our ultimate goal.[23]

[20] ' . . . sämmtliche Tänze sind autograph im Besitz von Johannes Brahms.' Nottebohm, *Thematisches Verzeichniss*, 215.

[21] Since Nottebohm dated only the dances found in B. 51 ('Nr. 2 bis 5, 8, 12, und 17 bis 20 wurden im Juli 1824 zu Zelesz in Ungarn geschrieben'), it appears that he examined either this dated manuscript (as well as the various undated sources in Brahms's possession), or else the Gotthard copy (from which the same information about the dances in B. 51 could be derived). Nottebohm's assertion that Brahms owned *autographs* of all the dances is incorrect; as we have seen, Nos. 11 and 16 are found only in copies.

[22] George Grove, *A Dictionary of Music and Musicians* (1883), 3: 380–1.

[23] The 'single-manuscript theory' has died hard. In his critical report for the *Gesamtausgabe* of the seventeen authentic two-hand Ländler, which would later become known as D. 366 (see above, n. 9), Julius Epstein stated that his reading was based upon an autograph that Brahms owned of all the pieces (*Franz Schubert's Werke: Erste kritisch durchgesehenen Gesammtausgabe. Revisionsbericht, Series 12*, report by Julius Epstein, 155; reprint ed., *Franz Schubert. Complete Works. Breitkopf & Härtel Critical Edition of 1884–1897*, 19: 155). All twenty pieces in the first edition, or only the seventeen within Epstein's purview? Reinhard van Hoorickx has taken the latter position. In his chronological listing of Schubert's dances, he cites Epstein's report as evidence that Brahms owned a 'fair copy' in Schubert's hand of D. 366, to which he gives the date 'Nov.–Dec. 1824 [?]' ('Franz Schubert [1797–1828]: List of the Dances in Chronological Order', 93). This supposition is almost certainly erroneous. The authentic two-hand version of No. 17 (found in B. 55) is significantly different from the version published in 1869.

Epstein's report compounds an earlier source of confusion, one that misled even the intrepid Otto Erich Deutsch. In 1857 Anton Schindler concluded his recollections of Schubert with an extensive catalogue of the composer's works, based upon two earlier ones by Ferdinand Schubert, but incorporating many additional pieces. One of these additions is a set of seventeen Deutsche, which is listed under the year 1823. Deutsch assumed that these dances were identical to the set which he identifd as number 366 in his thematic catalogue (*Schubert: Memoirs by His Friends*, 323). But reasons to doubt this identification abound. Most obvious, just as no single manuscript of all twenty dances is extant, neither is a single manuscript of the seventeen two-hand pieces to be found. More important, of the known autographs containing any of the dances, none is dated 1823 or inscribed 'Deutsche'. (The only dated source, B. 51, was written in July of the following year; moreover, none of the extant manuscripts includes a generic title except the copy B. 30, which is headed 'Ländler.') In all likelihood, Schindler's reference was to the seventeen Ländler of Op. 18, compiled from several manuscripts and published in early 1823. Commentary on D. 366 continues to be plagued by errors and misfortune. Rainer Riehn's recent list of works (*Musik-Konzepte, Sonderband: Franz Schubert*, 288) contains at least one typographical error—and this in the date of D. 366: '17 Ländler für Klavier. 1924 (D. 366).

# III

The impulse to couple the ninth and tenth Ländler, as we have seen, probably came, at least in part, from a desire to mimic the grouping of dances in Schubert's Op. 9. Though we may delight in discovering this recondite principle of organization, we should not overlook the more obvious reason to bring the pieces together: they make a tonally and motivically coherent set (see Example 2). Curiously, in spite of the physical discontinuity of these pieces in B. 34, Schubert's autograph actually emphasizes their kinship.[24] At some point after copying No. 9, Schubert crossed out its final phrase and fitted a new cadence on to some nearby staves; he subsequently used the original ending of this dance as the final cadence of No. 10. Not surprisingly, the endings of these pieces display sharp resemblances; the rhythms are similar, and the progression $I^6$–$ii^6_5$–V–I (which, unexpectedly, seldom occurs in Schubert's dances) is present in both. On the other hand, the final cadence of the later dance recalls the aggressive character and dactylic rhythm of the opening bars of the earlier one—which is to be expected, since it was conceived as an ending to that dance. In view of Brahms's penchant for creating in his own works what is loosely termed 'organic unity', it is not unlikely that his decision to publish Nos. 9 and 10 in succession was influenced as much by the relationships between them as by the opportunity to echo Schubert's Op. 9.

Indeed, a desire for coherence appears to have governed nearly all of Brahms's ordering decisions. In this regard the first six pieces merit study, for they lay bare in a most impressive way this overriding principle of organization (Example 3). Although these dances appear in the Gotthard copy, they were ultimately drawn from three manuscripts—the middle four pieces were copied from B. 51 (July 1824), No. 1 from B. 34 (late 1819 or early 1820), and No. 6 from B. 52 (apparently 1823 or 1824). Accordingly, the opening assortment comprises dances composed over a period of at least five years.

What is remarkable is the pains that Brahms took to arrange these pieces into a set rich in tonal and motivic relationships. As ordered in the edition, two dances in A major are followed first by three in A minor, and then by one in C major. This progression is not only coherent, but of a kind seldom found in Schubert's dance autographs, least of all in the sources for Brahms's edition. In B. 28, for example, one dance in G major is followed by four in Db major. By the same token, B. 34, B. 51, and B. 52 include such unfelicitous tonal juxtapositions as Db–B, D–C–eb, Eb–A, and A–bb–C. (One of the few autographs displaying long-range tonal planning is B. 47, the manuscript which served as the source for Brahms's edition of the *12 Ländler*. The tonal cohesion of that manuscript helps to explain why Brahms, in contrast to his later approach, did not reorder its dances and combine them with others; in this case, the composer's order satisfied the editor's requirements.)

---

[24] For a facsimile and transcription of the leaf containing these numbers, see Brodbeck, 'Brahms as Editor and Composer', 190–1.

EXAMPLE 3. Schubert, *20 Ländler*, Nos. 1–6.

The initial six dances in the *20 Ländler* seem fused in other ways, too. The profile of the melody beginning the first Ländler, for example, is echoed at the beginning of the second. Brahms would surely have noticed this relationship and might well have sought to emphasize it by publishing the dances consecutively. But why did he place No. 1 before No. 2, and not the other way around? Put briefly, the chosen order created an additional connection between dances not otherwise possible. The second dance, which begins on the downbeat, should end with one full bar. In Brahms's reading the first ending of part 2 is metrically correct, but the second ending contains only two beats. It appears that Brahms shortened this ending so that the third dance could follow without pause; the latter dance begins with a quarter-note anacrusis and hence 'fills out' the truncated final bar of No. 2. Now had Brahms merely desired a continuous performance of the Ländler, he could have juxtaposed the first dance with, say, No. 3. But that would have created a textural disjunction between consecutive pieces which was apparently unacceptable to him. By contrast, as Brahms ordered the dances the final chord of No. 2 leads smoothly to the initial chord of No. 3. With a single stroke Brahms fashioned both textural and temporal continuity, while effecting, in the bargain, a 'Schubertian' shift from major into parallel minor.

Similar alterations in the endings of other dances allow a continuous performance of all twenty Ländler.[25] Considering both this envisioned mode of performance and the motivic relation between the first two numbers, it is not surprising that later dances also share material. For example, variations of the melody in bars 9–12 of the third dance, which descends from E to A in a series of suspensions, occur in the fourth dance, first in bars 7–8 (in a faster rhythm) and later in part 2, where the original harmonic rhythm is restored. This ordering, moreover, draws attention to a cadential similarity: the upper voice in the closing bars of No. 4 is an augmentation of the cadential melody of the preceding dance.

The fourth dance, in turn, introduces ideas that are taken up in the following two pieces. The accompaniment in all three, for example, is characterized by 'rocking motion'; most often the interval of the third is used, and in each dance the motive F–A–F is conspicuous. The strongest relation occurs between Nos. 5 and 6, the start of the latter being a more elaborate version of the beginning of the second half of the former. The same two pieces, finally, are marked by quite similar cadences onto C; the eighth-note figurations seem as well to recall the active voice in the second half of No. 4.

Thus the first six dances unfold a coherent tonal progression and embrace a number of other trenchant relationships. But these are organized at an even higher level. Nos. 2–5 are simple binary forms, each composed of two repeated eight-bar periods; by contrast, the first dance is a ternary form of forty bars, and the sixth a rounded binary form of

---

[25]  See the second endings of Nos. 1, 6–8, 10, 12, 14, and 19. Actually the ending of No. 13 (♩.) and the beginning of No. 14 (♪) do *not* make a full bar; yet there is no reason to think that Brahms intended a metric disjunction here but nowhere else. In all likelihood he simply assumed that the performer would add the appropriate rests ( 𝄾 𝄾· ) at the end of the earlier dance. (Julius Epstein's reading of this piece in the old *Gesamtausgabe* [Series 12, No. 10] includes the altered second ending.)

forty-eight bars. Because both of the anomalous dances include a final repetition of part 1, they attain a greater degree of closure than do Nos. 2–5. They constitute, as it were, a temporal frame that causes the six dances to be taken in together.[26]

Brahms's edition begins, then, with a tightly knit ensemble of dances. The remainder of the set unfolds similarly; by choosing his pieces carefully, the editor ensured that every coupling would be felicitous. At the same time, the fusion of Nos. 13 and 14 (drawn respectively from B. 52 and B. 28) seems calculated as well to recall a pair of Ländler from Schubert's Op. 18—and in a manner analogous to the echoing of Op. 9 Nos. 22–4 in Nos. 9–11 (compare Examples 4 and 5). Though the eighth Ländler in the earlier collection begins in Bb minor, it ends emphatically in its relative key, Db major. No. 13 in Brahms's edition reverses this tonal shift; its final candence clinches the key of Bb minor, but the opening period is more readily apprehended in Db major.

By itself, of course, this similarity offers no reason to assume that Brahms associated the one dance with the other: neither the unfolding of the two keys nor the musical material itself correspond very closely. Yet a glance at the *ninth* Ländler in Op. 18 and the *fourteenth* dance in the later edition indeed raises the possibility that Brahms was attempting to echo the earlier print. Both pieces are in Db major; more important, each is characterized by chromatic neighbouring thirds and presents the same unusual succession of note values, albeit in different metric dispositions ( ♪♩ | ♩.. and ♪| ♩ ♩..).

In its fluid tonal relations, the set concluding the book recalls not a grouping of dances found in any earlier edition, but rather the one which opens the collection at hand. Here Brahms follows No. 16, drawn from B. 30, with four dances taken over in their original order from B. 51 (Example 6). The first dance, in Ab major, moves to the dominant before proceeding to its final cadence on the tonic. No. 17 turns matters round; the first period ends in the tonic, Eb major, the second includes a prolongation of the sub-dominant, Ab major. No. 18, in turn, re-establishes Ab major as a tonic. The axis between the two keys seems to have been broken when No. 19 sets out in C minor. Yet Ab major is tonicized in its first part, and Eb major is the goal of the first phrase of its second. No. 20, finally, follows in the tonic parallel of its immediate predecessor and closes out the edition.

Considering the placement of this set at the end of the collection, the succession of keys in the final two dances seems especially notable. The move from C minor to C major recalls the traditional closural sign of ending a minor-key work in the parallel major. The juxtaposition of these dances is important in another way as well. Of all the Ländler, No. 19 is probably the most agitated (Example 7). This ethos, deriving from the full texture, loud dynamics, and off-beat accents, is not matched by any other dance in the collection. Significantly, these features set off in stark contrast the thin texture (bare octaves) and quiet dynamics (*pp, con sordino*) of the beginning of No. 20. They enhance, that is, two 'natural' signs of closure in the final dance.

[26] The pianist Lili Kraus, in one of the few recordings of the dances, does indeed perceive these pieces as a unit; her 'Ländler Suite', fashioned out of a variety of Schubert's dances, opens with the first six numbers of Brahms's edition, and only then turns to other dances (Odyssey recording, 32 016 0380).

EXAMPLE 4. Schubert, *Walzer, Ländler und Ecossaisen*, Op. 18, Ländler Nos. 8–9.

EXAMPLE 5. Schubert, *20 Ländler*, Nos. 13–14.

EXAMPLE 6. Schubert, *20 Ländler*, Nos. 16–20: tonal organization.

EXAMPLE 7. Schubert, *20 Ländler*, Nos. 19–20 (arranged for piano two-hands by Brahms).

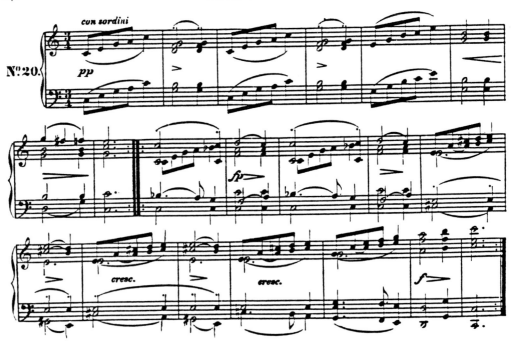

The structure of the last number is also telling. This piece follows a series of thirteen binary forms, each comprising two repeated eight-bar periods. The final dance is a binary form too, but its second part is composed of twelve bars, not the usual eight. The anomalous period thus thwarts the implication of a continuing sequence of comparable binary forms. Furthermore, owing to the presence in No. 20 of patent closural patterns, the second part suggests the opposite implication: that the series might not continue at all, that the collection has come to an end. The passage in question consists of three phrases in an anapestic grouping (Example 8*a*). Since the final phrase (bars 17–20) follows relatively long stretches of rhythmic mobility (the 'structural upbeats' of bars 9–16) and tonal instability (the prolongation of A major in bars 13–16), the full cadence is all the more decisive. The last phrase even completes two melodic processes. The dance is marked by several appearances of a rising motive, first occurring in bar 1, which generally is reversed by a falling interval. At the end, however, the rising line is extended upward to a high tonic, while the bass line descends along the scale to the note four octaves below (see Example 8*b*). This contrary motion in the outer parts coincides with a strong harmonic progression, and with it makes for an effective conclusion.

The appearance of this Ländler in last place, then, is not mere happenstance. Though Brahms had carefully arranged the preceding dances so as to create compelling tonal and motivic relationships, he had not thereby implied any specific ending. To ensure this feeling of completion, he needed to finish with a piece more strongly closed than its predecessors. This was to be found in No. 20. By ending with it Brahms imparted a sense of closure to the entire collection.

EXAMPLE 8. Schubert, *20 Ländler*, No. 20, bars 9–20.

In his role as editor Brahms naturally was constrained. He could only arrange dances, not compose them. The coherence of the *20 Ländler* is all the more remarkable, then, since it is due to Brahms's ingenuity in selecting and ordering dances that Schubert never intended to be performed together. Put differently, the origin of musical coherence was editorial, not compositional.

Would the composer have objected to Brahms's tinkering? It is fair to say 'No', if only because Schubert does not seem to have taken much interest in the fate of his dances. Most of the pieces, we know, were slight, casual works, and with few exceptions the manuscripts in which these 'written-out improvisations' were preserved amount to little more than random collections of occasional pieces. It is no wonder that the early editions are best described as potpourris, comprising diverse dances that in most instances were composed over a wide period of time.[27]

What sets Brahms's edition apart, then, is precisely what is most impressive about it: the seamless flow of one dance into the next and the web of relationships among these pieces. By contrast, the early editions were not designed to allow a continuous performance of all the numbers, and adjoining dances were not always tonally (much less motivically) related. In these respects, the *20 Ländler* find their parallel not in the editions of Schubert's lifetime but in Brahms's own works, not least of these being, as I have argued elsewhere, the Op. 39 Waltzes and the two books of *Liebeslieder*.[28] And since Brahms's selecting and ordering of the Ländler appear to have been strongly influenced by his own compositional and aesthetic preferences, the collection can be regarded as a kind of essay in criticism.

On the other hand, Brahms's editing evinces a different critical attitude as well—and an altogether modest and touching one. Notwithstanding the importance of his efforts to the set, Brahms, in customary fashion, withheld public announcement of his contribution. At no time did Schubert group the twenty Ländler together in a single manuscript; yet Brahms allowed his own arrangement of the set to be attributed to Schubert. In one sense, then, Brahms's occasional mimicking of typical Schubertian touches and copying of entire sets of dances from earlier prints are intellectual conceits: the work is to be passed off to an unknowing world as Schubert's own. But no less meaningful, these acts undoubtedly also constitute unselfish and heartfelt tributes to a composer whose music Brahms cherished.

---

[27] See Brodbeck, 'Brahms as Editor and Composer', 73–4, and 89–90.

[28] See my articles '*Primo* Schubert, *Secondo* Schumann: Brahms's Four-hand Waltzes, Op. 39', and 'Compatibility, Coherence, and Closure in Brahms's *Liebeslieder* Waltzes'.

# BRAHMS'S EDITIONS OF SCHUMANN

——

## LINDA CORRELL ROESNER

JOHANNES Brahms's editorial involvement with the music of Robert Schumann falls into three periods: the mid-1860s to early 1870s, when he brought out several hitherto unpublished Schumann compositions (a *Scherzo* in F minor, the *Presto passionato* in G minor, and five *Études symphoniques*); the late 1870s to early 1880s, when he undertook—unofficially—much of the editing of the Schumann *Gesamtausgabe*, the sole acknowledged editor of which was Clara Schumann; and the late 1880s to early 1890s, when he was instrumental in the publication of the 1841 version of Schumann's Symphony in D minor, Op. 120, and assumed editorial responsibility for the supplemental volume of the Schumann *Gesamtausgabe*. The present study will deal primarily with the first two periods, focusing on the editions themselves and on the published and unpublished correspondence between Brahms and Clara Schumann. It is important, however, to keep the third period in mind, not only because it rounds off Brahms's long editorial association with Schumann's works, but also because it proved to be a critical moment in his relationship with Clara Schumann. Brahms's 'creative' involvement with Schumann's music strained their friendship severely, but it also served as a focal point for their eventual reconciliation.[1]

Study of these editions and the sources upon which they were based affords insights into Brahms's editorial philosophy, Schumann's music, and the nineteenth-century performance practice of Schumann's music. Since the Schumann works that Brahms published in the 1860s and early 1870s were all piano pieces, and since the editorial dialogue between Brahms and Clara Schumann concentrated on piano music, this discussion will deal principally with compositions for that instrument. But it should be noted that Brahms's extensive contribution to the Schumann *Gesamtausgabe* included supervising the editorial work of the musicians who aided Clara Schumann with the orchestral, chamber, and choral works: Woldemar Bargiel, Ernst Franck, Robert Volkland, Ernst Rudorff, Albert Dietrich, and others.

## I

The two movements published by J. Rieter-Biedermann in November 1866 as *Scherzo und Presto Passionato für das Pianoforte*[2] represent Brahms's first editorial encounter with the music of Robert Schumann. Both movements were 'discovered' by Brahms in

---

[1] See Berthold Litzmann, ed., *Clara Schumann–Johannes Brahms: Briefe aus den Jahren 1853–1896*, 2:464–8, 476–97.

[2] See Kurt Hofmann, *Die Erstdrucke der Werke von Robert Schumann*, 334–5.

manuscripts either owned by him or to which he had access.[3] The *Scherzo* exists in only one source, Schumann's autograph of the Piano Sonata in F minor, Op. 14.[4] It was originally the second movement of a five-movement sonata containing two scherzos.[5] The *Presto passionato* is preserved in three autographs: an early draft,[6] a fair copy dated 27 October 1835,[7] and a manuscript transmitting an early version of the Piano Sonata in G minor, Op. 22, with the *Presto* as the finale.[8] Brahms was unaware of the draft but familiar with the other two manuscripts: he himself owned the fair copy of October 1835 (which, because of its present location, I shall call the 'Vienna' manuscript), while the manuscript of the early version of the G minor Sonata (which I shall call the 'Berlin' manuscript) was in the possession of Clara Schumann.

Brahms's edition of the *Scherzo*, since it is based on only one source, is straightforward: with a few exceptions it is almost a diplomatic copy of Schumann's manuscript. His edition of the *Presto passionato*, on the other hand, is a conflation of the two versions known to him. As such it can tell us much about Brahms's aesthetic judgement and his evaluation of his sources. I propose, therefore, to concentrate the following discussion on the *Presto passionato*.

Of the two manuscripts upon which Brahms based his edition of the *Presto*, the Vienna manuscript of October 1835 is the earlier. Although it is more carefully written than the autograph transmitting the entire sonata, the Berlin manuscript, there can be no doubt that it served as the model from which the finale of the Berlin manuscript was prepared, for this latter source contains revisions in all the places where they were marked for insertion in the Vienna manuscript. (Schumann did not enter these revisions into the Vienna manuscript itself, but wrote them on separate sheets; the pages containing the revisions are no longer extant.) There is also a later set of revisions within the Berlin manuscript. This source, therefore, represents Schumann's last thoughts on the movement, for in 1838 the composer rejected the *Presto passionato*, replacing it with the

---

[3] See Brahms's letter of 20 Oct. 1866 to Rieter-Biedermann, in *Brahms Briefwechsel*, 14:136. Here Brahms requests that Rieter ask Selmar Bagge, editor of the *Allgemeine musikalische Zeitung*, to publish an article explaining that Brahms found the pieces and that no one—not even Clara Schumann—was aware of their existence. The article, written by H[ermann] D[eiters], and entitled 'Nachgelassene Werke von Schumann', appeared in the *Leipziger Allgemeine musikalische Zeitung* on 3 July 1867. Clara may not have been aware of the 'existence' of the *Scherzo*, but she certainly knew of the *Presto*, since she had been instrumental in persuading Schumann to replace the movement— the original finale of the Piano Sonata in G minor, Op. 22—with an easier one. See Berthold Litzmann, *Clara Schumann: Ein Künstlerleben*, 1: 186, and Clara Schumann, ed., *Jugendbriefe von Robert Schumann*, 278.

[4] London, British Library, MS Add. 37056. This manuscript was purchased by the British Museum in 1905 from the Berlin autograph dealer Leo Liepmannssohn (Katalog 35 (26–7 May 1905), item 976). Brahms undoubtedly had access to this manuscript: it contains some annotations in his hand, and he referred to it in his preface to the 1866 edition.

[5] The first edition of Op. 14 appeared without the scherzos as the three-movement *Concert sans orchestre* published by Haslinger in 1836; the second edition, published as a 'grand Sonate' by Schuberth in 1853, included one of the scherzos. Schumann's autograph served as the engraver's model for the first edition only. For a discussion of this manuscript, see Linda Correll Roesner, 'The Autograph of Schumann's Piano Sonata in F Minor, Opus 14'.

[6] New York, private collection of Alice Tully; microfilm in New York Public Library, Toscanini Memorial Archives, *ZBT–88; Photogramm in Vienna, Österreichische Nationalbibliothek, PhA 1519–P.

[7] Vienna, Gesellschaft der Musikfreunde, A 288.

[8] Berlin, Deutsche Staatsbibliothek, Mus. ms. autogr. Schumann 38.

familiar finale of Op. 22. But had he retained this original finale, he may well have revised it further prior to publication, if one can judge from the extensive structural variants between the version of the first movement of the sonata in the Berlin manuscript and the published form of that movement.[9]

Brahms was well aware that the Berlin manuscript preserved the later version of the *Presto*, and even referred to its superiority.[10] None the less, in his edition he incorporated many of the melodic and figural details of the earlier version and chose to ignore some of the structural revisions Schumann had introduced into the later version.

Perhaps the most intriguing aspect of Brahms's edition of the *Presto* is that it stresses structural parallels that Schumann had attempted to de-emphasize in his last revisions of the movement—alterations made in the text of the Berlin manuscript. The movement is a sprawling sonata-like form in which much of the development section is recapitulated. Structural parallelism is inherent in such a design. Schumann's early compositional tendency to think in terms of additive blocks of musical material also invites such parallelism. The movement as edited and published by Brahms is shown in skeletal outline in Figure 1. One of the subtleties of the movement is the ambiguity or, more precisely, the overlapping of function at the end of the exposition and the beginning of

FIGURE 1. Schumann, *Presto passionato* in G minor, Op. posth., as edited by Johannes Brahms. Skeletal outline illustrating structural parallels.

| | [Exp.] | | | [Dev.] | | | | | | | | | Vivo molto | | |
|---|---|---|---|---|---|---|---|---|---|---|---|---|---|---|---|
| bar: | 1 | 35 | 69 | 99 | 107 | 121 | 129 | 137 | 151 | 159 | 183 | 195 | | | 219 |
| theme: | P | S | | K | S | P | K | S | P | (S) | anticip. of NT | NT | | | |
| key: | g | B♭ | cad. B♭ mod./seq. | B♭ | (B♭)⤳f | | C | (C)⤳g | | mod./seq. | f | F | B♭ | | mod. |

| | [Recap.] | | | | | | | | | | | [Coda] | | |
|---|---|---|---|---|---|---|---|---|---|---|---|---|---|---|
| | 247 | 273 | 307 | 337 | 345 | 359 | 367 | 375 | 389 | 397 | 409 | 423 | | |
| | P | S | | K | S | P | K | S | P | (S) | | S | + | P |
| | g | g | cad. g mod./seq. | G | (G)⤳d | | A | (A)⤳e | | mod./seq. | G ped. | g | | |

P=principal thematic and tonal area
S=secondary thematic and tonal area
K=cadential
NT=new theme
[⎯⎯]=altered (bars 159–79) or deleted (bars 337–44, 367–74) by Schumann in his last revision.

[9] See Linda Correll Roesner, 'Schumann's Revisions in the First Movement of the Piano Sonata in G Minor, Op. 22'.

[10] *Brahms Briefwechsel*, 14: 123.

the development. After the cadence in the new key at bar 69, Schumann departs from Bb major, returning to reinforce the key at bar 99 in a passage that sounds and functions like the typical closing gesture of a sonata exposition. The thematic material here is a variant of the secondary theme. After the statement of the secondary theme proper that enters in bar 107, Schumann moves away from Bb, and the development section appears to be under way. It is not until the whole block of material from bar 99 to 128 is repeated a tone higher, as bars 129–58, that we recognize the double function of the passage at bar 99—as both reinforcing the contrasting key of the exposition and thus acting in a closing capacity, and as beginning a developmental sequence. (It is interesting to note that in his early draft of the movement—which Brahms did not know—Schumann ended the exposition after the present bar 96, where there are four bars of first ending and a repeat sign.)

The passage from bar 99 to 106 (Example 1), which I have labelled 'K' because of its closing tonal function, is of some significance for our evaluation of Brahms's conception of the formal design of the movement; it also offers perspective on Schumann's ideas about form and symmetry. In Brahms's edition of the *Presto* this passage occurs four times, at bars 99, 129, 337, and 367. The last two occurrences, of course, appear during the recapitulation of the development section. In Schumann's early draft of the movement and in the Vienna manuscript this passage is absent; Schumann added all four statements at the time he prepared the Berlin manuscript from the Vienna manuscript, as can be seen by the indications in the Vienna manuscript at each place where the passage was to be inserted. Shortly after he had written the Berlin manuscript, however, Schumann apparently had second thoughts about the aesthetic and structural effect of four appearances of the passage. Consequently he crossed out—in the same brown ink as the main musical text of the Berlin manuscript—the statements at bars 129 and 367. That

EXAMPLE 1. Schumann, *Presto passionato*, Op. posth., bars 99–106.

is to say, he deleted the beginning of the second 'module' of each pair of 'modular blocks' of material, thus diminishing to a certain extent the repetitive effect and also cutting down somewhat on the tendency to overemphasize the tonal areas in question (C major and A major). By letting stand the first statement of each pair, Schumann reinforced the tonal weight at those junctures in the form, a reinforcement that is particularly important at bar 99 (less so at bar 337).

After this revision Schumann let the matter rest temporarily, but he returned to the Berlin manuscript at least twice at a later date to make further revisions, which he indicated by means of deletions and memoranda in red pencil and then either modified or executed in black ink.[11] Two of these revisions concern the passage in question: Schumann crossed out in red pencil bars 99–106 and 337–44. Since he had already—close to the time of writing the Berlin manuscript—deleted bars 129–36 and 367–74, the composer in effect reverted to the reading of the Vienna manuscript, where the passage was not present. Still not satisfied, Schumann returned to the problem once more, this time reinstating the passage in bars 99–106 and in 129–36: 'gilt' [*stet*] or 'das Ausgestrichene gilt' is written in black ink adjacent to both statements (black ink represents Schumann's last revision in the Berlin manuscript). Thus his 'final thoughts' on the matter, if we can use such a term to describe the working habits of a composer who routinely 'tinkered' with his works in this fashion, were to preserve the reinforcement of Bb major at bars 99 ff. and the sequential effect of repeating the block of material from bars 99–128 at bars 129–58. In the recapitulation of the development section the composer de-emphasized the structural parallels with the earlier part of the movement by omitting the passage in question: the crossed-out bars 337–44 and 367–74 were *not* marked by Schumann to be reinstated. Brahms, however, chose to preserve all four statements, as the word 'gilt', which he wrote lightly in pencil in the left-hand margin adjacent to bars 337 ff. and 367 ff., testifies.

Brahms's edition of the *Presto passionato* retains another structural parallel that Schumann had modified. In both the Vienna and Berlin manuscripts, bars 159–78—a modulatory, sequential passage in the development section based on the secondary theme—have the musical text of Brahms's edition. In the Berlin manuscript, however, Schumann crossed out the passage in red pencil and substituted another, which he wrote in black ink on a separate slip of paper, carefully indicating its placement with a capital 'A' and the instruction 'zum *letzten* Satz'. Brahms considered this revision to be an *ossia*, as his 'NB Ossia' in the left-hand margin indicates (see Illustration 1). Although the two passages (Example 2*a* and *b*) begin similarly, the revision is less sequential, somewhat modified tonally, and lacks the forceful passage in the left hand in bars 175–8 that so effectively prepares for the rhythmic anticipation of the new theme in bars 183 ff. One can imagine why Brahms wished to retain the original version, which, owing to its less rambling tonal plan, sharper melodic profile, and rhythmic drive, is altogether more

---

[11] I have speculated that the revisions in this manuscript in red pencil and black ink may not have been undertaken until spring 1837, about a year and a half after the manuscript was probably written (shortly after 27 Oct. 1835). See Roesner, 'Schumann's Revisions', 98–9.

EXAMPLE 2. (_a_) Schumann, _Presto passionato_, Op. posth., bars 159–79.

(b) Schumann, Finale ('Presto passionato') of early version of Piano Sonata in G minor, Op. 22 (Berlin, Deutsche Staatsbibliothek. Mus. ms. autogr. Schumann 38). Revision of the bars corresponding to *Presto passionato*, Op. posth., bars 159–79. (See over.)

[bar 180]

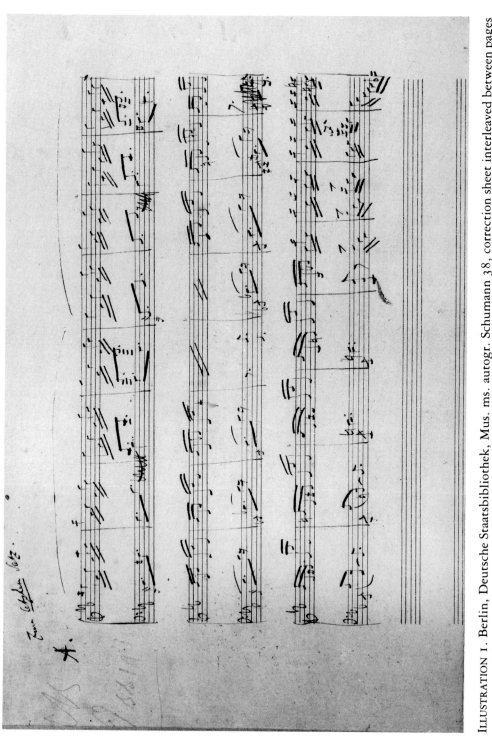

ILLUSTRATION 1. Berlin, Deutsche Staatsbibliothek, Mus. ms. autogr. Schumann 38, correction sheet interleaved between pages 12 and 13. (Robert Schumann, early version of Piano Sonata in G minor, Op. 22, Finale.) Reproduced with the permission of the Deutsche Staatsbibliothek, Berlin/Musikabteilung. (See Example 2b.)

compelling than Schumann's revision. But Schumann may have undertaken the revision because he wanted to reserve the stronger version for later in the movement (bars 397–416), where it serves as the culmination of the recapitulation and, expanded by six bars, ushers in the coda. By modifying the passage at bar 159 Schumann both reduced emphasis on the structural parallelism and intensified the climactic moment of the movement.

The structural regularity of the printed version of the *Presto* has an analogue in Brahms's consistent treatment of a thematic detail. In Brahms's edition the secondary theme appears in the exposition and recapitulation as shown in Example 3*a* (bars 35 ff.), and in a slightly modified form in the development section (Example 3*b*, bars 107 ff.). Brahms followed the Vienna manuscript with respect to this theme. In the Berlin manuscript, however, Schumann was more flexible. The first time the theme appears (bars 35 ff.) it has the melodic and rhythmic profile shown in Example 3*c*. Schumann had originally copied the reading of the Vienna manuscript into the Berlin manuscript, but then deleted it and substituted the reading in Example 3*c*. (This final version proves to be a modification of Schumann's early conception of the theme in his draft; see Example 3*d*.)[12] Schumann did not, in the Berlin manuscript, make the corresponding change in the recapitulation of this passage, nor did he alter the developmental form of the theme (Example 3*b*). I prefer to think, therefore, that the various forms of this theme were deliberate variations on Schumann's part—leading to a continuing unfolding of the

EXAMPLE 3. Schumann, *Presto passionato*, Op. posth.
(*a*) Bars 35–8. Vienna, Gesellschaft der Musikfreunde, A 288.

(*b*) Bars 107–10. All sources.

(*c*) Bars 35–8. Berlin, Deutsche Staatsbibliothek, Mus. ms. autogr. Schumann 38.

(*d*) Bars 35–8, early draft (New York Public Library, Toscanini Memorial Archives, microfilm ✻ZBT-88).

[12] In this connection it is interesting to note that in the final version of the first movement of Op. 22 Schumann reinstated what was apparently his earliest conception of the secondary theme. See Roesner, 'Schumann's Revisions', 104, n. 16.

theme—not the result of his neglecting to enter his revision in the later passage. Brahms apparently thought otherwise, but I find it puzzling that he should disregard an obvious correction in a manuscript that he considered to be the better source. His handling of this melodic detail and, in particular, his handling of Schumann's structural revisions in the *Presto* reveal Brahms the editor making decidedly *compositional* choices. It is possible that his preference for many of the readings of the Vienna manuscript reflects his greater familiarity with the text of the manuscript in his own collection.

# II

The question of the evaluation of sources comes up again in connection with the publication by N. Simrock in 1873[13] of five symphonic études that Schumann had left out of the two editions of the *Études symphoniques*, Op. 13, released during his lifetime. The five variations, together with a sixth, which was left incomplete, form part of an early version of Op. 13 that occupied Schumann compositionally from November 1834 to 18 January 1835.[14] This version of the *Études symphoniques* is documented by three extant manuscripts: six pages of sketches,[15] an autograph fair copy,[16] and a copyist's manuscript with additions and corrections in Schumann's hand.[17] The copyist's manuscript was prepared from Schumann's autograph fair copy: the composer's copying instructions in the autograph were followed to the letter. At the time of the 1873 edition of the five hitherto unpublished études, the copyist's manuscript was in Brahms's possession and the autograph fair copy in Clara's. Apparently neither Brahms nor Clara knew of the existence of the sketches.

An appraisal of the 1873 edition, usually attributed to Brahms,[18] must take into consideration Clara Schumann's reluctant participation in the editing process, as well as

[13] Hofmann, *Die Erstdrucke der Werke von Robert Schumann*, 336–7.

[14] See Georg Eismann, ed., *Robert Schumann: Tagebücher*, 1: 420–1; F. Gustav Jansen, ed., *Robert Schumanns Briefe*, 60. The date 18 Jan. 1835 appears at the end of Schumann's autograph fair copy (Morlanwelz-Mariemont, Belgium, Musée Royal de Mariemont, MS Aut. 1132c). Apparently this version of the work was initially offered to the publisher Haslinger on 3 Feb. 1836 (Schumann's entry in his *Briefverzeichnis* [Zwickau, Robert-Schumann-Haus, 4871 VII C, 10 A3, p. 270, no. 91] reads 'Mit Sonate [Op. 14] und Etüden'). The version of the work later published as the first edition (Vienna: Haslinger, June 1837; see Hofmann, *Die Erstdrucke der Werke von Robert Schumann*, 30–1) contains six variations not found in any of the early sources: Études 3, 6, 7, 8, 9, 11. These six variations may have been composed in September 1836 (see Wolfgang Boetticher, *Robert Schumann in seinen Schriften und Briefen*, 117). The only extant source for the first published version of the work is the engraver's model for the first edition, a manuscript in a copyist's hand with expression marks, corrections, and instructions to the engraver added by Schumann (Düsseldorf, Heinrich-Heine-Institut, MS 71.126; see also Manfred Hermann Schmid, *Musik als Abbild*, 90).

[15] New York, private collection of Alice Tully; microfilm in New York Public Library, Toscanini Memorial Archives, *ZBT–88.

[16] Morlanwelz-Mariemont, Belgium, Musée Royal de Mariemont, MS Aut. 1132c.

[17] Vienna, Gesellschaft der Musikfreunde, A 284. Wolfgang Boetticher, 'Neue textkritische Forschungen an R. Schumanns Klavierwerk', 57, 73, gave the false impression that this manuscript is completely autograph. But cf. Boetticher, *Robert Schumanns Klavierwerke*, 2: 257 f.

[18] Hofmann, *Die Erstdrucke der Werke von Robert Schumann*, 337.

Brahms's unwillingness to edit the pieces. There are many lacunae in the documentation, and we may never know all the details surrounding the publication of the études. Kalbeck states that Brahms persuaded Clara to give up her long-standing opposition and allow publication.[19] Apparently Brahms tried, unsuccessfully, as early as 1868 to convince Clara to release the études, the implication being that she would edit them.[20] Although Brahms did eventually see the études through the press, and therefore may be said to be 'answerable' for them,[21] he never signed the preface. Furthermore, for all that Brahms may have initiated the drive towards the publication of the études, he was singularly unhelpful in the initial stages of the publishing process.

Two unpublished letters written by Clara Schumann in the spring of 1873 to Fritz Simrock bear testimony to her reluctance to undertake the project and hint at unpleasant exchanges between Clara and Brahms over the études:[22]

[Baden-] Baden, 26 May 1873

Dear Herr Simrock,

It will be best if I copy out the Symphonic Études myself, since the copyist would find it difficult. I cannot do this, however, until I return [from a concert tour to Cologne, Aachen, and Düsseldorf], which will not be before the 9th or the 10th of June, because music writing tires the hand more than anything [else]. However, I ask you at least to get Brahms to write out the beginnings (only the first bar [of each]—he certainly knows them by heart) so that I can write them directly in the correct order. He will not refuse [to do] that; it would be truly uncivil. . . . I hope to find the afore-mentioned incipits here on 10 June. Please do provide them, otherwise I cannot begin to write. . . .[23]

Brahms sent the incipits to Simrock from his summer residence in Tutzing on 31 May. Presumably he wrote them out from memory, for he mentioned to Simrock that the copyist's manuscript in his possession had been revised by Schumann, but that it was buried in a trunk and could not be produced at that moment. He asked Simrock to provide him with a trial proof so that he could see whether his manuscript differed from

---

[19] *Brahms Briefwechsel*, 9: 142, n. 1. See also Clara's comments in her diary about her reluctance to undertake the project (Litzmann, *Clara Schumann*, 3: 293).

[20] *Brahms Briefwechsel*, 14: 153. On 17 March 1867, in the concert-hall of the Gesellschaft der Musikfreunde in Vienna, Brahms had performed the *Études symphoniques* 'zum Theile noch Manuscript'. The programme for this concert, in the collection of the Gesellschaft der Musikfreunde, is described in Otto Biba, *Johannes Brahms in Wien*, 37 (item 108). The manuscript mentioned in the programme is undoubtedly the copyist's manuscript owned by Brahms (Vienna, Gesellschaft der Musikfreunde, A 284).

[21] *Brahms Briefwechsel*, 9: 141–2, 144, 148, 152.

[22] Both letters transcribed from microfilm in the New York Public Library, Toscanini Memorial Archives, *ZBT–88.

[23] 'Das Beste wird sein, ich schreibe die Symphonischen Etüden selbst ab, da der Notenschreiber sich schwer herausfinden würde. Ich kann dies aber erst thun, wenn ich zurückgekehrt, was nicht vor dem 9. oder 10. Juni sein wird weil Notenschreiben die Hand mehr noch ermüdet als Anderes. Nun bitte ich Sie aber von Brahms wenigstens die Anfänge (den ersten Takt nur—er weiß sie ja auswendig) aufschreiben zu lassen damit ich sie gleich in der richtigen Reihenfolge schreibe. Das wird er nicht abschlagen, es wäre ja ungefällig. . . . Ich hoffe am 10. Juni hier die bewußten Anfänge zu finden. Bitte besorgen Sie sie ja, ich kann nicht eher anfangen zu schreiben. . . .'

Clara's.[24] Clara's second letter was written two weeks later in reply to a letter from Simrock.

[dictated] Baden-Baden, 14 June 1873

Dear Herr Simrock,

Do not believe that I had not thought about my promise concerning the Symphonic Études; but I do not know how I shall deliver them to you. It would be best if you were to release me entirely from my promise, for publishing them is so entirely against my intention. However, if you do not wish to desist in this matter, then I know of no better copy for you than the one made by Brahms, who in any event has resolved the few questionable passages better than anyone else could. For that reason ask him once again; he certainly does not need to give it [the manuscript] up, but only have it copied for you—either now or next winter, it is not of such great consequence. I cannot ask him about it, because he refused it to me last winter. . . .

P.S. In rereading your last letter I see that you say that the copy in Brahms's possession is one that was supervised and revised by Schumann; directly after this, however, [you say that] Brahms does not want to prepare a revision of the études and refer to the possible variant readings. But these are contradictory [statements]: if the copy is revised by Schumann, then he [Brahms] can certainly deliver it with confidence; if it is not, then Brahms, as I already said above, is certainly the one who can resolve the matter.

I also neglected to reply to the enquiry about your title, because I do not think that you can say: Second Collection, since there are certainly far too few [pieces] in relationship to the first edition. In any event, I must discuss the title with a musician. If I were able at the moment to do you another favour, then I would ask you very decisively to release me from the editing. Do it! The pieces seem to me to be really not of great musical consequence since the first collection is already so rich. . . .[25]

Despite her protestations, Clara did copy the five études from Schumann's autograph, and in the order that Brahms had supplied, an order based with one exception on the succession of the variations in the copyist's manuscript.[26] Clara's copy[27] served as the

---

[24] *Brahms Briefwechsel*, 9: 141–2.

[25] 'Glauben Sie nicht, daß ich nicht an mein Versprechen wegen der Symphonischen Etüden dachte; ich weiß aber nicht, wie ich es machen soll, Ihnen dieselben zuzustellen. Das Liebste wäre mir Sie entbinden mich ganz meines Versprechens, denn gebe ich sie heraus, so geschieht es doch ganz gegen meine Absicht. Wollen Sie aber nicht davon abstehen, so wüßte ich Ihnen doch keine bessere Copie als die von Brahms gemachte, der in jedem Falle die einigen fraglichen Stellen besser gelöst hat, als irgend ein Anderer es konnte. Fragen Sie doch noch einmal bei ihm darum an; er braucht es ja nicht herzugeben, sondern nur für Sie copieren zu lassen—ob nun jetzt oder nächsten Winter, darauf kommt ja auch nicht so viel an. Ich kann ihn nicht darum bitten, weil er es mir vorigen Winter abschlug. . . . P.S. Ich sehe eben bei nochmaligem Lesen Ihres Briefes, daß Sie sagen, die Brahms besitzt, sei eine von Schumann besorgte und revidirte; gleich hinterher aber, Brahms wollte nicht gern eine Revision der Etüden besorgen und etwaige Abweichungen angeben. Das sind doch Widersprüche; entweder die Abschrift ist von Schumann revidirt, dann kann er sie ja getrost hergeben, ist sie es nicht, dann ist Brahms ja doch der, der wie ich Ihnen schon oben sagte, darüber entscheiden kann. Ich vergaß auch auf Anfrage Ihres Titels zu erwidern, daß ich nicht meine, daß Sie sagen können: Zweite Sammlung, da es ja im Verhältniß zu der ersten Ausgabe viel zu wenige sind. Jedenfalls müßte ich mich über den Titel mit einem Musiker besprechen. Wüßte ich im Augenblick Ihnen einen andern Gefallen zu thun, so bäte ich ganz entschieden mir die Herausgabe zu erlassen. Thun Sie es! Die Sache scheint mir wirklich nicht von großem musikalischem Gewicht, da ja die erste Sammlung so reich schon ist. . . .'

[26] The question of the order of the variations in Schumann's early version of the *Études symphoniques* represented by all three of the early manuscripts is a complex one. Schumann often experimented with the order of pieces in his

engraver's model for the 1873 edition, but not until it had been 'corrected' by Brahms, who compared it with the manuscript prepared by Schumann's copyist and transferred into it all the corrections Schumann had made in the copyist's manuscript.[28] The source situation for these five études is thus somewhat unusual. We have two copies prepared from the autograph: Schumann's copyist's copy, which of course contains more than just the five études in question, and Clara's copy. Futhermore, we have Schumann's autograph revisions in his copyist's manuscript, and Brahms's copy of Schumann's revisions in Clara's manuscript.[29]

Clara's role in the publication of the five symphonic études was not limited to supplying the manuscript copy that eventually served as the engraver's model. Had Brahms been familiar with Schumann's autograph—and all the evidence suggests that he was not—he would have noticed that with very few exceptions it contains no dynamics. The dynamic structure of the 1873 edition, therefore, is almost exclusively Clara's, for it appears only in her manuscript copy. Furthermore, Schumann's autograph contains little in the way of articulation markings. The composer articulated the opening bar or so of each variation and thereafter provided only infrequent indications. In the études that are based on a repeated pattern, such as Variation I and the beginning of Variation II (left hand), Clara had merely to continue the opening slurring. But it is important to point out that a good deal of the articulation in this edition was supplied unilaterally and without comment by Clara (see, for example, bars 9–21 of Variation III, bars 29–43 of Variation IV, and almost all of Variation V, to list just some of the more prominent passages).

Would Brahms have concurred with these editorial additions had he known that they were indeed additions?[30] Certainly in his own earlier editions of the *Scherzo* and the *Presto passionato* he added nothing that was not suggested in the sources and adhered quite closely to Schumann's indications as he understood them, even when these involved notational eccentricities such as black note-heads without stems.[31] On the other

cycles of short pieces. Each of the early *Études symphoniques* manuscripts transmits a different order, and the copyist's manuscript also contains instructions in Schumann's hand specifying that the variations be recopied in yet another order. In the autograph in Clara's possession and in the copy owned by Brahms, the variation ultimately published as the fifth of the posthumous études formed the middle section of the étude that, without this middle section, became Étude 10 of the first edition (1837). But this variation (Posthumous 5) had originally been conceived as an independent variation and was not converted into a middle section until the time of Schumann's fair copy, which contains this revision. (Since the five posthumous variations are part of an earlier 'state' of Op. 13, their interpolation into a performance of a 'complete' Op. 13 seems inappropriate.)

[27] Düsseldorf, Heinrich-Heine-Institut, MS 54.1844.

[28] Brahms, however, neglected to enter a repeat sign at the beginning of bar 29 of Variation 4.

[29] Boetticher, 'Neue textkritische Forschungen', 73–4, attributed Schumann's revisions to Brahms. But cf. Boetticher, *Robert Schumanns Klavierwerke*, 2: 256 f.

[30] The copyist's manuscript in Brahms's possession would have been of little help to him in determining which expression marks Clara may have added to her copy. Schumann's instructions on the first page of the copyist's manuscript indicate that he planned to have another copy made; therefore he did not add many marks of articulation or expression to this copy. (Schumann often postponed decisions about expressive details.)

[31] See bars 35, 142, and 150 of the *Scherzo*. Schumann had originally specified note-heads without stems in the first movement of Op. 14 as it appears in this manuscript ('diese Köpfe ohne Striche'; bars 62–5, left hand, lowest notes on the first beat of each bar). This notational oddity did not find its way into the first edition, however.

hand, in his much later edition (1893) of the song 'Im Herbste' in the supplement to the Schumann *Gesamtausgabe*, Brahms modified—not radically, but without comment—the dynamic structure and accentuation, as a comparison of his edition with Schumann's autograph,[32] Brahms's model, reveals. The five symphonic études, as well as the *Scherzo* and the *Presto*, appeared in what were essentially second editions in this supplemental volume edited by Brahms, and we might expect to find a clue there to the question of whether Brahms was familiar with Schumann's autograph of the études and therefore would have recognized Clara's additions for what they were. However, with the exception of the additon or deletion of six cautionary accidentals and the restoration of one extension dot (Variation III, bar 2) that had been overlooked in the 1873 edition, the supplemental volume of the *Gesamtausgabe* reproduces the text of the 1873 edition. Moreover, in his preface to the *Gesamtausgabe* supplement, Brahms's only comment concerning the études was that they had been supplied from a copyist's manuscript corrected by Schumann.

The cavalier manner in which the 1873 edition of the études was prepared—the work of two unwilling editors, one who did not want the pieces to appear at all and the other who, for obscure reasons, did not want to take responsibility for choosing among and recording variant readings—is startling by modern standards, and even by the careful editorial procedures practised at the time in monumental editions such as the Bach Gesellschaft edition, so admired by Brahms. Under these circumstances, perhaps it is not surprising that the edition of the études appeared anonymously: neither editor may have wished to take responsibility. Most interesting of all, however, is that neither Brahms nor Clara seemed aware that these rejected *Études symphoniques* formed part of an earlier version of the work. The subject was never even mentioned.

# III

The collaboration of Clara Schumann and Johannes Brahms on the Schumann *Gesamtausgabe* is too large and complicated a topic to explore adequately in the present format.[33] It might be useful, however, to examine some of the points that came up for discussion, since they illuminate Brahms's editorial philosophy with regard to Schumann's works in a way that the editions of the *Scherzo*, *Presto*, and five *Études symphoniques* do not. Since these compositions were not published during Schumann's lifetime, the composer did not prepare them for publication or see them through the press. Brahms, therefore, could allow himself certain editorial liberties. But the new collected edition of Schumann's published *œuvre* was another matter. The correspondence between Clara Schumann and Brahms shows that Brahms had great respect for

---

[32] Cracow, Biblioteka Jagiellońska, Mus. ms. autogr. Schumann 23.

[33] Boetticher, 'Neue textkritische Forschungen', especially 72–6, deals with this collaboration. Some of his conclusions, however, are based on erroneous interpretation of the sources. A general discussion of Clara Schumann's position with regard to the editing of Schumann's works and her work on the Schumann *Gesamtausgabe* appears in Nancy B. Reich, *Clara Schumann: The Artist and the Woman*, 250–6.

Robert Schumann as an editor of his own works, and that he was sensitive to nuances of notation and expression in the first and early editions of Schumann's works. That much of this nuance was ultimately omitted from the *Gesamtausgabe*[34] cannot be easily explained.

Perhaps the thorniest problem is determining who really was responsible for the editorial decisions. The correspondence suggests that Brahms's role may have been the dominant one. It is possible that more sources will become available in the future, such as the early editions that were used as the engraver's model for the *Gesamtausgabe*, the proof-sheets, Clara's correspondence with Breitkopf & Härtel, the publisher of the edition, and the letters from Clara to Brahms that contain passages omitted from Litzmann's edition of their correspondence. This preliminary enquiry is based on the published Brahms–Clara Schumann correspondence and unpublished portions of Brahms's letters to Clara,[35] the published correspondence between Brahms and Breitkopf & Härtel,[36] and Brahms's personal copies of Schumann's piano music.[37]

The question of who was editorially responsible for the Schumann *Gesamtausgabe* is bound up with the issue of the quality and degree of dependability of the editions of Schumann's works that were to serve as copy-texts for the new collected edition. Here it was Brahms who insisted that the 'old editions', rather than more recent ones, must be used.[38] In designating 'old editions', though, Brahms apparently did not distinguish between first editions and later *Titelauflagen* printed from the plates of the first editions,[39] but only between the original engraved editions and later newly engraved prints.[40] The edition of the *Fantasiestücke*, Op. 12, in Brahms's collection, for example, is a *Titelauflage* from *c.* 1842.[41] Brahms made editorial annotations on this copy so that he could call Clara's attention to errors and inconsistencies in the musical text: the unpublished portion of his letter to Clara of February 1878 contains a list of all the passages he had marked in his edition.[42]

The search for early editions was carried out with industry by both Clara and Brahms. Clara pressed friends into service,[43] and Brahms even made use of rental libraries to

---

[34] Boetticher's study ('Neue textkritische Forschungen') includes a detailed discussion of corruptions in the text of the *Gesamtausgabe*.

[35] Berlin, Staatsbibliothek Preußischer Kulturbesitz, Mus. Nachlaß Clara Schumann 8, MS VI.1924.1859. I wish to thank Professor George Bozarth for calling my attention to this collection.

[36] In *Brahms Briefwechsel*, 14.

[37] Vienna, Gesellschaft der Musikfreunde, Nachlaß Brahms.

[38] Litzmann, ed., *Schumann–Brahms Briefe*, 2: 135.

[39] Boetticher, *Robert Schumanns Klavierwerke*, 1: 8, and 'Neue textkritische Forschungen', 60–1, remarks that worn plates in *Titelauflagen* used as the basis for the *Gesamtausgabe* resulted in errors of omission. He also states ('Neue textkritische Forschungen', 50–2) that the texts of the *Titelauflagen* contain many small changes when compared with those of the first editions.

[40] Litzmann, ed., *Schumann–Brahms Briefe*, 2: 135.

[41] Hofmann, *Die Erstdrucke der Werke von Robert Schumann*, 29.

[42] Litzmann, ed., *Schumann–Brahms Briefe*, 2: 134–6, letter 363. For a transcription of the unpublished portions of this letter, see Appendix, item 1.

[43] Heinrich von Herzogenberg, for example. See Litzmann, ed., *Schumann–Brahms Briefe*, 2: 139.

obtain editions for purposes of comparison.[44] Clara had in her possession Schumann's own copies of his first editions, a fact that Brahms apparently realized only after the search for old editions had begun.[45] The criteria used by Brahms to distinguish older from newer editions are not always clear. For example, in unpublished portions of his letters to Clara of February and April 1878,[46] Brahms mentions that one can tell the newer edition of the *Novelletten*, Op. 21, from the old edition by the typeface used in the pedal indications and by the fact that appoggiaturas in the new edition are written with a stroke ( ♪ ), whereas in the old edition they are not. On the first page of musical text of his copy of the *Novelletten* Brahms wrote a memorandum identifying the print as the new edition and citing as proof the strokes through the tails of the appoggiaturas. Yet the title-page, plate number, price, pagination, etc. of Brahms's copy are indeed those of the first edition.[47] One wonders what edition Brahms thought was the 'old edition', a copy of which was in Nottebohm's possession, according to his letter of April 1878.[48] If this apparent confusion over editions is representative, it may explain why so many *Titelauflagen* rather than first editions proper were used as engraver's models for the collected edition.[49]

Brahms not only determined the editions that would be used as the basis for the *Gesamtausgabe*, but took it upon himself as well to call Clara's attention to notational nuances in Schumann's works. For example, in a reference to *Carnaval*, Op. 9, Brahms alludes to Schumann's use of an accent placed to the side of a note to indicate that only that one particular note of the chord was to be accentuated (letter of March 1878).[50] In an unpublished list of errata, apparently to the first proofs of the *Gesamtausgabe* edition of *Carnaval* and the *Fantasiestücke*, Brahms elaborates on this point, telling Clara that the accents in bars 4 ff. of the 'Préambule' of *Carnaval* belong primarily to the upper notes of the chords in the left hand.[51] He also directs her attention to the fact that *sf* and *rfz* are not the same thing.[52] In an unpublished letter of February 1878 Brahms calls Clara's attention to Schumann's use of two different forms of appoggiatura in 'Warum?' (*Fantasiestücke*, Op. 12): ♪ and ♪ . He apparently assumed that Clara knew the difference between the two forms, but three years later he had to explain the difference to

---

[44] Two different lending libraries are mentioned in unpublished portions of letters to Clara of 15 Oct. 1879 and [end of] Oct. 1879 (Litzmann, ed., *Schumann–Brahms Briefe*, 2: letters 396 and 398, respectively).

[45] Litzmann, ed., *Schumann–Brahms Briefe*, 2: 169; but see ibid., p. 135, n. 1.

[46] Ibid., 2: 134–6, letter 363 (see Appendix, item 1); 141–2, letter 367.

[47] Hofmann, *Die Erstdrucke der Werke von Robert Schumann*, 54–5.

[48] Litzmann, ed., *Schumann–Brahms Briefe*, 2: 141. Possibly Brahms refers to the *Titelauflage* of c. 1842 (see Hofmann, *Die Erstdrucke der Werke von Robert Schumann*, 55). I have not seen this edition; Hofmann does not mention any re-engraving of the musical text.

[49] See Boetticher, 'Neue textkritische Forschungen', 60–1, nn. 87 and 88.

[50] Litzmann, ed., *Schumann–Brahms Briefe*, 2: 137.

[51] See Appendix, item 2. In the collection of letters in the Staatsbibliothek Preußischer Kulturbesitz this list of errata is appended to letter 363 (Feb. 1878), but it is clearly the 'Beilage' mentioned in Brahms's letter of Dec. 1878 (letter 377; Litzmann, ed., *Schumann–Brahms Briefe*, 2: 161). See n. 78, below. The placement of accents in 'Préambule' is inconsistent in the *Gesamtausgabe*.

[52] Cf. bar 43 of 'Préambule' in the first edition (*rfz*) and the *Gesamtausgabe* (*sf*). Was Clara's omission of Brahms's correction an oversight or deliberate?

her, this time with reference to the last bar of No. 5 of the *Gesänge der Frühe*, Op. 133. · In two unpublished postcards postmarked in Vienna we read the following:

[19 May 1881] I have nothing against the C♯, only against the manner of notation. Check to see if the appoggiatura has a stroke through it or not [♪] or [♪] (♪ ♪) and also if it is found in the first edition (<u>Arnold</u>). Doesn't the piece move you when you play it in the twilight and very slowly? . . .[53]

[23 May 1881] Well, d[ear] Cl[ara], that is certainly splendid and everything that I want. Without the stroke it means a long appoggiatura, and when I strike it slowly and raptuously I have nothing against it. (It indicates then [♩ ♩. ♩] ). So, cross out the little stroke in Härtel's [edition].[54]

The lists of corrections—largely unpublished—that Brahms sent to Clara cover everything from the faulty placement of expression marks in the early editions to mistakes in the *Gesamtausgabe* proofs. Brahms deals with questionable pitches or accidentals, inconsistencies in the articulation of parallel passages, the importance of retaining Schumann's deliberately general indications for the use of the sustaining pedal, and ugliness in the layout of the *Gesamtausgabe*. He objected, for example, to the placement of the 'Sphinxes' in the first proofs of *Carnaval*, Op. 9 (in the middle of a page), citing Schumann's careful positioning of them in the first edition. As a result, the text of the *Gesamtausgabe* was re-engraved to place the 'Sphinxes' in their proper position at the bottom of the page.[55]

The unpublished portions of Brahms's letters to Clara argue strongly in favour of seeing Brahms as the driving force behind the Schumann edition. All the major policy decisions were his. The published correspondence confirms this picture. Clara deferred to Brahms in almost every instance, even accepting, under weak protest, his contention that with the exception of the early piano works there was not much to be done on the Schumann edition.[56]

During the course of the work on the *Gesamtausgabe* Brahms gradually assumed more and more of the editorial responsibility. The impetus for this may well have been the new

[53] [19. Mai 1881] 'Ich habe nichts gegen das cis, nur gegen die Schreibart. Sieh nach ob der Vorschlag durchstrichen oder nicht . . . auch ob es sich in der ersten Ausgabe (<u>Arnold</u>) findet. Rührt Dich das Stück nicht sehr wenn Du es in die Dämmerung und recht langsam spielst? . . .'

[54] [23. Mai 1881] 'Nun, l[iebe] Cl[ara] das ist ja vortrefflich und Alles was ich wünsche. Ohne Strich bedeutet's einen langen Vorschlag und wann ich's langsam und schwärmerisch anschlagen darf habe ich nichts dagegen (Es heißt dann . . .). Also streiche das Strichelchen bei Härtels.' In the unpublished portion of an earlier letter, written in May 1881 (Litzmann, ed., *Schumann–Brahms Briefe*, 2: letter 431), Brahms had questioned the C♯ appoggiatura: '. . . I would have nothing against it if it were written differently (long, soft quarter note). So I think that it must simply be the chord struck in advance [♪].' ('. . . Ich hätte nichts dagegen wenn es anders geschrieben wäre (lange, weiche 1/4 Note). So denke ich es müßte einfach der Accord vorgeschlagen werden . . .').

[55] Litzmann, ed., *Schumann–Brahms Briefe*, 2: 162.

[56] Ibid., 2: 107, 121, 200, 202. In a letter of 3 Oct. 1879 (2: 184) Clara asks why they are bothering to revise the works if they are not going to correct questionable passages.

edition of *Carnaval*, which, together with the *Fantasiestücke*, Op. 12, and the *Novelletten*, Op. 21, was one of the first works to be engraved (in 1879). After thanking Brahms (in a letter of 5 April 1878) for his corrections,[57] Clara sent *Carnaval* and the *Fantasiestücke* to Breitkopf & Härtel on 7 May 1878.[58] In November she sent Brahms the proofs,[59] and in a follow-up letter (7 November 1878) wrote:

By now you have probably received my package of proofs and seen from it that I have laid aside my scruples; for [the sake of] my conscience you must at least allow me always to look at the things first before I send them to you; the final decision then will always remain yours.[60]

This letter speaks for itself, as does Brahms's reply in two letters written in December 1878. He complains about the engraving in Op. 9, comparing it unfavourably with Schumann's first edition, and, in a postscript, asks Clara to entrust him with the Schumann works *before* they are newly engraved, for he is not amused by only seeing them afterwards.[61] Subsequent letters document Brahms's control over how to deal with Breitkopf & Härtel, what should be sent to the publisher, and when it should be sent.[62] At one point, in October 1879, he strongly advises Clara not even to look at the piano works (that is, the exemplars that were to serve as the engravers' models?) before sending them to Breitkopf & Härtel, because the few things that she might possibly want to consider could wait until the arrival of the proofs.[63] Matters had progressed so far by May 1882 that Clara could write to Brahms informing him that Breitkopf & Härtel would, at her request, send him the first proofs [*Abzüge*] of Opp. 5 and 6; in this letter she asks Brahms to return the proofs to her and to tell her if the works are engraved according to his wishes.[64]

Passages in the correspondence such as these should not be construed to mean that Clara did not edit the pieces at all, only that she left many of the final editorial decisions to Brahms. Indeed, an unpublished letter of November 1880 from Brahms to Clara (see Appendix, item 4) deals with Clara's corrections in the two editions of the *Davidsbündlertänze*, Op. 6, and shows clearly that Brahms went over initial corrections that Clara had made, offering suggestions based on an important source in his own collection: a copy of the first edition (Friese, 1838), with corrections in Schumann's hand, that had served as the engraver's model for the second edition (Schuberth, 1850/51).[65]

It is difficult to reconcile Brahms's convictions about maintaining the stylistic integrity

[57] Ibid., 2: 141. These are probably the corrections Brahms sent in his letter of Feb. 1878 (No. 363; see Appendix, item 1).

[58] Ibid., 2: 142.

[59] Ibid., 2: 156.

[60] Ibid., 2: 159. 'Meine Sendung der Korrekturen hast Du nun wohl erhalten, und daraus gesehen, daß ich die Skrupel beiseite setze, für mein Gewißen mußt Du mir gestatten, daß ich wenigstens die Sachen immer erst ansehe, ehe ich sie Dir schicke, Dir bleibt dann immer die endgültige Entscheidung.'

[61] Ibid., 2: 160–4. The unpublished list of corrigenda at the end of letter 363 actually belongs with this letter, No. 377 (see Appendix, item 2).

[62] Ibid., 2: 191, 200, 202.

[63] Ibid., 2: 191.

[64] Ibid., 2: 251.

[65] Vienna, Gesellschaft der Musikfreunde, A 282.

of Schumann's music as expressed in its notation—as early as the preface to his 1866 edition of the *Scherzo* and the *Presto passionato* Brahms had made a point of mentioning his retention of Schumann's notational idiosyncrasies—with the corruptions in the musical text of the *Gesamtausgabe*. If, as the correspondence suggests, Brahms exerted final editorial control, why are the principles he advocated followed so inconsistently?

One answer might be found by taking into consideration the late nineteeth-century house style of Breitkopf & Härtel and the technical preferences of the house-editor, Friedrich Ferdinand Brißler. Thus far I have had the opportunity to examine only one edition that served as an engraver's model for the *Gesamtausgabe*, a *Titelauflage* of the 'Paganini Études', Op. 10.[66] It contains editorial emendations in Brahms's hand and a number of deletions or additions of cautionary accidentals in another hand. In the *Gesamtausgabe* the placement of many of the dynamic indications and accents is different from the placement in this model,[67] yet neither Brahms nor the other (house?) editor made any of these changes on the model. One must assume either that the changes were made by the engraver, following a house style, or that they were made by someone in the course of reading the proofs (Brahms? Clara? Brißler?). In a letter of [23] September 1880 to Breitkopf & Härtel, Brahms singled out Brißler for severe criticism; he referred to corruptions in the text of the *Gesamtausgabe*, and in the process clearly set forth his editorial philosophy with regard to Schumann's works:

Today I am returning R. Schumann's Symphony in B♭ major and the rest—with the urgent request to delay the edition further. The new score has become more disagreeable to the eye and more impractical for use owing to Herr Brißler's various instructions, entirely unanticipated as well as incomprehensible.

During his tenure I have already in particular requested, on the occasion of the new edition of Schumann's earlier piano works, that Herr Brißler respect the original, [that he] indicate his proposals, even when they concern formalities and apparently minor details, before the engraving, so that the proper editor in question can say yes or no.

In those fantastic pieces I could understand that the eccentric notation, often departing from the norm, provoked Herr Brißler's opposition. An orchestral score, however, Schumann wrote precisely in the same way as Mozart and Beethoven before him and we after him. On what grounds then is Herr Brißler qualified [to make] incursions and innovations that contradict all standard practice and that are so illogical and unmusical? . . . If Schumann or anyone occasionally departs from the norm or the custom, he has his reasons, and we and Herr Brißler have only to take care to appreciate and to respect these reasons. . . .[68]

---

[66] Vienna, Österreichische Nationalbibliothek, S.m. 5244.

[67] The placement of dynamics is of special significance for Schumann's piano music because the two hands often have separate dynamic markings. See Boetticher, 'Neue textkritische Forschungen', 62.

[68] *Brahms Briefwechsel*, 14: 309–11. 'Ich sende heute R. Schumanns B dur-Symphonie und Übriges zurück—mit der dringenden Bitte, die Herausgabe noch zu versögern. Die neue Partitur ist durch verschiedene, so unerwartete wie unbegreifliche Anordnungen des Herrn Brißler für den Anblick unerfreulicher und für den Gebrauch unpraktischer geworden. Ich habe schon seiner Zeit bei Gelegenheit der neuen Ausgabe der frühern Klaviersachen Schumanns angelegentlich gebeten, Herr Brißler möge has Original respektieren, seine Vorschläge, auch wo sie Äußerlichkeiten und anscheinende Kleinigkeiten betreffen, vor dem Stich anzeigen, damit der betreffende eigentliche Redakteur ja oder nein sagen kann. Bei jenen phantastischen Sachen war es mir begreiflich, daß die eigentümliche, vom Gewohnten oft abweichende Notation Herrn Brißler zum Widerspruch reizte. Eine Orchester-Partitur aber

If Brahms and Clara had to contend with Brißler's editorial ideas throughout their work on the *Gesamtausgabe*,[69] it is quite possible that a number of his modernizations and 'improvements' slipped into print.

When viewed from the perspective of the later nineteenth-century approach to editing piano music, which ranged from the routine editorial addition of expression markings and fingerings to the composing-out of 'latent' thematic content (Bülow's edition of the Beethoven sonatas), Brahms's editions of Schumann's posthumous works emerge almost as models of editorial sobriety. Even when he conflated versions and reinstated deletions, as he did in the edition of the *Presto*,[70] he rarely added anything that was not in the sources. Only in the edition of the five symphonic études do we find extensive editorial dynamics and articulation, and although Brahms must be implicated in the casual way in which this edition appeared, the additions can be demonstrated to be the work of Clara Schumann, not of Brahms.

It is much more difficult to come to grips with the reasons for the infelicities in the Schumann *Gesamtausgabe*. I have suggested that late nineteenth-century conventions of production might have played a part in this, but there are still too many gaps in our knowledge of how this edition was produced to be certain.[71] Perhaps more crucial is the role of Clara Schumann, the 'answerable' editor of the *Gesamtausgabe*. It is clear from the correspondence that she continually looked to Brahms for guidance. It is also evident that she was inclined to worry about details and to over-clarify.[72] Brahms's letter of December 1878, for example, implies that Clara elaborated on Schumann's pedalling indications in 'Paganini' from *Carnaval*.[73] At one point in her work on the Schumann edition Clara even laboured at adding metronome markings, but was dissuaded by Brahms and by the difficulty of the task.[74] On more than one occasion Brahms told Clara not to 'tifteln'.[75] Clearly the printed copies sent by Clara to Brahms for his comments contained editorial emendations that Brahms felt compromised the aesthetic position of Schumann's early editions. It is important to note, however, that his repeated advice to Clara to wait until the arrival of the proof-sheets before doing any necessary editing[76] is

schreibt Schumann genau in derselben Weise wie Mozart und Beethoven vor ihm und wir nach ihm. Auf was und wen beruft sich denn Herr Brißler für Einfälle und Neuerungen, die allem Gewohnten widersprechen, so unlogisch und unmusikalisch sind? . . . Wenn Schumann oder wer gelegentlich von Regel oder Gewohnheit abweicht, so hat er seine Gründe, und haben wir und Herr Brißler nur Acht zu geben, diese einzusehen und zu respektieren. . .' For Brahms's comment to Clara on the publisher's reply to this letter, see his unpublished letter of Nov. 1880 (Appendix, item 4).

[69] See Litzmann, ed., *Schumann–Brahms Briefe*, 2: 209, 214.

[70] He also reinstated one deletion in the *Scherzo*: bars 24–7 were crossed out by Schumann.

[71] Why, for example, was the intended critical commentary never issued? See Litzmann, ed., *Schumann–Brahms Briefe*, 2: 227; 182, n. 1.

[72] See e.g., ibid., 2: 184–7, for a discussion about the numbering of the pieces in the *Novelletten*, Op. 21.

[73] Ibid., 2: 163.

[74] Ibid., 2: 137, 142–3, 182, and the unpublished portion of letter 390 (Appendix, item 3).

[75] Including ibid., 2: 239; unpublished portion of letter 390.

[76] Ibid., 2: 145, 189, 191, 200, 202, etc.

contradicted by his lists detailing errata in the early editions and also by the editing that he himself did on the prints that served as the engravers' models.[77] Therefore, one should probably interpret Brahms's statements as an attempt to prevent Clara from over-editing. By logical extension, the corruptions in the *Gesamtausgabe* might partially be attributable to poor or hasty proof-reading on Brahms's part: he may have rectified only some of Clara's questionable editorial markings; perhaps he only made those corrections he considered to be of real importance.[78] In any event, Brahms certainly allowed errors, and particularly inconsistencies, to slip by. This can be seen in his editions of the posthumous works as well as in the Schumann *Gesamtausgabe*. But the nineteenth-century attitude towards inconsistencies was more casual than our late twentieth-century one. Inconsistencies in phrasing and expression marks are common in Schumann's own editions of his works, and Schumann is generally regarded highly as an editor of his own works; elsewhere I have advanced the hypothesis that he may have heard the details of expression differently at different times.[79] In several unpublished passages in his correspondence with Clara, Brahms mentions the inconsequentiality of small inconsistencies,[80] and he communicated his views on the matter to Ernst Rudorff during the preparation of the Chopin collected edition:

It is not of such great consequence if this or that passage is played according to the version of the French edition or that of the German edition. I don't want to compare myself with Chopin, but in my own things I also play a passage one time one way and another time a bit differently.[81]

Was Brahms a good editor? A proper assessment of his editorial ability will not be possible until his work on other monumental editions—Chopin, Schubert, Mozart—is taken into account, and until his editing of his own works is evaluated.[82] The decisions he made in conjunction with Schumann's music certainly reveal his interest in the editorial process and, in particular, his desire to bring to publication hitherto unpublished works that he considered to be of especial value. His love of the early (1841) version of Schumann's Symphony in D minor, Op. 120, and his subsequent involvement in the publication of this version, prompted a crisis in his relationship with Clara Schumann. The crisis in turn provided an occasion for Brahms himself to evaluate his editorial

---

[77] Ibid., 2: 189.

[78] Ibid., 2: 161, first sentence. In the second, unpublished, sentence of this letter Brahms tells Clara to use 'Pedale' instead of 'Ped.' in the following places in *Carnaval*, Op. 9: beginning of 'Préambule', bar 45 of 'Florestan', and bars 32–3 of 'Pantalon et Columbine'. In the first edition of Op. 9 all of the pedalling is marked 'Pedale' (Schumann's indication for the general use of the sustaining pedal, as the composer explained in a footnote in the first edition of the Piano Sonata in F♯ minor, Op. 11), yet Brahms singled out only these three places for reinstatement of the indication.

[79] 'The Sources for Schumann's *Davidsbündlertänze* Op. 6'.

[80] See e.g. the unpublished portion of letter 390 (Appendix, item 3).

[81] Ernst Friedrich Rudorff, 'Johannes Brahms. Erinnerungen und Betrachtungen', 142. 'Es kommt ja wirklich nicht so viel darauf an, ob diese oder jene Stelle nach der Version der französischen oder der deutschen Ausgabe gespielt wird. Ich will mich nicht mit Chopin vergleichen, aber ich spiele doch auch in meinen Sachen irgendeine Stelle das eine Mal so, das andere Mal ein bißchen anders.'

[82] Robert Pascall addresses the textual problems of Brahms's works in his paper in the present volume and also in 'Brahms and the Definitive Text'.

talents. The following extract is from a letter of 16 October 1891 which he wrote to Clara:

I am the editor of the symphony[83] and at the same time the only one who arranged for its publication and who was responsible for it. I could not put my name to it, first because I have no orchestra at my disposal in order to make the necessary experiments and aural tests; and then— because, to my sorrow, I know from experience that I am not a good editor. I have attempted it often enough and always with a great deal of love and diligence, but I cannot give myself an especially good testimonial and must admit that others are more suited to the task than I. . . .[84]

[83] The preface of this edition, which was published in 1891 as No. 4a of Series I of the *Gesamtausgabe*, was signed by Franz Wüllner.

[84] Litzmann, ed., *Schumann–Brahms Briefe*, 2: 497. 'Herausgeber der Symphonie bin ich und zugleich der einzige, der ihr Erscheinen veranlasst und zu verantworten hat. Meinen Namen konnte ich nicht voransetzen, zunächst weil ich kein Orchester zur Verfügung habe, um das Nötige zu versuchen und dem leiblichen Ohr zu beweisen; dann— weil ich leider die Erfahrung habe, daß ich kein guter Redakteur bin. Ich habe es oft genug versucht und stets mit aller Liebe und allem Fleiß, darf mir aber kein besonders gutes Zeugnis geben und muß anerkennen, daß andere geeigneter zu dem Geschäft sind.'

## APPENDIX

## Unpublished Portions of Letters from Johannes Brahms to Clara Schumann[*]

## I

Berthold Litzmann, ed., *Clara Schumann–Johannes Brahms. Briefe*, No. 363, 2: 134–6 (February 1878). [p. 135, after 'Nach solchem Exemplar muß wieder gestochen werden.']

Ich zeigte Dir die verschieden[en] Aenderungen namentlich b[ei] d[en] Bezeichnungen in der neuen Ausgabe. Hast Du nun im Carnaval [Op. 9] zweifelhafte oder falsche Noten gefunden? Hier sind einige Kleinigkeiten, nicht der Mühe werth.

Seite 6 fehlt zu Anfang [music] (oder zum Schluß des Theils [music] ) ['Pierrot', bar 8]

" " System 2 u[nd] 3 stimmen die Bogen nicht bei: [music] ['Pierrot', bar 19]

" " System 3 steht das 2^te *p* ein Viertel zu früh [music] ['Pierrot', bar 24]

S[eite] 7. Syst[em] 2 u[nd] 5 fehlen Punkte im Baß [music] [music] etc. ['Arlequin', bars 9, 31, 33]

S[eite] 14. S[ystem] 5. Takt 3 fehlt ein ♭ vor e [music] ['Papillons', bar 24]

S. 16. S. 1. T[akt] 3 im Baß [music] ? ['Chiarina', bar 15]

S. 17. S. 4. T. 1 versteh ich die Bezeichnung in der r[echten] H[and] nicht > statt [music] ? ['Estrella', bar 8]

S. 18. S. 3. T. 2. linke Hand letzte Note [music] fes? ['Reconnaissance', bar 11] wie auf S[eite] 19??

S.21 S. 5. T. 5 u[nd] 6 [music] der Bogen steht auf S. 23 nicht. ['Valse Allemande', bar 12; 'Paganini', bar 73]

S. 27. S. 6 vorletzte Takt r. H. [music] soll wohl c heißen? ['Marche des Davidsbündler', bar 81]

S. 29. S. 2. T. 4 u[nd] 5. lauter as? (S. 27 erst ♮ e dann ♭es) ['Marche des Davidsbündler', bars 139–40]

S. 29. S. 4. T. 2 natürlich [music] des (nur schlecht gestochen) ['Marche des Davidsbündler', bar 154]

[*] Berlin, Staatsbibliothek Preußischer Kulturbesitz, Musikabteilung, Mus. Nachlaß Clara Schumann 8, MS VI. 1924.1859. Published here with the permission of the library. I am grateful to Dr Otto Biba for his help in preparing these transcriptions for publication.

Fantasiestücke [Op. 12] I^tes Heft

Seite 8 System 1. Takt 7. ♪♪ Bogen zu lang. ['Aufschwung', bar 71]

"    "    "    5. Takt 1. 2. Bogen zu kurz ♪♪ ['Aufschwung', bars 91–2]

S. 10. S. 2 u. 3 fehlen die Punkte (wie auf S. 6 unten in der rechten Hand) ['Aufschwung', bars 132 ff., 25 ff.]

S. 11 S. 2. T. 3 u. 4 ♪♪ Bogen? ['Warum', bars 3–4]

S. 12 S. 4. T. 3 fehlt in der r. H. eine ♪♪ ['Grillen', bar 25]

S. 13 [recte, 12] S. 5 T. 6 u. 7 fehlt in der r. H. ein Bogen ♪♪ ['Grillen', bars 35–6]

II^tes Heft

S. 6 S. 3. T. 3 linke Hand ♪♪ (statt anders herum) ['In der Nacht', bars 142–3]

S. 9. S. 3. T. 5 fehlen in der l[inken] H[and] die ersten . . . Punkte ['Fabel', bar 5]

S. 10. S. 3. T. 1 steht ein unnützes ♮ vor h. ['Fabel', bar 32]

S. 12. S. 2. T. 4 u. 6 ist der Punkt über den 3^ten Achtel d in der l. H. richtig? Siehe S. 15. ['Traumes Wirren', bars 10, 12 (cf. bars 132, 134)]

S. 14. S. 2. T. 1 fehlt das ♮ vor a. ['Traumes Wirren', bar 75]

"    "    2. T. 3    "    das ♭ vor a. ['Traumes Wirren', bar 77]

S. 15. S. 4. T. 2 sollte der Bogen in der l. H. unter das ◁▷ in der Mitte stehen. ['Traumes Wirren', bar 130]

S. 18. S. 2. T. 3 fehlt in der l. H. ein Bogen ♪♪ ['Ende vom Lied', bar 40]

S. 19. S. 2. T. 1 u. 2 muß der Bogen von c auf c gehen ♪♪ ['Ende vom Lied', bars 68–9]

Die Novelletten sind früh zum zweiten Mal gestochen. Du kannst leicht die alte Ausgabe kennen. Das Pedalzeichen (gleich zu Anfang) sieht so aus Ped. In der zweiten: ℞.
Ich glaube zwar gewiß nicht . . . [p. 135]
[p. 135, after 'Ich finde einstweilen sehr wenig Fragliches oder Zweifelhaftes.']
Meine Bemerkungen hier sind natürlich ganz unnütz, die wenigen unterstrichenen vielleicht zu bedenken. Solches NB könnte ich mehr melden. Nun bin ich begierig ob Du denn mehr o[der] Wichtigeres in den Sachen gefunden hast??! Sonst aber siehst Du ein daß Du Härtels einstweilen zum Stechen geben kannst u[nd] ihnen nur ein Compliment dazu machen darfst wie sorgfältig bei ihnen gearbeitet wird. Vor allem aber . . . [p. 135]
[p. 136, after 'Laß mich wegen München hören.']
Und auch—ob Du besseren Augen o[der] Ohren hast als ich. Aber freilich, ich habe nur einstweilen u[nd] um anzufangen Obiges notirt. Das bitte zu bedenken!

Herzlichst dein
Johannes

## Translation

[p. 135, after 'Nach solchem Exemplar muß wieder gestochen werden.']

I showed you the various changes, in particular in the [expression] indications in the new edition. Have you then found questionable or wrong notes in *Carnaval* [Op. 9]? Here are a few minor details, not worth the effort.

Page 6 ♩ 𝄆 ♩ is missing at the beginning (or ≣ at the end of the section) [Pierrot', bar 8]

" " systems 2 and 3, the slurs are at variance: ≣ ['Pierrot', bar 19]

" " system 3, the 2nd *p[iano]* is a quarter note too early ≣ ['Pierrot', bar 24]

P[age] 7, systems 2 and 5, dots are missing in the bass ≣ ≣ etc.['Arlequin', bars 9, 31, 33]

P[age] 14, s[ystem] 5. in <u>bar</u> 3, a ♭ is missing before E ≣ ['Papillons', bar 24]

P. 16, s. 1, b[ar] 3, in the bass ≣ ? ['Chiarina', bar 15]

P. 17, s. 4, b. 1, I don't understand the indication in the r[ight] h[and] > instead of ≣ ? ['Estrella', bar 8]

<u>P. 18, s. 3. b. 2,</u> left hand, last note ≣ F♭? ['Reconnaissance', bar 11] as on p[age] 19??

P. 21, s. 5, b. 5 and 6 ≣ the tie is <u>not</u> on p. 23. ['Valse Allemande', bar 12; 'Paganini', bar 73]

P. 27, s. 6, penultimate bar, r. h. ≣ should probably read C? ['Marche des Davidsbündler', bar 81]

P. 29, s. 2, b. 4 and 5, simply A♭? (on p. 27, first E♮, then E♭) ['Marche des Davidsbündler', bars 139–40]

P. 29, s. 4, b. 2, of course ≣ D♭ ([it is] merely poorly engraved) ['Marche des Davidsbündler', bar 154]

<u>Fantasiestücke</u> [Op. 12], Book I

Page 8, system 1, bar 7 ≣ slur too long. ['Aufschwung', bar 71]

" " " 5, bar 1, 2, slur too short ≣ ['Aufschwung', bars 91–2]

P. 10, s. 2 and 3, the dots are missing (as on p. 6, underneath in the right hand) ['Aufschwung', bars 132 ff., 25 ff.]

<u>P. 11, s. 2, b. 3 and 4</u> ≣ tie? ['Warum', bars 3–4]

P. 12, s. 4, b. 3, a ♮ is missing in the r. h. ≣ ['Grillen', bar 25]

P. 13 [*recte*, 12], s. 5, b. 6 and 7, a slur is missing in the r. h. ['Grillen', bars 35–6]

Book II

P. 6, s. 3, b. 3, left hand (instead of the other way around) ['In der Nacht', bars 142–3]

P. 9, s. 3, b. 5, the first . . . dots are missing in the l[eft] h[and] ['Fabel', bar 5]

P. 10, s. 3, b. 1, there is a superfluous ♮ before B. ['Fabel', bar 32]

P. 12, s. 2, b. 4 and 6, is the dot over the 3rd 8th-note D in the l. h. correct? See p. 15. ['Traumes Wirren', bars 10, 12 (cf. bars 132, 134)]

P. 14, s. 2, b. 1, the ♮ is missing before A. ['Traumes Wirren', bar 75]

      "     "   b. 3, the ♭ "     "     before A. ['Traumes Wirren', bar 77]

P. 15, s. 4, b. 2, the slur in the l. h. should be under the ⎯⎯ in the middle. ['Traumes Wirren', bar 130]

P. 18, s. 2, b. 3, a slur is missing in the l. h. ['Ende vom Lied', bar 40]

P. 19, s. 2, b. 1 and 2, the tie must go from C to C ['Ende vom Lied', bars 68–9]

The *Novelletten* went through a second engraving early on. You can easily recognize the old edition. The pedal indication (right at the beginning) looks like this: Ped.   In the second [edition, like this]: 🎵.
Ich glaube zwar gewiß nicht . . . [p. 135]
[p. 135, after 'Ich finde einstweilen sehr wenig Fragliches oder Zweifelhaftes.']
My remarks here are naturally entirely superfluous; perhaps those few that are underlined should be taken into consideration. I could go on pointing out such NBs. At present I am curious [about] whether you have found more, or more important, [errors] in the things??! Generally, however, you understand that in the meantime you can give Härtels [something] to engrave and need only pay them a compliment about how carefully they work.
Vor allem aber . . . [p. 135]
[p. 136, after 'Laß mich wegen München hören.']
And also—whether you have better eyes or ears than I. But by all means, I noted down the above only provisionally and in order to make a start. That should be taken into consideration, please!

Most affectionately yours,
Johannes

## 2

Addendum to *Schumann–Brahms Briefe*, No. 377 (December 1878).
(In the collection of letters in the Berlin Staatsbibliothek Preußischer Kulturbesitz, this addendum erroneously follows letter 363.)

(Carnaval) [Op. 9] [The pagination in this list refers to an early proof and does not match that of the *Gesamtausgabe*.]

S[eite] 2, 8, 17 <u>Pedale</u> (statt Ped.) ['Préambule', bar 1; 'Florestan', bar 45; 'Pantalon et Colombine', bars 32–3]

Seite 2. System 2 [music notation] u.s.w. (geht hauptsächlich den oberen Ton an.) ['Préambule', bars 4 ff.]

S. 1 u.s.f. più statt piú (Letzteres doch falsch?)

S. 1. *sf* u[nd] *rfz* (nicht dasselbe)

S. 4. S. 5 [music notation] (<u>nicht</u> die Punkte unten u[nd] d[er] Bogen oben). ['Pierrot', bars 1 ff.]

S[eite] 5. Arlequin. Ich würde das lustige Stück Heute wieder so lustig schreiben. Solls anders so

muß Takt 9 u.s.w. geschrieben werden: [music notation] oder [music notation] (aber nicht

[music notation] wo dann eben [music notation] fehlen)

System 5 [music notation] gehört das *sf* <u>oben</u> [bars 25–6]

S[eite] 7. S[ystem] 1 u[nd] 2 muß genau bleiben. Ist unzweifelhaft deutlich u[nd] vorsichtig geschrieben u[nd] corrigirt.

S. 8. S. 4 etc. steht das *ff* schlecht [music notation] ['Coquette', bar 5]

S. 12. S. 2 [und] 5 [music notation] <u>braucht</u> wohl nicht col. 8$^{vo}$ zu bedeuten) ['Chiarina', bars 8, 32]

S. 14. S. 3 [music notation] würde ich den Bogen zusetzen ['Reconnaissance', bars 17–18]

<u>Fantasiestücke</u> [Op. 12] [Pagination corresponds to the *Gesamtausgabe*.]

S[eite] 4. S[ystem] 3 [music notation] würde ich den Bogen etwas über die Noten

hinausziehen lassen, weil er die 2. Noten <u>nicht</u> schweigen lassen soll. ['Aufschwung', bars 16–17]

S[eite] 5. S[ystem] 6 u[nd] S[eite] 5. S[ystem] 7 würde ich wohl die Bogen ändern u[nd] den späteren gleich machen

[music notation]

['Aufschwung', bars 67–8, 73–4]

S[eite] 6 (u[nd] 5) (Syst[em] 2) weiß ich nicht. Es ist merkwürdig daß das erste Mal der Bogen fehlt

u[nd] das 2$^{te}$ Mal da steht [music notation] ['Aufschwung', bars 55–6, 87–8; Brahms's example follows the readings of the first edition (cf. the *Gesamtausgabe*)]

Muß nicht S[eite] 15 S[ystem] I cis statt c in d[er] l. H.? ['In der Nacht', bar 105]

## Translation

(<u>Carnaval</u>) [Op. 9] [The pagination in this list refers to an early proof and does not match that of the *Gesamtausgabe*.]

P[age] 2, 8, 17 <u>Pedale</u> (instead of Ped.) ['Préambule', bar 1; 'Florestan', bar 45; 'Pantalon et Colombine', bars 32–3]

Page 2, system 2  etc. (applies mainly to the upper note.) ['Préambule', bars 4 ff.]

P. 1, etc. più instead of piú (the latter is certainly wrong?)

P. 1. *sf* and *rfz* (not the same thing)

P. 4, s. 5 ⟨music⟩ (<u>not</u> the dots underneath and the slur above). ['Pierrot', bars 1 ff.]

P[age] 5. Arlequin. Today I would notate the merry piece in just this merry way again. If it is to be otherwise, then bar 9 etc. must be written: ⟨music⟩ or ⟨music⟩ (but not ⟨music⟩ where then just now ⟨rests⟩ are missing)

System 5 ⟨music⟩ the *sf* belongs <u>above</u> [bars 25–6]

P[age] 7, system 1 and 2 must remain exact. It is unquestionably clearly and carefully written and proof-read.

P. 8, s. 4, etc. the *ff* is poorly placed ⟨music⟩ ['Coquette', bar 5]

P. 12, s. 2 and 5 ⟨music⟩ probably does not <u>have</u> to mean col. 8ᵛᵒ) ['Chiarina', bars 8, 32]

P. 14, s. 3 ⟨music⟩ I would add the slur ['Reconnaissance', bars 17–18]

<u>Fantasiestücke</u> [Op. 12] [Pagination corresponds to the *Gesamtausgabe*.]

P[age] 4, s[ystem] 3 ⟨music⟩ I would extend the slur a little beyond the notes, because it should <u>not</u> cause the 2nd notes to be silent. ['Aufschwung', bars 16–17]

P[age] 5, s[ystem] 6 and p[age] 5, s[ystem] 7, I would probably change the slurs and make the later ones uniform

['Aufschwung', bars 67–8, 73–4]

P[age] 6 (and 5) (system 2) I don't know. It is curious that the slur [tie] is missing the first time and present the second time ['Aufschwung', bars 55–6, 87–8; Brahms's example follows the readings of the first edition (cf. the *Gesamtausgabe*)]

On p. 15, s. 1 Shouldn't it be C♯ instead of C in the l. h? ['In der Nacht', bar 105]

# 3

*Schumann–Brahms Briefe*, No. 390, 2: 181 (September 1879).
[after '. . . denke ich zu Hause zu sein'.]

Aber ich will jetzt o[der] heute nur auf die Fragen antworten—habe nur leider kein altes Ex[emplar] der Fantasie [Op. 17] da! Nun schickst Du sie wohl an Woldemar [Bargiel]? Im Fall der aber viel NB. noch in die Sachen macht, so laß uns diese doch noch einmal besehen!!

1. (?) <u>Fantasie</u>. Ph. statt F ist wohl geändert weil auf derselbe Seite gleich darunter kommt <u>phantastisch</u> vorzutragen. Mir wäre lieber es bliebe beim Alten.

2. ♭ wohl unnöthig.

(7. In der alten Ausgabe steht doch Legen<u>denton</u>? Warum ändern?)

3. ♭ Wieder eine höchst überflüssige Neuerung bei Härtels; bei Noten die gebunden sind, also gar nicht angeschlagen werden, braucht man eine Vorzeichnung nicht zu wiederholen. Consequent sind sie auch nicht darin, siehe S[eite] 6 l[inke] H[and] etc. [I, bars 107–8] (Es steht doch nicht so in der alten Ausg[abe]?) (Steht S[eite] 9 Syst[em] I T[akt] 1 in der l. H. nicht etwa [I, bar 195]

4. Die ⁊ Pause würde ich stehen lassen. [I, bars 195 ff.]

5. Das g in der l. H. ist gewiß ein Fehler. <u>as</u>.

6. (Seite 5) das 8ᵗˡ würde ich lassen; verständlich ist es, steht 4 mal da, solcherlei könnte man viel tifteln.

8. Vom Metronom verstehe ich nichts u[nd] Du weisst daß ich sehr dafür bin darin nichts zu versuchen. Alles stehen zu lassen u[nd] etwa in spätere[n] krit[ischen] Bemerkungen weitere Weisheit los zu lassen.

9. (S[eite] 14) Die Bogen finde ich ganz richtig u[nd] verständlich; so subtile Sachen lassen sich nicht deutlicher schreiben.

10. (S. 17) Nur nicht tifteln!

11. (S. 18) g natürlich falsch (statt b). Für die zwei Fehler verdienst Du ein.

12. Den Bogen finde ich gut. So feine Stellen die sich wiederholen, schreibt oder bezeichnet man wohl ganz gern etwas verschieden (S. 19 steht's wieder).

13. Den Bogen hätte ich freilich auch gern anders. Lässt sich aber wohl nicht gut machen, daß es hübsch aussieht? Schaden thut's aber nicht.
Ich bin Heute . . . [p. 181]

## Translation

[after '. . . denke ich zu Hause zu sein.']
But now, or today, I merely want to answer the questions—only unfortunately I do not have an old exemplar of the Fantasie [Op. 17] here! Well, you are no doubt sending it to Woldemar [Bargiel]? In the event, however, that he is still writing many NBs in the things, let us surely have a look at this one again!!

1. (?) Fantasie. Ph instead of F has probably been changed because phantastisch occurs on the same page, directly underneath. I would prefer that it remain as in the old [edition].

2. ♭ probably superfluous.

(7. In the old edition it surely reads Legendenton? Why change it?)

3. ♭ Again an extremely superfluous innovation on the Härtels's part; when notes are tied, therefore
♭ not by any means intended to be sounded, one does not need to repeat an accidental. They [the

Härtels] are also not consistent in this regard; see p[age] 6, l[eft] h[and] 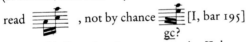 etc. [I, bars 107–8]

(It doesn't read that way in the old edition, does it?) (Does p[age] 9, system I, b[ar] 1 in the l. h.

read ▮ , not by chance ▮ [I, bar 195]
gc?
4. I would allow the 𝄾 rest to remain. [I, bars 195 ff.]

5. The G in the l. h. is certainly an error. A♭

6. (Page 5) I would leave the 8th note; it is intelligible, [and] occurs 4 times; one could quibble a lot about such things.

8. I understand nothing of the metronome and you know that I am very much in favour of attempting nothing in that quarter. [I would advise you] to leave everything alone and perhaps in the later critical commentary utter further wisdom [on the subject].

9. (P[age] 14) I find the slurs entirely correct and intelligible; such subtle things cannot be written more clearly.

10. (P. 17) Only don't quibble!

11. (P. 18) G is certainly wrong (instead of B♭). For the two errors you gain one.

12. I find the slur good. Such subtle passages that recur can probably quite readily be written or marked somewhat differently (it reappears on p. 19).

13. I confess that I also would have liked the slur otherwise. But can't it possibly be done well, so that it looks nice? But it doesn't do any damage.

Ich bin Heute . . . [p. 181]

# 4

November 1880 [unpublished]

Liebe Clara,

Ich fahre Heute Mittag u[nd] will Dir vorher noch die Corr[ekturen] zugehen lassen.

Zur Sinfonie [No. 1 in B♭ major, Op. 38] wäre nur zu bemerken daß auf Levis u[nd] m[einen] Brief Härtels keine eigentliche o[der] direkte Antwort gegeben haben, ein[e] indirekte aber durch diese Vorlage—worin eben keine Notiz davon genommen ist, sondern Brißler alles wie gewöhnlich hergerichtet hat. Beim Requiem war es auch so. Nun also—entweder—oder!?

Bei den Davidsbündler[n], alte Ausgabe, muß doch der Spruch hingesetzt werden; ich sehe kein Platz dafür. In Nr. 2 sind die ersten 3 Takte des 2<sup>ten</sup> Theils bei Sch[umann] auffallend geschrieben,

aber jedes mal gleich Es ist vielleicht ein Zufall oder ein Versehen, aber jetzt ist es verschieden geschr[ieben]. Vergleiche die 4 Stellen wo es kommt u[nd] lass immer dasselbe stehen (doch wohl das alte ursprüngliche).

In der neuen A[usgabe] Nr. 1 hast Du ein ⌢ zugesetzt. In m[einem] Correktur-Exemplar ist das ⌢ an beide Stellen deutlich von Sch[umann] gestrichen. Du hast vielleicht ein neueres Ex[emplar] von der Schubertschen Ausg[abe] wo hinein corrigirt (nachträglich) ist. In Nr. 4 sind die 8<sup>t[el]</sup> Pausen doch richtig die 2 g werden zusammen angeschlagen. In Nr. 6 zum Schluß meine ich wie [here an arrow points to the sentence in which Brahms speculates that Clara has a more recent copy of the Schuberth edition].

Ich habe nur das Corr[ektur]-Ex[emplar] von Sch[umann] da, kein eigentl[iches] von d[er] Schubertschen Ausg[abe]. In Nr. 15 würde ich mir doch nicht getrauen die Punkte fortzusetzen. Es steht beidemal deutlich der Bogen u[nd] Sch[umann] hat sie in beide Ausgaben durchgehen lassen!

Du siehst, da ist nicht viel zu bemerken o[der] ich hoffe es ist doch nichts übersehen.

Nun will ich aber das X. Couvert u[nd] dann m[einen] Koffer packen.

Zum 2<sup>t[en]</sup> Concert wünsche ich alles Glück u[nd] lass mich hören wie lustig es verlauft. Stockhausen hat wohl s[eine] Pläne aufgegeben? Herzogenbergs wollen in B[erlin] sein.

Alle herzlichste[n] Grüße von Deinem

Johannes

Deine Karte kommt auch soeben; in 8 Tagen spätestens denke ich zu Haus zu sein.

*Translation*

November 1880 [unpublished]

Dear Clara,

   I am leaving today at noon and beforehand still want to forward the proofs to you.

   With regard to the symphony [No. 1 in B♭ major, Op. 38], the only remark to be made would be that the Härtels have made no proper or direct reply to the letter that Levi and I wrote them, but instead an indirect reply through this copy [of the symphony]—in which absolutely no notice has been taken of it [the letter], but [in which] Brißler has touched up everything as usual. It was the same story with the Requiem. Well now—take it or leave it!?

   In the old edition of the *Davidsbündler[tänze]* the motto must indeed be inserted; [but] I see no place for it. In No. 2 the first 3 bars of the 2nd section are written in Sch[umann's edition] in a striking manner, but each time the same

Perhaps it is a chance occurrence or an oversight, but now it is written differently. Compare the 4 places where it appears and make the reading always the same (but indeed, the old, original [reading]).

   In the new edition, No. 1, you have added a ⌢. In my proof copy the ⌢ was clearly crossed out by Schumann in both places. Perhaps you have a more recent copy of the Schuberth edition where corrections were added (later). In No. 4 the 8th rests are indeed correct ; the 2 G's are to be sounded together. In No. 6 at the end I believe that [here an arrow points to the sentence in which Brahms speculates that Clara has a more recent copy of the Schuberth edition].

   I have here only Schumann's proof copy, no actual [copy] of the Schuberth edition. In No. 15 I would surely not venture to continue the dots. Both times the slur is clearly there, and Schumann tolerated them in both editions!

   You see, that is not much to note or I hope nothing has indeed been overlooked.

   Now, however, I want to pack the umpteenth envelope and then my suitcase.

   I wish you good luck for the 2nd concert, and let me know how merrily it turns out. Stockhausen has probably given up his plans? The Herzogenbergs want to be in B[erlin].

All heartfelt greetings from your

Johannes

Your postcard has just now also arrived; I plan to be home in 8 days at the latest.

# THE PUBLICATION OF
# BRAHMS'S THIRD SYMPHONY:
# A CRISIS IN DISSEMINATION

—

## ROBERT PASCALL

BECAUSE the vast majority of Brahms's works were published during his lifetime and with his close collaboration, it was widely assumed until recently that these published texts, unless revised or corrected in Brahms's personal copies (the *Handexemplare*), represent the exact and final wishes of the composer. Indeed, this assumption lay behind the decision of Eusebius Mandyczewski and Hans Gál to base nearly all their editions for the *Johannes Brahms Sämtliche Werke* on the *Handexemplare* and to place little value on readings in the other primary sources—autographs, copyists' manuscripts, and other contemporaneous editions. Studies in textual criticism undertaken during the last few years, especially by George Bozarth, Ernst Herttrich, and myself,[1] have shown this view to be erroneous for a number of Brahms's compositions. This paper, which will present a detailed account of the publication of Brahms's Third Symphony, seeks to exemplify the nature of the quality-control problems which beset editions of Brahms's works published during his lifetime. These problems were acute in the case of the Third Symphony: the initial issue of the first edition of this work is the most error-ridden of all such issues of Brahms's music. As we shall see, subsequent correction for later issues of the symphony did not entirely eradicate these errors, and at times compounded them and added to their number.

## I

Johannes Brahms announced his Third Symphony to his publisher Fritz Simrock in a letter of 15 September 1883 in the following terms: 'if I should once again find pages of notes from my youth, I will also send them to you. . . . By the way, don't overlook the pretty circus-gossip.'[2] These laconic, high-spirited remarks are typical of a mode of Brahmsian discourse which he used particularly with certain male colleagues. His

---

[1] George S. Bozarth, 'A New Collected Edition for Johannes Brahms'; Johannes Brahms, *Klaviertrios*, ed. Ernst Herttrich; Robert Pascall, 'Brahms and the Definitive Text'; also, George S. Bozarth, with Ernst Herttrich and Otto Biba, 'Provisional Editorial Guidelines (Richtlinien) for the Johannes Brahms, Gesamtausgabe der musikalischen Werke'.

[2] 'wenn ich etwa noch einmal Notenblätter aus meiner Jugendzeit finde, so will ich sie Ihnen auch schicken. . . . Nebenbei übersehen Sie die hübsche Zirkus-Plauderei nicht'. *Brahms Briefwechsel*, 11: 28–9.

mention of 'pages of notes' from his youth most likely refers to his reuse of a Sarabande and Gavotte from 1854–5 as the basis of the middle movement of his First String Quintet, Op. 88, a work which had appeared the previous year;[3] and these comments as a whole have been taken by most scholars, surely correctly, as indicating a similar reuse of earlier material somewhere in the Third Symphony.[4] While this symphony is not mentioned explicitly, it is unmistakably alluded to by his reference to the gossip about it which was rife at this time. Indeed, intense interest always surrounded the apex-genre of symphony in Brahms's private and public circles, and Brahms enclosed in this letter to Simrock a newspaper cutting of such gossip.[5] In Figure 1 I have registered the implications of this letter by the designation 'Models (unknown)'.

During October Brahms began to make preparations for the first performance of the Third Symphony, including the generation of a set of parts, and announced to Simrock his intention to publish the work 'round about spring'.[6] The set of parts must have been taken from the autograph score, since the manuscript copy of the score (which was later to serve as engraver's exemplar) was not completed before December, as we know from a letter to Joseph Joachim.[7] Brahms sent the five string parts to Simrock on 8 November to be printed for his private use, and these printed parts were to arrive back in Vienna by the 24th of that month, earlier if possible: 'Have the correcting done just in Leipzig,' wrote Brahms; 'a few mistakes are not going to matter!'[8] Brahms had used both of his regular copyists—Franz Hlaváček and William Kupfer—to prepare the initial set of orchestral parts (one copy of each part) for this symphony, for he was at this time in the process of replacing the former copyist with the latter, on grounds of age and speed.[9] Brahms's remark about Leipzig refers to the engraving and printing firm of C. G. Röder, leaders in the world of music printing at this time and the firm used by Simrock from 1870. Röder employed an in-house corrector, as we know from a detailed account of the working practices of the company, published by them in English in 1885.[10] Brahms's general opinion of the standards of this corrector may be deduced from this letter.

The first performance of the Third Symphony took place in Vienna on 2 December 1883 under Hans Richter, and during the next few months performances were given in Berlin (thrice), Wiesbaden (twice), Meiningen (twice at the same concert!), Leipzig, Cologne, Amsterdam, Dresden, Frankfurt, and Pest (on 2 April 1884). As Alfred von Ehrmann suggested, Brahms could well have written the two-piano, four-hand

---

[3] On the relationship of Op. 88 to these earlier pieces, see Hans Gál, *Johannes Brahms: His Work and Personality*, 163–8; Robert Pascall, 'Unknown Gavottes by Brahms'; and Johannes Brahms, *Kleine Stücke für Klavier*, ed. Robert Pascall.

[4] Christian Martin Schmidt has recently sought to argue otherwise, but takes no account of Brahms's habits of discourse with Simrock. See Johannes Brahms, *Sinfonie Nr. 3 F-Dur, Op. 90 Taschen-Partitur*, 157.

[5] Max Kalbeck, *Johannes Brahms*, 3: 387 n.

[6] *Brahms Briefwechsel*, 11: 34.

[7] Ibid., 6: 207.

[8] 'Korrigieren lassen Sie nur in Leipzig; es kommt ja auf ein paar Fehler nicht an!' Ibid., 11: 40.

[9] Ibid., 11: 38. In this letter Brahms noted that 'the old' copyist, Hlaváček, prepared the violin parts.

[10] This essay has been reprinted, with an introduction by A. Hyatt King, as 'C. G. Röder's Music-Printing Business in 1885'.

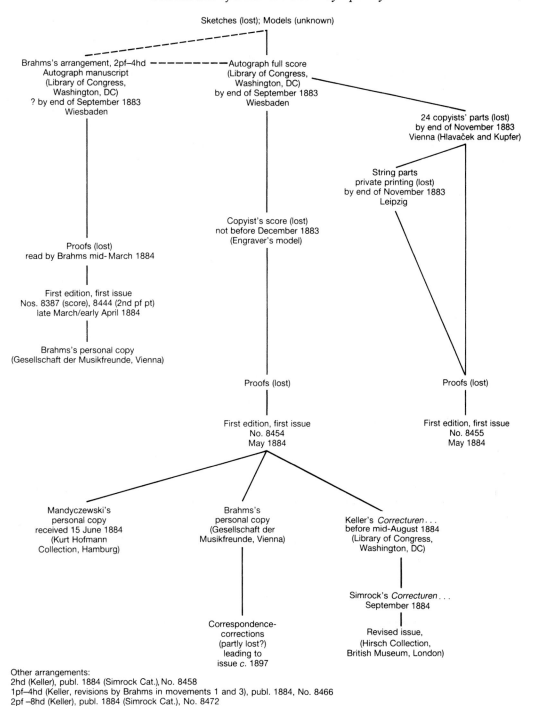

Sketches (lost); Models (unknown)

Brahms's arrangement, 2pf–4hd ——————→ Autograph full score
Autograph manuscript
(Library of Congress,
Washington, DC)
? by end of September 1883
Wiesbaden

Autograph full score
(Library of Congress,
Washington, DC)
by end of September 1883
Wiesbaden

24 copyists' parts (lost)
by end of November 1883
Vienna (Hlavaček and Kupfer)

String parts
private printing (lost)
by end of November 1883
Leipzig

Copyist's score (lost)
not before December 1883
(Engraver's model)

Proofs (lost)
read by Brahms mid-March 1884

First edition, first issue
Nos. 8387 (score), 8444 (2nd pf pt)
late March/early April 1884

Brahms's personal copy
(Gesellschaft der Musikfreunde, Vienna)

Proofs (lost)

Proofs (lost)

First edition, first issue
No. 8454
May 1884

First edition, first issue
No. 8455
May 1884

Mandyczewski's
personal copy
received 15 June 1884
(Kurt Hofmann
Collection, Hamburg)

Brahms's
personal copy
(Gesellschaft der
Musikfreunde, Vienna)

Keller's *Correcturen...*
before mid-August 1884
(Library of Congress,
Washington, DC)

Simrock's *Correcturen...*
September 1884

Correspondence-
corrections
(partly lost?)
leading to
issue *c.* 1897

Revised issue,
(Hirsch Collection,
British Museum, London)

Other arrangements:
2hd (Keller), publ. 1884 (Simrock Cat.), No. 8458
1pf–4hd (Keller, revisions by Brahms in movements 1 and 3), publ. 1884, No. 8466
2pf –8hd (Keller), publ. 1884 (Simrock Cat.), No. 8472

FIGURE I. Filiation of Primary Sources for Brahms's Third Symphony

arrangement during the previous summer at Wiesbaden, contemporaneously with the score.[11] This gives rise to interesting speculation about the relationship between the full orchestral version and the arrangement, since such an arrangement could naturally form a *Particell* stage in the compositional history of a symphony. Whether or not the arrangement had a compositional priority of this kind, it did have a publishing priority. As the correspondence and annotations on the autograph make clear, this arrangement was engraved from the autograph; Simrock received first proofs in the middle of February 1884, Brahms was able to proof-read the arrangement by mid-March, and the edition was ready by late March–early April.[12]

Brahms refers to his detailed plans for the engraving of the orchestral score and parts in a letter to Simrock in March 1884: 'On 2 April the symphony happens in Pest. Then I shall send you score and parts.' Brahms wrote to Simrock again on 29 March: 'I shall send you the whole ballast from Pest. The parts of course must be revised according to the score. . . . The paste-over in the first string parts does not stand—I shall correct it in the score.'[13] It was customary for individual parts, rather than the score, to be used as engravers' exemplars for the printing of the set of parts, although Brahms knew well the difficulties over discrepancy.

## II

The above information from correspondence in 1884 regarding the arrangement and the main text has occupied us in such detail for two reasons. In the first place, it is unequivocally clear that the publication dates for the Third Symphony given hitherto have been erroneous. And secondly, the dating confirmed by this evidence from the correspondence casts doubt on whether Brahms ever did see proofs for the main text, as was his normal practice.

Otto Erich Deutsch offered no month of publication for the arrangement, but March 1884 for the score and parts;[14] Kurt Hofmann placed publication of the arrangement in February 1884 and followed Deutsch in giving March for the main text.[15] But from the correspondence we know that the arrangement could not have appeared earlier than the last weeks in March, and the score and parts no earlier than the last weeks in May. This

---

[11] *Johannes Brahms: Weg, Werk und Welt*, 349. He bases his suggestion on a letter which Brahms wrote to an unnamed person in Wiesbaden to accompany a presentation copy of the arrangement. Kalbeck (*Johannes Brahms*, 3: 384) quoted this letter: 'I have often played the symphony to friends on two pianos with Brüll— each time it was a sorrow to me that modesty or whatever made me so restrained—I could certainly have played it there and to you also.' The letter remains suggestive rather than conclusive.

[12] Kurt Stephenson, ed., *Johannes Brahms und Fritz Simrock—Weg einer Freundschaft*, 193, and *Brahms Briefwechsel*, 11 : 51, 52.

[13] 'Am 2ten April ist die Symphonie in Pest. Dann schicke ich Ihnen Partitur und Stimmen', and 'Von Pest werde ich Ihnen den ganzen Ballast zuschicken. Die Stimmen müssen natürlich nach der Partitur revidiert werden. . . . Das Überklebte in den ersten Quartettstimmen gilt nicht—ich werde es in der Partitur korrigieren.' *Brahms Briefwechsel*, 11: 52, 53–4.

[14] 'The First Editions of Brahms', 123, 255.

[15] *Die Erstdrucke der Werke von Johannes Brahms*, 191.

revised dating is supported by the chronology of Simrock's plate-numbers. Furthermore, the arrangement must have appeared by 10 April, when Brahms requested that Simrock send complimentary copies of it to three friends;[16] and the publication of the score and parts must have been finished by the end of May, in time for materials to be ready for a performance of the work at the beginning of June in the Lower Rhenish Music Festival at Düsseldorf. By any standards, the score and parts were thus produced according to a very tight schedule; indeed, Simrock later alluded to this at the head of his published corrigenda list (see Illustration 2).

Brahms was corresponding with Simrock during April about other matters, and there is no mention in these letters of proofs for the score and parts. Some years earlier Röder had produced proofs for the Violin Concerto in about six weeks; but in 1884 Brahms left for Italy on 8 May, whence he travelled directly to the Rhine just in time for the Festival. He was in Düsseldorf from 1 to 6 June, as we know from his personal calendar-book.[17] While none of this is conclusive evidence, it remains more than probable that Brahms did not read proofs for the score and parts of his Third Symphony.

His previous experience with publishing symphonies had accustomed him to seeing mistakes in print. He corrected the First Symphony three times by letter after the first issue, and with the Second he specifically asked Simrock for a small initial print-run so that more mistakes could surface.[18] In the case of the Third Symphony, however, a real crisis in dissemination occurred: the initial printing of the score and set of parts was thoroughly error-ridden. Thus, with this composition the modern scholar is given a special and important opportunity to study a massive sample of characteristic errors and to witness some of the processes used to attempt to correct them.

## III

The process of correction began almost immediately. On 10 June Brahms wrote to Robert Keller, Simrock's valued house-editor, correcting errors in the viola, cello, and double-bass parts which he had noticed during rehearsals at Düsseldorf; he gave references to pages in the printed score.[19] Five days later he presented Eusebius Mandyczewski with a printed copy of the score (this copy now in the Kurt Hofmann Collection, Hamburg) which contains corrections introduced by both Brahms and

---

[16] *Brahms Briefwechsel*, 11: 56.

[17] Rudolf von der Leyen, *Johannes Brahms als Mensch und Freund*, 57. Brahms's personal calendar-books are in the Stadt- und Landesbibliothek, Vienna (Ia 79.559) and have been described in George S. Bozarth, 'Brahms's Lieder Inventory of 1859–60 and Other Documents of his Life and Work', 104–5.

[18] *Brahms Briefwechsel*, 10: 80.

[19] This letter, together with forty-one additional letters and postcards between Brahms and Keller and between Keller and Simrock, as well as the correction sheets for the Third Symphony, to be discussed presently, was acquired by the Library of Congress in 1982, and I am greatly indebted to Mrs Elizabeth Auman for providing me with copies of these materials. The entire extant Brahms-Keller correspondence, which also includes several letters and postcards in the Brahms estate in the Gesellschaft der Musikfreunde, Vienna, will be published in George S. Bozarth and Wiltrud Martin, eds., *A Working Relationship: The Correspondence between Johannes Brahms and Robert Keller*.

Mandyczewski, some of these at variance with corrections to be found elsewhere.[20] Brahms's own printed copy of the score, the *Handexemplar* (now in the archive of the Gesellschaft der Musikfreunde, Vienna), also shows corrections by Brahms, though we cannot date these entries. By mid-August 1884 Keller had read the printed score and parts for errors and sent twenty-eight pages of them to Brahms. This document, the first page of which is shown in Illustration 1, is an amazing tribute to Keller's acute eye and systematic expertise as a corrector. He identifies errors of all kinds, comments on suspected mistakes, and makes suggestions of his own for improvements. There are some 275 entries for the score and 672 for the parts (these totals have of course involved pragmatic decisions on what constitutes a separate entry).

Brahms's response was warm and enthusiastic. On 11 September he wrote to Keller: 'You can doubtless well imagine what a really special pleasure your missive was for me. . . . Of course it is very much to be wished that Herr Simrock takes appropriate notice of it and also puts the previous purchasers of the symphony in a position to be able to use your list.'[21] But Brahms by no means transferred all of these corrections into his own printed copy; he had, however, already written to Simrock, who then produced a three-page printed corrigenda list, also dated September (the first page of this list is reproduced in Illustration 2). Tallied according to principles similar to those employed with Keller's list, the Simrock corrigenda sheets record 52 corrections to the score and 225 to the parts. It is clear that the printed corrigenda list was not drawn by the printer directly from Keller's document: apart from the greatly reduced length of the Simrock list, some entries are expressed quite differently in the two lists, others vary in substance, and some of the corrections on the Simrock list are not present on Keller's.

No doubt Simrock reduced Keller's list for reasons of economy and appearance; furthermore, many of Keller's comments were not properly corrections. Indeed, Keller's suggested notational changes, especially with regard to cautionary accidentals, rest-shapes, and beaming, amount to a fundamental revision of Brahms's own graphic habits. And while Keller's recommendations may be desirable from the viewpoint of clarity and standardization, modern editors may well prefer to preserve the characteristics of Brahms's own writing style. (An example of this kind of unnecessary change is Keller's recommendation that cautionary B♭ be used in the fourth bar of the principal theme of the last movement each time that theme occurs.)

Keller's remaining annotations correct pitches, lengths of notes and rests, dynamics (including the placement of symbols and the extent of hairpins), staccato dots and accent signs, bowings, ties, slurs, and performance instructions (such as missing *arco* and *pizz*. indications). These are all characteristic errors for first issues of Brahms's works; some derive from copyists, others from engravers. Keller's method of work was to note

---

[20] I am much indebted to the kindness of Herr Kurt Hofmann in lending me a photocopy of this document, together with his own annotations.

[21] 'Sie können sich aber auch wohl ausmalen, eine wie ganz besondere Freude mir Ihre Sendung war. . . . Natürlich ist sehr zu wünschen daß Hr. Simrock gebührend Notiz davon nimmt u. auch die bisherigen Käufer der S[ymphonie] in den Stand setzt, Ihr Verzeichniß benützen zu können.'

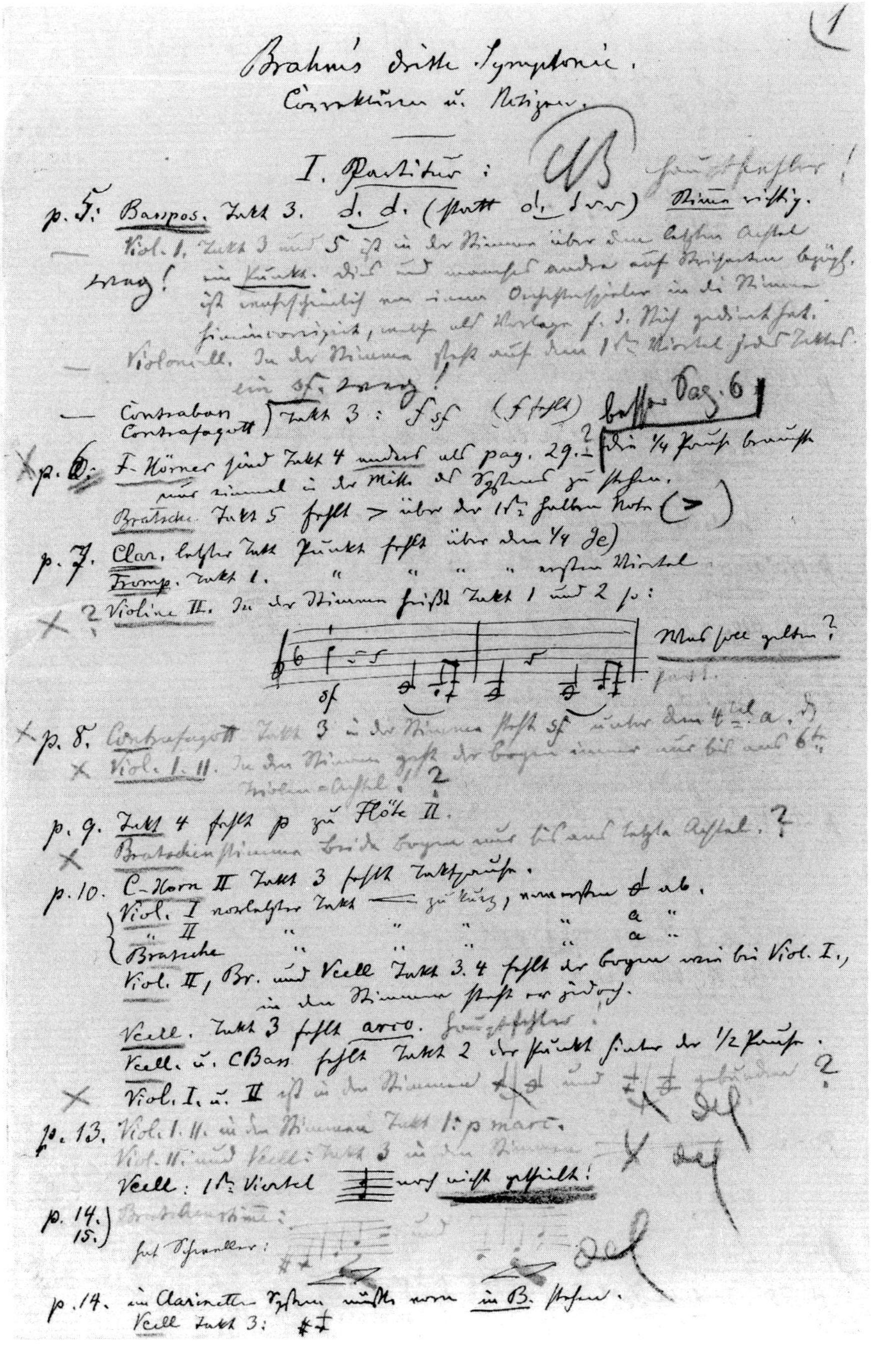

ILLUSTRATION 1. First page of Robert Keller's 'Brahms' Dritte Symphonie. Correkturen u. Notizen' (summer 1884). Reproduced with the permission of the Library of Congress, Washington, DC.

# Correcturen
## zu
## Brahms, Dritte Symphonie.

Da die Umstände seinerzeit eine sehr eilige Herausgabe der Partitur und Stimmen nöthig machten, so sind leider eine Menge Fehler und Ungenauigkeiten stehen geblieben, deren wichtigste und störendste hier mitgetheilt werden. Die Herren Orchesterdirigenten werden ersucht, Partitur und Stimmen gefälligst nach diesem Verzeichniss revidiren zu lassen.

*Berlin, September 1884.*          *N. SIMROCK.*

### Partitur.
#### Erster Satz.

Seite 5. Takt 3: Bassposaune muss den ganzen Takt f halten: ♩·♩·

—— 15. letzter Takt: Violine II das letzte Viertel Doppelgriff:

—— Takt 3: Contrabass erstes Viertel d statt h.

—— 18. vorletzter Takt: Violine II letztes Viertel e statt fis.

—— 19. letzter Takt: Flöte II 2tes Viertel dis statt h.

—— Takt 1: Bei allen 4 Hörnern muss das 3te u. 4te Viertel abgestossen (nicht gebunden) sein.

—— letzter Takt: Bratsche 5tes Viertel:    statt    gis   h

—— 22. letzter Takt: Bei Bratsche und Violoncello fehlt das ♮ vor dem ersten g.

—— 25. vorletzter Takt: Bratsche: Die 3te Viertelnote nicht mehr ges sondern f.

—— 29. letzter Takt: ——— fehlt bei Hoboen, Fagotten u. C-Hörnern.

—— Takt 2 müssen die F-Hörner so wie an der entsprechenden Stelle auf Seite 6 heissen.

—— Takt 4: Violine II eine 8ve tiefer, so:

—— 30. Takt 4: Violine I: ♭ vor a fehlt.

—— 32. Takt 3 u. 4: Violoncell falsch, muss bleiben wie Takt 1 u. 2.

—— 40. Takt 2: Violine II: ♯f statt ♮g.

—— 42. Takt 4: Bei allen spielenden Stimmen gleichmässig: f ———

—— letzter Takt: Das *dim.* im Streichquintett an den Anfang des Taktes.

#### Andante.

Seite 45. II. vorletzter Takt: Violoncell I: e statt c.

—— 49. II. letzter Takt: Violine II: 6tes Achtel fis statt h:

#### Poco Allegretto.

Seite 56. I. Takt 1: Violine II: Achtelpause hinter ♪ fort.

—— 57. II. Takt 4 zu 5: Violoncello fehlt der Bogen von

—— 58. I. vorletzter Takt: Violine I: gis statt fis.

—— 58. II. letzter Takt: Violine I: Das zweite 16tel e statt a.

—— 59. II. Takt 5 u. 6: Hörner müssen es halten, nicht auf c gehen: Beim Violoncell fehlt arco zum Beginn des as dur.

—— 63. II. Takt 1: Zur Bratsche fehlt arco.

—— Takt 5: Die Bratsche muss heissen:

—— 64. II. Takt 1: Violoncell: arco fehlt.

—— 65. II. Takt 5: C.Bass: arco fehlt.

#### Finale.

Seite 69. Takt 2: Bratsche: arco fehlt.

—— Takt 7: Horn I: ♭ vor e.

—— 72. Takt 1: Violoncell: Das 1te Viertel g tief (leere Saite).

—— 73. Takt 2: Violoncell: pizz. fehlt.

Seite 76. Takt 3: Contrabass und Contrafagott müssen diesen Takt pausiren!!

—— 77. Takt 6: Clarinette II: ♯ statt ♮ vor c.

—— 86. Takt 3: Hoboe II: ♮ vor das erste d.

—— Violoncello: ♮ statt ♯ vor c.

—— 87. Takt 3: Bratsche: ♮ statt ♯ vor c (letztes Achtel).

—— 88. letzter Takt: Horn I: ⌢ fort, Punkt über das Viertel.

—— Takt 1: Bratsche: ♯ vor c.

—— 90. Takt 2–5: Fagotte, Cfag., Veell. u. C.Bass Punkt u. marc. Zeichen unter jedes Achtel ♩

—— letzte Takte: stacc. Punkte beim Contrafagott fehlen.

—— 94. Takt 1 u. 2: Flöten doppelt gestrichen.

—— 97. Takt 2: Horn I: ♭ vor f.

—— letzter Takt: Violine II: letztes Achtel f statt des.

—— 98. Takt 1: Contrafagott ♮ vor c.

—— 103. Takt 2: Violoncell u. C.Bass: *dim.* statt *p*; im 3ten Takte *p espress.* und *arco.*

—— 106. letzter Takt: *cresc.* bei allen Streichinstrumenten.

—— 107. letzter Takt: *p* fehlt bei Violinen und Bratsche.

—— 108. Takt 3: *p* zu den Trompeten.

—— 109. Takt 4: *dim.* zur Bratsche.

—— letzter Takt: *pp* zum Contrafagott.

### In den Stimmen.
#### Violine I.

Seite 2. Zeile 7: Bogen von ♪ ♩. fort.

—— 3. —— 3. von unten: Takt 1 u. 2 falsch, muss so heissen:

*ben marc.*

—— 4. —— 1. letzter Takt: ⌣ unter den Punkten fort.

—— 6. Takt 2: (c fehlt in der Mitte.)

—— Takt 5 u. 7 muss der 2te Bogen fort.

—— 7. Takt 4 fehlt *cresc.*

—— letzte Zeile, letzter Takt *mp espress.* (statt *p*)

—— 5. Zeile 5. Takt 3: *p* fort.

—— 6. —— 4 von unten, letzter Takt; das vorletzte Achtel cis statt e.

—— 7. letzte Zeile : Stichnoten der Clarinette ↓ für das zweite ♩ ; ⌣ beim Eintritt der Viol., das zweite <> fort; 4 Takte vor dem Schluss fehlt *poco rit.*

—— 8. vorletzte Zeile: *pp espress.* statt *pp cresc.*

—— letzte Zeile: *p* statt *pp.*

—— 9. Zeile 4 von unten, Takt 1: Das Achtel muss c heissen statt h.

—— 11. —— 4 von unten: *p* statt *mp.*

—— 12. —— 4. Takt 1: *più f sempre.*

discrepancies within the score and between the score and the parts; his list does not seem to have been developed with reference to the engravers' exemplars or the autograph, nor does it mention them, and apparently he relied only on the printed materials (including the two-piano, four-hand arrangement, to which he does refer) and his acute eye. (Just how sharp his eye was may be noted in his observation of missing grave accents for the word 'più'.)

On the initial nine pages of his 'Correcturen u. Notizen'—those pages devoted to questions about the score itself and in relationship to the parts—Keller entered his queries mainly in dark brown ink, but highlighted those specifically concerning the parts by writing them in magenta ink. He addressed questions to Brahms directly—'<u>Was soll gelten</u>?' appears on page 1 after the first musical quotation—and drew Brahms's attention to certain entries with question marks in blue crayon and crosses in the margin in red crayon. Keller also designated certain mistakes, principally those concerning pitches and *arco* indications, as 'Hauptfehler' (again in blue crayon).

Brahms responded with verbal comments, deletions, crosses, underlinings, and specific alterations. His primary interest was the score, but even there he did not always supply the necessary decisions. The entry for page 9 of the score, for example, contains Keller's query and cross in the margin, but no response from Brahms. Brahms's only markings on page 1 of the Keller document are 'NB', 'weg!' (twice), and '<u>besser Pag. 6</u>' (all in pencil), three deletions ('del') towards the end of the page (in blue crayon), and some of the underlinings (also in blue crayon). Keller's query about lengthening the hairpins in the violins and viola on page 10 of the score received no decisive comment from Brahms, but according to the autograph score and the autograph of the arrangement, Keller was standardizing in the wrong direction here, and it is rather the cello hairpin that should be shortened. (This case is shown in Illustration 3*a* and *b*.) Thus Keller's document must be taken as representing an interim phase in the process of correction; it does not by itself deliver a definitive text, for it contains unnecessary alterations, possibly introduces some errors, and, although welcomed by Brahms, seems not to have been checked by him comprehensively. It is also incomplete. Simrock's published list is of similar status; it too is far from comprehensive and contains possible errors. For example, Simrock's entry for the score at page 42, bar 4 (bar 204; see Illustration 2) is very different from Brahms's annotations on Keller's document: 'Takt 4 *f* überall | $=$—nur im 4$^{\underline{tett}}$' (in pencil) and ' $=$ im 4$^{\underline{tett}}$' (in blue crayon; there are nine woodwind instruments playing here).[22]

Further errors in the printed edition came to light after September 1884 and were corrected. For example, Brahms sent a postcard to Keller, received by him on

---

[22] Keller's query reads as follows: '—<u>Takt 4</u> steht bei Bläsern *f*, beim Horn *mf*, beim Quartet in der | Partitur *sf* u[nd] in den Stimmen (Viol[ine] I. II u[nd] Br[atsche]) *rf* ! | Könnte das nicht regulisirt werden und wie? (*mf* $=$ überall?).' In addition to the two entries by Brahms already cited, there are two question marks in blue crayon in the left margin, probably entered by Keller; also in blue crayon Brahms has crossed out the '*m*', '*s*', '*r*', and '*m*' in Keller's '*mf*', '*sf*', '*rf*', and '*mf*', respectively, and entered '*f=*' before Keller's word 'überall'. It would seem that the entries in blue crayon represent Brahms's individual initial comments, and that the entry in lead pencil is his summary statement of the action to be taken. None of these comments, however, implies that the decrescendo hairpin should be applied beyond the strings.

ILLUSTRATION 3. Brahms's Third Symphony, first movement. a. Autograph score, bars 33–5. Reproduced with the permission of the Library of Congress, Washington, DC. b. Uncorrected first-issue plates, bars 33–4. Copy owned by the author.

29 October, which reads in full: 'So that you don't become too vain and hold yourself infallible, I am letting you know that in the F major score, on p. 11, at the A major, there is a necessary tenor clef missing for the bassoon [bar 36] and on p. 24 a♭ before E for the double-bass [bar 101]! Your heartily greeting J. Br.'[23]

This was by no means the end of Brahms's trouble with the symphony. He had recommended that Theodor Kirchner prepare the one-piano, four-hand arrangement, partly out of a desire to support Kirchner, partly out of a lack of enthusiasm for Keller's arrangements in general. But Simrock asked Keller. Brahms found elements to criticize in his arrangement of movements one and three, and wrote Keller a most tactful letter in October 1884. The upshot was that Brahms emended these two movements according to his own wishes, but not before Simrock had also become more fully involved in this difficult matter.

Simrock eventually did emend the plates for the score of the symphony, though with the present state of knowledge about the various printings of the symphony, this particular issue cannot be dated with accuracy. In 1889 the British Library acquired a copy of the score by purchase (Simrock frequently chose to send to major libraries, as 'deposit' copies, free specimens of the piano arrangements of large works, leaving the libraries to purchase their own copies of the full scores—a clear indication of the keenness of Simrock's business sense), and that copy was still printed from the uncorrected plates, with the published corrigenda list inserted.[24] In 1892 Brahms himself enquired of Simrock, because at that time he still had in his possession only 'a first printing [of the score] accompanied by a subsequent list of printers' errors.'[25] No response from Simrock is known, and any subsequent score of this work which may have come into Brahms's possession is not to be found today in his estate at the Gesellschaft der Musikfreunde in Vienna. A revised issue has, however, surfaced: a copy of the printed score acquired by Paul Hirsch in 1899 (now British Museum, Hirsch M 806). This copy includes more of Keller's corrections than appeared on Simrock's printed corrigenda list. Whether Simrock ever had the plates for the parts revised is not known.

# IV

The general problem for modern editors of Brahms's works is that for many of his compositions no definitive text, in a unified state, exists, because during the process of publication both revision *and* deterioration of the text occurred concurrently. In the print of the Third Symphony are to be seen many compositional improvements which Brahms made after preparing the autograph; he subsequently introduced these into the

---

[23] 'Damit Sie nicht zu eitel werden u[nd] sich für unfehlbar halten, melde ich, daß in der F dur-Partitur S[eite] 11 beim A dur ein nöthiges Tenorschlüßel für d[as] Fagott fehlt u[nd] S[eite] 24 ein ♭ vor e f[ür] d[as] Contrabass! Ihr herzlich grüßender J.Br.'

[24] I am much indebted to Nigel Simeone for this information and for generously sharing with me his bibliographical expertise.

[25] '. . . einen ersten Abzug, dem dann ein Bogen mit Druckfehler-Verzeichnis beibeliegt.' *Brahms Briefwechsel*, 12 : 90.

autograph and/or the copyist's score, for, as argued above, it is unlikely he saw the galley proofs. The most extensive of these is the deletion of trumpet, drums, and contrabassoon from the second movement. Evidence of another such compositional improvement exists on page 28 of Keller's list, where he refers to a B♭ drum roll (first movement, bars 201–2) which does not exist in the autograph. Although this drum roll is not in Brahms's characteristic notation for drums, it must surely stem from him; as a compositional improvement it has a certain piquancy, for indeed the work does not specify a drum in B♭ at all (as Mandyczewski and Keller both noted). A further small compositional improvement is shown in Illustration 3*a* and *b*: the ties in the upper strings, bars 33–4, have been deleted. While this improvement was made in the printed score, it was never taken over into the printed parts.

The deterioration in the musical text cannot receive further detailed amplification here. But in general one can note that Brahms could continue compositional revision and correction of deterioration after publication either by annotating his own copy and/or by writing to Keller, to Simrock, or even to Röder to request a change to the plates. The problems surrounding the annotations to his own copies I have discussed elsewere;[26] the chief problem with regard to his letters requesting changes is that we cannot know how many have been lost. Plates were freely emended without announcing the fact. Thus issues from the original plates of around 1897 should play an important part in establishing the definitive text of a Brahms work, since they should have picked up all the corrections Brahms made by letter (assuming that either Simrock or Röder heeded Brahms's requests, as in general they did). These issues from around 1897 will of course not necessarily be free from error, and modern editors must assess every variant between autograph, copyist's score and parts, and printed issues (whether corrected or not) in order to establish whether that variant is musically significant and consistent enough to be considered an improvement emanating from Brahms, or whether it seems arbitrary and inconsistent enough to have been an error. When no pre-publication materials survive, we must often work with our knowledge of copyists' and engravers' habits, developing our own acuteness of eye as best we may.

[26] 'Brahms and the Definitive Text', 59.

# THE ROLE OF TRIAL PERFORMANCES FOR BRAHMS'S ORCHESTRAL AND LARGE CHORAL WORKS: SOURCES AND CIRCUMSTANCES

—

## MARGIT L. McCORKLE

UNTIL recently Brahms scholarship has for the most part bypassed the study of primary musical sources, chronicling the origin and evolution of individual compositions mainly from circumstantial evidence found in the correspondence and in the anecdotal reminiscences of the composer's friends and colleagues.[1] In the 1920s Alfred Orel and Paul Mies opened the field of Brahms source studies with articles, respectively, on the extant sketches for the Haydn Variations and, more generally, on the nature of Brahms's 'workshop', but for decades these two studies remained virtually the only efforts to describe Brahms's method of composing.[2] During the late 1920s the *Johannes Brahms Sämtliche Werke* was also being published, based on the examination of some three hundred manuscripts; forty years later, from his experience as co-editor, Hans Gál gave his views on the usefulness of the primary musical sources in an assessment now widely accepted:

Occasionally one can learn something about his method of working from corrections in his manuscripts. Otherwise, one is confined to the very few instances of compositions or fragments thereof existing in different versions. One thing, however, can never be clearly determined; the various stages through which the invention itself had to pass.[3]

Although Gál's work with the sources was extensive, he did not study many of the more revealing manuscripts which illuminate the later stages of Brahms's compositional process.[4]

---

[1] Much of this information was first presented in Max Kalbeck's mammoth biography of Brahms.

[2] Alfred Orel, 'Skizzen zu Joh. Brahms' Haydn-Variationen', and Paul Mies, 'Aus Brahms' Werkstatt: Vom Entstehen und Werden der Werke bei Brahms'. For later studies concerning Brahms's sketches, alternative versions, and compositional process in general, see Imogen Fellinger's 'Zum Stand der Brahms-Forschung' and its sequel 'Das Brahms-Jahr 1983', as well as Siegfried Kross's *Brahms-Bibliographie*.

[3] Hans Gál, *Johannes Brahms: His Work and Personality*, trans. 156. The first sentence in the quotation reads somewhat differently in the text of the original German edition: 'Gelegentlich erfährt man etwas von seiner Arbeit aus Korrekturen in seinen Manuskripten, *die sehr aufschlussreich sein können*' (italics supplied).

[4] See the Critical Reports in the *Johannes Brahms Sämtliche Werke*.

From the start of his career Brahms composed for eventual publication. With this end in view, he put his works through rigorous paces, normally progressing through three distinct stages. He first solicited the reactions of his trusted musical confidants. Then, he sought opportunities for test performances. Finally, when he was satisfied with the results of these semi-private (or even public) trial performances, he released the revised performing materials to his publishers. While his compositions were usually fully intact musical entities by the time he introduced them to his circle of intimates, more often than not they were not finished in secondary detail until they had been subjected to a trial period in performance. The consequent revisions and refinements were essential to bringing about the desired aural effect.[5]

Brahms's letters to his friends, colleagues, and publishers refer continually to these steps towards publication and provide remarkably detailed accounts of the often complicated logistics of these painstaking preparations. The surviving manuscripts that were used as performing materials not only corroborate the information in the correspondence, but, more significantly, also yield fascinating glimpses of the composer-conductor shaping a dramatic aural experience from the inert notes on the page, breathing life, as it were, into the new creation.

Given the access we now have to materials which document these final stages—access not available to Gál and his collaborator Eusebius Mandyczewski—it is possible at last to study in depth this phase of Brahms's compositional process. The present paper will, I hope, serve as an introduction.

# I

Brahms's twenty major works for orchestra alone, with solo instruments, and with chorus, include four symphonies, two overtures, four concertos, a set of orchestral variations, two serenades, and seven large choral pieces (see Table 1). As a corpus, they span the heart of the composer's career, and their compositional histories reflect his life circumstances from novice, unestablished if not entirely unknown, to master of the highest classical art, lionized in Central Europe and England by all not partial to the Wagner–Liszt school.

Brahms brought to his earliest large-scale compositional efforts an inimitable personal style, sound training as a concert pianist, initial success as a published composer of piano pieces, songs, and a piano trio, and the public blessing of Robert Schumann, whose extravagant prophecy in 'Neue Bahnen' was soon to be fulfilled. He was already highly respected within a small circle of gifted and influential musicians, but as yet he held no professional position, knew, by his own admission, next to nothing about orchestras, and could hardly afford copyists' fees, let alone the cost of hiring a group of musicians for trial performances. Under the aegis of Schumann he had sold eight of his first ten opera to the prestigious firm of Breitkopf & Härtel; the Härtel brothers were, however,

---

[5] Paul Mies discussed the critical influence of Brahms's confrères on his works and the various phases of the publication process in his article 'Der kritische Rat der Freunde und die Veröffentlichung der Werke bei Brahms'.

conservative businessmen and sceptical about the return on their investment in the young man's talent. He had not yet attracted popular attention or enjoyed a *succès d'estime*, but the artistic merit and promise of his first published works had not escaped the notice of two other publishers of sounder musical instincts—J. Rieter-Biedermann, founder of an up-and-coming Swiss publishing house, and Fritz Simrock, young scion of the venerable Bonn music publisher N. Simrock.[6]

Thirty years later, Simrock held a virtual monopoly on Brahms's publications and spared no effort to keep his prize composer and dear friend in tow against the blandishments of Dr Max Abraham at C. F. Peters in Leipzig, while Breitkopf & Härtel rued their cavalier treatment of the young composer. Rumours of a new Brahms composition now precipitated a scramble among leading orchestras for the privilege of first performance—prompting Brahms to grumble that their interest was solely in obtaining 'Novitäten'. But even at the height of his career, he continued to seek the critical reaction of those in his circle whose judgement he valued, time and again asking for advice on technical matters where he felt uncertain. Moreover, he repeatedly insisted to his eager publishers that release of his works must wait until he had had sufficient opportunity to hear them performed and make his final revisions.[7]

In Table 1 Brahms's orchestral and major choral works appear together with the particulars of publisher and date of publication, dates and places of pre-publication performances, nature of performing materials (those surviving and those no longer extant), and other primary musical sources which aid in ascertaining the nature of this final stage in the compositional process.[8] The twenty compositions here under consideration might usefully be viewed in four groups. The First Piano Concerto and the two Serenades are clearly apprentice works; the five choral pieces from the 1860s and 1870s—the *German Requiem, Rinaldo*, the Alto Rhapsody, the *Schicksalslied*, and the *Triumphlied*—have in common not only genre, but also, to some extent, performing venues and personnel; the Haydn Variations and the First Symphony represent, in differing ways, the first achievement of technical and musical mastery; and the remaining works demonstrate the many-faceted richness of maturity.

# II

The compositional histories of the apprentice works reveal the dilemma of many a youthful composer—ambitious goals far in advance of his technical competence or

---

[6] The one other firm that took the risk of publishing music by the young Brahms was Bartholf Senff of Leipzig, which brought out his Piano Sonata in F minor, Op. 5, and the *Sechs Gesänge*, Op. 6.

[7] Brahms's relationship with his publishers is summarized in section II of the Introduction to Margit L. McCorkle, *Johannes Brahms Thematisch-Bibliographisches Werkverzeichnis*. For more detailed accounts, see the introductions to *Brahms Briefwechsel*, 9 and 14, and to Kurt Stephenson, ed., *Johannes Brahms und Fritz Simrock: Weg einer Freundschaft*.

[8] For descriptions of the sources cited, for listings and descriptions of related sources, and for full documentation of compositional histories, including information about the origin, first performance, and publication, see McCorkle, *Werkverzeichnis*.

## TABLE 1.

| Work Opus | Publication Publisher/Date | Performances prior to publication Date, Place/Conductor, Soloist |
|---|---|---|
| Serenade for Large Orchestra, Op. 11 | Breitkopf & Härtel/ Dec. 1860 (lith. MS score) Jan. 1861? (parts) | 3 March 1860, Hannover/J. Joachim |
| First Piano Concerto, Op. 15 | Rieter-Biedermann/ Apr. 1860 (solo part) Apr. 1862? (orch. parts) May 1864 (piano four-hand arr.) Early 1873? (two-piano arr.) Dec. 1874 (score) | Semi-private test: 30 Mar. 1858, Hannover/J. Joachim, Brahms 22 Jan. 1859, Hannover/J. Joachim, Brahms 27 Jan. 1859, Leipzig/J. Rietz, Brahms 24 Mar. 1859, Hamburg/J. Joachim, Brahms 20 Apr. 1860, Hamburg/G. D. Otten, Brahms |
| Serenade for Small Orchestra, Op. 16 | N. Simrock/Nov. 1860 (score, parts) | 10 Feb. 1860, Hamburg/Brahms 26 Nov. 1860, Leipzig/Brahms |
| *Ein deutsches Requiem*, Op. 45 | Rieter-Biedermann/ Oct. 1868 (choral parts) Nov. 1868 (score) Dec. 1868 (piano-vocal score) Jan. 1869 (orch. parts) Before Mar. 1871 (organ part) | Mvts. 1–3: 1 Dec. 1867, Vienna/ J. Herbeck, R. Panzer Mvts. 1–4, 6, 7: 10 Apr. 1868, Bremen/ Brahms, J. Stockhausen; also 27 Apr. 1868, Bremen/K. Reinthaler, F. Krolop (Brahms was present as listener) Mvt. 5: 17 Sept. 1868, Zurich/F. Hegar, I. Suter-Weber |
| *Rinaldo*, Op. 50 | N. Simrock/Aug. 1869 (score, parts, piano-vocal score) | 28 Feb. 1869, Vienna/Brahms, G. Walter |
| Alto Rhapsody, Op. 53 | N. Simrock/Jan. 1870 (score, parts, piano-vocal score) | 6 Oct. 1869, Karlsruhe/H. Levi, Amalie Boni-Bartel (test performance with orchestra?, without chorus) |
| *Schicksalslied*, Op. 54 | N. Simrock/Dec. 1871 (score, parts, piano-vocal score) | 18 Oct. 1871, Karlsruhe/Brahms |
| *Triumphlied*, Op. 55 | N. Simrock/Nov. 1872 (score, parts, piano-vocal score) | Mvt. 1: 7 Apr. 1871, Bremen/Brahms Complete work: 5 June 1872, Karlsruhe/H. Levi, J. Stockhausen |
| *Haydn Variations for Orchestra*, Op. 56a | N. Simrock/Jan. 1874 (score, parts) | 2 Nov. 1873, Vienna/Brahms 10 Dec. 1873, Munich/F. Wüllner |
| First Symphony, Op. 68 | N. Simrock/Oct. 1877 (score, parts, piano four-hand arrangement) | 4 Nov. 1876, Karlsruhe/O. Dessoff 8 performances between 7 Nov. 1876 and 16 Apr. 1877 in Mannheim, Munich, Vienna, Leipzig, Breslau, Cambridge, London/Brahms or J. Joachim; A. Manns and W. Cusins (in England) |

---

[a] Kalbeck lists Cologne (*Johannes Brahms*, 3: 211), but no other sources corroborate this assertion.

| Performance materials<br>Relevant sources | Function (present location) |
|---|---|
| Autograph score<br>MS parts | Conductor's score, *Stichvorlage* (D–brd–DS)<br>(Unknown) |
| Autograph score<br>MS score<br>Partly autograph solo part<br>MS parts<br>Autograph score, two-piano arr. | Conductor's score (D–ddr–Bds)<br>*Stichvorlage* (US–NYpm)<br>*Stichvorlage* (US–NYpm)<br>(Unknown)<br>*Stichvorlage* (US–Wc) |
| Autograph score<br>MS score<br>MS parts | (Unknown)<br>(Unknown)<br>(Unknown) |
| Autograph score<br>Partly autograph piano-vocal score<br>MS parts: mvts. 1–3 (Vienna)<br>MS parts: mvts. 1–4, 6, 7 (Bremen)<br>(mvts. 1–3 probably = Vienna<br>MS choral parts)<br>Printed parts: mvt. 5 (Zurich)<br>Corrected galleys for score:<br>mvt. 5 (Zurich) | Conductor's score, *Stichvorlage* (A–Wgm)<br>Rehearsal score, *Stichvorlage* (A-Gallspach, F. G. Zeileis Collection)<br>MS contrabassoon part (A–Wgm); other parts (unknown)<br>MS soprano, alto parts (D–Hamburg, Hofmann collection)<br><br><br>(Unknown)<br>Conductor's score? (D–Hamburg, Hofmann collection) |
| Autograph score<br>Partly autograph piano-vocal score<br>Printed parts | Conductor's score, *Stichvorlage* (US–Wc)<br>Rehearsal score, *Stichvorlage* (A–Wn)<br>(Unknown) |
| Autograph score<br>MS parts? | Conductor's score? (US–NYp)<br>(Unknown) |
| Autograph score<br>MS (Levi) piano-vocal score<br>MS parts | Conductor's score (US–Wc)<br>Rehearsal score, *Stichvorlage* (D–brd–Braunschweig, Heribert Esser)<br>(Unknown) |
| Autograph score<br>Copyist's score<br>Partly autograph piano-vocal score<br>Printed chorus and string parts<br>MS wind and percussion parts | Conductor's score for 1st mvt.? (Pl–Kj)<br>Conductor's score, *Stichvorlage* (unknown)<br>Rehearsal score for Karlsruhe performance (unknown)<br>(Unknown)<br>(Unknown) |
| Autograph score (Vienna)<br>MS parts (Vienna)<br>Autograph two-piano version (Op. 56b)<br>(Munich)<br>Printed score (Munich)?<br>Printed parts | Conductor's score, *Stichvorlage* (A–Wn)<br>(Unknown)<br>Conductor's study/rehearsal score (A–Wst)<br><br>Conductor's score? (unknown)<br>(Unknown) |
| Autograph score<br><br>MS parts | Conductor's score, *Stichvorlage*, mvts. 2–4 (US–NYpm)<br>(Mvt. 1: Autograph, and MS score, *Stichvorlage*, Unknown)<br>Violin and viola parts from Vienna performance (A–Wgm); other parts<br>(Unknown) |

| Work Opus | Publication Publisher/Date | Performances prior to publication Date, Place/Conductor, Soloist |
|---|---|---|
| Second Symphony, Op. 73 | N. Simrock/August 1878 (score, parts, piano four-hand arrangement) | 30 Dec. 1877, Vienna/H. Richter 6 performances between 10 Jan. and mid-June 1878 in Leipzig, Amsterdam, The Hague, Dresden, Düsseldorf/Brahms, F. Wüllner (Dresden), and J. Joachim (Düsseldorf) |
| Violin Concerto, Op. 77 | N. Simrock/Oct. 1879 (score, parts, violin-piano score) | 1 Jan. 1879, Leipzig/Brahms, J. Joachim 7(?) performances between 8 Jan. and 25 May 1879 in Budapest, Vienna, Cologne(?),[a] London, Amsterdam/Brahms, J. Hellmesberger (Vienna), A. Manns, W. Cusins (London), J. Verhulst (Amsterdam); J. Joachim |
| *Academic Festival Overture*, Op. 80 | N. Simrock/July 1881 (score, parts, piano four-hand arrangement) | Test performance: 6 Dec. 1880, Berlin/J. Joachim or Brahms? directed the Hochschule orchestra 4 Jan. 1881, Breslau/Brahms 7 performances between 13 Jan. and 20 Mar. 1881 in Leipzig, Münster, Krefeld, Amsterdam, The Hague, Haarlem, Vienna/Brahms; H. Richter (Vienna) |
| *Tragic Overture*, Op. 81 | N. Simrock/July 1881 (score, parts, piano four-hand arrangement) | Test performance: same as Op. 80 26 Dec. 1880, Vienna/H. Richter From Breslau to Haarlem, same as Op. 80 |
| *Nänie*, Op. 82 | C. F. Peters/Dec. 1881 (score, parts, piano-vocal score) | Test performance: 19 Oct. 1881, Meiningen/Brahms or H. von Bülow? (without chorus) 6 Dec. 1881, Zurich/Brahms |
| Second Piano Concerto, Op. 83 | N. Simrock/Jan. 1882 (two-piano arr.) July 1882 (score and parts) | Test performance(s): 18–21 Oct. 1881, Meiningen/ H. von Bülow, Brahms 9 Nov. 1881, Budapest/A. Erkel, Brahms 21 performances between 22 Nov. 1881 and 22 Feb. 1882 in Stuttgart, Meiningen, Zurich, Basel, Strasbourg, Baden-Baden, Breslau, Vienna, Leipzig, Berlin, Kiel, Hamburg, Münster, Utrecht, The Hague, Rotterdam, Amsterdam, Arnheim, Frankfurt a.M., Dresden/M. Seifriz, H. von Bülow, F. Hegar, A. Volckland, F. Stockhausen, B. Scholz, H. Richter, J.O. Grimm/Brahms |
| *Gesang der Parzen*, Op. 89 | N. Simrock/Feb. 1883 (score, parts, piano-vocal score) | 10 Dec. 1882, Basel/Brahms 7 performances between 17 Dec. 1882 and 18 Feb. 1883 in Zurich, Strasbourg, Bonn, Krefeld, Oldenburg, Schwerin, Vienna/Brahms |
| Third Symphony, Op. 90 | N. Simrock/May 1884 (score and parts, two-piano arr.) | 2 Dec. 1883, Vienna/H. Richter 13 performances between 4 Jan. and 2 Apr. 1884 in Berlin, Wiesbaden, Meiningen, Leipzig, Cologne, Düsseldorf, Barmen, Amsterdam, Dresden, Frankfurt a.M., Budapest/J. Joachim (1st Berlin performance), Brahms |

| Performance materials<br>Relevant sources | Function (present location) |
|---|---|
| Autograph score | Conductor's score, *Stichvorlage* for mvts. 2–4 (US–NYpm) |
| MS score, 1st mvt. | Conductor's score?, *Stichvorlage* (D–brd–private collection) |
| MS parts | (Unknown) |
| Printed score and parts<br>    (for Düsseldorf) | (Unknown) |
| | |
| Autograph score | Conductor's score, *Stichvorlage* (US–Wc) |
| MS solo part | Soloist's part for Leipzig, Budapest, Vienna? (unknown) |
| MS solo part | Soloist's part for London, Amsterdam, *Stichvorlage* (US–Wc) |
| MS orchestral parts | (Unknown) |
| | |
| Autograph score | Conductor's score, *Stichvorlage* (D–ddr–Bds) |
| MS score | Conductor's score?, *Stichvorlage* (D–brd–Hs) |
| Printed string parts | (Unknown) |
| MS other parts | (Unknown) |
| | |
| Autograph score | Conductor's score, *Stichvorlage* (US–STu) |
| Printed string parts | (Unknown) |
| MS other parts | (Unknown) |
| | |
| Autograph score | Conductor's score (Meiningen), *Stichvorlage* (D–ddr–LEm) |
| Galley proof of score | Conductor's score (Zurich)? (D–ddr–LEm) |
| Autograph piano-vocal score | (Unknown) |
| Printed string parts (Meiningen) | (Unknown) |
| MS other orch. parts | (Unknown) |
| Printed choral and orch. parts (Zurich) | (Unknown) |
| | |
| Autograph score | Conductor's score, *Stichvorlage* (D–brd–Hs) |
| Partly autograph two piano<br>    arr. (I=solo piano) | Soloist's part in Meiningen test, *Stichvorlage* (A–Wn) |
| Printed two-piano arr. | Soloist's part after publication, or did Brahms play from memory after<br>    the Meiningen test? (*Handexemplar*, A–Wgm, [VII 27 377/H 31 537]) |
| Printed string parts | (Unknown) |
| MS other orch. parts | (Unknown) |
| | |
| Autograph score | Conductor's score (D–brd–Krefeld, Stadtarchiv) |
| Printed choral and string parts | (Unknown) |
| Printed other orch. parts | (Unknown) |
| Autograph piano-vocal score | Rehearsal score? (S–Smf) |
| Printed piano-vocal score | Rehearsal score? (unknown) |
| Corrected galley of score | Score corrected from performances? (A–Wgm, [V 27 124/H 29 594]) |
| Autograph score | Conductor's score (US–Wc) |
| Printed string parts | (Unknown) |
| MS other parts | (Unknown) |

| Work<br>Opus | Publication<br>Publisher/Date | Performances prior to publication<br>Date, Place/Conductor, Soloist |
|---|---|---|
| Fourth Symphony,<br>Op. 98 | N. Simrock/May 1886<br>(two-piano arr.)<br>Oct. 1886 (score and parts) | 25 Oct. 1885, Meiningen/Brahms<br>23 performances between 1 Nov. and mid-June 1886<br>in Meiningen, Frankfurt a.M., Essen, Elberfeld,<br>Utrecht, Amsterdam, The Hague, Krefeld, Cologne,<br>Wiesbaden, Mannheim, Vienna, Berlin, Leipzig,<br>Dresden, Hamburg, Hannover, Breslau, London/<br>Brahms, H. von Bülow (Meiningen), J. Joachim (1st<br>Berlin performance), H. Richter (Vienna and<br>London), F. Wüllner (3rd Cologne performance) |
| Double Concerto,<br>Op. 102 | N. Simrock/June 1888<br>(score and parts) | Test performance: 23 Sept. 1887, Baden-Baden/Brahms,<br>J. Joachim, R. Hausmann<br>18 Oct. 1887, Cologne/same as above<br>8? performances between 17 Nov. 1887 and 21 Feb.<br>1888 in Wiesbaden, Frankfurt a.M., Basel, Leipzig,<br>Berlin, Hamburg?,[b] London/Brahms, H. von Bülow<br>(Berlin), G. Henschel (London); J. Joachim,<br>R. Hausmann |

---

[b] Kalbeck, again, mentions Hamburg in a series of concerts where Op. 102 was performed (*Johannes Brahms*, 4: 81–2); there are no corroborating sources for this assertion.

experience. In the spring of 1854 Brahms set out to compose a grand sonata for two pianos. Realizing, though, that the nature and scope of his musical ideas were symphonic, he attempted to recast the first movement as the opening of a symphony, only subsequently to find the best solution, a compromise of piano and orchestra joined as partners in a piano concerto.[9] Similarly, in 1857 Brahms started to draft a serenade for small orchestra which he later turned into a 'Sinfonie-Serenade', published in 1860 as 'Serenade für grosses Orchester', Op. 11. Between 1854 and 1859 one or the other versions of these two works was constantly under discussion or in circulation as he drew heavily on the advice and encouragement of those close to him. Seldom thereafter did the composer involve his musical confidants so much in the early stages of composition, never again revealing such self-consciousness, inexperience, and uncertainty in handling an orchestra.

In the 1850s and early 1860s Brahms most often turned for help to Joseph Joachim, whose judgement, taste, and practical experience he respected without reservation. The young virtuoso violinist had already composed works for orchestra, had served as concertmaster in Leipzig and Weimar, and presently had at his disposal the court orchestra in Hannover.[10] That he proved to be indispensable 'godfather' to Brahms's first orchestral works is documented in the extensive correspondence between the two friends. Others on whom Brahms relied at this time included the composer Julius Otto

---

[9] For detailed accounts of the history of this concerto, see Gustav Jenner, 'Zur Entstehung des D-moll Klavierkonzertes Op. 15 von Johannes Brahms'; Carl Dahlhaus, *Johannes Brahms—Klavierkonzert Nr. 1 d-moll, op. 15*; and Christopher Reynolds, 'A Choral Symphony by Brahms?' Dahlhaus includes reviews from the Leipzig and Hamburg concerts, but no discussion of the surviving manuscripts.

[10] By 1855 Joachim, only two years older than Brahms, had to his credit three overtures for orchestra and two works for violin and orchestra.

| Performance materials<br>Relevant sources | Function (present location) |
|---|---|
| Autograph score<br>MS parts/printed string parts from the<br>    Vienna performance (17 Jan. and<br>    after)/printed wind parts for the 3rd<br>    3rd Cologne performance in June | Conductor's score, *Stichvorlage* (CH–Zz)<br>(Unknown) |
| Autograph score<br>MS score<br>Printed string parts/MS other orch.<br>    parts<br>MS solo parts | Conductor's score? (A–Wgm)<br>Conductor's score, *Stichvorlage* (D–brd–private collection)<br>(Unknown)<br><br>(Unknown) |

Grimm, who conducted a choir in Göttingen until 1860, when he accepted the music directorship in Münster, and Albert Dietrich, who was music director in Bonn until 1861, when he took up the post of Hofkapellmeister in Oldenburg, where he stayed for the rest of his life. Like Joachim, both of these musicians were near Brahms's age, shared a musical affinity as adherents of Schumann's credo, and could offer the benefit of greater experience with choral and orchestral forces. Each participated closely in the evolution of Brahms's earliest large-scale works. Of Grimm's role in criticizing the D minor symphonic movement (later the initial movement of Op. 15), Brahms reported to Joachim: 'whatever good may be in it, I owe to Grimm, who stood by my side with the best advice. [What is] deficient and bad, which is probably not hidden very deeply, Grimm either overlooked or my stubbornness insisted on keeping.'[11] We are indebted to Dietrich for the information that the original slow Scherzo of the sonata for two pianos later became the funeral march (second movement) of the *German Requiem*, Op. 45.[12]

Eventually the enthusiastic reactions of his friends encouraged Brahms to test the concerto and the serenade. The piano concerto was first read by Joachim and his orchestra in Hannover. A disastrous performance followed in Leipzig, where orchestra, audience, and critics all received Schumann's protégé coldly, and the new concerto was even hissed. Joachim and Brahms then produced the work in a Hamburg Philharmonic concert to a decidedly warmer reception. Joachim stayed on to conduct the serenade (in the version for small orchestra) at a specially organized concert four days later; a year later he premièred the version for large orchestra at Hannover. All the while Brahms kept revising and polishing both scores, as the letters record.

---

[11] 'das Gute, was sich darin vorfinden sollte, Grimm verdanke, der mir mit dem besten Rat zur Seite stand. Das Mangelhafte und Schlechte, das wohl nicht so tief versteckt ist, hat Grimm entweder übersehen oder mein Eigensinn stehen lassen.' *Brahms Briefwechsel*, 5: 55–6.

[12] Albert Dietrich, *Erinnerungen an Johannes Brahms in Briefe besonders aus seiner Jugendzeit*, 45.

In 1860 the Härtel brothers accepted the serenade, but engraved only a set of parts (and the arrangement for piano duet), refusing to risk the cost of engraving the full score, much to Brahms's disappointment.[13] Breitkopf & Härtel expressed interest in the piano concerto, until they realized it was the work that had failed so miserably in Leipzig. Brahms then offered the concerto to Rieter-Biedermann, remarking wryly: 'I believe that the "Concerto" is a rather difficult undertaking. Furthermore, the more capable pianists now belong almost without exception to the New German school, which probably does not care about my things. Let us hope that at least the piano part will not be left on your hands. Would you want to circulate the orchestral parts in lithograph? For my part I have nothing against that.'[14] In the end he was pleased that the publisher engraved the orchestral parts soon after the solo piano part, and he was willing that the full score remain available only in manuscript and upon request to the publisher. Rieter was not disappointed in this venture; his keen interest in the young composer's career and his appreciation for Brahms's art were well repaid during the next decade, and by the early 1870s he considered the concerto popular enough to warrant engraving the full score.

The First Piano Concerto's protracted and problematic evolution is recorded in the multiple layers of revision in the autograph score. An assemblage of sections written down at various times on four different papers, the manuscript is partly a direct working draft, partly a revised fair copy. An unusual feature is the 'ghost' writing in it: partially erased experiments sketched in pencil are scattered about in the free spaces of the score, within the orchestral parts. Joachim's glosses are also visible (the manuscript functioned as conductor's score for the trial performances).

In April 1859, when Brahms wrote to Joachim about his intention of making a manuscript copy of the concerto for his friend, the latter responded: 'If you really intend to give me the manuscript of your concerto in remembrance of the Hamburg days, this would be a more than royal reward; but why are you thinking of copying it! I would think, and even hope, that you have more important things to do. Have it done by a good copyist in a philistine hand for the Herren Kapellmeister to use in public performance.'[15] Evidently no copy was made at that time, since Brahms had to borrow the autograph back in March 1860 for the second Hamburg performance.[16] Exactly when he returned

---

[13] The full score was published as a lithographic reproduction of a fair-copy manuscript prepared by the firm from the composer's autograph manuscript. The score continued to be sold in this form even after Simrock acquired the rights to this work in 1888. Only nine years after Brahms's death did N. Simrock finally print the score, which it then advertised as having been 'revised from handwritten notes by the composer'. Textual comparison shows, however, that, except for the correction of a few errors, and the introduction of several new errors, there is no difference between the Breitkopf print and the Simrock edition.

[14] 'Ich glaube, daß das "Konzert" ein etwas schwierigeres Unternehmen ist. Noch dazu gehören die tüchtigern Pianisten jetzt fast durchweg der neudeutschen Schule an, die sich vielleicht nicht um meine Sachen bekümmert. Die Klavierstimme bleibt wenigstens hoffentlich nicht liegen. Ob Sie die Orchesterstimmen durch Überdruck vielleicht verbreiten? Von meiner Seite habe ich nichts dagegen.' *Brahms Briefwechsel*, 14: 48.

[15] 'Willst Du mir wirklich zur Erinnerung an die Hamburger Tage das Manuskript Deines Konzerts schenken, so wäre dies ein mehr als königlicher Lohn; aber was fällt Dir von Abschreiben ein! Ich dächte doch, und hoffe es sogar, Du habest Wichtigeres zu tun. Lasse Dir's von einem guten Kopisten zum Gebrauch fürs öffentliche Spielen in philiströser Hand für die Herren Kapellmeister abschreiben.' *Brahms Briefwechsel*, 5: 244.

[16] Ibid., 5: 263.

the score is not known (the autograph manuscript now preserved in the Deutsche Staatsbibliothek, Berlin, came from Joachim's possession), nor is it known when he had the manuscript made that was used as the engraver's copy; variants between the engraver's model and the autograph manuscript suggest, however, that the model was copied from an intervening source.

In December 1860 Brahms offered to have two copies of the score prepared for Rieter-Biedermann's use. Rieter's response has not survived, but in March 1870 Brahms lent the publisher his own copy (autograph or copyist's manuscript?) with the request for its return; Brahms indicated that if Rieter wished to own a copy of the score, he should have it copied himself.[17] In a letter of 13 July 1872, the composer mentioned sending the score together with the two-piano arrangement which he had ready for engraving—the Piano Primo is the solo part, virtually identical to the published solo piano part—and asked whether publishing the score would not still be delayed awhile. Four days later he informed Rieter that the score of the concerto would need a lot of revision before being printed.[18] Over the years there had of course been further opportunity to revise and refine the work, based on experience gained from playing and conducting it.

Two years later Brahms requested that galley proofs of the score be sent in time for his use in a concert in Vienna on 2 November 1874. The concerto was to be repeated on 29 December in Breslau under the direction of Bernhard Scholz, who was to send the corrected proofs to Winterthur directly afterwards. Second proofs should not be necessary, Brahms added, though care must be taken to make all the designated changes.[19] But either the composer proof-read the galleys superficially, or the publisher was not careful enough, for the printed score contained many errors.[20]

The history of the publication of the First Serenade is by no means so complicated as that of the First Piano Concerto. The autograph score was undoubtedly the composer's working draft for orchestrating the version for large orchestra. Thereafter it was heavily revised as a result of discussions with Joachim and of trial performances; subsequently it was used as the copyist's model for the lithographed score.[21] Brahms's learning sessions with the orchestra are particularly evident in his efforts to lighten the bottom-heavy brass and lower strings and in the refinements he made in dynamics, phrasing, and articulation.

Relatively little is known about the Second Serenade, Op. 16, and the relevant musical sources have disappeared; it seems to have evolved quietly in the wake of the struggles with the concerto and the First Serenade. Its première was also its only test prior to publication. Joachim apparently was consulted merely about what would be the best placement of the musicians on the stage for the Hamburg performance.[22] In the letter

---

[17] Ibid., 14: 57–8, 184.  [18] Ibid., 14: 209, 211.

[19] Ibid., 14: 237, 239.

[20] In the *Revisionsbericht* for his edition of this concerto in the *Brahms Werke* (6: iii–iv), Hans Gál speculated that the relatively unreliable text for the piano part may have resulted from the long delay in the publication of the full score; it obviously had not undergone recent comparison with the carefully edited prints of the solo piano part and two-piano arrangement released many years before. However, the text of the orchestral parts is also not free of errors.

[21] See note 13.

[22] *Brahms Briefwechsel*, 5: 258.

transmitting the work to Simrock, Brahms insisted that an engraved score be published together with the orchestral parts.[23] Publication may well have been undertaken too hastily and editing rushed to meet the deadline of a commissioned performance in Leipzig on 26 November 1860, for at that performance, just after publication, and at others which followed, serious errors showed up in the score, numerous enough to cause Simrock to release a revised edition in 1875, with corrections in instrumentation, dynamics, and phrasing.

# III

After the concerto and two serenades were launched, nearly a decade passed before Brahms began to test a new series of large-scale works, and now vocal as well as instrumental forces were involved, in the *German Requiem*, *Rinaldo*, the Alto Rhapsody, the *Schicksalslied*, and the *Triumphlied*. During the intervening years Brahms had been building on his early achievements by gaining experience with instrumental and choral chamber music, developing more sophisticated contrapuntal techniques, and experimenting with new forms and styles.[24] He also broadened his horizons with sojourns in Austria (his first visit to Vienna took place in 1862), southern Germany, and Switzerland, and widened his circle of musical friends and colleagues. Clara Schumann, his muse of the 1850s, Joachim, and Dietrich continued to be among the first entrusted with new works, but others were enlisted to help produce trial performances.

The *German Requiem*, like the piano concerto whose original slow scherzo it contains in its second movement, also underwent a long gestation characterized by struggle with new compositional problems.[25] Here it was a matter of combining chorus and orchestra in a multi-movement work of major dimensions. The creative effort, together with the results of several trial performances, is evident on nearly every page of the autograph score, which was written down over a span of at least half a dozen years on a variety of papers.

In its initial version, the Requiem consisted of six movements. The first trial performance of movements 1–3 took place on 1 December 1867, at the second of that season's concerts of the Gesellschaft der Musikfreunde. Kalbeck reports that when rumours of a new Brahms composition reached Vienna, the conductor Johann Herbeck offered to programme part of the work as a novelty—the entire work would have been too much to impose on a subscription-concert audience. During the month of November, Brahms and Joachim had been on tour together, so the composer was not on hand to assist with rehearsals. As a result, the performance was poorly prepared and,

---

[23] *Brahms Briefwechsel*, 5: 258.

[24] Brahms's only completed works with orchestral forces during this period were his orchestrations of Schubert Lieder—'An Schwager Kronos' (D. 369), 'Memnon' (D. 541), 'Geheimes' (D. 719), 'Greisengesang' (D. 778), and 'Ellens Zweiter Gesang' (D. 838)—which were made in 1862; for further details, see Anh. Ia/12, 13, 15–17 in McCorkle, *Werkverzeichnis*.

[25] For a detailed account of the history of the Requiem, see Klaus Blum, *Hundert Jahre Ein deutsches Requiem von Johannes Brahms*.

under Herbeck's baton, came off badly. The worst mishap occurred at the fugal conclusion of the third movement, where the timpanist misread the dynamic markings and hammered away at the pedal-point, drowning out everything else and causing an uproar in the audience.[26] For Brahms the fiasco must have been painfully reminiscent of the début of his piano concerto in Leipzig.

From an exchange of letters between Brahms and Joachim in September 1867, we find that Brahms thought he had already sent the Requiem to his patient friend for critical reading. When he urgently requested its return for use in Vienna, Joachim had to remind him that he had given it to Dietrich to show to Karl Reinthaler, cathedral organist and director of the Singakademie in Bremen. The hope was that Reinthaler might be interested in mounting a full performance in Bremen cathedral, where, as Joachim pointed out, the resources, acoustics, and industry of the conductor were all favourable for a trial performance.[27]

After reading through the score—and despite the unpresentable appearance of the manuscript, for which Brahms apologized—Reinthaler was enthusiastic about the new work and offered to schedule it for Good Friday, 10 April 1868. His one reservation was that 'it lasts a long time for a choral work without solos'. He recommended that a solo be added to serve as a climax, with a pointed reference to the Christian resurrection and its meaning for man's redemption.[28] For the Good Friday performance, Reinthaler provided his own solution by inviting Amalie Joachim to sing Handel's aria 'I know that my Redeemer liveth' from the *Messiah*, after the fourth movement.[29] A month later Brahms composed a fifth movement of his own, 'Ihr habt nun Traurigkeit', a soprano solo on the theme not of redemption, but rather of consolation.[30]

To test a work the size of the Requiem was no small financial and logistical matter. For the Vienna and Bremen performances he needed, as he later recounted, three piano-vocal scores, twelve sets of string parts, and 200 choral parts.[31] Before he received a commitment from Reinthaler, he had thought of offering to play in a subscription concert or to give a benefit concert to raise the necessary funds to produce this work. Gratefully accepting Reinthaler's formal invitation, Brahms remarked: 'Without this, the work would have remained only written this year too. The purpose of the concert also suits me perfectly, since now the question of money can be dropped.'[32] He promised to send the complete choral parts and to be on hand during the preparations. With the choral parts he included the score of movements 4, 6, and 7 (the last three movements at the time), so that the viola and wind parts could be copied in Bremen. Of greatest

---

[26] Kalbeck, *Brahms*, 2: 234.

[27] *Brahms Briefwechsel*, 6: 47–9.

[28] Ibid., 3: 7–11.

[29] Dietrich, *Erinnerungen*, 62.

[30] In his reply to Reinthaler's recommendation (*Brahms Briefwechsel*, 3: 12), Brahms obliquely admitted his intention that the Requiem not be specifically Christian in its content and appeal.

[31] *Brahms Briefwechsel*, 14: 153.

[32] 'Ohne diese würde das Werk auch dies Jahr nur geschrieben sein. Sehr erwünscht ist mir auch der Zweck des Konzerts, da nun die Geldfrage auf sich beruhen kann.' Ibid., 3: 13.

importance, he reiterated, was to be able to rehearse as much and as often as possible; any extra money earned would be fine—especially to pay for extra rehearsals. A month before the concert he worried about whether the difficulties of the work were being taken seriously enough: 'in Bremen one goes rather more cautiously up to high "A" than in Vienna. I am now enclosing the score for the first three movements, as I sincerely wish and hope that you will have the strings take part in the chorus rehearsals; it would be very nice if the violins were acquainted with the thing from now on. Are the parts for the other movements ready and fairly correct?'[33] Whether or not his concern about the conduct of rehearsals was justified, the performance itself, directed by Brahms, was in every respect a triumph.[34]

In May and June 1868 manuscript materials for publishing the Requiem began arriving at Rieter-Biedermann's, first the corrected parts, then the full score and the piano-vocal score. Brahms was particularly anxious that the fifth movement had not yet been tested. He badgered Rieter all summer about arranging a performance, all the while keeping up a barrage of instructions about revisions, translation of the text, the format of the edition, etc.; he also requested galleys so that he could prepare the organ part and the arrangement for piano duet. By the end of September, Friedrich Hegar, conductor of the Tonhallegesellschaft in Zurich, had organized a private performance, and Brahms was finally able to hear the entire work and forward the revised fifth movement to his publisher.[35]

The surviving musical sources corroborate and supplement the information in the correspondence. The autograph score, the most significant source, reveals the successive stages of drafting and revision. Numerous passages were crossed out and rewritten; pitches, indications of tempo and expression, dynamics, phrasing, and articulation were altered in ink, pencil, and coloured crayons; rehearsal letters were entered and changed. Of the metronome markings inserted by Reinthaler and discussed by Brahms in a letter to Rieter on 1 October, the composer's advice was: 'In general, either every year [give] new metronome indications or [give] none at all.'[36] The 'notorious' fugal section over the pedal-point in the third movement was reworked—not the timpani part, but the strings, in order to lighten the texture.

The piano-vocal score which was used for rehearsals is also an interesting document, with paste-overs in the first and seventh movements and other revisions corresponding to those incorporated into the full score. The published piano reduction was prepared, except for the fifth movement, from the manuscript Brahms gave Clara Schumann for Christmas 1866; the differences, which appear as autograph corrections, represent the

---

[33] 'in Bremen geht man doch bedächtiger zum hohen a hinauf als in Wien usw. Ich schicke hierbei die Partitur der drei ersten Sätze, da ich herzlich wünsche und hoffe, Sie lassen das Streichquartett sich beteiligen an den Singproben; es wäre sehr schön, wenn die Geiger hernach die Sache kennten. Sind wohl die Stimmen der übrigen Sätze fertig und recht korrekt?' Ibid., 3: 17–18; cf. also 12–13, 15.

[34] Dietrich has described the joyful occasion, which attracted Brahms's friends from near and far and culminated in a festive supper in the Ratskeller after the concert (*Erinnerungen*, 61–5).

[35] *Brahms Briefwechsel*, 14: 152–62.

[36] 'Überhaupt entweder jedes Jahr neu metronomisieren oder gar nicht.' Ibid., 14: 164.

continuing evolution of the work during its trial period in 1867–8.[37] The extant copies from the set of manuscript parts show numerous pencilled alterations and refinements in both musical and literary text.

Brahms began work on his cantata *Rinaldo* within three years of publishing his First Piano Concerto and the two serenades. As he explained to Joachim in June 1863, the impetus was the 300-Thaler prize in the Aachen Liedertafel competition of that year. When the first part of the cantata was ready, Brahms sent it to Joachim who enthusiastically urged him on. But as the October deadline for submission approached, Brahms lost interest—the piece was not ready, and he had to turn his attention to starting the next season as the new director of the Wiener Singakademie.[38]

Both Joachim and Clara Schumann enquired about the work in the spring of 1864. Brahms returned to it, though, only after completing the Requiem, and then he composed a new concluding chorus (June 1868). As he was preparing for the trial performance in Vienna during the winter season 1868–9, Frau Schumann voiced her reservations about whether *Rinaldo* was a worthy sequel to the Requiem.[39] But already by September, the composer had been sure enough of his new piece to contact Fritz Simrock: 'I have recently written to Vienna about my *Rinaldo*, have made a piano-vocal score, and the copyist is now doing his part. In any case, I now want to hear the work this winter and—be rid of it. I don't believe, of course, that anything will have to be changed in the piano-vocal score and the choral parts; still I would like to consider a first performance as a test and have engraved only the parts needed for it.'[40]

When the planned trial performance with the Wiener Männergesangverein was cancelled, Brahms put off reading proofs for the parts which Simrock had obligingly supplied. He then had to press the publisher to get the necessary quantity of parts, still uncorrected, for the trial performance which did take place, with the Wiener Akademische Gesangverein, on 28 February 1869. This performance pleased the composer enormously, and he proceeded with preparations for publication.[41] There were, however, corrections and revisions resulting from this performance; the parts were collected from the Gesangverein and the requisite changes made in them. Writing to Simrock, Brahms noted that the piano-vocal score should serve as the model for placing rehearsal letters in the full score and parts and for the dynamic markings in the choral parts; the orchestral parts should be revised according to the full score; and a major revision in the final chorus, written on a paste-over in the score, should be observed. The

---

[37] For a comparative history of the two piano-vocal scores, see Friedrich G. Zeileis, 'Two Manuscript Sources of Brahms's German Requiem'.

[38] *Brahms Briefwechsel*, 6: 12–15.

[39] Berthold Litzmann, ed., *Clara Schumann–Johannes Brahms Briefe*, 1: 438, 442, 601.

[40] 'Ich habe dieser Tage nach Wien geschrieben, meines Rinaldo wegen, habe einen Klavierauszug gemacht, und der Kopist tut jetzt das Seinige. Das Werk will ich nun jedenfalls den Winter hören und—los sein. Ich glaube zwar nicht, daß im Klavierauszug und den Chorstimmen geändert wird, doch möchte ich eine erste Aufführung als Probe ansehen und nur die hierzu nötigen Stimmen stechen lassen.' *Brahms Briefwechsel*, 9: 57.

[41] Ibid., 9: 61–2, 68.

revised passage, bars 249–77, is actually written out on extra sheets, labelled 'Beilage' by Brahms, which were inserted into both full score and piano-vocal score. (Possibly there were paste-overs in the choral parts, which are no longer extant, although it is not entirely clear from Brahms's letter whether the correction was made during the rehearsals or after the performance.) Reluctantly he supplied metronome markings for the sections.[42]

Not much is known about the preparations for publishing the Alto Rhapsody. At the end of his summer's stay in Lichtental/Baden-Baden, Brahms, in a bitter mood, showed the piece to Clara Schumann, a few days after the wedding of her daughter Julie (22 September 1869).[43] In September Brahms also wrote to Hermann Deiters, mentioning the piece, confessing his uncertainty about publishing or performing 'this rather intimate music', and stating that he would soon be hearing it in Karlsruhe.[44] Indeed, the Rhapsody was given a trial performance of sorts there on 6 October at the dress rehearsal for the season's first subscription concert, with the assistance of the Hofkapellmeister Hermann Levi. But references to this event are ambiguous at best. In her diary Clara Schumann recorded that 'in the rehearsal Levi had Johannes's Rhapsody played for me (Frau Boni sang the alto solo)'. This wording raises the question of whether the work was given a hearing with piano or with orchestral accompaniment. The concert being rehearsed included a Schumann symphony and a Beethoven piano concerto with Frau Schumann as soloist; Levi joined her at the piano to accompany a vocal quartet that sang ten numbers from the *Liebeslieder* Waltzes. Thus both orchestra and soloist were on hand for testing the Rhapsody, but then so was the piano—only the male chorus was lacking.[45]

Despite the reservations expressed to Deiters, Brahms wrote Simrock, on the day before this test, 'In any case, I would like very much to have the work out quickly, and [I] am telling you about it now and sending the score right away; the piano reduction follows.'[46] Information in this letter and in related correspondence with Simrock, Levi, and Joachim causes some confusion about how many manuscripts once existed and what

---

[42] Ibid., 9: 67, 70, 73.

[43] Berthold Litzmann, *Clara Schumann. Ein Künstlerleben*, 3: 232. Clara Schumann was shaken by Brahms's 'Brautgesang' and speculated in her diary about his unsuspected feelings for Julie.

[44] '. . . die etwas intime Musik'. *Brahms Briefwechsel*, 3: 121.

[45] 'In der Probe ließ mir Levi Johannes' Rhapsodie vorspielen (Frau Boni sang das Altsolo).' Litzmann, *Clara Schumann*, 3: 232; cf. Kalbeck, *Brahms*, 2: 310. See also Walter Frisch's introduction to the facsimile edition of the autograph score; Frisch surmises from this that the piano was used, inaccurately translating this passage as 'In the rehearsal Levi allowed me to play through Johannes' Rhapsody' (p. 25 of the Introduction), although he then admits the ambiguity of the German. He reasons that, assuming the piano was used, the fact that in the manuscript the choral parts are written in close score would have made it possible for the pianist to play the choral parts as well. It is unlikely, at the very least, that Frau Schumann played from the score, for she was known to have difficulty reading a full score at sight, especially one in Brahms's hand (cf. *Brahms Briefwechsel*, 9: 84–5; Litzmann, ed., *Schumann–Brahms Briefe*, 1: 540).

[46] 'Jedenfalls möchte ich's gern rasch heraus haben, und melde es darum jetzt und schicke gleich die Partitur; der Klavierauszug folgt.' *Brahms Briefwechsel*, 9: 85–6.

sources were sent to whom and when.[47] Apparently, the single surviving source was used in the trial performance, but not as the engraver's model. Inexplicably, there is none of the usual exchange between Brahms and his publisher over matters of publication, no reference to the manuscript parts, to revisions, or to corrections at the proof-reading stage. When the piece was given its true première in March 1870, it had already been in print for three months.

For the two years following the Alto Rhapsody, Brahms continued to explore the choral-orchestral genre. In May 1870 he promised Grimm 'a second piece of the kind' for the winter concert season of 1870–1,[48] but completion of his planned work, the *Schicksalslied*, was delayed for a year by intervening political events. The triumphant campaigns of the German army in the Franco-Prussian War stirred the composer deeply and inspired him to write his 'Lied auf Paris', as he described the *Triumphlied* to Simrock in October.[49] In December he was calling his new work a 'Te Deum' in a letter to Reinthaler, who was quick to seize upon the idea of this piece being a 'twin brother to the Requiem'.[50] In February 1871 Brahms eagerly offered Reinthaler 'the first chorus in a Triumphlied' for the next Good Friday concert in Bremen. In March his exuberant anticipation of the performance knew no bounds: Reinthaler should get reinforcements from Dietrich's choir in Oldenburg, and they would need three trumpets and four horns in C to celebrate the German victories.[51]

[47] Ibid., 6:59; 7:49–50; 9:85–6, 88. I cannot entirely accept Frisch's reconstruction of events from these references because of his imprecision in dating several of the letters and describing their contents (the Brahms–Levi letters in question were published as 'undated', the letter from Brahms to Joachim was misdated by Andreas Moser, editor of the volume, as Frisch points out). The 'Quartett-Soirée' at which Brahms's Quintet in F minor, Op. 34, was performed and which Frisch associates with the trial performance of the Rhapsody, took place on 20 October, not two weeks earlier; Brahms's letter to Levi concerning the return of the original autograph and the manuscript copy of the Rhapsody score also refers to Brahms's promise to perform the quintet 'next Wednesday', and hence must be dated between 13 and 15 October, not the week of 27 September, a fact which substantially alters the reconstruction posited by Frisch. The letter to Joachim should probably be dated 'October', instead of 'November 1868'—Brahms stated that he sent the score for Clara Schumann 'at the moment of departure' ['im Moment der Abreise'], presumably from Baden-Baden on 19 October. The references to the nature of the source for the Rhapsody that Brahms was sending to Simrock are also not as clear as Frisch would have it. On 8 October Brahms wrote merely: 'The Rhapsody is being copied and can then perhaps be sent along [with the parts for the *Liebeslieder* Waltzes, Op. 52]' ['Die Rhapsodie wird kopiert und kann dann vielleicht mitkommen']—the reference is not to parts for the Rhapsody. What exactly was being copied and what was the nature of the copy is not clear. From what is said in the letter to Levi already cited, we may suppose that it was only the score that was being copied just then, not the parts. On 5 October Brahms announced to Simrock that he was going to enclose the 'prettiest score' ['die zierlichste Partitur'] of the Rhapsody when he returned the corrected galleys for the score of the *Liebeslieder* Waltzes; but when he sent off the galleys on the 7th, he did not enclose the promised score of the Rhapsody, as we have seen. On 15 October he did send a copy (singular) of the Rhapsody, promising again that the piano reduction would follow 'as soon as I have my manuscript' ['sobald ich mein Manuskript habe']. All of the foregoing leaves it uncertain whether Brahms ever did send Simrock his autograph of the Rhapsody score (I too erred in stating in my *Brahms Werkverzeichnis*, p. 222 under 'Zur Herausgabe', that Brahms sent the engraver's model on 5 October), and nothing is recorded to indicate precisely when the parts or the piano reduction were made and delivered to the publisher.

[48] '. . . ein zweites Stück der Art'. *Brahms Briefwechsel*, 4: 119.

[49] Ibid., 9: 98.

[50] '. . . den Zwillingsbruder des "Requiem" '. Ibid., 3: 32, 34.

[51] Ibid., 3: 37–9.

Following the splended première, Brahms wrote to Simrock (22 May), 'At the moment the *Triumphlied* has been left lying—but another Lied is ready just now. . . . Perhaps we shall try it out in Karlsruhe.'[52] Brahms evidently felt that the *Triumphlied* could benefit from further tests, and the *Schicksalslied* was waiting for its first try-outs. With both works Hermann Levi proved an invaluable musical collaborator. Brahms was invited to Karlsruhe, where Levi had been rehearsing the two pieces and where he now put his orchestra and chorus at Brahms's disposal. Moreover, Levi took on the preparation of the performing materials for the tests and for publication, prepared the piano-vocal score of the *Schicksalslied* (Brahms subsequently rewrote much of the piano reduction, to make it more difficult, he explained), copied the full score, corrected the parts for the *Triumphlied*, arranged to have the parts duplicated and the full score copied, and, in the role of factotum, communicated with Simrock in Brahms's stead, packing and sending off manuscripts as needed and forwarding instructions about the format of the publication.[53] Most importantly, though, Levi contributed to the composition of these works, as is documented in the extant manuscripts, suggesting small improvements in the orchestration and persuading Brahms to delete the chorus that originally concluded the *Schicksalslied*, thereby allowing the orchestra to have the epilogue to itself.

Brahms was feeling confident about these two works. Before the October test of the *Schicksalslied*, he sent Simrock all the performing materials except the wind and percussion parts, and already in September he could announce, 'I am now having the *Triumphlied* copied, and we can probably risk printing the choral parts immediately. For publication I must have a complete, good performance behind me.'[54] By the end of November he promised even more: 'Levi will now be sending you choral and violin [that is, string] parts for engraving; should the mentioned performance occur, it would also be good to engrave the piano reduction. But I absolutely must have permission to have all kinds of changes made in the plates afterwards! There will probably not be so many, but it is possible.'[55]

Copying took longer than expected, so Simrock evidently did not receive more than just the parts in advance. The performance had to be postponed while Levi tried unsuccessfully to interest his Grand Duke in helping to defray the cost of producing a patriotic piece for double chorus. He decided to go ahead with the *Triumphlied* anyhow and programmed it on his farewell concert at Karlsruhe, having in the mean time accepted a new position in Munich. Because of the special circumstances of this performance, it was agreed that Levi should conduct, but Brahms participated in the final

---

[52] 'Das Triumphlied ist den Augenblick liegen geblieben—aber gerade ist ein andres Lied fertig. . . . Vielleicht probieren wir es in Karlsruhe.' Ibid., 9: 102.

[53] Ibid., 7: 79–81, 83–4, 86–7.

[54] 'Das Triumphlied lasse ich jetzt ausschreiben, und wir könnten wohl riskieren, die Singstimmen sofort zu drucken. Für die Herausgabe muß ich eine Vollständige gute Aufführung hinter mir haben.' Ibid., 9: 105; cf. also 9:104–6.

[55] 'Nun wird Levi Ihnen Sing- und Violinstimmen schicken, um sie zu stechen; findet besagte Aufführung statt, so wäre es gut, auch den Klavierauszug zu stechen. Aber ich muß durchaus die Erlaubnis haben, nachher alles Mögliche in den Platten ändern zu lassen! Das wird nun zwar wahrscheinlich nicht gefährlich sein, aber möglich ist es.' Ibid., 9: 108.

rehearsals.[56] As the composer reported to Theodor Billroth in Vienna, the work was well rehearsed and powerfully performed; it made such a stunning impression, in fact, that he was tempted to reserve judgement until the next hearing of the piece.[57] Nevertheless, three weeks later all the performing materials were sent off to Simrock, with the caution, though, that the score was still not free of error and with instructions for the house editor to put a question mark beside all doubtful notes.[58]

The extant autograph manuscripts for the *Schicksalslied* and the *Triumphlied* did not serve as engraver's models. The autograph of the *Schicksalslied*, full of revisions and refinements, was undoubtedly used in the trial performance—the manuscript copy of the score was sent to Simrock before the test. The *Triumphlied* autograph, which contains many emendations for performance, would certainly have been available, if not actually in use during the trial performance in Karlsruhe, together with the manuscript copy of the score. Exactly what source was used for the performance of the first movement in Bremen is not known.

Thus, the Requiem, the *Schicksalslied*, and the *Triumphlied* were all tested under particularly favourable conditions. Carefully rehearsed by conductors sympathetic to the composer, they were enthusiastically presented and received. With *Rinaldo*, the situation was different. Although Brahms himself had been satisfied with the quality of the Viennese première, the audience and critics were decidedly cool. It was not until his next première in Vienna that he would finally enjoy a resounding popular and critical success in his adopted city.

# IV

*The Variations on a Theme by Haydn*, Op. 56a, is in every respect an anomaly. The 'first truly symphonic work of Brahms'[59] originated as a set of variations for two pianos which, when orchestrated, took on an independent existence in the orchestral repertoire and became a landmark in the composer's career. Brahms surely suspected this potential in his piano variations, but was not entirely convinced that it had been realized until he heard the trial performance of the orchestral version.[60]

Early in October 1873 Brahms sent the version for two pianos to Simrock, announced a trial performance for the orchestral version at the first Vienna Philharmonic concert of the season, and admitted that he was very confused about how to treat the two versions. The première went brilliantly, and within a week the autograph score was on its way to the publisher. Evidence in the score suggests that it served as both draft for the

[56] Ibid., 7: 95, 99, 105–6, 109–10.

[57] Otto Gottlieb-Billroth, ed., *Billroth und Brahms im Briefwechsel*, 198. For a further account of the Karlsruhe performance and the work's reception, see Klaus Häfner, 'Das "Triumphlied" op. 55, eine vergessene Komposition von Johannes Brahms'.

[58] *Brahms Briefwechsel*, 9: 123.

[59] Walter Niemann, *Brahms*, 271–2.

[60] *Brahms Briefwechsel*, 9: 149–50, 154. On the significance of this work in Brahms's *œuvre* and its genesis and evolution, see Donald M. McCorkle, ed., *Johannes Brahms, Variations on a Theme of Haydn for Orchestra, Op. 56a, and for Two Pianos, Op. 56b*.

orchestration of this work and as conducting score. One of the more significant revisions occurs already in the theme: originally strings doubled the winds, but these are crossed out entirely; whether this alteration was the result of the trial performance, or stemmed simply from a recollection of the characteristic sonority of the wind divertimento from which the chorale was borrowed, is unclear.[61]

The orchestral variations were immediately in demand, even before publication. The second performance was requested by Franz Wüllner in Munich; Brahms declined to come and conduct, but he sent Wüllner the autograph of his two-piano score to study, since the engraver's models for both versions (the autograph orchestral score and the copyist's manuscript for the two-piano version) had already gone to the publisher. Simrock in turn promised to deliver galleys of the orchestral parts in time for the rehearsals, and Brahms cautioned Wüllner to reserve a few hours for correcting the parts. He also engaged Wüllner and Simrock in a discussion over the relative merits of using a contrabassoon versus a bass trombone or tuba for the bass wind part, asking Wüllner's opinion (and that of Hermann Levi, now Wüllner's colleague in Munich), based on experience in performance.[62]

Three years were to pass before Brahms felt ready to test his next orchestral work, the long-planned First Symphony, Op. 68.[63] None of his other compositions had been through such a lengthy gestation. Intimidated by the legacy of Beethoven, Brahms had been engaged intermittently on this piece for at least twelve years, striving to produce an exemplary work in the form traditionally regarded as the *ne plus ultra* in musical art and craft. His old friends, Clara Schumann, Joachim, Dietrich, and Levi cheered his progress in the early 1860s. By the 1870s newer colleagues such as Franz Wüllner and the composer Max Bruch had started to press him about his symphonic project, offering their services in the first reading.

Finally, on 10 October 1876, following a summer of intensive compositional effort, Brahms was able to bring the whole symphony to Clara Schumann in Baden-Baden for a reading at the piano. At about the same time he approached Otto Dessoff, the new Hofkapellmeister in Karlsruhe, about a trial performance. (In 1875 Dessoff, a respected colleague of Brahms in Vienna, had left his post as conductor of the Wiener Hofoper orchestra and director of the Philharmonic concerts to assume the post in Karlsruhe; earlier in 1876 he had requested of Brahms the privilege of testing one of the composer's new works.) Brahms wrote to Dessoff from nearby Lichtental/Baden-Baden, explaining:

---

[61] Had the strings been retained in the orchestration of the theme, the result would have been a miscalculation of the relationship of theme to variations, as Michael Musgrave points out in his book *The Music of Brahms* (pp. 129–30): 'The association of [the wind-band sonority] with the model is a structural principle in the work, for the strings never take the varied form, only leading in the score when they have either a countersubject, as in variation 1 (the winds retaining the long notes), or a completely independent figure, as in the idiomatic writing of the last variation.'

[62] *Brahms Briefwechsel*, 15: 46–53.

[63] On the significance of this work in Brahms's *œuvre* and its genesis and evolution, see my introduction to the facsimile edition of the autograph score, and also Gieselher Schubert's remarks accompanying the Schott edition of this work.

'I always secretly preferred, of course, the thought of hearing the thing first in a small city which had a good friend, a good Kapellmeister, and a good orchestra.'[64]

Since Dessoff scheduled the new work for the first subscription concert of the season (4 November), he and Brahms had to work quickly with local copyists to prepare the performing materials in time for rehearsals. String parts for the first movement had already been copied in Vienna, but needed duplicating, while string parts for the remaining movements had to be copied and duplicated movement by movement, as Brahms handed over portions of the score being used as the master copy. When he sent the score of the second and third movements, Brahms asked for a word from Dessoff about them, noting: 'I have made things short and easy for the copyist (and myself?). I would hope it is not noticeable that they are shortened forcibly. The Finale requires this consideration.'[65] Dessoff expressed regret about the brevity of the third movement, whereupon Brahms sent him a supplement—two very short insertions and a third long one for the present bars 125–43, so that 'none of the earlier valuable bars are omitted'.[66]

Simrock was present for the début, but went away disappointed at not having extracted a promise for the early publication of this long-awaited work. Even before the Karlsruhe test, the symphony was committed for performances in Mannheim, Munich, and Vienna. When Simrock pressed Brahms to send the performing materials for engraving after the Vienna concert, so that the symphony might appear in February, the composer asked him not to announce the publication that soon: 'In case I really like the thing finally . . . we can occupy the engravers with it during the summer holidays!!'[67]

After Munich Brahms commissioned Dessoff to have the fourth movement of the score copied by Joseph Füller, a reliable copyist in Karlsruhe, adding: 'So that the confusion now goes no further, Herr F should also transpose the clarinets in the score to B♭.'[68] The autograph score reveals the cause for the confusion: at the beginning of the finale, the instrumentation is given as 'Clar. in B♭', although the part is actually written for clarinets in A. Since the manuscript parts for the clarinets are not extant, we cannot know whether they have the clarinets in A or B♭, and thus we cannot determine whether Brahms changed his mind about the clarinet timbre he wanted before or after hearing the work.

Those of Brahms's closest musical friends present at the first performances—Levi in Munich, Theodor Billroth in Vienna, and Clara Schumann in Leipzig—all found the symphony impressive, particularly the finale, but each had reservations about one or the

---

[64] 'Es war mir nämlich immer ein heimlich lieber Gedanke, das Ding zuerst in der kleinen Stadt, die einen guten Freund, guten Capellmeister und gutes Orchester hat, zu hören.' *Brahms Briefwechsel*, 16: 144. See also Frithjof Haas, 'Die Uraufführung der Ersten Sinfonie von Johannes Brahms in Karlsruhe'.

[65] 'Kurz und bequem habe ich's dem Copisten (und mir?) gemacht. Hoffentlich aber merkt man nicht, daß nur gewaltsam gekürzt ist. Das Finale verlangte die Rücksicht.' *Brahms Briefwechsel*, 16: 146.

[66] 'Es fällt keiner der so kostbaren Takte von früher weg!!!' Ibid., 16: 148.

[67] 'Im Fall mir das Ding wirklich schließlich gefällt, meine ich, wir werden die Stecher in den Sommerferien damit beschäftigen!!' Ibid., 10: 16.

[68] 'Damit es nun mit der Confusion nicht weiter gehe muß Hr. F. auch in der Part[itur] die Clarinetten nach B transponiren.' Ibid., 16: 150.

other movements: Levi thought the third movement too lightweight; to Billroth the first movement was not entirely sympathetic; and Frau Schumann expressed concern about the second movement.[69] From Clara's letter to Brahms of 12 February 1877, we learn that she thought she recognized in the Adagio an improvement over what she remembered of it from her previous, informal hearing, in October 1876.[70]

After its performance in Breslau, the symphony travelled to England with Joachim to be played under his direction at Cambridge University. This performance of the work, while still in manuscript, was the composer's acknowledgement of the honourary doctorate offered him by the university— he declined to travel abroad himself to receive the degree. From the descriptive programme notes written by Sir George Macfarren for the Cambridge concert and by Sir George Grove and again by Macfarren for the two subsequent performances in London, it is clear that the Adagio was then in a state considerably different from the one eventually published.[71] After getting the manuscript score back from England, and before turning it over to Simrock at the end of May, Brahms recast the form of the second movement by rearranging the existing musical materials and adding a motivic idea drawn from the first movement.

The surviving autograph score does not reveal much creative effort prior to the trial performances; the first movement is missing altogether, and the second movement is a fair copy. The third and fourth movements do, however, corroborate the events mentioned in the correspondence between Brahms and Dessoff—the revisions, 'Beilagen', etc., supplied during the copying process—and they also contain numerous emendations undoubtedly resulting from the series of performances that preceded publication. The extant violin and viola parts from the Vienna performance confirm the evidence from the British programme books about the penultimate state of the second movement.[72] In his instructions to Simrock, Brahms noted that he was not sending parts for the second movement—they should be engraved directly from the new score for the Adagio—and that the remaining parts needed to be compared with the score. In this

[69] See Levi's letter of 22 Nov. 1876 to Clara Schumann, in Litzmann, *Clara Schumann*, 3: 343; Billroth's letter of 15 Dec. 1876 to Eduard Hanslick, in Gottlieb-Billroth, *Billroth und Brahms*, 228, n. 1; and Clara Schumann's entry in her diary for 17 Dec. 1876, in Litzmann, *Clara Schumann*, 3: 347.

[70] Litzmann, ed., *Schumann–Brahms Briefe*, 2: 93.

[71] Discussions of this movement have appeared in S. T. M. Newman, 'The Slow Movement of Brahms's First Symphony: A Reconstruction of the Version First Performed Prior to Publication'; Robert Pascall, 'Brahms's First Symphony Slow Movement: The Initial Performing Version'; Margit L. McCorkle, 'Filling the Gaps in Brahms Source Research: Several Important Recent Manuscript Discoveries'; and Frithjof Haas, 'Die Erstfassung des langsamen Satzes der ersten Sinfonie von Johannes Brahms'.

[72] The second movement as reconstructed from the programme books and the Viennese string parts is so similar in crucial details to the version sketched on a sheet later used as a paste-over in the Third String Quartet, Op. 67, also completed in the summer of 1876, that I believe the penultimate version of the Adagio to have been the same as the original version. In light of this evidence, Newman's hypothesis (see note 71) that with this final revision Brahms reverted to the original version must now be dismissed. But what then are we to conclude about the reliability of Clara Schumann's recollection about the alteration that was supposed to have taken place between October and January (see note 69)? Possibly she simply heard the movement in a new light once it was adequately performed by an orchestra, rather than by Brahms on the piano. His informal performances of new works often left much to be desired.

instance he observed that the performance markings in the parts ought to deviate to some extent from those in the score and that the readings in the parts might well be more exact or more extensive. He asked that variants be signalled with question marks for his further consideration, rather than automatically altered—a direction which Simrock found thoroughly confusing.[73]

With the completion of his First Symphony Brahms had taken the final step towards full maturity as a composer of instrumental music and was now relieved of the heavy burden of proving himself worthy of the expectations of his contemporaries. By this time he had created for himself a settled life in Vienna, surrounded by a large group of loyal friends sympathetic to his art and esteemed by influential colleagues, with a dependable publisher, an established method of preparing works for publication, and growing financial security—all of these benefits contributing to the peace of mind essential to producing the masterpieces which flowed steadily from his pen over the next decade.

The nature of his relationships with friends and colleagues had inevitably changed with time and success. Now experienced, he no longer needed expert advice, though on occasion he still consulted with Joachim about technical matters when writing for strings. Nevertheless, not only his old friends, but also new admirers were privileged to preview the manuscripts and hear or play in the trial performances of Brahms's latest compositions. For the Second, Third, and Fourth Symphonies and for the Second Piano Concerto, the composer even invited a small group of acquaintances to the preliminary four-hand readings that took place in the Ehrbar piano salon in Vienna. Friendly reactions and encouragement were still important to him, and he seemed to find special nourishment in the appreciation for the subtleties of his art expressed by such discerning musical amateurs as Theodor Billroth, famous surgeon and dedicated *Liebhaber*, and Elisabet von Herzogenberg, his gifted former piano student who married the prolific *Kleinmeister* Heinrich von Herzogenberg, also a great admirer of Brahms's music.

The composer's major works were eagerly sought after by orchestras, and Brahms himself was equally in demand as interpreter of his music. For each concert season but two, from 1876 to 1888, he had ready a major new orchestral or choral-orchestral composition to introduce to avid audiences in the musical centres of Germany, Austria, Switzerland, Holland, and England. Among the most useful of his influential colleagues was the conductor-pianist Hans von Bülow, a convert from the Liszt–Wagner camp who

---

[73] *Brahms Briefwechsel*, 10: 35–6. In his essay 'Brahms and the Definitive Text', Robert Pascall indicates that the fourth movement in this manuscript was not used as the engraver's model, but he does not explain why he believes this to be so. Kalbeck reported seeing the manuscript in Simrock's possession and described its physical state: the first movement was a copyist's manuscript, the second through fourth movements were autograph, with the final two movements written on 'the same old, thick paper which Brahms was accustomed to buying in small batches from a second-hand dealer' (*Brahms*, 3: 90 n.). In the *Revisionsbericht* to his edition for the *Brahms Sämtliche Werke* (vol. 1), Hans Gál cited the same manuscript as being in the possession of N. Simrock, Berlin. There is nothing in the correspondence between Brahms and Simrock to help identify the source that served as the engraver's model. It is possible, of course, that Füller's copy of the fourth movement, with the transposed clarinet parts, was also submitted to Simrock, but, since the Füller copy has disappeared, no hard evidence exists to prove this.

put his well-drilled ducal orchestra at Meiningen at Brahms's disposal for tests of the Second Piano Concerto, *Nänie*, and the Fourth Symphony. Brahms conducted all the premières of his later works, except those of the Second Piano Concerto, in which he was the soloist, and the Second and Third Symphonies. The first readings of the two symphonies were given by the Vienna Philharmonic under the direction of Hans Richter, with whom Brahms must certainly have collaborated closely in rehearsal. While the new works were on tour, the composer normally guest-conducted, carrying along the manuscript score and sometimes also a set of parts or sending them on ahead when time between engagements permitted. Only England did he not visit, entrusting his manuscripts to Joachim or Richter for performances of the Violin Concerto, the Fourth Symphony, and the Double Concerto. On a few other occasions he lent his manuscripts to such respected colleagues as Richter, von Bülow, Wüllner, and George Henschel for pre-publication performances.

Although Fritz Simrock sometimes showed impatience, he had come to accept the deliberate pace with which Brahms's works progressed towards publication.[74] In his possessive devotion he eagerly tried to secure every new work as soon as possible and to co-operate to the utmost with the composer. From the Violin Concerto on, all trial performances were played from 'printed' string parts (that is, pulled proofs); Simrock was willing to print these, even though Brahms reserved the right to make whatever changes might be necessary once he had heard the compositions.[75] The organization testing the work would purchase the performing materials (parts other than those for the strings were still usually handwritten); these would at some point, according to the circumstances, be returned either to the composer or the publisher and in due course were replaced with the published parts. When the last concert of a season was over, Brahms would collect the performing materials and revise, correct, and refine the full score, based on his experience conducting and hearing the pieces. The score, parts, and other relevant manuscripts were then sent to the publisher, together with appropriate instructions for editing and engraving. As he grew busier Brahms tended to rely more heavily on Simrock's conscientious house editor Robert Keller to make the necessary textual comparisons of the sources and to control the mechanical process of correction.

---

[74] When Brahms evaded queries about his First Symphony, Simrock pleaded: 'Would you also do me the favour of telling me when I shall have the engraver's model—since for more extensive works, especially for you, I always have to have the best engravers reserved for me; but I must make an appointment ahead of time, since the *good* engravers are always engaged into the future; the score cannot be produced by two, but must be done by *one engraver-artist* uniformly and elegantly, which requires time and peace. Please let me have a word?' ['Auch mir täten Sie wohl den Gefallen, mir zu sagen, wann ich die Stichvorlagen haben soll—da ich für umfangreichere Werke, namentlich von Ihnen—stets mir die besten Stecher reservieren lasse; ich muß aber vorher anmelden, da die *guten* Stecher immer und längerhin besetzt sind; die Partitur kann nicht von Zweien, sondern muß einheitlich schön von *einem Stecherkünstler* hergestellt werden, erfordert also Zeit und Ruhe. Sagen Sie mir bitte ein Wort?'] Stephenson, ed., *Brahms und Simrock*, 94.

[75] Due to the added expense, a publisher would make such a concession only in exceptional cases, for a composition whose success could be predicted. This practice was not without precedent before Brahms: Fritz Simrock's father Peter Joseph Simrock had extended it to Mendelssohn; see Rudolf Elvers, ed., *Felix Mendelssohn Bartholdy, Briefe an deutsche Verleger*, 196–7, 200–1, 218–19.

The composer still received galleys, but typically read them more as composer-conductor-pianist than as systematic editor. In light of these normal final stages in the compositional process, the individual circumstances surrounding each work stand out more sharply.

## V

Brahms's Second Symphony, Op. 73, followed close on the heels of his First Symphony. Hardly had he finished writing it down than a date was fixed for its première in Vienna. Originally scheduled for 9 December 1877, the début had to be postponed three weeks because the parts could not be copied soon enough. From C. F. Pohl, then archivist of the Gesellschaft der Musikfreunde, we learn that three rehearsals were allotted to prepare for the premiére; a *Korrektur-Probe* or session for correcting the parts, a regular working rehearsal, and a dress rehearsal open to the public. After the dress rehearsal, Pohl reported to Simrock that 'the work is splendid and will find quick acceptance. The third movement already has its *Da capo* in its pocket [that is, it would be applauded until encored].'[76]

The performing materials were sent off to Simrock a week after the Dresden performance (6 March 1878) with the following directions: 'I wanted to correct the parts for you nicely, but I see that they must be looked at by expert eyes before they go to the engraver. However, it is simpler for Herr Keller to compare and correct them exactly from the score. What the players put in—fingerings, bowings, etc.—leave out, of course; this time let me have a proof of the parts to read.'[77] He also enclosed a manuscript copy of the score for the first movement for use by the engraver; the autograph score was so heavily marked up and so messy that Brahms had had a clean copy made, probably after the Dresden concert, and into it had entered his emendations.

The score and parts were in the second galley stage when Simrock printed enough parts for a performance in Düsseldorf. On 15 June Brahms wrote urgently asking that the printing be halted, for there were 'bad errors everywhere', as he had found out during the rehearsals.[78] Fortunately, the score had not yet been printed. As part of the proof-reading process, Brahms then sent galleys of the score to Dessoff and Joachim to have them double-checked.[79]

As is well known, Brahms turned again to Joachim during the composition of the Violin Concerto, Op. 77. In August 1878, while still drafting the first movement, he asked

---

[76] 'Das Werk ist herrlich und wird raschen Eingang finden. Der 3te Satz hat sein Da capo schon in der Tasche.' *Brahms Briefwechsel*, 10: 66.

[77] 'Ich wollte Ihnen die Stimmen schön korrigieren, sehe aber, daß sie doch, ehe sie zum Stecher gehen, von kundigen Augen besehen werden müssen. Da ist es denn doch einfacher, Herr Keller vergleicht und korrigiert sie genau nach der Partitur. Was von den Musikern zugesetzt ist, Fingersatz, Bogenstrich usw. fällt natürlich weg, und diesmal lassen Sie mich ja eine Korrektur der Stimmen lesen.' Letter of 12 Mar. 1878. Ibid., 10: 69.

[78] 'Es sind allerwärts sehr böse Fehler.' Ibid., 10: 75.

[79] Ibid., 10: 79–81; cf. Stephenson, ed., *Brahms und Simrock*, 120.

Joachim to peruse the solo part and tell him whether certain passages were practicable and playable; in September the two met to discuss the piece, and in November Brahms wrote that he was replacing the two middle movements of his projected four-movement work with a newly composed Adagio.[80]

The first performance of the concerto was scheduled for New Year's Day in Leipzig, but even as late as mid-December Brahms was not certain that the deadline could be met. The orchestral parts were ready, but Joachim had only just received the solo part and sections of the score. Brahms wrote on 17 December that he would come to Berlin a few days before the concert; they could try the piece together at the piano, and the Leipzig début could probably be risked, since Joachim was already acquainted with the 'main thing', and for one performance the rest of the notes would not matter much. As Brahms did not arrive in Berlin until late on 28 December, the first reading with orchestra in Leipzig four days later must have been precarious indeed.[81]

In January 1879 Brahms and Joachim took the concerto on tour, and the composer could soon report that the violinist was playing the work more beautifully with each concert.[82] Joachim then left for England, to introduce the concerto in London (using a copy of the solo part he had had made), while Brahms looked for an opportunity to try out the solo part (from his autograph manuscript) with a less accomplished violinist. He also hoped that Joachim would bring back the score and parts full of emendations, and indeed the collaboration between composer and violinist over improvements to the concerto continued on through the spring and summer, even into the proof-reading stage.

When he sent the performing materials to Simrock, Brahms repeatedly emphasized that the concerto must be given a careful, detailed editing. The independent solo part was the model for correcting the solo violin part in the full score and in the violin-piano score; on the other hand, *ossia* passages written into the full score had to be transferred to the independent solo part; the full score was used as the model for correcting the orchestral parts, which differed greatly from the score. Brahms also apologized for the messy appearance of the violin-piano score, which was nearly unreadable and which he felt ought to be copied before going to the engraver.[83]

An array of exceptionally interesting manuscripts for the concerto has been preserved, confirming the known facts about this work's complicated evolution. The autograph score is itself a multi-layered manuscript reminiscent of the autograph score for the First Piano Concerto. The original text was heavily annotated by both composer and editor: Brahms revised the orchestral accompaniment to keep it from overwhelming the solo violin; Keller transferred Joachim's revisions from the independent solo part into the full score. The fascinating cross-relationships among the extant sources—including a

---

[80] For a detailed account of the history of the Violin Concerto, see Günter Weiss-Aigner, *Johannes Brahms. Violinkonzert D-Dur*, which includes reviews of the first performance, but does not discuss the manuscripts.

[81] *Brahms Briefwechsel*, 6: 140–52.

[82] Ibid., 1: 90.

[83] Ibid., 10: 118, 120–22.

fragmentary solo part which Brahms originally sent to Joachim for criticism and the partly autograph violin-piano score—are deserving of thorough study.[84]

On 6 December 1880 Brahms borrowed Joachim's Hochschule orchestra to try out informally two new works before the coming winter's tour. During the previous summer he had composed the *Academic Festival Overture*, Op. 80, as an expression of his appreciation for the honourary doctorate bestowed on him by the University of Breslau, and, as happened often with him, at the same time had created a second, contrasting work in the same genre, the *Tragic Overture*, Op. 81. In the autumn the string parts for the two overtures had been sent to Simrock for engraving. Meanwhile, Brahms was busy announcing to colleagues that the new works would be available, under his baton, for their winter concerts.[85]

The revised and corrected score of the *Tragic Overture* went to the publisher early in March 1881. Materials for the *Academic Festival Overture* were held back, though, for use in a concert of the Vienna Philharmonic on 20 March, under Richter. Afterwards, both autograph score and a copyist's manuscript of the score were sent to Simrock for Keller's use. According to Brahms, Keller was to have the autograph for proof-reading and then send it back.[86] What he was to proof-read is not entirely clear, but the copy of the score may have needed checking. The autograph, with its many performance emendations, appears to have been used as the conducting score. The copy was evidently made after the tour and contains nearly all the refinements entered into the autograph. Subsequently, however, Brahms revised the copy further, and also entered a few new refinements into the autograph.

The fruits of the summer of 1881 were *Nänie*, Op. 82—a choral setting of a poem by Schiller, composed in memory of the painter Anselm Feuerbach, who had died the previous January—and the Second Piano Concerto, Op. 83. When informing Simrock about these new works, Brahms indicated that he might give one or the other to Dr Max Abraham of C. F. Peters, to whom he felt he owed the publication of a major work. Simrock was aghast, but, forced to choose between the two pieces, begged for the concerto. In a telegram on 17 September, Brahms agreed.[87]

In offering *Nänie* to Abraham, Brahms explained his usual procedures: 'It is a small piece for chorus and orchestra: "Nenie" by Schiller, which I— would like to hear in the meantime. In such a situation, Herr Simrock is always so kind as to engrave the string and choral parts for me. The respective choirs with which I test my works naturally purchase the parts—before actual publication, which then follows in due course. I do not

---

[84] Writings touching in greater or lesser detail on these relationships include Boris Schwarz, 'Joseph Joachim and the Genesis of Brahms's Violin Concerto', and reviews of the Library of Congress facsimile of the autograph score by Robert Pascall and Linda Correll Roesner.

[85] Cf. *Brahms Briefwechsel*, 6: 200, 203; 10: 156–7, 160; 15: 94.

[86] Ibid., 10: 168–70.

[87] Ibid., 10: 181–2, 184–5; Stephenson, ed., *Brahms und Simrock*, 171, 174.

know whether such a comfortable, deliberate slowness will suit you?'[88] Abraham replied that as soon as he received the composition he would have the parts engraved.[89]

The composer asked Abraham to forward the printed string parts for *Nänie* to Meiningen, where he was going to test the piano concerto in mid-October. Meanwhile he had received, read, and returned the corrected proofs of the parts. From Meiningen he sent the full score and the piano-vocal score for advance engraving.[90] Abraham was ready to publish the work before the end of November, but Brahms held him back, saying: 'I will be hearing the work only for the first time in Zurich, but am hoping that I can let you know immediately thereafter that everything is more or less in order and can go on its way—I have never yet pushed one of my poor creations out into the world in such a hurry, which you will be able to see with the new piano concerto, for example, whose score will scarcely appear before spring.'[91]

Final corrections and revisions resulting from the Zurich première on 6 December were entered into the galley proofs of the score. A few notes were changed, but mainly it was a matter of eliminating several dynamic markings. Brahms noted in the galleys that these corrections should also be made in the parts and the piano-vocal score.

The Second Piano Concerto was, as Brahms obliquely observed, by no means an easy work to prepare for publication. Ironically heralded by the composer as 'a tiny piano concerto with a tender little scherzo', this work was in fact enormous in conception, technically difficult, and untraditional in form, with its four movements including a passionate gipsy Scherzo.[92]

The string parts were engraved, corrected by Keller, and forwarded to Meiningen for a thorough test by the composer at the piano, with von Bülow on the podium. Upon his return to Vienna at the end of October, Brahms sent Simrock the two-piano arrangement for engraving (the Piano I, the solo piano part, was prepared by a copyist and corrected by the composer, who also wrote the reduction of the orchestral accompaniment for Piano II). A few days later Brahms promised to prepare the independent solo piano part

---

[88] 'Es ist ein kleines Stück für Chor und Orchester: "Nenie" von Schiller, das ich—einstweilen hören möchte. Herr Simrock hat für den Fall immer die Güte, mir die Violin- und die Singstimmen stechen zu lassen. Der oder die betreffenden Gesang-Vereine, mit denen ich probiere, schaffen sich natürlich die Stimmen an—vor der eigentlichen Herausgabe, die dann ganz gemächlich erfolgt. Ich weiß aber nicht, ob Ihnen so behagliche, überlegene Langsamkeit paßt?' *Brahms Briefwechsel*, 14: 328–9.

[89] Ibid., 14: 330, 335. Brahms later asked that 'Nenie' be spelled 'Nänie', because the 'e' looked so 'Berlinisch'.

[90] The extant autograph score and Brahms's letter to Abraham of 7 Oct. 1881 (*Brahms Briefwechsel*, 14: 333; original in an American private collection) document the most important alteration to result from the Meiningen trial performance (without chorus). In the letter Brahms asked to have the string parts corrected so as to make four bars out of the eighth and ninth bars after rehearsal letter F (the equivalent of bars 104 ff. in the final version); he enclosed the revised reading found in the published version of this letter (with the exception that the second and third bars of the cello/bass line, incorrectly transcribed, should read: E♮ B D♮ B | D♮ B C♯ [tied to C♯ in the next bar]). After the Meiningen test, Brahms further altered this passage in his score, to create a more interesting rhythmic effect for bars 104–7, the version published.

[91] 'Ich höre das Stück ja in Zürich zum ersten Mal, hoffe jedoch, Ihnen von dort aus sogleich melden zu können, daß alles so beiläufig in Ordnung und seinen Weg gehen kann.—So eilig habe ich aber noch nie eines meiner armen Geschöpfe in die Welt gestoßen, was Sie z.B. an dem neuen "Klavier-Konzert" sehen, dessen Partitur schwerlich vor dem Frühling erscheint.' *Brahms Briefwechsel*, 14: 336–7; cf. also 14: 331–2, 334–5.

[92] 'ein ganz ein kleines Klavierkonzert, geschrieben, mit einem ganz einem kleinen zarten Scherzo'. Ibid., 1: 154.

as soon as he received galleys of the two-piano arrangement—the full score was being lent out to the various conductors, who were rehearsing their orchestras in anticipation of the composer's forthcoming appearance as soloist with them.[93]

In a departure from his usual stance that all of the versions of a work should be published simultaneously, Brahms offered to read proofs for the two-piano arrangement and allow it to be published before the full score. Since the partly autograph manuscript of the arrangement was in Simrock's hands after 30 October and proofs did not arrive until sometime between the Zurich and Basel performances (that is, between 6 and 11 December), we may well wonder if Brahms played from memory for the Stuttgart and Meiningen performances of 22 and 27 November, and possibly for the Zurich performance as well. Following performances in Strassburg, Baden-Baden, and Breslau (14, 16, and 20 December, respectively), Brahms requested tempo changes in the two-piano edition already in press.

After the last concert of this long tour, Brahms was in no hurry to proceed further with publication, although he was also not willing to participate in or permit further performances from the manuscript. Finally at the end of March he let the parts and full score go off to Simrock. The string parts were all in order, but the wind parts needed revision from the score. In mid-April the independent solo part was ready for Keller's inspection.[94]

Both the autograph full score and the partly autograph score of the two-piano arrangement were thoroughly worked over; in successive layers one can see the original version, the composer's revisions and refinements, performance emendations, Keller's annotations, and the engraver's markings. Textual comparison reveals that, in accordance with Brahms's instructions, the solo piano part of the full score was corrected against the Piano I part of the two-piano arrangement.

The *Gesang der Parzen*, Op. 89, was Brahms's new composition for the 1882–3 season. In this case, the piano-vocal score and all the performing materials, except the full score, were engraved in advance of the trial performances. Simrock was naturally eager to offer them for sale soon after they were ready, but until the score was published Brahms permitted the sale of parts only to those organizations assisting in the trial performances. During the pause between concerts in Strassburg (20 December 1882) and Bonn (18 January 1883), Brahms let Simrock have a copy of the full score which he had had made; his instructions were to correct it against the revised parts and the piano-vocal score. The publisher, he added, should take his time, because a printed score was not needed for the next concerts. Three weeks later (15 January), however, he expressed the hope that a proof of the score could be ready by 20 January, in time for rehearsals for the Krefeld concert on 23 January.[95]

None of the surviving manuscripts for the *Gesang der Parzen* was used as engraver's

[93] Ibid., 10: 188–9, 191–3.
[94] Ibid., 10: 199–202.
[95] Ibid., 10: 224, 226–7, 229–30.

model; the autograph full score was probably the conductor's score for at least some of the trial performances, as was also the galley proof of the score. In comparison with corresponding manuscripts for other works, these sources are fair copies, with relatively few emendations.

The complicated publication history of the Third Symphony, Op. 90, is the subject of Robert Pascall's paper elsewhere in this volume.[96] Let it suffice here to mention a few details relevant to the relationship between trial performances and the process of revision. Half-way through the 1883–4 tour, Brahms modified the tempos of the first and second movements—he communicated these modifications to Simrock in a letter of 9 February 1883 in connection with the preparation of the two-piano arrangement for publication. Before the final concert of the tour, in Budapest, he asked Simrock for a new set of string parts for the finale, because he now regretted a larger revision pasted on to the parts he had been using.[97] The extant autograph score was evidently not the one sent to the publisher after the Budapest concert for use as the engraver's model; according to a letter Brahms had written to Joachim in November 1883, the score was to have been copied after the première in Vienna in December 1883.[98] This copy has not survived, but comparison of the autograph—the conductor's score for at least the first performance— with the printed score reveals such revisions as a change from B♭ clarinets to A clarinets in the second theme of the first movement and the addition or elimination of certain instruments, thus subtly influencing the colouration of various passages.

The Fourth Symphony, Op. 98, the composer's final work in this genre, was tested during the 1885–6 season. Rumours of a symphony-in-progress had begun to circulate in 1884, and friends and colleagues alike were awaiting its appearance with keen expectation. But when it was first informally introduced, in the two-piano arrangement at Ehrbar's establishment on 8 October 1885, those present—among them Billroth, Kalbeck, Hanslick, Richter, and Pohl—were noticeably reserved.[99] Elisabet von Herzogenberg, too, confessed to being baffled by the first movement's complexities when she first read the work in its two-piano arrangement.[100] Brahms himself was seriously concerned about its fate before he had tested it with an orchestra. He gave von Bülow to understand that the latter would be taking it on tour at his own risk. Even after satisfactory rehearsals in Meiningen, when Brahms conceded that the piece did not sound bad after all, the composer shuddered at the thought of the poor effect likely to result in the future from hurried preparations by less capable orchestras. Nevertheless, he was sufficiently convinced by the Meiningen readings to let Simrock have the string parts in

---

[96] See also Christian Martin Schmidt's introduction to his edition of the Third Symphony for Schott.

[97] *Brahms Briefwechsel*, 11: 47, 52, 54–5.

[98] Ibid., 6: 207–8.

[99] Kalbeck, *Brahms*, 3: 451–2. On the genesis and evolution of this work, see Christian Martin Schmidt's introduction to his edition of the Fourth Symphony for Schott.

[100] *Brahms Briefwechsel*, 2: 80–9.

November—the corrected parts for the first two movements came from Brahms at the beginning of the month, with the promise that the remainder would be sent from the Meiningen orchestra when their tour was over at the end of the month.[101]

Joachim requested the symphony in manuscript for a concert in Berlin on 1 February 1886. Brahms took this opportunity to ask Joachim's opinion of the work in general and to solicit his advice about several passages in particular. The composer indicated that he pencilled in temporary modifications of tempo which he characterized as exaggerations ('Übertreibungen') to aid conductors in preparing the unfamiliar work for first performance; unfortunately, Brahms added, the provisional was all too often made permanent where it did not belong, both in his and in others' printed works. His further remarks, in a letter of 20[?] January 1886, are a singular expression of his views about interpreting new works and giving directions for performance adequate enough to convey the effect he wished the music to make. Brahms and Joachim continued to exchange letters during February about problematical details in the symphony.[102]

Following the London début under Richter, the performing materials were forwarded to Franz Wüllner for his inspection of the parts. Since they had been thoroughly used by then, Brahms asked Simrock to pull new proofs of the strings parts and to engrave the wind parts. At the end of June he sent instructions to Keller about editing the symphony: many differences remained between score and parts, and if Keller were more of a string player than the composer, his suggestions about certain technical matters of articulation would be more than welcome.[103] The extant autograph manuscript, used as both conductor's score and engraver's model, shows numerous emendations in pencil for dynamics, phrasing, articulation, and tempo that were carried into the printed edition. If these are the 'exaggerations' about which he wrote to Joachim, did he simply overlook them during the process of publication or did he perhaps come to regard them as not so superfluous after all?

The Double Concerto, Op. 102, was composed in 1887 as a gesture of reconciliation toward Joachim—the two had been personally estranged, while still dealing with each other professionally, since Brahms had defended Amalie Joachim during the couple's divorce proceedings half a dozen years earlier. Brahms approached Joachim about the concerto in July and sent him the solo parts soon after, with the comment that the score was not yet properly written down on paper. Once again, as in the case of the Violin Concerto, Joachim contributed practical suggestions for the solo parts even before the work was ready to test.

By the end of August the first invitation for a public performance had been extended, and Brahms was soon trying to arrange an informal reading prior to the public one. The opportunity arose for Joachim, the cellist Robert Hausmann, and the composer to meet in Baden-Baden on 21–2 September, and there the first reading with piano took place, in

[101] Ibid., 2: 90; 11: 103–4, 107.
[102] Ibid., 6: 216–27.
[103] Ibid., 11: 119, 124.

the presence of Clara Schumann. The next day a private performance was given with the Kurhaus orchestra. The public première occurred in Cologne on 18 October, but before this Brahms revised the work; the close collaboration of Brahms, Joachim, and Hausmann on the evolving concerto continued as they presented it in another half-dozen concerts.[104]

Brahms had had his autograph manuscript of the score copied by his Viennese scribe, William Kupfer, before the tests. Because of this, we cannot know exactly which of the extant sources served as the conductor's score for which performances. The Kupfer copy, however, was the one used as the engraver's model. The autograph score appears to be the original draft of the composition, with various instrumental passages notated at different times. Substantial variants exist between the two scores, indicating that they were not revised in tandem; both are heavily annotated by Brahms and contain glosses in Joachim's hand. Kupfer's copy also shows Keller's editorial preparations for publication.

# VI

A pattern characteristic of the final stages of Brahms's compositional process emerges from the foregoing accounts of individual works. It is clear that Brahms was adamant about testing his works before publication, regardless of what this might entail in terms of time and cost. For most works the testing was not limited to a single performance, but constituted more of a process in itself, one which extended over a whole series of performances. Although a distinction may be drawn between more informal, private, or semi-private readings and public concerts, both types of trial performances provided Brahms with the necessary opportunity to hear his work, confront performance problems, and add finishing touches. To hear his composition in his mind and see it on paper was never enough; he needed to experience it in performance to see whether it came alive as he had imagined it. To be sure, in his earlier years he also needed the practical experience that could only be gained by working directly with orchestral forces in rehearsals and performance. Furthermore, the public performances introduced his music to audiences and critics and enhanced his chances of securing publication of his works. Once he became established as a composer, the problem of finding a publisher disappeared, and the question was only when the new work would be ready for publication. The function of the trial performance then was to help Brahms determine whether the new composition, as notated, achieved the desired effect, and, if it did not, how it should be altered. As a source of encouragement, technical advice, and practical assistance, Brahms's friends and colleagues proved invaluable, and he took full advantage of what each could contribute, without, however, allowing their views to affect unduly his own well-honed, instinctive judgement.

Almost without exception the extant musical sources contain valuable information about the final stages of correction, revision, and refinement; some reveal earlier stages as

---

[104] Ibid., 6: 229–33, 235–42; Litzmann, ed., *Clara Schumann*, 3: 493–5.

well. In his apprentice works, the composer's lack of experience shows up in a tendency to overscore the orchestra in opaque, bottom-heavy textures; his revisions lighten the texture. As a young composer, Brahms was also often over-fussy with performance directions, necessitating later revisions. In contrast, the revisions and refinements in works of his maturity are more subtle, serving to point up musical ideas through instrumental colouration, shading, and moulding through finer degrees of articulation, dynamic control, and modification of tempo. Beyond matters of detail, trial performances sometimes also prompted major alterations, such as the addition of a movement to the Requiem and the recasting of the second movement in the First Symphony.

The manuscripts of most of the works surveyed here have yet to be studied thoroughly to identify and explain the various layers of compositional activity. With information about the locations of sources now readily available, such studies should be undertaken. Moreover, these sources must assume a role in establishing critical texts far more significant than the one which the pioneers of Brahms scholarship assigned to them. It is in the manuscript sources that answers will be found, for Brahms clearly focused more attention on providing the publisher with accurate texts than on monitoring the process of publishing these texts, a task which in later years he seems to have been content to leave to the conscientious Keller, who undoubtedly did his best, as his letters to Brahms attest.[105] Working at a rate that produced at least one major orchestral composition each year (plus chamber works, piano pieces, songs, etc.), Brahms himself was preoccupied with composing and testing new works and frequently unable or disinclined to attend consistently to the details of publication. We also know how he loathed writing long, explanatory letters, and the pressure of external circumstances all too often made impossible the leisurely pace and undistracted attention necessary for thorough proof-reading. When errors came to his attention after publication, as for example, with the Third Symphony, he was greatly annoyed and demanded rectification in future issues (which, alas, seldom happened), but his manner of dealing with the publication process unquestionably contributed to these problems. Some of the errors can be found corrected in Brahms's personal copies, the so-called *Handexemplare*, and occasionally he emended the manuscripts which remained in his possession; the readings in these sources cannot, however, be necessarily regarded as definitive.[106]

Scholars have begun to reassess with a critical eye Brahms's skills as editor of his own compositions and of the works of others, and the effect this had on the quality of the printed musical texts; in fact, the need for a new critical edition of the complete works of

---

[105] See the correspondence between Brahms and Keller now in the possession of the Library of Congress, Washington, DC, and soon to be published in George S. Bozarth and Wiltrud Martin, eds., *A Working Relationship: The Correspondence between Johannes Brahms and Robert Keller*.

[106] The *Handexemplare* are preserved in the archives of the Gesellschaft der Musikfreunde in Vienna, as part of Brahms's estate. A few other printed scores with annotations by Brahms have turned up in various private and institutional collections; an annotated copy of the Requiem (first issue of first edition), for instance, was sold by the Gesellschaft der Musikfreunde in 1938 and has found its way into the library of the Riemenschneider Bach Institute, Baldwin-Wallace College, Berea, Ohio; an annotated copy of the Third Symphony, given by Brahms to Eusebius Mandyczewski, now belongs to Kurt Hofmann, Hamburg.

Brahms is now being considered seriously.[107] Perhaps we have traditionally expected too much from an inherently artistic nature when we have assumed that Brahms's active interest in the editorial process inevitably translated into systematic editing. His desire to have his compositions accurately preserved for posterity cannot be doubted, but the accounts given here show that a balance always had to be struck between compositional and editorial activities. And we are indeed fortunate that the proper choice was made.

[107] See the papers by Brodbeck, Pascall, and Roesner elsewhere in the present volume, and the Pascall article cited in note 73; cf. also the preface to my new edition of Brahms's piano variations, Opp. 9 and 21; the preface to George Bozarth's new edition of Brahms's organ works, and his articles 'Brahms's Organ Works: A New Critical Edition' and 'A New Collected Edition for Johannes Brahms'; and Camilla Cai's dissertation, 'Brahms' Short, Late Piano Pieces—Opus Numbers 116–119'. In 1983 the Johannes Brahms Gesamtausgabe e.V. was founded in Munich, under the chairmanship of Professor Friedhelm Krummacher of the Christian-Albrechts-Universität in Kiel. The publisher of the proposed edition will be G. Henle Verlag, Munich, and a Brahms Research Centre has been established in Kiel to lay the groundwork for this project.

# BRAHMS AS SONG
# COMPOSER

# BRAHMS'S EARLY SONGS: POETRY VERSUS MUSIC

——

## LUDWIG FINSCHER

BRAHMS'S song aesthetics have been reconstructed—from scattered remarks by the composer himself and from recollections of people close to him—by nearly everyone who has dealt with his songs, most recently and thoroughly by Christiane Jacobsen.[1] Certain principles which guided his selection of poems and his compositional procedures emerge from these reconstructions with reasonable certainty:

A perfect poem is not 'composeable'. In his well-known remark on Schubert—whom he admired as the greatest song composer of all—Brahms pointed out that, in his opinion, even Schubert in all his Goethe settings had only once produced something which added to the meaning and aesthetic quality of the poem: 'Schubert's Suleika songs are to me the only instances where the power and beauty of Goethe's works have been enhanced by the music. All other of Goethe's poems seem to me so perfect in themselves that no music can improve them' (1876).[2]

A poem must leave the composer something to do. It must have a spot (a weak spot) where music can enter (as indeed most of the poems composed by Brahms have).

A poem must have a special quality which lends itself naturally to music. This is not identical with the musicality of words and verses—indeed, this 'musical' quality in a poem works against is 'composeability'—but apparently is a matter of mood and substance. Schubert 'has found an element especially worth while for composing in many a poem by Schlegel' (1887).[3] Such qualitities are also independent from the aesthetic perfection of the poem. About Grabbe's 'Don Juan und Faust': 'It lacks musical substance, apart from the question of whether it is good or not. With "Egmont", "A Midsummer Night's Dream", or "Manfred" it is a wholly different thing' (1895).[4]

The composer must be spontaneously affected by the poem, but not to a degree that destroys the kind of objective detachment necessary for the act of composing. This is the reason why Brahms could never set to music poems by Klaus Groth in Low German, the language of Brahms's youth and therefore more than language to him. 'Plattdeutsch is too close to me; it is really

---

[1] *Das Verhältnis von Sprache und Musik in ausgewählten Liedern von Johannes Brahms, dargestellt an Parallelvertonungen*, 22–79 and *passim*.

[2] George Henschel, *Personal Recollections of Johannes Brahms*, 45.

[3] '. . . in manchem Gedicht von Schlegel einen für Komposition besonders wertvollen Gehalt gefunden'. Remark made to Gustav Wendt; Max Kalbeck, *Johannes Brahms*, 1: 220.

[4] 'Es fehlt an musikalischem Stoff in dem Gedicht, abgesehen davon, ob es was taugt oder nicht. Das ist mit "Egmont", "Sommernachtstraum" oder "Manfred" eine ganz andere Sache.' Remark made to Max Kalbeck; ibid., 4: 404.

something different from language for me. I have tried it, but it does not work' (1872?).[5] When Brahms did set poems in dialect, they were consistently in a dialect foreign to him, as the two Swabian folk-songs in Op. 7. Vice versa, High German is already an element of poetic stylization which he needed for composing.

The words, form, metre, and rhythm of a poem are to be preserved and mirrored strictly in its composition. Brahms once boasted of the unimpeachable grammatical correctness of his texts (to Max Kalbeck, *c*.1879–80).[6] Declamation seems to have had a special importance for him. On his walks he recited (loudly) poems on which he was working. In Schubert's songs he especially admired the effortless art of declamation: 'No composer understands correct declamation like he does. With him . . . the best always emerges so naturally, as if it could not be otherwise' (1887).[7] On the other hand, against Hugo Wolf: 'Well, if one does not care about the music, the declaiming of a poem is very simple' (1889).[8] 'Music' in this connection can only mean the melodic balance and regularity derived from the models of folk-song and strophic song which was one of the foundations of Brahms's song ideal. Declamation as one facet of poetic form has to be transformed into musical form in a way which is both 'natural' and 'regular'.

The composer has to trust the poem implicitly. 'Towards the work of art one has the obligation to assume the naïve, childlike point of view and to believe what the poet wants us to believe. [Otherwise,] one would have to throw away half of all poetry' (to Richard Heuberger, 1886).[9] But this also implies that the composer sets only the poem and nothing else. Speaking of his *Magelone* Romances, Op. 33: 'my music has, once and for all, nothing whatever to do with [Ludwig Tieck's] *Phantasus* and the love story of Peter. I have really set only the words to music, and nobody need be concerned about the landscape or the hospital or whatever else' (1875);[10] similarly, 'in the *Magelone* Romances one probably need not think much about continuity, let alone a connection with the novel' (1870).[11]

To judge a composer's work and intentions, one should read the poem and try to understand it thoroughly before listening to the music: 'Have [the songs of Schubert's *Die schöne Müllerin*] sung to you all together, not separately, but—do not forget to read the poems carefully first, to be able to experience the whole' (1856),[12] and later, more concerned with understanding than with

---

[5] 'Plattdeutsch steht mir zu nahe, das ist doch etwas anderes für mich als Sprache. Ich habe es versucht, es geht nicht.' Remark made to Klaus Groth; published in his 'Erinnerungen an Johannes Brahms' in Heinrich Miesner, *Klaus Groth und die Musik*, 64; cf. also Kalbeck, *Johannes Brahms*, 2: 380.

[6] Kalbeck, *Johannes Brahms*, 3: 342, n. 1.

[7] 'Kein Komponist versteht wie er richtig zu deklamieren. Bei ihm kommt . . . immer das Beste so selbstverständlich heraus als könnte es nicht anders sein.' Remark made to Gustav Wendt; Kalbeck, *Johannes Brahms*, 1: 220.

[8] 'Ja, wenn man sich um die Musik nicht kümmert, ist das Deklamieren eines Gedichtes sehr leicht.' Remark made to Richard Heuberger, *Erinnerungen an Johannes Brahms*, 41.

[9] 'Man ist dem Kunstwerk gegenüber verpflichtet, sich auf den naiven, kindlichen Standpunkt zu stellen und das zu glauben, was der Dichter zu glauben vorstellt . . . [Täte man das nicht,] müßte man die halbe Poesie wegwerfen.' Remark made to Richard Heuberger; ibid., 155.

[10] 'meine Musik hat nun einmal durchaus nichts mit dem "Phantasus" und der Liebesgeschichte vom Peter zu tun. Ich habe wirklich bloß die Worte in Musik gesetzt, und es geht niemand dabei die Landschaft oder das Hospital oder sonst was an.' Letter to J. Rieter-Biedermann, 10 Nov. 1875; *Brahms Briefwechsel*, 14: 256.

[11] 'Bei den Magelonen-Romanzen braucht man wohl nicht viel an einen Zusammenhang, und gar mit der Erzählung zu denken.' Letter to Adolf Schubring, Mar. 1870; *Brahms Briefwechsel*, 8: 219.

[12] 'Lassen Sie sie sich doch im Zusammenhang vorsingen, nicht einzeln, aber—vergiß nicht, auch die Gedichte ordentlich erst zu lesen, um das Ganze mit durchleben zu können.' Letter to Clara Schumann, 31 May 1856. The tell-tale slip of the tongue—the formal address 'Sie' at the beginning and the intimate 'vergiß nicht' later—is untranslatable. Berthold Litzmann, *Clara Schumann–Johannes Brahms Briefe*, 1: 189.

'experiencing', more rational than emotional: 'But do not immediately find something too rough; instead, read a poem twice if you do not like it' (1877).[13]

All these remarks come from different times in Brahms's creative career, but all are later than the early songs—Opp. 3, 6, and 7, and 'Mondnacht', WoO 21, composed between June 1851 and November 1853—which at the time Brahms found equal to his exacting standards and his incessant self-criticism.[14] Even the (predictably more emotional) remarks on song composition from his early years, collected and interpreted by Jacobsen,[15] are later than these songs. It might be worth while then to view some of the early songs in light of the principles summarized above.

If one looks at these songs in terms of their text treatment alone, they fall—conspicuously—into two groups: the Eichendorff songs, on the one hand, and all the remaining songs on the other. The texts of the latter group correctly reproduce the poetic version which Brahms knew or could have known, apart from details and with one major exception, all of which can easily be explained. There are a few rather obvious errors. In Alfred Meissner's 'Nachwirkung' (Op. 6 No. 3, April 1852), for example, Brahms changed the line 'in schweigender Nachtluft, beim säuselnden Winde' to 'in säuselnder Nachtluft, beim säuselnden Winde', without any discernible musical reason (the indentical melodic formula employed for both 'säuselnd' is also used for words in the first and second stanzas which are not identical).[16] The altered version is so much weaker than the original one that an oversight seems to be the only explanation. Likewise, some months later, in Eduard Ferrand's 'Treue Liebe' (Op. 7 No. 1, November 1852), Brahms apparently dropped one syllable in the second stanza: in the original poem, 'am Saume des Himmels' corresponds exactly with 'und blickte voll Sehnsucht' from the first stanza, but in his song Brahms writes 'am Saum des Himmels';[17] the first edition consistently differentiates between ♪. ♪♪ for the first stanza and ♩ ♪ for the second (since the autograph is lost, we do not know what Brahms himself actually wrote).

More interesting is the group of songs in which Brahms's variant readings make (or seem to make) musical sense. Comparatively simple are changes to avoid words which

[13] 'Aber finde nicht gleich etwas zu roh, lies ein Gedicht auch zweimal, wenn's Dir nicht gefällt . . .'. Letter to Clara Schumann, 24 Apr. 1877; ibid., 2: 95.

[14] The earliest of these songs—'Heimkehr', Op. 7 No. 6, dates from June 1851; 'Mondnacht' was composed by November 1853. A list of the correct dates, based on dated autographs of the songs and/or Brahms's handwritten *Werkverzeichnis* (Stadt- und Landesbibliothek, Vienna, HIN 32.866), was kindly provided by George Bozarth (cf. Table 1 in Bozarth's paper in the present volume). Since I prepared this paper, a manuscript has surfaced (now in the Library of Congress) which adds 'Der Überläufer', Op. 48 No. 2 (*Des Knaben Wunderhorn*) and the duet 'Klosterfräulein', Op. 61 No. 2 (Justinus Kerner) to the vocal works of this period, and Joachim Draheim has located in a private collection in Germany an autograph fragment of another song—a solo setting of Chamisso's 'Die Müllerin', Anh. III No. 13—which probably stems from July 1853 (see Johannes Brahms, *Die Müllerin*).

[15] *Das Verhältnis von Sprache und Musik*, 50–3.

[16] Alfred Meissner, *Gedichte* (Leipzig: F. L. Herbig, 1845; 2nd edn., 1846). Only a later edition (7th, from 1856), with no variant readings, is to be found in Brahms's extant library (Gesellschaft der Musikfreunde, Vienna); cf. Kurt Hofmann, *Die Bibliothek von Johannes Brahms*, 75.

[17] Eduard Ferrand (pseudonym for Eduard Schulz), *Gedichte* (Berlin: Stühr, 1834); not in Brahms's extant library.

are not easy to sing: 'hinauf' instead of 'herauf' in Bodenstedt's 'Lied' (Op. 3 No. 4, July 1853),[18] 'Eine Blume seh' ich' instead of 'eine Knospe seh' ich' at the end of Hoffmann von Fallersleben's 'Nachtigallen schwingen lustig ihr Gefieder' (Op. 6 No. 6, from the same month),[19] and 'bis ich mag bei der Liebsten sein' instead of 'eh ich mag . . .' in Uhland's 'Heimkehr' (Op. 7 No. 6, June 1851).[20] Whereas the alterations in the first and last of these three cases do not affect the poems seriously, the one in Op. 6 No. 6 is slightly more problematic: 'Blume' is certainly more easily sung than 'Knospe', but in Hoffmann von Fallersleben's poem 'Blume' is consistently used for flowers in bloom, while 'Knospe' (bud) is reserved for the final couplet where it reveals the essence of the poem: '*Eine* Knospe seh' ich, die nicht blühen will'.

A similar case is the companion piece to Op. 6 No. 6, 'Wie die Wolke nach der Sonne' (Op. 6 No. 5, again July 1853). Hoffmann von Fallersleben—who was a far from negligible poet—has linked the beginnings of the first and second stanzas by a kind of internal rhyme:

> Wie die Wolke *nach der Sonne*
> Voll Verlangen irrt und bangt
>
> Wie die Sonnenblume richtet
> *Nach der Sonn'* ihr Angesicht[21]

Brahms changed the second 'Nach der Sonn'' to 'Auf die Sonn'', a version slightly more singable. Perhaps the change was no more than the consequence of the introduction of a new melodic formula after the first two bars, where a recurring melodic formula had been combined with the first 'nach der Sonne'. But be that as it may, Brahms's version is weaker than the original.

Much more complicated is the situation in Robert Reinick's 'Juchhe' (Op. 6 No. 4, April 1852) in which Brahms altered what would later become so very important for him: the metrical system of the poem.[22] Reinick's otherwise unassuming lines produce their atmosphere of rapturous *joie de vivre* by a lilting alternation of iambic and anapaestic upbeats:

---

[18] Friedrich Martin Bodenstedt, *Ivan, der Sohn des Starost. Poetische Farbenskizze aus Rußland* (Berlin: Decker'sche Hofbuchdruckerei, 1842); later in *Gedichte* (Bremen: Schlodtmann, 1852); neither book in Brahms's extant library. Variant reading: Bodenstedt has 'und steigst du herauf, so steigt sie herab'; changed by Brahms probably to avoid the assonance. The title 'Lied' is not in Bodenstedt.

[19] August Heinrich Hoffmann von Fallersleben, *Buch der Liebe* (Breslau: Adesholz, 1836; 2nd edn., 1843); not in Brahms's extant library.

[20] Ludwig Uhland, *Gedichte* (Stuttgart-Tübingen: Cotta, 1839). A copy is extant in Brahms's library; cf. Kurt Hofmann, *Die Bibliothek von Johannes Brahms*, 117. There are many editions of Uhland's extremely popular poems in the nineteenth century, but no variant readings.

[21] Cf. n. 19.

[22] Robert Reinick, *Lieder von Robert Reinick, Maler* (Berlin: Reimarus, 1844). A copy is extant in Brahms's library; cf. Kurt Hofmann, *Die Bibliothek von Johannes Brahms*, 88. There are some later editions—Reinick was a rather popular *poeta minor* in this time—but, as far as I can tell, there are no variant readings for his poems.

Wie ist doch die Erde so schön, so schön!

Das wissen die Vögelein,

Sie heben ihr leicht Gefieder,

Und singen so fröhlich Lieder

In den blauen Himmel hinein.

Wie ist doch die Erde so schön, so schön!

Das wissen die Flüß und Seen,

Sie malen im klaren Spiegel

Die Gärten und Städt' und Hügel,

Und die Wolken, die d'rüber geh'n!

Und Sänger und Maler wissen es,

Und es wissens viel and're Leut'!

Und wers nicht malt, der singt es,

Und wers nicht singt, dem klingt es

Im dem Herzen vor lauter Freud!

Whereas the alternation is more or less flexible within each line, the beginning of every line, except the fifth one in each stanza, is iambic, with one exception—the second line of the third stanza, which creates a slight accelerando towards the end of the poem. Brahms has set the poem strophically (A A A')—true to his principle (later formulated) that everything which can be set strophically should be. Moreover, he has rendered it in an overall rhythmic scheme of single eighth-note upbeats (no doubt derived from the predominant iambic line openings), which in the chosen $\frac{6}{8}$ metre works both at the beginning and in the middle of most bars ( ♪ | ♫ ♪ ♫ ♪ ♫ ). The anapaestic (two-eighth) anacrusis of the last line in the first two stanzas (given identical music by Brahms) is very effectively set apart from this scheme, as a triumphant climactic gesture: 'in den 'blauen Himmel hinein' and 'und die Wolken, die d'rüber geh'n'. Finally, Brahms decided to repeat the second line of each stanza (because it is so much shorter than the first?) and to build towards a climax in stanzas one and two by fulfilling and at the same time negating the repetitive formula of the third and fourth lines:

sie heben ihr leicht Gefieder: new rhythmic pattern, $\frac{6}{8}$ throughout, onomatopoetic
sie heben ihr leicht Gefieder: repeated without change
und singen so fröhliche Lieder: repeated sequentially
und singen, und singen: sudden shift to D♭, the melody broken up as if the voice were choked by
                  excitement and tension, then the piano alone leading to the climax: 'in den
                  blauen Himmel . . .'

Brahms's ambitious exploitation of the parallelism of lines three and four of the poem already leads to difficulties in the second stanza, because the poet has replaced parallelism with a single sentence filling the two lines (and creating, necessarily, an enjambment):

Sie malen im klaren Spiegel
Die Gärten und Städt' und Hügel.

Brahms circumvents the problem rather than solving it, reciting:

Sie malen im klaren Spiegel
Die Gärten und Städt' und Hügel,
Sie malen im klaren Spiegel
Die Gärten und Hügel

—a version in which especially the excited breaking up of the second line does not make much sense any more.

The third stanza presents a different problem, which Brahms solves by a small, but significant change of text and metre. He must have decided early in the process of composing this song to repeat the pattern of the first two stanzas up to the middle of stanza three and to expand the second half of the stanza to serve as a climactic coda for the whole song, focusing on the final line, 'in dem Herzen vor lauter Freud'. Again his decision to employ a repetitive pattern starting with the third line leads to difficulties. Brahms abandons text repetition here, but retains the melodic repetition, now intensified harmonically, first by shading the passing E♭ major into minor, then by changing the former shift to C major into a shift to B major. The juxtaposition of B♭ and B major prepares strikingly for the last line of text, on which the coda is going to expand, but the rhythmic pattern forces the composer to recite 'im Herzen' instead of 'in dem Herzen', thereby abandoning a most important element of the poem's own rhythmic and metric pattern. This in turn makes it necessary to abandon the anapaestic anacrusis of the final climactic expansion: 'im Herzen vor lauter Freud / vor lauter Freud / dem klingt es / im Herzen / vor lauter, lauter Freud'. The loss of the change from iambic to anapaestic, which in itself worked as a kind of climax for the first two stanzas, is counterbalanced musically and emotionally by the beautiful turn from the exuberant first outburst 'im Herzen vor lauter Freud' to the introverted final repetition and the return of the piano postlude. But the fact remains that the composer, judged according to his later rules, has not quite overcome the difficulties which the poem presented for stropic composition.

More easily explained is the one major interference with another poem which appears in this group of early songs. Of Johann Baptiste Rousseau's 'Der Frühling' (Op. 6 No. 2, April 1852) Brahms set the first, second, and fourth stanzas, but left out the third:

> Es zuckt und bebt im Blute was,
> Die Wimper [sic] werden tränennaß,
> Es pochet leis im Herzen.
> O Mensch, du fühlest Frühlingslust,
> Und Liebe hebet deine Brust,
> Und wecket süße Schmerzen![23]

This stanza is neither better nor worse than the other three, and its strong emotional turn could have appealed to the young composer. But perhaps it was this very emotionality which prevented him from composing it. The first and second stanzas, and again the beginning of the fourth stanza, depict nature's phenomena in spring, and only the end of the last stanza turns towards the human heart, an ideal sequence of lyrical events which enables the composer to echo and dwell upon the poem's 'open' final turn—'Du triffst *vielleicht* das Rechte'—in the beautiful piano postlude, which is so much more poetic than the whole poem. The third stanza, which anticipates this final turn and which ruins it through overemphasis, would have forced the composer to a quite different treatment of the poem and would have presented a serious obstacle to strophic composition. For once in this group of early songs, Brahms's predilection, already strong, for simple strophic forms, his attempt at a kind of 'poetic' treatment of the piano (derived much more from Schumann's songs than from Schubert's), and his acute perception of the musical possibilities of a poem led to a definite improvement of the poem through composition, albeit at the expense of the poem's integrity and the poet's intention.

The poems of Meissner and Ferrand, Reinick, Rousseau, and Bodenstedt, and even those of Hoffmann von Fallersleben and Uhland found in Opp. 3, 6, and 7 were works of more or less solid craftsmanship and more or less original poetic inspiration, but clearly not too perfect to be set to music, works which could indeed be improved through composition and which in this way were consistent with Brahms's later song aesthetics. But when he turned to Eichendorff, he was confronted with a different kind of poetry altogether: poems perfect in their own right. On the other hand, Eichendorff was, as the old Brahms put it, 'probably the youthful enthusiasm of us all' (1895).[24] Indeed, the poet's influence on the young composer seems to have gone far beyond that of youthful enthusiasm. To Max Kalbeck he remarked in 1885 that in his youth he had composed 'the

---

[23] Johann Baptist Rousseau, *Spiele der lyrischen und dramatischen Muse* (Aachen: Cremer, 1826; 2nd edn., Frankfurt am Main: Schmerber, 1829) and *Gesammelte Dichtungen*, vol. 2 (Berlin: Schlesinger, 1845). In this last edition, musical settings of the poem are mentioned (as is frequent in the nineteenth century): 'Komponirt von Reissiger und Julius Weiß'. Not in Brahms's extant library.

[24] 'Wohl unser aller jugendliche Schwärmerei'. Letter to Heinrich von Herzogenberg, 8 Aug. 1895; *Brahms Briefwechsel*, 2: 270.

complete Eichendorff and Heine',[25] and in a letter to Otto Dessoff (1878) he wrote similarly: 'I composed enough of [Geibel] (let alone Eichendorff and others) as a boy. But fortunately, when the time came for printing them, I was shy enough to consider other compositions better and let mine alone'.[26] Perhaps even more important is the way in which the young composer tried to relive the romantic dream of the wayfaring artisan and artist. Kalbeck has lovingly described how Brahms and Reményi on their first concert tour disdained the railroads most of the time and walked their way through Germany, and how, some months later, the young composer en route to the Schumanns wended his way on foot down the romantic Rhine valley, from the region of Mainz to Düsseldorf—approximately 200 kilometres—with rucksack and walking-stick, knocking at the doors of other members of his 'guild', like a real travelling craftsman or one of Eichendorff's students, poets, and good-for-nothings who are always on the road. The prosaic fact that Eduard Marxsen, Brahms's music teacher in Hamburg, had still followed the artisan tradition of declaring his student free after he had completed his studies, like an apprentice roofer or carpenter, must have mingled in a strange way with his poetic vision of the Romantic poet. The young composer, traditional artisan and Romantic poet at the same time, consciously or unconsciously played a role of which Eichendorff had written again and again, enacting a tale which had long been told— ironically at the very moment when the old and disillusioned poet opened his unfinished memoirs with a highly topical description of the new age:

On a fine warm autumn morning, I came from the other end of Germany by railway in a headlong rush, as if at danger of a life's sentence I had speedily to finish the very journey which was my sole purpose. These steam voyages shake the world (which now really consists of nothing more than railway stations) incessantly like a kaleidoscope in which the landscapes, flashing past, continuously make new faces before one has grasped a single physiognomy, and in which the flying salon continuously forms new assemblies before one has really recovered from the old ones.[27]

A romantic youth so deeply absorbed in Eichendorff's poetic world must have had a special relation to Eichendorff's novels and poems. Witness to this are the Eichendorff songs which Brahms thought fit for publication. In contrast to all the other songs in Opp. 3, 6, and 7, these are not so much settings of poems as musical evocations of the poems and of the Eichendorff world.

---

[25] 'den ganzen Eichendorff und Heine . . .' Kalbeck, *Johannes Brahms*, 1: 133.

[26] 'daß ich ihn [Geibel] (und gar Eichendorff und andere) als Knabe hinreichend komponiert habe. Als die Zeit des Druckens kam war ich zum Glück gescheut genug andere Compositionen für besser zu halten und meine liegen zu lassen.' Letter to Dessoff, June 1878; *Brahms Briefwechsel*, 16: 181.

[27] 'An einem schönen warmen Herbstmorgen kam ich auf der Eisenbahn vom andern Ende Deutschlands mit einer Vehemenz dahergefahren, als käme es bei Lebensstrafe darauf an, dem Reisen, das doch mein alleiniger Zweck war, auf das allerschleunigste ein Ende zu machen. Diese Dampffahrten rütteln die Welt, die eigentlich nur noch aus Bahnhöfen besteht, unermüdlich durcheinander wie ein Kaleidoskop, wo die vorüberjagenden Landschaften, ehe man noch irgendeine Physiognomie gefaßt, immer neue Gesichter schneiden, der fliegende Salon immer neue Sozietäten bildet, bevor man noch die alten recht überwunden.' Joseph von Eichendorff, *Erlebtes*, final version of 1857, beginning of first chapter, quoted from *Neue Gesamtausgabe der Werke und Schriften in vier Bänden*, ed. Gerhard Baumann and Siegfried Grosse, 2: 1019.

There are two exceptions to this: 'In der Fremde' (Op. 3 No. 5, November 1852) and 'Mondnacht' (WoO 21, by November 1853) which Brahms composed in obvious competition with two of the greatest Schumann songs. Whereas 'Mondnacht' raises no serious textual problems[28] (and is obviously quite inferior to Schumann's setting), 'In der Fremde' is a most remarkable demonstration of artistic subtlety prompted by competitive energy. Brahms's song, as has frequently been remarked, uses Schumann's, not Eichendorff's version of the text, up to the double bar separating the two four-line stanzas (in the original poem, there is no additional space at this point).[29] On the other hand, Brahms's setting provides an object lesson in faithfulness to the form and metre of this 'two-stanza' version (quite in contrast to Schumann's irregular treatment of the poem) and is an astonishing (and, in my opinion, highly successful) attempt to capture and stress all the infinite subtleties of the poem (again in contrast to Schumann's setting, which focuses more on the general mood of the poem). It is highly suggestive, in view of Brahms's later song aesthetics and song technique, that the balance of form and expression, general mood and poetic detail, is achieved by the strictest adherence to strophic form, in combination with the most careful attention to details of verse, metre, declamation, and poetic content. The fusion of these elements is most obvious in the handling of the enjambment between the sixth and seventh lines:

> Da ruhe ich auch, und über mir
> Rauschet [Schumann and Brahms: Rauscht] die schöne Waldeinsamkeit.

This stands in demonstrative contrast to Schumann's version, and in striking contrast to the handling (or rather, non-handling) of the enjambment in the second stanza of Reinick's 'Juchhe'.[30] Clearly, the special circumstances of competition sharpened the young composer's wits to an exceptional degree. But the very sophistication and superb craftsmanship of this song forbids us from regarding the eccentricities of text treatment in the remaining Eichendorff settings as mere negligence, and allows us to view them as the result of an internalization of Eichendorff's poetic world from which the songs surface as arrested moments of an internal monologue—a kind of song composition which Brahms was to abandon when he left off setting Eichendorff poems.

[28] Only in stanza 3 did Brahms change 'flog durch die stillen Lande' to 'flog durch die stillen Räume'. Max Friedlaender assumed this was only a slip in writing or printing and 'corrected' it in the edition he prepared for Peters (cf. Max Friedlaender, *Brahms' Lieder*, 198 [English trans., 251]). The *Brahms Werke* uses the word 'Räume'.

[29] Cf. the edition mentioned in n. 27 and the *Historisch-kritische Ausgabe*, ed. Wilhelm Kosch, August Sauer, Hermann Kunisch, and others (begun in 1908 and still in progress). Brahms owned a copy of the second 'expanded and revised' edition ('Zweite vermehrte und veränderte Auflage') of *Gedichte von Joseph Freiherr von Eichendorff* (Berlin: M. Simion, 1843), from which he apparently worked (cf. Kurt Hofmann, *Die Bibliothek von Johannes Brahms*, 25, and see n. 37 below). He acquired a copy of the third edition (Berlin, 1850) on 24 Dec. 1853, which he gave to Clara Schumann in August 1855, that is, while he was living at the Schumann's home in Düsseldorf (cf. George S. Bozarth, 'Brahms's Lieder Inventory of 1859–60 and Other Documents of his Life and Work', 106, n. 22). The designation 'vermehrte und veränderte Auflage' in all editions of the Eichendorff poems which appeared during the poet's lifetime refers to the addition of poems and regroupings of them, not to variant readings within single poems.

[30] This is not the place to give a detailed comparison of Schumann's and Brahms's songs. There is a very good comparative analysis in Christiane Jacobsen, *Das Verhältnis von Sprache und Musik*, 365–99, which, however, seems to me to underrate the quality of Brahms's setting.

Perhaps it is significant that the three remaining Eichendorff songs are all settings of poems originally integrated into novels: 'Lied' (Op. 3 No. 6, December 1852) comes from *Viel Lärmen um nichts* (1832), 'Parole' (Op. 7 No. 2, November 1852) from *Dichter und ihre Gesellen* (1834), and 'Anklänge' (Op. 7 No. 3, March 1853) from *Ahnung und Gegenwart* (1815). In each of his settings Brahms took into account, in various ways and to differing degrees, the context of the poem in the novel.

'Lied' is a title invented by Brahms. In *Viel Lärmen um nichts* the poem of course has no title at all; in the first edition of Eichendorff's collected poems (1837), where it is entitled 'Erinnerung' (together with another poem), the fourth stanza, present in the novel and in Brahms's setting, is missing. Brahms must therefore have drawn his text from the novel. Moreover, he seems to have kept in mind the situation in which the poem is sung in the novel. The singer is a girl in disguise, Countess Aurora, who calls herself a hunter named Florentin. A hunting party hears her sing the first three stanzas in the woods, before she appears:

Here Leontin suddenly sprang up, and also the prince, who, pleasantly surprised, turned his gaze toward the rock, for suddenly a wondrously beautiful singing sounded towards them from the forest. They could understand something like this: [here follows the song].

Florentin enters after the third stanza, and after some dialogue the party breaks up, Florentin disappears again, and the prince remains alone.

But high up on the cliffs, Florentin appeared again, waved his hat, and sang after them as they departed:

> Muntre Vögel in den Wipfeln,
> Ihr Gesellen dort im Tal,
> Grüßt mir von den fremden Gipfeln
> Meine Heimat tausendmal!

Eichendorff probably deleted this final stanza because its direct appeal to the 'Gesellen' who have just left the scene linked the poem too closely with the novel. But in doing so he changed the character of the poem completely, finishing it on that note of dreamlike confusion and unreality so very dear to him:

> Ach, hier auf den fremden Gipfeln:
> Menschen, Quellen, Fels und Baum,
> Wirres Rauschen in den Wipfeln,—
> Alles ist mir wie ein Traum.

Brahms apparently saw in the four-stanza version the opportunity to create a song which combines strophic and cyclic form, using the third stanza for contrast rather than (semi-)closure (A A′ B A″). The 'A' stanzas are unified by the incessant sixteenth-note movement of the right hand, illustrating the 'lindes Rauschen in den Wipfeln'; the contrast for the third stanza is achieved by a turn from the tonic A major to the submediant F major, by sudden cessation of the sixteenth-note motion, and by a tortuous (perhaps a bit too tortuous) chromatic line in the voice. But because he had made the mysterious rustling of the leaves the unifying accompaniment motif for the main sections of the song, Brahms was apparently at a loss to know how to handle the third line of this stanza, 'Wirres Rauschen in den Wipfeln'. His solution was singularly radical: he simply left the line out, putting in its place a two-bar piano interlude imitating bugle-calls—the only piano interlude in the whole song—and setting the fourth line of the stanza to these bugle sounds, thereby hinting at the dream atmosphere of which the text speaks (and perhaps at the confusion of which the deleted line speaks?) by deploying 'confused' imitations of these calls and shifting suddenly to E major (which prepares the return to the tonic in the ensuing fourth stanza). This is a very strange moment, perhaps one of the strangest in Brahms's songs: the poem ruined by the deletion of a poetically superb line, and the bugle-calls creating an atmosphere which is not even latent in the poem, but which is part of the scene in the novel in which the poem is supposed to be sung.[31] Immediately before the song ends there is another hint at the scene of the poem. After the forte outburst of the last line—'Meine Heimat tausendmal'—the melody drops into the lowest register and to piano, with the accompaniment marked *piano ritardando e diminuendo*—it is Florentin, high on the cliff, his song dissolving into the blue sky above the romantic landscape into which the prince dreams himself as he listens to Florentin's last stanza:

Down there [the prince] saw his two friends, already far away, between vineyards and flowering gardens, walking into the resplendent land, and castles, turrets, and hills glowing purple hued; and a soft breeze refreshingly wafted up [to him] the sound of the morning bells and larks and sweet fragrances, as if this were, in the glistening distance, the country of youth. But high up on the cliffs, Florentin appeared . . .

'Parole' and 'Anklänge' are linked as the second and third song of Op. 7 (published in 1854), although the former was written in November 1852, the latter in March 1853. At first sight, 'Parole' seems to present only minor problems. This time Brahms seems to have taken the poem from Eichendorff's collected poems (1837)—presumably using his copy of the second edition (1843)—rather than from *Dichter und ihre Gesellen* (1834). The title 'Parole'—originally 'Die Parole'—comes from the collected poems; in the novel, two stanzas are added which are introduced as an improvised sequel to the actual poem (which again is a song, performed by one of the novel's protagonists). The relationship between the poem and the novel is different from that of 'Lied': the original five stanzas work as a complete and independent poem, and the two additional stanzas are part of the narrative which follows the singing of this song—a rhymed dialogue. Thus Eichendorff could republish the original five stanzas as a separate poem without any difficulty and without change. Brahms interfered with the poem in only one apparently insignificant detail: at the beginning of the very last line he added the emphatic

---

[31] Could it be that the conspicuously clumsy declamation which pervades the whole song is an attempt both to characterize the mode of very emotional speaking (in short, breathless phrases) and to create a kind of folk-song simplicity and regularity counterbalancing this emotionality and the extreme chromaticism of the melodic line?

exclamation 'O'—'O grüßt mir ihn tausendmal!'[32] This is easily explained; every line of the poem, apart from this last one, begins with an iambic anacrusis, and the whole song, including the piano prelude and postlude, is developed from this rhythm. In accordance with the poem's character (both within the novel and as a separate entity) and the general character of Op. 7, the rhythmic and melodic simplicity of the vocal line creates a quasi-folk-song atmosphere.[33]

The metric and rhythmic uniformity which Brahms achieves is, however, detrimental to the aesthetic quality of the poem: after nineteen iambic lines, the dactylic opening of the last line gives a very strong additional accent to the already emphatic 'grüßt' and makes the whole last line—'grüßt mir ihn tausendmal'—appear as the climax towards which the poem has developed. It is no coincidence that Brahms puts his musical accent not on 'grüßt' but on 'tausendmal', but this is against the spirit and form of the poem. The music of the composition has destroyed the music of the poem.

But there is one more problem connected with Brahms's reading of the text. The song's principal tonality is E minor, which in the end—predictably, after the outburst on 'tausendmal'—turns to E major. The piano prelude, however, is in C major, firmly based on a bourdon C–G and with a figure in the right hand which could be understood as bugle-calls—'The notes ring out, rising like clear bugle-calls, and are repeated, as if the assembly were being sounded in the wood.'[34] But the 'real' bugle-calls which Brahms intends appear in the setting of the third and fourth stanzas, where their connection with

[32] The end of the second line of the first stanza reads 'ihr Haar' in all of Eichendorff's versions, but 'das Haar' in Brahms's song—scarcely more than an error on Brahms's part.

[33] The one aspect of Brahms's later song aesthetic which is already evident in the early opera of songs is the arrangement of the songs into well-organized and meaningful groups (see also the paper by Imogen Fellinger in the present volume). This explains, at least partly, why songs comparatively far apart chronologically appear together in single opera. In Op. 3, published in December 1853, the only rules of arrangement seem to be grouping according to poet and a certain predilection for unusual keys—the two Hoffmann von Fallersleben poems (both in B major) and the two Eichendorff poems (in F♯ minor/major and A major) are grouped together; the two remaining songs are in E♭ minor—but there is no ready explanation why the two Eichendorff songs, written in November and December 1852, were put after the remaining four songs, written between January and July 1853.
In Op. 6, also published in December 1853, the overall ordering is more obvious. First come four songs composed in April 1852, in A minor/major, E major, A♭ major, and E♭ major, then two Hoffmann von Fallersleben songs written in July 1853, in B major and A♭ major with a middle section in E major. Op. 7, released in November 1854, is more complicated. For the first time, poems by one and the same poet (Eichendorff) are put together, although they were composed at different times, and there is a clear-cut sequence of keys—F♯ minor, E minor/major, A minor/major, E minor (Phrygian), A minor (Aeolian), B minor/major—which corresponds with the individual mood of each poem and with the 'story' that Brahms's arrangement of the texts—rather naïvely—relates: the deserted maiden who seeks her beloved in death; the deserted maiden who finds consolation in the voices of the forest; the lonely maiden who (in Brahms's musical interpretation of the poem) spins her bridal gown for a marriage which will never come; two Swabian peasant girls in the most depressive moods, and finally the homecoming boy—'Welt, geh nicht unter, Himmel, fall nicht ein, bis ich mag bei der Liebsten sein!' Damsels in distress—but the rescuing hero comes. And this arrangement is the only discernible reason why the oldest extant Brahms song—'Heimkehr', written in June 1851, nearly two years before 'Anklänge'—was put at the end of Op. 7. It is a nice touch that this very song is the only one in the three early song opera which, according to the criteria governing these opera, is not so much a song as a dramatic scene.

[34] Max Friedlaender, *Brahms' Lieder*, 8; English trans., 11

the hunter's world is obvious.[35] Why did the composer use a distinctly separate motive—obviously *not* meaning 'bugle-calls'—for the C major introduction, one which reappears in the short postlude to the first and second stanzas and in the longer E major postlude to the whole song? The explanation seems to be, again, the situation in which the song is sung in the novel:

Apart from the merry little crowd, however, there stood leaning against the mast in the middle of the ship a most beautiful youth in graceful hunter's dress; in his arm he carried a zither which he had found in the cabin, and at his feet sat another pretty boy. One could think that they both were schoolboys, travelling on their recess, and it was charming to see how the merry pictures swiftly flew away in the changing landscape, now in the cool shades of the cliffs, now in the bright evening sun. The one at the mast looked brightly from under his traveller's hat into the green and sang . . .

It is of no importance for the understanding of Brahms's song that the young hunter singing the poem is—of course—a girl in disguise. But it may be of importance that the singer is accompanying herself on a zither.[36]

Of all the Eichendorff songs, the strangest is the companion piece to 'Parole' in Op. 7, 'Anklänge'. The poem was first printed in *Ahnung und Gegenwart* (1815); here it is called 'eine alte Romanze' and is a long ballad about a girl who betrays her beloved knight for a hunter and therefore is slain by her first lover, who comes back as a ghost. The whole poem was republished under the title 'Der Reitersmann' among the 'Romanzen' in the collected poems of 1837, but in the same collection a second version was printed as the second of three poems which under the title 'Anklänge' open the section 'Frühling und Liebe'. This poem is a variation of the first two stanzas of the original romance:[37]

| 1815 | 1837 |
|---|---|
| Hoch über den stillen Höhen | Hoch über stillen Höhen |
| Stand in dem Wald ein Haus, | Stand in dem Wald ein Haus, |
| Dort war's so einsam zu sehen | So einsam war's zu sehen |
| Weit über'n Wald hinaus. | Dort über'n Wald hinaus. |

---

[35] The supposed relation of these hunting calls (and even of the middle section of 'Anklänge') to Schubert's 'Rückblick' ('Wie anders hast du mich empfangen') from the *Winterreise*, stressed by Kalbeck (*Johannes Brahms*, 1: 228) and Friedlaender (*Brahms' Lieder*, 8; English trans., 11), is very difficult to discern—quite apart from the fact that it would hardly make musical and literary sense. George Bozarth has noted a musical similarity between 'Anklänge' and Schubert's 'Die liebe Farbe' from *Die schöne Müllerin* ('Brahms's Duets for Soprano and Alto, op. 61', 192, n. 5).

[36] For further discussion of this song, see the paper by George Bozarth in the present volume.

[37] Kalbeck's description of the different versions of the poem and of their printing history is confused; Friedlaender's description is not quite correct and (as in his evaluation of the other Eichendorff songs) influenced by the edition of Eichendorff's poems published by the poet's oldest son, Rudolf, an edition of highly questionable reliability. I am relying on the two editions mentioned in n. 27 and 29. In his copy of the second edition of Eichendorff's collected poems (cf. n. 29), Brahms made a note of, among other things, the page numbers 215 and 445 (in that order). Page 215 contains the first of the 'Anklänge' poems (with this title) and the initial stanza of 'Hoch über stillen Höhen'; on p. 445 are the first six stanzas of 'Der Reitersmann'.

| | |
|---|---|
| D'rinn saß ein Mädchen am Rocken | Ein Mädchen saß darinnen |
| den ganzen Abend lang, | Bei stiller Abendzeit, |
| Der wurden die Augen nicht trocken, | Tät seidne Fäden spinnen |
| Sie spann und sann und sang. | Zu ihrem Hochzeitskleid. |

The 1837 version is a strange poem, even without Brahms's music: a genre-painting mysteriously oscillating between sadness and peace, loneliness and comfort. But apparently it was not this ambiguity which attracted the composer. The song is saturated with sadness to a degree which finds no justification in the text; indeed, the final return to A minor and to the melodic line of the beginning for the repetition of the last line and the melancholy arrest of the melody on the final word, 'Hochzeitskleid', are in open contrast to the literal meaning of the text; the timid intimation of A major in the very last bars makes the whole composition even more enigmatic. The reviewer for *Signale für die musikalische Welt* laid the blame on the poem:

Some [of the poems in Op. 7] are even so simple that they are done an undeserved honour by the composition of Herr Brahms. Thus one reads, for example, this poem by Eichendorf [sic]: . . . Perhaps one *reads* a thing like that while browsing through the book, but it is not worth while to be set to music. Nevertheless, this has been done by Brahms in as attractive a way as possible— only, at the end one thinks: now it will come! But there comes nothing.[38]

It is probably nearer the truth, though, to assume that Brahms once again was inspired not so much by the poem itself as by the context of the poem's original version in the novel, and that in this case he deliberately composed what lay behind the poem, not what was said in it. In doing so, he took a position quite opposite to that of his later song aesthetic. And the quintessence of the Eichendorff songs seems to be that the young Brahms was concerned with the poems not so much as poems, but rather as emanations of a poetical world in which he was still trying to live. It is surely no coincidence that the mature composer never returned to this poetical world of his youth.

---

[38] 'Einige . . . sind sogar so simpel, daß ihnen durch die Composition des Herrn Brahms eine unverdiente Ehre angethan wurde. So lese man z.B. dieses Gedicht von Eichendorf [sic]: . . . . So etwas *liest* man wohl im Umblättern, aber es in Musik zu setzen, ist nicht der Mühe werth. Gleichwohl ist dies hier von Brahms in möglichst anziehender Weise geschehen—nur meint man am Schlusse: jetzt wird's kommen! Es kommt aber eben nichts mehr.' Ker. [Louis Köhler], 'Sechs Gesänge . . . von Johannes Brahms', 65. In this same review one of Brahms's later principles of song composition is nicely formulated: 'Where Brahms depicts *strong* feelings . . . he has always been most dear to us. Would that this master dedicate himself only to those poems which draw him into themselves forcefully! Today so many songs are written that we advise all composers never to follow the first impression upon reading a poem by setting it immediately to music, but: only fill with music *those* poems which, after having been read, refuse to withdraw from the composer's mind—this is, which *demand* music from him. The "la bourse ou la vie" of a poem must be: "compose me, or else you will be unhappy".' ['Wo Brahms *starke* Gefühle . . . schildert, da ist er uns immer am liebsten gewesen. Möge dieser Meister sich nur solchen Poesien hingeben, die ihn mit Gewalt in sich hineinziehen! Es werden jetzt so viele Lieder geschrieben, daß wir allen Componisten rathen, nie dem ersten Eindrucke des Lesens eines Gedichtes sofort mit der Composition zu folgen, sondern: nur *die* Poesien mit Musik zu erfüllen, die, nachdem sie gelesen wurden, sich nicht von dem Geiste des Musikers trennen wollen,—die also Musik von ihm *verlangen*. Das "la bourse ou la vie" eines Gedichtes muß heißen: "componire mich, oder du bist unglücklich!"']

# BRAHMS'S *LIEDER OHNE WORTE*: THE 'POETIC' ANDANTES OF THE PIANO SONATAS

———

## GEORGE S. BOZARTH

LATE in the year 1853 Johannes Brahms provided a glimpse into his compositional process, as reported by fellow composer Albert Dietrich in his memoirs: 'He told me in the course of our conversation that, when composing, he liked to recall folk-songs, and that melodies then spontaneously presented themselves.' To demonstrate this link between 'folk-song' and original composition, Dietrich recounted that Brahms had had in mind Robert Burns's poem 'Mein Herz ist im Hochland' ['My heart is in the Highlands'] when composing the A minor melody for the $\frac{6}{8}$ passage in the finale of the Piano Sonata in C major, Op. 1, and that the words for an Old German song—'Mir ist leide, daß der Winter beide Wald und auch die Haide hat gemachet kahl'—had provided the foundation for the theme of the Andante variations in the Piano Sonata in F♯ minor, Op. 2.[1] To these instances can be added four others, all in pieces marked Andante and all well known: The theme of the variations in the Sonata in C major is labelled 'Nach einem altdeutschen Minnelied' and below the melody appears a text which begins 'Verstohlen geht der Mond auf'. At the head of the second movement of the Piano Sonata in F minor, Op. 5, appear the initial three lines of a poem by C. O. Sternau, 'Der Abend dämmert, das Mondlicht scheint'. The first of the four Ballades, Op. 10, is entitled 'Nach der schottischen Ballade: "Edward" in Herders "Stimmen der Völker"'. And the first of the three Intermezzi, Op. 117, is preceded by the opening three lines of a Scottish folk-poem 'Schlaf sanft, mein Kind', also from Herder's collection. Max Kalbeck cited all of these instances in his Brahms biography, duly demonstrating those cases where it is actually possible to sing the opening lines of the poem to the initial phrases of Brahms's melodies and describing in general terms the 'poetic' nature of Brahms's early piano sonatas.[2] Although other commentators have taken up the topic, few have done much more than reiterate Kalbeck's observations. To explore the relationship between word and tone in the 'poetic' Andantes of the three Piano Sonatas and to speculate on how extramusical influences extend beyond the two Andantes in the formally unorthodox Sonata in F minor, Op. 5, is the purpose of this paper.

---

[1] *Erinnerungen an Johannes Brahms*, 3 (trans., 3–4).
[2] *Johannes Brahms*, 1: 71, 89, 120–2, 190–1, 212–13, 278–80.

# I

Recent years have witnessed a number of attempts to move beyond the Schenkerian notion that the content of music is in no way, either directly or indirectly, verbal or literary, that analyses of 'musical content' should focus on the 'composition-technical' aspects of a work, on its 'structural content' or 'congeneric meaning' alone, and that one need not be concerned with the presumed 'experiential', 'expressive', or 'extrageneric content' of a musical work.[3] As Leo Treitler has pointed out, Schenker's conception of what constitutes the proper study of music was developed in reaction to a nineteenth-century mode of interpretation termed 'musical hermeneutics' by its chief exponent Hermann Kretzschmar.[4] Schenker's restrictive definition of 'musical content' placed him squarely in the autonomist camp of the Viennese music critic, aesthetician, and Brahms advocate Eduard Hanslick, who had written in the treatise *Von Musikalisch-Schönen* (1854) that musical forms or procedures are the sole content and subject of music and that what is beautiful in music is not contingent upon or in need of a subject introduced from without, but resides entirely in the pitches and their artistic combination.[5] To Hanslick, the nature of music is specifically musical, not representational; a musical idea has its own intrinsic beauty, which can be enchanced no further by its presumed ability to represent feelings, thoughts, or situations. Yet, as Morris Weitz has stressed, Hanslick's position was not entirely that of the autonomist. Hanslick never denied the expressivity of music, the ability of music to suggest certain 'dynamic properties' of feeling. Musical sounds may, according to Hanslick, be characterized as 'graceful, gentle, violent, vigorous, elegant, fresh', for all of these properties may be inherent in particular melodic, harmonic, and rhythmic events. But, if I may borrow Weitz's example, 'to say of a melody . . . that it is graceful, is not to say that it represents or symbolizes anything graceful or even any feeling of gracefulness . . . but rather that its lingering character, as sound, is graceful . . . . The gracefulness is presented in the sounds, it is not represented by them.'[6]

In his own critical writings on music for *Die Presse*, Hanslick often resorted to evocative terminology, and in the light of these essays it would be hard to imagine him advocating a discourse on music limited solely to discussion of syntactical relationships.[7]

---

[3] Cf. Leo Treitler, 'History, Criticism, and Beethoven's Ninth Symphony', 198–202 (on the restrictive nature of Schenker's analytical approach); Edward T. Cone, 'Schubert's Promissory Note: An Exercise in Musical Hermeneutics' (including references to and discussion of earlier writings on music and meaning); Wilson Coker, *Music and Meaning*, 61 ('congeneric' and 'extrageneric' meaning). Cf. also the history of analysis and critique of Schenkerian analytical method (with a focus on its shortcomings for assessing Lieder) in Joseph Kerman, 'How We Got Into Analysis, and How to Get Out'.

[4] Cf. *Führer durch den Konzertsaal*.

[5] 'Tönend bewegte Formen sind einzig und allein Inhalt und Gegenstand der Musik' and 'ein Schönes, das unabhängig und unbedürftig eines von Außen her kommenden Inhaltes, einzig in den Tönen und ihrer künstlerischen Verbindung liegt', 38 and 37, respectively (trans., 48 and 47). For a discussion of the historical context of Hanslick's position, see Anthony Newcomb, 'Those Images That Yet Fresh Images Beget', 227–32.

[6] Ibid., trans., p. xi.

[7] A brief sample of Hanslick's evocative writing—an excerpt from his review of the première of Brahms's Second Symphony—appears in Newcomb, 'Those Images', 230.

But if discussions of 'expressive content' are to be anything more than neo-Kretzschmarian musings, they need to be based on careful and consistent analytical observation. Edward T. Cone has defined the task and pointed the way: 'the locus of expression in a musical composition is to be sought neither in its wider surfaces nor in its more detailed motivic contours, but in its comprehensive design, which includes all the sonic elements and relates them to one another in a significant temporal structure. In other words, extrageneric meaning can be explained only in term of congeneric [meaning]. If verbalization of true content—the specific expression uniquely embodied in a work—is possible at all, it must depend on close structural analysis'.[8]

Since Brahms has traditionally been considered the foremost exponent of absolute music in the late nineteenth century, a composer who thoroughly rejected the programmatic approach of Liszt and whose compositions are free of extramusical implications, he has received scant attention among writers on 'meaning in music' and music 'between absolute and programmatic'.[9] But can a composer who conjures up Wertherian images to explain the tragic mood of his Third Piano Quartet, Op. 60 (1855),[10] who writes to Clara Schumann concerning the slow movement of the First Piano Concerto, Op. 15, 'I am painting a gentle portrait of you' (1856),[11] who evokes the name of his beloved Agathe von Siebold in musical pitches in his Second String Sextet, Op. 36 (1864)[12]—can such a composer be considered totally inimical to the views of the heteronomist camp? Such tempting clues have encouraged scholars to begin to explore the possibility that there exists in Brahms's music a realm between the autonomist and heteronomist extremes; the resulting studies have yielded new ways of viewing certain of Brahms's instrumental works.[13] Yet much of this work has been, of necessity, highly speculative. The 'poetic' Andantes offer the advantage of well-documented links to

---

[8] 'Schubert's Promissory Note', 235. Compare also Cone's response, 'Beethoven's Orpheus—or Jander's?', to Owen Jander's article 'Beethoven's "Orpheus in Hades": The *Andante con moto* of the Fourth Piano Concerto'.

[9] Cf. Walter Wiora, 'Zwischen absoluter und Programmusik', and Ludwig Finscher, ' "Zwischen absoluter und Programmusik": Zur Interpretation der deutschen romantischen Symphonie'; see also Anthony Newcomb, 'Once More "Between Absolute and Program Music": Schumann's Second Symphony'.

[10] Kalbeck, *Brahms*, 1: 232.

[11] 'Male ich an einem sanften Porträt von Dir', Berthold Litzmann, ed., *Clara Schumann-Johannes Brahms Briefe*, 1: 198.

[12] Kalbeck, *Brahms*, 2: 157 ff.

[13] Cf. the general discussion in Constantin Floros, *Brahms und Bruckner*; also, on specific works, James Webster, 'Brahms's *Tragic Overture*: The Form of Tragedy' (which experiments 'with an interpretation of the "notes themselves", in their "purely musical" meanings, as embodying or articulating relationships which can be understood as analogous to tragic ones'); Christopher Reynolds, 'A Choral Symphony by Brahms?' (which places analytical observations in the service of speculation on musical 'depiction' and compositional connections between the First Piano Concerto and the *German Requiem*); and A. Peter Brown, 'Brahms' Third Symphony and the New German School' (which attempts to revive the long-standing debate about the 'meaning' of the F–A♭–F motive, advancing the notion that it is derived from 'Faust'). At the time of publication, Kenneth Hull had recently completed work on a dissertation focusing on the 'meaning' of Brahms's Fourth Symphony (Ph.D., Princeton University); in a paper entitled 'Quotation, Allusion, and Model in Brahms's Fourth Symphony' (presented at the 1985 National Meeting of the American Musicological Society in Vancouver) Hull explored the relationship of the symphony's finale to Schumann's 'Süßer Freund', the sixth song in *Frauenliebe und -leben*, and Beethoven's *An die ferne Geliebte*.

external literary works and therefore provide a solid starting-point for a consideration of 'extramusical' promptings in Brahms's 'absolute' music.

## II

The chronology of the four Andantes in the piano sonatas and the movements which surround them is given in Table 1, together with that of contemporaneous songs and instrumental works.[14] The songs are included so as to place the 'poetic' Andantes within the context of their vocal counterparts and view all of these works as manifestations of Brahms's very personal involvement with Romantic poetry.[15] Although the Sonata in C major, Op. 1, was the second of the extant piano sonatas to be completed (and, according to the title on the autograph manuscript, the fourth sonata actually composed[16]), its Andante pre-dates the composition of the Sonata in F♯ minor, Op. 2, by seven months (and, among the extant instrumental works, postdates only the Scherzo, Op. 4). The date of composition for the two Andantes in the Sonata in F minor, Op. 5, is unknown, but, according to Brahms's handwritten *Werkverzeichnis*, both movements were written earlier than the sonata's three fast movements. Thus, at least three of the four Andantes initally existed independent of the works in which they eventually found a place. Put another way, at least two of the three piano sonatas were composed 'from the inside out', and in both cases it can be shown that the movements subsequently composed drew upon and were conditioned by the melodic and tonal characteristics and procedures of their 'poetic' slow movements.

The relationship between the Andante variations in the Piano Sonata in C major, Op. 1, composed as an independent piece in April 1852, and the pseudo-folk-poem 'Verstohlen geht der Mond auf', from the *Deutsche Volkslieder* of Kretzschmer and Zuccalmaglio,[17] is simple and straightforward. (Brahms's attribution of the poem to the tradition of the Minnesingers was purely the product of the young composer's imagination, as is the *Barform* structure of his theme. See Example 1 for the original folk-song and for Brahms's theme; in the case of this and all subsequent movements under discussion, the reader should make reference to the edition of the piano sonatas in volume 13 of the *Johannes Brahms Sämtliche Werke*. Example 2 provides the complete text of the folk-song.) Not only does the number of thematic statements (four) match the number of strophes in the poem, but the whole musical composition, both in its gross features and in its details, closely follows the progress of the poem. (The movement consists of a theme [bars 1–12], three variations [bars 12–26, 26–56, and 56–71], and a postlude [bars

---

[14] This chronology for Brahms's early compositions is based entirely on documentary evidence, drawing upon dated manuscripts, correspondence, and Brahms's handwritten *Werkverzeichnis* (Vienna, Stadt- und Landesbibliothek HIN 32.866).

[15] Although I will comment on certain of the early songs as relevant to my topic, I would recommend to the reader the fuller discussion of these works by Ludwig Finscher elsewhere in this volume.

[16] The autograph is now owned by the Österreichische Nationalbibliothek, Vienna.

[17] August Kretzschmer and Anton Wilhelm von Zuccalmaglio, *Deutsche Volkslieder mit ihren Original-Weisen*, 1: 56–7. This is the famous collection on which Brahms drew for the majority of his folk-song arrangements.

TABLE I. Brahms's extant compositions, 1851–4

| Date | Songs | Instrumental Works |
|---|---|---|
| June 1851 | 'Heimkehr', Op. 7 No. 6 (Uhland) | |
| Aug. 1851 | | Scherzo, Op. 4 |
| Apr. 1852 | 'Spanisches Lied', Op. 6 No. 1 (Heyse) | Andante, 'Verstohlen geht der Mond |
| | 'Der Frühling', Op. 6 No. 2 (Rousseau) | auf', Op. 1, mvt. 2 |
| | 'Nachwirkung', Op. 6 No. 3 (Meissner) | |
| | 'Juchhe', Op. 6 No. 4 (Reinick) | |
| Aug. 1852 | 'Volkslied', Op. 7 No. 4 | |
| | 'Die Trauernde', Op. 7 No. 5 (Volkslied) | |
| Sept. 1852 | 'Klosterfräulein', Op. 61 No. 2 (duet; Kerner) | |
| Nov. 1852 | 'In der Fremde', Op. 3 No. 5 (Eichendorff) | Sonata in F♯ minor, Op. 2 |
| | 'Treue Liebe', Op. 7 No. 1 (Ferrand) | |
| | 'Parole', Op. 7 No. 2 (Eichendorff) | |
| Dec. 1852 | 'Lied', Op. 3 No. 6 (Eichendorff) | |
| Jan. 1853 | 'Liebestreu', Op. 3 No. 1 (Reinick) | |
| Mar. 1853 | 'Anklänge', Op. 7 No. 3 (Eichendorff) | |
| Spring 1853 | | Allegro, Scherzo, and Finale for Sonata in |
| | | C major, Op. 1 (entitled 'Vierte Sonate') |
| July 1853 | 'Liebe und Frühling' I and II, Op. 3 | |
| | Nos. 2 and 3 (Hoffmann von Fallersleben) | |
| | 'Lied', Op. 3 No. 4 (Bodenstedt) | |
| | 'Wie die Wolke nach der Sonne', Op. 6 No. 5 | |
| | (Fallersleben) | |
| | 'Nachtigallen schwingen lustig', Op. 6 No. 6 | |
| | (Fallersleben) | |
| Summer 1853? | 'Die Müllerin' (Chamisso), Anh. III/13 | |
| Oct. 1853 | | Scherzo for 'F.A.E.' Sonata, WoO 2 |
| | | Allegro, Scherzo, and Finale for Sonata in |
| | | F minor, Op. 5 ('Andante u. Intermezzo |
| | | früher') |
| by Nov. 1853 | 'Mondnacht', WoO 21 (Eichendorff) | |
| by Dec. 1853 | 'Der Überläufer', Op. 48 No. 2 (*Des Knaben Wunderhorn*) | |
| | [possibly 'Liebesklage des Mädchens', Op. 48 No. 3 (*Des Knaben Wunderhorn*)] | |
| Jan. 1854 | | Piano Trio in B major, Op. 8 |
| June 1854 | | *Variations on a Theme by Schumann*, Op. 9 |
| Summer 1854 | | Ballades for Piano, Op. 10 |

72–85].) Note, for example, how the theme itself appears throughout in the bass-baritone register that we might associate with the poet himself; how the minor mode which persists through the second variation combines with the ominous triplet motive (bars 12 ff.), the cadential dissonances (bars 16, 25), and the Neapolitan digressions of variation 1 (bars 20, 24) to create a mood appropriate for the stealthily rising moon, while registral changes chart its course; how descending melodic arabesques in variation 2 respond to the poet's request that the moon shine down into his beloved's window (bars 26 ff.); and how 'celestial' chords near the end of variation 2 suggest shimmering moonlight and

EXAMPLE 1. (*a*) The folk-song 'Verstohlen geht der Mond auf' as published in the
*Deutsche Volkslieder* of Kretzschmer and Zuccalmaglio (1: 56–7). (*b*) Brahms, Piano
Sonata in C major, Op. 1, II, bars 1–12.

(*a*)

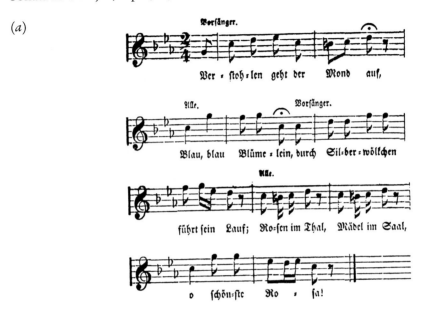

(*b*)

Example 2. Niederrheinisches Volkslied, 'Verstohlen geht der Mond auf': Poem related to the Andante of the Piano Sonata in C major, Op. 1 (movement 2).

Brahms's source: August Kretzschmer and Anton Wilhelm von Zuccalmaglio, *Deutsche Volkslieder mit ihren Original-Weisen*, 2 vols. (Berlin, 1838, 1840), 1: 56f.

Verstohlen geht der Mond auf,
Blau, blau Blümelein!
Durch Silberwölkchen führt sein Lauf;
Rosen im Thal, Mädel im Saal,
  o schönste Rosa!

Er steigt die blaue Luft hindurch,
Blau, blau Blümelein!
Bis daß er schaut auf Löwenburg;
Rosen im Thal, Mädel im Saal,
  o schönste Rosa!

O schaue Mond durchs Fensterlein,
Blau, blau Blümelein!
Schön' Trude lock' mit deinem Schein;
Rosen im Thal, Mädel im Saal,
  o schönste Rosa!

Und siehst du mich und siehst du sie,
Blau, blau Blümelein!
Zwei treu're Herzen sahst du nie:
Rosen im Thal, Mädel im Saal,
  o schönste Rosa!

Stealthily the moon rises,
blue, blue little flower!
Through silver clouds it makes its way;
Roses in the valley, maiden in the hall,
  o most beautiful Rosa!

It climbs through the blue air,
blue, blue little flower!
Until it looks down upon the Löwenburg;
Roses in the valley, maiden in the hall,
  o most beautiful Rosa!

O moon, look through the little window,
blue, blue little flower!
Entice beautiful Trude with your glow;
Roses in the valley, maiden in the hall,
  o most beautiful Rosa!

And if you see me and if you see her,
blue, blue little flower!
Two truer hearts have you never seen;
Roses in the valley, maiden in the hall,
  o most beautiful Rosa!

blissful love (bars 47–9, 51–3). Of a slightly more sophisticated nature is Brahms's affective and selective use of the major mode. In the theme, a momentary shift to Eb major (which is not necessarily implied by the G in the original tune) seems prompted by the word 'schönste' (bar 11). In the second variation, as the moonlight shines into the beloved's window, the theme sings forth in Bb major (*ben cantando*), before tentatively returning to G minor and ultimately sinking back into C minor (bars 30–3, 38–41). And, later in the same variation, the poet's beckoning of the moon to entice the fair Trude with its glow calls forth a tonal shift into a deep, warm Ab major (bars 42 ff.), which is eventually punctuated by the washes of soft treble chords previously mentioned, as the poet's thoughts seem to linger on his beloved.

With the final variation, marked *con grand' expressione,* the mode at last shifts to C major, as the focus of the poem changes from the rising moon to the pure love of the poet and his beloved. The theme, in strong bass octaves, is joined by an elliptical melody which takes flight in the treble (bars 56 ff.). A shift to Ab major occurs once again, and in the same register as before, at the end of the second *Stollen* (bars 63–4), after which the melody moves back into C major, now also starting in a rich, low register and culminating with the first subdominant harmony of the movement (bars 65 ff.). The true hearts are united in free counterpoint—the baritone seemingly pressing its suit of the soprano—only to be interrupted momentarily by impetuous triplet chords which build to a climax and then subside into a broad, 'textless' apotheosis-postlude now rich in subdominant-related harmonies (bars 72 ff.). Baritone and soprano melodies sing a duet in strict imitation, harmonized with the sort of 'melting' seventh chords which were to become a hallmark of Brahms's music, and set over an ever-constant pedal tone. The movement closes with echoes of the opening phrase of the theme (bars 80–3), sung in parallel sixths, as Bb resolves to A, Ab to G, as the tempo progressively slackens to *Adagio*, and as the volume gradually diminishes to the barely audible.

Although these sentiments and their musical analogues may seem extreme, they are no more unabashed than those found in the Lieder of the adolescent Brahms. In the earliest extant song, 'Heimkehr', Op. 7 No. 6 (Ludwig Uhland), dating from June 1851, the poet declares that no obstacle—neither trembling footbridge, crumbling cliff, perishing world, nor falling sky—will prevent him from reaching his beloved, and Brahms's triplet accompaniment creates the same excitement and sense of virility as does the extension at the end of variation 3 (bars 69 ff.) in the Op. 1 Andante. Similar piano parts accompany the vocal lines of two songs composed in April 1852, the same month as the Andante: 'Nachwirkung', Op. 6 No. 3 (Alfred Meissner), the song of a poet whose 'sick, feverish mind is reeling' and whose 'heart is pounding' with longing for his departed beloved, and 'Juchhe', Op. 6 No. 4 (Robert Reinick), an exclamatory ode to the beauty of spring. Joy in spring overflows another work from that month, 'Der Frühling', Op. 6 No. 2 (J. B. Rousseau), whose simple message is that 'spring is here in all its beauty, and now perhaps you will find the right love' (the poet addresses himself, of course), and whose introductory and accompanimental material is cut from cloth of the same pattern as the beginning of the final variation in the Op. 1 Andante.

# III

In the 'poetic' Andante of Op. 1, harmonic, modal, and tonal events are used merely to highlight certain local references to beauty and to the poet's beloved. The same approach can be seen in the songs stemming from early 1852. In the 'Spanisches Lied', Op. 6 No. 1 (Paul Heyse), for example, at the mention of 'mein Geliebte' (bar 5, echoed in bar 7), the A minor of the brown-skinned Iberian maiden singing the song is momentarily replaced by its relative major (cf. 'o schönste Rosa' in the Op. 1 variations, bars 11–12).[18] In this song, however, Brahms also explores the potential of harmony as a means to reveal the state of mind behind the words: when the girl reiterates her decision not to awaken her lover at the end of each stanza, the augmented harmony, as well as the size and direction of the melodic skips in her vocal line, betray her lack of resolve.

The song 'Parole', Op. 7 No. 2 (Joseph von Eichendorff), composed seven months later, in November 1852, is the first in which Brahms employs larger-scale tonal planning to underscore the central issue of a poem, in this case, the distance between the young girl singing the song and her absent beloved, and the anxiety which results from the lovers' separation. By placing the singer in the tonic minor and centring thoughts of the distant beloved on the flattened supertonic (and later the subdominant), and by continually modulating between these tonal areas and avoiding root-position tonic harmonies in both areas, Brahms effectively renders the psychological flux of the poem into musical terms. Only after the young girl has told the streams and the birds to carry her greetings 'tausend mal' to her beloved is the tension allowed to resolve, with a varied repetition of the introduction, at last in the tonic major.[19]

With 'Parole' Brahms began to realize the potential of harmonic and tonal means for conveying psychological states. In the same month he created an even more subtle word-tone synthesis along the same lines, this one another set of Andante variations without words—the slow movement of the Piano Sonata in F♯ minor, Op. 2. For this movement Brahms took as his poetic model a genuine Minnelied poem, 'Mir ist leide', a quintessential *Winterlied* written by the Swiss poet Count Kraft von Toggenburg and preserved in the magnificent Manesse manuscript at the University of Heidelberg.[20] With

---

[18] Cf. also 'Der Frühling', Op. 6 No. 2 ('der Winter ist zeronnen', bars 18 ff.).

[19] On a smaller scale, Brahms uses a harmonic shift between tonic minor and submediant major to set the lines 'aber Vater und Mutter sind lange tot / es kennt mich dort keiner mehr' in the song 'In der Fremde', Op. 3 No. 5 (Eichendorff), composed the same month as 'Parole'.

[20] Although Dietrich's recollections are not always to be trusted, his account of the connection between the Andante in Op. 2 and von Toggenburg's poem receives independent confirmation from a document in Brahms's hand cited in an inventory of the collection of Antonia Speyer-Kufferath and Edward Speyer, prepared *c.*1931. The document is reported to contain the poem 'Mir ist leide', labelled ' "Lied von Toggenburg" Op. 2', together with the Sternau poem upon which Brahms based the first of the Andantes in Op. 5, here entitled 'Liebeslied' (the present location of the document is unknown; I would like to thank Margit McCorkle for calling the Speyer-Kufferath inventory to my attention). Moreover, preserved with the letter Brahms wrote to Clara Schumann on 21 Aug. 1855 (Staatsbibliothek Preußischer Kulturbesitz, Berlin) is a sheet of paper, in an unidentified hand (Marie Schumann?), labelled 'Beilage z. 21. Aug. 55' and containing the initial eight lines from strophe 1 of 'Mir ist leide', entitled 'Lied von Toggenburg' and inscribed at the end 'Zu dem Andante in h moll', and all three strophes of the Sternau poem, entitled 'Liebeslied. (C. O. Sternau)' and inscribed at the end '(Zum Andante in As dur)'. It seems very likely that the

this Andante, though, Brahms sought neither 'to set the poem to music' nor even to reflect its overall formal scheme. Instead, he created a theme—no Minnelied melody is extant—and three variations which freely draw upon the changing moods and content of the poem and vividly render its underlying psychological tensions into musical terms. (The theme extends through bar 18; the three variations are bars 19–36, 37–67, and 68–87.)

The opening verse of von Toggenburg's Minnelied advances the central issue of the poem: 'Mir ist leide' (see Example 3). All else that follows provides explanation and elaboration of this pregnant declaration, as the poet makes various attempts, through various means, to find release from his personal isolation and its concomitant tensions and thereby to resolve his suffering. But in nature he finds only the bleakness of winter; the sight of his beloved only causes further pain; and recounting her attributes leads to recollection of her high station, and thus her inaccessibility. The poet wishes 'to sing more with good hopes', to move beyond himself and enter into a relationship with his ideal beloved, but, as the subjunctive mode implies, all his efforts come to naught.[21]

Brahms's musical response to the poem is direct and powerful. The Andante begins with a head motive, plus 'choral' response (cf. the theme of the Op. 1 variations), which renders von Toggenburg's initial declaration into musical terms and, like the opening verse of the poem, provides the material on which all subsequent elaborations will draw (see Example 4): a constricted, isolated four-note motive establishing a solemn B minor tonic and immediately linked to the tensions of a diminished seventh harmony, as the initial melodic rise from B is halted by a precipitate drop to A♯ and the soprano enters on G. The first attempt at moving beyond the 'isolation' of the poet's opening harmonies then ensues. For a moment, both escape from the tonic and integration of at least one of the diminished chord's dissonances (the G) seem at hand, as the phrase moves through E minor and on to C major. Yet each step of the harmonic path is immediately retraced and the attempt to transcend the tonic and diminished seventh proves as fruitless as the poet's effort to find solace in nature.

---

Speyer document was the original enclosure, which, when subsequently separated from Brahms's letter, was replaced by the Berlin copy. The Schumanns and the Speyers were well acquainted; in 1921 Marie Schumann gave the Speyers the autograph of Brahms's song 'Junge Lieder I', Op. 63 No. 5, which the composer had presented to her mother on 24 Dec. 1873, and the letter from Brahms to Clara Schumann which had accompanied the song manuscript. No mention of the 1855 enclosure was made in Litzmann's edition of the Schumann-Brahms correspondence. Although in his letter of 21 August Brahms refers to 'the little verses which I prudently enclosed' (1: 134), he writes in the past tense; the enclosure was probably sent with a slightly earlier (now lost?) letter.

Exactly when and how Brahms came to know von Toggenburg's Minnelied is unknown. Prior to 1852, it had appeared in Friedrich Heinrich von der Hagen's *Minnesinger* of 1838 (1: 22–3), and, in a modernized version, in Ludwig Tieck's *Minnelieder aus dem schwäbischen Zeitalter* of 1803 (pp. 207–8). The text as recorded on the 1855 enclosure provides no clue, for its reading varies from both Tieck's and von der Hagen's, which, for the first strophe at least, are in agreement.

I am indebted to Professor Diana Behler of the University of Washington for assistance with the translation of this poem.

[21] On the use of 'Leit' and its variants in Minnelieder to describe the sufferings of the lover, see Vickie L. Ziegler, *The Leitword in Minnesang: Stylistic Analysis and Textual Criticism*, 175–8.

Example 3. Kraft von Toggenburg, 'Mir ist leide' (Minnelied): Poem related to the Andante of the Piano Sonata in F♯ minor, Op. 2 (movement 2).

| | |
|---|---|
| Mir ist leide. | It is painful to me |
| das der winter beide. | that winter |
| walt vñ ouch die heide. | has made fallow |
| hat gemachet val. | both forest and heath; |
| sin betwingen. | its firm grip allows |
| lat niht blůmen entspringen. | neither flowers to bloom |
| noch die vogel singen. | nor birds to sing |
| ir vil sůssen schal. | their very sweet songs. |
| alsus verderbet mich ein selig wib. | In like manner, a blessed woman destroys me, |
| dú mich lat. | has left me |
| ane rat. | without giving the counsel |
| den si hat. | of which she is possessed; |
| des zergat. | because of this my joy, |
| an frŏiden gar min lip. | even my life, has perished. |
| | |
| Miner swere. | From my sufferings |
| schiere ich ane were. | I would leave off without hesitation |
| solde ich die seldebere. | if I could see, without feeling pain, |
| schowen ane leit. | the one who brings happiness. |
| dú vil here. | This very noble lady |
| hat schŏne zuht vñ ere. | is of high breeding and honor; |
| der wnsch vñ dannoch mere. | any wish, and yet still more, |
| ist gar an si geleit. | is indeed her companion. |
| rose wengel mv́ndel rot si hat. | Rosy cheeks and a little red mouth has she, |
| val har lang. | full long hair, |
| kele blank. | a white neck, |
| siten kranc. | slender waist: |
| min gedanc. | my thought is |
| an ir vil hohe stat. | of her very high station. |
| | |
| Ich wil singen. | I want to sing |
| mere vf gůt gedingen. | more with good hopes, |
| sol mir wol gelingen. | but if I succeed, |
| das mv̊s an ir geschehen. | that must happen through her. |
| si kan machen. | She can make |
| trurig herze lachen. | sad hearts laugh, |
| grosse sorge swachen. | lessen great worry; |
| des mv̊s man ir ieheh. | one must grant her that. |
| wurde mir ir werder trost geseit. | If her worthy comfort would be given me, |
| seht fúr war. | see, verily, |
| offē bar. | obviously, |
| minú iar. | the rest of my life |
| wolde ich gar. | I would indeed consider |
| mit frŏiden sin gemeit. | full of joy. |

Poem as transcribed in Friedrich Pfaff, ed., *Die große Heidelberger Lieerhandschrift*, cols. 36–7.

EXAMPLE 4. Brahms, Piano Sonata in F♯ minor, Op. 2, II, bars 1–18.

Mir ist leide · das der winter · beide walt vñ ouch die heide

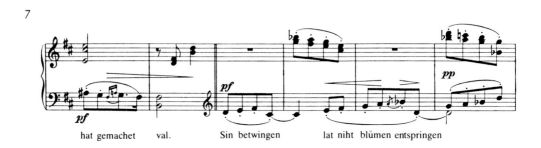

hat gemachet val. · Sin betwingen · lat niht blümen entspringen

noch die vogel sin – gen · ir · vil süssen schal.

The second phrase of the theme (bars 9–18) follows a similar course, but now moves to E♭ major and its dominant, thereby integrating both initial pitches of tension (the A♯ now spelt enharmonically as B♭), as the poet's thoughts turn to the songbirds of spring and a decorated melody sounds forth. But E♭ major is immediately inflected to G minor, the dominant seventh to the original diminished seventh, and we become painfully aware of how fragile, how illusory progress has been. The theme ends on a half-cadence, with the dissonant G resounding bleakly amidst the upper voices (as a ninth in the dominant harmony), disturbing even this temporary respite.

Further attempts to escape the tonic minor and either resolve or gain integration for the dissonance of the diminished chord dominate the harmonic progress of the rest of the composition. In variation 1 (bars 19–36), a reiterated, unresolving, and unrelenting G (an upper pedal extending out of the dissonant pitch in the preceding half-cadence) hovers fatefully over all harmonies, rendering the poet's song as desolate as winter, as joyless as his life. In the second half of the variation, the G is replaced by B♭, only to be restored for the final half-cadence on F♯, where the G again functions as it had at the end of the theme.

Subsequent modulatory efforts include a momentary shift to G major at the point when the poet first sings of how he would leave off from his sufferings, if only seeing his beloved were not so painful (beginning of variation 2, bar 37); brief contacts with E minor, C⁷, and B♭ harmonies during the same passage in the poem (bars 39, 41, and 42); and a glorious duet of parallel, then imitative tenths in E♭ major, as the poet sings of his beloved's high breeding, honour, and physical beauty (bars 50 ff.; this resolution, of course, recalls the brief E♭ major in the theme, when the poet spoke of the songbirds of spring, bar 13). As before, these harmonies integrate at least one of the diminished seventh chord's pitches of tension; it would seem that the poet is trying all means of reconciling his dissonant elements. But the diminished seventh harmony always reasserts itself (bars 43, 46–7, and 54), providing a musical equivalent for the subjunctive mode of the poem. It begins to seem as if the poet will never escape this harmony and move beyond his original B minor (note the disconsolate sounding G♮–F♯ echoes in the cadential extension, bars 44–5).

After the shift back to diminished seventh harmony in bar 54, the diminished harmony suddenly finds easy, stepwise (rather than common-tone) resolution into a bright, exultant D major (bars 56–8). Now at last the poet effects his escape, and to the major key 'relative' to his own B minor. For two bars of reiterated, *grandioso* chords, he remains in this 'uplifted' state, and there would seem little doubt that at last we are in the presence of the beloved lady whose high station the poet describes at this point in the Minnelied and whose ability to give counsel, and thereby 'uplift' the poet, had been noted in the first stanza. But even now one senses a certain uneasiness: is this D major really a tonic, or perhaps just a dominant of G minor? Soon the irony of the moment is brutally revealed. Resolution is not to be found in this tonal realm, the poet will find no relief from his suffering: the head motive, 'Mir ist leide', now in D minor (and thus on *her* tonic pitch), breaks into the final resounding D major chord (bar 58), the off-beat rhythm of variation 1 returns for two loud diminished seventh chords (bar 59), these events are reiterated, and all the poet's hopes become illusions as the variation ends, like all others so far, on F♯, dominant of B minor, reached once again by resolving G♮ to F♯.

As the poet expresses his desire 'to sing more with good hopes', and then recounts his beloved's powers to make him happy the rest of his days (beginning of stanza 3), Brahms shifts to B major, parallel key to the poet's own sorrowful minor. But, as before, the diminished seventh harmony soon intrudes. Twice the poet's hopefulness reasserts itself, as the diminished chord's G is forcefully resolved upwards to G♯ (bars 69 and 71, the latter harmonized as a shift from E minor to E major). The progression to C major which occurred in the original theme is preserved here (bar 72), and then once more the positive G♯ replaces G (bar 73) and continues to hold sway until after the cadence on B major at bar 75 (compare this extension to the disconsolate G♮–F♯ echoes at the parallel point in variation 2, bars 44–5). Yet this joy is not to be. Despite further attempts to gain and retain B major—and a moment when it seems that success is at hand (the broad $I_4^6$–$V^7$ at the final climax, bar 84)—the dominant is once again left unresolved, and the final pitches heard are the sombre G♮ resolving to F♯ (bars 86–7).

As in Op. 1, this set of 'wordless' variations is followed by a 'textless' postlude, here a full Scherzo-Trio-Scherzo which begins *attacca* after the Andante and provides resolution for that movement's final half-cadence (Example 5). Furthermore, since the Scherzo proper is built from the same melody, harmonic progression, and formal scheme as the theme of the Andante variations, it functions in effect as a fourth variation, now sardonic and self-deprecatory in mood (and strikingly reminiscent of the thematic transformations effected by Berlioz in the *Symphonie fantastique*). The initial section comes to a full close on a unison tonic: the tensions of the diminished harmony find resolution, but in the end there is little to show for the effort.

A stately, but graceful Trio follows, replete with the sonorities that Brahms the song composer typically employed to create an *altdeutsch* atmosphere: 'horn-call' duets; exclusive use of triadic chords in root position or second inversion; and open fifths as bass sonorities and as full chords (Example 6). The tonal shift to D major recalls the crucial moment in the Andante and finalizes the association of the Trio with the Minnesinger's beloved. But the fair lady appears not only in her idealized form, but also in relationship to the poet: both dominant and subdominant change into minor (bars 25–6, 28–9), and haunting open fifths on the dominant follow moments of tonic minor (bars 31 ff.). The Trio ends, however, in D major, with the third of the tonic chord resounding brightly on top (bars 61–2). Again, though, Brahms reveals resolution as illusion: a restatement of the 'horn-call' anacrusis, in D major, is brought to an abrupt halt on F♯; A♯ rumbles in the bass, G brutally sounds against F♯, and with mounting tension the varied reiteration of these clashing pitches of the diminished seventh and dominant harmonies leads back to the B minor Scherzo.

The Scherzo resumes as in the beginning, but is soon intensified by the injection of a high, persistent tremolo (bars 81 ff.), first on G, then on B♭, recalling variation 1 of the Andante. For a moment all hangs in the balance. Then G♯ asserts itself, as in variation 3, and the hopeful parallel major of the poet's key is heard. Soon, however, B minor returns, the left hand descends through the diminished seventh harmony, and the movement ends with a terrifying sense of finality.

# IV

On 26 December 1853 Brahms sent the engraver's model of his Piano Sonata in F minor to Bartolf Senff, who published the work in February 1854 as the composer's Op. 5. Accompanying the manuscript was a letter requesting that Senff add the opening three

EXAMPLE 5.  Brahms, Piano Sonata in F♯ minor, Op. 2, III, bars 1–8.

EXAMPLE 6. Brahms, Piano Sonata in F♯ minor, Op. 2, III, bars 22–36.

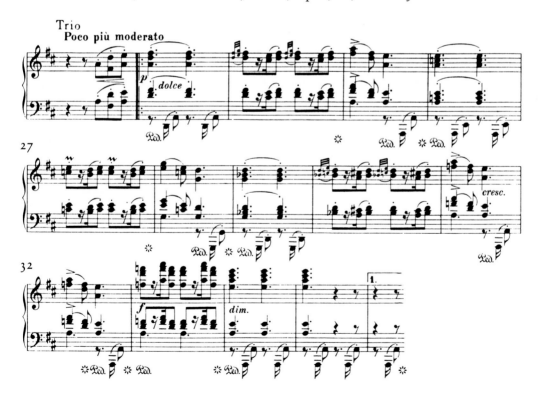

lines of C. O. Sternau's poem 'Der Abend dämmert, das Mondlicht scheint' in parentheses and small type above the first of the sonata's two Andantes. The package containing the manuscript was already sealed, Brahms explained, and he did not wish to delay sending it off in order to make the entry himself. The verses, he added, are 'perhaps necessary or pleasant for an appreciation of the Andante'.[22] Sternau's atmospheric verses are in fact much more than that: they constitute the beginning of a poem upon which the entire slow movement is modelled (see Example 7). Moreover, Sternau's poem provides the key which unlocks a series of extrageneric associations that extend well beyond this single Andante.

The two Andante movements, it will be recalled, were composed before the rest of the movements of Op. 5, and they can stand alone as a pair of 'character pieces', the second a variation of the first.[23] (The titles 'Rückblick' and 'Intermezzo' on the second Andante are both creations of Brahms, the latter added, however, only in the engraver's model.) With the first of these Andantes Brahms made no attempt to follow the declamation of his poetic model, nor is the opening melody at all 'singable'. Although the overall ABA′ design of the movement is derived from the poem, the music only occasionally reflects the lower-level organization of the poem. Instead, melodic construction, texture, harmony, and variation procedure combine to create tonal analogues which convey the mood, imagery, and meaning of the poem: twilight descends to a measured chain of melodic and harmonic thirds in A♭ major (see Example 8); the moonlight shines forth to a broadening texture of ascending treble and descending bass moving towards a half-cadence on the dominant; a tonal shift to C♭ major introduces the realm of the 'two hearts in love', thus fully revealing the 'meaning' of the entwined thirds; and the extension of this phrase closes the period with rolling arpeggios, which Brahms typically uses in songs of bliss (cf. 'Wie bist du, meine Königen,' Op. 32 No. 9). Likewise, a duet of interlocking sixths, played *äußerst leise und zart* and arrayed over a soft tonic pedal on D♭, exquisitely renders into music the intimate love scene at the centre of the poem (see Example 9).[24] The full intensity of the lovers' passion is expressed in the strong, rising

---

[22] 'NB. Ich habe die "Sonate" schon zugesiegelt und mag mich nicht mehr aufhalten; so bitte ich Sie folgenden kleinen Vers über das *erste* Andante in Paranthese *klein* setzen zu lassen. Es ist zum Verständnis des Andante vielleicht nötig oder angenehm: [the lines by Sternau follow].' *Brahms Briefwechsel*, 14: 5.

The engraver's model for Op. 5 is now owned by the Staats- und Universitätsbibliothek, Hamburg. The manuscript is in Brahms's hand, except for the Scherzo, which was copied out by Julius Otto Grimm. At the beginning of the second movement (p. 9) one can see the Sternau verses added in small script (but not in parentheses), with the direction '(Sehr kleine Schrift)' (a facsimile of the page appears in Christiane Jacobsen, *Johannes Brahms: Leben und Werk*, 129).

[23] Among Brahms's songs there are four instances where two songs were composed on common melodic material and published together: the two 'Liebe und Frühling' (Hoffmann von Fallersleben), Op. 3 Nos. 2 and 3 (July 1853); 'Scheiden und Meiden' and 'In der Ferne' (Ludwig Uhland), Op. 19 Nos. 2 and 3 (Oct. 1858); 'Regenlieder' and 'Nachklang' (Klaus Groth), Op. 59 Nos. 3 and 4 (1873); and 'Sommerabend' and 'Mondenschein' (Heine), Op. 85 Nos. 1 and 2 (May 1878).

[24] In his essay 'Brahms and the Waltz', Ernest Newman termed parallel thirds and sixths 'those great instruments of the sentimental, that seem to symbolize the soulful German sweethearts clasping hands and gazing into each other's eyes'.

Example 7. C. O. Sternau, *Junge Liebe* (*Young Love*): Poem related to the first Andante of the Piano Sonata in F minor, Op. 5 (movement 2).

| | |
|---|---|
| Der Abend dämmert, das Mondlicht scheint, | Twilight is falling, moonlight shines, |
| Da sind zwei Herzen in Liebe vereint | there two hearts are united in love |
| Und halten sich selig umfangen. | and keep themselves enclosed in bliss. |
| Es weht und rauschet durch die Luft, | It wafts and rustles through the air, |
| Als brächten die Rosen all ihren Duft, | as if the roses were yielding all their fragrance, |
| Als kämen die Englein gegangen. | as if the little angels came on foot. |
| | |
| Ich küsse Dich zum ersten Mal, | I kiss you for the first time, |
| Ich küsse Dich viel tausend Mal. | I kiss you many thousand times. |
| Ich küsse Dich immer wieder; | I kiss you again and again; |
| Auf Deine Wangen lange Zeit | Down your cheeks, for a long time, |
| Rollt manche Träne der Seligkeit | roll many tears of blissfulness |
| Wie eine Perle nieder. | like pearls. |
| | |
| Die Stunde verrauscht, der Morgen scheint, | The hours pass away, the morning appears, |
| Wir sind noch immer in Liebe vereint | we are still united in love |
| Und halten uns selig umfangen. | and keep ourselves enclosed in bliss. |
| Es weht und rauschet durch die Luft, | It wafts and rustles through the air, |
| Als brächten die Rosen all ihren Duft, | as if the roses were yielding all their fragrance, |
| Als kämen die Englein gegangen. | as if the little angels came on foot. |

Poem according to Kalbeck, *Brahms*, 1: 120–1.

EXAMPLE 8.  Brahms, Piano Sonata in F minor, Op. 5, II, bars 1–10.

EXAMPLE 9. Brahms, Piano Sonata in F minor, Op. 5, II, bars 37–44.

sequential melody, accompanied by ardent triplets, which rounds out the central binary unit (bars 68 ff.). When the time for parting arrives, foreshadowed by an inflection from Db major to Db minor (bars 100 ff.), the initial melody returns, but now varied: the accompanimental pattern of the love-scene lingers, as do the lovers in the poem, their duet coloured by both a bittersweet tinge of minor (marked *sostenuto*, bar 109) and 'awakening' melodic seconds (bar 110).

On first perusal, the coda would seem merely to function as a 'textless' postlude, another grand apotheosis of a poet's love, as in the Op. 1 Andante (the coda uses the melody, key, and texture of the central love scene; see Example 10*a*). Yet there may well be another way to 'read' this section, for, as Adolf Schubring pointed out as long ago as 1862, the melody here bears a strong resemblance to the German 'folk-song' 'Steh' ich in finst'rer Mitternacht'. In this sentimental song a young soldier on midnight watch in a foreign land recalls his affectionate parting from his now distant beloved and wonders whether she remains true to him (see Examples 10*b* and 11).[25] This association would account for the retrospective nature of the coda and would also explain why Brahms chose to end the movement in Db major, presumably the key of the soldier's memories of his beloved, rather than Ab major, which now appears only to have been an illusory 'home' key. Such an interpretation of the coda is also consistent with the poetic content of the ensuing 'Rückblick'.[26]

---

[25] 'Schumanniana Nr. 8: Die Schumann'sche Schule: IV. Johannes Brahms', 103. I wish to thank Walter Frisch for calling my attention to Schubring's article. Professor Frisch examines Schubring's critical writings on Brahms's early works in 'Brahms and Schubring'. Also cf. Walter Niemann, *Brahms*, 188 (trans., 222). The text of this 'folk-song' is attributed to Wilhelm Hauff by Schubring and in Friedrich Silcher's *100 Volkslieder*, 76.

   Although Max Kalbeck did not connect Brahms's melody to this folk-song, he did note its similarity to Hans Sachs's 'Dem Vogel, der heut' sang' in Act 2 of Wagner's *Die Meistersinger*. Kalbeck speculated on how Wagner's melody might well have been based on Brahms's (*Brahms*, 1: 216–17, 2: 120), yet such a resemblance need not suggest more than common folk origins. The similarity of countermelody and accompaniment, however, strengthens Kalbeck's case.

[26] Detlef Kraus, in his essay 'Das Andante aus der Sonate Op. 5 von Brahms: Versuch einer Interpretation', tried to match just the initial three lines of stanza one of Sternau's poem (that is, the lines present in the 'motto' published at the head of the movement) with various points in the Andante: 'Der Abend dämmert' = bars 1 ff.; 'das Mondlich scheint' = bars 11 ff.; 'da sind zwei Herzen in Liebe vereint' = bars 37 ff.; 'und halten sich selig umfangen' = bars 68 ff. Kraus's approach is not unperceptive, but it encounters one major problem, which he readily admits: how does one account for the reprise of the opening section (bars 105 ff.)? Kraus can only credit the reprise to the demands of 'the inner logic of the piece', noting that 'for Brahms the musician, form was always a *conditio sine qua non*'. Taking the entire poem into consideration allows a fuller and more consistent explanation for the influence of word on tone in this movement.

EXAMPLE 10. (a) Brahms, Piano Sonata in F minor, Op. 5, II, bars 144–50. (b) Friedrich Silcher, 'Steh' ich in finst'rer Mitternacht'.

Max Kalbeck was the first to suggest that the second Andante in Op. 5 may also have been based on a Sternau poem—the three-stanza lyric entitled 'Bitte' which Brahms entered into an early notebook of poetry directly after 'Der Abend dämmert'.[27] The poem is indeed a 'Rückblick', recalling a blessed and blissful love which lasted, however, only one short year (see Example 12). Furthermore, the words of Sternau's poem can actually be sung to Brahms's Andante, and virtually all details of musical punctuation, form, texture, harmony, and melody can be attributed to the influence of the poem. Noteworthy are the transformation of the radiant $\hat{3}$–$\hat{1}$ that crowns the final, full Db major chords in the first Andante into the isolated, unsupported $\hat{5}$–$\hat{3}$ dyad in Bb minor which begins this loveless recollection (see Example 13); the reminiscent contour of the ensuing melody which now, however, instead of entwined thirds, consists merely of the pitches of the tonic minor chord; the muffled, fateful drum rolls in the bass which echo the hollow fourths ($\hat{8}$–$\hat{5}$) in the melody; the solidly established key areas which bespeak the irreversibility of the poet's situation; the extremely literal rendition of the line 'an dem verstummt des Herzens Schlag' by means of washes of proto-impressionistic sound (hollow fifths which create, but do not contain thirds), ending in halting chords, then silence (Example 14); and the deepened gloom of the recapitulation, with its rumbling dominant pedal and its poignant mixture of major and minor mode at the cadence.

As the autograph manuscript reveals, the first section of the piece (bars 1–12) was originally to be repeated. In that state the formal scheme of the 'Rückblick' would have been identical to that of the A section in the first Andante, thereby providing, in effect, the final varied A section 'missing' from the initial Andante. With the shift into Bb minor for the second Andante, the progression Ab major–Db major–Bb minor latent in the tonally ambiguous opening gesture of the first Andante finds its projection across the full span of the two movements. The second Andante continues the slower tempo with

In his remarks on the coda, Kraus sees Brahms drawing upon the folk-song 'Steh' ich in finst'rer Mitternacht' for the quiet mood in which the section begins and for the repetitive accompanimental notes, which Kraus suggests portray the lover's warmly beating heart and growing rapture. Schubring, in 'Schumanniana Nr. 8', interprets the coda in the following manner: 'Brahms allows his lovers . . . repeatedly to make their sweetest farewell, to call to each other their last "Ade" from the distance (cf. the two last lines [of the third section, bars 138–43, in the] top voice: "Ade, Ade"; in the lower voice, footsteps becoming ever fainter); the male lover is left behind, "in the darkness of midnight, he stands so lonely on his still watch"; all [is] quiet—lightly he hums to himself Hauff's "Schildwachtlied"; "his heart beats warmly, he thinks about the distant love", and ever more loudly he sings forth into the night with joy: "She loves me truly, she is good to me". [Schubring then cites the entire fourth stanza of the Hauff's poem.] The situation is now a different one from when the loved one descended to him—and for this reason the A flat major Andante closes with a pious Adagio in D flat major' ['läßt Brahms seine Liebenden . . . wiederholt den zärtlichsten Abschied nehmen, sich die letzten Ade noch aus der Entfernung zurufen (vergleich . . . Oberstimme: Ade, Ade, in der Unterstimme verhallende Schritte); der Liebende bleibt allein zurück, "in finstrer Mitternacht, steht er so einsam auf der stillen Wacht"; Alles still—leise summt er das Hauff'sche Schildwachtlied vor sich hin; "sein Herz schlägt warm, denkt er ans ferne Lieb", und laut und immer lauter jubelt er dann in die Nacht hinaus: "Sie liebt mich treu, sie ist mir gut". . . . Die Situation ist jetzt eine andere, als da die Liebste zu ihm herabstieg—und deshalb schließt das As dur-Andante mit einem frommen Adagio in Des dur']. Schubring's substitution of 'stillen' for 'fernen' in the first stanza is crucial, for it led him to view the distance between the lovers and the time since their last meeting as considerably less than the poem implies. Neither Kraus nor Schubring consider the Andante in relationship to the second Andante in the sonata.

²⁷ *Brahms*, 1: 121. This notebook is now owned by the Stadt- und Landesbibliothek, Vienna (HIN 55.734).

Example 11. Wilhelm Hauff, 'Steh' ich in finst'rer Mitternacht'.

| | |
|---|---|
| Steh' ich in finst'rer Mitternacht<br>So einsam auf der fernen Wacht:<br>So denk' ich an mein fernes Lieb,<br>Ob mir's auch treu und hold verblieb. | I stand in the darkness of midnight,<br>so lonely on a foreign guard;<br>thus I think about my distant love,<br>whether she also remains true and pleased with me. |
| Als ich zur Fahne fortgemüßt,<br>Hat sie so herzlich mich geküßt,<br>Mit Bändern meinen Hut geschmückt,<br>Und weinend mich an's Herz gedrückt. | When I had to go forth to my company,<br>she kissed me so affectionately,<br>adorned my hat with ribbons,<br>and crying pressed me to her heart. |
| Sie liebt mich noch, sie ist mir gut,<br>Drum bin ich froh und wohlgemuth.<br>Mein Herz schlägt warm in kalter Nacht,<br>Wenn es an's treue Lieb gedacht. | She loves me still, she is good to me,<br>therefore I am happy and cheerful.<br>My heart beats warmly in the cold night,<br>when it thinks about my true love. |
| Jetzt bei der Lampe mildem Schein<br>Gehst du wohl in dein Kämmerlein,<br>Und schickst dein Nachtgebet zum Herrn,<br>Auch für den Liebsten in der Fern'. | Now by the mild light of the lamp<br>you are probably going into your little room,<br>and will send your evening prayer to the Lord,<br>also for your beloved far away. |
| Doch wenn du traurig bist und weinst,<br>Mich von Gefahr umrungen meinst:<br>Sei ruhig, bin in Gottes Hut,<br>Er liebt ein treu Soldatenblut. | Yet if you are sad and cry,<br>if you think me encircled by danger,<br>be at peace, I am in God's care,<br>He loves a true-blooded soldier. |
| Die Glocke schlägt, bald naht die Rund',<br>Und löst mich ab zu dieser Stund';<br>Schlaf' wohl im stillen Kämmerlein,<br>Und denk' in deinen Träumen mein. | The clock strikes, soon the patrol will draw near,<br>and relieve me at this hour;<br>sleep well in your quiet little room,<br>and think of me in your dreams. |

Poem according to Friedrich Silcher, *100 Volkslieder für eine Singstimme mit Begleitung des Pianoforte*, 76.

Example 12. C. O. Sternau, *Bitte (Request)*: Poem related to the second Andante of the Piano Sonata in F minor, Op. 5 (movement 4).

| | |
|---|---|
| O wüßtest du, wie bald, wie bald<br>Die Bäume welk und kahl der Wald,<br>Du wärst so kalt und lieblos nicht<br>Und sähst mir freundlich ins Gesicht! | O, if only you knew how soon, how soon<br>the tree withers and the forest is barren,<br>if you would not be so cold and loveless<br>and would look me in the face in a friendly manner! |
| Ein Jahr ist kurz und kurz die Zeit,<br>Wo Liebeslust und Glück gedeiht,<br>Wie bald kommt dann der trübe Tag,<br>An dem verstummt des Herzens Schlag. | A year is short, and short is the time,<br>for the delight and bliss of love to thrive,<br>how soon then comes the sad day<br>for the silencing of the heart's beat. |

O schau mich nicht so lieblos an,          O, do not look at me so lovelessly,
Kurz ist die Zeit und kurz der Wahn!        short is the time and short the delusion!
Der Liebe Seligkeit und Glück               The blessedness and bliss of love
Bringt keine Träne dir zurück!              brings back no tears to you!

Poem according to Kalbeck, *Brahms*, 1: 121.

EXAMPLE 13.  Brahms, Piano Sonata in F minor, Op. 5, II, bars 186–91, and IV, bars 1–8.

EXAMPLE 14. Brahms, Piano Sonata in F minor, Op. 5, IV, bars 19–25.

EXAMPLE 15. Brahms, Piano Sonata in F minor, Op. 5, IV, bars 37–53.

which the first Andante closed, and the two movements are also linked by the 'textless' codetta which ends the 'Rückblick' with one last reference to the soldier's song of the first Andante, now cast in a shape grotesquely warped by the insistent inclusion of the dissonant ♭2̂ and set over the ominous bass motive (Example 15; see bars 38–42). After a brief pause, the opening melody reappears, but remains in its isolated, 'loveless' state. In the end, only a solo line is left to descend to a deep, solitary tonic. The plagal cadence which ends the movement provides one last ironic touch: just such a cadence had closed the 'apotheosis' coda of the first Andante.

# V

Charles Rosen notes elsewhere in the present volume that 'there is a precedent for almost everything in Brahms', and indeed much effort in this collection of papers is devoted specifically to linking Brahms to his musical tradition.[28] But with a composer so steeped in Romantic poetry and for whom song was a central and lifelong preoccupation, one is well advised to consider poetic as well as musical models, whenever possible. In the Andantes of the early piano sonatas, the model poems predetermine both the formal structure and the 'expressive content' of the music. Particular situations and specific emotions, as well as general moods and feelings, find tonal analogues that are often quite original and arresting. The relationship between text and music is as in song, but here with actual words suppressed. In subsequent works, even among the piano pieces of Brahms's final years, other 'poetic' Andantes can be identified. (I will make mention of these movements near the end of this study.) Still, pieces with such clear links to poetry form only a small part of Brahms's instrumental *œuvre*. While an understanding of the fusion of word and tone in these pieces may be important in itself—and, as with Lieder, instructive to the performer—study of these Andantes might not seem central to an understanding of Brahms's instrumental music in general. Not at least until one recalls the cases cited near the outset of this paper—the autobiographical remarks Brahms made about the Piano Quartet, Op. 60, the relationship of the slow movement in the First Piano Concerto to Clara Schumann, and the Agathe cypher in the String Sextet, Op. 36—or considers, for instance, that movements in two of the Violin Sonatas are based on melodies from Brahms's settings of Klaus Groth poems.

But how is one to deal with such 'extramusical' promptings, beyond merely citing their existence, as many writers have done? The task may well prove impossible, particularly in cases where the role of 'abstract' musical models seems every bit as important as the influence of poetic ones. Yet with the Sonata in F minor, Op. 5, we may have an opportunity to undertake such exploration. Not only did its three Allegro movements grow up around and draw musical material from its two 'poetic' Andantes— the implication being that the 'meaning' of the musical material might also have been

---

[28] Also cf. Charles Rosen, 'Influence: Plagiarism and Inspiration', 91–100; James Webster, 'Schubert's Sonata Forms and Brahms's First Maturity'.

taken over from the Andantes into the fast movements—but the musical form of the opening and closing Allegros is quite unorthodox, seeming to draw upon no specific historical models.

The first movement of this work, as Walter Frisch has noted in a penetrating analysis, is 'a highly unusual sonata structure . . . novel and without precedent'.[29] Certain of its gross features seem to conform to the norms of Classical sonata structure, but analysts have generally been at a loss to account for such events as an exposition which ends in the submediant major (D♭) and a development which for the most part remains in that key and concerns itself chiefly with the presentation of a full-blown 'new' theme (bars 90 ff.). And how is one to explain all those short thematic episodes separated by pauses (bars 1–6, 7–16, 16–22), and such unusual tonal features as the sudden modal shifts and 'bizarre harmonic syntax' (Frisch) which dominate the transition from first to second thematic group (bars 23–38)?

Frisch has convincingly demonstrated how the movement 'unfolds not as an essay in thematic development', but as successive transformations of the two contrasting yet intimately related motives that together comprise the opening musical gesture of the

EXAMPLE 16. Brahms, Piano Sonata in F minor, Op. 5, I, bars 1–11.

[29] *Brahms and the Principle of Developing Variation*, 40 and 52. Frisch's analysis appears on pp. 36–52.

movement—*x* (A♭–G–F–D♭), with its mercurial upward leap, and the more stable *y* (A♭–G–F–G), which circles about a central pitch (see Example 16). I think he comes closest to the mark when he describes the various subsequent manifestations of these motives as 'a series of discreet character studies'.[30] We have already seen how the two Andantes in this sonata paint a portrait of love and eventual betrayal, and it would not seem out of order to posit that the 'character' introduced and examined musically in the first movement is that of the poet of the Andantes. We need not pursue this hypothesis very far before it begins to provide a means for explaining those musical events in the movement which have heretofore remained puzzling.

The initial two phrases stand in stark contrast to each other, but close inspection reveals them actually as two strongly differentiated facets of the same 'character'. In the first phrase, the upwardly surging *x*, set over a strong, descending chromatic bass, initially dominates (bars 1–4), but in the end it is the more stable *y* which emerges in a broad statement in parallel sixths and double octaves (bars 5–6). The next phrase (bars 7–11) immediately begins to develop *y*; the mood is both serious and agitated, as the motive is sounded in the dominant *minor*, repeated, fragmented, and metrically altered. In the third phrase (bars 12–16), the motive moves to the still more remote secondary dominant minor (G minor). Bars 7–16 are dominated throughout by sombre low and middle registers and never rise in volume above piano, with the duple right hand, in triple metre, brooding above a pedal of droning fifths played as triplets in duple metre. On the one hand, our poet seems flamboyant, striving, and, as things subsequently develop, erratic in nature; on the other hand, he reveals a serious, restrained, introspective side to his personality.

The strong duality of personality presented here provides the decisive clue to the identity of our poet: at the time Brahms composed the Sonata in F minor, he signed all his compositions 'Johannes Kreisler, jun.', a *nom de plume* taken from a fictional Kapellmeister created by E. T. A. Hoffmann, and we know that Brahms strongly identified his own character with that of Kreisler, whose personality, we read in the novel *Kater Murr*, was extremely volatile and whose music was 'fragmentary, "bizarre" . . . and painfully expressive', but who, upon seeing his reflection in a lake, recognized that 'the person who is going next to me down there is a calm, thoughtful man who, no longer buzzing wildly around in vague, endless spaces, holds firmly to the established path'.[31] The opening episodes of the Sonata in F minor can thus be interpreted as representing the dual nature of the Brahms–Kreisler personality, with the introspective side of our poet-composer rendered by musical means quintessentially 'Brahmsian'.

The two facets of personality delineated here by Brahms echo, of course, those created by Robert Schumann in Florestan and Eusebius, themselves modelled on the twins Vult and Walt in Jean Paul Richter's novel *Die Flegeljahre* (published 1804–5). It should be remembered that Brahms is said to have undertaken his first serious study of Schumann's

---

[30] *Brahms and the Principle of Developing Variation*, 39.

[31] Cf. Siegfried Kross, 'Brahms and E. T. A. Hoffmann', and also the relevant chapters in Floros, *Brahms und Bruckner*. The passages from *Kater Murr*, also quoted in Kross's article, are taken from the translation by Leonard J. Kent and Elizabeth C. Knight.

music in Mehlem during September 1853, shortly before meeting Schumann for the first time. The initial movement of Op. 5, as well as the other two fast movements, was composed soon after, while Brahms was residing with the Schumanns in Düsseldorf.[32]

The rest of the first movement can be seen as a working out of the fundamental conflicts in the Brahms–Kreisler personality, as symbolized and embodied in the motives *x* and *y*. At times, *x* predominates, as in the *fest und bestimmt* transition (bars 23–38), where it is heard on two contrasting metrical levels and in a series of disjointed chord progressions and unprepared modal shifts. On other occasions, *y* seems to gain the upper hand, as, for example, in the lyrical second theme (Example 17), where the appoggiaturas of *y* exert a tempering influence on *x*, an effect that lingers even into the codetta, where the accelerando and hemiolas of *x* (bars 56–9, 62–5) are quelled by a chromatic, inverted, sostenuto variant of *y* (bars 60–1, 66–8).

EXAMPLE 17.  Brahms, Piano Sonata in F minor, Op. 5, I, bars 39–47.

In the manuscript of the Sonata, Op. 5, now owned by the Staats- und Universitätsbibliothek in Hamburg, the Hoffmannesque pseudonym is signed at the end of the last movement, while the double bars that end movements 1, 2, 4, and 5 are each embellished into an elaborate *B*. (Kross is incorrect when he states on p. 193 that such a *B* appears at the end of each movement; none is to be found at the end of movement 3, for that movement in the Hamburg manuscript, as noted earlier, is not autograph, but was copied by Julius Otto Grimm.)

To Kross's list of Brahms manuscripts signed 'Johannes Kreisler jun.' (or some variant of this; cf. p. 193) must be added the autographs of the Sonata in F♯ minor, Op. 2 (the present location of this manuscript, once owned by Albert Dietrich, is unknown, but a description of it appeared in Liepmannssohn Katalog 38 [May 1909; auction of items from the Dietrich estate]) and the *Lieder und Gesänge*, Opp. 3 and 6 (once owned by Julius Otto Grimm, now in the Library of Congress, Washington, DC, and the Gesellschaft der Musikfreunde, Vienna, respectively). Furthermore, the autograph of the Rondo after Weber (Anh. Ia/1, No.2) which Kross cites is dated 'März 1852'.

[32] The clearest documentary evidence of the Brahms–Kreisler dual personality is provided by the autograph of the Schumann Variations, Op. 9, and a letter from Brahms to Clara Schumann written during the summer of 1854, both items to be cited later in this paper. The theme of duality of personality held a particular attraction for the nineteenth century; cf., for instance, E. T. A. Hoffmann's *Die Doppeltgänger* (*The Doubles*, 1822) and Robert Louis Stevenson's *Doctor Jekyll and Mr. Hyde* (1886). For a discussion of Hoffmann's artist-hero Johannes Kreisler, see, in addition to Kross's 'Brahms and E. T. A. Hoffmann', Horst S. Daemmrich's *The Shattered Self: E. T. A. Hoffmann's Tragic Vision*, particularly 39–46; for a summary and discussion of Richter's *Die Flegeljahre*, see Dorothea Berger, *Jean Paul Friedrich Richter*, 96–125; on Schumann and Richter, especially *Die Flegeljahre*, see Edward A. Lippman, 'Theory and Practice in Schumann's Aesthetics', and Eric Sams, 'Schumann and the Tonal Analogue'.

EXAMPLE 18. Brahms, Piano Sonata in F minor, Op. 5, I, bars 90–109.

As Frisch has noted, the more tranquil motive *y* achieves its grandest transformation in the 'new' theme of the development section (Example 18),[33] and for a moment we seem to be privy to the poet's sincerest and most intimate aspirations. Their precise nature is left ambiguous, although the soaring sequential theme, spun out over an ascending chromatic bass (the 'positive' inversion of the bass in the opening phrase) and accompanied by throbbing chords, bears clear kinship to many another Romantic 'love' theme (cf., for instance, the slow movement of Schumann's Second Symphony).[34] And

---

[33] *Brahms and the Principle of Developing Variation*, 49.

[34] In a letter to Clara Schumann written on 8 Dec. 1855, Brahms declared the Second his favourite Schumann symphony, and the Adagio his favourite movement. In the slow movement of the Symphony in C major, Newcomb hears 'a mood of melancholy pathos and suffering' ('Once More "Between Absolute and Program Music" ', 243). Brahms heard something more: 'Such an Adagio only a German can compose, [for] only his deeply serious eye [can] still look [forth] full of love amidst great suffering' ['Solch Adagio kann nur ein Deutscher komponieren, nur sein tiefernstes Auge blickt noch voll Liebe in größtem Schmerz'] (Litzmann, ed., *Schumann-Brahms Briefe*, 1: 160).

indeed, when it again emerges, first as the theme of the love-scene in the central section of the initial 'poetic' Andante, then in the grand coda of the same movement, as the distant lover recalls those precious moments, and finally in the codetta of the second Andante, there transformed into a reminiscence of love lost, the association of theme and meaning becomes complete (cf. Examples 9, 10*a*, and 15).

One should also note that all of these full statements of the *y*-derived theme are in D♭ major (except, of course, the one in the 'Rückblick', which is appropriately transposed into B♭ minor). Thus, both theme *and* key are associated with the realization of the poet's aspirations—defined by the first Andante as the union of the poet's true nature, the stable, 'Brahmsian' side of his personality, with an ideal beloved. This in turn explains why it is always the 'warm embraces' (Frisch) of D♭ major, whether as a momentary harmony (as at the end of the transition, bars 35 and 37, here emphasized by dramatic registral shifts), a temporary tonal plateau (as at the end of the exposition, bars 68–70), or a full key area (the 'new' theme in the development), that provide the poet with moments of repose amidst his struggles.

Framing the lyrical theme in the development are two boldly striving passages based on the initial phrase of the movement. The second of these, labelled *maestoso* (bars 119 ff.), seems to be leading back to the opening episode and key when suddenly the quiet, pulsating accompaniment of the central theme is recalled (bars 123 ff.). Still under its influence, the recapitulation begins pianissimo, *misterioso* (bars 131 ff.). In the coda, the opening phrase is heard again, now in a bright, triumphant F major (bars 200 ff.). An inflection to D♭ major and its subdominant occurs (bars 202–3), but exerts little influence. As the movement closes, *y* is entirely absent; we are left with a cadential formula derived from the impetuous *x*.

The vigorous Scherzo which follows the love-apotheosis of the second movement is, like the first movement, cast in the poet's F minor. Moreover, while its treble melody reiterates the shape of the initial Andante theme, its rising chromatic bass, with many small tensions immediately resolved, recalls the bass of the grand D♭ major theme of the first movement, a bass which itself was derived from the opening phrase of that movement, as already noted. Thus, the series of interrelated 'character studies' continues. Not surprisingly, the contrasting key established in the chordal Trio is again D♭ major.

At the beginning of the finale—that is, after the reflection on lost love presented in the 'Rückblick'—we find the poet in a sardonic mood of mounting agitation (again the rising chromatic bass) and momentary outbursts. Like the 'Rückblick', this section ends on a bleak unison tonic. Suddenly the mood changes: a broad theme is spun forth, *con espressione* and full of life from its quivering accompaniment (Example 19). Again the bass rises below a soaring melodic sequence, but all motion is now diatonic. The poet at last sings forth in the tonic major, and a sense of wholeness, of well-being seems to permeate his theme. Though a certain sadness lingers (the A and D minor between the F major poles of the first phrase), the poet now seems to be moving away from his brooding and back into the mainstream of life. The initial pitches of the theme provide confirmation for this interpretation: F–A–E, *Frei aber einsam*, was the motto Joseph

EXAMPLE 19. Brahms, Piano Sonata in F minor, Op. 5, V, bars 37–51.

Joachim used to express his attitude towards bachelorhood, a motto woven into the famous 'F–A–E' Sonata which Brahms, Robert Schumann, and Albert Dietrich composed for Joachim during the same month that Brahms was completing the Sonata in F minor, Op. 5. Note in this case how the motto is isolated rhythmically, how its two harmonies connected by an ambivalent dyad (F major moving to A minor) perfectly translate into musical terms its two adjectives linked by the conjunction *aber*, and how the ties joining the dyad to its common pitches on either side provide a musical equivalent of the motto's hyphenation.[35]

The sardonic mood that opened the movement eventually returns, and now in the key

---

[35] On the origins of this motto, see Joachim's letter to Robert Schumann, 29 Nov. 1853, in Johannes Joachim and Andreas Moser, *Briefe von und an Joseph Joachim*, 1: 109. Cf. also Michael Musgrave, '*Frei aber Froh*: A Reconsideration'; Reynolds, 'A Choral Symphony by Brahms?', 4; and A. Peter Brown, 'Brahms' Third Symphony and the New German School'.

EXAMPLE 20. Brahms, Piano Sonata in F minor, Op. 5, V, bars 140–7.

of the love scene, D♭ major (bars 78 ff.), but it is ultimately replaced by a hymn-like theme that enters in the same key and is again derived from the head motives of the first movement and from the D♭ major themes (Example 20). Yet, instead of leaping upwards, as does *x*, or circling on itself, as does *y*, here the descending $\hat{3}$–$\hat{2}$–$\hat{1}$ is followed by a controlled drop to $\hat{5}$, all set over stable diatonic chords and a pedal-point. (The sequential repetition of this four-note cell in bars 141–2 restates the actual pitches of the original statement of *x* in movement 1, but now with D♭ in the lower octave; *y* provides the cadential formula, bars 146–7, as it had in the first phrase of movement 1, but here in inversion; and the ascending bass line of bars 144–7 recalls the descending bass that opened the sonata; cf., Example 16.) The poet finally seems at one with himself, at least while in the key of D♭ major. Emotional intensity is then generated by renditions of this melody in stretto (bars 164 ff.). The sardonic melody attempts a reappearance, at first briefly over the hymn-like melody (bars 195 ff.), and then as an independent section (bars 215 ff.), but even *its* mood has changed, for its rising bass is now diatonic rather than chromatic. At last the hymn-like theme returns (bars 249 ff.), now in the home key and major mode, and in one form or another, and with mounting intensity, it dominates the rest of the movement. A final plagal cadence in F major recalls the plagal cadences which closed the two Andantes and brings this musical essay to an end.[36]

[36] Anthony Newcomb's analysis of Schumann's Second Symphony (in 'Once More "Between Absolute and Program Music" ') as a kind of *Bildungsroman* in music, a 'quasi-dramatic evolution and interaction' of themes organized according to a plot archetype of 'suffering leading to healing or redemption' (a plot which had also served Beethoven in his Fifth and Ninth Symphonies) yields results similar to the present assessment of Brahms's Sonata in F minor. Newcomb observes that 'the manner in which one theme is generated by and interacts with another . . is laden with metaphorical meaning' and advises that the analyst 'think of the thematic units partly as characters in a narrative, transformed by the requirements of various different contexts, while remaining recognizably related to their previous selves' (pp. 236–7). The thematic units 'interact with each other, with the plot archetypes, with their own past guises, and with conventions of musical grammar and formal schemes analogously to the way the characters in a novel interact with each other and with the moral and legal conventions that shape the situations'. The overall construction of Brahms's sonata also finds precedent in Schumann's symphony, which, as Newcomb observes, displays a 'limited reliance on tonal effects and restricted tonal spectrum' and has an 'end-accented' organization that 'throws considerable weight on [the work's] last movement', which serves to 'draw together the threads of the entire symphony that has gone before'. It is not surprising that the young Brahms would be so fond of this work (cf. n. 34). (As for connections between this symphony and earlier works, a topic treated by Newcomb, Brahms remarked to Frau Schumann in his letter of 8 Dec. 1855 that 'an echo of this beautiful Adagio in Bach's *Musical Offering* will interest you, if you do not know of it [already]'. The reference, no doubt, is to the descending chromatic line present in Bach's theme and in the counterpoint of the fugal section at the middle of Schumann's movement.)

# VI

After Op. 5 Brahms abandoned the genre of piano sonata, but not the composition of 'poetic' Andantes. In the Ballades, Op. 10, composed in the summer of 1854, the Scottish ballad 'Edward' exercised a powerful influence over musical events even beyond the first Andante. In the 'Little Variations on a Theme by Him [Robert Schumann] for Her [Clara Schumann]', Op. 9, composed during the same summer, 'Brahms' and 'Kreisler' rejoined their struggle: in the autograph, the mercurial Allegros are initialled *Kr*, the pensive Andantes, *Br*,[37] and in a letter of mid-August, Brahms wrote to Clara Schumann that he often argued with himself, 'which means that Kreisler and Brahms are quarreling . . . usually each has his own opinion and they fight it out, but this time both are utterly confused, and neither knows what he wants'.[38]

In 1892, near the end of his career as a composer, Brahms again created a cycle of 'poetic' Andantes, the Intermezzi, Op. 117, which he called 'three lullabies to my sorrows'.[39] The first two pieces form a musically related pair which draw formal and dramatic inspiration from J. G. von Herder's 'Lullaby of an Abandoned Mother' ('Wiegenlied einer unglücklichen Mutter', translated from the Scottish ballade 'Lady Anne Bothwell's Lament' and published in *Stimmen der Völker in Liedern*), which begins 'Schlaf sanft mein Kind'. The E♭ major Intermezzo 'sets' strophes 1–3, the B♭ minor

For discussion of extramusical reference in Schumann's music, see Thomas Alan Brown, *The Aesthetics of Robert Schumann*; Edward A. Lippman, 'Theory and Practice in Schumann's Aesthetics'; Leon Plantinga, *Schumann as Critic*; and Eric Sams, 'Schumann and the Tonal Analogue', among others.

[37] The autograph of Op. 9, which Brahms sent to Clara Schumann in 1854, is now owned by the Gesellschaft der Musikfreunde in Vienna. The title reads: 'Kleine Variationen über ein Thema von Ihm. / Ihr zugeeignet'. On the Variations, Op. 9, cf. Kross, 'Brahms and E. T. A. Hoffmann', 193, 195 (facsimile of p. 7 of the autograph); Floros, *Brahms und Bruckner*, 115–43; and Oliver Neighbour, 'Brahms and Schumann: Two Opus Nines and Beyond'. One is reminded of the first edition of Schumann's *Davidsbündlertanze*, Op. 6, in which the individual pieces were signed by either Eusebius or Florestan, or by both, and in which indications of their behaviour were occasionally given. These indications were deleted for the second edition.

[38] 'Ich habe oft Streit mit mir, das heißt, Kreisler und Brahms streiten sich. Aber sonst hat jeder seine entschiedene Meinung und sicht die durch. Diesmal jedoch waren sie beide ganz konfus, keiner wußte, was er wollte, höchst possierlich war's anzusehen.' These remarks were written on 15 Aug. 1854 and appear in Litzmann, ed., *Schumann-Brahms Briefe*, 1: 9. On this occasion, Brahms was torn between continuing a trip on his own to the Black Forest or travelling to Ostende to be with Clara. Kross ('Brahms and E. T. A. Hoffmann', 199) is in error when he states that soon after Brahms wrote this letter 'Kreisler disappears completely from the biography of Brahms'. As late as 1860 Brahms signed the *Avertimento* outlining the bylaws for his women's choir in Hamburg 'Johannes Kreisler jun. alias: Brahms', and consideration of the conflicting aspects of the Brahms–Kreisler personality may well prove useful for 'interpreting' Brahms's First Piano Concerto (1854–9), as Kross himself suggests.

[39] 'Drei Wiegenlieder meiner Schmerzen' (Rudolf von der Leyen, *Johannes Brahms als Mensch und Freund*, 82). To Fritz Simrock, who had inquired about publishing the first of the Op. 117 pieces as a song, hoping this lullaby might becomes as popular as the famous Brahms 'Wiegenlied' (Op. 49 No. 4), Brahms wrote: 'It is unfortunately quite impossible to issue the thing as a lullaby. It would have to be entitled "Lullaby of an Unfortunate Mother" [Herder's title] or of a disconsolate bachelor, or with figures by [the artist Max] Klinger: "Sing Lullabies of my Sorrow!" ' ['Es geht leider durchaus nicht, daß man das Ding als Wiegen- oder Schlummerlied ausgibt. Es müßte dann ja dabeistehen "Wiegenlied einer unglücklichen Mutter" oder eines trostlosen Junggesellens, oder mit Klingerschen Figuren: "Singet Wiegenlieder meinem Schmerze!" '; *Brahms Briefwechsel*, 12: 89].

Intermezzo, strophes 4–7, while the final Andante, the Intermezzo in C♯ minor, can be shown to be informed (as Kalbeck was the first to suggest) by the structure and emotional content of yet another Scottish poem translated by Herder, a love-lament which begins 'O weh! o weh, hinab ins Thal'. (These two poems appear one after the other in Herder's collection and, like the two Sternau poems which Brahms 'set' in Op. 5, were copied by the composer into one of his poetry notebooks.[40])

The foregoing observations have demonstrated amply, if not exhaustively, the nature of the tonal analogues Brahms created to convey the 'expressive content' of his poetic models in the Andantes of the Piano Sonatas and to sketch the dual Kreisler–Brahms personality in the F minor Sonata. In these works there can be no doubt that 'the return, change, modification, and modulation of the motives are conditioned by their relation to a poetic idea', which is, of course, how Franz Liszt defined 'programme music'.[41] But this is also how a song composer sensitive to achieving word-tone synthesis proceeds, and in this sense one must view the young Brahms not as a composer of instrumental music who occasionally wrote songs, but rather as a tone poet whose lyric muse found expression principally through song, both with and without words.

Writing of Brahms's early songs in the famous essay 'Neue Bahnen', Robert Schumann observed how 'the poetry of [these works] would be understood even without words'.[42] This description applies equally to the early Andantes. And indeed herein lies the difference between Brahms 'the absolutist' and those contemporaries who composed 'programme' music. It is not that experience—personal or poetic—played no part in the inspiration and composition of Brahms's works, that his compositions were conceived only in 'abstract' terms and are thus devoid of 'extrageneric meaning'. All evidence, and most importantly the music itself, speaks against this. But in these works 'meaning' is translated from verbal into musical terms, and when the translation is complete and successful, appreciation of 'the beautiful' need no longer be dependent upon knowledge of the original 'experience', 'programme', or poetic model. The composition transcends its prosaic (or even poetic) underpinnings, escaping the verbal sphere and ultimately existing solely in the realm of music. Of the nature of this process, one finds no clearer description than that which Gustav Mahler provided to Max Marschalk, in explanation of his First Symphony:

---

[40] Stadt- und Landesbibliothek, Vienna (Ia 79.564, fo. 7ᵛ).

[41] 'In der Programm-Musik dagegen ist Wiederkehr, Wechsel, Veränderung und Modulation der Motive durch ihre Beziehung zu einem poetischen Gedanken bedingt.' *Franz Liszt Gesammelte Schriften*, 4: 69, trans. Roger Scruton in 'Programme Music', 15: 283. Liszt continued: 'All exclusively musical considerations, though they should not be neglected, have to be subordinated to the action of the given subject' ['Alle exklusiv musikalischen Rücksichten sind, obwohl keineswegs außer Acht gelassen, denen der Handlung des gegebenen Sujets untergeordnet']. To yield the prerogatives of music to this extent seems never to have been Brahms's aim, even in the early instrumental works.

[42] '. . . Lieder, deren Poesie man, ohne die Worte zu kennen, verstehen würde . . .', 185 (reprint, 2:301–2; trans., 253).

The real-life experience [is] the *reason* for the work, not its content . . . I find it banal to compose programme-music . . . despite the fact that the *reason* why a composition comes into being at all is bound to be something the composer has experienced, something real, which might after all be considered sufficiently concrete to be expressed in words . . . [But] as long as I can express an experience in words, I would never try to put it into music. The need to express myself musically—in symphonic terms—begins only on the plane of *obscure* feelings, at the gate that opens into the 'other world', the world in which things no longer fall apart in time and space.[43]

In the early Brahms works examined here the relationship between word and tone (and, one senses, between experience and music) is at times established in a very straightforward manner, and in such instances one blushes right along with the adolescent composer, so blatant are the tonal analogues, even for a listener without detailed foreknowledge of the underlying 'text'. To the degree that these works lack subtlety because of too direct and lasting a reliance upon their poetic models, they must be considered immature. Thus, for example, although the 'programme' offered here for the opening Allegro of the Sonata in F minor may help to account for the awkwardness of the transition in the exposition (and, one hopes, lead to a more intelligent and 'convincing' performance), the passage may none the less remain musically unsatisfying for many. The 'programme' can inspire the creation of music, and even suggest the emotional progress of the whole composition and many of its details, but ultimately the music must be judged on its own merits.

In the mid-1850s, after the publication of his first ten opera, Brahms experienced a compositional crisis. Although he was at work on the First Piano Concerto, various chamber pieces, and additional sets of variations for piano (the two in Op. 21 probably stem from this time), he seems all the while to have been conscious of shortcomings in his compositional skills. To provide himself with new models and to enchance his technique, he undertook close study of the music of his predecessors and of the art of counterpoint. In the rich series of works which followed, both directly and later in his career, experience—actual, emotional, poetic—continued to provide impetus for composition, as evidence already cited indicates. But now, with a more assured technique and a more mature emotional outlook, the master composer could create works which move well beyond the experience from whence they sprang. In these later works, verbal thought is transcended and music exists fully in its own terms—as 'sounds artistically combined', as musical essence which 'steals gently through the mind, / blossoming like spring flowers / and hovering like fragrance'.[44]

---

[43] Alma Mahler and Knud Martner, eds., *Selected Letters of Gustav Mahler*, 179.

[44] These lines are from Klaus Groth's poem 'Wie Melodien zieht es mir', so sensitively set to music by Brahms in 1886 (Op. 105 No. 1).

# CYCLIC TENDENCIES IN BRAHMS'S SONG COLLECTIONS

## IMOGEN FELLINGER

AFTER the funeral for Clara Schumann in Bonn on 24 May 1896, Brahms spent several days at the Hagerhof near Honnef on the Rhine in the circle of friends of the von Beckerath, the von der Leyen, and the Weyermann families. Here a private chamber music festival took place, and on 25 May, apart from the festival proper, Brahms first performed his *Vier ernste Gesänge*, Op. 121, and some of his *Choralvorspiele*, published posthumously as Op. 122.[1] At that time he made two important remarks regarding the texts of his vocal compositions and the grouping of his songs. In conversation with Gustav Ophüls, he mentioned that he had long wished to see prepared a collection of the poems he had set to music. Ophüls agreed to compile such a collection and shortly thereafter began work on his *Brahms-Texte: Vollständige Sammlung der von Johannes Brahms komponierten und musikalisch bearbeiteten Dichtungen* [*Brahms Texts: A Complete Collection of the Poems composed or musically arranged by Johannes Brahms*]. Hoping to establish the origins of Brahms's texts, Ophüls considered a wide variety of sources available to him, and he intended to discuss the final arrangement of the texts and the information about sources with Brahms. But the composer's final illness, which began at the end of June, prevented the execution of this plan. Instead of visiting Brahms, Ophüls wrote to him about several philological questions, but Brahms did not reply.[2] At the end of October, however, Rudolf von der Leyen received a letter from Brahms requesting that he explain to Ophüls that, although he had thought he and Ophüls were in agreement about the nature of the collection, apparently they were not. He reiterated his belief that the texts he had set to music 'would form a fine selection of poems; if simply written together, one could look at them with pleasure'. But he objected in the strongest terms to 'modern philological hairsplitting', which he felt was no concern of musicians.[3] Brahms obviously had in mind merely an anthology of the poems, not a scholarly tome. Accordingly, Ophüls recopied the whole volume, omitting all

---

[1] Cf. Gustav Ophüls, *Erinnerungen an Johannes Brahms*, 27–30 (new edn., 19–21).

[2] Ibid., 45–6 (28–9).

[3] 'Ich glaubte nämlich, er meine, wie ich, die von mir komponierten Texte gäben auch an sich eine recht hübsche Auswahl Gedichte; einfach zusammengeschrieben, könnte man sie mit Vergnügen betrachten'; 'moderne philologische Wortklauberei'. Ibid., 63–4 (37–8).

philological remarks. In December he sent the manuscript to Brahms.[4] The volume was published in 1898, the year after Brahms's death, by N. Simrock.[5]

The second remark Brahms made during these days at the Hagerhof was related to the first and concerned the performance of his songs. In a discussion with Heinz von Beckerath (1876–1964), son of Brahms's friend Alwin von Beckerath, 'Brahms complained that most male and female singers group his songs together [on their programmes] in a quite arbitrary manner, considering only what suits their voices, and not realizing how much trouble he had always taken to assemble his song compositions like a bouquet.' Beckerath speculated that the reason Brahms had made Ophüls wait so long for a reaction to his collection of Brahms's texts was because Ophüls had arranged them by author rather than by opus number. He said he had wanted the established succession of his song texts to be kept, so that one could read the texts 'to remember the music'. Brahms 'spoke of "Lieder-Sträuße" [bouquets of songs] which Ophüls had plucked apart'. Heinz von Beckerath sympathized with Brahms's complaint, noting that his songs were virtually never performed according to opus number, with the possible exception of the *Magelone* Romances, Op. 33. He observed the 'subtle tactfulness and poetic feeling' with which Brahms had bound his 'bouquets of songs' together and expressed the opinion that individual songs would profit greatly from being sung within the succession of songs established by the composer.[6]

There seem to be several reasons why singers selected and grouped Brahms's songs arbitrarily and tended to perform only certain ones, such as 'Feldeinsamkeit', Op. 86 No. 2, and 'Die Mainacht', Op. 43 No. 2. To begin with, during Brahms's lifetime it was not common to present whole cycles of songs, except on rare occasions, as when Julius Stockhausen first sang Schubert's *Die schöne Müllerin* and Schumann's *Dichterliebe* in their entirety in Vienna in 1857 and 1861. (On 30 April 1861 Brahms accompanied Stockhausen in presentations of these cycles, together with Beethoven's *An die ferne Geliebte*, in Hamburg; his own cycle, the *Magelone* Romances, Op. 33, was begun shortly after this.) As a rule, single songs or a selection of songs from such cycles were performed. The same was true for songs grouped within a single opus number. Heinz

---

[4] This manuscript is now owned by the Staats-und Universitätsbibliothek Hamburg. It should be emphasized that Brahms was not opposed to the inclusion of philological remarks, as is clear from his last letter to Ophüls, in December 1896, after he had received the revised manuscript. Brahms was now ready to answer Ophüls's questions, but thought 'that one should take care not to disturb the quiet reading of others with [such remarks]'. He apparently did not want philological comments included between the texts, but would condone them at the end of the volume. Ibid., 68–9 (40–1).

[5] A revised edition of this book was issued by the Deutsche Brahms-Gesellschaft in 1908, another in 1923, and in 1983 a newly edited and expanded version, prepared by Kristian Wachinger, was released.

[6] 'Brahms beklagte mir gegenüber, daß die meisten Sänger und Sängerinnen sich die Lieder ganz willkürlich zusammenstellten, wie sie gerade ihrer Stimme lägen, und garnicht beachteten, wie er sich stets große Mühe gegeben hätte, seine Liederkompositionen wie zu einem Bouket zusammenzustellen.' Von Beckerath continues: 'Mit welch feinem Taktgefühl und welch poetischem Empfinden hat er seine Liedersträuße zusammengebunden.' Regarding Ophüls's *Brahms-Texte*: 'sagte Brahms, er würde sich gefreut haben, die Texte, so wie er sie zusammengestellt hatte, durchzulesen und sich dabei an die Musik zu erinnern. Er sprach von Blumensträußen, die ihm Ophüls auseinandergepflückt hätte . . .' Heinz von Beckerath, 'Erinnerungen an Johannes Brahms', 4.

von Beckerath, however, noted an exception to this: the famous singer Raimund von Zur Mühlen (1854–1931), a pupil of Stockhausen, mostly sang full opera of Brahms's songs.[7]

Second, certain songs seem to have become favourites with audiences (and to have remained so ever since), and for this reason singers conscious of public taste may well have programmed these songs more often than others. And indeed those songs singled out by prominent critics such as Eduard Hanslick may have enjoyed greater local popularity from the very beginning.

Third, the nature of concert programming in the nineteenth century, at least in the early years of Brahms's compositional career, precluded the performance of large groups of songs. The singer often appeared only as an 'assisting artist' who performed a song or two between instrumental works. Even the 1861 Stockhausen–Brahms concert in Hamburg was 'mixed', including two pieces from Schumann's *Kreisleriana* (not the whole cycle) interspersed among the sixteen songs of Schumann's cycle *Dichterliebe*, in addition to the Beethoven cycle and Brahms's Second Serenade, Op. 16. Only in the later years of the century did this practice began to change, with the advent of vocal virtuosi such as Stockhausen, George Henschel, and Amalie Joachim, and later Hermine Spies and Alice Barbi. It should also be noted that when opera of songs were published, they were issued not only as a whole, but also in editions of individual songs and selections of songs, as well as in transposed keys and even in arrangements for solo pianoforte, without voice.[8]

From Brahms's remarks to von Beckerath and his criticism of Ophüls's edition of his texts, it would seem that he laid special emphasis on the sequence of texts within his opera and attached importance to the succession of his songs as he had determined it when ordering them for publication. And it might well be concluded that in performance, songs should not be selected to stand on their own or within groups devised by the singer, but rather should be left in relationship to the songs amongst which they are found within an opus. (Presumably, performance of Brahms's songs grouped by poet, except where that grouping is the composers, would also not have met with his approval.)

It is reasonable also to inquire how Brahms organized his opera of songs, how he meant the term 'bouquet' to be understood. Literally 'flowers picked and fastened together in a bunch',[9] this term is also commonly used figuratively in such phrases as 'bouquet of poems' or 'bouquet of Lieder'. But does this imply an organization tight enough to warrant the designation 'cyclic'? (It should be mentioned that Brahms himself never, to the best of our knowledge, used the term 'cycle', even for the *Magelone* Romances, which is a genuine song cycle.) Brahms probably chose his word well, and it would seem that for him 'bouquet' did not correspond with 'cycle'. The term implies a

---

[7] Ibid.

[8] Three of Theodor Kirchner's arrangements of Brahms songs for solo piano, all of them 'perennial favourites'— 'Wie bist du, meine Königin', Op. 32 No. 9; 'Des Liebsten Schwur', Op. 69 No. 4; and 'Minnelied', Op. 71 No. 5— have been republished in Joachim Draheim, ed., *Johannes Brahms und seine Freunde*, 98–107.

[9] Cf. *Webster's Seventh New Collegiate Dictionary*, 99.

looser conception, though one in which connective elements might well exist. And there would seem to be no limits on the nature of these unifying elements, for the flowers in a bouquet may come from different meadows or gardens and be assembled according to any number of criteria—all small flowers or all large ones, flowers of one kind or colour or of very different kinds and colours, etc.

So how did Brahms assemble and order his songs? As the outlines of a chronology for Brahms's songs begin to emerge, it would seem that he composed songs in small clusters or singly, especially through the 1860s and to some extent in subsequent decades; apparently he would become interested in a particular volume of poetry or in the lyrics of a particular poet and would set one or more of these poems to music within a relatively short period of time.[10] These would be kept for a while in his portfolio and circulated individually or in small groups to such friends as Clara Schumann, Elisabet von Herzogenberg, and Theodor Billroth; opera of songs seem to have been assembled only shortly before being sent to the publisher. For example, in a letter to Rieter-Biedermann on 23 October 1871, we read of the songs released two months later as Opp. 57 and 58:

During a few restless days in Karlsruhe [Hermann] Levi and I gathered together songs for you. . . . There are 16 songs, 8 to each opus and of course [Opp.] 56, 57 [thus opus number '56' was subsequently reserved for the Haydn Variations]. They could appear in 2 volumes or in 4 (4 in each). The first is called *Lieder und Gesänge von G. Fr. Daumer*, the second just *Lieder und Gesänge* by J. Br. . . . The order, which Levi perhaps forgets (losing the slip of paper regarding this), or which I—, makes me somewhat apprehensive; yet if you keep the 'Lieder', we will be able to order them quickly.[11]

From these remarks and others in his letters to his publishers, it is clear that he attached great importance to the established succession of songs within each opus. The division of an opus of songs into separate volumes, though, seems merely to have been a practical concession to the publisher. Thus he wrote to Breitkopf & Härtel on 5 october 1864 when offering them his *Lieder und Gesänge von Platen und Daumer*, Op. 32, together with the first six of his *Magelone* Romances: 'The first collection contains 9 songs, but these will not create, I think, too big a volume. Should you wish to divide them, please leave the first 4 and the remaining 5 together. But I believe, since they will also appear separately, it would be better to keep them all together.'[12] Breitkopf refused the

---

[10] Cf. George S. Bozarth, 'Brahms's "*Liederjahr* of 1868" ', 218, as well as *The Lieder of Johannes Brahms—1868–1871*, 24–68, and 'Brahms's Lieder Inventory of 1859–60 and Other Documents of his Life and Work', 98–102, for evidence on the chronology of Brahms's songs up to 1871; *Johannes Brahms, Three Lieder on Poems of Adolf Friedrich von Schack*, Introduction, on his Schack songs; and 'Brahms's Duets for Soprano and Alto, op. 61', 191–6, 203–6, on his Mörike settings.

[11] 'Während einiger unruhigen Tage in Karlsruhe haben Levi und ich "Lieder" für Sie zusammengesucht. . . . Es sind 16 Lieder, je 8 auf ein Opus und zwar 56, 57. Sie können nun in 2 Heften oder in 4 (zu je 4) erscheinen. Das erste heiße: "Lieder und Gesänge von G. Fr. Daumer", das zweite bloß "Lieder und Gesänge" von J. Br. . . . Etwas besorgt macht mich die Reihenfolge, die Levi vielleicht vergessen (den betreffenden Zettel verloren) oder die ich—doch falls Sie die "Lieder" behalten, werden wir das rasch ordnen können.' *Brahms Briefwechsel*, 14: 199.

[12] 'Die erste Sammlung enthält 9 Lieder, doch geben diese, wie ich denke, kein zu umfangreiches Heft. Sollten Sie sie zu teilen wünschen, so bitte, die ersten 4 und die übrigen 5 beisammen zu lassen. Ich glaube jedoch, da die Lieder wohl auch einzeln erscheinen, sie bleiben besser zusammen.' *Brahms Briefwechsel*, 14: 107.

collection because of the difficult piano accompaniments, but when Rieter-Biedermann published it in January 1865 in two volumes, the division approved by Brahms was the one used.

The nature of most of the autographs and scribal copies which served as the engravers' models for his songs confirms that he composed his songs individually or in small groups and organized them into opera only at the time of publication: the manuscripts usually consist of songs written on a variety of papers and with their number within the opus subsequently assigned. The engraver's model for the earliest of his song collections, the *Sechs Gesänge*, Op. 3, for instance, consists of six separate manuscripts, one for each song.[13] Above the beginning of the first song Brahms wrote the title of the opus and the sequence of the six songs in it (there is no separate title page);[14] on each separate song he entered the proper number; and, at the end of Nos. 1 and 4, in parentheses, he designated the text incipits for Nos. 2 and 5, respectively. These indications were probably added shortly before the manuscripts were sent to the publisher. (Nos. 1 and 4, 'Liebestreu' and 'Lied aus dem Gedicht "Ivan" ', both in E♭ minor, are on the same type of paper and, though separated in the published version, were originally paginated continuously.[15]) Likewise, Brahms entered a table of contents for the *Sechs Gesänge*, Op. 6, on the title-page of the engraver's model before sending it to the publisher Bartholf Senff in Leipzig.[16] Again the single songs are separate manuscripts, with the exception of Nos. 5 and 6, settings of Hoffmann von Fallersleben's 'Wie die Wolke nach der Sonne' and 'Nachtigallen schwingen', both composed in July 1853 and found here paired in a gathering of two bifolia.[17]

In some cases Brahms had second thoughts about the order of his songs within an opus, even after he had sent them to the publisher. In the case of the *Lieder und Gesänge von G. F. Daumer*, Op. 57, mentioned earlier, he reversed the fifth and seventh songs— 'Die Schnur, die Perl' und Perle' became No. 7, 'In meiner Nächte Sehnen', No. 5— giving the final order for that opus and its companion, Op. 58, in a letter to Rieter-Biedermann on 10 November 1871.[18] In this way he created a strong connection between the dramatic last song in volume one, 'Ach, wende diesen Blick', and the equally

---

[13] This collection of manuscripts was acquired by the Library of Congress, Washington, DC, in 1981.

[14] Brahms later crossed out this table of contents and entered a dedication (of the manuscript, not the published opus) to his friend Julius Otto Grimm.

[15] No. 1: pp. 1–2; No. 4: pp. 3–5. The songs in this manuscript appear in pairs on three different types of paper— Nos. 1 and 4 are on one type, Nos. 2 and 6 are on a second type, Nos. 3 and 5 on a third—yet these pairs correspond with neither the order in which the songs were composed—Nos. 5 and 6 in Nov. and Dec. 1852, respectively, No. 1 in Jan. 1853, and Nos. 2–4 in July 1853—nor the poets being set—No. 1 is by Robert Reinick, No. 2–3 by Hoffmann von Fallersleben, No. 4 by Friedrich Bodenstedt, and Nos. 5–6 by Eichendorff. This would suggest either that Brahms was using all of these types of paper interchangeably during this period or that some of these manuscripts are copies of earlier manuscripts, perhaps prepared especially as engraver's models.

[16] This source was acquired by the Gesellschaft der Musikfreunde in Vienna in 1982.

[17] In the engraver's model for the *Lieder und Romanzen*, Op. 14, now owned by the Staatsbibliothek Preußischer Kulturbesitz Berlin (West), Brahms indicated the order of the songs with roman numbers entered on the songs in red chalk pencil.

[18] *Brahms Briefwechsel*, 14: 203–4.

dramatic, though more excited first song of the second volume, 'In meiner Nächte Sehnen', which provides the climax of the collection.

Evidence of the regrouping of songs at stages earlier than publication also exists. The four songs on poems by Klaus Groth published as Nos. 3–4 and 7–8 in the *Lieder und Gesänge*, Op. 59, for instance, apparently originally formed a small cycle which Brahms sent to the poet in April 1873, as the correspondence between composer and poet attests.[19] On 27 April Doris Groth wrote to Brahms: 'Since the 24th [of April] I have spent some time each day with the wonderfully beautiful cycle of songs by you and by Klaus. How tenderly, how ingeniously you have ordered these 4 songs. How great and magnificent is the first; the second one I have sung for Klaus today . . . he was quite touched by it; how deeply they are felt, these songs, and the last repeats the first and returns us to the past.'[20] Brahms had arranged the four songs in a cycle, or at least Frau Groth perceived this to be the case, with the two 'Regenlieder'—'Walle, Regen, walle nieder' and 'Regentropfen aus den Bäumen'—functioning as the first and last songs and with the other two—'Mein wundes Herz' and 'Dein blaues Auge'—in the middle. The order of the two interior songs cannot be determined, nor can the stage of composition which all four songs had reached, since the only extant evidence of the Groth manuscripts is a photocopy of the first page of the first 'Regenlied'.[21] But remarks in Klaus Groth's letter to Brahms on 24 January 1874,[22] written after he had received a copy of the printed edition of Op. 59 (published in December 1873), suggest that Brahms had made alterations since the preceding spring, perhaps in the second of the 'Regenlieder', since in the published collection this song serves a different function than it had in the earlier cycle: originally the final song of a foursome, now it is the fourth song in a collection of eight, forming a 'Nachklang' (the title Brahms gave it in Op. 59) to the other 'Regenlied' which precedes it, and thus ending the first volume of the collection. Its new function is as last (varied) strophe or as coda, epilogue to the first 'Regenlied', rather than as final, independent song in a cycle. As published in Op. 59, the two 'Regenlieder' are linked directly by textual and musical means and by proximity; the remaining two Groth songs, which appear as Nos. 7 and 8, form the end of the second volume of the collection. Or shall we call it a cycle? To his publisher Rieter-Biedermann, Brahms wrote regarding

---

[19] These songs, which include the two 'Regenlieder', could therefore not have been composed, as Max Kalbeck maintained, during the rainy summer of 1873 in Tutzing on the Starnberger See, where Brahms had been staying since 14 May, but must have already been finished by April of that year, when Brahms sent them to Klaus Groth and the correspondence ensured. Cf. Imogen Fellinger, 'Zur Entstehung der "Regenlieder" von Brahms'; also see Max Kalbeck, *Johannes Brahms*, 2: 437, and Volquart Pauls, ed., *Briefe der Freundschaft Johannes Brahms–Klaus Groth*, 75 ff.

[20] 'Seit dem 24sten habe ich jeden Tag ein wenig Zeit mir gestohlen für den wunderbar schönen Zyklus Lieder von Ihnen und von Klaus. Wie zart, wie sinnig haben Sie diese 4 Lieder aneinander gereiht. Wie ist das erste groß und herrlich, das zweite habe ich heute Klaus vorsingen können . . . er war ganz getroffen; wie tief sind sie empfunden, diese Lieder, und das letzte gibt zum Schluß das erste wieder und versetzt uns zurück in die Vergangenheit.' Pauls, *Brahms–Groth*, 77.

[21] This photocopy is owned by the Klaus Groth-Museum in Heide; cf. Margit McCorkle, *Johannes Brahms Thematisch-bibliographisches Werkverzeichnis*, 253.

[22] Pauls, *Brahms–Groth*, 81.

Op. 59: 'There has been a frightful cleaning out at my home, and so that this does not lead to a complete nothing, I am sending you "pro novitate", "on approval" some extremely lovely, recommendable, agreeable, here and there difficult, moral, god-fearing, briefly first-class songs. Op. 59, 2 volumes is what I would like to deliver . . . The two volumes differ in size, but I wish the order, which you will call a disorder, to be kept.'[23] Brahms may often have had strong reasons for ordering his songs as he did, though his publishers may not always have been able to discern them.

Another opus which seems to have undergone regrouping is the *Vier Lieder*, Op. 43. In a letter on 26 June 1868, Brahms inquired of Rieter-Biedermann how strongly he desired to publish the two songs that Stockhausen had sung in Zurich, 'Von ewiger Liebe' (translated by Leopold Haupt and Heinrich Hoffmann von Fallersleben from a Wendish folk-poem) and 'Die Mainacht' (Ludwig Hölty); he continued: 'I have long promised the young Simrock something and, if I take two [songs] out of the centre, I can only order the remaining songs badly.'[24] On 5 July Brahms wrote again to Rieter: 'I am busy with ordering a small group of songs and, since I am happy to give you the 2 you desire, I fear I am forced to throw the poets into complete confusion.'[25] On 9 August Brahms announced to Rieter a 'Liederheft', to be designated Op. 43; it contained the two desired songs, 'a long "vom Herrn von Falkenstein" ', and 'Ich schell mein Horn', a solo version of the first of the *Fünf Lieder* for male choir, Op. 41, which Brahms felt should be 'shown to the public in this manner'.[26] This group of songs was sent off to the publisher the following day.[27] At the same time Brahms sent four volumes of songs to Simrock, published as Opp. 46–9.[28] As can be surmised from the correspondence, Brahms had originally placed 'Von ewiger Liebe' and 'Die Mainacht' amidst other songs he intended to be published by Simrock, probably arranged together with other settings of poems by Hölty (Opp. 46 Nos. 3 and 4, Op. 49 No. 2), as well as with the other settings of folk-poems in Opp. 47–9. Thus, in Op. 43 Brahms combined a folk-song-like dialogue, an ode, an old German lamentation, and a ballad.

As we have seen, some songs were grouped by poet—the pairs of Eichendorff and Hoffmann von Fallersleben songs in Opp. 3 and 6, and the two pairs of Groth songs in

[23] 'Es ist schändlich aufgeräumt bei mir, und damit das nicht bis zu völliger Null geht, schicke ich hier "pro novitate", "zur Ansicht" einige besonders liebliche, empfehlenswerte, angenehme, nur stellenweise diffizile, moralische, gottesfürchtige, kurz "Lieder" prima Sorte. op. 59, 2 Hefte wünschte ich damit zu liefern. . . . Die Hefte sind an Umfang verschieden; ich wünschte aber doch die Ordnung so zu lassen, die Sie eine Unordnung nennen werden.' *Brahms Briefwechsel*, 14: 222.

[24] 'Ich habe dem jungen Simrock lange was versprochen und kann eine Anzahl "Lieder" schlecht ordnen, wenn ich so 2 aus der Mitte herausnehme.' *Brahms Briefwechsel*, 14: 157. Wilhelm Altmann, editor of this volume of letters, incorrectly identified the two desired songs as Op. 43 Nos. 3 and 4, but it was Nos. 1 and 2 which Stockhausen sang in concert with Brahms in Hamburg on 11 Mar. 1868 (the première, from manuscript; cf. Kalbeck, *Brahms*, 2: 217) and surely these same two songs which he performed in Zurich, probably at a private concert.

[25] 'Ich bin dabei ein Häufchen "Lieder" zu ordnen und, da ich Ihnen gern die gewünschten 2 gebe, so werde ich wohl die Dichter überhaupt durcheinander werfen.' Ibid., 158.

[26] 'ein langes "vom Herrn von Falkenstein" und eines enthält, das nach Nr 1 der "Männerchöre" [Op. 41] gesetzt ist, aber durchaus auch so dem Publico gezeigt werden muß'. Ibid., 159–60.

[27] Ibid., 161.

[28] *Brahms Briefwechsel*, 9: 56 f. and 14: 159.

Op. 59. In other cases, similarity of content reinforces common poetic source—the two Groth 'Regenlieder' in Op. 59, the first two Uhland songs in Op. 19, and the two Heine settings, 'Sommerabend' and 'Mondenschein', in Op. 85 (Nos. 1 and 2) (in all three cases the songs share musical material as well); and the two 'Junge Lieder' on poems by Felix Schumann and the three 'Heimweh' songs on poems by Klaus Groth, all in Op. 63 (Nos. 5–6 and 7–9, respectively).[29] Larger numbers of songs by single poets and on common themes occur in the *Lieder und Gesänge*, Op. 32—Nos. 1 and 3–6 by August von Platen and Nos. 2 and 7–9 by Georg Friedrich Daumer—and, as already noted, all of the songs collected together in Op. 57 are on poems by Daumer. Likewise, all but one of the poems in the *Lieder und Romanzen*, Op. 14, are folk-songs from collections by Karl Simrock, Johann Gottfried Herder, and Kretzschmer and Zuccalmaglio, several dealing with medieval romance (the one exception, 'Ein Sonett', No. 4, is also taken from Herder's collection), and all five of the *Romanzen und Lieder*, Op. 84, are dialogues (three on poems by Hans Schmidt, the other two on Lower Rhenish folk-song texts). The acknowledged cycles, of course, are the *Magelone* Romances, Op. 33 (Ludwig Tieck) and the *Vier ernste Gesänge*, Op. 121, on biblical texts (which is actually more in the tradition of the Baroque cantata than the Romantic song cycle), as well as the two sets of *Liebeslieder* Waltzes, Opp. 52 and 65 (Daumer) and the eleven *Zigeunerlieder*, Op. 103 (translated from the Hungarian by Hugo Conrat), all three opera for vocal quartet.[30]

The opening and closing songs of Brahms's 'bouquets' often seem linked by size and/or tonality. It is probably true that Brahms began his first published opus of songs

[29] Adjoining songs by single poets also occur in Opp. 7 (Nos. 2 and 3 by Eichendorff), 46 (Nos. 1 and 2 by Daumer; Nos. 3 and 4 by Ludwig Hölty), 47 (Nos. 1 and 2 by Daumer), 48 (Nos. 2 and 3 from *Des Knaben Wunderhorn*), 58 (Nos. 1–3 by August Kopisch; Nos. 6 and 7 by Friedrich Hebbel), 63 (Nos. 1–4 by Max von Schenkendorf), 69 (Nos. 1–4 on folk-poems translated by Josef Wenzig, beginning with a pair of 'Klage'), 72 (Nos. 1 and 2 by Karl Candidus), 85 (Nos. 3–4 by Siegfried Kapper), 95 (Nos. 2–4 by Friedrich Halm), 96 (Nos. 1, 3, and 4 by Heine), and 97 (Nos. 1 and 2 by Christian Reinhold). Amongst Brahms's duets are the two 'Weg der Liebe' drawn from Herder's *Stimmen der Völker* (Op. 20 Nos. 1 and 2), the two 'Klänge' by Groth (Op. 66 Nos. 1 and 2), the three settings of Hans Schmidt poems (Op. 84 Nos. 1–3), and the two Lower Rhenish folk-songs (Op. 84 Nos. 4 and 5); his *Sechs Quartette* for solo voices, Op. 112, begin with two settings of poems by Franz Kugler and continue with four 'Zigeunerlieder' on poems translated from the original Hungarian by Hugo Conrat; and in his choral works we find four 'Lieder aus dem Jungbrunnen' by Paul Heyse in Op. 44 (Nos. 7–10) and four more in Op. 62 (Nos. 3–6), together with two settings of poems from *Des Knaben Wunderhorn* (Nos. 1 and 2), and a pair of 'Nachtwache' songs on poems by Friedrich Rückert in the *Fünf Gesänge für gemischten Chor a cappella*, Op. 104 (Nos. 1 and 2).

[30] Brahms entitled his songs variously 'Lieder', 'Gesänge', 'Romanzen', and 'Gedichte', sometimes employing more than one of these terms in the title of an opus. The term 'Lieder' he used mainly for strophic and varied strophic songs (Opp. 47–9, 85, 86, 94–7, and 105–7); the designation 'Gesänge' he reserved for songs in a more elevated or artificial style (Opp. 3, 6, 7, 43, 46, 69–72, 91, as well as the *Vier ernste Gesänge*, Op. 121). Mixed groupings were called 'Lieder und Gesänge' (Opp. 32, 57–9, and 63). It should be noted, though, that chronology also seems to be a factor: all of the early songs (Opp. 3, 6, and 7) and the four opera published in 1877 (Opp. 69–72) are called 'Gesänge'; three of the opera published in 1868 (Opp. 47–9) and all the later songs (Opp. 94–7, published 1884 and 1886, and 105–7, published 1888) are entitled 'Lieder'; and all of the songs published 1871–4 are designated 'Lieder und Gesänge' (Opp. 57–9 and 63). 'Romanzen' suggests archaic themes of medieval romance (the *Lieder und Romanzen*, Op. 14, the *Magelone* Romances, Op. 33, and the *Romanzen und Lieder*, Op. 84). Brahms used the title 'Gedichte' only once, for Op. 19, which begins with a poem by Ludwig Hölty, continues with three poems by Ludwig Uhland, and ends with a poem by Eduard Mörike.

(Op. 3) with the impressive 'Liebestreu' in order to introduce himself to the public as a song composer with one of the most important songs then in his portfolio, but we also find ambitious songs heading such collections as the Platen-Daumer songs of Op. 32 ('Wie rafft ich mich auf in der Nacht'), the Daumer group, Op. 57 ('Von waldbekränzter Höhe'), and the mixed collection, Op. 59 ('Dämm'rung senkte sich von oben'). Opp. 32 and 57 also end with large-scale songs ('Wie bist du meine Königin' and 'Unbewegte laue Luft', respectively), and within the latter of these two opera, the dramatic succession of songs seems very carefully regulated: after the initial 'Lebhaft' of 'Von waldbekränzter Höhe' follow two quieter, slower, more lyrical songs—'Wenn du nur zuweilen lächelst' and 'Es träumte mir'; the fourth song, 'Ach, wende diesen Blick', is also slow, but dramatically much more intense than the two songs that precede it, for its function is to move the opus toward its climax in the fifth song, 'In meiner Nächte Sehnen'; the sixth and seventh songs—'Strahlt zuweilen auch ein mildes Licht' and 'Die Schnur, die Perl' an Perle'—restore a certain calmness, and the final song of the collection, 'Unbewegte laue Luft', opens in a quiet, sultry mood. A dramatic outburst, however, ensues at 'Aber im Gemüte schwillt heißere Begierde mir' and, despite melodic and harmonic echoes of its slow initial section, the song ends the collection 'Lebhaft', albeit at an intense pianissimo.

The *Magelone* Romances, Op. 33, begin and end with songs in the key of E♭ major. Likewise, the first and last of the *Lieder und Gesänge*, Op. 63—'Frühlingstrost' (Schenkendorf) and 'Ich sah als Knabe Blumen blühn' (Groth)—are in the same key (A major). All of the other collections open and close in different keys, but this does not necessarily speak against cyclic tendencies. Certain collections seem focused on one mode—the *Sechs Gesänge*, Op. 7, the first five of which speak of young women separated from their beloveds, are all in minor keys (the final song, in which the young man sings of overcoming all obstacles to reach his distant sweetheart, begins in minor but ends in a resounding major); the songs in Opp. 46 and 63 are all in major. Other collections show internal groupings by mode. For example, the tightly knit and progressive key scheme of the songs in Op. 57:

| 1 | 2 | 3 | 4 | 5 | 6 | 7 | 8 |
|---|---|---|---|---|---|---|---|
| G major— | E♭ major— | B major— | F minor— | E minor— | E major— | B major— | E major |

Three major tonalities surround two minor ones; the keys of the initial three songs are related by a descending major third and a descending diminished fourth; the final three songs establish a plateau on E major, reached through E minor, the relative minor of the opening G major. Such modal 'nesting' also occurs in the *Sechs Lieder*, Op. 85 (B♭ major—B♭ major—A minor—B minor—G major—B major), the *Vier Gesänge*, Op. 43 (B minor—E♭ major—B♭ major—C minor), and the *Vier Gesänge*, Op. 70 (G minor—B major—B major—A minor).

Thorough exploration of the key schemes of Brahms's 'bouquets' of songs, duets, and vocal quartets—let alone his collections of short keyboard pieces—exceeds the scope of the present paper and must be undertaken as a study in itself, but the evidence presented here is suggestive, and should encourage such exploration. One would do well to consider first the nominal cycles such as the *Magelone* Romances, the *Liebeslieder* Waltzes, and the *Zigeunerlieder* (as well as the Op. 39 Waltzes), and then compare findings with other opera;[31] the most likely candidates as 'cycles' would, of course, be the Platen-Daumer songs of Op. 32 and the Daumer songs of Op. 57, but one should not ignore the other opera of songs. With groups of songs composed at separate times and subsequently brought together for publication, the most fruitful area of investigation would seem to be key relationships; with collections containing songs all composed at about the same time, motivic and other relationships may well be found to compliment and reinforce key relationships. In each case, discussion of musical means will need to be related closely to interrelationship of content among the poems involved. Evidence of compositional process may add a further dimension; changes in the order of the songs, as noted in Op. 57 and as also occurred, at least twice, in the *Liebeslieder* Waltzes, Op. 52, and in the keys of individual songs may provide clues. Though we might suspect from the beginning that Brahms's collections of songs are indeed not true cycles—as we have come to define that term in light of the song cycles of Beethoven, Schubert, and Schumann—we should not be surprised if we find that this master of motivic unity, developing variation, and formal architecture in instrumental music used similar means to fashion the details and the larger dimensions of his song collections.

[31] For further discussion of cyclic tendencies in Brahms, compare the papers by David Brodbeck and Ludwig Finscher in the present volume. A further study by the author is in preparation.

# BRAHMS'S SYMPHONIC
# MUSIC

# 'FORM' AND THE *TRAGIC OVERTURE*: AN ADJURATION

—

## CLAUDIO SPIES

THERE is nothing new about 'forms' with whose aid pieces of music are easily and lazily categorized or typified, tagged, pigeon-holed, and conveniently stored away without further—or even prior—hearing, and without further thought. We were all initiated into the non-mysterious stolidities of 'form', particularly the most fictitious one of all, 'Sonata Form'. Nor is there, I hasten to add, anything new in the notion that such 'forms'—and especially 'Sonata Form'—*are* fictions to whose specifications and proclaimed norms very few pieces of music worth any further thought actually conform in an appreciable way. What is *still* new, by refreshing contrast, and in no danger, moreover, of relinquishing its novelty, is the better than one-hundred-year-old overture that has given rise to these musings. It is almost as if Brahms had decided to compose this piece as a potent rebuttal of notions propounded by the tenets of *Formenlehre*, although the *Tragic Overture* is by no means unique among his works in this respect. Neither, indeed, is the usage, which had by that time become Brahms's characteristic—we are speaking, after all, of Op. 81—whereby materials whose distinguishing traits and marked susceptibility to compositional elaboration and transformation are intimately involved with, and plausibly responsible for, generating the design of a work—more obviously so, at any rate, than those associable segments or sections that habitually have been issued name-tags or alphabetical denominations, in conformity to precepts of *Formenlehre* but in defiance of musical common sense.

One such section promulgated by *Formenlehre* is the 'transition' or 'bridge-passage' following initial statements of thematic material in the tonic. It is said to be destined to convey the music away from the tonic and help establish whatever non-tonic area is reserved for whatever material is to be stated there. The means for this harmonic transfer are said to be clearly derived from materials heard near the beginning of the movement, and it is asserted that sequences designed to arrive eventually on the dominant of whatever 'second key' may be in store for us should abound. The later bridge-passage is therefore presumably a mere retread of this music, shifted by however many necessary hundreds of bars, deftly transposed, adapted to, and stuck between inspired 'first' and 'second' themes in the never-never land of 'Recapitulation'. If we were to search the *Tragic Overture* for passages roughly fitting these descriptions, we would be hard-pressed to find any. Near the beginning, for example, there are two places (at rehearsal letters *A* and *C*, bars 21 and 41) where emphatic D minor cadences coincide both with downward registral shifts and sudden textural changes, ushering in varieties of sequential writing which might well mislead an indoctrinated *Formenlehrling* into applying the 'bridge-passage' misnomer. That it *is* a misnomer is made evident by the further emphatic D minor cadences to which both places lead, successively twenty-one and twenty-four bars later (at letters *C* and *D*, bars 41 and 65). The music has not gone where that 'transition' was supposed to take it; a bridge is meant, I think, to get you to the other side, not to return you to the one you started from. In the end, it is only after a *third* emphatic D minor cadence that the harmony begins gradually to move away from the tonic sphere, but it does so with musical means so sharply different from anything heard in all sixty-five preceding bars of the overture that this 'bridge' might as well have turned into a magic carpet. As for that later, supposedly parallel bridge-passage, conjectured to occur in a similar location within the 'recapitulation', no stretch of the imaginations of even the devoutest of 'form's' adherents could dream up its existence in this piece, since an unexpected 'recapitulation' occurs, in fact, where the 'development' should begin (bars 185 ff.), and nowhere else does the opening of that 'first theme' subsequently return, save for one spot fifty-one bars from the end (bars 379 ff.), where it is followed by its own brief 'development'. Furthermore, the deceptive return to the tonic (albeit in the wrong mode), once the 'development' appears to have suddenly subsided, takes place precisely through a related portion of the strange passage (bars 264 ff.) which, for lack of anything better, we had likened to a magic carpet, but which has now changed into one of those very bridges that oddly returns to where it began! Nevertheless, as if to restore deluded confidence to believers in 'form', and to appear to resolve ambiguity for sceptics, Brahms permits both these transformative passages to lead into the material (beginning, respectively, at bars 106 and 300) doggedly categorized as 'second theme', each in its anticipated key, though in some other important respects not at all alike, and accordingly eroding somewhat further any sense in which 'recapitulation' could here be taken literally. For whatever it may be worth, the term may actually be applied to only one relatively brief segment in the overture, if certain qualifications are kept in mind: the passage occupying bars 300–64 corresponds to the previous passage between bars 106 and 171; both involve the 'second theme group', and both present those materials in the same succession. The circumstance that neither of them precedes or follows similarly related passages cannot, however, be deemed trivial.

Rather than dwell on further instances showing how little the conventional concept and nomenclature of 'sonata form' bear upon the unfolding of the *Tragic Overture*, let us take the opposite tack, and approach some aspects of the composition's coherence and continuity in its own terms, as it were, by examining certain of its materials, resources, and details, their different—though also recurring—uses, and the strong links between the materials themselves and compositional decisions that determine the design of the piece. From the beginning of the overture, for example, until letter *C* at bar 41, it may be seen that the bass line moves exclusively through diatonic scales or within such collections, and by arpeggiating triads or, in one instance, a diminished seventh. There is a forcefully articulated octave ascent (between As) in bars 16–19, immediately preceding the first of the three D minor cadences mentioned earlier. There is also a singular emphasis placed on the bass motion F–B♭, giving rise to a conspicuous augmented triad first in bars 27–8 and more prominently in bars 59–60. Once the second D minor cadence has been heard at bar 41, the bass motion, confined for the next fourteen bars to rising arpeggiations of triads in first inversion, is now exclusively chromatic. A crucial transformation, however, must take place before such chromatically ascending arpeggiations can support a coherent harmonic design. To this end, the initial F–A–D–F in bars 42–3 must first become F♯–A–D–F♯ in the next two bars, in order to proceed, in turn, to sixth chord arpeggiations based on G, and then on G♯ and A. In other words, only *major* triads in first inversion can connote a local dominant function through their lowest pitches, since these may be heard as leading-tones. The resulting chain of local deceptive resolutions ($V^6$–$VI^6$) not only fills in the bass line's F–A, which has been of prime importance from the start in the bass's surface, but also replicates, in each successive step, the harmonic configuration that appears from the very beginning to be prototypical— both linearly, in the rising arpeggio that begins at the end of bar 2, and in simultaneity on the opening quarter of bar 1. The augmented triads F–A–C♯, mentioned in connection with the bass motion F–B♭, now assume the added significance of flanking the chromatically rising bass, and we recognize in bars 59–60 a variant of the overture's opening simultaneities.

Such marked exclusiveness of diatonic or chromatic motion in the bass lines of adjacent segments of music is transferred, moreover, to an area that is not a direct parallel to the one described above. The melody that begins in bar 106 is supported until bar 117 by a rigorously diatonic bass, consisting of all seven elements of the F major collection within the span of an octave. Then, between bars 118 and 129, the bass covers the span of a twelfth (F–C, two octave-shifts notwithstanding) in direct chromatic ascent from which only one element, between A♭ and B♭, is necessarily omitted in bar 126–7, inasmuch as the upper line has at this point taken on its own chromatic rise from F to A♭. You will notice—as I did not, until a gifted pupil of Brahms brought it to my shamed attention—that the chromatic motion from bar 118 on begins with exactly the same pitch-class configurations as in bars 42–7 (see the circled portions of Examples 1*a* and *b*, which show the successive F–A–D, F♯–A–D, G–B♭–E♭ relations in both). At the same time, coupled with the strictly diatonic bass in bars 106–17, there is a contrasting upper line that fills in the chromatic hexachord spanning C–F (bar 113), as well as an abundance of embellishing neighbours in inner parts (bars 114–17). I cannot help adding a comment, perhaps gratuitously offered, on the melody's distinctiveness in opening with the inversion (at transposition o) of the overture's first upper-line interval. One might also be inclined to notice that the bass line's motif in bar 1 is verticalized in bars 106–7 in such a way that the bass will not leave its F until the tune above has returned to its initial A!

So far, we have cast a glance at a few details, and have observed how so simple a resource as the contrast between diatonic and chromatic motion in a bass line provides means for coherence within adjacent, and therefore also among non-contiguous, parts of the overture. For the remainder of this paper, I shall carry these observations a step or

EXAMPLE 1.  Brahms, *Tragic Overture*, Op. 81.

(*a*) Bars 42–51.

(*b*) Bars 118–20.

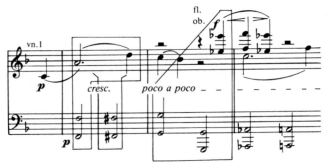

two further, expecting no more, however, than that they will cover the composition's vast and complex interrelations only to the slightest extent. First, let us return to that odd, seemingly 'unprepared' music beginning at letter *D* (bar 66), following the third D minor cadence—about which we shall presently have more to say. To begin with, there is a telling octave descent between As in a momentarily transferred inner voice (violin 1); it brings to mind the rising octave framed by the same pitch-class already noted in the bass at bars 16–19, but it also foreshadows a longer-range bass octave descent that begins at bar 82. It is important to hear how the music arrives at the registrally extreme Cs in that bar. While for fifteen preceding bars the harmonic field has remained strictly within the D minor collection, while rhythmic activity is restrained throughout to evenness of note-values in all parts except horns and bassoons, and while, in fact, the only prominent contour is found in the patterned scalewise ascent by half-notes of the oboe, the chromatic contrary motion from bar 80 sets a precedent in the composition—a precedent that will ultimately be reflected in the simultaneous upward chromatic motion in outer parts following letter *R* (bars 366–79).

Once converged upon, the Cs of bar 82 each touch off significant linear deployments: the bass's octave descent is symmetrically divided into a four-element portion of a whole-tone collection (C–Bb–Ab–Gb) on the one hand, and chromatic filling-in for the remaining segment—Eb being the only missing pitch-class—while the top line (flute, and octave-doubling clarinet and bassoon) displays both a Db upper neighbour to C and an enharmonic retrograde of the chromatic segment Bb–Bb–C, first heard in bars 80–2. Furthermore, the piccolo's high C is held in reserve until the neighbouring motion around C is chromatic in all represented registers—until, in short, the dominant function of C is undeniably established. But what happens at bar 84 in the trombones and tuba adds a further thread to the gathering tangle of connections: Example 2 summarizes the neighbouring effect upon Eb of the descending arpeggiation (as if a 'sixth chord') as well as the relation between the bass motion Gb–F and the downward arpeggio over it (which *is*, over a Gb, in first inversion). The first trombone-tuba arpeggio, Fb–Db–Ab–Fb, appears as a triad in first inversion, but it occurs over a bass Ab and is therefore perceived as a 'six-four' neighbour. The subsequent Bb–Gb–Eb–Bb arpeggio turns the tables by being registered in second inversion, but since it is placed over a bass Gb, it is heard in first inversion. Furthermore, some larger tables have been neatly turned: now a sixth-chord chromatic motion can *descend*, inasmuch as the triads involved are *minor*!

The story of the upper-line C–Db–C neighbour again takes us back to bar 1, and opens up a view of the initial 'dominant' simultaneity, with its carefully left out C#, as lacking that crucial pitch-class only because the ensuing arpeggio includes C#, and because the resulting crudity of that ambivalence would, I imagine Brahms to have imagined, have been excessive for the composition's opening. A little later, in bars 36–8, the dyad Db–C is repeated more than any other within the syncopated homophony leading to the second D minor cadence. (Those high Dbs were themselves anticipated in the flutes' C#s in bars 26–7, acting there, however, as lower neighbours to D.) Moreover, the alternating wind fragments in bars 51–9 go back and forth between C# and C# before settling on C#—in the

EXAMPLE 2. Brahms, *Tragic Overture*, Op. 81, bars 84–92.

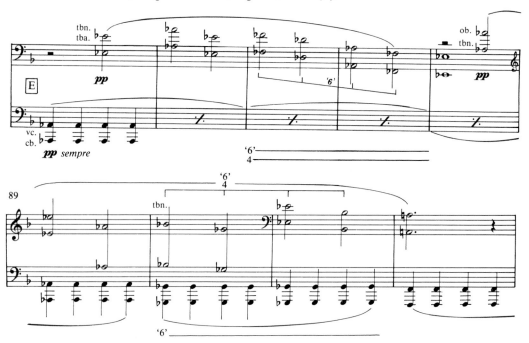

context of the augmented triad mentioned above—so as to proceed to the third D minor cadence. Later still, beginning at letter *G* (bars 142 ff.), there is much Db and Bb neighbouring of Cs in connection with the relentlessly approaching, yet always elegantly postponed, cadence to F. There is, then, something 'motivic' in the C–C♯/Db relation, since Brahms puts it to such evident structural use.

Having already gone back several times to the first bar, I must return to it once more to bring up two additional features whose far-ranging consequences affect the timing of certain sections in the overture. First of all, the two opening simultaneities, and in particular their spacing and registration, provide the context for assigning a hierarchy among the three D minor cadences to which I have so often alluded. Notice that in the initial simultaneity the lowest pitches are the Fs, and that there are no Fs above middle C; a span of three octaves and a fifth is occupied by the Ds and As, with As topmost. Notice also that the first and second horns play the same pitch successions in bars 1, 4, and 6, and that their octave Ds are prolonged after the opening bar, in order to conform articulatively and dynamically to the strings. I remark, in passing, on the registral distinctness of bars 2–6, which in three respects, at least, underlines the isolation of the opening simultaneities' upper reaches. Those heights will not, however, remain silent for longer than seven bars, so that from bar 10 on the orchestra is spread out over all its available registers. Nevertheless, at the first D minor cadence (bars 20–1) the uppermost register is not represented in a closure on D; in fact, the registral gap between the dominant simultaneity and the succeeding downbeat is very much akin to the one between bars 1 and 2. From a purely registral point of view, something similar happens at the second D minor cadence, although here the upper Ds *are* articulated on the downbeat at bar 41, and the registral skip occurs immediately *thereafter*. It is not until the third cadence is approached, however, that closure in the upper register is made manifest through iterance at two different octave levels (bars 60–5). A transposed variant of the arpeggiating tune first heard in bars 2–6 now brings about that closure three times; it is abetted, moreover, by three additional bars (66–8) in which the registral skip, in one further application, now 'clinches' the closure by highlighting the one feature that certifies it: the two horns—with octave-doubling bassoons—play the *retrograde* of the pitch successions assigned them in bars 1, 4, and 6! The ear is thereby informed not only of the greater importance Brahms attaches to this articulative juncture, for which the prior D minor cadences were, retrospectively, preparatory, but it is also guided into the succeeding texture through singularly deft dovetailing, as well as being forcefully reminded of the source for all these connections and relations in the composition's first few bars.

Lastly, the reappearances of the two simultaneities of bar 1, respectively found in bars 185 and 379, are timed to connote practically anything but what such recurrences might lead the unthinking to infer. In neither instance are they intended to announce any extensive return, let alone a 'recapitulation'; for one thing, their internal make-up is significantly changed each time, as an outgrowth of the local contexts which give rise to these recurrences, and, I suspect, for more 'global' reasons as well. The most obvious change at bar 185 is the large registral switch between Ds and Fs, so that the initial simultaneity is anchored here—*and only here*—on the tonic. The self-evident fifths by contrary motion between outer parts were overridden in Brahms's mind by the necessity of changing the heavily stressed bass Fs in the preceding bars to the requisite D, and I sense that the composer must have 'heard' the reference to Beethoven's Eighth Symphony in those preceding bars—thereby allowing the upper registers to retain their F–A dyads. There are two non-trivial details here: first, the horns do not play their characteristic pitch successions until the echo, two bars later, and then, in bars 191–2, unmistakably convey that this passage can be neither a 'repeated exposition' (except for the unhearing) nor a 'recapitulation' (except for those who might have fallen asleep); secondly, it is enlightening to corroborate the dexterousness with which Brahms avoids consecutive fifths in any of the double lines given to instruments of a kind that are involved in the three places under discussion. The second recurrence, in bar 379, is heralded by the chromatically rising, register-expanding bars (366 ff.), to which I have referred before. The spacing at bar 379 is altered again, so as to place Ds in closer registral contiguity to As, and, in somewhat of a registral feint, to move the bass's F up an octave. The immediate effect of that shift is to expand the ensuing vertiginous descent in bars 380–3 to cover five octaves, from highest to lowest As. Yet it is this huge A frame that bar 379 prepares and reinforces—it had been set up differently at bars 364–5—so that the purpose of the return in bar 379 is not so much to recall as to propel, just as its prototype had done, to begin with, and the music initiated by it is a long-held-back elaboration of the falling fourth between the two simultaneities. A subsequent 'developmental' recurrence of materials associated with the first eighty-odd bars of the piece—whose details of reinterpretation, reworking, and rerhythmicization may well provide me with the substance of an even longer disquisition—serves to guide those framing As to their ultimate Ds at the close. None the less, to call this concluding section of the overture a 'coda', as the still invoked 'form books' would have us do, is arrant nonsense, bygone pastimes of pinning on the donkey's tail notwithstanding.

To sum up, then, we have seen in a few places how Brahms will enable elaboration or transformation of given pieces of material to encompass long time-spans and changing contexts, and how resources or properties inherent in musical materials—more so, of course, than 'themes' or tunes themselves—set up the incredibly rich and varied relational networks that are his unique and uniquely exhaustive concern to exploit throughout this overture, in a continuously evolving process. That process, in all its complexities of transformation and timing, is necessarily ignored by the purveyors of 'form'. Consequently, the music is both massively misrepresented and completely misunderstood by those who continue, in turn, to teach and to be taught the tidy fiction of 'musical form'. It is time that the record be rid of its warps and set aright! Above all, it is a matter—for those of us whose primary interest is musical composition, whether or not we be practitioners of the art—of taking in the *Tragic Overture* precisely as the composer made it: carefully notated, elegantly crafted, conveying its wealth of relations, and provided with every necessary detail to insure either its practical application to performance or its precise communicability as an object for quiet reflection and study. As such, this work gives eloquent evidence of its composer's extraordinary mind and of that mind's powerful, subtle, and sometimes uniquely recondite musical workings; it needs no thoughtless props or silly tags to be understood, since it is comprehensible on its own musical terms. What it does need, along with most of Brahms's other larger works, is considerably more thoroughgoing theoretical analysis and investigation of a kind perhaps lightly adumbrated here, yet insufficiently supplied.

# D-LIGHT REFLECTING: THE NATURE OF COMPARISON

## JOHN RAHN

To recognize a pitch as D requires only a workable memory for pitch identity. To recognize that a pitch is D in two different environments requires additionally an ability to distinguish one environment from another, which again depends only on memory to identify and compare various ingredients such as pitch, rhythm, and instrument. But to appreciate what a D is doing in different environments, or what (obversely) those different environments are doing to that D, needs, if not creative thought ($νοηδιζ$), at least some thinking over ($διανόια$).[1]

Consider, for example, the initial forty-four bars of Brahms's Second Symphony. The D chromatically inflected in the cellos in bar 1 later appears in the same octave as, successively, a timpani roll, a trombone note, a timpani roll, a trombone note, and another trombone note (bars 32–44). At some point during this succession, though, we become aware that this D has changed its personality. Previously courted and embellished by C♯, it has now become attracted to that pitch, and at last succumbs to it at bar 42 in the second trombone. The woodwinds here remind us of the former relationship between D and C♯ without contradicting the new (bars 35 and 39). In retrospect, the seeds of the fall to C♯ were sown in the fourth phrase (over the A pedal, bars 14 ff.), and the later D—even the timpani's D—largely serves C♯ as affectionate upper neighbour, a C♯ which in turn more largely serves D as lower neighbour over the first forty-four bars, as it had in bar 1 (see Figure 1).

Just as the pitch D (or any other pitch) is variously flavoured by (and contributes to the flavour of) all the other ingredients during each part of the repast, at each course, each dish, each mouthful—flavoured also by our memories and anticipations of previous and subsequent morsels and by our emergent organization of our experience, our 'theory of the meal'—just so does each musical piece we have digested incorporate itself into each musician, influencing his taste, infusing his experience of other pieces with its particular savour. This kind of influence of musical events upon each other must be especially strong between pieces as close in style, instrumentation, metre, and key as are Brahms's Violin Concerto and Second Symphony.

It would be tedious merely to enumerate likenesses and differences between the two works. There are local trivia, such as the family resemblance between the theme of the

---

[1] ΠΟΛΙΤΣΙΑ (Respublica), books 6 and 7. The immediate reference is from 511 d 6 to 511 e 4 (the end of book 6).

FIGURE 1.

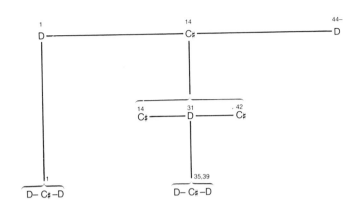

symphony's last movement and the theme of the concerto's first movement, or the curious but still trivial result of overlaying bars 1–8 of the concerto's first movement onto bars 2–9 of the symphony's first movement. There are also resonances between larger spaces, such as, in the first movements of the two works, a rough correspondence in general musical function starting with the recapitulation (from bar 302—or 298—in the symphony, bar 381 in the concerto) and continuing to the end; for example, that marvellous horn solo before the coda of the symphony (bars 455–77) which parallels in place and function the somewhat less exciting cadenza in the concerto (bars 526 ff.). But what does it do for us to recognize the cadential nature of the horn solo, or to hear that solo ringing in the background of the concerto's cadenza?

In making comparisons what, if anything, are we talking about? Not, directly, about the concerto or the symphony, but about their intermodulation; our perception of each modulates, warps, and informs our perception of the other, forming a third entity which is the pattern of their interaction and the object of comparative discourse. For practical purposes, we may hypostatize this pattern of interaction, and from it we may even form an idea of some essential nature—call it 'D-ishness'. This D-ishness, the essence of at least these two pieces considered together, would lie in that realm of the intelligible inaccessible except to creative intelligence; that is, pretty inaccessible. According to one rather frivolous theory of Plato's cave metapor,[2] the composer—in this case, Brahms—gets an idea of D-ishness (which resides outside the cave, with the Good) and makes an image of it, that is, a piece. The orchestra then parades the image behind the low wall to our rear so that we perceive its fire-lit shadow (the performance) as we sit shackled to our expensive seats.

The pattern of interaction, of course, is neither the image nor the essence, and indeed it does not fit well into the cave metaphor, for it is less ethereal than D-ishness and maybe more useful. If the pieces each imperfectly imitate D-ishness, the individuating imperfections of imitation are what create the intermodulation. (If they were each to

---

[2] This theory was advanced by my wife, Suzanne Rahn, in private conversation.

imitate D-ishness perfectly, only D-ishness would then be present.) This pattern of interaction would then hold information both on the individuality of each piece and on the whole which they are considered to imitate imperfectly.

Thus we know that whatever D-ishness is, its logic does not prevent two imitations of it from sharing a structure of differently effected musical functions. One such function includes the elaboration of the last large-scale cadence (tonic six-four, dominant seventh, tonic five-three). But the interaction between the symphony's horn solo and any particular violin cadenza in the concerto is not limited to this common description. All the details of sound, organization, and context that individuate each of them must contribute to the pattern of their interaction in our perception of them. The context that helps individuate any section, and in whose creation that section participates, ramifies outwards from that section to embrace the entire piece. The inextricability of a section from its context, and of the context from the piece, means that talk of the interaction of any two sections (such as the horn solo and violin cadenza) may lead to a kind of blind-men-and-the-elephant situation. Our elephant is the intermodulation of the two pieces. We have to examine him holistically.

But we have to start somewhere. For example, both the symphony and the concerto have sections which can be called 'dominant motors'. The dominant motor in the first movement of the symphony (bars 402–23) is melodically but not rhythmically related to the movement's second theme; the dominant motor in the first movement of the concerto (bars 84–90) is rhythmically but not melodically related to a beautiful and unique section in that movement (bars 102–19) in which the large hemiolas of the kind found in the dominant motor are now more explicit, counterpointed in the violin against the triple metre in the winds. Neither of these two related sections in the concerto shows the kind of complexity of play with rhythm against metre found in the symphony's dominant motor (see Figure 2), where the tune is in canon at a distance of three beats, but one beat late with respect to the metre, and the wind accompaniment is offset one sixteenth-note too early with respect to the tune. The effect is static but vertiginous.

(By the way, Figure 2 does not show how Brahms breaks the stasis and gets out of the symphony's dominant motor. The perceived downbeat is shifted from the second beat of

FIGURE 2. Brahms, Symphony No. 2 in D major, Op. 73, I, bars 404 ff.: rhythm against metre in the 'dominant motor'.

the written bar to the first via four bars [bars 420–3] divided up into groups of 1 + 5 +
5 + 1 beats. The written downbeat [perceived third beat?] of the first group is isolated by
the dramatic halt of the wind ostinato, and on a crashing dissonance [bar 420]: the E and
D of the E-root dominant seventh chord against a melodic passing-tone C♯ in the bass.
The two groups of five are truncated hemiolas, each 2 + 2 + 1 [where the final single
beat stands for two beats], arpeggiating E-root dominant seventh and A-root dominant
seventh, respectively. The A-root dominant seventh of D, prolonged in the background
of the entire dominant motor section, resolves on the written third beat [of bar 423] on to
a first-inversion D-root tonic. This resolution stands alone, for looking back after the
next bar or so, one perceives the perceived downbeat to have shifted, finally, to the
written downbeat, one beat later [bar 424].

Another way of describing this process is as a recursive function of accelerating
application. The function right-shifts the perceived downbeat to beat 2 with respect to
the previous perceived downbeat. Thus the dominant motor starts by shifting [from 1] to
2, then to 2 of 2 [written 3] at the resolution [bar 423], then very quickly to 2 of 2 of 2
[written 1] on the next beat [bar 424]. This last shift is perceivable only in retrospect, but
undeniable after a bar or two more have passed [by bar 425].

Of course the situation is not as simple as this description makes it out to be. For
example, new 'felt downbeats' do not entirely displace their predecessors, which persist
by metric inertia at least. Even a merely metrical model of this music should show
multiple layers of coexistent, mutually contradictory perceived metres fading in and out
of our perceptual foreground.)

A third section of the concerto (bars 27–40) has a similar degree of complexity in
playing rhythms against each other and against the metre, but serves an opposite overall
effect: instead of vertiginous stasis, increasing compression released by expansion. Figure
3 shows the numbers of beats between accents, within the bass part, between the bass
part and the treble and the treble part and the bass, and within the treble part itself. The
accented notes are at first all F♯s and are always the highest pitches in their small, local
phrases.

One could continue following some quality to its manifestation at some other place in
either piece, running one's index finger over the loops and whorls of the elephant's hide.
The elephant is many-dimensional; the description, one-dimensional. Narrative or
expository prose has to present a sequential model of what is in this case a non-sequential
object. The whole pattern of interaction in our perception of the two pieces, which is
palpable, definite, and present to our intuition, is expressible here only through shadows
and images, through one-dimensional tracks on multi-dimensional surfaces. Other
modes of discourse—dialogues, dramas, poetry, mathematics, choreography, sculpture,
music—are capable of producing objects in a multiply dimensioned space, objects which
could more fully and precisely characterize musical pieces and their interaction in our
perception.[3]

---

[3] See Benjamin Boretz, 'What Lingers On (, When the Song Is Ended)'. The present paper is a kind of trope on
Boretz's. (As for the actual substantiality of intermodulations, or the essentiality of D-ishness, let me remark, as
Socrates did in a similar context, that though it may be a useful assumption, god knows if it is true.)

FIGURE 3. Brahms, Violin Concerto in D major, Op. 77, I, bars 28–41.

'Clearly, in knowing what is in a poem we know immediately and not in discursive terms, our knowing being intermediate between a proposition and a sensation, partaking, in a way, of character of both.'[4] If this is true of a poem, or musical composition, it is true *a fortiori* of that much more tenuous musical object of knowledge that arises when we compare two works of art. Our mode of knowing is as weird as what we know, in a similar fashion. My metaphors and discourse here have tried to characterize any musical comparison as an object (essence, elephant) as substantial as possible, while emphasizing its fluidity and complexity. It is impossible properly to know the parts (of a comparison or of a piece) without knowing the whole, or to know the whole without knowing the parts. Worse, the relations among the parts (including the greatest part, the whole) largely comprise those parts, even within one piece of music. A representation of such knowledge will distort it least when in a medium which, unlike discursive prose, and more like music, poetry, and so on, offers a comparable range of dimensional richness, of fluidity, allusiveness, complexity, and dependence on context.

If the comparison (of two works by Brahms), as a musical object, is such a slippery character ontologically and epistemologically, so hard to know and grasp, so elusive of adequate representation, what shall we say of the notions of *œuvre*, style, or period? When they appear, especially in scholarly prose, that least ambiguous, most impoverished medium, can they be well represented, can they well represent their musical constituents? The process of abstraction, as musicians often remind theorists, runs the danger of leaving behind, discarded, precisely those ingredients which give an object the flavour of music.

Under one view of the matter, 'musical style' (for example) would be an n-ary relation constituted by means of, or analysable into, binary relations that are comparisons of the

---

4 Delmore Schwartz, 'Poetry as Imitation', 106.

kind described here. The prospect of such a construction is daunting. There is something musical about musical style, but while a comparison maintains intimacy with its musical pieces and tastes, as it were, like a metapiece or hyperpiece, musical style does not itself feel like a piece of music, and has little really to do with any individual composition. I must leave it to musicological monophysites, better men than I, to demonstrate that the body of musical constructs, from individual piece through comparisons to concepts like style, is all one substance, all musical, all divine.

# MUSICAL LANGUAGE AND STRUCTURE IN THE THIRD SYMPHONY

## ROBERT BAILEY

THE year 1983 marked two anniversaries—the sesquicentenary of Brahms's birth, and also the centenary of Wagner's death. No composition seems more appropriate for discussion in this context than the Third Symphony, which also celebrated its one-hundredth anniversary in 1983.

The entire musical world, and particularly that of Wagner's native Germany, felt a sense of shock and loss at the news of his death in February 1883. Both Bruckner and Brahms seem to have reflected this in their symphonic composition. The case of Bruckner is well known: he was at work on his Seventh Symphony when the news reached him, and he recast the slow movement as a memorial to the deceased master, adding for symbolic purposes the intruments most closely associated with Wagner and in fact invented by him—the so-called 'Wagner tubas'. In the summer of 1883 Brahms completed his Third Symphony, a work which can to some extent also be regarded as a memorial to the deceased composer, a memorial of Brahms's own particular sort, for he accomplished it through two musical evocations. The first of these occurs in the first movement of the symphony and sounds curiously reminiscent of the Sirens at the end of the opening scene of *Tannhäuser* (Examples 1 and 2). *Tannhäuser* was an opera of special significance for Brahms. For several years he had owned Wagner's autograph of the second scene of Act 1 in the version Wagner had composed afresh for the Paris performances of 1861, and he also had in his permanent possession a copy of the score of the earlier 'Dresden' version (now in the Gesellschaft der Musikfreunde in Vienna), to which his musical reference in the Third Symphony clearly relates. Brahms's woodwind figuration for the sustained chords is strangely reminiscent of the figuration Wagner appended to his own concluding harmony.

Brahms's second reference occurs towards the conclusion of his second movement (Example 3). Brahms frequently indulges in short passages of this sort in inner movements of large-scale instrumental pieces: for a moment he seems to depart from the context of the movement, bringing in a short section apparently different from anything else in the movement, and then allowing the original context to resume. (The second movement of the Fourth Symphony affords another equally striking example.) The

EXAMPLE 1. Brahms, Symphony No. 3 in F major, Op. 90, I, bars 31–5.

EXAMPLE 2. Wagner, 'Sirens' passage from *Tannhäuser*, Act 1, scene 1.

EXAMPLE 3. Brahms, Symphony No. 3 in F major, Op. 90, II, bars 106–15.

beginning of the passage under consideration here seems to evoke a section from the so-called 'Immolation Scene' at the end of *Götterdämmerung* (Example 4). The melody which is continuous in the Brahms is divided by Wagner between Brünnhilde and an orchestral counterpoint.

There is yet another evocation in the Third Symphony, something more like a direct quotation: as the main subject of the first movement Brahms uses a melody found in the first movement of Schumann's Third Symphony (Examples 5 and 6). In Schumann's movement, this passage serves as a curious addition to the recapitulation and has no counterpart in the exposition. Schumann placed his melody in two different registers, scoring it first for the cellos and then for the violas in the higher register—a registral disposition at times reflected in Brahms's treatment of it.

This last reference leads to the important question of Brahms's formal models for the symphony—a genre he approached with great hesitation, as is well known. In terms of the design of the whole symphony, Brahms does not utilize the Classical model, but recalls the model provided by Schumann. This applies to the inner movements in particular and to the lack of contrast between a large-scale scherzo and a large-scale slow movement, along the lines of pieces like Beethoven's Ninth Symphony and Schubert's C major Symphony. It was really Bruckner who pursued this idea. Brahms looked instead to a later generation and constructed his inner movements as small-scale intermezzi, basing them (as Schumann had done in some noteworthy cases) on principles derived from strophic song composition. Moreover, in the Third Symphony Brahms paired the

EXAMPLE 4. Wagner, 'Immolation Scene' from *Götterdämmerung*, Act 3, scene 3.

EXAMPLE 5. Schumann, Symphony No. 3 in E♭ major, Op. 97, I, bars 444–54.

two inner movements together by placing them in the same key, albeit with opposite modes—second movement in C major, third movement in C minor (see Figure 1). Like Kalbeck before him, Christian Martin Schmidt also regards these two movements as paired together and has pointed out that the autograph for this symphony, now owned by the Library of Congress, was actually put together by Brahms in three parcels—the two outer movements, Parts 1 and 3, the pair of inner ones, Part 2.[1] Grouping two (or more) movements together to form a single unit of the total symphonic design larger than that provided by an individual movement later became a characteristic procedure in Mahler's symphonic composition.

With this pair of movements in C major and C minor, we confront a crucial principle

---

[1] Johannes Brahms, *Sinfonie Nr. 3 F-Dur, Op. 90: Taschen-Partitur*, ed. Christian Martin Schmidt, 194, n. 90. The autograph of the Third Symphony is written on two types of sixteen-staff paper; movements 1 and 4 are on one type, movements 2 and 3 on another. Moreover, the inner two movements are paginated together, separately from each of the outer two movements. Cf. the facsimile of his manuscript in *Johannes Brahms. Opus 24, Opus 23, Opus 18, Opus 90.*

EXAMPLE 6. Brahms, Symphony No. 3 in F major, Op. 90, I, bars 1–6.

of later nineteenth-century tonal construction—the principle of modal mixture. Modal mixture is ultimately responsible for the calculation of many aspects of this symphony and determines the layout of its three Parts—a layout which in some ways can be likened to that of a traditional first-movement design: presentation of the tonic in the first movement (a movement in which the dominant is conspicuous by its absence),

FIGURE 1. Brahms, Symphony No. 3 in F major, Op. 90.

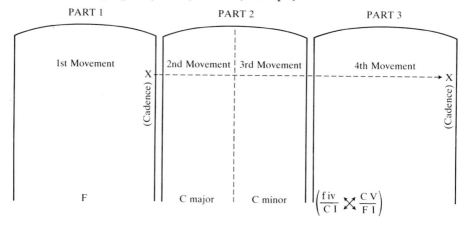

FIGURE 2. Brahms, Symphony No. 3 in F major, Op. 90, IV.

EXPOSITION

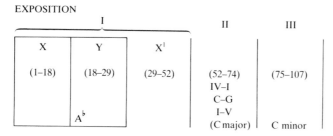

| | I | | II | III |
|---|---|---|---|---|
| X | Y | X¹ | | |
| (1–18) | (18–29) | (29–52) | (52–74) | (75–107) |
| | | | IV–I | |
| | | | C–G | |
| | A♭ | | I–V | |
| | | | (C major) | C minor |

DEVELOPMENT

| X | Y expanded |
|---|---|
| (108–148) | (149–172) |
| | ⟿ F |

RECAPITULATION

| I | II | III |
|---|---|---|
| X¹ | | |
| (172–194) | (194–216) | (217–252) |
| | ⎛ IV–I ⎞ | |
| | ⎜ F–C ⎟ | |
| | ⎝ I–V ⎠ | |
| F minor | F major | F minor |
| | | ↑ |
| | | root position |

CODA

| X expanded | Y shortened; initiates cadence |
|---|---|
| (253–280) | (280–309) |
| | F major |
| | ↑ |
| | root position |

exploration of the dominant at the beginning of Part 2 and its prolongation with change of mode in the latter portion, and then the finale which brings F and C into direct confrontation and provides the necessary tonal and modal resolutions for them.

This approach to large-scale design in turn calls forth an unusual and highly imaginative structure for the finale (see Figure 2). The exposition falls into three clearly defined sections, and Brahms begins the first of them with two sharply contrasted strophes—a procedure he also follows in the first movement; but whereas the two strophes are tonally differentiated here, they are both in the tonic in the first movement. After their initial statement, Brahms deploys these two strophes separately—X to initiate the development and Y to conclude it, and likewise X to initiate the coda and Y half-way through it. These two strophes are also differentiated in that X presents the main material of Section I, while Y remains utterly independent.

Section I is an excellent example of another typical later nineteenth-century procedure—presenting the tonic *by implication* rather than by direct statement of its root-position triad. The first root-position F triad in this movement does not occur until Section III (at bar 82), where it is indecisive since the local tonic of this section is C minor. F emerges more definitively at the culmination of the development (in the retransition), where the A♭ of Strophe Y is resolved to the tonic, but the mode of F is now major. As far as F triads are concerned, root position here quickly gives way to six-four position, the mode reverts to minor, and F proceeds on to a C major triad to inaugurate the recapitulation (bars 167–72).

There is no longer any possible ambiguity in Section I of the recapitulation, not only because of the strong reinforcement of F in the immediately preceding passage, but also because Strophes X and Y do not appear here. The omission of X is crucial, for in its initial presentation it works to some extent around the potential ambiguity of the relationship between F minor and C:

$$
\begin{array}{ccc}
V & \to & I \\
C & : & F \\
I & \leftarrow & iv
\end{array}
$$

The cadential progression of the second movement has already presented the latter interpretation (Example 7). The same possible ambiguity occurs in Section II of the exposition between C and G, though both elements are in the major mode. When this section returns in the recapitulation, C and G are naturally transposed to F and C, now likewise both in the major mode, but the definitions of the role of F as tonic alluded to above make this section less susceptible to ambiguity of interpretation than its counterpart in the exposition.

The coda expands on X and Y, which had been omitted from the recapitulation, and thus effectively balances their appearance at the beginning of the movement. The initial segment of the coda, then, is Strophe X in a newly harmonized version complete with root-position triads, but it begins off-tonic in B minor. When its main subject returns at the original pitch-level (bars 260–6), it is likewise harmonized with root-position triads,

EXAMPLE 7. Brahms, Symphony No. 3 in F major, Op. 90, II, bars 131–4.

but only those of C and A♭. F returns to this melodic context with the ensuing augmentation of the subject (bars 267–71), now shortened and without root-position triads, but with the *major* mode, which in turn alters the subject itself so that the characteristic F minor elements are 'resolved' to F major. The subject's initial four-note motive then appears in the bass and initiates a recall of the primary cell from the first movement (but not yet at the tonic pitch-level).

In bar 280, the material of Strophe Y returns in unambiguous F *major*, root-position F triads are present, and the recall leads to the primary cell from the first movement once again—now at the tonic pitch-level and in counterpoint with the initial four-note motive of the finale with a tonic pedal below (Example 8)—and this serves as an introduction to the descending cadential passage from the first movement which now likewise concludes the finale.

EXAMPLE 8. Brahms, Symphony No. 3 in F major, Op. 90, IV, bars 297–301.

EXAMPLE 9. Brahms, Symphony No. 3 in F major, Op. 90.
(*a*) I, bars 220–4.

(*b*) IV, bars 302–9.

By virtue of these recalls from the first movement at the end of the finale, this symphony is 'cyclic' in the customary meaning of the term. None of Brahms's other symphonies makes such obvious reference to the understood norm of cyclic procedure—the straightforward recurrence of thematic material. By allowing the cadential portion of the first movement to return and serve again as conclusion for the last movement, Brahms creates something more than a mere thematic recall, something which also concerns the structure of the whole symphony. The element most strongly and unequivocally associated with the tonic over the course of the symphony (namely, the cadence of the first movement) returns at the conclusion of the symphony in order to reinforce the definition of F as tonic. At the same time, Brahms builds in one other subtle detail. The passage at the end of the first movement is constructed in such a way as to leave an important melodic element unresolved, and that resolution is supplied only at the end of the finale when the passage returns. At the end of the first movement, the main theme descends through three registers in the violins (see Example 9a). But with the penultimate note, the violins reach their lowest note on the open G string and therefore shift up to a higher register to join in the final chord. At the conclusion of the finale, however, Brahms gives the third statement of the theme to the violas, and they carry the melodic descent all the way down to the low F, thereby achieving the full melodic resolution lacking at the end of the first movement (Example 9b).

A noteworthy feature of the first movement's exposition (Figure 3) is the strophic construction of its individual parts—a principle at work on the larger scale in the inner movements, which are constructed like strophic songs. Strophic organization of expositions, or portions of expositions, often occurs in later nineteenth-century sonata form. Parallel strophes in the exposition provide a basis for foreshortening in the recapitulation, where the repetition is typically removed. In the first movement's exposition, then, Brahms has set up the first section (see Figure 3, where this section is labelled 'A') in three strophes, the second and third of which employ exactly the same thematic material; inevitably, this repetition is removed in the recapitulation. Thus, two contrasting strophes appear at the beginning, and we have seen that this also occurs at the beginning of the finale. Here, both strophes are in the tonic, and they differ not only in thematic materials but also in modal treatment—Strophe I presents both modes of F, while Strophe II with its new materials is confined to the *major* mode of F. The beginning of Strophe I provides a classic example of the differentiation between melodic and harmonic materials so often at work in later nineteenth-century music: the tonic triads here are all *major* triads, but the melodic materials present both F major and F minor (Example 10; cf. Example 6). The central cell for this movement is the *minor* third, F/A♭, and it employs three characteristic extensions of this cell (Example 11)—the first a kind of *Urmotiv* that simply duplicates the initial F an octave higher, the second a form which falls back a sixth to A♮ rather than A♭ and thus incorporates modal mixture into a configuration otherwise associated with the minor mode.

The central cell opens the symphony as a kind of large-scale upbeat to the main theme. It is associated with F *minor* by virtue of its A♭, and it also serves as the bass line for the

FIGURE 3. Brahms, Symphony No. 3 in F major, Op. 90, I, Exposition.

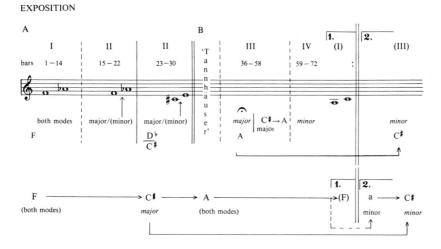

EXAMPLE 10. Brahms, Symphony No. 3 in F major, Op. 90, I, bars 1–5.

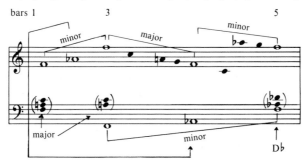

EXAMPLE 11. Central cell and three characteristic extensions.

main theme that comes in against it—first in F *major*, then in F *minor*. By such means, both modes of the tonic are presented at the opening of Strophe I, where the first triad other than the tonic is a D♭ major triad, prefiguring the first structural tonal change from F to D♭. At the same time, this harmonic juxtaposition is parallel to the corresponding appearance of the D♭ (C♯) triad after the extended A major triad in Strophe III.

As we have noted, Strophe II restricts the mode of F to major and thereby projects on a larger-scale formal level the tensions of the fundamental cell of the minor third. Strophe II is repeated (bars 23–30), but now in D♭, and the process of arrival at D♭ projects the characteristic ambiguity implicit in the solitary interval of a third. A given third can naturally assume either of two positions in a triad, and thus F/Ab can serve as the lower third of an F *minor* triad, as it does by implication at the beginning of the movement, or it can become the upper third of a Db *major* triad. It is precisely through restatement of the F/Ab that Brahms arrives at Db (cf. bars 21–2). And if the mode of this new key, spelled enharmonically as C♯ major, is then mutated to the minor mode, its bottom third, C♯/E♮, can also serve as the upper third of an A major triad. And by exactly the same means that Brahms had shifted from F to Db, he later moves from Db (C♯) to A.

The second section of the exposition (labelled 'B' in Figure 3) begins with the *Tannhäuser* evocation (bars 31–5), serving here as a kind of symbolic introduction to the most unusual passage in this movement—an extended section over an open-fifth pedal on A with no substantive change of harmony (Strophe III, bars 36–43). The first change of harmony does not occur until bar 44, when Brahms suddenly brings back the C♯ major triad and quickly modulates back to A major (bar 46). The final strophe, however, changes the mode once again, now to A *minor* (bars 61 ff.), and the lower third of its triad returns to F major for the repetition of the exposition. The concluding third of the first ending, A/C, is thus followed immediately by the F/Ab at the beginning of the exposition. This same juxtaposition of thirds, A/C and F/Ab, also occurs at the end of the F major statement of Strophe II (bars 19–22) in connection with the modulation to Db.

The key of Db assumes much greater weight in the exposition than it might otherwise have done, considering the relatively brief space allotted to it, precisely because it appears in connection with the repetition of an entire strophe *just heard in the tonic*. In any case, the exposition as a whole moves through a complete circle of major thirds—F, Db(C♯), and A, and on around to F once more as the exposition begins again. The repetition of the exposition is thus absolutely necessary to complete the circle, and precisely because Brahms will later reverse direction in the circle as he goes from the second statement of the exposition into the development. An essential compositional point of the movement is lost when the exposition's repetition is arbitrarily omitted in performance.

Db(C♯) is the only key in the exposition which Brahms confined exclusively to its major mode; its minor mode he withholds for the development. We have seen that the exposition's one long stable tonal plateau—on A major at the beginning of Strophe III—was finally interrupted by a harmonic shift to a C♯ major triad. That shift also foreshadows the tonal plan at the beginning of the development, where Brahms modulates directly from A minor to C♯, but now as C♯ *minor*. The material recalled in C♯ *minor* is the initial portion of Strophe III in A *major*. The circle of major thirds has

FIGURE 4. Brahms, Symphony No. 3 in F major, Op. 90, I, Development and Retransition.

indeed reversed its direction and eventually returns to F at the beginning of the recapitulation.

Like the exposition, the development (Figure 4) is clearly divided into two parts—the first moving quickly from A minor to C♯ minor, as we have seen, and finally back to A (at bar 90), but now in the major mode, to be followed by a circle-of-fifths move to G (bars 91–7). Brahms articulates the beginning of the second part with an arresting arrival at E♭, which is short-lived and in fact serves merely as a pivot between G♮ and G♭. In terms of the tonal scheme of the movement so far, the *major* third is thus converted to a *minor* third, which was absent from the exposition but will become prominent in the recapitulation:

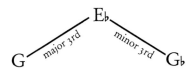

E♭ returns at bar 112 to initiate the retransition, which moves rapidly through a descending sequence of thirds no longer confined to the major mode:

$$E\flat \;—\; C\flat \;—\; A\flat \;—\; F$$

major     minor     minor
3rd       3rd       3rd

The tonic at the beginning of the recapitulation is thus immediately approached through a segment of the circle of *minor* thirds—C♭, A♭, F—leaving the D, which would complete this circle, to serve as an area of further tonal contrast in the recapitulation itself.

The recapitulation (Figure 5) begins with not one but two statements of the primary

FIGURE 5. Brahms, Symphony No. 3 in F major, Op. 90, I, Recapitulation.

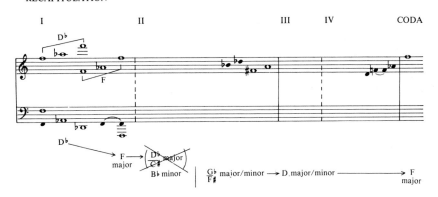

cell (in its first extension) in two different registers—the first harmonized as a progression in Db, the second as one in F. The two possible harmonic interpretations of the tonic form of the fundamental third—F/Ab—are thus brought together here in two successive statements. We have seen that the recapitulation is characteristically shortened by omitting the exposition's repetition of Strophe II. The single statement of the strophe is now modified so that it progresses through a sequence of major and minor thirds not unlike the one prepared for this purpose in the retransition. Strophe II's original move toward Db major is now deflected to Bb minor, which with the third Bb/Db effects a modulation to Gb(F#) major. The latter immediately changes mode so that its lower third, F#/A, can support a modulation to D major for Strophe III, otherwise analogous to Strophe III in the exposition. Strophe IV likewise appears in D minor, but its final third, D/F♮ (analogous to the A/C♮ of the exposition's first ending), continues by adding an additional minor third (Ab) to precipitate the return of the tonic at the beginning of the coda.

The later nineteenth-century formal archetype of sonata form represents considerable revision of its Classical model. It is a full-fledged ternary structure instead of a binary one, and it does not provide for a repetition of the exposition. Finally, the exposition is customarily divided into three parts rather than two and provides for three key areas rather than the traditional two. This is in turn determined and supported by new developments in tonal language.

The Third Symphony is a decisive work in Brahms's creative career. Its outer movements are both in sonata form and represent two different possibilities in the transition from the earlier archetype to the later one. The first movement is still binary, and it has a repeated exposition which Brahms took great care to make absolutely essential in accordance with his modern musical language. And while that exposition is in two parts, it none the less contains three key areas. The finale, on the other hand, is a ternary movement, with no repetition of the exposition, and it is perhaps typical that from this particular perspective, Brahms's finales have on the whole been more 'progressive' or 'advanced' up to this point in his career than his first movements. As far as the latter are concerned, Brahms took the decisive step with his next symphony, the Fourth.

Meanwhile, we have seen that the symphony as a whole consistently involves the principle of modal mixture, to which Schoenberg drew attention when he talked about the 'transition from twelve major and twelve minor keys to twelve chromatic keys'. Schoenberg continued by saying that 'this transition is fully accomplished in the music of Wagner, the harmonic significance of which has not yet by any means been theoretically formulated'.[2] Not yet theoretically formulated, perhaps—but certainly absorbed by Brahms! And thus it seems singularly appropriate that in the Third Symphony he should have constructed a major masterpiece which embodies that principle and that he should

---

[2] Arnold Schoenberg, *Harmonielehre*; trans. *Theory of Harmony*, 389.

at the same time have evoked, by means of purely musical reference, precisely the two composers of the previous generation who played the largest role in his symphonic practice at this time—Schumann in terms of overall design and Wagner in terms of musical language.

# THEMATIC STRUCTURE AND FORMAL PROCESSES IN BRAHMS'S SONATA MOVEMENTS

## SIEGFRIED KROSS

How closely the music of the young Brahms imitated the style of Beethoven's middle period has often been noted. This orientation was in accordance not only with his education in a classicist tradition under the tutelage of Eduard Marxsen, but also with the rather strongly romanticized image of Beethoven then prevalent. At the time, this was thought to be progressive. More conservative musicians were oriented towards Mozart, who, however, was also romanticized. What Brahms knew about the music of Chopin, Schumann, and others of that generation is unknown, but it did not influence him in his first attempts to combine knowledge of tradition with his own expressive impulses. That Brahms, from an environment so influenced by Beethoven, put up a fierce resistance to taking cognizance of Schumann's works is shown by the incident with the pianist Louise Langhans-Japha, who wanted to make him familiar with Schumann's *Das Paradies und die Peri*.[1] After coming to know both Schumann and his work, Brahms became conscious of the fact that his former refusal to study Schumann's music seriously was due to his former environment. 'They only showed him to me from this side,' he remarked, pointing to an empty sheet of music paper.[2]

To investigate the topic of thematic structure and formal processes, it is not necessary to discuss in detail the question of the young Brahms's continuity or discontinuity with the Beethovenian tradition. Suffice it to note that in his Piano Sonata in C major, Op. 1— the autograph shows that it was actually the fourth of his numbered piano sonatas[3]— Brahms used that type of theme which by its expansive three-step format propels the work forwards towards its finale and accounts for much of the dynamism of the music (Example 1). This is the developing type of theme which since the 1740s had gradually been supplanting the Baroque technique of 'spinning forth' material and can be seen in its most precise and purest form in the theme of the first movement of Mozart's Symphony in G minor, K. 550, where it determines the propulsive and conclusively 'logical' character of the piece. But this potent type of theme, with its expansive third step, is already present in the works of Handel: in his Concerto Grosso, Op. 6 No. 1, such a

---

[1] Max Kalbeck, *Johannes Brahms*, 1: 36.
[2] 'Man hatte ihn mir bisher nur von der Seite gezeigt'. Ibid., 1: 103.
[3] This autograph is owned by the Österreichische Nationalbibliothek, Vienna.

EXAMPLE 1. Brahms, Piano Sonata in C major, Op. 1, I, bars 1–6.

theme appears in the grosso as well as the concertino, clearly demonstrating Handel's progressiveness, even as he works within forms that were already becoming antiquated.

Allusion to the thematic similarity of Brahms's Opus 1 and Beethoven's *Hammerklavier* Sonata and to the parallelism of its key disposition with that of the *Waldstein* Sonata is present in nearly all descriptions of this work. One should add, though, that the complex manner in which Brahms propels his opening theme—by metrically displacing its motivic units, and thereby immediately developing them—goes beyond thematic expansion of the Classical type, where the third step of the theme is usually made dynamic by the changing combination of its manifold parts and is linked with the subsequent phrase by displacement of its final tone from the main accent (first beat) on to a secondary accent (third beat). In his very first published work, Brahms the great experimenter with rhythm already reveals himself, and at a time before he had come to know the more complex rhythms of Schumann.

Without dealing in detail with Brahms's formal principles and tendencies and their relationship to the Beethovenian tradition, I would like to note that the proportions of the various sections of the first movements in his early sonatas correspond to those in Beethoven. While Mozart's development sections, as a rule, are shorter than the respective expositions,[4] the proportions of exposition-development-recapitulation in the works of Haydn, especially his later symphonies, tend towards 1 : 1 : 1. After the extreme case of the *Eroica* first movement (150 : 247 : 294 bars, or 1 : 1.65 : 1.96), Beethoven stabilized these proportions, and Brahms fashioned the first movement of his Opus 1 in exactly the same proportions, except that the recapitulation is shortened by ten bars in favour of the coda (87 : 86 : 77 + 21 bars).

The Piano Sonata in F♯ minor, Op. 2, also composed before his intensive study of Schumann, shows no essential deviations from the thematic plan and form of the Sonata, Op. 1, although the three-step format of its first theme appears in a more potent form: the expansive third step is itself presented in three steps, and in an especially audible manner (Example 2). But even this thematic structure can be traced back at least to Handel (compare, for example, the theme in his Concerto Grosso, Op. 6 No. 1, cited

---

[4] For example, in the *Jupiter* Symphony, K. 551, the proportions of exposition, development, and recapitulation are 1 : 0.56 : 1; in the Symphony in G minor, K. 550, 1 : 0.64 : 1.35; and in the Symphony in E♭ major, K. 543, 1 : 0.58 : 1.1 (without the slow introduction).

EXAMPLE 2. Brahms, Piano Sonata in F♯ minor, Op. 2, I, bars 1–8.

already). It is also not significant that the development section here is only half as long as the exposition (due to the inner structure of the themes), for, of course, a general statement on proportional relationships for the works of a composer has only statistical value and is not called into question by considerable deviations in individual cases (such as can also be found in Haydn, Mozart, and Beethoven), especially since 'the norm' results as much from the stabilization of proportional relations in later works as from earlier individual exceptions.

In the compositions which follow the Sonata, Op. 2, the stabilization of proportional relations is already apparent. Although the first movement of the Sonata in F minor, Op. 5, was composed in October 1853, during Brahms's first visit to Schumann, it clearly stands within the tradition of Beethovenian thematic and formal practices (even discounting its often-noted but superficial allusions to the *Appassionata*). The opening theme is organized into two phrases, and each is clearly cast in expansive three-step format, both procedures found in themes of Classical works (Example 3). But Brahms's motives and sequential disposition charge the theme with moments of tension which subsequently will be applied to forming larger structures. Contributing to these moments of tension is the contrary motion between upper voice and bass in bar 1, which is immediately echoed in each of the next two bars and, on a larger scale, seems to generate the overall contrary motion of bars 1–4, as treble and bass establish the tonal frame of the first theme by moving progressively further apart, the chromatic progression in the bass spanning a fourth from initial tonic to closing $I_4^6$–V (the final C in the descent at first rapidly quit). These elements—contrary motion, emphasis of the fourth, and chromatic progression—by nature 'pre-thematic', find varied reiteration in bars 17–21, but, more importantly, seem to legislate and legitimate most of the rest of the

EXAMPLE 3.  Brahms, Piano Sonata in F minor, Op. 5, I, bars 1–6.

exposition, accumulating in a manner truly remarkable. Although the overall form of Brahms's movement adheres rather closely to Beethovenian proportions (72 : 66 : 85 bars), the manner of discourse within the movement is original.[5]

The piano style of the young Brahms is clearly orchestral and reaches beyond the possibilities of the piano, even though he conceived his works for that instrument. Even the experienced pianist Clara Schumann was misled: once, while listening from outside the room, she thought she heard piano duet playing, but found only Brahms by himself.[6] It is interesting to see the different reactions of the Schumanns towards Brahms's instrumental writing: while the pianist Clara noted in her diary that in Brahms's *Phantasie* in D minor for Piano, Violin, and Violoncello (Anh. IIa No. 6) 'here and there the sound of the instruments was not suitable to their characters . . .',[7] the composer Robert recognized in the piano sonatas that Brahms 'made an orchestra of lamenting and loudly rejoicing voices out of the piano'. Schumann acknowledged the mixing of genres, calling the sonatas 'veiled symphonies', but then stressed the possibilities for future growth: 'When he will direct his magic wand to where the masses of choir and orchestra will lend him their powers, we can look forward to even more wondrous glimpses of the secret world of spirits.'[8]

Indeed, shortly thereafter, in the spring of 1854, Brahms began working on a

---

[5] The similarities with Liszt's Sonata in B minor about which Walter Frisch has written in *Brahms and the Principle of Developing Variation*, 47–9, seem to me superficial.

[6] Kalbeck, *Brahms*, 1: 218.

[7] 'der Klang der Instrumente war hier und da nicht immer ganz ihrem Charakter angemessen . . .' Berthold Litzmann, *Clara Schumann: Ein Künstlerleben*, 2: 282.

[8] 'Wenn er seinen Zauberstab dahin senken wird, wo ihm die Mächte der Massen, im Chor und Orchester, ihre Kräfte leihen, so stehen uns noch wunderbarere Blicke in die Geisterwelt bevor.' 'Neue Bahnen', 185 (reprint, 2: 301).

EXAMPLE 4. Brahms, Piano Concerto in D minor, Op. 15, I, bars 1–11.

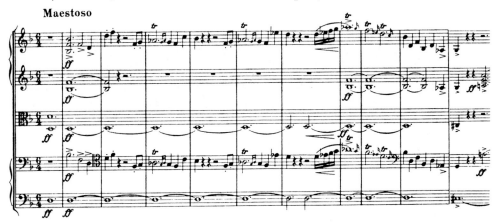

composition which reached so far beyond his style of piano writing up to that time that he proved unable to master the work as a sonata for two pianos. Though it may not have been his intention, Brahms was compelled by purely musical reasons to fulfil Schumann's predictions at a time when he did not believe himself equal to the task. This first attempt at composing a symphony failed, and he could save the piece only by a partial retreat to the piano, by reworking portions of the composition into a piano concerto, later to become Op. 15.[9] It is a pity that for this work, like most others, he destroyed all intermediate stages; he never showed any appreciation for those music philologists who find sketches and unfinished versions of works as interesting as the definitive ones.

Nevertheless, we may assume that the first thematic complex in the planned symphony is identical in musical substance with those in the Piano Concerto, Op. 15, and we may therefore suppose that Brahms also based this symphony on the expansion type of theme (Example 4). This type, however, does not occur at the very beginning of the work, but only in the secondary phase of the first theme (bars 3–10), as it also does in the Piano Quintet in F minor, Op. 34. Again the theme is charged with moments of tension, which here relate exclusively to the tonal structure of the movement. Brahms begins with a timpani roll on the tonic D. But the listener's expectation of a piece in D is thwarted when the theme sounds emphatically in B♭ major, making the fundamental tone the basis of a submediant sixth chord. In each section of the three-step theme, Brahms adds as the longest note an A♭, emphasizing this in the third phase with an accent and a trill, thus transforming the fictitious tonic of B♭ major into a dominant seventh chord. This type of transformation of tonic into dominant became one of his most important, though often misinterpreted means for shifting the tonal centre to the subdominant region (for example, at the beginning of the *German Requiem*, Op. 45, and the First Symphony, Op. 68). Yet in this case, although the added seventh transforms the submediant chord, which

[9] Cf. Siegfried Kross, 'Brahms the Symphonist', 129–30.

EXAMPLE 5. Accumulation of structural semitones in Brahms, Piano Concerto in D minor, Op. 15, I, bars 1–26.

bar   1    2    4    12    13              21    23   24    26

had suggested B♭ major as tonal basis, into a dominant six-five chord which prepares for E♭ major—all the more because the A♭ is emphasized by occurring as the peak of the phrase—Brahms does not cadence in that key, but rather moves to an A major six-five chord, which belongs to the tonic of D minor, as yet not perceptible. The second occurrence of the theme confirms A major as an important tonal plateau, but leads to a series of diminished chords. The main key is manifested only at bar 26, and then as a six-four chord. The cadence from submediant B♭ major to the dominant A major, with its Neapolitan effect, and the chain of harmonic changes that it sets off (see Example 5) produces an accumulation of structural semitones, of multiple leading-tones that legitimates all such relationships in the rest of the movement. Although this is the first example of such procedures in the works of Brahms (as already observed and described by Edwin Evans in the early 1930s[10]), it works within a tradition of using double leading-tones, from above as well as below, already established in the eighteenth century (cf. the themes of Bach's Musical Offering and the G minor Fugue in the *Well-Tempered Clavier*, Book 1).

Since the symphonic version of Op. 15 has not survived, we cannot know whether the theme that introduces the solo part in the concerto (bars 91 ff.) was also present in the symphony. Furthermore, one might wonder whether Brahms could also have experimented with three contrasting themes in the symphonic version. The possibility is not remote, given a work whose formal problems are so clearly connected with the characteristic monumentality of the genre of symphony. This might well have been the case, although the introduction of the third theme might have resulted as the solution to another problem inherent in transforming a symphony into a concerto, that is, how to introduce the solo instrument after a complete orchestral exposition, without repeating the entire exposition. All three thematic complexes in the concerto show the same three-step format, though each is constructed in its own very different way, relative to its individual character, therefore allowing the movement to unfold.

The struggle for the creation of his first symphonic composition, a work which he lamented 'cannot be born',[11] caused the young Brahms a creative crisis: 'I have no judgement and no power over the piece any more'.[12] The creation of a symphonic form which would become constantly more intense, reaching a climax only in its finale, had become such a problem for Brahms that he drew the conclusion that 'if one dares to

[10] *Historical, Descriptive and Analytical Account of the Entire Works of Brahms.*
[11] 'Schicke meinen unglückseligen, nicht geboren werden könnenden 1ten Satz . . .' *Brahms Briefwechsel*, 5: 196.
[12] 'Ich habe kein Urteil und auch keine Gewalt mehr über das Stück.' *Brahms Briefwechsel*, 5: 195.

compose symphonies after Beethoven, they must look completely different'.[13] Not until the mid-1870s would he achieve this 'completely different' conception; as late as the first years of that decade he remarked to Hermann Levi, 'I shall never compose a symphony! You have no idea what it feels like always to hear such a giant (Beethoven) marching behind one.'[14] Yet even at that time he had not left the field entirely, although he still had not found a conclusive resolution for the problems which had become evident in the Op. 15 symphony-concerto; as early as 1862 references to the work completed in 1876 as the First Symphony appear in his correspondence.[15]

The compositional studies which Schumann had recommended to Brahms, with quite another goal in mind, and in which Brahms immersed himself in the 1850s indeed appeared to take him in another direction. In the tradition of the Romantic and Cecilian movements, Schumann had prescribed the study of Renaissance vocal polyphony, 'in order to get the spirit of song'.[16] But Brahms took up another aspect of this music; it was voice-leading, the problem of equality of voices, that captivated him. He was especially fascinated by the possibility of intensifying this equality by means of strict canon, and in this way linking together melody and bass in the service of developing identical material. Brahms's exploration of this principle can be seen in the small motet 'Schaffe in mir, Gott, ein rein Herz', Op. 29 No. 2, as well as in the fifth movement of the *German Requiem*, composed at a later date. How naïvely proud he sounded when he wrote to Clara Schumann on 3 February 1855: 'I can now make canons in every possible artful form.'[17] But when one sees how intensively he had tried to found the formal development of his earlier works upon the structure of his theme, one realizes that in making this remark Brahms was touching upon a compositional issue basic to him. It would therefore seem that his study of canon was only superficially directed towards choral composition, where closed canonic forms were traditionally considered suitable, and that this study was undertaken in more general service to his compositional art. Indeed, his practice of testing new compositional techniques first in choral works was one that continued until his very last works.[18]

After his failed attempt at symphonic composition and the counterpoint studies that followed, Brahms prepared with great care his path to the genres which he considered the most difficult and problematic, the string quartet and the symphony. From chamber

[13] 'Ach, Gott, wenn man wagt, nach Beethoven noch Symphonien zu schreiben, so müssen sie ganz anders aussehen!' Kalbeck, *Brahms*, 1: 339.

[14] 'Ich werde nie eine Symphonie komponieren! Du hast keinen Begriff davon, wie es unsereinem zu Mute ist, wenn er immer so einen Riesen (Beethoven) hinter sich marschieren hört.' Ibid., 1: 165.

[15] *Brahms Briefwechsel*, 5: 314–15, 8: 15, and Berthold Litzmann, ed., *Clara Schumann–Johannes Brahms Briefe*, 2: 78.

[16] 'damit man hinter den Gesangsgeist komme.' Kalbeck, *Brahms*, 1: 186.

[17] 'Kanons kann ich jetzt in allen möglichen künstlichen Formen machen.' Litzmann, ed., *Schumann–Brahms Briefe*, 1: 73.

[18] Brahms even studied the rhythmical problem of dislocation of musical material from accented beat in a canon (Op. 37 No. 1). His abstractions from the real choral texture in his early works finally went so far that the compositions proved practically unperformable (cf. *Brahms Briefwechsel*, 4: 55; 5: 191).

works with piano (the two Quartets, Opp. 25 and 26; the Quintet, Op. 34; and the Horn Trio, Op. 40) and compositions with fuller complements of strings (the two Sextets, Opp. 18 and 36) he went on to the transparent settings for string quartet (Op. 51 Nos. 1 and 2) and, via a series of choral-orchestral works (the *German Requiem*, Op. 45; *Rinaldo*, Op. 50; the Alto Rhapsody, Op. 53; the *Schicksalslied*, Op. 54; and the *Triumphlied*, Op. 55) and the orchestral *Variations on a Theme by Haydn*, Op. 56, finally achieved his First Symphony.

The truly decisive work, the one which manifests the change in Brahms's manner of basing musical form on thematic structure, is the Piano Quartet in G minor, Op. 25. Special attention has been paid to this work in recent years within the context of scholarly discussion of Schoenberg's writing.[19] In a radio lecture on the occasion of the Brahms centenary in 1933, Schoenberg spoke provocatively about 'Brahms the Progressive', contradicting the tendency prevalent at the time (and still quite common) to represent Brahms as a Classical traditionalist.[20] The Op. 25 quartet was clearly a special work for Schoenberg—in 1937 he arranged it for orchestra—and he seems to have been one of the first to realize its key position in Brahms's creative output. But little attention has been paid to Schoenberg's perception of the decisive change in the relationship between thematic structure and formal processes that occurred in this work, a change that may well have prompted Joseph Joachim's perceptible irritation with the piece when he first saw it;[21] indeed, the literature that has followed from Schoenberg's remarks has dealt almost exclusively with the question of what he could have meant by his oracular term 'developing variation' and what importance this compositional method may have had in the music of Brahms.[22] 'Locus ab auctoritate est infirmissimus,' wrote Thomas Aquinas, referring to Boethius.[23] If the principle of 'developing variation' can be found at work from Brahms's Op. 1 to Op. 121, and in Beethoven and Mozart, as Schoenberg himself emphasized, as well as in Handel, one must wonder what significance a methodical investigation really has if it is unable to come to grips with the reorientation particular to Brahms's understanding of musical form.[24]

[19] Cf. Frisch, *Brahms and the Principle of Developing Variation*, 66–77; Klaus Velten, *Schönbergs Instrumentationen Bachscher und Brahms'scher Werke als Dokumente seines Traditionsverständnisses*, 82–6; Carl Dahlhaus, 'Zur Problemgeschichte des Komponierens' in *Zwischen Romantik und Moderne*, 47–9 (trans., 49–51); Peter Gülke, 'Über Schönbergs Brahms-Bearbeitung'.

[20] Due to the small number of people who heard this broadcast in 1933, Schoenberg's provocative idea made little impact at the time; it gained wider circulation only after the publication of this talk in English in 1950 and with my first reference to it in a commemorative article in 1958 ('Brahms in heutiger Sicht. Zum 125. Geburtstag am 7. Mai', 271–2).

[21] *Brahms Briefwechsel*, 5: 311.

[22] Cf. Siegfried Kross, 'Kontinuität und Diskontinuität im heutigen Brahms-Bild', 218.

[23] *Summa Theologiae* 1, 8, in *Topica Ciceronis Commentariae Libri VI* (Migne Patr. Lat. 64, 1166, etc.).

[24] I am of course aware of the recent writings of Walter Frisch on the topic of 'developing variations'. Although I appreciate many of the details of his work, in the basic matter of what can be considered a manifestation of the principal of 'developing variation' I am in disagreement with him. The problem of defining 'developing variation' begins with Schoenberg, who never stated clearly what he meant by the term. The difficulty with Frisch's approach, as I see it, is that he interprets the term so broadly that it becomes applicable to virtually all of Brahms's works, thereby obscuring the coherence of groups of compositions previously delineated on historical and stylistic grounds.

Viewed superficially, the theme of the first movement of Op. 25 again appears to be of the three-step type (Example 6). But it is remarkable that the beginning of the melody is sounded only in octaves, unharmonized except at the cadence, and in a rhythmically indifferent manner.[25] The intervals themselves are therefore the material which receives undivided attention: the initial ascending minor sixth, D–B♭, with its upper tone on an unaccented beat, is an unstable interval with the effect of a suspension and must be resolved downwards on to the fifth, A, like an *Überschlag* in the theory of ornamentation in the eighteenth century; the outline of the fifth above the dominant, with leading-tones above and below the top note, is expected (D–B♭–G♯–A), but Brahms leaves out the resolution to A in favour of a half-step from leading-tone to tonic, F♯ to G. The next two steps in this three-step theme are inversions of the first bar and, with their initial intervals of a fourth (F♮–C, C–G), demonstrate that the first tone of the theme was actually a substitute for F♮. This opening D may be required to accentuate the dominant, which has cadential function and which provides the root of the outline of the fifth, and to avoid F♮ beside the *subsemitonium modi* F♯ later in the bar. All the more forcefully then does the F♮ appear on the downbeat of the following bar, serving as part of a secondary dominant leading to the mediant (F[7]–B♭). In this bar, the central tone D is attained by half-step motion from E♭, the seventh of the secondary dominant. The resolution of the suspension B♭–A left pending in the first bar now arrives by means of a further inversion of the main motive in bar 3. It is true that the cadence at bar 4 leaves out the third of the chord, but the six-four suspension at the onset of the bar clearly establishes major mode. This is, however, immediately displaced in the next bar, where the main motive is sounded in inversion and in D minor. The double change from F♯ to F♮, within such a narrow space of time, the encircling of the (dominant-like) central D by E♭ and C♯, and the outline of the fifth with leading-tones established above and below the central D all create a wealth of tonal tensions and, in consequence, a series of semitone steps founded within the theme but subsequently used to form structures in the further course of the movement (compare, for example, the quite visible complexes beginning at bar 11 and again at bars 30 ff.).

In a manner far more radical than in former works, and notwithstanding all prior

EXAMPLE 6. Brahms, Piano Quartet in G minor, Op. 25, I, bars 1–4.

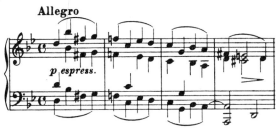

[25] Velten, *Schönbergs Instrumentationen*, 67.

attempts to base form on elements of theme, the thematic and formal structures in Op. 25 depend on each other. The border between the theme and its development or elaboration has become fluid. The theme itself no longer has the effect of expansion, although the three-step format is still recognizable. Rather, the parts of the theme already develop on their own, with nearly every interval taking part in forming the structure. Such a design must have consequences for the function of the other parts of the overall form of the movement. If the exposition of the themes has already become elaboration, if the development of the different complexes of themes has already resulted from the setting free of pre-thematic structural elements, then the development and recapitulation sections of the movement can no longer function as *confutatio* and *peroratio*. And indeed the exposition of Op. 25, with its 160 bars, is the dominating section of this 'sonata' form (the whole movement is only 373 bars long).

Although the exposition unmistakably ends with the dominant cadence at bar 160, writers on this work have not agreed on this point, for only if one fully appreciates the developmental character of the exposition can one comprehend why Brahms begins the development section with a fictitious recapitulation (bars 161–70). The repetition of the initial theme as opening of the development (instead of as beginning of the recapitulation) is necessary for the creation of the form, and ought not to be misconstrued as some kind of coda to the exposition. The development section no longer serves to split up and elaborate the themes. On the contrary, Brahms's technique of assembling his theme allows the theme less to materialize as pregnant *Gestalt* than to crystalize as a unity in a kind of micro-genesis (*Aktualgenese*) during the process of recognition. It may therefore appear as a whole in the development section without disturbing the formal function of that section. But the Beethovenian proportions of exposition versus development which remained intact in the compositions of the young Brahms can no longer be maintained. In this first work where Brahms's new idea of form becomes manifest, the proportions between exposition and development are 1 : 0.48; in subsequent works they stabilize at 1 : 0.7.

An altered relationship between exposition and development must logically have consequences for the structure of the recapitulation, all the more because Brahms has begun the development with a complete statement of the main theme in the tonic. Brahms's solution in this case is to create a recapitulation in four sections, each interrupted by periods developmental in character (see Figure 1). Form in this movement thus does not result from arbitrary decisions by the composer and is not a matter simply of constructing clearly designed sections; on the contrary, form is a consequence of the construction of the opening theme and has become a process interdependent with motivic structure. Beethoven's idea of form has been abandoned.

In 1979 James Webster conclusively demonstrated, using other methods, that during this phase of his compositional career Brahms drew upon the music of Schubert for his models; Webster furthermore suggested that it was probably Schumann who had encouraged this.[26] The observations of this current study would seem to corroborate

---

[26] James Webster, 'Schubert's Sonata Form and Brahms's First Maturity', Part 1, p. 18, and Part 2, p. 52.

FIGURE I. Design of the Recapitulation in the Piano Quartet in G minor, Op. 25, I.

| Partial Recapitulation | Developmental Section | Partial Recapitulation | Transition | Partial Recapitulation | Developmental Section | Partial Recapitulation |
|---|---|---|---|---|---|---|
| b. 237–46 ≈ 11–20 | b. 247–58 | b. 259–79 ≈ 21–41 | b. 279–81 | b. 281–303 ≈ 79–98 | b. 304–15 | b. 316–42 ≈ 113–40 |

these positions, though I can introduce no new documentary evidence to support the notion of Schumann as mediator. One should not forget, though, that Schumann introduced to the musical world not only Schubert's 'Great' C major Symphony, but also his 'Tragic' Symphony and numerous other works. Before his own study of Schubert's works, Schumann had had to give up several attempts at large-scale compositions due to insoluble problems. But it is probably not by chance that shortly after his study of Schubert he created his own first finished symphony and then, in close succession, several other cyclical works, one of them the Symphony in D minor about which Brahms was so enthusiastic. In the context of the present paper, I cannot go into detail about how greatly Schubert's technique of composition using pre-thematic structural elements influenced Schumann, but suffice it to say that without the technique of thematic connection which Schumann developed in his D minor Symphony it is hard to imagine Brahms's First Symphony coming into being. Brahms and Schumann must both have been conscious of the basic problem Schubert had had to solve in order to find his own compositional identity, that is, how to develop musical forms in a manner independent of Beethoven. This might well lead one, in spite of much current literature to the contrary, to view the late music of Schubert as more progressive, more capable of future development than that of Beethoven. At some point Brahms must have realized that to establish his own artistic talents he too must insulate himself from the Beethovenian tradition, must struggle to liberate himself from it, and this explains his intense irritation when others sought to relate his works, especially his symphonies, to those of his illustrious predecessor.[27]

As demonstrated, the tonal disposition and harmonization of intervals in the theme of the Op. 25 quartet clearly preconditioned the shaping of the form of the movement, or put another way, the formal processes found their bases in the structural elements of the theme. This type of interrelationship is not unique to this composition, but can also be discerned in its twin, the Piano Quartet in A major, Op. 26. These workings begin already in bars 4–5, but are most clearly visible in the group beginning at bar 13; both passages develop out of the opening shifting harmonies—A Major–F♯ minor–D major–F♯ major–B minor—which outline, among other things, the semitonal series A–A♯–B. There is a certain similarity here to Op. 25, for again the minor second becomes a structural element. At the same time, though, it is clear that this kind of progressive revelation of formal possibilities depends upon the specific thematic material.

With the Op. 26 quartet, the proportions of the parts of the sonata form are in the

[27] Cf. Kalbeck, *Brahms*, 3: 109.

relation 1.0 : 0.7 : 1.35. In most subsequent compositions Brahms retains these pro-portions, right on through the works of his final period. The development sections in his sonata movements remain about a third shorter than the expositions, with recapitulation and coda in nearly all cases about twice as long as development. The disparity in length between development on the one hand and recapitulation and coda on the other, however, creates a new problem, because the extra length is not caused by expansion of the coda. Furthermore, these movements have nothing in common with Beethoven's finale apotheoses, with their agogic accents which render the texture broader and broader while the inner tempo of harmonic changes (the harmonic rhythm) becomes progres-sively slower. On the contrary, Brahms aims at formal and textural concentration; canonic formations very often occur directly before or during the coda.[28]

If the thesis is correct that Brahms's chamber works with piano and with fuller string combinations, irrespective of their own aesthetic value, represent steps towards emancipation along the way to the string quartet and symphony, the dependence of formal processes on the structure of themes must be visible in these works in a special way. However interesting these works may be in detail—in the first movement of the String Sextet in G major, Op. 36, for instance, the generation of the longer second period (bars 17 ff.) from the basic elements of the first period, an accumulation of fifths linked by leading-tones (G–D and E♭–B♭, over B–B♭; then in the second period, extended to A–E♭) appearing in framework largely of contrary motion (first violin versus second viola and violoncello)—I wish to leave them aside and proceed now directly to the string quartets.

In the opening movement of the Quartet in C minor, Op. 51 No. 1, the Classical three-step theme can still be seen (Example 7). But in contrast to the opening theme of the First Piano Concerto (Op. 15), where a separate motive precedes the developmental portion of the theme, here the motive for development is an inseparable part of the first step; the further steps grow out of the first by means of fragmentation, elaboration, and development, as they had in Op. 25. The rising chromatic tones of the theme—F♯–G–A♭–A♮–B♭—find closure in the A♭–G of the cadence (bar 7) and the G♭–F of the extension of the cadence (bar 9). The secondary phrase (bars 11–14) is derived from this, and when the second violins pick up the secondary phrase (bar 15), the first violin's countermelody clarifies this structural connection. For the first time in Brahms's music, the initial complex is bound to the second, contrasting complex by musical elements which are not yet themes. With the first and second themes developed from the same motivic material, the dialectic principle of sonata, with its contrasting themes, is cast in doubt. But the Piano Quartet, Op. 25, had already so fundamentally broken with Classical tradition that in the C minor String Quartet no further reproportioning of overall form was necessary (the ratio remains 1.0 : 0.7 : 1.5, now becoming a characteristic of Brahms's music).

When the dialectic sonata principle is weakened in favour of structural unity of themes, with form now generated by thematic-motivic process, the cyclical form of the

---

[28] Cf. Matthias Rohn, *Die Coda bei Johannes Brahms.*

EXAMPLE 7. Brahms, String Quartet in C minor, Op. 51 No. 1, bars 1–10.

work as a whole cannot remain unaffected. Obviously the creation of a cyclic form consisting of movements contrasting in character can no longer be derived from the idea of contrast in the initial movement when indeed that first movement is laid out along other lines. It should come as no surprise, though, if whole movements, like the thematic sections within the first movement, now become linked by shared material.

This is the way Brahms chose in the C minor String Quartet: the two outer movements are linked to each other, as are also the two inner ones. The finale begins with a variant of the motive which in the first movement was split off from the first step of the theme and developed in the second and third steps (Example 8*a*). Repetition of tones and falling seconds are common to both Scherzo and Romance. But since the theme of the Romance is developed over the first theme of the opening movement, here transferred into the bass (Example 8*b*), the unity of the whole work, by means of pre-thematic, motivic material, is assured. As if to reconfirm this, Brahms again and again lets the chromatic elements which structured the opening theme of the first movement shimmer through, most remarkably in the Trio of the Scherzo, thereby emphasizing in a most impressive manner the common substance, or perhaps one should call it the common structure.

Most interesting in this connection is Brahms's First Symphony. From a letter Clara Schumann wrote to Joseph Joachim, we know that at first (in 1862) the opening movement began directly with the Allegro section; the slow introduction was not

EXAMPLE 8. Brahms, String Quartet in C minor, Op. 51 No.1.

(*a*) IV, bars 1–2                                   (*b*) II, bars 1–4

composed until later.[29] It is unfortunate that the letter from Clara Schumann to Brahms giving her reaction to this movement does not survive. But from her letter to Joachim we can tell that she regarded the opening of the movement as too direct, and Brahms must eventually have come to share her opinion.

In the introduction to this symphony, Brahms allows two basic lines to extricate themselves from the pedal bass inexorably marking the basic metre (Example 9). These lines remain without any thematic contours. The first interval added to the empty octave is the minor seventh which, as so often in Brahms, turns the tonic into a dominant, but here without leading it to subdominant regions. The two lines are developed, the one directed upwards in the violins and cellos, the other moving in contrary motion and linked with a lower third in the woodwinds and viola. Thus we have a two-part counterpoint filled out to three parts and set over a pedal-point. The real thematic nucleus, not yet discernible as such, though, lies in the upward-moving line. Once again the principle of identity of bass and melody is apparent, for this line, sounded, as it is, in both violins and cellos, appears in both functions. In the course of further development, the contrary motion generated by the winds and violas evolves its own formal energy.

Not until the ninth bar can thematic contours be heard—a descending diminished seventh leading sequentially to a major sixth—but these are more motivic than thematic. At bars 21 to 24 one encounters what appears to be simply a gradual preparation for the repetition of the introductory complex on the dominant, but which indeed proves to be an anticipation of the main theme (Example 10). This slow introduction, though composed *after* the main theme, thus has the formal function of preparing for the main theme by laying out its structural elements, although the legitimation of these elements is revealed only upon the exposition of the theme. In the works from Op. 25 on, the growth of form had occurred from structural elements in the themes. Now the theme itself is no longer a given, but likewise comes about through a process of growth. Such a

[29] Litzmann, *Clara Schumann*, 3: 123–4. The early date is confirmed in a letter from Joachim to Brahms (*Brahms Briefwechsel*, 5: 318–19).

EXAMPLE 9.  Brahms, Symphony No. 1 in C minor, Op. 68, I, bars 1–4. String parts only.

stepwise formation of themes is uncharacteristic of Beethoven, which makes understand-able Brahms's furious reaction to being apostrophized as his successor. One experiences this gradual unveiling (which may well replicate the actual compositional genesis of this material) in a temporally irreversible manner, so that the main theme, when it finally appears in full at bar 42 (Example 11), seems, as Hermann Kretzschmar has observed, like 'a secondary, artificial product of counterpoint'[30]—triadic melody, from bars 21–4, over rising chromatic line, from the thematic nucleus at bars 1 ff., now barely perceptible in the cello part.

The theme of Brahms's First Symphony thus proves to be a mere derivative of a motivic nucleus which does not itself appear as a theme. In this work more radically than in any of his earlier ones, Brahms moved the 'centre' of the composition forward, making a developmental process out of even the creation of the main theme. This procedure is used again in the finale—the opening motive of its slow introduction later expands into its main theme—thereby establishing that movement as coequal to the initial one, and in the process avoiding the risk of disappointing the expectations of a public oriented towards Beethoven's ideal of apotheosis at the end.[31] (This explains why Brahms went to such great lengths to guarantee that his First Symphony would not be performed at the end of concert programmes, where its finale would bear an additional burden.)

Problems inherent in motivically linking all other movements of a work to the opening one have been discussed with respect to the C minor String Quartet; with the First Symphony, however, they are of a different type. In the second movement, the

---

[30] Hermann Kretzschmar, *Führer durch den Konzertsaal*, Abt. 1, 1: 738. Cf. Kross, 'Brahms the Symphonist', 132 f.

[31] Cf. *Brahms Briefwechsel*, 3: 141, 15: 69.

EXAMPLE 10. Brahms, Symphony No. 1 in C minor, Op. 68, I, bars 21–4.

EXAMPLE 11. Brahms, Symphony No. 1 in C minor, Op. 68, I, bars 38–46.

EXAMPLE 12. Brahms, Symphony No. 1 in C minor, Op. 68, II, bars 1–7.

chromatic motion of the first movement is woven seamlessly into the thematic development that extends the second musical gesture (bar 5) and leads on to a dotted melody fashioned over a bass derived from the main theme of the first movement as it had appeared in its rudimentary state in bar 21 of the introduction (Example 12). Such a process is unimaginable with Beethoven's themes and only intelligible if one comprehends the building of themes as a process, for the integrated parts of the slow introduction to the first movement are by no means mere quotations of themes to come. Unity of substance also binds the third movement, a scherzo, to the whole: the material from bar 21 of the opening introduction underlays the falling dotted eighths at bars 11 ff.; moreover, the chord separating the first phrase of the Scherzo theme from the second (bars 4–5) is expanded step by step until the characteristic two chromatic lines in contrary motion become audible at bars 22–5 and even more so at bars 29–32. That a 'process' is at work is undeniable.

Unity between slow introduction and first movement as audible as in the case of Brahms's First Symphony can be found in works of the Classical period, but now that this unity encompasses slow movement, Scherzo, and finale as well, certain problems arise. On the one hand, the unity of substance between all portions of a cyclical work emphasizes their connection. But it also threatens the variety necessary within the unity, the tension needed to give life to an artistic organism. Thus the creation of themes which will allow such close connections as the ones discussed here and yet make possible variety, without reducing the material itself to insignificance, is extremely difficult. Only a few solutions will succeed, and therein perhaps lies the reason why Brahms composed only four symphonies and never seriously attempted another.

Within the limits of this paper I must forgo discussion of such problems in Brahms's other symphonies. Though such an investigation might enrich our knowledge, it would not in principle reveal new problems. Thus the finale of the Third Symphony only proves what our interpretation of Brahms's earlier sonata movements has suggested, that Brahms did not employ Beethoven's method of intensifying all the way to the end. Although this finale shows, more than in his other symphonies, a tendency towards contrasting themes (cf. bars 19–40)—or perhaps because of this—Brahms allowed the movement to die away pianissimo and close out the cyclic form with a return to the initial motive of the first movement, which had provided the structural basis for the entire symphony. This is clearly a revocation of the idea of symphony as developed in its most distinctive type by Beethoven, not a continuation of the Beethovenian tradition.

In the 1880s Brahms once again made studies in choral texture, which for him always indicated a confrontation with new textural principles. These studies produced a strange piece—'Stand das Mädchen', Op. 93a No. 2, which Brahms also published in a version for solo voice and piano at the beginning of the *Sieben Lieder*, Op. 95 (in this position, it seems to provide a new beginning after the songs of deep resignation bound together in the *Fünf Lieder*, Op. 94). Linkage of bass and melody to the point of identity is no longer the issue, as it had been in earlier works; the focus now is on identity of thematic structure and formal process. The song consists of a single motive which appears alternately in ternary and quaternary versions (see Example 13). There is great artistic merit in how closely Brahms is able to accommodate the different variants to the syntax and expression of the text. But what is most impressive is how totally and tightly the motivic workings in this piece are organized.[32] From here on, we may truly speak of the shaping force of 'developing variation' in the works of Brahms. At this point, though, the thematic structure only allows the shaping of relatively small forms.

With his Fourth Symphony, Brahms moved decidedly beyond the procedure found in 'Stand das Mädchen', taking a decisive step which led him to the very limits of what is possible within tonal music. I am speaking, of course, of the famous chain of thirds

---

[32] Siegfried Kross, *Die Chorwerke von Johannes Brahms*, 410–11.

EXAMPLE 13. Motives and motivic transformations in Brahms's *Das Mädchen* ('Stand das Mädchen'), Op. 93a No. 2.

which is the basis of the opening theme. Sequences of several thirds can be seen in other works as well, but here *all* steps of the diatonic scale appear moving downwards and upwards again in an uninterrupted sequence of thirds, every tone separated from its reappearance by the maximum distance and thus all tones being sounded before any single one recurs.

In January 1874 Philipp Spitta had sent Brahms a manuscript of the Bach cantata *Nach dir, Herr, verlanget mich* (BWV 150);[33] the idea to treat the chaconne theme of the final chorus of this cantata symphonically was apparently born in a discussion of this movement which Brahms had with Hans von Bülow and Siegfried Ochs,[34] the fruition of this idea occurring, of course, in the finale of the Fourth Symphony. The principle of the chaconne, with its uniform formal structure constructed, however, without the permanent presence of the bass, may have led Brahms to the possibilities of formal

[33] *Brahms Briefwechsel*, 16: 52, 54, 60. Cf. Kross, 'Brahms the Symphonist', 142, 139.
[34] Cf. Richard Specht, *Brahms*, 293 (trans., 270). On the question of authenticity, cf. Alfred Dürr, *Die Kantaten von Johann Sebastian Bach*, 628; on the conversation, see Alfred von Ehrmann, *Johannes Brahms*, 366.

organization which he tested in 'Stand das Mädchen'. Brahms's transformed version of Bach's chaconne bass (he altered it chromatically) could be combined with the thirds-based theme from the first movement. Brahms's thoughts still revolved around the problems of structural bonding of melody and bass. A new dimension was added here, though, since the theme of thirds had implications for vertical stratification as well. To begin the chaconne finale with the subdominant rather than the tonic was not a free decision on the part of the composer, but resulted from the structure of the thematic material. These processes have already been described so often that this remark can suffice.[35]

With the Fourth Symphony, Brahms must have realized that he had not only exhausted the possibilities for shaping musical forms from ongoing thematic processes, but also reached the limits for shaping pieces formally based upon concentrated thematic material deployed horizontally and vertically. Indeed, the principle of stratification of thirds was the only possibility within traditional tonality for utilizing the same material horizontally and vertically. In both genres for which Beethoven had set the standards for his successors—the symphony and the string quartet—Brahms had found solutions to formal problems which proved able to sustain his conception of form, without being dependent on Beethoven. From this point of view, one must hold that Ludwig Speidel's characterization of Brahms as the 'greatest living follower' of Beethoven and the other Classical masters misses the mark.[36] On the contrary, Brahms believed that tradition needed continually to be given new legitimacy, and the pains he took to do this were scarcely matched by any other creative musician of his time. Indeed, no other contemporary composer seems to have been as conscious of the boundaries of the possibilities for formal shaping in tonal music, and perhaps this is what makes Brahms's music especially relevant for our own times.

[35] Cf. Kross, 'Brahms the Symphonist', 143, and 'Brahms, der unromantische Romantiker', 39f.; Rudolf Klein, 'Die Doppelgerüsttechnik in der Passacaglia der IV. Symphonie von Brahms'.
[36] Ludwig Speidel, 'Johannes Brahms †', 385.

# Bibliography

## CORRESPONDENCE

*Johannes Brahms Briefwechsel.* 16 vols. Rev. edns. Berlin: Deutsche Brahms-Gesellschaft, 1912–22; repr. Tutzing: Hans Schneider, 1974.

I, II. *Johannes Brahms im Briefwechsel mit Heinrich und Elisabet von Herzogenberg.* Ed. Max Kalbeck. 2 vols. 4th rev. edn. 1921. Translated into English by Hannah Bryant. London: John Murray, 1909; repr. New York: Da Capo Press, 1986.

III. *Johannes Brahms im Briefwechsel mit Karl Reinthaler, Max Bruch, Hermann Deiters, Friedrich Heimsoeth, Karl Reinecke, Ernst Rudorff, Bernhard und Luise Scholz.* Ed. Wilhelm Altmann. 2nd rev. edn. 1912.

IV. *Johannes Brahms im Briefwechsel mit J. O. Grimm.* Ed. Richard Barth. 1912.

V, VI. *Johannes Brahms im Briefwechsel mit Joseph Joachim.* Ed. Andreas Moser. 2 vols. Vol. 1: 3rd rev. edn., 1921. Vol. 2: 2nd rev. edn., 1912.

VII. *Johannes Brahms im Briefwechsel mit Hermann Levi, Friedrich Gernsheim sowie den Familien Hecht und Fellinger.* Ed. Leopold Schmidt. 1910.

VIII. *Johannes Brahms Briefe an Joseph Victor Widmann, Ellen und Ferdinand Vetter, Adolf Schubring.* Ed. Max Kalbeck. 1915.

IX, X. *Johannes Brahms Briefe an P. J. Simrock und Fritz Simrock.* Ed. Max Kalbeck. 2 vols. 1917.

XI, XII. *Johannes Brahms Briefe an Fritz Simrock.* Ed. Max Kalbeck. 2 vols. 1919.

XIII. *Johannes Brahms im Briefwechsel mit Th. Wilhelm Engelmann.* Ed. Julius Röntgen. 1918.

XIV. *Johannes Brahms im Briefwechsel mit Breitkopf & Härtel, Bartholf Senff, J. Rieter-Biedermann, E. W. Fritzsch und Robert Lienau.* Ed. Wilhelm Altmann. 1920.

XV. *Johannes Brahms im Briefwechsel mit Franz Wüllner* Ed. Ernst Wolff. 1922.

XVI. *Johannes Brahms im Briefwechsel mit Philipp Spitta, Otto Dessoff.* Ed. Carl Krebs. 1920.

Bozarth, George S., and Wiltrud Martin, eds. and trans., *A Working Relationship: The Correspondence between Johannes Brahms and Robert Keller.* Washington, DC: Library of Congress, forthcoming.

Elvers, Rudolf, ed., *Felix Mendelssohn Bartholdy: Briefe an deutsche Verleger.* Berlin: Walter de Gruyter, 1968.

Gottlieb-Billroth, Otto, ed., *Billroth und Brahms im Briefwechsel.* Berlin and Vienna: Urban & Schwarzenberg, 1935.

Joachim, Johannes, and Andreas Moser, eds., *Briefe von und an Joseph Joachim.* 3 vols. Berlin: Julius Bard, 1911–13.

Litzmann, Berthold, ed., *Clara Schumann–Johannes Brahms: Briefe aus den Jahren 1853–1896.* 2 vols. Leipzig: Breitkopf & Härtel, 1927.

Orel, Alfred, ed., *Johannes Brahms und Julius Allgeyer. Eine Künstlerfreundschaft in Briefen.* Tutzing: Hans Schneider, 1964.

Pauls, Volquart, ed., *Briefe der Freundschaft Johannes Brahms–Klaus Groth.* Heide in Holstein: Westholsteinische Verlagsanstalt Boyens & Co., 1956.

Spengel, Annemarie, ed., *Johannes Brahms an Julius Spengel. Unveröffentlichte Briefe aus den Jahren 1882–1897*. Hamburg: Gesellschaft der Bücherfreunde, 1959.

Stephenson, Kurt, ed., *Johannes Brahms und Fritz Simrock: Weg einer Freundschaft: Briefe des Verlegers an den Komponisten*. Hamburg: J.J. Augustin, 1961.

—— ed., *Johannes Brahms in seiner Familie. Der Briefwechsel*. Veröffentlichungen aus der Hamburger Staats- und Universitätsbibliothek, vol. 9. Hamburg: Ernst Hauswedell, 1973.


BOOKS, ARTICLES, AND DISSERTATIONS

Abdy-Williams, Charles F., *The Rhythm of Modern Music*. London: Macmillan, 1909.

Ambros, August Wilhelm, *Geschichte der Musik, Dritte vermehrte und verbesserte Auflage von Heinrich Reimann*. 5 vols. Leipzig: F. E. C. Leuckart, 1891.

(Anonymous), *Katalog der Bibliothek von Richard Wagner in Wahnfried*. Manuscript (completed 1888), Richard-Wagner-Archiv, Bayreuth.

(Anonymous), 'Recensionen. Kammermusik. Johannes Brahms. Quartett für Pianoforte, Violine, Viola und Violoncello. Op. 26. Bonn, Simrock. Pr. 16 Frcs.' *Allgemeine musikalische Zeitung* 37 (9 Sept. 1863): 625–8.

Babbitt, Milton, 'Responses: A First Approximation'. *Perspectives of New Music* 14–15 (1976): 3–23.

Bate, W. Jackson, *The Burden of the Past and the English Poet*. Cambridge, MA: Harvard University Press, Belknap Press, 1970.

Beckerath, Heinz von, 'Erinnerungen an Johannes Brahms: Brahms und seine Krefelder Freunde'. *Die Heimat* 29 (Nov. 1958).

Bellermann, Heinrich, 'Einige Bemerkungen über die consonierende Quarte bei den Componisten des 16. Jahrhunderts'. *Allgemeine musikalische Zeitung* 58 (1870): 273–5.

—— *Der Contrapunkt*. 4th edn. Berlin: Julius Springer, 1901.

—— *Die Mensuralnoten und Taktzeichen des XV. und XVI. Jahrhunderts*. 2nd edn. Berlin and Leipzig: Walter de Gruyter, 1930.

—— ed. and trans., *Franconis de Colonia Artis Cantus Mensurabilis Caput XI*. Berlin: Weidmanische Buchhandlung, 1874.

—— Review of Gustav Nottebohm, *Beethoveniana*. *Allgemeine musikalische Zeitung* 61 (1873): 809.

—— Review of Gustav Nottebohm, *Beethoven's Studien. Erster Band. Beethoven's Unterricht bei J. Haydn, Albrechtsberger und Salieri*. *Allgemeine musikalische Zeitung* 61 (1873): 810–12.

—— 'Über die Eintheilung der Intervalle in Consonanzen und Dissonanzen bei den ältisten Mensuralisten'. *Allgemeine musikalische Zeitung* 58 (1870): 81–2, 89–91, 97–8.

—— 'Zur Quintenfrage'. *Allgemeine musikalische Zeitung* 58 (1870): 281–3, 329–32, 337–9.

Berger, Dorothea, *Jean Paul Friedrich Richter*. Twayne's World Authors Series: Germany, ed. Ulrich Weisstein, vol. 192. New York: Twayne Publishers, Inc., 1972.

Bernstein, Jane A., 'An Autograph of the Brahms "Handel Variations" '. *The Music Review* 34 (1973): 272–81.

Biba, Otto, *Johannes Brahms in Wien*. Catalogue of an Exhibition held at the Gesellschaft der Musikfreunde, 19 April–30 June 1983. Vienna: Gesellschaft der Musikfreunde, 1983.

Bloom, Harold, *The Anxiety of Influence*. London and New York: Oxford University Press, 1973.

Blum, Klaus, *Hundert Jahre Ein deutsches Requiem von Johannes Brahms: Entstehung, Uraufführung, Interpretation, Würdigung*. Tutzing: Hans Schneider, 1971.

Böhme, Franz M., *Altdeutsches Liederbuch*. Leipzig: Breitkopf & Härtel, 1877.

Boetticher, Wolfgang, 'Neue textkritische Forschungen an R. Schumanns Klavierwerk'. *Archiv für Musikwissenschaft* 25 (1968): 46–76.

—— *Robert Schumann in seinen Schriften und Briefen*. Berlin: Hahnefeld, 1942.

—— *Robert Schumanns Klavierwerke: Neue biographische und textkritische Untersuchungen, Teil I, Opus 1–6, Teil II, Opus 7–13*. Wilhelmshaven: Heinrichshofen, 1976 and 1984.

Boretz, Benjamin, 'What Lingers On (, When The Song Is Ended)'. *Perspectives of New Music* 16/1 (1977): 102–9.

Bozarth, George S., 'A New Collected Edition for Johannes Brahms'. *The American Brahms Society Newsletter* 6/1 (Spring 1988): (4)–(8), based in part on 'Toward a New Edition of Brahms's *Magelone Romanzen*', a paper read at the International Brahms Festival-Conference, Detroit, MI, 1980.

—— 'Brahms's Duets for Soprano and Alto, Op. 61: A Study in Chronology and Compositional Process'. *Studia Musicologica* 25 (1983): 191–210.

—— 'Brahms's Lieder Inventory of 1859–60 and Other Documents of his Life and Work'. *Fontes Artis Musicae* 30 (1983): 98–117.

—— 'Brahms's "*Liederjahr* of 1868" '. *The Music Review* 44 (1983): 208–22.

—— 'Brahms's Organ Works: A New Critical Edition'. *The American Organist*, 22/6 (June 1988): 50–59.

—— 'Brahms's Posthumous Compositions and Arrangements: Editorial Problems and Questions of Authenticity'. In *Brahms: Biographical, Documentary and Analytical Studies*, vol. 2, ed. Michael Musgrave, 59–94. Cambridge: Cambridge University Press, 1987.

—— 'Johannes Brahms und die Liedersammlungen von David Gregor Corner, Karl Severin Meister und Friedrich Wilhelm Arnold'. *Die Musikforschung* 36 (1983): 179–99.

—— 'The Lieder of Johannes Brahms—1868–71: Studies in Chronology and Compositional Process'. Ph.D. diss., Princeton University, 1978.

—— 'Synthesizing Word and Tone: Brahms's Setting of Hebbel's "Vorüber" '. In *Brahms: Biographical, Documentary and Analytical Studies*, ed. Robert Pascall, 77–98. Cambridge: Cambridge University Press, 1983.

—— in consultation with Ernst Herttrich and Otto Biba, 'Provisional Guidelines (Richtlinien) for the Johannes Brahms, Gesamtausgabe der musikalischen Werke'. Typescript.

Brand, Friedrich, *Das Wesen der Kammermusik von Johannes Brahms*. Berlin: Deutsche Brahms-Gesellschaft, 1937.

Breslauer, Peter, 'Motivic and Rhythmic Contrapuntal Structure in the Chamber Music of Johannes Brahms'. Ph.D. diss., Yale University, 1984.

Braus, Ira, 'Brahms's *Liebe und Frühling II*, Op. 3 No. 3: A New Path to the Artwork of the Future'. *19th-Century Music* 10 (1986–7): 135–56.

—— 'Rhetorical Text Organization and Harmonic Anamoly in Selected Lieder of Johannes Brahms'. Ph.D. diss., Harvard University, 1988.

Brinkmann, Reinhold, 'Anhand von Reprisen'. In *Brahms-Analysen: Referate der Kieler Tagung 1983*, ed. Friedhelm Krummacher and Wolfram Steinbeck, 107–20. Kassel: Bärenreiter, 1984.

Brodbeck, David, 'Brahms as Editor and Composer: His Two Editions of Ländler by Schubert and His First Two Cycles of Waltzes, Opera 39 and 52'. Ph.D. diss., University of Pennsylvania, 1984.

—— 'Compatibility, Coherence, and Closure in Brahms's *Liebeslieder* Waltzes'. In *Explorations in Music, the Arts, and Ideas: Essays in Honor of Leonard B. Meyer*, ed. Eugene Narmour and Ruth A. Solie, 411–437. Stuyvesant, NY: Pendragon Press, 1988.

—— 'Dance Music as High Art: Schubert's Twelve Ländler, Op. 171 (D. 790)'. In *Schubert: Critical and Analytical Studies*, ed. Walter Frisch, 31–47. Lincoln, NE: University of Nebraska Press, 1986.

—— '*Primo* Schubert, *Secundo* Schumann: Brahms's Four-Hand Waltzes, Op. 39'. *The Journal of Musicology* 7 (1989): 58–80.

Brown, A. Peter, 'Brahms' Third Symphony and the New German School'. *The Journal of Musicology* 2 (1983): 434–52.

Brown, Maurice J. E., 'The Dance-Music Manuscripts'. In *Essays on Schubert*, 217–43. New York: St Martin's Press, 1966.

Brown, Thomas Alan, *The Aesthetics of Robert Schumann*. New York: The Philosophical Library, 1968.

Cai, Camilla, 'Brahms' Short, Late Piano Pieces—Opus Numbers 116–119: A Source Study, an Analysis, and Performance Practice'. Ph.D. diss., Boston University, 1985.

Citron, Marcia, 'Metric Conflict in Brahms'. Revision of a paper read at the annual meeting of the American Musicological Society, Chicago, IL, 1973.

Coker, Wilson, *Music and Meaning*. New York: Free Press, 1972.

Cone, Edward T., 'Beethoven's Orpheus—or Jander's?' *19th-Century Music* 8 (1984–5): 283–6.

—— *Musical Form and Musical Performance*. New York: W. W. Norton, 1968.

—— 'Schubert's Promissory Note: An Exercise in Musical Hermeneutics'. *19th-Century Music* 5 (1981–2): 233–41.

—— 'The Uses of Convention: Stravinsky and his Models'. *The Musical Quarterly* 57 (1962): 287–99.

Cooper, Grosvenor, and Leonard Meyer, *The Rhythmic Structure of Music*. Chicago: University of Chicago Press, 1960.

Creelman, C. D., 'Human Discrimination of Auditory Duration'. *Journal of the American Acoustical Society* 34 (1962): 582–93.

Czesla, Werner, 'Studien zum Finale in der Kammermusik von Johannes Brahms'. Ph.D. diss., University of Bonn, 1968.

Daemmrich, Horst S., *The Shattered Self: E.T.A. Hoffmann's Tragic Vision*. Detroit: Wayne State University Press, 1973.

Dahlhaus, Carl, *Johannes Brahms—Klavierkonzert Nr. 1 d-moll, Op. 15*. Meisterwerke der Musik, ed. Ernst Ludwig Waeltner, vol. 3. Munich: Wilhelm Fink Verlag, 1965.

—— *Die Musik des 19. Jahrhunderts*. Neues Handbuch der Musikwissenschaft, vol. 6. Wiesbaden: Akademische Verlagsgesellschaft, 1980. Trans. J. Bradford Robinson as *Nineteenth-*

*Century Music.* California Studies in 19th-Century Music, ed. Joseph Kerman, vol. 5. Berkeley, Los Angeles, and London: University of California Press, 1989.

—— *Zwischen Romantik und Moderne: Vier Studien zur Musikgeschichte des späteren 19. Jahrhunderts.* Berliner Musikwissenschaftliche Arbeiten, ed. Carl Dahlhaus and Rudolf Stephan, vol. 7. Munich: Musikverlag Emil Katzbichler, 1974. Trans. Mary Whittall as *Between Romanticism and Modernism: Four Studies in the Music of the Later Nineteenth Century.* California Studies in 19th-Century Music, ed. Joseph Kerman, vol. 1. Berkeley, Los Angeles, and London: University of California Press, 1980.

—— *Schönberg und Andere: Gesammelte Aufsätze zur neuen Musik.* Mainz: B. Schott, 1978. Trans. Derrick Puffett and Alfred Clayton as *Schoenberg and the New Music.* Cambridge: Cambridge University Press, 1987.

—— 'Wagner und Bach'. Programmhefte der Bayreuther Festspiele 1985, ed. Wolfgang Wagner, 1–18. Bayreuth, 1985.

Davis, Shelley, 'H. C. Koch, the Classic Concerto, and the Sonata-form Retransition'. *The Journal of Musicology* 2 (1983): 45–61.

Deiters, Hermann, 'Nachgelassene Werke von Schumann'. *Leipziger Allgemeine musikalische Zeitung* 27 (3 July 1867): 215–17.

Dietrich, Albert, *Erinnerungen an Johannes Brahms in Briefe besonders aus seiner Jugendzeit.* Leipzig: Otto Wigand, 1898. Trans. Dora E. Hecht as *Recollections of Johannes Brahms.* London: Seeley and Co., 1899.

Deutsch, Otto Erich, 'The First Editions of Brahms'. *The Music Review* 1 (1940): 123–43, 255–78.

—— *Schubert: Memoirs by His Friends.* New York: Macmillan, 1958.

Doflein, Erich, 'Historismus in der Musik'. In *Die Ausbreitung des Historismus über die Musik,* ed. Walter Wiora, 9–38. Studien zur Musikgeschichte des 19. Jahrhunderts, vol. 14. Regensburg: Bosse, 1969.

Downs, Philip G., 'Beethoven's "New Way" and the *Eroica*'. In *The Creative World of Beethoven,* ed. Paul Henry Lang, 83–102. New York: W. W. Norton, 1971.

Dunsby, Jonathan, *Structural Ambiguity in Brahms.* Ann Arbor: UMI Research Press, 1981.

Dürr, Alfred, *Die Kantaten von Johann Sebastian Bach.* Kassel: Bärenreiter-Verlag, 1971.

Ehrmann, Alfred von, *Johannes Brahms: Weg, Werk und Welt.* Leipzig: Breitkopf & Härtel, 1933.

Eichendorff, Joseph von, *Historisch-kritische Ausgabe.* Ed. Wilhelm Kosch, August Sauer, Hermann Kunisch, *et al.* Regensburg: Josef Habbel, 1908– .

—— *Neue Gesamtausgabe der Werke und Schriften in vier Bänden.* Ed. Gerhart Baumann and Siegfried Grosse. Stuttgart: J. G. Cotta'sche Buchhandlung Nachf., 1957–8.

Eismann, Georg, ed., *Robert Schumann: Tagebücher, Band I, 1827–1838.* Leipzig: VEB Deutscher Verlag für Musik, 1971.

Epstein, David, *Beyond Orpheus: Studies in Musical Structure.* Cambridge, MA, and London: The MIT Press, 1979.

Evans, Edwin, *Historical, Descriptive and Analytical Account of the Entire Works of Brahms.* 4 vols. London: William Reeves, 1912–38.

Fellinger, Imogen, 'Brahms's View of Mozart'. In *Brahms: Biographical, Documentary and Analytical Studies,* ed. Robert Pascall, 41–57. Cambridge: Cambridge University Press, 1983.

Fellinger, Imogen, 'Das Brahms-Jahr 1983. Forschungsbericht'. *Acta Musicologica* 56 (1984): 145–210.

—— 'Brahms und die Musik vergangener Epochen'. In *Die Ausbreitung des Historismus über die Musik*, ed. Walter Wiora, 147–63. Studien zur Musikgeschichte des 19. Jahrhunderts, vol. 14. Regensburg: Bosse, 1969.

—— 'Das Brahms-Jahr 1983. Forschungsbericht'. *Acta Musicologica* 56 (1984): 145–210.

—— *Über die Dynamik in der Musik von Johannes Brahms*. Berlin and Wunsiedel: Max Hesse, 1961.

—— 'Zum Stand der Brahms-Forschung'. *Acta Musicologica* 55 (1983): 131–201.

—— 'Zur Entstehung der "Regenlieder" von Brahms'. In *Festschrift Walter Gerstenberg zum 60. Geburtstag*, ed. Georg von Dadelsen and Andreas Holschneider, 55–9. Wolfenbüttel and Zurich: Möseler, 1964.

Feuerbach, Ludwig, *Grundsätze der Philosophie der Zukunft*. Ed. Gerhart Schmidt. Frankfurt am Main: Klostermann, 1967.

Finscher, Ludwig, ' "Zwischen Absoluter und Programmusik": Zur Interpretation der deutschen romantischen Symphonie'. In *Über Symphonien: Beiträge zu einer musikalischen Gattung. Festschrift Walter Wiora zum 70. Geburtstag*, ed. Christoph-Hellmut Mahling, 103–15. Tutzing: Hans Schneider, 1979.

Floros, Constantin, *Brahms und Bruckner: Studien zur musikalischen Exegetik*. Wiesbaden: Breitkopf & Härtel, 1980.

—— 'Studien zu Brahms Klaviermusik'. *Brahms-Studien* 5 (1983): 25–63.

—— Hans Joachim Marx, and Peter Petersen, eds., *Brahms und seine Zeit: Symposion Hamburg 1983*. Hamburger Jahrbuch für Musikwissenschaft, vol. 7. Hamburg: Laaber-Verlag, 1984.

Forte, Allen, 'The Structural Origin of Exact *Tempi* in the Brahms-Haydn Variations'. *The Music Review* 18 (1957): 138–49; reprinted in Donald M. McCorkle, ed., *Johannes Brahms, Variations on a Theme of Haydn*, 185–200. New York: W. W. Norton, 1976.

Franco of Cologne, *Ars cantus mensurabilis*. In *Source Readings in Music History*, ed. Oliver Strunk, 139–59. New York: W. W. Norton, 1950.

Friedlaender, Max, *Brahms' Lieder*. Berlin and Leipzig: N. Simrock, 1922. Trans. C. Leonard Leese. London: Oxford University Press, Humphrey Milford, 1928.

Frisch, Walter, 'Brahms and Schubring: Musical Criticism and Politics at Mid-Century'. *19th-Century Music* 7 (1983–4): 271–81.

—— *Brahms and the Principle of Developing Variation*. Berkeley and Los Angeles: University of California Press, 1984.

—— 'Brahms, Developing Variation, and the Schoenberg Critical Tradition'. *19th-Century Music* 5 (1981–2): 215–32.

Gál, Hans, *Johannes Brahms: Werk und Persönlichkeit*. Frankfurt am Main: Fischer Bücherei, 1961. Trans. Joseph Stein as *Johannes Brahms: His Work and Personality*. New York: Alfred A. Knopf, 1971.

Geiringer, Karl, 'Brahms als Musikhistoriker'. *Die Musik* 25 (1933): 571–8. Also issued in *Johannes Brahms Festschrift*. Berlin: Max Hesse, 1933.

—— 'Brahms as a Musicologist'. *The Musical Quarterly* 69 (1983): 463–70.

—— 'Brahms as a Reader and Collector'. *The Musical Quarterly* 19 (1933): 158–68; reprinted in *Brahms: His Life and Work*, 3rd edn., 369–79. New York: Da Capo Press, 1982.

—— in collaboration with Irene Geiringer. *Brahms: His Life and Work*. 3rd edn. New York: Da Capo Press, 1982.

—— 'The Brahms Library in the "Gesellschaft der Musikfreunde," Wien'. *Notes* 30 (1973): 7–14.

Gerber, Rudolf, 'Formprobleme im Brahms'schen Lied'. *Jahrbuch Peters* 39 (1932): 23–42.

Getty, D. J., 'Discrimination of Short Temporal Intervals: a Comparison of Two Models'. *Perception and Psychophysics* 18 (1975): 1–8.

Giebeler, Konrad, 'Die Lieder von Johannes Brahms: Ein Beitrag zur Musikgeschichte des 19. Jahrhunderts'. Ph.D. diss., University of Münster, 1959.

Gombrich, E. H., *Art and Illusion: A Study in the Psychology of Pictorial Representation*. Princeton: Princeton University Press, 1960.

Grove, George, *A Dictionary of Music and Musicians*. 4 vols. London: Macmillan, 1883.

Gülke, Peter, 'Über Schönbergs Brahms-Bearbeitung'. *Beiträge zur Musikwissenschaft* 17 (1975): 5–14.

Haas, Frithjof, 'Die Erstfassung des langsamen Satzes der ersten Sinfonie von Johannes Brahms'. *Die Musikforschung* 36 (1983): 200–11.

—— 'Die Uraufführung der Ersten Sinfonie von Johannes Brahms in Karlsruhe'. In *Johannes Brahms in Baden-Baden und Karlsruhe*, ed. Joachim Draheim, *et al.*, 129–32. Karlsruhe: Badische Landesbibliothek Karlsruhe, 1983.

Häfner, Klaus, 'Das "Triumphlied" op. 55, eine vergessene Komposition von Johannes Brahms'. In *Johannes Brahms in Baden-Baden und Karlsruhe*, ed. Joachim Draheim, *et al.*, 83–102. Karlsruhe: Badische Landesbibliothek Karlsruhe, 1983.

Hagen, Friedrich Heinrich von der, *Minnesinger: Deutsche Liederdichter des zwölften, dreizehnten und vierzehnten Jahrhunderts*. Leipzig: Joh. Ambr. Barth, 1838.

Hancock, Virginia, *Brahms's Choral Compositions and His Library of Early Music*. Ann Arbor: UMI Research Press, 1983.

—— 'Brahms's Links with German Renaissance Music'. In *Brahms: Biographical, Documentary and Analytical Studies*, vol. 2, ed. Michael Musgrave, 95–110. Cambridge: Cambridge University Press, 1987.

—— 'Brahms's Performances of Early Choral Music'. *19th-Century Music* 8 (1984–5): 125–41.

—— 'Sources of Brahms's Manuscript Copies of Early Music in the Archiv of the Gesellschaft der Musikfreunde in Wien'. *Fontes Artis Musicae* 24 (1977): 113–21.

—— 'The Growth of Brahms's Interest in Early Choral Music, and its Effect on His Own Choral Compositions'. In *Brahms: Biographical, Documentary and Analytical Studies*, ed. Robert Pascall, 27–40. Cambridge: Cambridge University Press, 1983.

Hanslick, Eduard, *Vom Musikalisch-Schönen*. 2nd edn. Leipzig: Rudolph Weigel, 1858. Trans. Gustav Cohen as *The Beautiful in Music*; ed., with an introduction, by Morris Weitz. The Library of Liberal Arts. Indianapolis and New York: The Bobbs-Merrill Company, 1957.

Harrison, Max, *The Lieder of Brahms*. London: Cassell and New York: Praeger Publishers, 1972.

Hauptmann, Moritz, *The Nature of Harmony and Metre*. Trans. W. E. Heathcote. London: Sonnenschein, 1888. [Original German ed., 1853.]

Helms, Siegmund, *Die Melodiebildung in den Liedern von Johannes Brahms und ihr Verhältnis zu Volksliedern und volkstümliches Weisen*. Kassel: Bärenreiter, 1967.

—— 'Johannes Brahms und Johann Sebastian Bach'. *Bach-Jahrbuch* 57 (1971): 13–81.

Henschel, George, *Personal Recollections of Johannes Brahms: Some of His Letters to and Pages from a Journal Kept by George Henschel*. Boston: Richard G. Badger, The Gorham Press, 1907; repr. New York: AMS, 1978. Rev. edn., without letters, published in George Henschel, *Musings and Memories of a Musician* (London: Macmillan, 1918; repr. New York: Da Capo Press, 1979), 44–131, and in Helen Henschel, *When Soft Voices Die: A Musical Biography* (London: John Westhouse Publishers, 1944), 147–78.

Herttrich, Ernst, 'Johannes Brahms—Klaviertrio H-Dur Opus 8. Frühfassung und Spätfassung—ein analytischer Vergleich'. In *Music, Edition, Interpretation. Gedenkschrift Günter Henle*, ed. Martin Bente, 218–36. Munich: G. Henle Verlag, 1980.

Heuberger, Richard, *Erinnerungen an Johannes Brahms. Tagebuchnotizen aus den Jahren 1875 bis 1897*. Ed. Kurt Hofmann. Tutzing: Hans Schneider, 1971.

Hoffmann, E. T. A., *Lebens-Ansichten des Katers Murr nebst fragmentarischer Biographie des Kapellmeisters Johannes Kreisler in zufälligen Makulaturblättern*. 1820–1. Ed. Herbert Kraft and Manfred Wacher. Berlin: Aufbau Verlag, 1958. Ed. and trans. Leonard J. Kent and Elizabeth C. Knight as *The Life and Opinions of Kater Murr, with the Fragmentary Biography of Kapellmeister Johannes Kreisler on Random Sheets of Scrap Paper* in *Selected Writings of E. T. A. Hoffman*, vol. 2. Chicago and London: University of Chicago Press, 1969.

Hofmann, Kurt, 'Brahmsiana der Familie Petersen. Erinnerungen und Briefe'. *Brahms-Studien* 3 (1979): 69–105.

—— *Die Bibliothek von Johannes Brahms: Bücher- und Musikalienverzeichnis*. Schriftenreihe zur Musik. Hamburg: Karl Dieter Wagner, 1974.

—— *Die Erstdrucke der Werke von Robert Schumann*. Tutzing: Hans Schneider, 1979.

—— *Die Erstdrucke der Werke von Johannes Brahms*. Tutzing: Hans Schneider, 1975.

—— *Johannes Brahms in den Erinnerungen von Richard Barth. Barths Wirken in Hamburg*. Hamburg: Schuberth, 1979.

Hoorickx, Reinhard van, 'Franz Schubert (1797–1828): List of the Dances in Chronological Order'. *Revue Belge de Musicologie* 25 (1971): 68–97.

Horstmann, Angelika, *Untersuchungen zur Brahms-Rezeption der Jahre 1860 bis 1880*. Hamburg: Karl Dieter Wagner, 1986.

Hull, Kenneth, 'Quotation, Allusion, and Model in Brahms's Fourth Symphony'. Paper read at the annual meeting of the American Musicological Society, Vancouver, BC, 1985.

Jacobsen, Christiane, *Das Verhältnis von Sprache und Musik in ausgewählten Liedern von Johannes Brahms, dargestellt an Parallelvertonungen*. Hamburger Beiträge zur Musikwissenschaft, vol. 16. Hamburg: Karl Dieter Wagner, 1975.

—— ed., *Johannes Brahms: Leben und Werk*. Wiesbaden: Breitkopf & Härtel, 1983.

Jacobsthal, Gustav, 'Die Mensuralnotenschrift des XII. und XIII. Jahrhunderts'. *Allgemeine musikalische Zeitung* 58 (1870): 253-4, 261–2, 270–1, 279, 285–7.

Jander, Owen, 'Beethoven's "Orpheus in Hades": The *Andante con moto* of the Fourth Piano Concerto'. *19th-Century Music* 8 (1984–5): 195–212.

Jansen, F. Gustav, ed., *Robert Schumanns Briefe, Neue Folge*. 2nd edn. Leipzig: Breitkopf & Härtel, 1904.

Jenner, Gustav, *Johannes Brahms als Mensch, Lehrer und Künstler*. Marburg: Elwert, 1905.

—— 'Zur Entstehung des D-moll Klavierkonzertes Op. 15 von Johannes Brahms'. *Die Musik* 12 (1912): 32–7.

Johnson, Douglas, 'Nottebohm'. In *The New Grove Dictionary of Music and Musicians*, 6th edn., ed. Stanley Sadie, 13: 429–30. London: Macmillan, 1980.

Johnson, Janet, 'Brahms's Mozart: Sources of Classicism in the First Movement of Op. 15'. M.A. thesis, University of California at Los Angeles, 1979.

Kalbeck, Max, *Johannes Brahms*. 4 vols. Rev. edns. Berlin: Deutsche Brahms-Gesellschaft, 1912–21; repr. Tutzing: Hans Schneider, 1976.

Kamien, Roger, 'The Opening Sonata-Allegro Movements in a Randomly Selected Sample of Solo Keyboard Sonatas Published in the Years 1742–1774 (Inclusive)'. Ph.D. diss., Princeton University, 1964.

—— 'Style Change in the Mid-18th-Century Keyboard Sonata'. *Journal of the American Musicological Society* 19 (1966): 37–58.

Ker. [Louis Köhler], 'Sechs Gesänge für eine Singstimme mit Pianoforte componirt von Johannes Brahms. Op. 7'. *Signale für die musikalische Welt* 13 (1855): 65–6.

Kerman, Joseph, 'How We Got into Analysis, and How to Get Out'. *Critical Inquiry* 7 (1980): 311–31. Also appeared as 'The State of Academic Music Criticism', in *On Criticizing Music: Five Philosophical Perspectives*, ed. Kingsley Price, 38–54. Baltimore and London: Johns Hopkins University Press, 1981.

—— 'Notes on Beethoven's Codas'. In *Beethoven Studies*, vol. 3, ed. Alan Tyson, 141–60. Cambridge: Cambridge University Press, 1982.

—— *The Beethoven Quartets*. 1966. New York: W. W. Norton, 1979.

—— and Alan Tyson, 'Beethoven'. In *The New Grove Dictionary of Music and Musicians*, 6th edn., ed. Stanley Sadie, 2: 354–414. London: Macmillan, 1980.

King, A. Hyatt, 'C. G. Röder's Music-Printing Business in 1885'. *Fontes Artis Musicae* 13 (1966): 53–9.

Klein, Rudolf, 'Die Doppelgerüsttechnik in der Passacaglia der IV. Symphonie von Brahms'. *Österreichische Musikzeitschrift* 27 (1972): 641–8.

Koch, Heinrich Christoph, *Musikalisches Lexicon*. 2nd, rev. and expanded edn. Ed. Arrey von Dommer. Heidelberg: Academische Verlagsbuchhandlung von J. C. B. Mohr, 1865.

Komma, Karl Michael, 'Das "Scherzo" der 2. Symphonie von Johannes Brahms'. In *Festschrift für Walter Wiora zum 30. Dezember 1966*, ed. Ludwig Finscher and Christoph-Hellmut Mahling, 448–57. Kassel: Bärenreiter, 1967.

Kraus, Detlef, 'Das Andante aus der Sonate Op. 5 von Brahms: Versuch einer Interpretation'. *Brahms-Studien* 3 (1979): 47–51.

Kreissle von Hellborn, Heinrich, *Franz Schubert*. Vienna: Carl Gerold's Sohn, 1865; repr. Hildesheim: Georg Olms Verlag, 1978.

Kretzschmar, Hermann, *Führer durch den Konzertsaal*. 4th edn. Leipzig: Breitkopf & Härtel, 1913.

Kross, Siegfried, 'Brahms and E. T. A. Hoffmann'. *19th-Century Music* 5 (1981–2): 193–200.

—— *Brahms-Bibliographie*. Tutzing: Hans Schneider, 1983.

—— 'Brahms der unromantische Romantiker'. *Brahms-Studien* 1 (1974): 25–43.

—— 'Brahms the Symphonist'. In *Brahms: Biographical, Documentary and Analytical Studies*, ed. Robert Pascall, 125–45; in German, *Brahms-Studien* 5 (1983): 65–89.

—— 'Brahms the Symphonist'. In *Brahms: Biographical, Documentary and Analytical Studies*, ed. Robert Pascall, 125–45; in German, *Brahms-Studien 5* (1983): 65–89.

—— *Die Chorwerke von Johannes Brahms*. 2nd edn. Berlin and Wunsiedl: Max Hesse, 1963.

—— 'Kontinuität und Diskontinuität im heutigen Brahms-Bild'. *Österreichische Musikzeitschrift* 38 (1983): 218–27.

Krummacher, Friedhelm, and Wolfram Steinbeck, eds., *Brahms-Analysen: Referate der Kieler Tagung 1983*. Kieler Schriften zur Musikwissenschaft, vol. 28. Cassel: Bärenreiter 1984.

Kurth, Ernst, *Romantische Harmonik und Ihre Krise in Wagners 'Tristan'*. Berne and Leipzig: P. Haupt, 1920; 2nd edn., Berlin: Max Hesse, 1923; repr. of 2nd edn., Hildesheim: Georg Olms Verlag, 1968.

Lamberton, Elizabeth Jean, 'Brahms's Piano Quintet, Op. 34, and Duo-Piano Sonata, Op. 34 *bis*: A Critical Study'. M.A. thesis, University of British Columbia, 1978.

Larsen, Jens Peter, Howard Serwer, and James Webster, eds., *Haydn Studies*. New York: W. W. Norton, 1981.

Lewin, David, 'Vocal Meter in Schoenberg's Atonal Music, with a Note on a Serial Hauptstimme'. *In Theory Only* 6 (1982): 12–36.

Leyen, Rudolf von der, *Johannes Brahms als Mensch und Freund*. Düsseldorf and Leipzig: K. R. Langewiesche, 1905.

Liepmannssohn, Leo, *Lager-Katalog 35 von 26. und 27. Mai 1905*. Berlin: Leo Liepmannssohn, 1905.

—— *Lager-Katalog 38 von Mai 1909*. Berlin: Leo Liepmannssohn, 1909.

Lippman, Edward, 'Theory and Practice in Schumann's Aesthetics'. *Journal of the American Musicological Society* 17 (1964): 310–45.

Liszt, Franz, *Franz Liszt Gesammelte Schriften*. 6 vols. Ed. L. Ramann. Leipzig: Breitkopf & Härtel, 1880; repr. Hildesheim: Georg Olms Verlag, 1978.

Litzmann, Berthold, *Clara Schumann: Ein Küstlerleben nach Tagebüchern und Briefen*. 3 vols. 8th (vol. 1), 7th (vol. 2), 5th/6th (vol. 3) rev. edns. Leipzig: Breitkopf & Härtel, 1923–5.

Mach, Ernst, 'Untersuchungen über den Zeitsinn des Ohres'. *Sitzungsberichte der kaiserlichen Akademie der Wissenschaften: mathematisch-naturwissenschaftliche Classe* 51 (1865): 133–50.

Mahler, Alma, and Knud Martner, eds., *Selected Letters of Gustav Mahler*. Trans. Eithne Wilkins, Ernst Kaiser, and Bill Hopkins. New York: Farrar, Straus, Giroux, 1979.

Mandyczewski, Eusebius, 'Die Bibliothek Brahms'. *Musikbuch aus Oesterreich* 1 (1904): 7–17.

—— *Zusatz-Band zur Geschichte der k. k. Gesellschaft der Musikfreunde in Wien: Sammlungen und Statuten*. Vienna: Gesellschaft der Musikfreunde, 1912.

Mast, Paul, 'Brahms's Study, Octaven u. Quinten u. A., with Schenker's Commentary Translated'. *The Music Forum* 5 (1980): 1–196.

Mauro, Rosemarie P., 'The *Gesang der Parzen* of Goethe and Brahms: A Study in Synthesis and Interpretation'. M.A. thesis, University of Washington, 1986.

May, Florence, *The Life of Johannes Brahms*. 2 vols. 2nd edn., rev. London: William Reeves, 1948; repr. Neptune City, NJ: Paganiniana, 1981.

McCorkle, Donald M., in collaboration with Margit L. McCorkle, 'Five Fundamental Obstacles in Brahms Research'. *Acta Musicologica* 48 (1976): 253–72.

McCorkle, Margit L., *Johannes Brahms Thematisch-Bibliographisches Werkverzeichnis*. From preliminary work in collaboration with Donald M. McCorkle. Munich: G. Henle Verlag, 1984.

—— 'Filling the Gaps in Brahms Research'. *The Musical Times* 124 (1983): 284–6.

—— 'Filling the Gaps in Brahms Source Research: Several Important Recent Manuscript Discoveries'. Paper read at the annual meeting of the American Musicological Society, Ann Arbor, MI, 1982.

Mies, Paul, 'Aus Brahms' Werkstatt: Vom Entstehen und Werden der Werke bei Brahms'. *Simrock-Jahrbuch* 1 (1928): 42–63.

—— 'Der kritische Rat der Freunde und die Veröffentlichung der Werke bei Brahms'. *Simrock-Jahrbuch* 2 (1929): 65–83.

—— *Stilmomente und Ausdrucksstilformen im Brahms'schen Lied*. Leipzig: Breitkopf & Härtel, 1923; repr. Niederwalluf bei Wiesbaden: Martin Sändig, 1975.

Miesner, Heinrich, ed., *Klaus Groth und die Musik. Erinnerungen an Johannes Brahms. Briefe, Gedichte und Aufzeichnungen nebst einem Verzeichnis von Vertonungen Grothscher Dichtungen*. Heide/Holstein: Heider Anzeigen, Westholsteinische Verlagsanstalt, 1933.

Mitschka, Arno, *Der Sonatensatz in den Werken von Johannes Brahms*. Gütersloh: (n.p.), 1961.

Morik, Werner, *Johannes Brahms und sein Verhältnis zum deutschen Volkslied*. Tutzing: Hans Schneider, 1965.

Musgrave, Michael, ed., *Brahms 2: Biographical, Documentary and Analytical Studies*. Cambridge: Cambridge University Press, 1987.

—— '*Frei aber Froh*: A Reconsideration'. *19th-Century Music* 3 (1979–80): 251–8.

—— 'The Cultural World of Brahms'. In *Brahms: Biographical, Documentary and Analytical Studies*, ed. Robert Pascall, 1–26. Cambridge: Cambridge University Press, 1983.

—— *The Music of Brahms*. London, Boston and Henley: Routledge & Kegan Paul, 1985.

Neighbour, Oliver, 'Brahms and Schumann: Two Opus Nines and Beyond'. *19th-Century Music* 7 (1983–4): 266–70.

Newcomb, Anthony, 'Once More "Between Absolute and Program Music": Schumann's Second Symphony'. *19th-Century Music* 7 (1983–4): 233–50.

—— 'Those Images That Yet Fresh Images Beget'. *The Journal of Musicology* 2 (1983): 227–45.

Newman, Ernest, 'Brahms and the Waltz'. In *A Musical Motley*, 254–62. 2nd edn. London and New York: John Lane, 1920.

Newman, S. T. M., 'The Slow Movement of Brahms' First Symphony: A Reconstruction of the Version First Performed Prior to Publication'. *The Music Review* 9 (1948): 4–12.

Niemann, Walter, *Brahms*. Berlin and Leipzig: Schuster & Loeffler, 1920. Trans. Catherine Alison Phillips. New York: Alfred A. Knopf, 1929; repr. New York: Cooper Square Publishers, 1969.

Nottebohm, Gustav, *Beethoveniana*. Leipzig: C. F. Peters, 1872; repr., with an introduction by Paul Henry Lang, New York and London: Johnson Reprint Corp., 1970.

—— *Beethoven's Studien. Erster Band. Beethoven's Unterricht bei J. Haydn, Albrechtsberger und Salieri*. Leipzig and Winterthur: J. Rieter-Biedermann, 1873; repr. Niederwalluf bei Wiesbaden: Martin Sändig, 1971.

—— *Thematisches Verzeichniss der im Druck erschienenen Werke von Franz Schubert.* Vienna: Friedrich Schreiber, 1874.

Ophüls, Gustav, *Brahms-Texte: Vollständige Sammlung der von Johannes Brahms komponierten und musikalisch bearbeiteten Dichtungen.* Berlin: N. Simrock, 1898; 2nd edn., rev. and enlarged, Berlin: Deutsche Brahms-Gesellschaft, 1908; 3rd edn., Berlin: Deutsche Brahms-Gesellschaft, 1923; 4th edn., rev. and enlarged, ed. Kristian Wachinger, Ebenhausen bei München: Langewiesche-Brandt, 1983.

—— *Erinnerungen an Johannes Brahms.* Berlin: Deutsche Brahms-Gesellschaft, 1921; new edn., Ebenhausen bei München: Langewiesche-Brandt, 1983.

Orel, Alfred, 'Johannes Brahms' Musikbibliothek'. *Simrock-Jahrbuch* 3 (1930–4): 18–47; repr. in Kurt Hofmann, *Die Bibliothek von Johannes Brahms*, 139–66.

—— 'Skizzen zu Johannes Brahms' Haydn-Variationen'. *Zeitschrift für Musikwissenschaft* 5 (1922–3): 296–315.

Osmond-Smith, David, 'The Retreat from Dynamism: A Study of Brahms's Fourth Symphony'. In *Brahms: Biographical, Documentary and Analytical Studies*, ed. Robert Pascall, 147–65. Cambridge: Cambridge University Press, 1983.

Pascall, Robert, 'Brahms and the Definitive Text'. In *Brahms: Biographical, Documentary and Analytical Studies*, ed. Robert Pascall, 59–75. Cambridge: Cambridge University Press, 1983.

—— 'Brahms and Schubert'. *The Musical Times* 124 (1983): 286–91.

—— ed., *Brahms: Biographical, Documentary and Analytical Studies.* Cambridge: Cambridge University Press, 1983.

—— 'Brahms's First Symphony Slow Movement: The Initial Performing Version'. *The Musical Times* 122 (1981): 664–7.

—— 'Formal Principles in the Music of Brahms'. Ph.D. diss., Oxford University, 1973.

—— 'Musikalische Einflüße auf Brahms'. *Österreichische Musikzeitschrift* 38 (1983): 228–35.

—— Review of Johannes Brahms, *Concerto for Violin, Op. 77 by Johannes Brahms: Facsimile of the Holograph Score. Music and Letters* 62 (1981): 95–7.

—— 'Ruminations on Brahms's Chamber Music'. *The Musical Times* 116 (1975): 697–9.

—— 'Some Special Uses of Sonata Form by Brahms'. *Soundings* 4 (1974): 58–63.

—— 'Unknown Gavottes by Brahms'. *Music and Letters* 57 (1976): 404–11.

Pevsner, Nikolaus, *Studies in Art, Architecture, and Design.* 2 vols. New York: Walker and Company, 1968.

Pfaff, Friedrich, ed., *Die große Heidelberger Liederhandschrift.* Heidelberg: Carl Winter's Universitätsbuchhandlung, 1909.

Plantinga, Leon, *Schumann as Critic.* New Haven: Yale University Press, 1967.

Plato, ΠΟΛΙΤΣΙΑ (Respublica). In *Platonis Opera.* Ed. John Burnet. Oxford: Oxford University Press, 1949.

Plyn, Franz Hermann Wolfgang, 'Die Hemiola in der Instrumentalmusik von Johannes Brahms'. Ph.D. diss., Rheinische Friedrich-Wilhelms-Universität (Bonn), 1984.

Popper, Karl R., *The Poverty of Historicism.* London: Routledge & Kegan Paul, 1957.

Reich, Nancy B., *Clara Schumann: The Artist and the Woman.* Ithaca and London: Cornell University Press, 1985.

Réti, Rudolf, *The Thematic Process in Music*. New York: Macmillan, 1951.

Reynolds, Christopher, 'A Choral Symphony by Brahms?' *19th-Century Music* 9 (1985–6): 3–25.

Richter, Jean Paul Friedrich, *Die Flegeljahre*. 4 vols. 1804–5. Published in section 1, vol. 10 of *Jean Pauls Sämtliche Werke*. Historisch-kritische Ausgabe. Berlin: Preußische Akademie der Wissenschaften in Verbindung mit der Akademie zur Erforschung und zur Pflege des Deutschtums, 1934 ff. Trans. as *Walt and Vult, or The Twins* by Eliza B. Lee. Boston: Munroe and New York: Wiley, 1846.

Riehn, Rainer, 'Werkverzeichnis'. *Musik-Konzepte, Sonderband: Franz Schubert* (Dec. 1979): 285–302.

Riemann, Hugo, 'Die Taktfreiheiten in Brahms' Liedern'. *Die Musik* 12 (1912): 10–21.

—— *Geschichte der Musiktheorie im IX.-XIX. Jahrhundert*. 3 vols. in 1. Leipzig: Max Hesse, 1898.

Roesner, Linda Correll, Review of Johannes Brahms, *Concerto for Violin, Op. 77 by Johannes Brahms: Facsimile of the Holograph Score. Current Musicology* 30 (1980): 60–72.

—— 'Schumann's Revisions in the First Movement of the Piano Sonata in G Minor, Op. 22'. *19th-Century Music* 1 (1977–8): 97–109.

—— 'The Autograph of Schumann's Piano Sonata in F Minor, Opus 14'. *The Musical Quarterly* 61 (1975): 98–130.

—— 'The Sources for Schumann's *Davidsbündlertänze*, Op. 6: Composition, Textual Problems, and the Role of the Composer as Editor'. In *Mendelssohn and Schumann: Essays on Their Music and Its Context*, ed. Jon W. Finson and R. Larry Todd, 53–70. Chapel Hill, NC: Duke University Press, 1984.

Rohn, Matthias, *Die Coda bei Johannes Brahms*. Schriftenreihe zur Musik, vol. 25. Hamburg: Karl Dieter Wagner, 1986.

Rosen, Charles, 'Influence: Plagiarism and Inspiration'. *19th-Century Music* 4 (1980–1): 87–100. Also in *On Criticizing Music: Five Philosophical Perspectives*, ed. Kingsley Price, 16–37. Baltimore and London: Johns Hopkins University Press, 1981.

—— *Sonata Forms*. New York and London: W. W. Norton, 1980.

—— *The Classical Style: Haydn, Mozart, Beethoven*. New York: The Viking Press, 1971.

Rudorff, Ernst Friedrich, 'Johannes Brahms: Erinnerungen und Betrachtungen'. *Schweizerische Musikzeitung* 97 (1957): 81–6, 139–45, 182–7.

Rufer, Josef, *Composition with Twelve Notes Related Only to One Another*. Trans. Humphrey Searle. London: Barrie and Jenkins, 1954.

Sams, Eric, 'Brahms and his Clara themes'. *The Musical Times* 112 (1971): 432–4.

—— *Brahms Songs*. BBC Music Guides. London: BBC Publications, 1972.

—— 'Schumann and the Tonal Analogue'. *Proceedings of the Royal Musical Association* 96 (1969): 103–13. Repr. in *Robert Schumann: The Man and His Music*, ed. Alan Walker, 390–405. London: Barrie & Jenkins, 1972.

Schachter, Carl, 'The First Movement of Brahms's Second Symphony: The Opening Theme and its Consequences'. *Musical Analysis* 2 (1983): 55–70.

Schauffler, Robert Haven, *The Unknown Brahms*. New York: Dodd, Mead, 1933.

Schenker, Heinrich, *Beethoven, Die letzten Sonaten: Sonate A dur Op. 101*. Ed. Oswald Jonas. Vienna: Universal-Edition, 1972.

—— *Harmony*. Ed. and annotated Oswald Jonas, trans. Elisabeth Mann Borgese. Chicago and London: University of Chicago Press, 1954.

Schmid, Manfred Hermann, *Musik als Abbild*. Tutzing: Hans Schneider, 1981.

Schmidt, Christian Martin, *Verfahren der motivisch-thematischen Vermittlung in der Musik von Johannes Brahms dargestellt an der Klarinettensonate f-Moll op. 120,I*. Berliner musikwissenschaftliche Arbeiten, ed. Carl Dahlhaus and Rudolf Stephan, vol. 2. Giebing: Katzbichler, 1971.

Schoenberg, Arnold, 'Brahms the Progressive'. 1933. In *Style and Idea*, 398–441.

—— 'Composition with Twelve Tones (1)'. 1941. In *Style and Idea*, 214–45.

—— 'Criteria for the Evaluation of Music'. 1946. In *Style and Idea*, 124–36.

—— *Fundamentals of Musical Composition*. Ed. Gerald Strang with the collaboration of Leonard Stein. London: Faber and Faber, 1967.

—— *Harmonielehre*. Rev. edn. Vienna: Universal-Edition, 1922; repr. 1966. Trans. Roy E. Carter as *Theory of Harmony*. Berkeley and Los Angeles: University of California Press, 1978.

—— 'National Music (2)'. 1931. In *Style and Idea*, 172–4.

—— *Preliminary Exercises in Counterpoint*. Ed. Leonard Stein. London: Faber and Faber, 1963.

—— *Structural Functions of Harmony*. Rev. edn. with corrections. Ed. by Leonard Stein. New York: W. W. Norton, 1969.

—— *Style and Idea: Selected Writings of Arnold Schoenberg*. Ed. Leonard Stein. New York: St Martin's Press, 1975.

—— 'The Orchestral Variations Op. 31: A Radio Talk, 1931'. *The Score* 27 (1960): 27–40.

—— 'Twelve-Tone Composition'. 1923. In *Style and Idea*, 207–8.

Schubring, Adolf, 'Schumanniana Nr. 8: Die Schumann'sche Schule: IV. Johannes Brahms'. *Neue Zeitschrift für Musik* 56 (1862): 93–6, 101–4, 109–12, 117–19, 125–8.

Schumann, Clara, ed., *Jugendbriefe von Robert Schumann*. Leipzig: Breitkopf & Härtel, 1898.

Schumann, Robert, 'Neue Bahnen'. *Neue Zeitschrift für Musik* 39 (1853): 185–6; included in *Robert Schumann: Gesammelte Schriften*, ed. Martin Kreisig, 2: 301–2. Leipzig: Breitkopf & Härtel, 1914; repr. Wiesbaden: Breitkopf & Härtel, 1969. Trans. Paul Rosenfeld in *Robert Schumann: On Music and Musicians*, ed. Konrad Wolff, 252–4. New York, Toronto, and London: McGraw-Hill, 1964.

Schwarz, Boris, 'Joseph Joachim and the Genesis of Brahms's Violin Concerto'. *The Musical Quarterly* 69 (1983): 503–26.

Schwartz, Delmore, 'Poetry as Imitation'. *Perspectives of New Music* 24/1 (1985): 102–6.

Scruton, Roger, 'Programme Music'. In *The New Grove Dictionary of Music and Musicians*, 6th edn., ed. Stanley Sadie, 15: 283–7. London: Macmillan, 1980.

Shamgar, Beth, 'On Locating the Retransition in Classic Sonata Form'. *The Music Review* 42 (1981): 130–43.

Sisman, Elaine R., 'Haydn's Hybrid Variations'. In *Haydn Studies*, ed. Jens Peter Larsen, Howard Serwer, and James Webster, 509–15. New York: W. W. Norton & Co., 1981.

—— 'Tradition and Transformation in the Alternating Variations of Haydn and Beethoven'. *Acta Musicologica* 62 (1990).

—— 'Brahms and the Variation Canon'. *19th-Century Music* 14 (1990).

Specht, Richard, *Johannes Brahms: Leben und Werk eines deutschen Meisters*. Hellerau: Avalun-Verlag, 1928. Trans. Eric Blom. London: Dent and New York: Dutton, 1930.

Speidel, Ludwig, 'Johannes Brahms †'. *Signale für die musikalische Welt* 55 (1897): 385–8.

Stahmer, Klaus, 'Musikalische Formung in soziologischem Bezug. Dargestellt an der instrumentalen Kammermusik von Johannes Brahms'. Ph.D. diss., University of Kiel, 1968.

Stravinsky, Igor, *Poetics of Music in the Form of Six Lessons*. Trans. Arthur Knodel and Ingolf Dahl. Cambridge: Harvard University Press, 1947.

Tieck, Ludwig, *Minnelieder aus dem schwäbischen Zeitalter*. Berlin: Realschulbuchhandlung, 1803; repr. Hildesheim: Georg Olms Verlagsbuchhandlung, 1966.

Tovey, Donald Francis, 'Brahms's Chamber Music'. 1929. In *Essays and Lectures on Music*, 220–70. London: Oxford University Press, 1949.

—— *Essays in Musical Analysis*. 7 vols. Vol. 1: Symphonies; vol. 2: Symphonies (II), Variations and Orchestral Polyphony; vol. 3: Concertos; vol. 5: Vocal Music; vol. 6: Supplementary Essays. London: Oxford University Press, 1935–9.

—— *Essays in Musical Analysis: Chamber Music*. Ed. Hubert J. Foss. London: Oxford University Press, 1944.

Treitler, Leo, 'History, Criticism, and Beethoven's Ninth Symphony'. *19th-Century Music* 3 (1979–80): 193–210.

—— 'Meter and Rhythm in the *Ars Antiqua*'. *The Musical Quarterly* 65 (1979): 524–58.

Velten, Klaus, 'Das Prinzip der entwickelnden Variation bei Johannes Brahms und Arnold Schönberg'. *Musik und Bildung* 6 (1974): 547–55.

—— 'Entwicklungsdenken und Zeiterfahrung in der Musik von Johannes Brahms: Das Intermezzo op. 117 Nr. 2'. *Die Musikforschung* 34 (1981): 56–9.

—— *Schönbergs Instrumentationen Bachscher und Brahms'scher Werke als Dokumente seines Traditionsverständnisses*. Kölner Beiträge zur Musikforschung, ed. Heinrich Hüschen, vol. 85. Regensburg: Gustav Bosse Verlag, 1976.

Wackernagel, Philipp, *Das deutsche Kirchenlied*. Stuttgart: S. G. Liesching, 1841.

—— *Kleines Gesangbuch geistlicher Lieder*. Stuttgart: S. G. Liesching, 1860.

Wagner, Cosima, *Die Tagebücher*. 2 vols. Ed. and with commentary by Martin Gregor-Dellin and Dietrich Mack. Munich and Zurich: Piper, 1976.

Wagner, Richard, *Sämtliche Schriften und Dichtungen*. 15 vols. Leipzig: Breitkopf & Härtel, 1912–14.

Walker, Alan, 'Brahms and Serialism'. *Musical Opinion* 82 (1958): 17–21.

Webster, James, 'Brahms's *Tragic Overture*: The Form of Tragedy'. In *Brahms: Biographical, Documentary and Analytical Studies*, ed. Robert Pascall, 99–124. Cambridge: Cambridge University Press, 1983.

—— 'Traditional Elements in Beethoven's Middle-Period String Quartets'. In *Beethoven, Performers, and Critics*, ed. Bruce Carr and Robert Winter, 94–133. Detroit: Wayne State University Press, 1980.

—— 'Schubert's Sonata Form and Brahms's First Maturity'. Part 1, *19th-Century Music* 2 (1978–9): 18–35; Part 2, ibid., 3 (1979–80): 52–71.

—— 'Sonata Forms'. In *The New Grove Dictionary of Music and Musicians*, 6th edn., ed. Stanley Sadie, 17: 497–508. London: Macmillan, 1980.

Weinmann, Alexander, *J. P. Gotthard als später Originalverleger Franz Schuberts*. Wiener Archivstudien, vol. 2. Vienna: Ludwig Krenn, 1979.

Weiss-Aigner, Günter, *Johannes Brahms: Violinkonzert D-Dur*. Meisterwerke der Musik, vol. 18. Munich: Wilhelm Fink Verlag, 1979.

Wellesz, Egon, *The Origins of Schoenberg's Twelve-Note System*. Washington, DC: Library of Congress, 1958.

Winter, Robert, 'Cataloguing Schubert'. *19th-Century Music* 3 (1979–80): 154–62.

—— 'Paper Studies and the Future of Schubert Research'. In *Schubert Studies: Problems in Style and Chronology*, ed. Eva Badura-Skoda and Peter Branscombe, 209–75. Cambridge: Cambridge University Press, 1982.

Winterfeld, Carl von, *Der evangelische Kirchengesang*. 3 vols. Leipzig: Breitkopf & Härtel, 1843–7.

—— *Johannes Gabrieli und sein Zeitalter*. 3 vols. Berlin: Schlesinger, 1834.

Wiora, Walter, 'Zwischen absoluter und Programmusik'. In *Festschrift Friedrich Blume zum 70. Geburtstag*, ed. Anna Amalie Abert and Wilhelm Pfannkuch, 381–8. Kassel: Bärenreiter, 1963.

Wirth, Helmut, 'Nachwirkungen der Musik Joseph Haydns auf Johannes Brahms'. In *Musik, Edition, Interpretation: Gedenkschrift Günter Henle*, ed. Martin Bente, 455–62. Munich: G. Henle Verlag, 1980.

Wörner, Karl, *Das Zeitalter der thematischen Prozesse in der Geschichte der Musik*. Regensburg: Gustav Bosse Verlag, 1969.

Wolff, Christoph, 'Von der Quellenkritik zur musikalischen Analyse: Beobachtungen am Klavierquartett A-Dur op. 26 von Johannes Brahms'. In *Brahms-Analysen: Referate der Kieler Tagung 1983*, ed. Friedhelm Krummacher and Wolfram Steinbeck, 150–65. Kieler Schriften zur Musikwissenschaft, vol. 28. Cassel: Bärenreiter, 1984.

Zeileis, Friedrich G., 'Two Manuscript Sources of Brahms's German Requiem'. *Music and Letters* 60 (1979): 149–55.

Ziegler, Vickie L., *The Leitword in* Minnesang: *Stylistic Analysis and Textual Criticism*. University Park and London: Pennsylvania State University Press, 1975.


MUSIC, INCLUDING FACSIMILE EDITIONS

Bach, Johann Sebastian, *Cantata No. 4: Christ lag in Todesbanden*. Norton Critical Scores. Ed. Gerhard Herz. New York: W. W. Norton, 1967.

Brahms, Johannes, *Alto Rhapsody Opus 53 for contralto, men's chorus, and orchestra. A facsimile edition from the composer's autograph manuscript in the Music Division of The New York Public Library*. Introduction by Walter Frisch. New York: The New York Public Library, 1983.

—— *Concerto for Violin, Op. 77, by Johannes Brahms: A Facsimile of the Holograph Score*. Preface by Yehudi Menuhin; Foreword by Jon Newsom. Washington, DC: Library of Congress, 1979.

—— *Dein Herzlein mild*. University of Pennsylvania Choral Series No. 25. Ed. Henry S. Drinker. Philadelphia, 1938.

—— *Intermezzi Opus 119 Nr. 2 und 3: Faksimile des Autographs*. Commentary by Friedrich G. Zeileis. Tutzing: Hans Schneider, 1975.

—— *Johannes Brahms Autographs: Facsimiles of Eight Manuscripts in the Library of Congress.* Introduction by James Webster; Notes about the Manuscripts by George S. Bozarth. Music in Facsimile, vol. 1. New York and London: Garland Publishing, 1983.

—— *Johannes Brahms. Opus 24, Opus 23, Opus 18, Opus 90.* New York: Robert Owen Lehman Foundation, 1967.

—— *Johannes Brahms sämtliche Werke.* 26 vols. Ed. Hans Gál and Eusebius Mandyczewski. Leipzig: Breitkopf & Härtel, 1926–8; repr. Ann Arbor: J. W. Edwards, 1949, and Wiesbaden: Breitkopf & Härtel, 1964.

—— *Klaviertrios.* Ed. Ernst Herttrich. Munich: G. Henle Verlag, 1972.

—— *Klaviervariationen, Opus 9 und 21. Variations for Piano, Opp. 9 and 21.* Ed. Margit L. McCorkle. Munich: G. Henle Verlag, 1987.

—— *Kleine Stücke für Klavier.* Ed. Robert Pascall. Vienna: Doblinger, 1979.

—— *Lieder für eine Singstimme mit Klavierbegleitung.* Ed. Max Friedlaender. Leipzig: C. F. Peters, n.d.

—— *Die Müllerin.* Ed. Joachim Draheim. Wiesbaden: Breitkopf & Härtel, 1983.

—— *Oktaven und Quinten u. a.* Ed. and with commentary by Heinrich Schenker. Vienna: Universal-Edition, 1933.

—— *Die Orgelwerke. The Organ Works.* Ed. George S. Bozarth. Munich: G. Henle Verlag, 1987.

—— *Piano Concerto, D major, Op. 15.* Ed. Paul Badura-Skoda. Eulenburg Miniature Scores. London: Ernst Eulenburg, 1963.

—— *Sinfonie Nr. 1 C-Moll, Op. 68: Taschen-Partitur.* Ed. Gieslher Schubert. Mainz: Goldmann Schott, 1981.

—— *Sinfonie Nr. 3 F-Dur, Op. 90: Taschen-Partitur.* Ed. Christian Martin Schmidt. Mainz: Goldmann Schott, 1981.

—— *Sinfonie Nr. 4 e-moll, Op. 98: Taschen-Partitur.* Ed. Christian Martin Schmidt. Mainz: Goldmann Schott, 1980.

—— *Symphony No. 1: A Facsimile of the Autograph Manuscript in the Pierpont Morgan Library.* Introduction by Margit L. McCorkle. New York: Dover Publications, 1986.

—— *Three Lieder on Poems by Adolf Friedrich von Schack: A Facsimile of the Autograph Manuscripts . . . in the Collection of the Library of Congress.* Introductory essay and translations by George S. Bozarth. Washington, DC: Library of Congress, 1983.

—— *Variations on a Theme of Haydn for Orchestra, Op. 56a, and for Two Pianos, Op. 56b.* Ed. Donald M. McCorkle. Norton Critical Scores. New York: W. W. Norton, 1976.

—— *et al., Johannes Brahms und seine Freunde.* Ed. Joachim Draheim. Wiesbaden: Breitkopf & Härtel, 1983.

Eccard, Johannes, *et al., Geistliches Chorlied.* Ed. Gottfried Grote. 2 vols. Berlin: Merseburger, 1967.

Isaac, Heinrich, *et al., Antiqua Chorbuch.* 10 vols. Ed. Helmut Mönkemeyer. Mainz: Schott, 1951–2.

Kretzschmer, August, and Anton Wilhelm von Zuccalmaglio, *Deutsche Volkslieder mit ihren Originalweisen.* 2 vols. Berlin: Vereins-Buchhandlung, 1838, 1840; repr. Hildesheim: Georg Olms Verlag, 1969.

Mozart, Wolfgang Amadeus, *Wolfgang Amadeus Mozart: Neue Ausgabe sämtlicher Werke.* Kassel: Bärenreiter, 1955 ff.

Scandello, Antonio, *et al., Der Schulchor.* Ed. Egon Kraus. 6 vols. Mainz: Schott, 1963–7.

Schubert, Franz, *Franz Schubert: Neue Ausgabe sämtlicher Werke.* Kassel: Bärenreiter, 1964 ff.

—— *Franz Schubert's Werke: Kritisch durchgesehenen Gesammtausgabe.* Leipzig: Breitkopf & Härtel, 1884–97; repr. *Franz Schubert. Complete Works.* 19 vols. New York: Dover Publications, 1965.

Schumann, Robert, *Robert Schumann's Werke.* 31 vols. Ed. Clara Schumann. Leipzig: Breitkopf & Härtel, 1879, 1881–93; repr. Westmead, Farnborough, Hants, England: Gregg International Publishers, 1968.

Schütz, Heinrich, *Heinrich Schütz. Neue Ausgabe sämtliche Werke.* Kassel: Bärenreiter, 1955 ff.

Silcher, Friedrich, *100 Volkslieder für eine Singstimme mit Begleitung des Pianoforte.* Revised by Alfred Dörffel. Leipzig: C. F. Peters, n.d.


SOUND RECORDINGS

Schoenberg, Arnold, Interview with Halsey Stevens (no date given). *The Music of Arnold Schoenberg*, vol. 3. Issued in Great Britain by CBS as BRG 72359 and in the United States by Columbia as M2L 309 (1965).

# Index